MW01055974

The Runciman Mission to Czechoslovakia, 1938

The Runciman Mission to Czechoslovakia, 1938

Prelude to Munich

Paul Vyšný

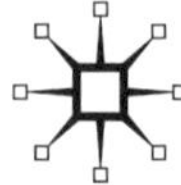

First published 2003 by
PALGRAVE MACMILLAN
Houndmills, Basingstoke, Hampshire RG21 6XS and
175 Fifth Avenue, New York, N. Y. 10010
Companies and representatives throughout the world.

PALGRAVE MACMILLAN is the global academic imprint of the Palgrave Macmillan division of St Martin's Press, LLC and of Palgrave Macmillan Ltd. Macmillan® is a registered trademark in the United States, United Kingdom and other countries. Palgrave is a registered trademark in the European Union and other countries.

ISBN 0–333–73136–0

This book is printed on paper suitable for recycling and made from fully managed and sustained forest sources.

A catalogue record for this book is available from the British Library.

Library of Congress Cataloging-in-Publication Data

Vyšný, Paul, 1944–
The Runciman mission to Czechoslovakia, 1938: prelude to Munich / Paul Vyšný.
p. cm.
Includes bibliographical references and index.
ISBN 0–333–73136–0 (cloth)
1. Czechoslovakia – Foreign relations – Great Britain. 2. Great Britain – Foreign relations – Czechoslovakia. 3. Runciman, Walter Runciman, Viscount, 1870–1949. 4. Europe – Politics and government – 1918–1945. I. Title.

DB2078.G3 V96 2002
327.437041'09'043–dc21

2002028753

10 9 8 7 6 5 4 3 2 1
12 11 10 09 08 07 06 05 04 03

Printed and bound in Great Britain by
Antony Rowe Ltd, Chippenham and Eastbourne

Contents

Maps vi

Preface ix

1 A Quarrel in a Far-Away Country 1

2 Avoiding a Commitment 24

3 Seeking a Solution 43

4 Choosing a Mediator 71

5 Deadlock in Prague 101

6 The Mission Takes Shape 128

7 Adrift in Central Europe 147

8 A Glimmer of Hope 165

9 Anxiety in London 187

10 Mounting Despair 214

11 Turning the Screw 243

12 The Last Resort 263

13 The Collapse of Mediation 285

14 The Reckoning 310

Conclusion 341

Appendix 1: The Runciman Report 344

Appendix 2: Ashton-Gwatkin's Parodies 351

Bibliography 353

Index 364

List of Maps

1 National minorities in Czechoslovakia, 1918–38 vii
2 German minority in Bohemia and Moravia, 1918–38 viii

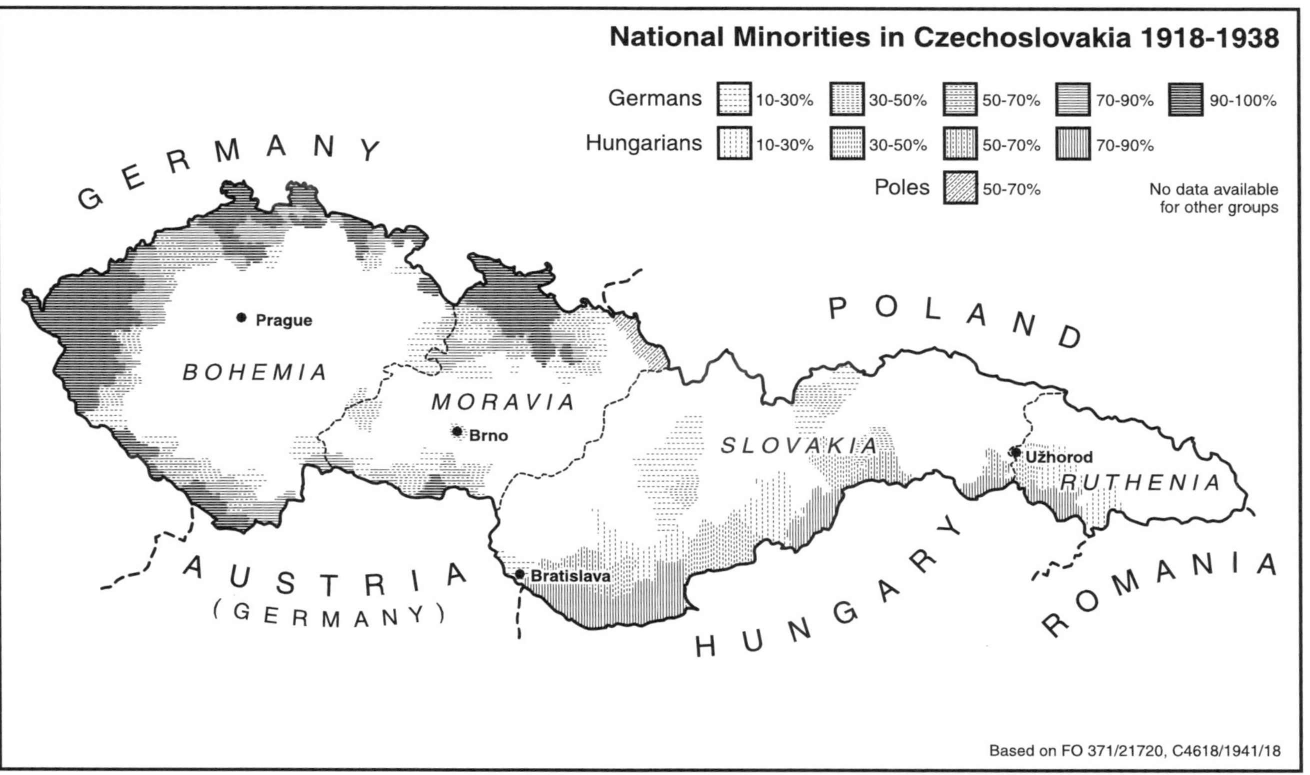

National Minorities in Czechoslovakia 1918-1938
Germans
10-30%
30-50%
50-70%
70-90%
90-100%
Hungarians
10-30%
30-50%
50-70%
70-90%
Poles
50-70%
No data available for other groups
GERMANY
POLAND
BOHEMIA
MORAVIA
SLOVAKIA
RUTHENIA
Prague
Brno
Bratislava
Užhorod
AUSTRIA
(GERMANY)
HUNGARY
ROMANIA
Based on FO 371/21720, C4618/1941/18

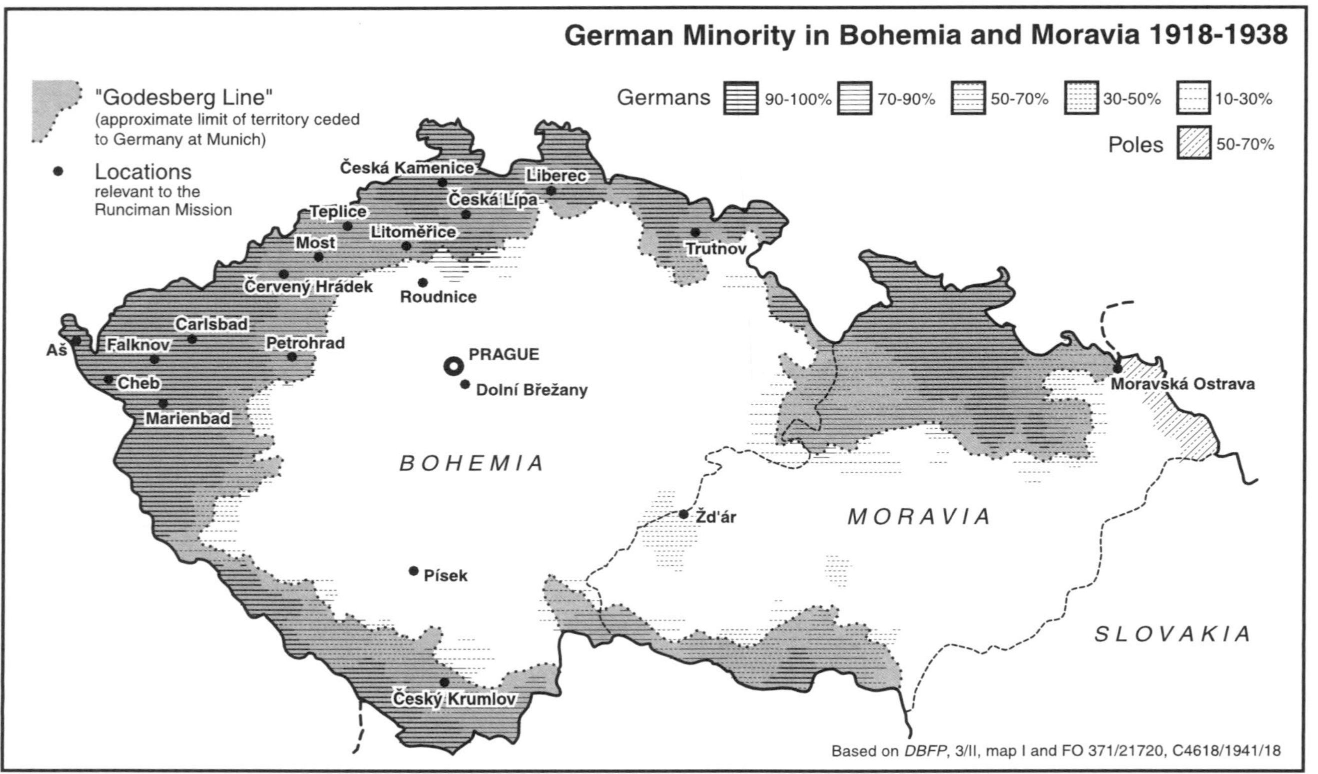

German Minority in Bohemia and Moravia 1918-1938
"Godesberg Line"
(approximate limit of territory ceded to Germany at Munich)
Locations relevant to the Runciman Mission
Germans
90-100%
70-90%
50-70%
30-50%
10-30%
Poles
50-70%
Česká Kamenice
Liberec
Česká Lípa
Teplice
Litoměřice
Most
Trutnov
Červený Hrádek
Roudnice
Carlsbad
Aš
Falknov
Petrohrad
PRAGUE
Cheb
Dolní Břežany
Marienbad
Moravská Ostrava
BOHEMIA
Žd'ár
MORAVIA
Písek
SLOVAKIA
Český Krumlov
Based on DBFP, 3/II, map I and FO 371/21720, C4618/1941/18

Preface

Much has been written about 'appeasement' and it is not the intention of this work to offer yet another general analysis of Britain's policy towards Nazi Germany in the 1930s nor to re-examine in their entirety the events surrounding the Munich Conference of September 1938. The aim of this book is, more simply, to study one particular aspect of the developments that preceded the Munich Agreement – the British attempt at mediation in, what was known as, the 'Sudeten German problem'. The international ramifications of the political and ethnic tensions within Czechoslovakia during the spring and summer of 1938 were such as to threaten to plunge Europe into war, and the object of the mission in question was, therefore, to preserve peace. That formidable task was entrusted by the British government to Lord Runciman of Doxford.

The Runciman Mission formed a key component of the developing British response to the heightened danger in Central Europe following the *Anschluss* of Austria in March 1938. In its anxiety to avoid becoming entangled in the problems of Czechoslovakia, the British government was compelled, paradoxically, into greater involvement. At a loss to know how to proceed, it resorted to mediation. This ill-prepared and conceptually flawed initiative, which followed a period of severe British diplomatic pressure on the Prague government, failed in its objective and served only to prepare the ground for Czechoslovakia's destruction at Munich. Indeed, Runciman's controversial report on his Mission provided Neville Chamberlain with the required public justification for forcing the cession of the Sudeten territories to Germany.

The study of Runciman's activity in Czechoslovakia and his interaction with those attempting to control developments from London provides an illuminating insight into the aims and methods of British foreign policy at that critical juncture. With inadequate understanding of the situation in Central Europe and in the absence of clear objectives – other than to avoid war with Germany – the Mission became little more than a convenient vehicle for applying further pressure for concessions on the Prague authorities. Runciman was manipulated into that position not only by Sudeten German separatists, exploiting his presence in Czechoslovakia, but also by those on the British side, sympathetic towards the expansion of German influence in Central Europe, hoping to secure a basis for a lasting rapprochement between Britain and Germany. It was the determined pursuit of that objective by Runciman's chief assistant (though not by Runciman himself) that sowed the seeds of Chamberlain's fateful flying visits to Hitler.

I would like to acknowledge the support received from the University of St Andrews, and also to record my thanks to all who gave assistance in the research for and preparation of this book – not least to the succession of students who attended my Special Subject on the origins of the Second World War. Extracts from the Runciman Papers appear by permission of the Special Collections Librarian, Robinson Library, University of Newcastle upon Tyne. Material from the Stopford Papers is reproduced by permission of the Trustees of the Imperial War Museum, London. Quotations from the Neville Chamberlain Papers appear by permission of the Special Collections Librarian at the University of Birmingham Library. Crown copyright material in the Public Record Office is reproduced by permission of the Controller of Her Majesty's Stationery Office, London. I am also grateful to the following for granting access to private papers in their care: Crewe and Templewood Papers, the University of Cambridge Library; Caldecote, Christie and Vansittart Papers, Churchill College, Cambridge; Mason-Macfarlane and Stronge Papers, the Department of Documents at the Imperial War Museum, London; Samuel Papers, the House of Lords Record Office, London; and Lothian Papers, the National Archives of Scotland, Edinburgh. Thanks are also due to the Royal Archive at Windsor, and to the Franklin D. Roosevelt Library, Hyde Park, New York for responding to specific queries. Every effort has been made to trace other copyright-holders and apologies are offered for any inadvertent omissions.

For ease of identification, places inside former Czechoslovakia are referred to by their Czech or Slovak names with the German or other names given in parenthesis only when first mentioned. An exception is made for those place names, such as Prague or Carlsbad, that have an accepted English form.

Finally, this book is dedicated to Helen, Stephen, Nicholas and Catherine, in gratitude for their forbearance during the years of its preparation.

PAUL VYŠNÝ

1
A Quarrel in a Far-Away Country

The name of Lord Runciman of Doxford was first officially linked with the crisis in Czechoslovakia by Neville Chamberlain in the House of Commons on 26 July 1938. The Prime Minister announced that the 67-year-old shipping magnate and former Cabinet minister had been appointed 'an investigator and mediator'[1] in a dispute between the government of the Czechoslovak Republic and an opposition political movement representing the German minority population, the Sudeten German Party (SdP). The Parliamentary statement was not unexpected as news of Runciman's forthcoming mission had been carried in the *News Chronicle* the previous day.[2] British involvement in the developing crisis in Central Europe – which was described by Chamberlain a few weeks later, in an unfortunate phrase, as 'a quarrel in a far-away country between people of whom we know nothing'[3] – was prompted principally by the fear of being dragged unwillingly into war with Germany.

The unhappy situation in Czechoslovakia, which Runciman was sent to resolve, had its roots deep in Central European history. Czechs and Germans had lived side by side in that quintessential heart of Europe, Bohemia, and the adjacent territories of Moravia and (Southern) Silesia, since at least the twelfth century.[4] During the following 700 years, both peoples were caught up in the turbulent developments of that region, including the Hussite Wars of the fifteenth century and the Thirty Years' War of the seventeenth. However, important though these events subsequently became in the forging of national consciousness, it was not until that identity emerged as a political force in the mid-nineteenth century that the modern period of Czech–German relations began. It was the revolutionary year of 1848 – heralding the arrival of modern nationalism in Central Europe – which formed the effective starting point of this troubled relationship. In that year, the Czech national leader, František Palacký, refused to attend the Pan-German Frankfurt Parliament on the grounds that he was 'a Czech of Slav descent',[5] thus drawing the first modern political distinction between the Czech and German populations of Central Europe.

At that time, the territories of Bohemia, Moravia and Silesia – known collectively as the Historic Provinces of the Bohemian (or Czech) Crown or the Bohemian Lands – were integral parts of the Habsburg Empire, ruled by an essentially German government from Vienna. Despite the changes introduced in 1867, when the Habsburg Austrian Empire acquired its dualist structure and became the Austro-Hungarian Empire, the situation remained substantially unaltered until that, by then ramshackle, multinational state finally disintegrated under the pressures of war in 1918.

Throughout this period, the Czechs remained in an inferior position relative to their German neighbours. Although outnumbering the German population of the Bohemian Lands by a ratio of about 2:1, they considered themselves to be both politically and economically disadvantaged. Consequently, a bitter struggle ensued between the two national groups, focused largely on inter-related economic and linguistic issues. The Germans were determined to protect their privileged position, if necessary within ethnic sub-divisions of Bohemia and Moravia, whereas the Czechs fought to preserve the territorial integrity of the Historic Provinces, within which they sought to exploit their numerical preponderance. In social and economic terms the Czechs achieved considerable advances, establishing their own middle class alongside that of the Germans. They failed, however, to achieve their political objective of gaining autonomous status for the Bohemian Lands within a reformed Habsburg Empire.

Up until 1918 it was the Germans who narrowly maintained the upper hand in this conflict, but in the independent Czechoslovak state, which came into being in that year, the roles were reversed. The Czechs were now the dominant group, and the Germans became a minority population, complaining of discrimination in political, financial and cultural matters. The situation deteriorated further at the onset of the Depression and developed into a full-blown crisis following the triumph of National Socialism in neighbouring Germany in 1933.

The German inhabitants of the Bohemian lands – known as the Sudeten Germans[6] – were primarily concentrated along the northern, western and, to a lesser extent, southern borders of the territory, in areas referred to as the Sudetenland. At the time of the formation of the Czechoslovak state in October 1918, this population numbered over three million. In the aftermath of defeat, which provided the opportunity for the Czechs, in conjunction with the neighbouring Slovaks, to establish their new state, the Germans also attempted to establish national territories. Four such units, aspiring to self-determination, briefly came into existence during the autumn of 1918,[7] but none survived for more than a few weeks, as Czech troops gradually occupied the areas concerned establishing the authority of the new Czechoslovak government. They met with little resistance from the demoralised German population. Bloodshed did occur, however, early in 1919, when, at several locations, Czech troops opened fire on German demonstrators protesting against being excluded from participating in parliamentary elections in the neighbouring new Austrian Republic. Although more than fifty Germans were killed overall,[8] the violence did not give rise to further unrest. Once the Paris Peace Conference had resolved to maintain the historic frontier of Bohemia as the western border of Czechoslovakia,[9] thus ensuring the inclusion of the Germans in the newly formed republic, that population accepted the inevitable. Most Sudeten Germans became citizens of the new state with much reluctance; but some, those with industrial interests in particular, saw positive economic advantage in remaining within Czechoslovakia.[10]

Although the formal Czechoslovak claims made at the Peace Conference extended beyond the historic territory of the Bohemian Lands and the Slovak ethnic regions of former Hungary, the Foreign Minister, Edvard Beneš, had more realistic aims. As far as the western frontiers of the new state were concerned, in order to avoid raising the issue of self-determination for the German population, he sought the preservation of the 1914 boundary. Thanks largely to the support of the French representatives, who, seeking to create a strong ally in Central Europe, argued for the construction of a strategically and economically viable Czechoslovakia, Beneš secured this objective. Similar considerations determined the frontiers of Slovakia and the inclusion of Ruthenia (or Sub-Carpathian Ukraine).[11] As a result, in addition to over three million Germans, Czechoslovakia contained, at its formation, three-quarters of a million Hungarians in southern Slovakia, almost half a million Ruthenians in Ruthenia, 76 000 Poles in Silesia and a Jewish population of 180 000. Czechs and Slovaks together numbered less than nine million.[12]

Critics of the Czechoslovak government subsequently maintained that the claims made on its behalf at the Peace Conference were founded on tendentious evidence accompanied by false promises. The Czechoslovak case was based on the claim that the size of the German minority in Bohemia itself was closer to $1\frac{1}{2}$ million than the $2\frac{1}{2}$ million recorded by the Austrian census of 1910. This assertion was unrealistic, as was proved by the census of 1921 which substantially corroborated the previous Austrian figures, and was clearly produced for propagandistic purposes. However, the Peace Conference was not swayed by the Czechoslovak submission, basing its decisions on the more accurate Austrian census results.[13] The accusation of unfulfilled undertakings was founded on references, made by Beneš, to Czechoslovakia becoming a 'sort of Switzerland'. It is unlikely that Beneš had in mind the introduction of a cantonal system on the Swiss federal model, indeed he specifically mentioned that the new state would be predominantly 'Czecho-Slovak' in character. More probably, as Beneš subsequently maintained, he used the term simply as a synonym for a state based on liberal democratic institutions and the respect of minority rights.[14] However, the terminology was undoubtedly ill-chosen and provided Beneš's opponents with valuable political ammunition for use against him in the 1930s.

Beneš's statement was made in connection with negotiations concerning specific provisions for the protection of national minorities in the succession states of Central Europe – the Minorities Treaties. He promised the introduction of a system of proportional representation in all elections to fully reflect the ethnic composition of the electorate; the provision of publicly-funded schools for each nationality; the bilingual administration of justice; and the exercise of local administration in the language of the majority of the population concerned. More generally, although Czech (or Slovak) was to be the official language of the state, German was to serve as the second language.[15] These undertakings fully satisfied the Peace Conference, being considered to offer more than the minimum provisions required. A Minorities Treaty, containing most of these points, was concluded with Czechoslovakia in the autumn of 1919.[16]

The provisions of the Minorities Treaty were duly incorporated in the Czechoslovak Constitution approved by a nominated provisional National Assembly in February 1920. As the Assembly consisted only of Czech and Slovak representatives, the minority nationalities, including the Sudeten Germans, objected to being excluded from participation in determining the fundamental political structure of the new state. Although the Constitution itself did not define Czechoslovakia as a 'National State', it was, nevertheless, clearly based on the concept of *Czechoslovak* nationality. Despite the undertaking (known as the Pittsburg Agreement) given to Slovak representatives in the United States by T.G. Masaryk, prior to becoming the first President of Czechoslovakia in 1918, promising substantial autonomy for Slovakia, the new state was founded on a unitary basis. No official distinction was made between Czechs and Slovaks, who were considered subdivisions of a single nation. The other ethnic groups, although constitutionally guaranteed full equality of individual citizenship, were nevertheless accorded the status of national minorities – which many of Czechoslovakia's Germans found particularly objectionable.

A further source of grievance for many Sudeten Germans was provided by the application of the language laws. In terms of language status, the situation was a reversal of that which had prevailed in the Habsburg Empire, with Czech now the official language of the state in Bohemia and Moravia. The practical effect was the imposition of the Czech language on many who had little interest in it. Additional problems arose in the related area of education, with Germans accusing the Czechoslovak authorities of excessive enthusiasm in opening Czech schools in German areas whilst closing German schools in Czech districts.

The social and economic reforms introduced in the early years of the new republic also provoked unfavourable reactions from the German minority. Most prominent was the issue of land reform. In view of the fact that, prior to

1918, a substantial proportion of the land in the Historic Provinces was in the hands of a small number of German landowners, and because most of the small farmers seeking additional land were Czech, it was inevitable that reform would result in the transfer of land from German to Czech ownership. Consequently, it also led to accusations of Czech colonisation of German areas, with the incoming Czech population introducing the Czech language and setting up Czech schools in previously purely German communities.[17]

The multitude of grievances, real and perceived, felt by the Sudeten Germans did not, however, prevent their participation in the politics of the new state. The local elections of 1919 established German local authorities in German areas. In the first parliamentary election, held in 1920, five German political parties secured 72 out of 281 seats in the lower house, the Chamber of Deputies, a slightly higher proportion than the size of the German minority as recorded in the census of the following year. Similar results were achieved also in the general elections of 1925 and 1929. Although initially all the German parties chose to be in opposition, in 1926 the Agrarians and the Christian Socials entered the government coalition (gaining, respectively, the portfolios of Public Works and Justice), thus initiating a period of 'activism'. Only the Nationalists and the Nazis maintained their hostility towards the new state. The strongest German party, the Social Democrats, though not entering the government, signalled their positive attitude by establishing links with their Czechoslovak counterparts, who were also in opposition to the right-of-centre administration. In the general elections of 1929, the German 'activist' parties secured more than three times the number of votes obtained by the parties hostile towards Czechoslovakia.[18] Following those elections, the German Social Democrats also joined the administration (obtaining the Social Welfare portfolio) on the insistence of their Czechoslovak colleagues, who otherwise refused to enter the government. The German Christian Socials lost their representation in the Cabinet, but retained their 'activist' attitude.

The onset of the Great Depression, which began to affect Czechoslovakia in the early 1930s, exerted a profound influence on inter-ethnic relations in Central Europe. Although the entire Czechoslovak economy began to suffer from the collapse of international trade, it was the German areas that bore the brunt of the hardship. The Sudeten German industries, mainly engaged in consumer goods manufacturing such as textiles and glass, being more dependent on exports than the Czech-owned industrial sector, were more severely affected by the slump. Consequently, levels of unemployment became far higher amongst Germans than amongst Czechs, and the Sudeten German districts became gripped by economic despair.[19]

As was the case in neighbouring Germany, the economic hardship stimulated the growth of political extremism in the Sudeten German areas. In parallel with the rise of National Socialism in Germany, culminating with Hitler's coming to power in Berlin in 1933, the German Nazis and

Nationalists in Czechoslovakia gained strength at the expense of the German 'activist' parties. The Czechoslovak authorities reacted to the rising tide of extremism by proscribing both the German National Socialist Party and the German Nationalist Party in the autumn of 1933. The banned parties were soon replaced by a new organisation, the Sudeten German Home Front (*Sudetendeutsche Heimatfront*), under the leadership of Konrad Henlein. Although Henlein, a prominent figure in the German nationalist *Turnverband* gymnastics association, vigorously denied any links with National Socialism and professed loyalty to Czechoslovakia, the Sudeten German Home Front was, in reality, established by Nazi sympathisers and from 1935 secretly received funding from Berlin.[20] Henlein and his followers shared the outlook and also imitated the style of Hitler's Nazis, adopting paramilitary uniform and, in May 1937, the Hitler salute.[21] However, the new movement was not monolithic and free from internal tensions. Henlein's closest associates in the leadership came mostly from the elitist pan-German *Kameradschaftsbund* (KB) organisation and not infrequently clashed over policy with the more militant and radical former members of the banned Sudeten German Nazis.[22]

The Third Reich's rejection of the Versailles settlement which concluded the First World War, combined with the expansionist nature of its National Socialist ideology, were factors self-evidently not conducive to the development of cordial relations between Berlin and Prague. The predictable tensions were further exacerbated by the influx of refugees from Nazi Germany who sought safety from persecution in Czechoslovakia.[23] Prior to 1933 however, relations between Prague and Berlin had been more harmonious if not entirely cordial. The governments of Weimar Germany had no plans for territorial expansion in Central Europe, and despite being suspicious of the pro-French attitude exhibited by Beneš, generally regarded Czechoslovakia with less antipathy than Poland. Nevertheless, Weimar Germany was not prepared to follow up the 1925 Locarno Agreement, guaranteeing Germany's western borders, with a similar agreement in the east, though arbitration treaties were concluded with both Czechoslovakia and Poland. Trading relations during the period were also generally amicable, though the proposal for an Austro-German customs union, made in 1931 but blocked by Britain and France, greatly alarmed the Czechoslovak government which feared economic and ultimately political domination by Germany. As far as the Sudeten Germans were concerned, Weimar Germany gave little encouragement to the irredentist tendencies amongst them by giving general support to the 'activist' attitude. Weimar politicians saw greater advantage in the German minority remaining within Czechoslovakia than in its incorporation in Germany.[24] The Nazi regime, however, viewed the matter very differently.

The Czechoslovak government reacted to Hitler's rise to power by reinforcing its alliance with France, dating from 1925, with the addition of a treaty with the Soviet Union. The new alliance, concluded in May 1935 following Hitler's announced intention to rearm Germany, specified that the Soviet Union would only be obliged to defend Czechoslovakia from attack if France did so first.[25] Internally, the Czechoslovak authorities increased their military preparedness and, in particular, began constructing fortifications along the vulnerable border with Germany – in the Sudetenland. The militarisation of the frontier zone, provided for under the State Defence Law of 1936, enacted in response to Germany's reoccupation of the Rhineland, and other measures aimed at restricting the number of German employees in firms applying for defence contracts, served inevitably only to exacerbate relations between the central authorities and the local German population.[26]

A further source of grievance for Czechoslovakia's German minority was their under-representation in the various branches of government service. Particularly strong feelings were aroused by the replacement of the local police in German areas with the mainly Czech-staffed state police, a measure justified on the grounds of the strategic importance of the Sudeten territories. However, the disproportionately small number of Germans employed in other areas of government service, including the post office and the railways, was more difficult to excuse. Moreover, in addition to claiming that the German minority bore the brunt of the economic hardship resulting from the combined impact of the depression and discrimination in employment, many Sudeten Germans accused the authorities of practising discrimination also in the provision of unemployment relief. Although the Czechoslovak government rejected this particular accusation, the under-representation of the German minority in state service was irrefutable. The problem was not easy to resolve however, as the authorities remained unconvinced of the loyalty of the German minority – particularly after the rise of the Henlein movement.[27]

The first real test of the strength of Henlein's new organisation came at the general election of 1935. The Czechoslovak authorities insisted that the use of a designation which included the word 'Front' was unacceptable in a democratic contest, and the movement therefore entered the election under the name of the Sudeten German Party (*Sudetendeutsche Partei*) – using the initials SdP. The new title was chosen to reinforce Henlein's claim to represent the entire German population of Czechoslovakia.[28] Although amongst Czechs and Slovaks the election results showed no significant move towards political extremism, the Sudeten Germans swung decisively towards the SdP. Henlein's party obtained $1\frac{1}{4}$ million votes – over 60 per cent of the German vote – securing 44 of the 300 seats in the Chamber of Deputies. (In terms of electoral support the SdP was the largest party, gaining 750 000 more votes than the Czechoslovak Agrarians who, however, secured one more seat in the lower house.) This amounted to a substantial defeat for the 'activist' German parties, who polled only 600 000 votes between them, obtaining 22 seats in the lower chamber.[29]

The 'activists', nevertheless, continued their policy of participation in the government, retaining two seats in the Cabinet (the Ministry of Health and Minister without portfolio); and the SdP, despite its parliamentary strength, remained in opposition.

Although Henlein himself (emulating Hitler) had not sought a parliamentary mandate, the election outcome confirmed his increasing significance on the Central European political scene. He soon followed up the electoral success of the SdP by seeking to draw international attention to its cause. In particular, Henlein made considerable effort to develop links with persons in Britain considered potentially useful or sympathetic. Between 1935 and 1938 he visited London on at least four occasions during which he publicised his party's grievances and established contact with Foreign Office personnel and others influential in British public life.[30] Prior to 1935 the British government had shown little interest in the Sudeten Germans. Indeed as late as April of that year, only a month prior to the general election in Czechoslovakia, Anthony Eden, then Lord Privy Seal (but in effect occupying the number two position in the Foreign Office), visited Prague during a tour of the region, but made no reference to the German minority.[31] Henlein's intervention was soon to change that outlook.

The SdP leader's main engagement during his visit to London in December 1935 was to speak to the Royal Institute of International Affairs. Henlein complained of Czechoslovak discrimination against the German minority, but he did so in impeccably reasoned terms, accepting that there were faults on both sides. He expressed loyalty towards the Czechoslovak state and maintained that his party sought merely to secure for the Sudeten Germans the implementation of the Minorities Treaty and the realisation of their constitutional rights. In response to questions, Henlein denied having links with German National Socialism or receiving any funds from Germany.[32] Similar assurances were repeated in interviews with the *Daily Telegraph* and, a few months later, with the London *Evening Standard*.[33] They were also given over lunch with members of the Foreign Office to Lord Stanhope, Parliamentary Under-Secretary, and to two permanent officials, Orme Sargent and Clifford Norton, who observed that their visitor gave 'a strong impression of sincerity and honesty'.[34]

The most significant contact made by Henlein in London was with Sir Robert Vansittart, the Permanent Under-Secretary of State at the Foreign Office. The two men did not actually meet until Henlein's return to Britain in July 1936, but Vansittart was sufficiently persuaded by reports of the SdP leader's previous visit to suggest to Eden, then Minister for League of Nations Affairs, that he should ask Beneš at the forthcoming meeting of the League 'to give these fellows a straighter deal'.[35] Although on that particular occasion the message was not delivered, owing to Beneš's absence from Geneva, having been elected to succeed Masaryk as President,[36] he was to hear similar advice frequently repeated by British representatives during the coming years.

Despite his habitual antipathy towards Germany, Vansittart formed a very positive assessment of Henlein. He noted after their first meeting that the SdP leader made 'a most favourable impression', adding that Henlein was 'moderate, honest and clear-sighted'. However, in addition to his reasoned statement of limited aims, accompanied by complaints of disproportionate economic hardship suffered by the German minority in Czechoslovakia, Vansittart's visitor also began to apply pressure on the British government. Henlein impressed on his host that if his policies failed to achieve any concessions from the Czechoslovak authorities by the autumn, he would be replaced as party leader by more radical forces, leading to the direct involvement of Germany, and hence to war.[37] This warning was reiterated a few days later by the SdP's foreign policy adviser, Heinrich Rutha, who accompanied Henlein. During a separate meeting at the Foreign Office with Lord Cranborne, Parliamentary Under-Secretary, Rutha additionally indicated that he favoured autonomy for the German areas within a Swiss-style federal structure.[38]

Vansittart duly conveyed Henlein's warning to the Czechoslovak Minister in London, Jan Masaryk, son of the country's founder-president, urging a positive response to those Sudeten German grievances which were 'legitimately curable' in order to forestall the considerable danger of Germany's involvement.[39] Masaryk sought to counter Henlein's influence by drawing attention to the nature of Henlein's movement, and, stressing that his father had 'put all his eggs in the democratic basket', pointed to the incompatibility of parts of a democratic state being governed on a totalitarian basis. That, Masaryk argued, would be the inevitable outcome if autonomy were granted to the Sudeten German areas.[40]

Faced with two sharply contradictory accounts of the 'perplexing situation' in Czechoslovakia, Eden – who had become Foreign Secretary in December 1935 – decided it would be unwise to become further involved in mediating between the conflicting parties beyond the 'friendly suggestions' given to Masaryk by Vansittart. The British Minister in Prague, Sir Joseph Addison, was nevertheless instructed to keep a close eye on the situation and to advise on any further action.[41] Addison, who had been at his post in Czechoslovakia since 1930, responded with a lengthy despatch full of characteristically pungent criticism of the 'Czech' authorities, whose ill-judged domestic policies, he argued, were motivated by 'hatred and the spirit of revenge'. The possession of such views was not calculated to enamour the British Minister to the Czechoslovak authorities, although they would have heartily agreed with his further assertion that the introduction of a Swiss-style federal structure was 'quite impossible' as it would inevitably result in the disintegration of the state. Addison estimated that 85 to 90 per cent of the German minority were Nazis who sought union with Germany, the realisation of which was just a matter of time. His advice therefore was simple: Britain should 'take no further active interest in the matter'.[42]

Although Addison's caustic report caused much amusement in the Foreign Office, the nature of his advice was unwelcome and his competence questioned. Vansittart was critical of Addison's general attitude, noting that he had contributed little over the last six years towards resolving the problems of Czechoslovakia. Eden was even more disparaging, accusing Addison not only of neglecting to warn London of the developing crisis but also of failing to appreciate the full international danger inherent in the situation.[43] Others, however, promptly rallied to Addison's defence, circulating extracts from his despatches demonstrating his consistent contention that Czechoslovakia was a 'fictitious country founded on several injustices and maintained by the continuance of injustice'.[44] Owen O'Malley, Head of the Southern Department, which was responsible for Czechoslovakia, also maintained that he was kept fully informed by Addison. O'Malley added his analysis of the situation, predicting German subversion of Czechoslovakia rather than a direct attack. He advised that the ineffective appeals for justice for the Sudeten Germans be replaced by stronger warnings that Britain, and probably France also, would in no circumstances defend Czechoslovakia against a German attack.[45] For the moment, however, that advice was not followed.

In addition to receiving reports, adequate or otherwise, from Britain's official representative in Prague, Vansittart was also supplied with information by his own network of agents. One of his most valuable sources of information concerning Germany and Czechoslovakia was Group Captain Grahame Christie, a former British Air Attaché in Berlin, who, after retiring from the service, became a businessman resident in Germany.[46] Following a visit to Czechoslovakia in May 1936, Christie supplied Vansittart with a lengthy report on the Sudeten German situation in which he maintained that Henlein enjoyed 'little sympathy' amongst Nazi leaders in Germany. He was strongly critical of the Czechoslovak government's failure to respond positively to Henlein's desire for 'conciliation and co-operation', warning that if the authorities persisted in their policy, the SdP would be forced into 'whole-hearted irredentism', resulting in the military intervention of Germany. Christie's attitude evidently differed little from that being proclaimed by Henlein himself, whom he met during his visit to Czechoslovakia.[47]

Christie was not only helpful to Vansittart as a source of intelligence; he also acted as a convenient intermediary with Henlein and was directly responsible for facilitating the SdP leader's visits to London.[48] From Henlein's point of view these visits were a considerable success. Although his attempt to open up a direct line of communication with the British government by corresponding with Sargent was rebuffed, in order to avoid causing offence in Prague,[49] Henlein not only succeeded in establishing contact with senior Foreign Office personnel but also in creating a very favourable personal impression. His presence in Britain, added to his electoral success in Czechoslovakia, had the desired effect of bringing the SdP's case to the attention of the government and public alike. Henlein's visits also reinforced the belief held in the Foreign Office that it was the Czechoslovak authorities who were primarily at fault not the SdP.[50] That assessment, though prevalent, was not unanimous. R.A. Gallop, of the Southern Department, commenting on an early report of Henlein's activity in 1934, observed with remarkable prescience: 'His idea is probably to form a cadre which can – at the right moment – go Nazi, but which will remain camouflaged till then.'[51] Three years later, Henlein himself characterised the SdP's mode of activity in near-identical terms.[52]

Indeed, Henlein's journeys beyond the borders of Czechoslovakia were not restricted to visiting London – he was also a not infrequent visitor to Berlin. What was possibly his first meeting with Hitler took place at the Berlin Olympic Games in August 1936. Although the meeting was brief, it was of considerable symbolic value to Henlein, as he disclosed during a subsequent, and longer, conversation with the German Minister of Foreign Affairs, Constantin von Neurath. The SdP leader's visit to Germany coincided with a period of internal disputes within the party between the Nazi radicals and Henlein's closest associates from the *Kameradschaftsbund*, which was only resolved by the mediation of Berlin. In this connection, Neurath informed his visitor that, contrary to the belief of the radical faction, there was no immediate prospect of direct German military involvement in Czechoslovakia.[53] Although during that particular visit Henlein appears not to have received any specific instructions from the German government, it would not be so on a future occasion.

The authorities in Prague responded to the rising tide of the SdP by concluding an agreement with the German 'activist' parties – the Agrarians, Social Democrats and Christian Socials (who had re-entered the government in 1936[54]). The initiative came from the 'activists', who, in an attempt to counteract the growing strength of the SdP, presented a series of demands to the Czechoslovak government. The outcome, known as the Agreement of 18 February 1937, reaffirmed existing minority rights and contained specific undertakings on matters such as the awarding of public works contracts to local contractors, greater employment of minority nationalities in the public service, and improved educational provision for these groups.[55] The measures were easily characterised as being exceedingly modest, and Henlein lost little time in doing so.

Within a few weeks, the SdP produced its own proposals for reform, tabling a series of six parliamentary bills which included provision for equality of opportunity in public service employment and protection against administrative malpractice. More significant, however, were measures aiming to divide the population into autonomous national associations, with compulsory registration of members and protection against the enforced transfer (of individuals and property) from one group to another. In the eyes of their critics, these SdP proposals exhibited clear totalitarian overtones, envisaging not only the division of the population into national groups but also that each national association would be headed by an extra-parliamentary leader.[56] Predictably, the Czechoslovak government was strongly opposed to legislation of this nature and there was little prospect of the bills being enacted.

While this inconclusive manoeuvring was taking place in Prague, British foreign policy makers were beginning to devote increasing attention to the situation in Czechoslovakia. The issue was discussed at a meeting in the Foreign Office in late February 1937, when it was again decided to take no action apart from encouraging Czechoslovakia to seek good relations with Germany. It was feared that more active intervention might result in committing Britain to assist Czechoslovakia if talks failed.[57] The informal encouragement to Beneš was to be offered by Britain's new Minister in Prague. Doubtless much to the relief of the authorities in London and Prague alike, Addison retired from that position in the autumn of 1936. He was briefly succeeded by Charles Bentinck, who in turn, in March 1937, was followed by Basil Newton, previously Minister at the Berlin Embassy.[58] Newton retained his new post until the German occupation of Bohemia and Moravia in March 1939, and was destined therefore to play a key role as the crisis over Czechoslovakia unfolded. His standing instructions on arrival in Prague were, whenever possible, to urge upon the government the 'importance of a far-reaching settlement' of the Sudeten German problem, not in order to facilitate an agreement with Germany, but because it would enhance Czechoslovakia's reputation 'for humane and generous treatment of her minorities'.[59]

Although the Foreign Office took some encouragement from the agreement reached by the Czechoslovak government with the 'activist' parties, this soon gave way to disappointment when it became apparent that a similar understanding with the SdP was not in prospect.[60] It was also believed in London that more effective leverage might be exerted on the Czechoslovak authorities if that were carried out in concert with France, Czechoslovakia's principal ally. The French government, however, was disinclined to join the British, particularly when the Foreign Office suggested that the desired settlement with Henlein should include the admission of the SdP to the Czechoslovak Cabinet. The French Foreign Minister, Yvon Delbos, refused to countenance the British idea, pointing out that it would be equivalent to bringing pressure to bear on the Austrian Chancellor, Kurt von Schuschnigg, to take Austrian Nazis into his government, thus enabling them to undermine it from within.[61]

Whilst the Foreign Office was seeking more effective means of influencing developments in Central Europe, representatives of the Sudeten

Germans continued to travel to London in the hope of securing British support. The visitors came not only from the SdP but also from one of the 'activist' parties. In February 1937, Wenzel Jaksch, a prominent member of the German Social Democrats, was received at the Foreign Office by O'Malley, but Vansittart dismissed him as insignificant.[62] Nevertheless, Jaksch returned to London in November to address the Royal Institute of International Affairs on 'activist' policy in Czechoslovakia.[63] Even more intensive was the activity undertaken in London by the SdP, who, during the previous year, established Walter Brand, a close associate of Henlein, as permanent representative in western Europe.[64] Another of Henlein's close colleagues, Rutha, also travelled to Britain twice during 1937, in February and July. On each occasion, as during his previous visit, he had a meeting in the Foreign Office with Cranborne.[65] The most significant visitor, however, was Henlein himself, who arrived in London in October.

Henlein's visit also followed a familiar pattern; he gave an interview to the *Daily Telegraph*,[66] and addressed the Royal Institute of International Affairs. At Chatham House, Henlein repeated his assurances of moderation and loyalty to Czechoslovakia, stressing that 'at no time had Germany sought to influence or dictate the policy of his party – or vice versa'. He denied that the SdP's parliamentary bills were totalitarian in nature and that they posed a threat to the 'activist' parties.[67] Henlein also renewed his contact with Vansittart. The two men were seated alongside at a dinner, during the course of which they conversed, in German, for almost three hours. Vansittart characterised the discussion as both 'interesting and depressing', noting that although Henlein remained a 'relatively moderate' man, he was 'more excited and embittered' than previously.

Henlein complained to Vansittart about the deteriorating situation of the Sudeten Germans, adding that well over 90 per cent of them now favoured incorporation in Germany. He saw three possible outcomes: autonomy within Czechoslovakia, autonomy within Germany, or complete absorption into Germany. The SdP leader maintained that he would continue to strive for the first solution, as it alone would avoid a cataclysmic world war which would not only destroy the Sudetenland but civilisation in general. He also made the astonishing observation (some five months before the event itself took place) that the authorities were unlikely to make any significant concessions to the Sudeten Germans until Czechoslovakia's position had been weakened by the German absorption of Austria. Having made the Permanent Under-Secretary's flesh creep by such revelations, Henlein then offered a solution. He stressed that only an appeal from Britain or France – made directly to Beneš – had any prospect of securing the concessions required from the Czechoslovak side. Henlein added that such a move would need to be made without delay, as he could not restrain his followers' desire to join Germany for much longer.[68]

Vansittart was clearly shaken by Henlein's table-talk, and lost little time in drawing Eden's attention to the 'important and disturbingly illuminating conversation'.[69] However, not everyone at the Foreign Office was quite so impressionable. Christopher Bramwell, of the Southern Department, suggested that evidently 'Berlin was fast tightening its grip' over Henlein and that his lurid statements, which had to be taken 'with a large lump of salt', were designed to persuade Britain and France to intensify their pressure on Beneš.[70] That was an isolated view however, and in its scepticism unrepresentative of the Foreign Office.

Henlein's latest visit to London did indeed result in increasing British pressure on the Czechoslovak authorities, although immediately following his return to Czechoslovakia, Henlein overplayed his hand somewhat by appearing to claim the support of the British government. He did so in an open letter, addressed to Beneš, concerning an incident at Teplice (Teplitz) on 17 October, during which Czechoslovak police clashed with SdP members of parliament following a political meeting. In his indignant protest, Henlein not only demanded immediate steps towards administrative autonomy for the Sudeten Germans but also claimed that he had 'met with the greatest understanding' during his recent visit to London.[71] An embarrassed Foreign Office hastened to assure the Czechoslovak government that Henlein was referring to sympathy expressed in the press and by Members of Parliament, and that the British government itself had merely advised cooperation and moderation.[72] Nevertheless, the irritation caused in London by Henlein's claim did little to reduce the practical impact of his visit.

The Teplice incident, coming on top of the warning given by Henlein in London, and being followed by an intensive German press campaign against Czechoslovakia,[73] convinced the Foreign Office that the situation in Central Europe was deteriorating. In addition, Henlein's urging that an approach be made to Beneš in person reinforced the belief that the main stumbling block to progress was the President himself.[74] During an audience with Beneš on 9 November, Newton, in the tactful language of diplomacy, duly relayed his government's concern that a 'disunited and distraught' Czechoslovakia could not constitute an effective 'deterrent to German aggression in Central Europe' and observed that the failure to resolve the Sudeten German problem provided a 'temptation to extremists in Germany'. Britain suggested therefore, that the 'policy of pin-pricks' towards the German minority be abandoned, 'unnecessary irritation' avoided, and that they be 'deprived of [their] grievances' through improvements in economic and social conditions.[75]

Beneš responded to Newton's unsolicited advice with an undertaking to increase recruitment into the public service from the German minority.[76] Predictably, this was received with disappointment in London,[77] where Foreign Office attention was already turning towards other means of alleviating the situation, in particular towards some form of autonomy for the

Sudeten Germans. However, as Beneš indicated to Newton, 'autonomy' was 'a vague phrase and mischievous', because it meant different things to different people.[78] The Foreign Office therefore sought Newton's advice on the matter.[79] He distinguished three types of autonomy. The first – territorial autonomy – which was demanded by some 'extremists' amongst the Sudeten Germans, would, in Newton's view, result in a 'geographical absurdity' and the probable incorporation of the areas concerned into Germany and Austria. The remaining two forms – personal autonomy and cultural autonomy – were, Newton explained, elements of the SdP's recent proposals, the six parliamentary bills, (although he confessed to have some difficulty fully comprehending these on account of their 'vagueness'). In practical terms, however, he believed that most of Henlein's grievances could be alleviated by making the Agreement of 18 February 1937 enforceable in law and applicable also to the SdP; by extending autonomy in the field of education; by holding local elections (postponed in the wake of the Teplice incident[80]); and by the appointment of German officials in German districts. The British Minister was fully aware that such measures would not satisfy the SdP, but they would at least provide a breathing space.

Newton then turned to the wider question of German intentions in Central Europe, which he interpreted as being 'to manoeuvre Czechoslovakia into her orbit'. That deduction flowed from the observed inconsistency between Germany's 'violent tirades' concerning the treatment of the Sudeten Germans and the friendly relations with Poland and Italy, despite the fact that German minorities in those countries, Newton noted, received 'far worse treatment' than did the minority in Czechoslovakia. He suggested therefore that Czechoslovakia was now in a state of 'unstable equilibrium' and that it was in Britain's interest to move it into a 'position of natural stability'. This prompted Newton to pose the question: 'Would it not be in [the Czechs'] real interests to get on better terms with Germany, even at some cost to their independence?'[81]

Newton's question remained, for the moment, unanswered but much of his exposition concerning the issue of autonomy was incorporated into a Foreign Office briefing paper prepared for Franco-British ministerial talks held in London in late November 1937. The memorandum amounted to a counsel of despair. It concluded that even after a scheme of autonomy acceptable to both parties concerned was devised, some inducement would need to be offered to the Czechoslovak government to implement it. The only inducement likely to be effective was a British guarantee of Czechoslovakia, given in conjunction with France and Germany. That, however, was rejected out of hand as being 'in the highest degree unlikely' to be acceptable to British public opinion.[82]

The discussions between the British and French governments demonstrated clear differences in perception. Whereas Chamberlain and Eden placed emphasis on urging Beneš to make concessions to the Sudeten

Germans, their respective counterparts, Camille Chautemps and Yvon Delbos, wished to see calls for moderation also being addressed to Germany. Moreover, unlike his hosts, Delbos expressed fears that Germany was intent on annexing the Sudeten territories and argued that allegations of Czechoslovak mistreatment of the German minority served merely as a convenient pretext. The most the French Foreign Minister would agree to was, on his forthcoming visit to Prague in December, to urge Beneš to avoid the 'appearance of provocation', but he refused to press for Sudeten German autonomy.[83]

Whilst the British government searched fruitlessly for an effective policy towards Czechoslovakia, Henlein was addressing a revealing memorandum to Hitler concerning the policies and the problems of the SdP. The document, prepared during November 1937, accused Czechoslovakia's political leaders of anti-German attitudes and actions, as evidenced by their provision of a base 'for the Western Powers in the very heart of the German *Lebensraum*'; by their alliance with the Soviet Union; and by their association with forces hostile to the Reich and National Socialism, such as 'political Catholicism and the Vatican, Jewry and Freemasonry, Bolshevism and Refugee Emigration'. Henlein also pledged his party's support for Germany, emphasising that the SdP was 'imbued with National Socialist principles' and organised as a 'National Socialist Party, based on the Führer concept'.

Doubtless these were precisely the sentiments that Hitler wished to hear, but the real purpose of the memorandum was to account for the disunity within the SdP and to seek support against the dissident elements in the party. Henlein explained that operating within a democratic parliamentary system the SdP was obliged to 'camouflage its profession of National Socialism', adding:

> The apparent lack of unity of the Sudeten German Party is intensified by the circumstance that at heart it desires nothing more ardently than the incorporation of the Sudeten German territory, nay the whole of Bohemian, Moravian, and Silesian area, within the Reich, but that outwardly it must stand for the preservation of Czechoslovakia and for the integrity of its frontiers, and must try to display some apparently genuine aim in the sphere of internal politics to justify its political struggle.

That however, created further problems. It had become 'senseless to advocate autonomy' of the Sudetenland as that territory had become the fortified frontier of Czechoslovakia. Hence, Henlein sought clarification of the SdP's role and guidance on future actions.[84]

Although several months were to elapse before Henlein received a response to his initiative, unbeknown to him, Hitler had discussed the future of Czechoslovakia earlier in November at a meeting of the Commanders-in-Chief of the three armed services and the Ministers of War and Foreign Affairs. Hitler outlined to this exclusive audience his thoughts on military expansion during the 1943–45 period. The first objective, he declared, 'must be to overthrow Czechoslovakia and Austria simultaneously'. Hitler added the observation that Britain, and possibly France also, had 'already tacitly written off the Czechs'.[85]

Hitler's belief that Britain had abandoned Czechoslovakia would not have been undermined by the outcome of the visit to Germany made by Lord Halifax, Lord President of the Council (in effect Minister without portfolio). Halifax, who was ostensibly attending an International Sporting Exhibition in his capacity as Master of the Middleton Hounds, met Hitler on 19 November 1937. During the course of their conversation, Halifax indicated that Britain would not object to alterations to the *status quo* in Central Europe providing that any changes were the outcome of peaceful evolution.[86] Halifax was articulating the views of the Prime Minister, who shortly afterwards disclosed (in a letter to his sister Ida) that he did not see why 'we shouldn't say to Germany, give us satisfactory assurances that you won't use force to deal with the Austrians and Czecho-Slovakians and we will give you similar assurances that we won't use force to prevent the changes you want if you can get them by peaceful means'.[87] Within three months of undertaking his visit to Germany, Halifax had replaced Eden as Foreign Secretary.

The first clear public indication of Hitler's attitude towards the Sudeten Germans and other German minorities outside the Reich was given in a speech to the Reichstag in February 1938, in which he declared Germany's interest in over ten million fellow-nationals who lived in two states adjacent to Germany. That interest included the protection of those who were 'unable to ensure for themselves the right to a general freedom, personal, political, and ideological'. Although Hitler did not refer to Czechoslovakia by name, the inference was obvious when he added a commendation to Poland for having concluded a non-aggression treaty with Germany in 1934, when, under the leadership of Marshal Piłsudski, there had been 'no western parliamentarianism in Warsaw'.[88] Within a month of Hitler's speech, one of the two countries alluded to, Austria, was annexed to Germany, and Czechoslovakia alone remained.

The Czechoslovak government viewed this development with the utmost concern, despite calming assurances received from Berlin.[89] The *Anschluss* of Austria on 13 March 1938 resulted in Germany establishing a potential stranglehold on the western part of Czechoslovakia not least because, through the extension of its territory, Germany outflanked Czechoslovakia's defensive fortifications, which were incomplete along the southern frontier with former Austria. (Newton likened the new geographical situation of Bohemia and Moravia to 'the butt end of a champagne cork' protruding into German territory.[90]) Internally also the situation deteriorated, with the *Anschluss* bringing about the end of

Sudeten German 'activism'. Two of the three German parties that participated in the Czechoslovak government, the German Agrarians and the Christian Socials, succumbed to pressure from a jubilant SdP, merging with it in late March and their ministers resigning from the government. The third party, the German Social Democrats, remained in sole opposition to the SdP, but even they ceased to be represented in the Czechoslovak Cabinet.[91]

Having just digested Austria, Hitler was not yet ready to move against Czechoslovakia. He nevertheless agreed to see Henlein only two weeks after the *Anschluss*. The meeting took place on 28 March 1938 in the presence of Hitler's deputy, Rudolf Hess, the new Foreign Minister, Joachim von Ribbentrop, and the head of the agency responsible for German minorities outside the Reich, the *Volksdeutsche Mittelstelle*, Werner Lorenz. Henlein was accompanied by his deputy, K.H. Frank. During the course of a three-hour conversation, Hitler assured Henlein of his rightful position as Sudeten German leader, and indicated his intention to resolve the Sudeten German issue in the near future. The SdP leader was instructed, in the interim, to continue making demands unacceptable to the Czechoslovak government. Henlein summarised Hitler's wishes in the words: 'We must always demand so much that we can never be satisfied.'[92] He would closely adhere to these instructions over the coming six months.

The *Anschluss* also gave rise to increased anxiety in London. Although the fate of Austria itself did not greatly perturb the British government, which registered no more than a perfunctory protest concerning the annexation[93] and rejected a call by the Soviet government for an international conference,[94] the heightened tension in Central Europe caused much concern. Consequently, the question of Czechoslovakia moved to the top of the British government's political agenda.

Notes

1 *Parliamentary Debates*, 5th series, *House of Commons* (hereafter cited as *HC Deb.*), vol. 338, cols 2957–8.

2 *News Chronicle*, 25 July 1938. The information had come from Paris, where, on 20 July, the Foreign Secretary, Lord Halifax, accompanying the King and Queen on an official visit, had informed the French government of the projected British initiative. (E.L. Woodward and R. Butler, eds, *Documents on British Foreign Policy, 1919–1939*, (hereafter cited as *DBFP*), Third Series, I, no. 523.)

3 Radio broadcast, 27 September 1938. See *The Times*, 28 September 1938; N. Chamberlain, *In Search of Peace; Speeches 1937–1938*, (ed. A. Bryant; London, 1939), p. 275.

4 E. Wiskemann, *Czechs and Germans; A Study of the Struggle in the Historic Provinces of Bohemia and Moravia*, (2nd edn, London, 1967), p. 4.

5 See F. Palacký (ed.), *Gedenkblätter*, (Prague, 1874), p. 149. For an English translation see 'Letter sent by František Palacký to Frankfurt', *Slavonic and East European Review*, XXVI (1948), p. 304.

6 The term Sudetenland (*die Sudetenländer*) was originally applied by Austrian Germans to the Historic Provinces of the Empire; hence their German inhabitants were referred to as Sudeten Germans (*Sudetendeutsche*). See J.W. Bruegel, *Czechoslovakia before Munich: The German Minority Problem and British Appeasement Policy*, (Cambridge, 1973), p. 22.

7 Most significant was the province of German-Bohemia (Deutsch-Böhmen) centred on Liberec (Reichenberg). A second unit, consisting of the German districts of Northern Moravia and Silesia, centred on Opava (Troppau), styled itself Sudetenland. Two further units, the Bohemian Forest District in southern Bohemia and the territory of German Southern Moravia, sought incorporation into adjacent Austria. *Ibid.*, pp. 22–3.

8 Wiskemann, *Czechs and Germans*, p. 84. The incidents took place on 4 March 1919.

9 D. Perman, *The Shaping of the Czechoslovak State: Diplomatic History of the Boundaries of Czechoslovakia, 1914–1920*, (Leiden, 1962), pp. 165–76.

10 Wiskemann, *Czechs and Germans*, pp. 85–6.

11 Perman, *The Shaping of the Czechoslovak State*, pp. 121–55.

12 *Statistická příručka Československé republiky*, (Prague, 1928), III, p. 275. Census of 1921.

13 Wiskemann, *Czechs and Germans*, pp. 87–9; H.W.V. Temperley, ed., *A History of the Peace Conference of Paris*, (6 vols, London, 1920–24), V, pp. vii, 155.

14 Bruegel, *Czechoslovakia before Munich*, pp. 48–9.

15 The full text of Beneš's note appears in Wiskemann, *Czechs and Germans*, pp. 92–3.

16 Bruegel, *Czechoslovakia before Munich*, p. 51. For details of the Czechoslovak Minorities Treaty see Temperley, ed., *History of the Peace Conference*, V, pp. 461–70.

17 Wiskemann, *Czechs and Germans*, pp. 147–60.

18 The Social Democrats, Agrarians, and Christian Socials secured 17 per cent of votes for the Chamber of Deputies; the Nationalists and Nazis gained just over 5 per cent. (J. Rothschild, *East Central Europe between the Two World Wars*, (Seattle, 1974), p. 116.)

19 Wiskemann, *Czechs and Germans*, pp. 165–96. Wiskemann describes the Sudeten German territory as 'a gigantic distressed area without hope of recovery' (p. 190).

20 Bruegel, *Czechoslovakia before Munich*, pp. 103–20, 131–2. The German government supplied Henlein with 300 000 marks for the 1935 general election and thereafter made regular payments of 15 000 marks per month. See Memorandum by Stieve, 27 February 1935, *Documents on German Foreign Policy*, (hereafter cited as *DGFP*), Series C, III, no. 509 and Memorandum by Woermann, 19 August 1938, *ibid.*, Series D, II, no. 375.

21 Wiskemann, *Czechs and Germans*, p. 264; Bruegel, *Czechoslovakia before Munich*, p. 152. Early in 1938, the German Minister in Prague, Ernst Eisenlohr, looking back over the development of the SdP noted: 'What seemed so terrible to the Czechs in the Sudeten German Party – and not wrongly so from their point of view – was not only its numerical strength, the ideological similarity with National Socialism, the "undemocratic" Führer principle, and the totalitarian claim, ... but it was above all the fact that this party does not claim to represent material or religious interests but the entire German section as such, by emphasising the racial ideal.' (Eisenlohr to Foreign Ministry, 4 February 1938, *DGFP*, D/II, no. 53.)

22 R.M. Smelser, *The Sudeten Problem, 1933–1938: Volkstumspolitik and the Formulation of Nazi Foreign Policy*, (Folkestone, 1975), pp. 53–66. The extent to which Henlein was an agent of the German government in Berlin is a matter of controversy amongst historians. Bruegel maintains that Henlein was a faithful 'henchman of Hitler' from the outset. (*Czechoslovakia before Munich*, p. 109.) Smelser, however, argues that Henlein did not fall under the control of Berlin until late in 1937. (*The Sudeten Problem*, pp. 252–3.)

23 Bruegel, *Czechoslovakia before Munich*, pp. 103–4.

24 *Ibid.*, pp. 86–102. For a more detailed study of the relationship see F.G. Campbell, *Confrontation in Central Europe; Weimar Germany and Czechoslovakia*, (Chicago, 1975).

25 Royal Institute of International Affairs, *Documents on International Affairs*, (hereafter cited as RIIA, *Documents*), 1935, I, pp. 138–9.

26 Wiskemann, *Czechs and Germans*, pp. 239, 241.

27 *Ibid.* pp. 200, 269–70.

28 Bruegel, *Czechoslovakia before Munich*, p. 122.

29 For table of results see Rothschild, *East Central Europe between the Two World Wars*, p. 126.

30 Henlein visited London in December 1935, July 1936, October 1937 and May 1938. (He may also have visited London earlier in 1935. See Public Record Office, Hadow to Hoare, 21 December 1935, R 7759/234/12, FO 371/19493.) For a discussion of Henlein's visits see K.G. Robbins, 'Konrad Henlein, the Sudeten Question and British Foreign Policy', *Historical Journal*, XII (1969), pp. 674–97.

31 Record of Anglo-Czechoslovak Conversation, Prague, 4 April 1935, W.N. Medlicott and M.A. Dakin, eds, *DBFP*, Second Series, XII, no. 693.

32 *International Affairs*, XV (1936), pp. 561–72; Memorandum by Bramwell, 10 December 1935, R 7511/234/12, FO 371/19493.

33 See the *Daily Telegraph*, 10 December 1935 and the London *Evening Standard*, 17 March 1936.

34 Memorandum by Norton, 10 December 1935, R 7511/234/12, FO 371/19493.

35 Minute by Vansittart, 16 December 1935, *ibid.*

36 Minute by Hankey, 21 December 1935, *ibid.*

37 Record of Interview between Vansittart and Henlein, enclosed in Eden to Addison, 27 July 1936, R 4395/32/12, FO 371/20374. The meeting took place on 20 July. Henlein's warning had come to the attention of the Foreign Office some months previously. (Hadow to Eden, 31 January 1936, R 675/32/12, FO 371/20373.) For Henlein's account of his visit to London, see Stein to Foreign Ministry, 21 July 1936, *DGFP*, C/V, no. 465.

38 Memorandum by Cranborne, 23 July 1936, R 4460/32/12, FO 371/20374.

39 Eden to Addison, 5 August 1936, *ibid.*

40 Masaryk to Vansittart, 28 July 1936, R 4705/32/12, FO 371/20374.

41 Eden to Addison, 5 August 1936, R 4460/32/12, FO 371/20374.

42 Addison to Eden, 25 August 1936, R 5216/32/12, FO 371/20375. Addison's critique of the internal policies of the 'Czech rulers' drew attention to the multitude of ethnic tensions within the state (including that between Czechs and Slovaks); to the discontent felt by all the minority nationalities (including the Slovaks); and, in particular, to the oppression suffered by the Sudeten Germans. He added that Czechoslovakia 'presents to the outside world the semblance of a bulwark of democracy, freedom and liberty, whereas it is in fact a "Polizeistaat" similar to other States where arbitrary rule prevails'.

43 Minutes by Vansittart, 10 September 1936, and Eden, 15 September 1936, *ibid.* Eden added: 'Whatever the faults of the Czechs, they are tough and they have a good fighting record.'
44 'Sir J. Addison's reports on the Sudetendeutsche question in Czechoslovakia', 7 October 1936, R 6487/32/12, FO 371/20375.
45 Memorandum by O'Malley, 13 October 1936, R 6724/32/12, FO 371/20375. A detailed memorandum concerning the German minority in Czechoslovakia (beginning in the fifth century) was prepared in the Foreign Office early in 1936. (Memorandum by McDermott, 8 April 1936, R 971/971/12, FO 371/20376.)
46 N. Rose, *Vansittart: Study of a Diplomat*, (London, 1978), pp. 135–6. See also T.P. Conwell-Evans, *None so Blind*, (London, 1947).
47 Memorandum by Christie, June 1936, R 3662/32/12, FO 371/20374. Christie's general attitude towards Germany's role in Central and Eastern Europe was revealed in the following sentence: 'Many of us may feel that an Interessen-Gemeinschaft of States (I.G.) stretching from the Baltic to the Black Sea might not be the least satisfactory solution to the German and Danubian problems, provided the structure is confederative and the hegemony of Berlin does not superimpose itself too severely upon the Slav, Magyar and other non-Germanic peoples.'
48 Copy of letter from Christie to unknown addressee, 26 September 1935, Christie Papers, CHRS 180/1/11; Christie to Vansittart, 16 June 1937, Christie Papers, CHRS 180/1/21A, Churchill College, Cambridge. The Christie Papers also contain a number of letters from Henlein to Christie dating from December 1935 to December 1937 (CHRS 180/1/11 and CHRS 180/1/19). See also L. Thompson, *The Greatest Treason: The Untold Story of Munich*, (New York, 1968), pp. 22, 275.
49 Henlein to Sargent, 19 December 1935, and Sargent to Addison, 31 December 1935, R 32/32/12, FO 371/20373.
50 See, for example, memorandum by McDermott on the 'German minority in Czechoslovakia', 8 April 1936, R 971/971/12, FO 371/20376. It commends Henlein's 'moderation' (without a trace of irony) as being 'almost too good to be true', whilst castigating the Czechoslovak government for 'continuing and intensifying their discrimination against Germans'.
51 Minute by Gallop, 2 November 1934, R 6108/1070/12, FO 371/18382.
52 See below p. 16.
53 Memorandum by Neurath, 14 August 1936, *DGFP*, C/V, no. 508.
54 A representative of the Christian Socials became Minister without portfolio.
55 E. Beneš, *Mnichovské dny*, (Prague, 1968), pp. 12–15; Bruegel, *Czechoslovakia before Munich*, pp. 148–9.
56 Wiskemann, *Czechs and Germans*, pp. 257–60.
57 J. Harvey, ed., *The Diplomatic Diaries of Oliver Harvey, 1937–1940*, (hereafter cited as *Harvey Diaries*), (London, 1970), pp. 18–19.
58 For further details see below p. 133.
59 Eden to Newton, 12 March 1937, *DBFP*, 2/XVIII, no. 279.
60 Minute by Sargent, 5 May 1937, R 2886/188/12, FO 371/21128.
61 Memorandum by Bramwell, 21 October 1937, R 7101/188/12, FO 371/21131.
62 Minutes by O'Malley, 20 February 1937, and Vansittart, 23 February 1937, R 903/188/12, FO 371/21127.
63 Report by Hadow, 12 November 1937, R 7634/188/12, FO 371/21131.
64 R. Luža, *The Transfer of the Sudeten Germans: A Study of Czech–German Relations, 1933–1962*, (New York, 1964), p. 65, n. 11. Brand, a member of the KB faction,

was forced out of the party leadership by internal disputes. He divided his time between Paris and London.

65 Memoranda by Cranborne, 11 February 1937, R 1072/188/12, FO 371/21127, and 16 July 1937, R 4896/188/12, FO 371/21130.

66 See the *Daily Telegraph*, 15 October 1937.

67 Report by Hadow, 15 October 1937, R 6899/154/12, FO 371/21125.

68 Memorandum by Vansittart, 18 October 1937, *DBFP*, 2/XIX, no. 253.

69 Minute by Vansittart, 19 October 1937, R 6982/188/12, FO 371/21131.

70 Minute by Bramwell, 19 October 1937, *ibid.*

71 Open letter from Henlein to Beneš, 18 October 1937, R 7016/188/12, FO 371/21131. The letter was published in the Reich German press but suppressed by censorship within Czechoslovakia. Henlein's opponents claimed that the Teplice incident was exploited by the SdP in order to deflect attention from the arrest of Rutha, Henlein's close associate, for alleged homosexual offences against minors. Rutha later committed suicide whilst in detention. (Bruegel, *Czechoslovakia before Munich*, pp. 158–9).

72 Newton to Eden, 9 November 1937, R 7540/188/12, FO 371/21131. Following representation from Masaryk, Sargent suggested that 'balance' might be restored in a Parliamentary answer to a planted question. Vansittart also wished to correct Henlein's 'cheating', but Eden was opposed. (Minutes by Sargent, 6 November 1937, Vansittart, 9 November, and Eden, 19 November 1937, R 7574/188/12, FO 371/21131.)

73 Memorandum by Bramwell, 21 October 1937, R 7107/188/12, FO 371/21131.

74 Minute by Ingram, 26 October 1937, *ibid.*

75 Eden to Newton, 6 November 1937, R 7376/188/12, FO 371/21131; Newton to Eden, 9 November 1937, *DBFP*, 2/XIX, no. 305.

76 Newton to Eden, 9 November 1937, R 7540/188/12, FO 371/21131.

77 Minute by Nichols, 16 November 1937, *ibid.*

78 Newton to Eden, 9 November 1937, *ibid.*

79 Sargent to Newton, 11 November 1937, R 7357/188/12, FO 371/21131.

80 Newton to Eden, 9 November 1937, R 7540/188/12, FO 371/21131.

81 Newton to Sargent, 22 November 1937, R 7807/188/12, FO 371/21132.

82 Foreign Office memorandum, 26 November 1937, R 8248/188/12, FO 371/21132.

83 Record of Franco-British conversations, 29 and 30 November 1937, *DBFP*, 2/XIX, no. 354; *Documents Diplomatiques Française, 1932–1939*, (hereafter cited as *DDF*), Série 2, vol. VII, no. 287.

84 Report for Hitler enclosed in Henlein to Neurath, 19 November 1937, *DGFP*, D/II, no. 23. The memorandum itself is unsigned.

85 Memorandum by Hossbach, 10 November 1937, *DGFP*, D/I, no. 19. For an outline of the controversy surrounding the 'Hossbach Memorandum' see R. Boyce and E.M. Robertson, eds, *Paths to War: New Essays on the Origins of the Second World War*, (London, 1989), p. 5.

86 Report by Halifax on his visit to Germany, 17–21 November 1937, *DBFP*, 2/XIX, no. 336; Memorandum on Halifax's conversation with Hitler on 19 November 1937, *DGFP*, D/I, no. 31.

87 Neville Chamberlain to Ida Chamberlain, 26 November 1937, *DBFP*, 2/XIX, no. 349.

88 N.H. Baynes, ed., *The Speeches of Adolf Hitler*, (2 vols, London, 1942), II, pp. 1404–6. Speech delivered on 20 February 1938. Poland contained a German

minority of just over one million. (A. Polonsky, *The Little Dictators: The History of Eastern Europe since 1918*, (London, 1975), p. 158.)
89 Masaryk to Halifax, 12 March 1938, *DBFP*, 3/I, no. 63.
90 Newton to Halifax, 16 May 1938, *DBFP*, 3/I, no. 221.
91 Bruegel, *Czechoslovakia before Munich*, pp. 170–2.
92 Henlein's report on meeting with Hitler, 28 March 1938 [?], *DGFP*, D/II, no. 107.
93 Henderson to Neurath, 11 March 1938, *DBFP*, 3/I, no. 47.
94 Maisky to Halifax, 17 March 1938, *DBFP*, 3/I, no. 90; Halifax to Maisky, 24 March 1938, *DBFP*, 3/I, no. 116.

2
Avoiding a Commitment

The main features of British policy towards Czechoslovakia in 1938 were determined, within days of the German annexation of Austria, during a series of ministerial meetings between 18 and 22 March. The first and most significant of these was a meeting of the Cabinet Committee on Foreign Policy (established in response to the German re-militarisation of the Rhineland in 1936), consisting of the Prime Minister, the Foreign Secretary and a small number of other senior members of the Cabinet.[1] The Committee considered a paper from the Foreign Secretary, entitled 'Possible Measures to Avert German Action in Czechoslovakia', based on three key assumptions: that Germany would continue to seek the incorporation of the Sudeten Germans into the Reich; that the SdP (in Halifax's words, 'now suspected of being in Nazi pay') would continue to grow in influence; and that the military position of Czechoslovakia had been substantially weakened by the annexation of Austria. The problem of Czechoslovakia itself was divided into two components: the situation of the German minority and the security of the state itself. Concerning the former, Halifax reasoned that it was incumbent upon the Czechoslovak authorities to satisfy both the British government and public opinion 'not only that the Sudeten Germans enjoy the treatment to which they are entitled, but also such treatment as will leave the German government with no reasonable cause for complaint'.

The main attention of the paper was focused on the second aspect of the problem, the protection of Czechoslovakia. Halifax identified three possible policy alternatives. The first was a 'grand alliance' of states to resist aggression as envisaged by Winston Churchill. This he immediately rejected as impractical on account of the time required to bring it into being, during the course of which Germany might act against Czechoslovakia. The second option was an indirect commitment to Czechoslovakia, with Britain undertaking to assist France, conditional upon satisfactory treatment of the Sudeten Germans, to be determined by a commission of enquiry with either British or international membership. The third alternative outlined was not to offer any new commitment but to seek to persuade France and Czechoslovakia, as Halifax explained, 'that the best course would be for the latter to make the best terms she can with Germany while she can perhaps still do so in more favourable conditions than would obtain later'.

Considering, more generally, Germany's possible intentions, Halifax questioned the wisdom of risking a major war in order to stop German expansion in Central Europe. Although he conceded that such a risk might be justified on the grounds that Czechoslovakia formed a further step towards Germany's objective of hegemony over continental Europe, which would eventually lead to a clash with Britain, the Foreign Secretary thought otherwise. He doubted whether the annexation or subjection of Czechoslovakia would 'necessarily be a source of over-powering strength to Germany'.

Although Halifax's preference for no further commitment emerges clearly from the paper, he indicated that he would have fewer objections to giving a conditional guarantee to France if the commission of enquiry 'would not be debarred from recommending a drastic solution of the Sudetendeutsch problem, even a plebiscite under neutral supervision and control'. He justified this attitude by citing a recent dispatch from Prague, in which Newton argued that '"having regard to her geographical situation, her history and the racial divisions of her population, Czechoslovakia's present political position is not permanently tenable"'.[2] The Foreign Secretary added that he would be prepared to risk seeking to deter Germany if Britain were 'to go to great lengths in bringing the Czechoslovak government to agree to measures which will settle the Sudeten question in conformity with the realities of the situation, unpleasant as those realities may be'. He would do so because 'in that event Germany would have less reason to risk the hazards of war in order to obtain what she could have some hope of obtaining by peaceful negotiation'.[3] In effect, Halifax indicated that even if a conditional undertaking were given to France, as far as Czechoslovakia was concerned, the outcome would be much the same as if no guarantee were given. He evidently considered that Britain could best avoid a war with Germany by inducing the Czechoslovak government to accept the as yet unspecified demands of Berlin concerning the Sudeten Germans.

The subsequent discussion in the Foreign Policy Committee[4] provided a further revealing insight into the minds of those directing British foreign policy. Chamberlain himself had few doubts concerning German intentions, observing that although the seizure of the whole of Czechoslovakia would not be in accordance with Hitler's policy of including all Germans – but not other nationalities – in the Reich, it was 'most likely that Germany would absorb the Sudeten German territory and reduce the rest of Czechoslovakia to a condition of dependent neutrality'. Later in the discussion, Halifax again questioned the assumption that if Germany thereby gained control over Central Europe, it would necessarily come into conflict with Britain and France. He believed, however, that if Britain were to associate itself more closely with France and the Soviet Union, Germany would fear encirclement and a settlement would prove more difficult. Halifax's underlying supposition distinguished 'between Germany's racial effort, which no one could question, and a lust for conquest on a Napoleonic scale, which he himself did not credit'. The discussions revealed another characteristic fear held in Whitehall circles that, in the event of a war over Czechoslovakia, the British Commonwealth would disintegrate. Chamberlain also discounted the possibility of the United States becoming actively involved in European affairs.

As far as the policy alternatives outlined by Halifax were concerned, no support was given to the idea of protecting Czechoslovakia by the formation of a 'grand alliance'. In fact, not one of the Cabinet ministers present uttered a single word in defence of Czechoslovakia. It was left to the Cabinet Secretary, Sir Maurice Hankey (who had played a prominent secretarial role at the Paris Peace Conference[5]), to remind the Committee that the frontiers of Bohemia were historic ones and that during the formation of the state at the end of the First World War 'it had been recognised that Czechoslovakia could only continue to exist if the whole territory were maintained as one unit'. Hankey's remarks, however, fell on deaf ears.

Even the second alternative, that of an indirect guarantee to Czechoslovakia by undertaking to assist France, attracted very little support, although there was wide agreement that the security of France was of considerable concern to Britain. This point was made succinctly by Oliver Stanley, the President of the Board of Trade, who stated that 'we are not vitally interested in the fate of Czechoslovakia, but we are vitally interested in that of France'. He was inclined therefore, to support the idea of giving a new but limited commitment to France, conditional upon Britain being satisfied that the German minority in Czechoslovakia was being 'properly treated'. This would best be achieved by having a 'British representative continuously on the spot'. Other members of the Committee, however, opposed the idea of giving such support to France. Their underlying fear was articulated by Chamberlain, who expressed his intense dislike of being placed in a situation where the decision to involve Britain in a war with Germany rested with the French government.

In that connection, military considerations were obviously of paramount importance. Although a full up-to-date assessment of the military situation following the annexation of Austria was not yet available – a report by the Chiefs of Staff was under preparation – the Minister for Co-ordination of Defence, Sir Thomas Inskip, stated categorically that, in the event of an attack by Germany, Czechoslovakia would be overrun in 'less than a week' and that no available military force could prevent this. A British naval blockade of Germany could not be effective in time to save the situation.

The belief that Czechoslovakia was indefensible was shared by Chamberlain who added that, despite the quality of the French army, France was also in an otherwise 'hopeless position'.

In view of these attitudes, there remained only the third alternative outlined – that of doing nothing. This inaction commended itself to Halifax on the grounds that the existing arrangements left the British government, in theory at least, with considerable freedom of manoeuvre, allowing it to determine whether or not to assist France according to the circumstances. He considered that situation to have the advantage of placing restraints on both France and Germany by keeping them 'guessing' of British intentions. Those present at the meeting failed to point out that this attitude, though perhaps prudent in dealings with a potential enemy, was hardly appropriate to a relationship between allies.

Concerning the Sudeten German question itself, Chamberlain declared that he was 'disturbed' by the fact that Halifax contemplated a solution of the problem without directly involving Germany. He recalled that Hitler, in conversation the previous year with the Aga Khan, had stated that he wished to see the German areas of Czechoslovakia receive autonomy similar to the arrangement between the United Kingdom and Eire. Chamberlain added cautiously, however, that since then Hitler 'might have changed his mind', but felt nevertheless that such a solution was worth exploring. Later in the discussion, he ventured the opinion that Germany would not resent the suggestion from Britain that the problem should be resolved by negotiation. 'If Germany could obtain her *desiderata* by peaceable methods', Chamberlain argued, 'there would be no reason to suppose that she would reject such a procedure in favour of one based on violence.' When the Chancellor of the Exchequer, Sir John Simon, rejoined that this would encourage the German minority to demand incorporation in Germany, Chamberlain agreed that 'ultimately this would no doubt be so' but he thought that 'in the first place our objective should be the retention by Czechoslovakia of the Sudeten areas with some measure of local autonomy'. Evidently, British ministers were not only aware that the tension concerning the Sudeten Germans was being orchestrated from Berlin, but also had no doubts concerning Hitler's real intentions towards Czechoslovakia. This was six months before the demand for the incorporation of the Sudetenland in Germany was actually articulated by Hitler, and at a time when the SdP itself was asking for no more than autonomy for the German areas.

Summarising the discussion, Halifax concluded that 'we must decline to undertake fresh commitment in regard to Czechoslovakia'. The reality was, he continued, 'that there was no country able, or indeed willing, to help' and, ultimately, this would 'compel Czechoslovakia to make a settlement with Germany if she was to survive'. The Foreign Secretary added that Britain might 'vigorously impress on Germany' the importance of 'an orderly settlement of the Sudeten question' and that every effort was being made to persuade the Czechoslovak authorities to adopt 'a fair and reasonable attitude'. As far as Czechoslovakia and France were concerned, Halifax continued, 'we should have to point out frankly and clearly that this was a very bad wicket on which to bat'. Although no formal decision was taken, mainly due to the absence of the military assessment by the Chiefs of Staff, and although it was agreed to continue the discussion at a further meeting in three days' time, the issue was in fact resolved – the integrity and independence of Czechoslovakia would not be guaranteed.

That was the message conveyed by Halifax on his return to the Foreign Office following the Cabinet Committee meeting. On hearing the news, Sir Alexander Cadogan, who had replaced Vansittart as Permanent Under-Secretary of State earlier in the year, noted in his diary, with evident satisfaction: 'FPC unanimous that Czechoslovakia is not worth the bones of a single British Grenadier. And they're quite right too!'[6]

The memorandum presented by Halifax to the Foreign Policy Committee was, of course, not his work alone, but prepared in conjunction with his senior advisers, including Cadogan. As was to be expected in the aftermath of the German annexation of Austria, the Foreign Office had been plunged into a flurry of activity assessing the implications for British foreign policy. During the week preceding the Foreign Policy Committee meeting, three separate papers were produced examining various aspects of the new situation.[7] Cadogan admitted that they were 'dictated by the embarrassment in which we find ourselves as the result of the Germans taking a step which had long been foreseen, and taking it unexpectedly, rapidly and efficiently'.[8]

Concerning Czechoslovakia, most significant was the paper by William Strang, head of the Central Department (to which responsibility for Czechoslovakia had been transferred at the beginning of 1938). It was used by Halifax as the basis for his, much shorter, memorandum for the Cabinet Committee. Strang's paper provided a detailed assessment of the Sudeten German problem and its international ramifications. It even contained a possible scenario for the German 'nominally "peaceful"' liquidation of Czechoslovakia:

(i) The Czechoslovak Government would be prevailed upon to allow the Germans in Czechoslovakia to organise themselves more fully than at present on a racial basis ...;

(ii) That Sudetic German Ministers should be admitted into the Czechoslovak Government;

(iii) That the Sudetic German party, being progressively more and more organised on the lines of the National Socialist party, with uniforms, storm-troopers and the rest, should, by its own action and through the action of its Ministers in the Government, acquire predominant influence in Czechoslovakia, which would thus become a kind of vassal State of Germany;

(iv) That the Sudetic German regions should become to all intents and purposes autonomous and self-governing;

(v) This might be followed by the incorporation of the German districts in the Reich, and the dismemberment of Czechoslovakia, the Czech population of Bohemia and Moravia enjoying a kind of autonomy within the Reich, and the Slovaks perhaps returning to Hungary whence they came.[9]

Though not accurate in matters of detail, this prediction was nevertheless to be substantially borne out by subsequent events.

Strang's advice to Halifax also contained three policy options. Two of these, the 'grand alliance' and the indirect conditional guarantee, were taken up by Halifax; but the third was significantly different. Strang did not consider the possibility of no action being taken; his third option was a direct British commitment to Czechoslovakia. He immediately ruled this out, however, on the grounds that it would be 'difficult to obtain public support for the assumption of obligations in regions remote from our direct interests'. Halifax was evidently in total agreement and did not consider this alternative even worth putting to his Cabinet colleagues. Unlike Halifax however, Strang came down in favour of an indirect guarantee in the form of a conditional commitment to France, which was the 'least objectionable' of the possibilities considered. The commitment would be conditional upon the Czechoslovak authorities satisfying Britain and France that everything possible had been done to remove the grievances of the German minority, which could be verified by a joint British–French, or purely British, commission of enquiry.

The two other Foreign Office papers prepared in response to the German annexation of Austria were of less direct use to Halifax, one because its recommendations were not to his liking, the other because it was not specifically concerned with Czechoslovakia. The first of these was written by Sir Orme Sargent, the Assistant Secretary of State superintending the Central Department. It indeed presented, what Cadogan termed, a 'gloomy picture',[10] arguing that the danger of war in Europe had greatly increased and that Hitler was intent on dismembering Czechoslovakia and gaining hegemony over Central Europe. To counter this, Sargent offered suggestions for mobilising British diplomatic resources, advocating closer co-operation with Britain's continental friends and allies, principally with France, but also Belgium, Greece and Turkey, coupled with a determined effort aimed at arousing the interest of the United States of America. He further proposed developing relations with countries such as Japan, Italy, the Soviet Union and Poland, in order to assure their neutrality. Other states that considered themselves threatened by German expansion – including, by inference, Czechoslovakia – should be offered assistance, mainly in the form of military equipment. The only alternative envisaged by Sargent was an alliance with Germany in order to protect British interests by assisting to promote those of Germany at the expense of others. That, however, was clearly repugnant to Sargent as it would involve 'withdrawal from the League [of Nations], abandonment of our special relations with France, and the loss of our reputation in the world at large and especially in the United States'.[11]

In the last of the three papers, Gladwyn Jebb, private secretary to Cadogan, rejected Sargent's idea of an anti-German alliance, on the grounds that it might precipitate a war for which Britain was unprepared. If an early war with Germany was to be avoided, he argued, Britain and France must secure the friendship of Italy and detach it from its alliance with Germany. Jebb believed that this could be achieved by encouraging Franco's victory in the Spanish Civil War and, subsequently, by guaranteeing Italy against Germany. As far as Czechoslovakia was concerned, it would have to be sacrificed to Germany, for Mussolini's support could not be gained to oppose this. Only following the German absorption of Czechoslovakia was Italy likely to consider opposing further German expansion. Jebb believed that an equilibrium could then be achieved between an enlarged Germany ('the new Holy Roman Empire') and the West European powers including Italy.[12]

Although the general tenor of Jebb's thinking was in tune with Halifax's ideas – particularly concerning a rapprochement with Italy – the method suggested by Jebb did not commend itself to the Foreign Secretary. Sargent's proposals however, found even less favour with Halifax – as was evident from the Foreign Secretary's remarks to the Foreign Policy Committee. Halifax did not share Sargent's fears concerning German intentions and hence did not accept his conclusions.

Much more to the liking of the Foreign Secretary was undoubtedly the advice offered by Cadogan in a memorandum accompanying the other papers. Cadogan conceded that Hitler probably intended absorbing the Sudeten Germans into Germany, but considered that not to constitute adequate grounds for unleashing a European war. Looking further ahead, he did not believe that the annexation of Austria and the possible incorporation of the Sudetenland were necessarily the first steps in an eastwards expansion of Germany. German hegemony over Central and South-Eastern Europe was improbable, though German economic domination over the area was a distinct possibility. Cadogan did not see why that should be particularly distressing for Britain, which had other markets elsewhere. More immediately, Cadogan was opposed to any commitment being given to safeguard Czechoslovakia, unless the Chiefs of Staff report was much more encouraging than he expected it would be. Instead, he also favoured efforts to reach an understanding with Italy, and simultaneously advocated an intensification of British rearmament, particularly in terms of air power. Cadogan's outlook, at least in the medium term, was pessimistic: 'If we stand aside from Central Europe, we and the French may lose face, but the reverse may steel us to efforts that may make good some of our present deficiencies.'[13] He evidently envisaged the dismemberment of Czechoslovakia by Germany as a form of catharsis, essential for Britain's ultimate well-being.

The Foreign Office, however, was not the only source of advice concerning the new situation in Central Europe; the Prime Minister also had clear views on the matter. Chamberlain claimed that his first reaction following the *Anschluss* was to favour the idea of a 'grand alliance' to protect Czechoslovakia made public by Churchill, but which, he wrote to his sister Ida on 20 March, 'had occurred to me long before he mentioned it'. Despite its initial appeal, he soon rejected the plan on ground of practicability:

> You have only to look at the map to see that nothing that France or we could do could possibly save Czecho-Slovakia from being over-run by the Germans if they wanted to do it. ... Therefore we could not help Czecho-Slovakia – she would simply be a pretext for going to war with Germany. That we could not think of unless we had a reasonable prospect of being able to beat her to her knees in a reasonable time and of that I see no sign. I have therefore abandoned any idea of giving guarantees to Czecho-Slovakia or to France in connection with her obligations to that country.[14]

Having made up his mind in this way, Chamberlain found to his 'great satisfaction' that 'Halifax had come independently to the same conclusion'.[15]

But within the Foreign Office, Halifax's senior advisers were less unanimous. Sargent's wish to see positive action taken to protect Czechoslovakia received vigorous support from Vansittart, who now occupied the position of Chief Diplomatic Adviser (a much less influential position than he had held previously[16]). Cadogan, on the other hand, continued to argue against a guarantee on the grounds that 'we *must* not precipitate a conflict now – or we shall be smashed'.[17] This argument, similar to that advanced by Chamberlain, carried the day.

Although, understandably, the immediate preoccupation of ministers and Foreign Office personnel in London was with the wider strategic implications of the developments in Central Europe, it is nevertheless surprising that the idea of using a guarantee as an inducement to the Czechoslovak authorities to settle the German minority problem – considered the key to the solution of the wider international crisis – received so little attention. Despite the fact that (as previously mentioned) this possibility was raised in Halifax's memorandum for the Foreign Policy Committee, the proposal found little support during the Committee meeting. However, the idea was developed further the following day by Sir William Malkin, the Legal Adviser to the Foreign Office, who suggested Czechoslovakia should be offered protection only if it negotiated a settlement with Germany, and, conversely, should receive British support if Germany refused to negotiate.[18] But the proposition was taken no further, for anxious though the British government was to see the Sudeten German problem resolved, it was not prepared to pay the price of guaranteeing Czechoslovakia's existence. Other means would have to be found to attain that objective.

The seeds of one such attempt made during the summer of 1938 to resolve the problems of Czechoslovakia – the Runciman Mission – were, in fact, contained within the preconditions Halifax attached to considering, albeit only briefly, an indirect guarantee. The stipulation in question was the proposed establishment of a commission of enquiry into the Sudeten German problem, first suggested by Strang. The idea, which was prompted by an interview with Beneš published in the *Sunday Times* in early March,[19] found influential support in the Foreign Office. It was not only taken up and developed by Cadogan,[20] but also further elaborated by Halifax in his paper for the Foreign Policy Committee. The Foreign Secretary interpreted Beneš's remarks as indicating that 'the Czechoslovak Government might be prepared to receive a neutral commission, with powers to examine and report upon the situation of the German minority'. Expanding a little on the idea, Halifax added that an

> Anglo-French Commission would perhaps not be desirable, but if it were found necessary to include a French member, it might be well to include some neutral members also, say of Swedish or Swiss nationality, as well as a United States member, who might perhaps be Mr. Hoover – possibly as Chairman.[21]

Nevertheless, despite the attention it received, the contemplated commission of enquiry, being linked to an indirect guarantee of Czechoslovakia, disappeared from consideration following the decision not to adopt that policy.

A further explanation for the, albeit temporary, abandonment of the idea of a commission of enquiry may be found in a fuller consideration within the Foreign Office of Beneš's press interview. Commenting on the suggestion of the Labour peer and former cabinet minister, Lord Noel-Buxton, that the Sudeten German problem should be resolved by a plebiscite and the subsequent transfer of territory to Germany,[22] Ivo Mallet, of the Central Department, argued that this was based on a misinterpretation of Beneš's words. In his interview with the *Sunday Times*, Beneš had indicated a willingness to supply the British and French governments with information concerning the nationalities, but he also stressed that the Sudeten German question constituted 'an internal issue which can never be the subject of direct official negotiation or discussion with a foreign Power'.[23] Mallet believed that the statement did not constitute an offer to accept the 'mediation of a friendly Power', as Noel-Buxton argued. He went on to speculate that if British mediation were refused by the Czechoslovak authorities 'we should, I suppose, wash our hands of them and thereby give a false justification to the German invasion, which would undoubtedly follow'.[24] Mallet's reasoning presumably applied equally to the proposed commission of enquiry, favoured by his Foreign Office superiors, which was also inspired by Beneš's interview. Neither Halifax nor Cadogan recorded their reactions to Mallet's arguments, but the idea of a commission of enquiry was not considered again until the end of May, when new avenues towards a solution were being urgently explored.

In addition to the commission of enquiry, Strang's paper also explored four further possible solutions. The first was a suggestion that the Czechoslovak authorities should negotiate a settlement of the Sudeten German problem directly with Berlin, and enter into a new treaty with Germany, similar to those concluded by Germany with Poland and Belgium. But the price demanded by Germany was likely to be substantial, and might include the renunciation of Czechoslovakia's alliances with France and the Soviet Union. Nevertheless, Strang argued that, in view of Czechoslovakia's weakness, it might be prudent 'to make the best of a bad job' and wise for Britain and France to urge such a course. On the other hand, however, in the light of the recent experience of Austria in negotiations with Germany, Strang conceded that it would be difficult to recommend the same procedure to Czechoslovakia. An additional problem arose from the insistence of the Czechoslovak authorities that the German minority question was an internal matter and therefore of no direct concern to Germany. This attitude effectively disposed of another possible solution advanced by Strang, that of recourse to the 1925 Arbitration Treaty between Germany and Czechoslovakia, whereby unresolved disputes were to be resolved by international adjudication.

The remaining alternatives analysed in the paper also failed to stand up to scrutiny. Hitler's reported suggestion to the Aga Khan that Germany would guarantee the independence of Czechoslovakia in exchange for Sudeten German autonomy was, as Strang saw it, fraught with problems. Not only would the negotiation of Sudeten autonomy be far from easy, but it would also be most difficult subsequently to establish the truth concerning any alleged breaches of that autonomy, upon the maintenance of which the German guarantee would be conditional. Furthermore, if Britain and France were also to become guarantors of Czechoslovakia, Strang considered that for Britain this would constitute 'an embarrassing addition to existing commitments'. The last possibility examined, that of a plebiscite to determine whether the Sudetenland should be incorporated in Germany, was also problematical. Strang observed that, in order for a plebiscite to be valid, pressurisation and intimidation of the electorate would have to be guarded against, possibly by the supervision of neutral troops. In addition, due to the complex distribution of the German and Czech nationalities within the area concerned, any transfer of territory determined by a plebiscite would have to be accompanied by an exchange of population.[25]

The resolution of Czechoslovakia's German minority problem was also concerning the Prime Minister. He, however, adopted a much less complicated approach than Strang. Chamberlain proposed simply to say to Hitler, as he wrote to his sister on 20 March, 'tell us exactly what you want for your Sudeten Deutsch. If it is reasonable we will urge the Czechs to accept it and if they do you must give assurances that you will let them alone in future'. Chamberlain added that in those circumstances he might even be willing to guarantee, jointly with Germany, the independence of Czechoslovakia. He also observed that his idea of approaching Germany did not greatly appeal to the Foreign Office, 'they don't want us to approach Hitler but to tell Beneš to go to him direct'.[26]

Opinion within the Foreign Office was not, in reality, as unanimous as Chamberlain indicated. Although it was principally Halifax who favoured pressuring the Czechoslovak authorities to negotiate directly with the German government, at least two of his advisers – Strang[27] and Sargent – expressed reservations in view of the recent experience of Austria. Sargent minuted his objections in forthright terms, maintaining that the proposed policy was based on the false premise of Germany's readiness to fight a prolonged major war. Arguing that Germany had not directly involved itself in the problem of Czechoslovakia, he added:

> If we now go to Berlin with an offer to coerce (for that is what it is) the Czech[oslovak] Gov[ernmen]t to submit to German demands, we shall be practically inviting the German Gov[ernmen]t to open the question and having opened it they will naturally be under the temptation to force it to a conclusion by whatever means are available to them. ... In thus intervening without accepting any responsibility for the result of our intervention, we are ... weighing down the scales most unfairly against the weaker party. What chance in such conditions will Czechoslovakia have of a fair deal with Germany, when at our bidding Beneš, following in Schuschnigg's footsteps, goes alone and unsupported to interview Hitler at Bergtesgaden [*sic*]?[28]

The Prime Minister, however, disagreed with Halifax's preferred mode of action for a different reason. As Chamberlain indicated to his sister, he envisaged the approach to Germany being a continuation of the discussions between Halifax and Hitler in November 1937, and offering an opportunity to 'restore the confidence' Hitler had shattered by annexing

Austria. Encouraged by improved relations with Italy and on the basis of other information received, he believed that the German government would respond positively to such an initiative, which would at least postpone a crisis and perhaps even avert it.[29] Evidently, Chamberlain hoped that a negotiated solution of the Sudeten German problem would provide a basis for an understanding between Britain and Germany and therefore wished to see Britain seize the initiative. He was looking beyond the immediate problems of Czechoslovakia towards the greater goal of a settlement between Britain and Germany. Nevertheless, Chamberlain had not given direct voice to these ideas two days previously during the meeting of the Foreign Policy Committee. Although he made the suggestion at that meeting that Britain might appeal to Germany for a negotiated solution of the Sudeten German problem, he gave no indication of dissenting from Halifax's summing up 'that the best course would be for Czechoslovakia to make the best terms she could with Germany'.[30]

That advice was reiterated in a memorandum presented to the Foreign Policy Committee on 21 March[31] – the second of the three crucial meetings of ministers which determined British policy towards Czechoslovakia. This meeting was less directly concerned with Czechoslovakia itself than had been the case three days previously. The major decision not to guarantee Czechoslovakia, either directly or indirectly, having been effectively taken, it remained only to be decided how best to inform France. This delicate matter was discussed at some length by members of the Committee who had before them a draft memorandum for the French government prepared by the Foreign Secretary.[32] The document argued that Britain and France must persuade Czechoslovakia, in its 'own interests and in the interest of European peace, to enter into early negotiations with the German Government' to seek to resolve the Sudeten German problem.

In his opening remarks, however, Halifax amended the text deleting this and other references. Taking his cue from Sargent, Halifax explained that he sought to avoid the criticism that Britain 'wished to drive Dr. Beneš into a visit to Berchtesgaden'.[33] The Foreign Secretary also deleted a lengthy reference to a possible direct British approach to Germany under the terms of the Czechoslovak Minorities Treaty, in order to see 'justice done' to the German minority. The deleted section further suggested that Berlin might be informed of the British government's willingness 'to contribute all that lay within [its] power' to resolve the Sudeten German question.[34] The paragraph substituted by Halifax indicated merely that any approach to Germany would be the subject of prior consultation between London and Paris, adding that the agreement of Germany was a prerequisite for any solution.[35]

Having made the indicated changes to the memorandum, the Foreign Secretary proceeded to justify his opposition to giving a guarantee to France concerning Czechoslovakia. Halifax considered the deterrent value of such an undertaking to be questionable; he did not see how the *status quo* could be restored following a German attack; and, lastly, did not wish Britain to undertake any commitment, either direct or indirect, towards Czechoslovakia. He added that he found the idea of a conditional guarantee to France, advocated by Stanley at the previous meeting of the Committee, equally unacceptable.

Stanley responded with a spirited defence of his proposal, arguing that the document under consideration would have a 'catastrophic' effect on France, which caused Halifax to remark (pointedly perhaps) that this view was also shared by Vansittart. But Stanley's voice was an isolated one, although Malcolm MacDonald, the Dominions Secretary, and Sir Samuel Hoare, the Home Secretary, who were opposed to any new guarantee, both sought to see included in the memorandum a re-affirmation of Britain's existing commitment to France under the Treaty of Locarno. Even Chamberlain found Halifax's draft document 'stiff and unsympathetic', but, while not wishing to cause France unnecessary offence, he remained resolutely opposed to Britain undertaking any further commitments. As a result of the discussion, Halifax agreed to 'warm up' the document, but again emphatically rejected the idea of any guarantee being included.[36]

At the meeting on 21 March, the Foreign Policy Committee also considered a first draft of a statement to be made by the Prime Minister in the House of Commons on 24 March. The draft, prepared by the Foreign Secretary, emphasised in particular the dangers inherent in a guarantee being given to Czechoslovakia, which might result in Britain being dragged automatically into war.[37] It was again Stanley who offered pungent criticism of the document, arguing that it was too negative in tone, and suggesting that emphasis be given to Britain's obligations towards Czechoslovakia under the Covenant of the League of Nations. In response, Halifax observed that if the draft 'gave the impression of sloppiness and defeatism' it would have to be reconsidered. It was agreed that Chamberlain and Halifax would produce a revised version in consultation with other members of the Committee.[38]

The ministers also had before them one further document, the crucial report of the Chiefs of Staff on the new military situation concerning Czechoslovakia. This report concluded that 'no pressure that we or our possible allies can bring to bear ... could prevent Germany from invading and over-running Bohemia and from inflicting a decisive defeat on the Czechoslovakian Army'. The territorial integrity of Czechoslovakia could only be restored, the report argued, following the defeat of Germany, which would take considerable time. Moreover, any British involvement in a war against Germany would probably result not in a limited European war but in a 'world war', as both Italy and Japan are likely to become involved.[39] The Chiefs of Staff report was not discussed in any detail by the Foreign Policy Committee, although Halifax referred to its conclusion that it was 'hopeless to prevent Germany overrunning Czecho-Slovakia', and it is doubtful whether most members of the Committee could have familiarised themselves thoroughly with this 15-page document as it was only made available during the course of the meeting itself.[40] Moreover, it should be noted that the decision not to guarantee Czechoslovakia had, in effect, been made three days previously, without the benefit of formal military advice.

The last of the three key meetings of ministers which determined British policy towards Czechoslovakia was the meeting of the full Cabinet on 22 March, which ratified the decisions taken earlier by the Foreign Policy Committee. For the benefit of ministers who were not members of the Committee, Halifax again outlined the essence of the problem as he saw it, pointing out that, following the *Anschluss* of Austria, Czechoslovakia had become highly vulnerable to attack and that there was 'grave anxiety about Czechoslovakia especially owing to the French commitments to that country'. Initially he himself and, he thought, the Prime Minister also, had felt 'some sympathy' towards the idea of a direct or indirect guarantee of Czechoslovakia. However, in view of the assessment of the military situation by the Chiefs of Staff (placed before the Cabinet), and which Halifax described as an 'extremely melancholy document', he was unable 'to recommend a policy involving a risk of war'. He suggested, therefore, that Britain, with French assistance, 'should endeavour to induce' the Czechoslovak authorities to resolve the Sudeten German problem. Developing further the reconsideration of policy announced during the Foreign Policy Committee meeting the previous day, Halifax stressed that he envisaged a settlement between the Czechoslovak government and the Sudeten Germans themselves, although Britain and France might subsequently urge Germany to accept the outcome.[41]

The decision not to undertake to defend Czechoslovakia having been formally taken, it remained only to inform, in suitably phrased terms, those concerned. On the day following the Cabinet meeting, 23 March, Halifax authorised the British Ambassador in Paris, Sir Eric Phipps, to transmit to the French government the considerably re-written and 'warmed up' memorandum considered previously by the Foreign Policy Committee.[42] The *aide-mémoire* noted that, although Britain would honour its existing commitments, it was unable to add to them, suggesting instead that the two governments jointly use 'their good offices with the Government of Czechoslovakia to bring about a settlement' of the Sudeten German problem. The outcome envisaged in London 'would be compatible with ensuring the integrity of the Czechoslovak State', and would retain the German minority 'within the frontiers of Czechoslovakia'. France was assured of the 'high importance' Britain attached to the 'closest collaboration', and was urged to consider further joint action in the search for a solution.[43]

In addition to this written communication, Halifax, acting on Chamberlain's suggestion that the British views might be conveyed to French ministers verbally,[44] furnished Phipps with certain other arguments which he 'hesitated to commit to paper'. These points concerned the inadvisability of issuing warnings to Germany concerning Czechoslovakia, the inadequacy of British and French military preparations, and the economic vulnerability of Czechoslovakia. Halifax also indicated that, prior to the problem of the Sudeten Germans being resolved, it would 'be necessary, at some stage, to bring the German Government into the negotiations' because 'good relations' between Germany and Czechoslovakia could only be established if Berlin was satisfied with the implemented solution. It would, therefore, 'sooner or later be necessary to approach the German Government on this matter'. Although this point was not mentioned in the *aide-mémoire*, Halifax stressed the importance of bringing it to the attention of the French government in order to forewarn of British intentions.[45]

When Phipps duly transmitted these views to the French Foreign Minister, they met with a hostile reception. Joseph Paul-Boncour strongly objected to the proposed approach to Germany, arguing that it would be resented by the Czechoslovak authorities and, moreover, would constitute a dangerous precedent for other countries with German minorities. The French government, which believed that the minorities in Czechoslovakia received better treatment than was the case elsewhere, continued to favour a joint warning being given by Britain and France to Germany concerning the likely consequences of aggression against Czechoslovakia.[46] This proposition, which had been made in more general terms earlier in the year, prior to the annexation of Austria, was rejected by the British government, which was not prepared to threaten to go to war.[47]

When an outline of the new British policy was communicated to Czechoslovakia itself, no indication was given of the proposed involvement of Germany. Newton was instructed to transmit the decision, reached with the 'greatest regret', not to undertake specifically to protect Czechoslovakia but to add that the British government, 'within the limits of their ability, will do everything to assist the Czechoslovak Government, who can be assured of their sympathy and goodwill towards a solution of their difficulties'. Meanwhile, the Czechoslovak authorities were urged 'in the interests of international peace' to take every possible step 'to remove the causes of friction or even conflict arising out of the present minority problem'. Halifax also envisaged that the two governments would, at some future date, enter into an 'exchange of views' on the matter.[48]

Although, understandably, the Czechoslovak government was not informed of the intended direct involvement of Germany in negotiations concerning the Sudeten Germans, it is clear from Halifax's instructions to Phipps that this plan was a definite one, despite the fact that only the previous day Halifax had indicated to the Cabinet that it was no more than a possibility. Indeed, the Cabinet conclusions specifically stated that Britain and France would approach Germany, with a view to urging it to accept any settlement reached in Czechoslovakia, only 'if circumstances should render this advisable'.[49] The discrepancy between the official policy of the Cabinet and the intentions of the Foreign Secretary is significant. The policy formally adopted by the Cabinet in March 1938 resembled a compromise between Chamberlain's idea of Britain itself seeking a solution of the Sudeten German problem through negotiations with Germany, and Halifax's original suggestion that Britain should avoid direct involvement and merely pressure the Czechoslovak government into negotiating with Hitler. It appeared as if both these ideas were being set aside and a third alternative adopted – that of pressuring the Czechoslovak government into negotiations with the Sudeten Germans. This policy was officially to remain in force until it was overtaken by the events of September 1938, but the real attitude of those directing British foreign policy already pointed clearly in the direction of Munich. Chamberlain's plan for negotiating directly with Germany over Czechoslovakia was not abandoned but merely postponed whilst, hopefully, the preliminaries of a settlement were arranged between the Czechoslovak government and representatives of the Sudeten Germans. Moreover, the distinction between the Czechoslovak authorities negotiating with the SdP instead of the German government was one of form rather than of substance, for British policy-makers were aware that the SdP was not independent of Berlin. Pressuring the Czechoslovak government to negotiate with the SdP, however, would be less damaging to its susceptibilities than the alternative of being forced into direct negotiations with Germany, and the former course might therefore be less difficult to achieve.

The logical assumption underlying British policy appeared to be the belief that the Sudeten German problem could be resolved by compromise acceptable to both the SdP (and therefore the German government) and the government of Czechoslovakia. It is clear, however, from the deliberations held in London during March 1938, that many of those responsible for policy formulation were themselves not convinced that a compromise solution was possible, but, in their anxiety to avoid a war with Germany, were prepared to explore any avenue, no matter how unpromising. And besides, even if it proved impossible to achieve a solution acceptable to both Czechoslovakia and Germany, it was believed in London that the alternative of Czechoslovakia capitulating to German demands, thus compromising its existence as an independent sovereign state, would not necessarily be prejudicial to British interests, providing that peace was maintained.

But this was not a view shared by all. Within the Foreign Office, Sargent had become acutely depressed by the developing British attitude, which (in the eyes of one observer) made him contemptuous of the government and full of anxiety for the future.[50] He minuted:

> One thing I think we must accept as a fact, and that is that Hitler will never be *satisfied* with a compromise solution, e.g. cultural, local autonomy, etc. Even if Hitler were to accept it as a *pis aller* for the time being, once he started absorbing Central Europe, he cannot afford to have an independent and bitterly hostile Czech[oslovak] State on his flank. ... We must, I think therefore, take it that Hitler will be compelled in self defence to break up Czechoslovakia as it is at present and to take control of the Czech nucleus himself.
>
> For this reason, I fear that no compromise solution to the Czech[oslovak] problem is by itself going to restore security and confidence. For Europe will continue to be kept on tenter-hooks awaiting the day when to use Mr. Newton's somewhat ominous phrase Czechoslovakia 'adjusts her position to the circumstances of post-war Europe' by which, I suppose, he means Gleichschaltung with the Reich.[51]

Despite this pertinent advice, the search for the elusive compromise was to occupy much of the attention of the British government throughout the spring and summer of 1938. Yet already in March, the outlines of future developments in British policy concerning Czechoslovakia were discernible. The solutions contemplated in London included not only the initially preferred one of pressuring the Czechoslovak government into making concessions to the Sudeten Germans, but also the subsequently adopted policies of attempted British mediation inside Czechoslovakia (as yet in the embryonic form of a commission of enquiry) and, ultimately, direct negotiations with Germany. For the time being, however, the two last-mentioned options were to remain in reserve, and the British government was to expend every effort in implementing the first alternative, that of pressuring the Czechoslovak authorities into an agreement with the SdP. But one crucial decision had definitely been taken – Britain would not undertake to defend Czechoslovakia in the event of German aggression.

Notes

1 In addition to Chamberlain, who was in the chair, and Halifax, the Committee consisted of Sir John Simon (Chancellor of the Exchequer), Sir Samuel Hoare (Home Secretary), Malcolm MacDonald (Dominions Secretary), Sir Thomas Inskip (Minister for Co-ordination of Defence), Lord Hailsham (Lord President of the Council), W. Ormsby-Gore (Colonial Secretary) and Oliver Stanley (President of the Board of Trade). R.A. Butler (Parliamentary Under Secretary in the Foreign Office) attended on occasions. Sir Maurice Hankey was secretary. (FPC Minutes, 18 March 1938, FP (36) 26th Meeting, CAB 27/623.)

2 See Newton to Halifax, 15 March 1938, *DBFP*, 3/I, no. 86.

3 Memorandum by Halifax, 'Possible Measures to Avert German Action in Czechoslovakia', 18 March 1938, appendix I to FPC Minutes, 18 March 1938, FP (36) 26th Meeting, CAB 27/623.
4 FPC Minutes, 18 March 1938, FP (36) 26th Meeting, CAB 27/623.
5 Hankey had not only been secretary to the British delegation, but had also acted in a similar capacity for the supreme body of the Conference, the Council of Four (Clemenceau, Lloyd George, Orlando and Wilson). See S. Roskill, *Hankey: Man of Secrets*, (3 vols, London, 1970–74), II (1972), pp. 43–101.
6 D. Dilks, ed., *The Diaries of Sir Alexander Cadogan, O.M., 1938–1945*, (London, 1971), p. 63.
7 'Memoranda on the Situation Created by the German Absorption of Austria and on the possibility of German Action in Czechoslovakia', C 1866/132/18, FO 371/21674.
8 Memorandum by Cadogan, 17 March 1938, *ibid.*
9 Memorandum by Strang, 17 March 1938, *ibid.* Strang added, however, that the process described, which would take some considerable time to complete, would probably be interrupted by a crisis, resulting in a German ultimatum to Czechoslovakia and possibly in the outbreak of war between the two countries.
10 Memorandum by Cadogan, 17 March 1938, C 1866/132/18, FO 371/21674.
11 Memorandum by Sargent, 13 March 1938, *ibid.* Oliver Harvey, Halifax's Private Secretary at the Foreign Office, noted in his diary on 15 March 1938 that Sargent had 'put up a paper urging that we should give an indirect guarantee to Czechoslovakia'. (Harvey, ed., *Harvey Diaries*, p. 116.) Sargent appears not to have been as specific as that.
12 Memorandum by Jebb, 17 March 1938, C 1866/132/18, FO 371/21674.
13 Memorandum by Cadogan, 17 March 1938, *ibid.*
14 Neville Chamberlain to Ida Chamberlain, 20 March 1938, Chamberlain Papers, NC 18/1/1042, University of Birmingham Library.
15 Neville Chamberlain to Hilda Chamberlain, 27 March 1938, Chamberlain Papers, NC 18/1/1043.
16 Until the beginning of 1938, Vansittart held the post of Permanent Under-Secretary of State. His tough anti-German posture was unwelcome to his political superiors, Chamberlain and Eden, and resulted in his removal from that key position in the Foreign Office. This was achieved through the creation of a new post, that of Chief Diplomatic Adviser – a virtual sinecure. In his new post Vansittart's access to official papers was limited and, as Harvey (then Eden's Private Secretary) noted in his diary, Vansittart functioned as an adviser 'only if and when asked'. (Harvey, ed., *Harvey Diaries*, p. 66. See also I. Colvin, *Vansittart in Office*, (London, 1965), pp. 169–74.)
17 Dilks, ed., *Cadogan Diaries*, p. 63.
18 Memorandum by Malkin, 19 March 1938, C 1970/1941/18, FO 371/21712.
19 *Sunday Times*, 6 March 1938.
20 Minute by Cadogan, 17 March 1938, C 1866/132/18, FO 371/21674.
21 Memorandum by Halifax, 'Possible Measures to Avert German Action in Czechoslovakia', 18 March 1938, appendix I to FPC Minutes, 18 March 1938, FP (36) 26th Meeting, CAB 27/623. Presumably, Halifax had in mind Herbert Hoover, the former President of the United States.
22 'Memorandum on the suggestion for a plebiscite in the Sudetenland', by Noel-Buxton, undated, C 1957/1941/18, FO 371/21712 and C 2707/1941/18, FO 371/21714.

23 *Sunday Times*, 6 March 1938.
24 Minute by Mallet, 28 March 1938, C 1957/1941/18, FO 371/21712.
25 Memorandum by Strang, 17 March 1938, C 1866/132/18, FO 371/21674.
26 Neville Chamberlain to Ida Chamberlain, 20 March 1938, Chamberlain Papers, NC 18/1/1042.
27 Memorandum by Strang, 17 March 1938, C 1866/132/18, FO 371/21674.
28 Minute by Sargent, 19 March 1938, C 1933/132/18, FO 371/21674. A marginal note by Cadogan poses the question, 'What about the "10,000,000 Germans" outside the Reich?' (See above, p. 17.) The reference to Berchtesgaden concerns the visit made there by the Austrian Chancellor, on 12 February 1938, during which he was forced by Hitler, under threat of a German invasion, to agree with the appointment of the leader of the Austrian National Socialists, Artur Seyss-Inquart, to the key post of Minister of the Interior. See K. Schuschnigg, *Austrian Requiem*, (London, 1947), pp. 20–32.
29 Neville Chamberlain to Ida Chamberlain, 20 March 1938, Chamberlain Papers, NC 18/1/1042.
30 FPC Minutes, 18 March 1938, FP (36) 26th Meeting, CAB 27/623.
31 FPC Minutes, 21 March 1938, FP (36) 27th Meeting, CAB 27/623. Attendance at this meeting was identical with that of 18 March.
32 FPC Papers, FP (36) 56, CAB 27/627.
33 FPC Minutes, 21 March 1938, FP (36) 27th Meeting, CAB 27/623.
34 FPC Papers, FP (36) 56, CAB 27/627.
35 FPC Minutes, 21 March 1938, FP (36) 27th Meeting, CAB 27/623.
36 *Ibid.*
37 Memorandum by Halifax, 'Situation in Central Europe – Czechoslovakia', FPC Papers, 21 March 1938, FP (36) 58, CAB 27/627.
38 FPC Minutes, 21 March 1938, FP (36) 27th Meeting, CAB 27/623.
39 'Report of the Chiefs of Staff Sub-Committee on Military Implications of German Aggression against Czechoslovakia', FPC Papers, FP (36) 57, CAB 27/627.
40 FPC Minutes, 21 March 1938, FP (36) 27th Meeting, CAB 27/623.
41 Cabinet Minutes, 22 March 1938, Cabinet 15 (38), CAB 23/93.
42 Halifax to Phipps, 23 March 1938, *DBFP*, 3/I, no. 108.
43 Halifax to Phipps, 23 March 1938, *DBFP*, 3/I, no. 106 and enclosure.
44 FPC Minutes, 21 March 1938, FP (36) 27th Meeting, CAB 27/623. Halifax pointed out that normal diplomatic practice also required an *aide-mémoire*.
45 Halifax to Phipps, 23 March 1938, *DBFP*, 3/I, no. 107.
46 Phipps to Halifax, 24 March 1938, *DBFP*, 3/I, no. 112.
47 The French Ambassador, Charles Corbin, put this suggestion to the then Foreign Secretary, Anthony Eden, on 18 February 1938. (Memorandum by Corbin, 18 February 1938, *DBFP*, 2/XIX, no. 557.) The negative British reply was sent a week later. (Memorandum for the French Government, 25 February 1938, *DBFP*, 2/XIX, no. 592).
48 Halifax to Newton, 23 March 1938, *DBFP*, 3/I, no. 110.
49 Cabinet Minutes, 22 March 1938, Cabinet 15 (38), CAB 23/93.
50 Harvey, ed., *Harvey Diaries*, p. 123.
51 Minute by Sargent, 21 March 1938, C 1809/132/18, FO 371/21674. (Emphasis in original.) Sargent was citing Newton's words. (See Newton to Halifax, 15 March 1938, *DBFP*, 3/I, no. 86.)

3
Seeking a Solution

The British government's decision not to guarantee Czechoslovakia, far from resolving the issue, marked only the beginning of a growing British involvement in Central Europe, because the danger of war persisted as long as the Sudeten German dispute remained outstanding. The increasing British interest in the problems of Czechoslovakia was signalled publicly by the Prime Minister in the House of Commons on 24 March. This laboriously prepared statement was, in its final form, somewhat less negative in tone than the earlier draft considered by the Foreign Policy Committee on 21 March.[1]

Chamberlain announced that Britain would not issue a guarantee to Czechoslovakia either directly or indirectly – by pledging support to France. He did so on the grounds that the automatic nature of such commitments removed the decision to go to war from the control of the British government, which was unacceptable in a geographical location where Britain's vital interests were not involved. However, this refusal to undertake to protect Czechoslovakia was mitigated by a reference to a speech made by Eden (whilst still Foreign Secretary) indicating that Britain did not rule out assistance, under the terms of the League of Nations Covenant, to any victim of aggression. Chamberlain observed that this 'might' be applicable in the case of Czechoslovakia, adding that, in the event of war, 'it would be well within the bounds of probability' that other countries, including Britain and France, 'would almost immediately become involved'. For the moment, however, diplomacy was to be employed in preserving peace by seeking a solution to the Sudeten German problem. In this connection, Chamberlain expressed gratitude to the German government for assurances given, and to the Czechoslovak government for 'addressing themselves to the practical steps that can be taken within the framework of the Czechoslovak constitution to meet the reasonable wishes of the German minority'. He then provided the first public indication of a more active British involvement in Central Europe by stating that his government would 'be ready to render any help in their power, by whatever means might seem most appropriate', towards resolving difficulties between Germany and Czechoslovakia.[2]

The Prime Minister's ambiguous statement, which disguised the full extent of his determination not to assist Czechoslovakia in maintaining its integrity and independence, met with a generally satisfactory reception.[3] Even in Czechoslovakia, not inconsiderable comfort was derived from the increased British interest, which seemed to be heralded by Chamberlain's declaration. Particularly welcome in Prague was the reference to Britain's obligations under the Covenant of the League of Nations. The absence of a specific guarantee was not regarded as a serious set-back, as, in the light of the traditions of British foreign policy, it was considered to have been an unrealistic expectation.[4] Beneš remarked to Newton that 'he looked forward to a growing recognition of identity of interest of Great Britain and Czechoslovakia in resisting German aggression' and Kamil Krofta, the Minister for Foreign Affairs, expressed satisfaction with 'British sympathy and understanding'. In London, Masaryk also professed to be on the whole encouraged by the statement and believed that it might have a deterrent effect upon Germany.[5]

The cosmetic surgery carried out on the Prime Minister's statement had evidently been too successful, and had given rise to unwelcome interpretations. Even Sargent noted with concern that the Commons statement had 'confirmed Dr. Beneš in his uncompromising attitude', and suggested that a corrective should immediately be sent to Prague.[6] But it was not only the attitude in Prague that caused anxiety. During meetings of the Cabinet and the Foreign Policy Committee, Halifax also expressed concern over the apparent French 'misinterpretation' of the Prime Minister's words.[7] Phipps and Newton were duly instructed to bring to the attention of the French and Czechoslovak governments respectively, that Chamberlain's statement was being given 'too broad an interpretation', particularly concerning the possible involvement of Britain in any conflict. That contingency, Halifax declared, was no more than a 'probability', and should not be 'assumed to be in the nature of a certainty'.[8]

The other significant element of the Prime Minister's statement – the offer of British mediation between Czechoslovakia and Germany – received much less attention. In making the vaguely expressed offer, Chamberlain indicated, in effect, that he had not abandoned his idea of involving Berlin in the search for a solution of the Sudeten German problem. This offer did not come as a surprise to the Czechoslovak authorities, for Masaryk appears to have learned of the general tenor of British thinking somewhat earlier. He reported to Prague on 19 March, the day following the first of the three crucial ministerial meetings in London, that, although Britain was unlikely to guarantee the independence of Czechoslovakia, it was probable that an offer would be made to mediate between Germany and Czechoslovakia concerning the Sudeten German problem.[9]

The tentative suggestion of British mediation between Prague and Berlin was not the only offer under consideration. The alternative form of mediation, between the Czechoslovak government and the SdP, was also being aired in London. On the day following Chamberlain's statement in the House of Commons, Hoare developed the idea during an informal conversation with Masaryk. A few days previously, Masaryk had approached Hoare requesting 'direct, blunt, concrete advice – not vague admonitions of the advisability of "doing something"' concerning the course of action his government should pursue in search of a settlement of the German minority problem.[10] During the meeting, Hoare, 'as an old friend and as an individual', suggested that, if he were in Beneš's position, he would ask France and Britain to give him 'their good offices in helping to make a really satisfactory arrangement' for the Sudeten Germans. He added that it would be desirable for Beneš to take the initiative in order to avoid the suggestion 'of any dictation from outside'. Masaryk indicated that this advice coincided with his own thinking.[11] Believing that Hoare's suggestion had been inspired by Chamberlain and possibly Vansittart, Masaryk lost no time in passing the information to his government.[12] The Home Secretary had indeed conveyed official British thinking, though there is no evidence to suggest that he was acting under instructions. But Hoare's advice certainly met with Halifax's approval – who declared it to be 'admirable'.[13] Furthermore, when informing Newton of the development, Halifax added that it would be 'useful' if Newton could bring about such an approach.[14]

Having rejected the option of guaranteeing Czechoslovakia, the British government appeared to be slowly gravitating towards what was considered the less hazardous alternative of some form of mediation, although the concept remained imprecise. Chamberlain was thinking in terms of Britain mediating between Czechoslovakia and Germany, whereas Halifax and his Foreign Office advisers had in mind a commission of enquiry operating within Czechoslovakia. These ideas, whilst not mutually incompatible, indicated a degree of confusion and absence of co-ordination, perhaps hardly surprising in the immediate aftermath of the annexation of Austria. Nevertheless, a consensus seemed to be emerging that it would be in Britain's interest to act as 'honest broker' in the Czechoslovak crisis, but exactly how this role might be performed was far from clear.

Concern about the lack of clarity in Britain's approach is evident in a lengthy Foreign Office memorandum, entitled 'The German Minority in Czechoslovakia: The Next Step', prepared at the end of March. This anonymous document is remarkable not for the solutions it offered – it offered few – but for the many pertinent questions it raised. At the outset, the paper drew attention to the great complexity of the situation in Czechoslovakia, which was such that neither the Foreign Office nor the Prague Legation were 'competent to draw up any concrete scheme of reform'. Therefore:

> If it is in our minds to make concrete proposals, it would seem necessary, as a first step, to despatch an investigator to study the question on

> behalf of His Majesty's government, with the consent of the Czechoslovak government, and to report his conclusions and recommendations.

But any on the spot investigation would of necessity be a lengthy operation, and, in the potentially explosive situation following the *Anschluss*, time was in short supply. The danger was further compounded, the memorandum added, by the encouragement Beneš appeared to derive from Chamberlain's Commons declaration and his probable belief that Czechoslovak independence could only be preserved by a victorious war against Germany.

In the light of this situation, the memorandum urged that the Czechoslovak government 'be informed, in the most emphatic terms', that 'drastic concessions' to the German minority were essential, and its attention drawn to the military unpreparedness of both Britain and France for a war with Germany. The question remained, however, with whom were the Czechoslovak authorities to negotiate – with Henlein or with Hitler? In view of the recent Austrian experience, negotiating directly with Hitler was not to be recommended. Coming to terms with Henlein was therefore preferable, particularly since, it was believed, satisfying Henlein would also satisfy Hitler.

The Foreign Office analysis of the available concessions was far from encouraging. One possibility, the full application of the Minorities Treaty, was immediately rejected on the grounds of irrelevance, as it would not satisfy the Sudeten Germans. Other measures considered included the holding of communal elections postponed in 1937, the appointment of more Germans to the administration of German areas, and the removal of discrimination in the awarding of defence contracts. It was doubtful, however, whether even these concessions would prove sufficient. There remained, therefore, the more radical step of granting autonomy to the German minority, which was believed to be the least that would satisfy the German government and the Sudeten Germans. It was noted, however, that Beneš was resolutely opposed to the idea, claiming it would result in the disruption of the country.

Addressing the question of whether the Czechoslovak government's attitude could be changed, the memorandum reasoned that 'advice without either pressure or bribes is unlikely to be accepted'. Bribery, however, was not practicable, for having refused to guarantee Czechoslovakia, Britain had nothing else to offer. The only alternative, therefore, was to apply 'considerable pressure' in order to induce the government 'to face the question of autonomy'. But the introduction of autonomy would necessitate changes in the Czechoslovak constitution, whereas in his parliamentary statement Chamberlain had spoken of attempting to solve the minority problem '"within the framework of the ... constitution"'. Nevertheless, if the proposals in preparation by the Czechoslovak authorities failed to satisfy the German minority, should Britain insist on a revision of the constitution?

The answer to that question, the Foreign Office paper continued, depended on the view taken of Germany's intentions:

> If we think that Germany is resolved to break up the Czechoslovak State as it exists to-day whatever concessions are granted to the German minority ... then we might confine ourselves to insisting on the concessions which in our view are reasonable and adequate and such as would satisfy public opinion in this country and the world at large. In fact, the concessions would be made, not in the hope of solving the Czech–German conflict, but in order to secure as good a tactical position as possible for ourselves and the Czechs when the time came for Hitler to proceed to action. If, on the other hand, we think that it is possible to reach a settlement of the Sudetendeutschen problem with Germany then we should boldly tackle the problem from the base upwards and work for the reconstitution of Czechoslovakia on a federal basis.

However, even if the Czechoslovak constitution were to be re-written, would a federal system be viable? The memorandum was pessimistic:

> Are we not compelled to the conclusion that if Germany demands autonomy, it may be precisely because she counts upon the fact that the centrifugal force which would thereby be liberated would lead more or less quickly to the complete disintegration of the Czechoslovak State, and thereby facilitate the partition of its members without violence and, above all, without affording the rest of Europe a pretext for accusing Germany of aggression.

Furthermore, finding a suitable form of federal structure would not be a simple matter, though the Swiss cantonal model was probably the most appropriate, particularly since it was recalled that Beneš himself had given an undertaking at the Paris Peace Conference that Czechoslovakia would adopt such a constitution. In addition, the memorandum drew attention to a further concession likely to be demanded by Germany – the neutralisation of Czechoslovakia – but the implications of this were not considered.[15] That particular avenue was to be explored in detail on a later occasion.

This insightful document appears to have served as a basis for a discussion between Halifax and his Foreign Office advisers on 1 April, although few of the questions raised by the memorandum would seem to have been answered. The meeting endorsed the view that Britain lacked the expertise to recommend any specific proposals for reform, and agreed that an approach should be made to France with a view to applying joint pressure on Beneš to negotiate a settlement with Henlein.[16] Halifax evidently hoped that pressure on the Czechoslovak authorities would be adequate to induce concessions acceptable to the SdP and to the German government, thus obviating the need for more direct British involvement.

The Foreign Secretary explained this latest thinking to two meetings of ministers early in April. The Cabinet, meeting on 6 April, was informed that Britain could not suggest a settlement because of lack of information. Furthermore, Halifax explained: 'It was not sufficient to bear in mind the justice of any plan that might be drawn up; it was also necessary to remember that the settlement had to have value with Germany.' The 'right course' therefore was to approach the Czechoslovak government, jointly with France, urging it 'to come to terms with the Sudeten-Deutsch and with Germany while this was still possible'. However, the Cabinet discussion was perfunctory and, although approved in principle, elaboration of the policy was remitted to the Foreign Policy Committee.[17]

When the Committee met the following day, Halifax explained that, as far as developments inside Czechoslovakia were concerned, he did 'not contemplate doing anything more than encouraging the Czecho-Slovak government to make every effort to reach a settlement with the Sudeten Germans'. Clearly, any thought of on the spot mediation either by a commission of enquiry, which Halifax himself had suggested three weeks previously, or by an individual investigator, mentioned in the 'Next Step' memorandum, had been abandoned, at least for the moment. However, the related idea of Britain interceding between Czechoslovakia and Germany was still very much under consideration, and formed the main topic of discussion at the meeting. The crucial issue was not whether Britain should approach Germany, but precisely when the approach should be made. Halifax, though not contemplating an immediate approach, envisaged that London might give a semi-official indication to Berlin that the Czechoslovak authorities were giving 'careful consideration to the problem' and express the 'hope that Germany would exercise patience in the matter'. If this were done prior to the details of the Czechoslovak proposals being known, it would avoid the danger of the British government appearing to support a particular scheme which it might find 'unable to carry into effect'. The alternative case was made by Hoare, who argued that Germany should not be approached until after Britain had been informed of the contents of the Czechoslovak reform programme. That would avoid giving Germany the impression that Britain was 'on her side' and, by keeping Germany uncertain of possible British action, might lead to a 'fair and reasonable' settlement. The disagreement between Halifax and Hoare remained unresolved, and the discussion closed with Chamberlain suggesting that Britain should 'refrain from making any approach to Germany at the moment'. The Prime Minister did not explain why he took this attitude, which was all the more surprising since it was he who had initiated the move to involve Germany only three weeks earlier.

The general underlying desire to avoid direct involvement in the Sudeten German problem also surfaced when Viscount Hailsham, the Lord President of the Council, supported by Stanley, expressed disquiet over the advice Hoare had given Masaryk, believing that the offer of good offices 'might become a dangerous commitment'. Halifax explained that he interpreted the advice as meaning that, if the Czechoslovak government went as far as possible to meet the wishes of the Sudeten Germans, then Britain and France might recommend the proposals to Germany, and Hoare confirmed that he had not suggested to Masaryk that Britain would support 'any proposals'. Although Halifax had approved Hoare's advice only a few days previously, the Foreign Secretary now stated that 'such a policy would need careful consideration' and he would 'prefer to suspend judgement on it for the time being'.[18] The view clearly prevailed within the Foreign Policy Committee that it was essential to avoid Britain being placed in a position of supporting any particular Czechoslovak reform proposal because of the fear of such support developing into a commitment.

It was felt, nevertheless, that attempts to defuse the potentially explosive situation in Czechoslovakia had to be continued, preferably in conjunction with France. Halifax therefore proposed to seek French co-operation in urging Beneš to reach a settlement with Henlein. He envisaged this joint approach being made as soon as possible, combined with a request for London to be kept informed of developments. Halifax also suggested that the British government should 'thereafter continue to watch the situation very closely and be ready at any appropriate moment and in any appropriate manner to use ... [its] influence to assist to secure a settlement'. This proposed action was approved by the Foreign Policy Committee and communicated to Paris a few days later.[19]

A more fundamental point to emerge from the Committee discussion, however, was one relating to the crucial unanswered question raised in the Foreign Office 'Next Step' memorandum – namely, the question of Germany's intentions towards Czechoslovakia. Simon enquired whether Halifax thought that if the Czechoslovak government 'produced a scheme which impartial persons would regard as fair and reasonable was there any real chance that Herr Hitler would accept that scheme', particularly in view of his declared intention of bringing all Germans within the Reich. Halifax found this question 'very difficult to answer', adding that 'Germany did not want war and if she could gain her ends by recourse to other methods, such as economic pressure, she might be expected to do so'.[20] Halifax, in effect, conceded that he believed Germany did intend to bring about the breakup of Czechoslovakia, albeit without necessarily going to war, yet he ignored the advice offered in the 'Next Step' memorandum, that, if that were the case, Britain should aim at securing the best possible tactical position. Although the Foreign Secretary thought it unlikely that Czechoslovakia's difficulties could be solved without detaching the Sudeten

Germans, he was nevertheless basing his policy on just that premise. With the assistance of France, the Czechoslovak authorities were to be coerced into granting far-reaching concessions to the German minority, ostensibly in order to preserve the independence and integrity of the state. Halifax, however, patently believed that the independence and integrity of Czechoslovakia could not be preserved, as any concessions granted to the Sudeten Germans were unlikely to be deemed sufficient by Germany, despite a possible British request for moderation. This was a policy devoid of logic, and based, at best, on a pious hope of Hitler's reasonableness and, at worst, on a cynical disregard for Czechoslovakia's continued existence as an independent state.

The shape of the emerging British policy towards Czechoslovakia was certainly not to everyone's liking. Foremost amongst the critics within the Foreign Office was, predictably, Vansittart, who was becoming increasingly concerned about the lack of balance in British government thinking, which sought to single out only the Czechoslovak side for severe pressure for concessions. This caused him, in early April, to pose the crucial question – 'shall we have the courage to drive the Germans equally hard, and if so how?'[21] – but the point went unanswered. Vansittart developed his views in greater detail a week later. In a memorandum for Halifax, Vansittart pointed out that, although he concurred with the general policy of 'putting considerable pressure on Czechoslovakia to produce a reasonable settlement', he attached 'vital importance' to the word 'reasonable'. He 'most earnestly' hoped that Czechoslovak independence and integrity would not be sacrificed simply to avoid conflict with Germany. Such a step by Britain, Vansittart added, 'would be not only an immediate confession of weakness but I think also of immorality'. The alternative policy favoured by Vansittart was that Britain

> should fix some point in the line of least resistance beyond which we should not go, and that this in reality is a much smaller risk than compelling Czechoslovakia to immolate herself, losing all our political credit and giving Germany an easy ride to domination of Europe which will ultimately turn against ourselves.[22]

However, Vansittart's strictures and advice went unheeded, despite being discussed by Halifax and his advisers (including Vansittart) on 12 April.[23] By that date, the next stage of British policy towards Czechoslovakia had already been determined. The previous day, Halifax had instructed Phipps to inform the French government of the urgent need for concerted Franco-British pressure to be brought to bear on Czechoslovakia to reach a settlement of the German minority problem. The Foreign Secretary did not indicate the exact nature of the desired settlement, although he stressed the importance of making the Czechoslovak authorities 'realise the necessity of making drastic concessions to the German minority', adding that 'superficial measures, though they might have been adequate in the past, will no longer meet the case'.[24] It was precisely these unspecified 'drastic' measures, alluded to in the 'Next Step' memorandum, which gave Vansittart cause for concern. Halifax, nevertheless, still claimed to envisage – at least for the benefit of the French government – a solution not involving partition or the loss of sovereignty, for he referred to the Sudeten German dispute as a problem 'on the settlement of which the continued existence of Czechoslovakia as an independent state within her present frontiers may well depend'.[25]

A few days earlier the door had been closed even more firmly, for the time being at least, on the idea of British mediation in Czechoslovakia. One factor contributing to Halifax's decision may have been the lack of interest shown in Hoare's advice to Masaryk concerning British good offices.[26] The Czechoslovak authorities were, however, keen to enlist British and French support and aimed to achieve this by presenting their proposals to the British and French governments for approval, prior to making them known to the SdP.[27] When notice of this intention arrived at the London Foreign Office, it gave rise to considerable concern. Sargent minuted that the apparent intention of the Czechoslovak government to 'draw up a scheme for the Sudetendeutschen to take or to leave, instead of attempting to negotiate a settlement with them' was not at all what Hoare had had in mind.[28] On 9 April, Halifax instructed Newton to bring this point to the attention of the Czechoslovak authorities, explaining that the British government did 'not possess enough knowledge of the complexities of the Sudeten German problem and of its interaction on Czechoslovak internal politics to adjudicate on the merits of any solution' proposed. Halifax added that to do so would require sending out 'a special investigator to take evidence on the spot – a course which in the present circumstances I do not favour'.[29] Although he offered no explanation, Halifax probably concurred with the 'Next Step' memorandum, which drew attention to the danger of the inevitable delay.

Thus, within a period of about a month following the annexation of Austria, British policy towards Czechoslovakia began to crystallise. Taking the negative decision not to guarantee Czechoslovakia's independence was relatively straightforward, but bringing about a settlement of the Sudeten German problem was considerably more difficult. One obvious possibility was for Britain to play the role of mediator, but both contemplated forms of mediation had drawbacks. Mediation between the parties concerned inside Czechoslovakia was considered impracticable and dangerous as the Foreign Office, lacking the necessary expert knowledge of the situation, would require time to remedy this deficiency, and the resulting delay would only exacerbate the crisis. Mediation between Czechoslovakia and Germany, aiming to bring together representatives of the two governments, was considered unwise in view of the recent experience of Austria. In addition, any attempt to play the role of an 'honest broker' carried with it the feared risk of increased British involvement. The alternative policy of pressuring the Czechoslovak authorities into making concessions to the Sudeten Germans was considerably more attractive as it avoided that danger. Here also there were two main possibilities. The Czechoslovak government could be coerced into dealing directly with Berlin, but again the recent example of Austria militated against this. The alternative option of pressuring the Czechoslovak authorities to achieve a negotiated settlement with the SdP showed no evident drawbacks and was therefore adopted by the British government. In addition, it was believed that this policy would more likely be successful if the co-operation of France could also be secured. But developments within Czechoslovakia were shortly to indicate that pressure alone was insufficient to produce the required changes, and, despite the effort to avoid it, more direct British involvement in the Sudeten German problem would soon be considered necessary.

Whilst the British government was casting about for an effective policy in Central Europe, inside Czechoslovakia itself the dispute between the government and the SdP continued to develop and the intractability of the situation was becoming increasingly evident. In response to the suggestion made to Masaryk by Hoare in late March, that the Czechoslovak government, in the words of Halifax, 'ought to try and put its house in order', the authorities in Prague began to prepare new proposals for resolving the problem.[30] The outcome, which was communicated to London and Paris in late April, included measures to prevent the loss of national identity, a new language law, proportionate budgetary provision for ethnic groups, proportionate allocation of official posts, educational autonomy, provision for compensation for administrative injustices, and the establishment of inspectorates to ensure impartiality in national matters.[31] Within the Foreign Office these proposals were received with little enthusiasm, but greater encouragement was taken from indications of a change in Beneš's attitude towards the constitutional structure of Czechoslovakia; he now appeared receptive to the concept of creating a 'State of Nationalities'.[32] This had emerged during the course of a conversation with Newton on 22 April, when the President indicated agreement with the British Minister's personal suggestion for the creation of the 'United States of Bohemia and Slovakia', in which the concept of national minorities would be replaced by a partnership of all national groups.[33]

Any slender hopes of successful negotiations based on the Czechoslovak government's proposals were almost immediately extinguished, however, by the nature of the SdP's demands. During a party gathering in Carlsbad on 24 April, Henlein outlined his basic prerequisites for a settlement. His demands, the 'eight points', were summarised by Newton:

(1) Full equality of status between Czechs and Germans.
(2) Guarantee of that equality by recognition of the Sudeten Germans [*Volksgruppe*] as a legal personality [*Rechtspersönlichkeit*].

(3) Definition and recognition of the German regions within the State.
(4) Full self-government for those regions.
(5) Legal protection for every citizen living outside the region of his own nationality.
(6) Removal of injustices inflicted upon the Sudeten Germans since 1918 and the reparation of the damages caused thereby.
(7) Recognition and realisation of the principle: Within the German regions German officials.
(8) Full liberty to profess the German nationality ('Volkstum') and the German political philosophy.[34]

The most significant of the demands was the final eighth point, which amounted to an open espousal of German National Socialism. That, in particular, was unacceptable to the Czechoslovak authorities, who were not prepared to allow the SdP openly to profess National Socialism at the inevitable expense of the freedom of others.[35] In the Central Department of the London Foreign Office, however, Frank Roberts was undisturbed by Henlein's requirements, noting that they were 'what might have been expected and only amplify the demands already made'. Referring to a further demand contained in Henlein's speech (though not actually included in the eight points), that Czechoslovakia should revise its foreign policy and cease to oppose the eastwards expansion of Germany, Roberts observed that this may cause 'greater difficulty as it means a revision of Czech[oslovak] alliances'.[36] His more senior colleague, Ivo Mallet, was rather less sanguine and did not see how the British could induce the Czechoslovak government to make further concessions beyond those already contemplated.[37] However, only Vansittart appeared to be fully aware of the implications of Henlein's words, concluding that 'he is completely in the hands of the German Nazi Party'.[38] This view was in sharp contrast with Vansittart's otherwise sympathetic attitude towards the Sudeten German leader, and it was not to be long-lasting.

Although Henlein's Carlsbad demands convinced the Czechoslovak authorities of the futility of negotiating with the SdP until the completion of local government elections in June,[39] the British government persisted in its belief that urgent action was required in Czechoslovakia. Pressure on Prague to make concessions was maintained and the co-operation of France continued to be sought. Consequently, the subject of Czechoslovakia featured prominently at a conference of British and French ministers, held in London on 28 and 29 April. During the discussions, the new French Prime Minister, Edouard Daladier, sought to persuade his hosts to adopt an attitude more supportive of Czechoslovakia and more critical of Germany. Chamberlain and Halifax, however, restated their refusal to issue a guarantee, even in the event of the Czechoslovak authorities introducing the required reforms. Arguing that the German claims were 'rather like mushrooms, in that they grew in the dark', the British ministers proposed that they be brought out into the open by asking the German government what was required. They also urged that co-ordinated British and French diplomatic pressure be exerted on the Czechoslovak government for maximum concessions to be granted to the German minority. The French ministers accepted these proposals, though Britain alone was to make a *démarche* in Berlin.[40]

The agreed co-ordinated diplomatic initiative was carried out in Prague and Berlin on 7 May, although the actual meeting between the British Ambassador, Sir Nevile Henderson, and the German Foreign Minister took place four days later, on Ribbentrop's return from a visit to Italy. Henderson informed the German government of the 'influence' Britain was bringing to bear on the Czechoslovak authorities in favour of a settlement of the German minority problem. He added that such a step would more likely be effective if 'the German government could indicate the lines of a settlement which in their view would be satisfactory to the Sudeten-Deutschen'.[41] Ribbentrop, predictably, declined to respond directly to the British request, claiming the matter was one for Henlein to determine, but adding that, in his opinion, the points contained in the SdP leader's Carlsbad speech should serve as a basis for discussion.[42]

The main thrust of the joint British–French diplomatic initiative was made in Prague. Newton impressed on Krofta the extreme gravity of the situation, warning that, in the event of war, Czechoslovakia's allies would be unable to prevent the country being overrun by Germany. He reinforced the point by stating that, even in the event of ultimate victory, 'the question would still have to be decided whether the Czechoslovak State could be re-established in its present form'. In view of these factors, Newton emphasised the need for urgency in commencing negotiations with the SdP and stressed that a 'supreme effort' was required in order to achieve a 'comprehensive and lasting settlement'. The British government, he added, 'would be ready at any appropriate time and in any appropriate manner to use their influence to assist' in achieving this objective.[43] A similar, though less menacing, message was conveyed by the French Minister in Prague, François de Lacroix, who added that the British approach to Berlin would more likely be effective if additional concessions were made by the Czechoslovak authorities.[44]

Newton also informed Krofta of the British reaction to the recent Czechoslovak proposals. Although reluctant to express a firm opinion before Henlein's response was known, the British government took the view that the measures outlined did not come close enough to the Carlsbad demands or to the concept of a 'State of Nationalities' which Beneš was believed to have accepted.[45] It is significant that although Newton was instructed to indicate that it was Henlein's reaction which had to be gauged first, during Cabinet discussion of the issue it was observed that 'however reasonable these proposals might be Herr Hitler might want more'.[46] This reference to Hitler provides further confirmation of the British government's awareness of the relationship between the SdP and the German government. A few weeks later, however, Henlein paid another visit to London during which, thanks to his accomplished air of sincerity, he again succeeded in convincing many of his listeners of his independence from German control. In doing so he was carrying out the instructions of Ribbentrop, whom he visited in Berlin en route for London.[47]

This, Henlein's final visit to London, was arranged through Vansittart, who had last met the SdP leader the previous October. The initiative came from Henlein,[48] who was in fact complying with Hitler's wish, expressed during their meeting on 28 March 1938, when Hitler complimented Henlein on his 'great success ... in England' and asked him to visit London again, as soon as possible, 'and to continue to use his influence with a view to ensuring non-intervention by Britain'.[49] After consulting Halifax and Chamberlain, Vansittart encouraged the SdP leader to come but stipulated, in order not to offend the Czechoslovak authorities, that the visit was to be a 'purely private one'. Consequently, during his stay in London between 12 and 14 May, Henlein was not received by members of the government[50] – though he did, of course, meet Vansittart – and arrangements were also made for him to meet individual Members of Parliament.[51]

As on his previous visits, Henlein's most significant discussions were those held with Vansittart. The talks were held over dinner at Vansittart's London home on 13 May, with Christie (who had also helped facilitate Henlein's earlier trips to Britain) the only other person present.[52] The conversation lasted about four hours, concentrating mainly on Henlein's Carlsbad demands. Vansittart subsequently reported to Halifax that he had found Henlein 'far more reasonable and amenable than had dared to hope'. Vansittart advised his guest against introducing the 'extraneous matter of foreign policy' into 'the perfectly legitimate question' of rectifying the internal grievances of the German minority. Commenting on the Carlsbad demands, Vansittart indicated that it would be 'quite unworkable to set up a Nazi State within the boundaries of a democratic State', and he also counselled Henlein 'to drop all mention of reparations' as it had an 'ugly ring' in British ears. Otherwise, Vansittart had no criticism to offer to his 'old friend' other than to observe that his guest was 'no longer ostensibly the moderate Henlein' whom he had known previously. Henlein brushed aside this mild rebuke by blaming the Czechoslovak authorities for their tardiness in attempting to resolve the outstanding problem, adding that his policy of 'conciliation' had not achieved appreciable results.[53]

Henlein had anticipated Vansittart's criticism of his Carlsbad programme and, earlier in the day, over lunch with Churchill and the Liberal leader Sir Archibald Sinclair (with the Oxford physicist Professor F.A. Lindemann acting as interpreter), appeared to restate his demands in a considerably more moderate form. Henlein outlined a vision of local autonomy for the German areas operating within the existing political system and posing no threat to the security of Czechoslovakia.[54] The programme was a pale shadow of that proclaimed in his Carlsbad speech and contained none of the points unacceptable to the Czechoslovak government. Even the Czechoslovak Minister in London signified that he would be 'contented with a settlement on these lines'.[55] Evidently, Henlein had once again succeeded in playing the role of – in Vansittart's words – a 'wise and reasonable man'[56] remarkably well.

In reality, despite his apparent moderation, Henlein remained equivocal concerning the Carlsbad demands. When questioned by Churchill and Sinclair and, later the same afternoon, at a meeting with back-bench Members of Parliament arranged by Harold Nicolson (a prominent National Labour Member), Henlein did his utmost to allay British fears by claiming that the measures demanded were entirely consistent with democracy.[57] Nevertheless, at no time did he actually repudiate the Carlsbad programme. Furthermore, a menacing undertone was detectable in his utterances. He informed Churchill and Sinclair that he saw three possible solutions to the Sudeten German problem: 'The first was some sort of autonomy within the Czech[oslovak] State. The second was a plebiscite probably leading to the Anschluss. The third was war.'[58]

Evaluation of the outcome of Henlein's last visit to London was mixed. Vansittart later claimed that it had been his intention to subject the SdP leader to pressure from anti-appeasers in order that 'he should be disillusioned from any idea ... that England was not interested in the Czech crisis'[59] but that 'Henlein got off the string sufficiently to see the appeasers who undid our handiwork'.[60] Masaryk, whom Henlein visited on Vansittart's urging,[61] appears, however, to have believed that the anti-appeasers were successful. He informed the Foreign Ministry in Prague that 'all those who have spoken with Henlein have assured him that England will march if we are attacked. It appears that he is going away from here disabused, and that he is softening.'[62] But Masaryk's belief was directly contradicted by the German Ambassador in London, Herbert vom Dirksen, who reported to Berlin that Henlein had made a 'favourable impression' in London. Dirksen added that, thanks to 'the quiet and reasonable manner' in which he explained the SdP demands, Henlein won the 'extensive sympathy and even confidence' of those whom he met.[63] The German Ambassador's assessment was nearer the truth than Masaryk's and is supported by Vansittart's observation that Henlein was 'pleased by his visit'.[64] Certainly, Henlein's visit to London did not result in any appreciable changes in his policies or in those of the German government.[65]

As far as the formulation of British foreign policy was concerned, however, the outcome of Henlein's visit was unambiguous. It was determined by Vansittart's report to Halifax which noted that Henlein had stressed 'that what was above all necessary was a *quick* settlement', thus confirming Vansittart's supposition that the SdP leader was in danger of being subjected to 'extremist pressure', mainly from Germany. Vansittart took the view that this pressure might be counteracted if the Czechoslovak authorities seized the opportunity. The alternative, he argued, would be the 'dismemberment of Czechoslovakia', constituting a step towards the German domination of Europe.[66] Summarising Vansittart's observations for the Cabinet, Halifax expressed matters more succinctly by stating that two conclusions had emerged: 'Henlein had no instructions from Berlin', and 'Beneš could get an agreement of a useful character if he would only act quickly'.[67] Hence Newton was instructed to impress on Beneš the urgent need 'to come forward at once with a good offer'.[68] Henlein's visit to London evidently further confirmed the British view that speedy action was required in Czechoslovakia.

This belief was substantially reinforced almost immediately by the events of the weekend of 19 to 22 May, termed the 'May Crisis', when, in response to reported German troop movements towards the Czechoslovak frontier, the authorities in Prague resorted to partial mobilisation. The crisis commenced on 19 May, three days prior to local elections in parts of Czechoslovakia, when reports of German troop concentrations in Saxony, southern Silesia and northern Austria began to reach the British and Czechoslovak authorities.[69] These rumours were preceded by an intensification of hostile German propaganda aimed at Czechoslovakia.[70] Enquiries made in Berlin the following day by the British Ambassador produced official denials of the troop concentrations.[71] The Czechoslovak Minister in Berlin, Vojtěch Mastný, was also informed by the German Minister of Foreign Affairs that no aggressive military dispositions were being made towards Czechoslovakia. Accusing the Czechoslovak government of responsibility for initiating the rumours, Ribbentrop warned that if this continued the troop concentrations 'would take place with lightning speed'.[72] The atmosphere of crisis was further heightened by an incident outside Cheb (Eger), close to the German frontier, in which Czechoslovak security forces shot dead two Sudeten Germans who refused to stop at a check-point.[73] The following morning, 21 May, Czechoslovakia, without consulting its allies, mobilised one class of reservists, together with certain specialist troops, and moved them into the frontier regions.[74]

The threat of war not only caused alarm in Prague, but also gave rise to great concern in London and Paris. On 21 May, Britain and France issued warnings to Germany. The new French Foreign Minister, Georges Bonnet, announced that France would honour its treaty commitments to Czechoslovakia,[75] and Halifax warned Ribbentrop of the likely involvement of Britain.[76] By 23 May, however, the crisis appeared to have passed its peak. The local elections in Czechoslovakia had taken place the previous day and the country had remained largely calm. In Prague, it was widely believed that only the decisive action by the government, accompanied by the diplomatic support of Britain and France, had averted war.[77] Sections of the British and French press also reflected this attitude, despite Halifax's direct appeal for journalistic moderation.[78] This belief was shared by Vansittart, who wrote to Halifax, on 23 May, expressing the hope that the conclusion would be drawn from recent events 'that the best way to deal with Germany is with firmness'.[79]

Despite the apparent success of its diplomatic intervention in the crisis, the British government, although much relieved that war had been avoided, remained uneasy about the weekend's events. Neither the British nor the French had, in reality, been as resolute as appeared at first sight. The French government, irritated by the lack of consultation over the partial mobilisation, urged caution on the Czechoslovak authorities, and exhorted them to reverse the call-up as soon as possible.[80] The British government also urged its Czechoslovak counterpart to act with circumspection.[81] Moreover, during the height of the crisis on 22 May, after an emergency meeting of the Cabinet,[82] Halifax cautioned the French not to read too much into the warning given in Berlin. He explained that, although Britain would aid France if it were attacked by Germany, it should not be assumed that Britain would become involved in assisting Czechoslovakia.[83]

The German government, meanwhile, continued to protest its innocence, claiming that the military had gained control of Czechoslovakia and were pursuing policies dangerous to Germany.[84] When Halifax sought Newton's comment on this allegation, the British Minister responded with a spirited defence of the Czechoslovak authorities, pointing out that Berlin 'cannot seriously maintain that the enrolment of one class of Czech[oslovak] reservists was an act of aggression against Germany'.[85] Nevertheless, the German point of view gradually gained credence, thanks to the fact that no conclusive evidence of potentially aggressive German troop movements could be found.[86] In London and Paris responsibility for the crisis began to be placed increasingly on the Czechoslovak authorities.[87] However, whether the German troop movements were real or imaginary, merely routine in character or aggressive in intent, is, in a sense, immaterial, for the atmosphere of crisis itself was real enough and the consequences which stemmed from it were also significant. Two such outcomes were particularly important as far as the future of Czechoslovakia was concerned.

One significant development took place in Berlin, where the May Crisis appears to have stiffened Hitler's resolve to dispose of Czechoslovakia. Hitler spent most of the crisis weekend at Berchtesgaden where, amongst other matters, he worked on the directives for 'Operation Green' – the plan for the destruction of Czechoslovakia. Up to that time, these military directives had resembled contingency plans, to be implemented at some unspecified future date when conditions were considered right.[88] A few days later, however, on 30 May, Hitler issued a new directive for 'Operation Green' in which he stated: 'It is my unalterable decision to smash Czechoslovakia by military action in the near future.' In a covering letter, General Wilhelm Keitel, the Chief of the Supreme Headquarters of the Armed Forces, gave the date of execution as 'October 1, 1938 at the latest'.[89] This change of policy was brought about by Hitler's belief that he and Germany had suffered loss of face in climbing down – or appearing to climb down – when confronted with the apparent resolution of Britain and France.[90]

The effects of the May Crisis on the British government were very different in character. In London, the crisis served to reinforce the awareness that the Sudeten German problem was an international, and not purely an internal Czechoslovak issue, and caused the British government to redouble its efforts to find a peaceful solution. With this object in mind, and in order to familiarise the British diplomatic representatives in Czechoslovakia and Germany with details of Foreign Office thinking, and vice versa, Halifax despatched Strang, the Head of the Central Department, on a brief visit to Prague and Berlin. No arrangements were made for Strang to have any contacts with German or Czechoslovak Ministers or officials, nor with any representatives of the Sudeten Germans.[91] Strang visited (what Henderson termed) 'the front trenches'[92] in Prague on 26 and 27 May and in Berlin on the two following days.

One of the main topics of discussion at the Prague Legation was a possible plebiscite in the Sudeten German areas, which, together with the neutralisation of Czechoslovakia, was being studied in the Foreign Office. The policy held considerable appeal in London as it offered the prospect of avoiding the necessity to express an opinion on the Czechoslovak government's proposals. As Strang candidly explained, Halifax was wary of endorsing 'Beneš' plan (however good it might be) and then having to run away from it because the Germans rejected it'. The speedy use of a plebiscite on the questions of 'acceptance of the [Czechoslovak] plan' or 'union with Germany', would avoid that danger. But Halifax was also aware of the practical problems of implementation and of the difficulty in securing Beneš's agreement, particularly since any British guarantee of the truncated and neutralised post-plebiscite Czechoslovak state was out of the question. Newton showed little enthusiasm for the idea, preferring instead some form of autonomy for the German minority accompanied by the neutralisation of Czechoslovakia, although he added that the question of a plebiscite might be referred to the British investigator, if one were sent. The reluctance to embark on a plebiscite was shared by the Berlin Embassy.[93]

Newton had considered the issue of a plebiscite a few days earlier. Writing at length to Halifax on 16 May, he concurred with the view of the Versailles peace-makers in 1919 that Bohemia (including, by implication, also Moravia and Silesia) formed a 'natural region' in terms of economic, geographical, political and strategic considerations, and questioned therefore 'whether any attempt to divide it up would provide a permanent solution'. More explicitly, Newton doubted whether there was 'any half-way house between a Czechoslovakia within her present frontiers and the abandonment to Germany of the whole area covered by the Historic Provinces'.[94] Although not indicating which of these alternatives he preferred, Newton clearly believed that the cession of the predominantly German districts to Germany would not resolve the problem, and conducting a plebiscite in these areas would therefore be pointless.

During his discussions in Prague, Strang linked the question of a plebiscite with the possible neutralisation of Czechoslovakia. Being unwilling to offer any guarantee of protection, the Foreign Office could only suggest that Czechoslovakia 'would have a better chance of survival as a neutralised State'. Newton agreed that, in addition to the question of the Sudeten German minority itself, consideration had also to be given to Czechoslovakia's foreign relations. He reasoned that 'even if there were not a single German in Czechoslovakia, the root problem of German–Czech relations would still remain, viz. a Slav State thrust into the heart of Germany having treaties of mutual assistance with powerful States East and West'. Neutralisation, therefore, might remove the 'sting' from the Sudeten German issue. Newton added that the Czechoslovak authorities themselves might prefer autonomy for the German population, accompanied by the neutralisation of the state, to the alternative of a plebiscite and dismemberment.[95]

Newton had also considered the question of neutralising Czechoslovakia on a previous occasion. In a despatch sent on 12 April, he envisaged three possible international orientations of Czechoslovakia in Europe:

(a) The present position, where she is a nominally independent Power, but is actually buttressed by France and in some sense by Great Britain;
(b) A neutralised position; or
(c) A position within the German orbit.

The present situation, being in Newton's opinion 'not permanently tenable', it was obviously desirable to 'move Czechoslovakia towards the second position', otherwise, nothing 'short of a world war' would preserve it from German domination. Three different forms of neutrality were available, arranged by Newton in order of desirability: the Swiss model, where the country would be 'immunised against aggression'; the Belgian model, receiving guarantees but giving none; or finally, the Polish model, retaining the alliance with France.[96]

Newton's radical suggestion met with some hostility in the Foreign Office. Sargent emphatically rejected Newton's reasoning, describing the examples cited as 'most misleading', and argued that as far as Czechoslovakia was concerned it was 'difficult to see any clear line of demarcation between a policy of "neutrality" and entering into the German orbit'. He therefore strongly urged that no initiative be taken to deprive Czechoslovakia of its international treaties 'merely in order to propitiate Germany'.[97] This view was echoed, with equal force, by Vansittart, who accused Newton of being 'defeatist' and of advocating a policy which could not 'by any stretch of the imagination' be seen as being in Czechoslovakia's interest. Moreover, pressing the Czechoslovak government into abandoning its alliance with France and the Soviet Union, he argued, would have a 'disastrous effect' on Britain's relations with those countries.[98]

But Vansittart's views concerning the neutralisation of Czechoslovakia soon underwent modification. Some weeks later, at the end of May, he informed Halifax that, although he rejected the Swiss model as being incompatible with the integrity of Czechoslovakia, neutrality itself was a 'conceivable solution'. Vansittart stipulated, however, that this 'must be guaranteed by Russia as well as France and Germany'.[99] The day before Vansittart recorded this softening of his attitude towards neutralising Czechoslovakia, Halifax himself raised the subject for the first time with a Czechoslovak representative. During a meeting with Masaryk on 25 May, the Foreign Secretary, 'speaking in a purely personal capacity and as a friend', suggested that the Czechoslovak government might give consideration to the idea of neutrality. He added that, in order to avoid the impression of external dictation, 'this might be represented as [a] contribution ... to the peace of Europe'.[100]

The possible neutralisation of Czechoslovakia was under active consideration in the Foreign Office. Acknowledging Newton's authorship of the view that it was Czechoslovakia's existing external links which were at the crux of its relations with Germany, the memorandum identified the need to find a 'face-saving' device for extricating the country from its alliances with France and the USSR. Neutralisation linked with a combined international guarantee offered a possible solution, providing it removed Germany's grievance, left Czechoslovakia with an effective international guarantee, and freed France from its potentially embarrassing alliance with Czechoslovakia. The paper's tentative conclusion envisaged Czechoslovakia severing its alliances with France and the USSR and also with Romania and Yugoslavia, its partners in the Little Entente. In their place Czechoslovakia would receive undertakings to individually respect and collectively guarantee its independence and integrity from Britain, Germany, France, Italy and possibly the USSR as major powers, and from Poland and Hungary as neighbouring states.[101] The proposal, however, did not become an 'approved line of policy',[102] although neutralisation was not actually rejected. Despite Newton's advice to the contrary, the Foreign Office continued to pay more attention to Czechoslovakia's internal problems than to its international orientation, hoping that a solution of the former would ease its strained relations with Germany.

The persisting intractability of the Sudeten German dispute, and the threat of war associated with it, continued to propel the British government towards a more direct involvement in the search for a solution. Consequently, the general offer of British and French 'good offices', made late in March, began, two months later, to assume a more concrete form. Indeed, the possibility of on the spot investigation of the Sudeten German problem was the second major topic of conversation during Strang's visit to British diplomatic representatives in Prague and Berlin at the end of May.

Strang outlined several alternatives. The first plan, preferred by the Foreign Office largely on account of its simplicity, envisaged Britain appointing an investigator, possibly with supporting staff, who would 'tour the Sudeten country' and provide the British government with 'a first hand review of the existing situation'. Strang added that the investigator would be free 'to submit any suggestions for a solution that might occur to him', and might also report on the feasibility of any scheme referred to him from London. The second alternative, which Strang described as being 'a much more serious matter than the first, and ... in the nature of an arbitration', involved the appointment by Britain of 'a commission of enquiry composed either of British subjects or of "neutrals" or both', with specific instruction 'to propose a solution' after conducting on the spot investigation. Strang noted, however, that this proposal was unlikely to be acceptable to Germany, as the outcome would probably be less favourable to the Sudeten Germans than a solution extracted directly from the Czechoslovak authorities with the strong support of Berlin. The third suggestion was a variation of the second, with the appointment of the commission of enquiry jointly by the British and German governments, and was open to similar objections. The fourth alternative outlined by Strang envisaged the convening of an international conference 'attended by the Powers chiefly concerned' which would establish an international commission for the purpose of finding a solution. The last option, different in character from the other four, originated not from the Foreign Office but from a Labour Member of Parliament, Philip Noel-Baker, who suggested the creation of an international commission to investigate violations of the Czechoslovak–German frontier. The major difficulty foreseen here was the probability of Germany's refusal to co-operate.[103]

Britain's diplomats in Prague and Berlin gave a generally positive response to Strang's suggestions. Newton expressed the view, endorsed by Henderson, that it was 'better for us to go on doing something than to do nothing'. As for the alternatives outlined, both Newton and Henderson were less than specific, but generally favoured the despatch of an investigator or a commission of enquiry. Henderson, however, added the proviso that any such action would have to be undertaken purely under British auspices and restricted to Czechoslovak territory. Although Britain's representatives in Central Europe agreed on the need for closer British involvement in the problems of Czechoslovakia, they appeared uncertain about the precise nature of the policy, failing to distinguish between the simple process of investigation and reporting and the more involved proposal of arbitration. Indeed, Newton appears to have summed up their imprecision admirably, when, metaphorically crossing his fingers, he observed that: 'If we try first one thing, then another, some solution may emerge.'[104]

Plans for a more active British policy towards Czechoslovakia had, in fact, been initiated prior to Strang's visit to Central Europe. At the time of the May Crisis, on 22 May, Henderson was asked to establish whether Germany would object to an observer being sent to the German areas of Czechoslovakia 'to report direct on actual situation' to London.[105] The State Secretary at the German Foreign Ministry, Ernst von Weizsäcker, replied that Ribbentrop took the view that if the presence of a British observer would 'have the effect of avoiding further incidents it would be useful'.[106] This idea of combining what was envisaged as a purely fact finding exercise with that of pacification had not been contemplated in the Foreign Office.[107] Instructing Henderson not to raise the matter again until the plan had been further studied in London, Halifax explained that Britain could give no assurance that the intervention of an observer would 'avert further incidents'. Halifax added, however, that he was considering placing an observer 'in Prague in readiness to proceed to investigate any incident which might threaten serious consequences'.[108] As the consent of the Czechoslovak government was required for such action, Newton was asked to discuss the matter with Strang during his visit to Prague.[109]

However, before Newton's response was known, the Foreign Office put forward a further idea. Adopting the formula suggested by Noel-Baker,[110] Halifax instructed Henderson and Newton, on 27 May, to enquire of the governments in Berlin and Prague respectively whether they would welcome the establishment of an international commission to investigate incidents of 'alleged violations of Czech and German territory ... or of internal disorder'. It was envisaged that the commission would operate both in Germany and Czechoslovakia.[111] The response from Berlin was predictable. Weizsäcker indicated that Germany would have no objection to the establishment of a commission of enquiry providing it was 'purely British' and its activities were 'confined to Czechoslovak territory and internal disorder'. It should not be concerned with frontier incidents.[112] The Czechoslovak Minister of Foreign Affairs responded somewhat more positively, observing that, if the situation on the Czechoslovak–German frontier were to deteriorate, a commission of enquiry would be welcome. Krofta added that the investigation of internal disorder might also be possible, 'but subject to reservation that Germany had no right to intervene in the internal affairs of Czechoslovakia'.[113]

On 2 June, Newton was informed that the proposed international commission to investigate frontier violations had been abandoned because of German objections. In its place Halifax was now considering appointing two British observers who, by operating in the Sudeten German districts of Czechoslovakia, 'might serve usefully to preserve peace by calming local agitation, by dispelling rumours regarding the misbehaviour of Czech officials and troops if these are unfounded, and by checking such misbehaviour if they are not'. The Foreign Secretary added that the observers' presence might also demonstrate to Germany that Britain was anxious to assist in finding a solution to the problem.[114] Beneš responded by indicating unofficially to Newton that, as Czechoslovakia had 'nothing to hide', he did not object to the idea of British observers, providing that their appointment was not made public, that they investigated both sides in the dispute and consulted fully with the Czechoslovak authorities.[115] On receipt of the formal positive response from Czechoslovakia on 8 June, the British government appointed two observers: Major R. Sutton-Pratt, who was made Assistant Military Attaché in Prague, and Peter Pares, the British Consul in Liberec (Reichenberg). No press announcement was made of this development.[116] Newton, however, was reluctant to move Pares from Liberec, one of the main centres of German population in Czechoslovakia, where he had established valuable local contacts.[117] The alternative name, proposed in London by Sargent, was that of Ian Henderson, British Consul at Innsbruck, who was duly appointed an observer on 10 June, and attached to the staff of the British Legation in Prague.[118] The observers took up their posts with minimum delay. Sutton-Pratt's first report to London, concerning incidents which he described as being of a 'minor nature', was made on 20 June.[119]

The concept of an international commission enquiring principally into incidents on both sides of the Czechoslovak–German frontier, which became diluted on the prompting of Berlin into the appointment of two British observers on Czechoslovak territory, was not however the only line of policy being pursued in London. The quite distinct, and more significant, idea of a commission mediating between the Czechoslovak government and the SdP also remained in the forefront of Foreign Office thinking.[120]

Although the British government remained anxious not to become too deeply involved in the Sudeten German imbroglio, developments inside Czechoslovakia, despite their apparently positive character, militated otherwise. In the immediate aftermath of the May Crisis, on 23 May, Henlein informed the Czechoslovak Prime Minister, Milan Hodža, that, although the SdP was prepared to remain in contact with the authorities, it would not open negotiations until the state of partial mobilisation was ended.[121] The government refused to comply with this demand, despite British and French pressure, but it did agree to some reduction of troop levels and to a withdrawal of troops and aircraft from the immediate vicinity of the frontier.[122] These measures appeared to satisfy the SdP, and during the last few days of May their representatives held several meetings with Hodža. At one of these meetings, on 30 May, the SdP tabled specific proposals. Thanks to assurances received by Vansittart from Henlein – indicating that he would 'not go beyond those demands which I discussed and to which I confined myself in my London talks' – it was believed in the Foreign Office that these proposals were based not on the eight points stipulated by Henlein at Carlsbad in April, but on the more moderate requirements outlined during his recent visit to London. Henlein's London desiderata did not include the contentious issues of control of Czechoslovak foreign policy, reparations, and the right of the Sudeten Germans collectively to profess National Socialism.[123]

The commencement of these talks, however, did little to ease British apprehension concerning the Sudeten German dispute. It was realised that, in the not unlikely event of failure, conditions in Central Europe were likely to become even more dangerous to peace than they had been before the negotiations. As a result, not only was pressure applied on Prague to respond positively to the SdP's proposals, but simultaneously contingency plans were prepared for the event of a breakdown. These plans involved mediation.

Notes

1 Harvey, ed., *Harvey Diaries*, p. 123; Dilks, ed., *Cadogan Diaries*, pp. 64, 66.
2 *HC Deb.*, 333, cols 1399–407, 24 March 1938.
3 Harvey, ed., *Harvey Diaries*, pp. 123–4.
4 Newton to Halifax, 25 March 1938, C 2139/1941/18, FO 371/21713; Beneš, *Mnichovské dny*, pp. 45–6.
5 Hoare to Halifax, 25 March 1938, H/VI/6, FO 800/309 and also Templewood, Viscount, (Samuel Hoare), *Nine Troubled Years*, (London, 1954), pp. 194–5.
6 Minute by Sargent, 11 April 1938, C 2164/1941/18, FO 371/21713.
7 Cabinet Minutes, 6 April 1938, Cabinet 18 (38), CAB 23/93; FPC Minutes, 7 April 1938, FP (36) 29th Meeting, CAB 27/623.
8 Halifax to Phipps, 11 April 1938, *DBFP*, 3/I, no. 135; Halifax to Newton, 12 April 1938, *DBFP*, 3/I, no. 139.
9 'Czechoslovakia: Foreign Policy', 22 March 1938, C 1955/1941/18, FO 371/21715. Commenting on this report in the Foreign Office, Strang minuted that it was 'pretty well what we would have expected M. Masaryk to report. If so it was a good report.' Minute by Strang, 1 April 1938, *ibid.*
10 Masaryk to Hoare, 14 March 1938, Templewood, *Nine Troubled Years*, pp. 293–4.
11 Hoare to Halifax, 25 March 1938, H/VI/6, FO 800/309; Templewood, *Nine Troubled Years*, pp. 294–5. See also Halifax to Newton, 2 April 1938, *DBFP*, 3/I, no. 123. Hoare reported that Masaryk was fearful of some British move which might 'weaken the moral resistance of the Czech[oslovak] Government against the annexation of the German districts'. Agreement with the Sudeten Germans would only be possible, Masaryk argued, if Britain and France 'continued to take an interest in the integrity of the country' and made this clear to

Germany. If, however, it appeared that 'annexation was only a question of time' no agreement would be possible.

12 Newton to Halifax, 2 April 1938, *DBFP*, 3/I, no. 122; Newton to Cadogan, 2 April 1938, C 2471/1941/18, FO 371/21714: Czechoslovak Legation to Hoare, 1 April 1938, H/VI/9, FO 800/309.

13 Halifax to Hoare, 28 March 1938, H/VI/7, FO 800/309; Templewood, *Nine Troubled Years*, p. 295.

14 Halifax to Newton, 2 April 1938, *DBFP*, 3/I, no. 123.

15 'The German Minority in Czechoslovakia: The Next Step', final text, 31 March 1938, C 2510/1941/18, FO 371/21714. (No indication of authorship given.)

16 Harvey, ed., *Harvey Diaries*, pp. 125–6.

17 Cabinet Minutes, 6 April 1938, Cabinet 18 (38), CAB 23/93.

18 FPC Minutes, 7 April 1938, FP (36) 29th Meeting, CAB 27/623.

19 *Ibid.*; Halifax to Phipps, 11 April 1938, *DBFP*, 3/I, no. 135.

20 FPC Minutes, 7 April 1938, FP (36) 29th Meeting, CAB 27/623.

21 Minute by Vansittart, 2 April 1938, C 2254/1941/18, FO 371/21713.

22 Memorandum by Vansittart, 8 April 1938, C 3065/1941/18, FO 371/21715.

23 *Ibid.* See also Dilks, ed., *Cadogan Diaries*, p. 68.

24 Halifax to Phipps, 11 April 1938, *DBFP*, 3/I, no. 135.

25 *Ibid.*

26 Templewood, *Nine Troubled Years*, p. 295. Hoare received a letter from Beneš which was 'friendly and optimistic' but which 'omitted any mention of my suggestion of Anglo-French intervention'. He concluded therefore that Beneš believed 'he could deal successfully with the crisis without the help of other governments'.

27 Newton to Halifax, 5 April 1938, *DBFP*, 3/I, no. 127.

28 Minute by Sargent, 8 April 1938, C 2634/1941/18, FO 371/21714.

29 Halifax to Newton, 9 April 1938, *DBFP*, 3/I, no. 133.

30 Cabinet Minutes, 6 April 1938, Cabinet 18 (38), CAB 23/93; Newton to Halifax, 2 April 1938, *DBFP*, 3/I, no. 122.

31 Newton to Halifax, 19 April 1938, *DBFP*, 3/I, no. 150; 'Memorandum on the Nationality Policy of the Czechoslovak Republic', *DBFP*, 3/I, no. 160.

32 Minute by Mallet, 25 April 1938, C 3315/1941/18, FO 371/21716; Minute by Roberts, 25 April 1938, C 3378/1941/18, FO 371/21716.

33 Newton to Halifax, 19 and 23 April 1938, *DBFP*, 3/I, nos 150, 156. Newton explained that in using the term 'United States' he was not advocating federalism.

34 Newton to Halifax, 25 April 1938, *DBFP*, 3/I, no. 157. For details of the speech see K. Henlein, *Heim ins Reich. Reden aus den Jahren 1937 und 1938*, (Reichenberg, 1939), pp. 68–104.

35 Newton to Halifax, 26 April 1938, *DBFP*, 3/I, no. 158.

36 Minute by Roberts, 25 April 1938, C 3371/1941/18, FO 371/21716.

37 Minute by Mallet, 25 April 1938, *ibid.*

38 Memorandum by Vansittart, 25 April 1938, C 3510/1941/18, FO 371/21716.

39 Newton to Halifax, 26 April 1938, *DBFP*, 3/I, nos 158, 161.

40 Record of Franco-British conversations, 28 and 29 April 1938, *DBFP*, 3/I, no. 164; *DDF*, 2/VII, no. 258.

41 Henderson to Halifax, 12 May 1938, *DBFP*, 3/I, no. 209.

42 Henderson to Halifax, 12 May 1938, *DBFP*, 3/I, no. 206. See also Memorandum by Ribbentrop, 11 May 1938, *DGFP*, D/II, no. 154.

43 Newton to Halifax, 9 May 1938, *DBFP*, 3/I, no. 195. See also Halifax to Newton, 4 May 1938, *DBFP*, 3/I, no. 171.
44 De Lacroix to Bonnet, 7 May 1938, *DDF*, 2/VII, no. 296; Beneš, *Mnichovské dny*, p. 58, and document no. 6, Record of Krofta's conversations with British and French Ministers, 7 May 1938, pp. 364–9.
45 Newton to Halifax, 9 May 1938, *DBFP*, 3/I, no. 195; Halifax to Newton, 4 May 1938, *DBFP*, 3/I, no. 171.
46 Cabinet Minutes, 6 April 1938, Cabinet 18 (38), CAB 23/93. The minutes do not record which member of the Cabinet made this point.
47 Memorandum by Weizsäcker, 12 May 1938, *DGFP*, D/II, no. 155.
48 Note by Vansittart, 16 May 1938, *DBFP*, 3/I, appendix II (1); Dilks, ed., *Cadogan Diaries*, p. 76. I. Colvin in *Vansittart in Office*, (London, 1965), p. 207 states that Henlein approached Vansittart through Robert Hadow, First Secretary at the British Legation in Prague.
49 Henlein's report on meeting with Hitler, 28 March 1938 [?], *DGFP*, D/II, no. 107.
50 *The Times*, 16 May 1938, reported that Henlein had also met the Dominions Secretary, Malcolm MacDonald, but this was denied by R. A. Butler in the House of Commons. *HC Deb.*, 336, col. 5, 16 May 1938,
51 Note by Vansittart, 16 May 1938, *DBFP*, 3/I, appendix II (1).
52 There is conflicting evidence concerning Henlein's movements in London. Vansittart claimed that Henlein dined with him and Christie on 13 May, but *The Times*, 14 May 1938 reported that: 'Last night [i.e. 13 May] Herr Henlein was one of a party of 10 who dined privately at Claridge's Hotel.'
53 Note by Vansittart, 16 May 1938, *DBFP*, 3/I, appendix II (1).
54 Note by Churchill, 15 May 1938, *DBFP*, 3/I, appendix II (2); W.S. Churchill, *The Gathering Storm* (*The Second World War*, vol. I), (London, 1948), p. 223.
55 Note by Churchill, 15 May 1938, *DBFP*, 3/I, appendix II (2).
56 Note by Vansittart, 16 May 1938, *DBFP*, 3/I, appendix II (1).
57 Nicolson recorded in his diary that it was put to Henlein that 'we do not understand certain points in his Carlsbad speech such as that in which he claims a directing voice in Czech foreign policy, and that in which he expresses sympathy for Nazi *Weltanschauung*. He explains the first by saying that what he meant was that the Sudetens could not approve of a pro-Russian and anti-German policy, and would claim the right to protest against anything in the nature of allowing Czecho-Slovakia to be used for an attack upon Germany. But they did not claim more than to voice their opinion in this respect. They did not claim to overrule the majority. On the second point he said that they approved of the social and class legislation of the Nazis, but not their anti-God and anti-semitic measures.' H. Nicolson, *Diaries and Letters, 1930–1939*, (London, 1966), p. 341. Henlein gave similar assurances to Churchill and Sinclair, see note by Churchill, 15 May 1938, *DBFP*, 3/I, appendix II (2).
58 Note by Churchill, 15 May 1938, *DBFP*, 3/I, appendix II (2). Henlein made the same point at Nicolson's tea party. Nicolson, *Diaries and Letters*, pp. 340–1.
59 *The Times*, 15 June 1953, letter from Vansittart. He added that 'never at any time did Henlein receive anything but warnings against any violence or encroachment anywhere'. The intention of warning Henlein was confirmed by Nicolson, also in a letter to *The Times*, 5 June 1953, in which, referring to his diary entry for 11 May 1938, he stated that Vansittart had indicated that: 'What is required is that he [Henlein] should be made to realise that if he insists on

the Sudetenland being united with Germany, it means a European war in which we are bound to be involved.'

60 Lord Vansittart, 'A Morally Indefensible Agreement', *The Listener*, XL, no. 1032 (4 November 1948), p. 676. See also Lord Vansittart, *Bones of Contention*, (London, 1945), p. 111. According to a report in *The Times*, 14 May 1938, Henlein 'paid calls in the city', and (as previously mentioned) attended a dinner party at Claridge's Hotel. Wheeler-Bennett (who is however somewhat inaccurate concerning Henlein's visits to London) implies that Henlein met Geoffrey Dawson and J.L. Garvin, respectively editors of *The Times* and the *Observer*, both strong supporters of Chamberlain's foreign policy. See J.W. Wheeler-Bennett, *Munich: Prologue to Tragedy*, (London, 1966), p. 54.

61 Note by Vansittart, 16 May 1938, *DBFP*, 3/I, appendix II (1).

62 Masaryk to Krofta, 14 May 1938, cited in W.V. Wallace, 'The Making of the May Crisis of 1938', *Slavonic and East European Review*, XLI (1962–63), p. 371.

63 Report by Dirksen, 10 June 1938, *DGFP*, D/II, no. 250.

64 Note by Vansittart, 16 May 1938, *DBFP*, 3/I, appendix II (1).

65 Henlein's report to Hitler is not known, indeed there is considerable confusion about when this took place. See Robbins, 'Konrad Henlein, The Sudeten Question and British Foreign Policy', p. 696, n. 99.

66 Note by Vansittart, 16 May 1938, *DBFP*, 3/I, appendix II (1). (Emphasis in original.)

67 Cabinet Minutes, 18 May 1938, Cabinet 24 (38), CAB 23/93. Perhaps Halifax was also influenced by the report from Churchill that Henlein had 'offered to give his word of honour that he had never received orders or even recommendations ... from Berlin'. Note by Churchill, 15 May 1938, *DBFP*, 3/I, appendix II (2).

68 Halifax to Newton, 16 May 1938, *DBFP*, 3/I, no. 220.

69 Henderson to Halifax, 19 May 1938, *DBFP*, 3/I, nos 232, 233; Newton to Halifax, 20 and 21 May 1938, *DBFP*, 3/I, nos 238, 244, 245; *Master of Spies. The Memoirs of General Frantisek Moravec*, (London, 1975), pp. 125–7.

70 Memorandum by Weizsäcker, 14 May 1938, *DGFP*, D/II, no. 159; Circular to Certain German Missions Abroad, 18 May 1938, *DGFP*, D/II, no. 165; Henderson to Halifax, 10 May 1938, *DBFP*, 3/I, no. 237; Newton to Halifax, 24 May 1938, *DBFP*, 3/I, no. 304.

71 Henderson to Halifax, 20 and 21 May 1938, *DBFP*, 3/I, nos 240, 255. German denials of troop movements were received with scepticism in view of the precedent set by the annexation of Austria.

72 Minute by Ribbentrop, 20 May 1938, *DGFP*, D/II, no. 174. See also Newton to Halifax, 21 May 1938, *DBFP*, 3/I, nos 246, 251.

73 Newton to Halifax, 21 and 23 May 1938, *DBFP*, 3/I, nos 251, 291.

74 Newton to Halifax, 21 and 22 May 1938, *DBFP*, 3/I, nos 247, 272.

75 Phipps to Halifax, 21 and 22 May 1938, *DBFP*, 3/I, nos 257, 261.

76 Halifax to Henderson, 21 and 22 May 1938, *DBFP*, 3/I, nos 250, 264.

77 Newton to Halifax, 22 May 1938, *DBFP*, 3/I, no. 283; Beneš, *Mnichovské dny*, pp. 84–7.

78 Halifax had appealed to the British press during the evening of 22 May. Halifax to Henderson, 24 May 1938, *DBFP*, 3/I, no. 305.

79 Memorandum by Vansittart, 23 May 1938, C 4851/1941/18, FO 371/21721.

80 Phipps to Halifax, 21, 22, 23 and 24 May 1938, *DBFP*, 3/I, nos 256, 266, 296, 301; Bonnet to de Lacroix, 21 May 1938, *DDF*, 2/VII, no. 402.

81 Phipps to Halifax, 21 and 23 May 1938, *DBFP*, 3/I, nos 256, 286; Halifax to Newton, 22 May 1938, *DBFP*, 3/I, no. 262; Halifax to Phipps, 22 and 23 May 1938, *DBFP*, 3/I, nos 279, 292.

82 Cabinet Minutes, 22 May 1938, Cabinet 25 (38), CAB 23/93. The Cabinet also resolved that Halifax should not see Masaryk that evening lest the German press might conclude that 'special consideration' was being given to the Czechoslovak case.

83 Halifax to Phipps, 22 May 1938, *DBFP*, 3/I, no. 271.

84 Memorandum by Weizsäcker, 21 May 1938, *DGFP*, D/II, no. 185; Henderson to Halifax, 21 and 22 May 1938, *DBFP*, 3/I, nos 255, 268.

85 Halifax to Newton, 22 May 1938, *DBFP*, 3/I, no. 277; Newton to Halifax, 24 and 25 May 1938, *DBFP*, 3/I, nos 302, 304, 306.

86 Henderson to Halifax, 23 and 25 May 1938, *DBFP*, 3/I, nos 287, 289, 316 (enclosure from Mason-MacFarlane); Henderson to Strang, 7 June 1938, *DBFP*, 3/I, no. 380 (enclosure from Mason-MacFarlane). Vansittart, however, remained convinced that the threat had been real and minuted, on 29 May: 'Our own intelligence are quite right and the Embassy in Berlin is wrong: there were German concentrations – that is incipient ones – because there *was* an intention to march in. When the latter idea was abandoned the troop movements were obliterated ... so far as possible.' (Minute by Vansittart, 29 May 1938, C 5063/1941/18, FO 371/21722. Emphasis and ellipsis in original.)

87 For details of the 'May Crisis' and for the controversy which surrounds it see Laffan, *Crisis over Czechoslovakia*, pp. 122–46; G.L. Weinberg, 'The May Crisis, 1938', *Journal of Modern History*, XXIX (1957), pp. 213–25; B. Celovsky, *Das Münchener Abkommen: 1938*, (Stuttgart, 1958), pp. 209–25; W.V. Wallace, 'The Making of the May Crisis of 1938', *Slavonic and East European Review*, XLI (1962–63), pp. 368–90; D.C. Watt, 'The May Crisis of 1938: A Rejoinder to Mr. Wallace', *Slavonic and East European Review*, XLIV (1965–66), pp. 475–80; W.V. Wallace, 'A Reply to Mr. Watt', *Slavonic and East European Review*, XLIV (1965-66), pp. 481–6; H.B. Braddick, *Germany, Czechoslovakia and the 'Grand Alliance' in the May Crisis, 1938*, (Denver, 1969); I. Lukes, 'The Czechoslovak Partial Mobilisation in May 1938: A Mystery (almost) Solved', *Journal of Contemporary History*, 31 (1996), pp. 699–720. Also of interest is the account given by the then Chief of Czechoslovak Military Intelligence, General F. Moravec, *Master of Spies*, pp. 125–8.

88 'Memorandum on Operation "Green"', 22 April 1938, *DGFP*, D/II, no. 133; Keitel to Hitler, 20 May 1938, *DGFP*, D/II, no. 175.

89 'Directive for Operation "Green"', 30 May 1938, *DGFP*, D/II, no. 221. See also Baynes, ed., *Speeches of Adolf Hitler*, II, p. 1571.

90 See entry in Jodl's diary in International Military Tribunal, *Trial of the Major War Criminals*, (XLII vols, Nuremberg, 1947–9), XXVIII, p. 372. Hitler himself also made this point in subsequent speeches. See Baynes, ed., *Speeches of Adolf Hitler*, II, pp. 1495, 1571.

91 Halifax to Henderson and Newton, 24 May 1938, *DBFP*, 3/I, no. 299. Halifax informed the Cabinet that he was sending Strang to Prague 'to obtain some idea of the atmosphere in that city' and also to Berlin. (Cabinet Minutes, 25 May 1938, Cabinet 26 (38), CAB 23/93.)

92 Henderson to Cadogan, 2 June 1938, C 5617/1941/18, FO 371/21724.

93 Notes by Strang, 29 and 30 May 1938, *DBFP*, 3/I, nos 349, 350.

94 Newton to Halifax, 16 May 1938, *DBFP*, 3/I, no. 221.

95 Notes by Strang, 29 May 1938, *DBFP*, 3/I, no. 349.
96 Newton to Halifax, 12 April 1938, *DBFP*, 3/I, no. 140. See also Newton to Halifax, 11 April 1938, *DBFP*, 3/I, no. 134. Newton previously raised the question of neutralising Czechoslovakia in the immediate aftermath of the annexation of Austria. (See Newton to Halifax, 15 March 1938, *DBFP*, 3/I, no. 86.)
97 Minutes by Sargent, 14 and 22 April 1938, C 2989/1941/18 and C 2984/1941/18, FO 371/21715.
98 Minute by Vansittart, 14 April 1938, C 2989/1941/18, FO 371/21715.
99 Minute by Vansittart, 26 May 1938, C 5235/1941/18, FO 371/21723.
100 Halifax to Newton, 25 May 1938, *DBFP*, 3/I, no. 315.
101 'Memorandum on the Possibility of Neutralising Czechoslovakia', *DBFP*, 3/I, appendix IV. See also C 5235/1941/18, FO 371/21723. The memorandum is undated, but minutes were attached on 26 and 27 May 1938.
102 This was pointed out in a covering letter by Sargent when copies of the memorandum were sent to Phipps, Henderson and Newton, 9 June 1938, C 5235/1941/18, FO 371/21723.
103 Notes by Strang, 29 May 1938, *DBFP*, 3/I, no. 349.
104 Notes by Strang, 29 and 30 May 1938, *DBFP*, 3/I, nos 349, 350.
105 Halifax to Henderson, 22 May 1938, *DBFP*, 3/I, no. 281.
106 Henderson to Halifax, 23 May 1938, *DBFP*, 3/I, no. 294.
107 Minute by Mallet, 26 May 1938, C 5009/1941/18, FO 371/21722.
108 Halifax to Henderson, 25 May 1938, *DBFP*, 3/I, no. 310.
109 Halifax to Newton, 25 May 1938, *DBFP*, 3/I, no. 311.
110 *HC Deb.*, 336, col. 1396, 26 May 1938; Halifax to Newton, 27 May 1938, *DBFP*, 3/I, no. 325.
111 Halifax to Henderson and Newton, 27 May 1938, *DBFP*, 3/I, no. 326.
112 Henderson to Halifax, 28 and 31 May 1938, *DBFP*, 3/I, nos 337, 352.
113 Newton to Halifax, 29 May 1938, C 5094/1941/18, FO 371/21722.
114 Halifax to Newton, 2 June 1938, C 5334/4839/18, FO 371/21773. See also note 3 to document no. 349, *DBFP*, 3/I, pp. 410–11.
115 Newton to Halifax, 4 June 1938, C 5520/4839/18, FO 371/21773. See also note 3 to document no. 349, *DBFP*, 3/I, pp. 410–11.
116 Halifax to Newton, 8 June 1938, C 5555/4839/18, FO 371/21773. See also note 3 to document no. 349, *DBFP*, 3/I, pp. 410–11.
117 Newton to Halifax, 8 June 1938, C 5582/4839/18, FO 371/21773.
118 Minute by Sargent, 9 June 1938 and Halifax to Newton, 10 June 1938, *ibid*; Halifax to Newton, 15 June 1938, C 5701/4839/18, FO 371/21773.
119 Report from Sutton-Pratt, 20 July 1938, C 6226/4839/18, FO 371/21773.
120 Halifax to Phipps, 30 May 1938, *DBFP*, 3/I, no. 347.
121 Newton to Halifax, 24 and 25 May 1938, *DBFP*, 3/I, nos 298, 307, 308.
122 Halifax to Newton, 27 and 30 May 1938, *DBFP*, 3/I, nos 329, 345; Halifax to Phipps, 27 May, 1938, *DBFP*, 3/I, no. 330; Newton to Halifax, 27, 28, 29 and 31 May 1938, *DBFP*, 3/I, nos 332, 339, 340, 351.
123 Memoranda by Vansittart, 26 and 31 May 1938, C 5260/1941/18 and C 5261/1941/18, FO 371/21723. Vansittart responded with a message expressing satisfaction over Henlein's declared intention of adhering to his modified demands and also urged a speedy commencement of negotiations. (See also Halifax to Newton, 31 May 1938, *DBFP*, 3/I, no. 353.)

4
Choosing a Mediator

Although the British government considered Henlein's modified demands, outlined during his visit to London in May 1938, as reasonable, and Halifax exhorted the Czechoslovak authorities to accept them as a basis for discussion since 'it should not be impossible to reach a solution along these lines',[1] the Foreign Secretary was far from sanguine about the outcome. At the end of May, he indicated to his French counterpart that it would 'be wise to be prepared for a possible breakdown in these negotiations' and suggested that Britain and France should have in readiness 'proposals for bringing the two parties together again'. The plan Halifax had in mind was for mediation by a small international commission, – 'presided over by a strong chairman, with special qualifications for the delicate task' ahead. British membership of the commission would not be insisted on – indeed, this proposed method of mediation was preferred precisely in order to limit British involvement. Halifax also stressed that the British government did 'not wish to be manoeuvred into the position of an arbitrator'.[2] But the determination to avoid becoming directly involved in the problems of Czechoslovakia could not be sustained. As had been the case with the proposed international commission on Czechoslovak–German frontier violations, it was again Germany which, albeit on this occasion indirectly, induced a change of attitude in London.

The British Ambassador in Germany was unenthusiastic about the plan and advised Halifax, on 1 June, that it was unlikely to find favour in Berlin. Henderson cited a stipulation, made by Hitler in conversation some three months previously, that Germany could not '"allow third parties to interfere in the settlement of her relationship with countries with large German populations"'. He believed Hitler would only agree to secret talks with Britain, and possibly France, 'with a view to drawing up a settlement which he would impose on Henlein' and which Britain and France 'would be expected to press on Czechoslovakia'.[3] The following day, Henderson reiterated his opposition to the proposed commission in a letter to Cadogan. Although he understood and sympathised with the British government's unwillingness to be manoeuvred into arbitration, the Ambassador anticipated that, ultimately, such a role would be unavoidable. 'If deadlock ensues', Henderson speculated, 'my belief is that what you will decide will be to instruct me to see Hitler and to try to get him to agree to induce Henlein to accept something provided ourselves or the French can persuade Beneš to accept something else.'[4] In effect, Henderson was offering his services as a mediator, at least at the Berlin end of the proceedings. News of Henderson's proposed approach was received 'with satisfaction' by Newton,[5] but the idea was not taken up by the Foreign Office.

Although London showed little interest in Henderson's offer to intercede with Hitler, the Ambassador's advice did result in a change of policy. Roberts minuted on 2 June that, failing German agreement concerning an international commission, Henderson's suggestion of secret talks with Berlin would have to be adopted.[6] Reasoning at greater length two days later, Mallet concurred with this view. He believed that Germany might 'give away a good deal more in secret' than it would if pressure for concessions were applied publicly. 'What is essential', Mallet concluded,

> is that we ourselves should devise and have ready a plan for overcoming a deadlock which we think fair and practical and which we will be prepared both to press on the Czechs and to propose to the Germans as the limit of what we consider the Czechs could reasonably be asked to grant.[7]

Sargent, however, was prepared to take a more robust stand towards Berlin. Although accepting Henderson's interpretation of Hitler's likely attitude, he foresaw the possibility of Henlein and Hodža jointly requesting British assistance, in which case Hitler's objections to British mediation would have to be ignored. Concerning Henderson's suggestion of direct secret talks with Germany, Sargent believed they would be 'full of pitfalls – the chief of course is that we have not sufficient technical knowledge to carry on such negotiations – in vacuo'. Talks with Hitler might, however, be considered in the future, if the British government acquired the necessary information about the problem. That could be achieved by the appointment of a single British adviser, a move which, Sargent believed, would be easier and quicker to accomplish than resorting to an international commission. He added:

> The objection, of course, is that a single British adviser would commit H.M. Government more directly than would an international Commission. In fact that is why we proposed the latter. But it looks as though in the end we may have to abandon this cover and ourselves assume a greater measure of direct responsibility.[8]

This was not the first occasion on which the idea of employing an individual British adviser or mediator had been considered in the Foreign Office.

It had first been raised at the end of March in the (previously discussed) 'Next Step' memorandum,[9] to which Sargent himself may have contributed that suggestion. He certainly advocated a similar idea in late April, arising from a visit to Czechoslovakia by Captain Victor Cazalet, a Conservative Member of Parliament. Cazalet not only met members of the government, including Beneš and Hodža, but also conferred with Henlein, whom he found 'essentially honest and rather simple-minded'.[10] Commenting on Cazalet's report, Sargent noted that 'the presence of an impartial intermediary in Czechoslovakia at the present time might be very useful'. He went on to suggest, tentatively, 'I wonder whether it would not be possible to find some unofficial Englishman who enjoyed the confidence of both Henlein and Hodža, and send him out privately to Prague on the chance of his being able to act as unofficial mediator'.[11] Cadogan's response was less than enthusiastic, although he conceded that an unofficial mediator 'might do no harm'. He was also unable to put forward any suitable names.[12] Halifax, however, was a little more positive, minuting: 'I think the idea of a "mediator" is worth keeping in mind, but I don't think we are quite there yet. And he would not be an easy person to find.'[13]

Despite Halifax's expression of mild approval, over a month was to elapse before Sargent's idea was pursued further. Even during Strang's (previously discussed) visit to Central Europe in the aftermath of the May Crisis, no reference was made to the possibility of mediation by an individual British figure, although the idea of sending a British investigator was considered alongside that of a commission of enquiry. By early June, however, the attitude in the Foreign Office had changed, although there remained still a marked lack of enthusiasm for direct British mediation. On 8 June, Cadogan recorded his agreement with Sargent's recently repeated suggestion, minuting that, if all else failed, 'we should not be deterred from attempting mediation alone'.[14] The following day, Halifax also concurred with this view, noting, with evident reluctance: 'I agree that in the last resort, if deadlock occurs and if the international comm[ission] is not likely to be acceptable, we might [have] to be prepared to act alone – to try and resolve the deadlock.'[15]

The decision had been made, albeit reluctantly, at the highest level in the Foreign Office, that, should circumstances in Czechoslovakia warrant it, and should the proposed international commission be unacceptable, Britain would mediate directly in the Sudeten German dispute. A week later the idea of an international commission had been totally abandoned and mediation by a British individual was substituted. Although a meeting of the Cabinet took place on 15 June, at which Czechoslovakia was discussed and ministers were informed of the decision to send British observers to that country, no mention appears to have been made then of mediation.[16] The issue was, however, discussed by the Cabinet Foreign Policy Committee the next day, when Halifax outlined the proposal for mediation by a 'distinguished person'. After a short discussion, in which 'the names of two such persons were mentioned', the Foreign Secretary agreed to 'think the matter over in the light of the views expressed by his colleagues'.[17] Later that day, Mallet recorded that 'it is now proposed that in the event of a breakdown of negotiations, a single British mediator should be sent out to try and reconcile the two parties'. Acknowledging the part played by the Berlin Ambassador in this change of policy, Mallet observed that 'this does not meet the German objections to interference and publicity, but comes nearer to what Sir N. Henderson thinks the Germans might agree to than any other suggestion that has been made'.[18]

There remained, however, two further important matters to be settled: the consent had to be obtained of the parties concerned and a mediator had to be chosen. For the moment, until it became more certain that mediation would be required, no mention was made of the proposed British initiative to the protagonists. The process of finding a suitable potential mediator, however, started immediately in the knowledge that, as Cadogan noted on 8 June, 'if a breakdown comes, we shall want to act quickly'. Although Cadogan was again unprepared to put forward any names,[19] the following day, Halifax was less reticent. He listed three suggestions: the journalist and politician, Lord Lothian; Sir Horace Rumbold, a former diplomat; and Richard Feetham, a South African judge with experience of chairing government commissions.[20]

The Foreign Secretary's candidates found little favour with Sargent on the grounds that 'however eminent these three persons may be in their respective walks of life, none of them has had any practical experience of administration, and still less of dealing with problems of government in the face of racial or religious hatreds and jealousies'. In Sargent's opinion such experience was most likely to be found amongst Indian Governors, and he therefore privately contacted the India Office for suggestions. The India Office also supplied three names: Lord Hailey, Sir Geoffrey de Montmorency, and Sir Herbert Emerson, all present or former Governors of Indian provinces.[21] The next day, the Foreign Secretary added a further name, Sir Laurie Hammond, an ex-governor of Assam. Accepting Sargent's point about the suitable qualifications of Indian Governors, Halifax, himself a former Viceroy of India, suggested that further consultation should be undertaken with the India Office.[22] In the Foreign Office, however, Vansittart was unimpressed by the growing list of candidates, arguing that most of them would 'look slightly *pour rire* in foreign eyes – some of them more than slightly, and rightly'. He himself, however, had no suggestions to make.[23]

On 18 June, Halifax sought Newton's opinion of the new contingency plan, referring to the possible use of an 'independent British expert' to try and achieve a reconciliation in Czechoslovakia. The Foreign Secretary indicated that he had in mind a person 'with practical experience of administration and of minority problems, such as an ex-Governor of an Indian Province', but also mentioned the possibility of appointing an 'outstanding figure, without necessarily any expert knowledge'.[24] Newton gave a general welcome to the proposal but advised that 'it would be better to avoid choosing anyone whose experience is limited to India or Colonial Empire, since, however foolishly, the connection might be considered derogatory by both sides'. He added that 'experience of the problems of Ireland, French Canadians, Palestine or Danzig' would be useful qualifications for a prospective mediator providing that his previous record had not 'compromised him with either side'. Newton was rather more positive towards the alternative idea of selecting an 'outstanding figure' for the role of mediator, pointing out that the appointment of such a person would be advantageous as his 'impartiality and judgement could more readily be accepted by both parties'. He also suggested that the prominent person should 'be assisted by a man with practical experience of administrative and racial problems'. Although he appreciated that there might be 'political and practical objections', Newton further envisaged that the expert might have to remain in Czechoslovakia for 'some time' in order to supervise the execution of any agreement reached through the process of mediation.[25] Something rather similar to Newton's formula, of an eminent person accompanied by an expert – albeit not in the area of nationalities disputes – was later adopted when the Runciman Mission was appointed, although Mallet commented, on the receipt of Newton's despatch, that 'if we could find one person who combined all qualities it would be simpler'.[26]

Halifax also sought Newton's advice about informing the Czechoslovak authorities of the contemplated British initiative.[27] Newton cautioned against any reference being made to the possibility of mediation until the negotiations between the government and the SdP had failed beyond doubt. He feared that 'if the Czechoslovak government felt they could fall back upon a kind of court of appeal in which there was no German element it may be that they would make less effort to reach agreement direct in the belief that they will get better terms than by direct negotiations'. Newton added that the agreement of the SdP would also be required before any mediation could be attempted.[28] Mallet concurred, but suggested that Newton should be asked to watch the situation carefully 'so that we may be ready to step in as soon as a deadlock is reached'. This reasoning was approved, and Newton instructed accordingly.[29]

There were, however, two other parties involved in the Czechoslovak crisis; Germany and France. As far as the former was concerned, Newton's statement that the SdP could 'hardly be regarded as independent agents'[30] prompted Mallet to advise that the Foreign Office 'ought, therefore, before deciding on this scheme, to consider whether the German government are likely to approve of it'. He believed it desirable to involve Germany and to attempt 'through Sir. N. Henderson, to bring about a triangular agreement'.[31] This suggestion also appears to have met with general approval, though Sargent added that 'it would be necessary to word our communication in such a way as not to give the German government the power of direct veto'.[32] Cadogan concurred, minuting that Berlin should not be informed until it became necessary. 'We should then,' he suggested, 'simply *inform* the German Gov[ernmen]t that we are putting in, or offering, a mediator to try and bring Henlein and the Czech[oslovak] Gov[ernmen]t together again.'[33] For the time being, Germany was to remain ignorant of the plan for British mediation taking shape in London. France was also kept uninformed of the development; a fact to which Sargent drew attention on 27 June.[34] Two days later, Halifax instructed Phipps to outline the proposal to the French Minister of Foreign Affairs, explaining that he was 'trying to obtain the assistance of some outstanding figure whose name would be known, not only in England, but also abroad'.[35]

In London efforts continued to identify a suitable mediator. Newton's objections to colonial administrators were sustained in the Foreign Office and, as noted by Sargent on 22 June, the search was extended 'among "outstanding figures" without any particular knowledge'. Five such persons were listed by Sargent as being under consideration (though imperial experience still featured largely amongst their qualifications): Sir Montagu Butler, Master of Pembroke College, Cambridge, and a former Indian Governor; Sir Francis Humphrys, a former Indian civil servant and diplomat; Field Marshal Sir Philip Chetwode, former Commander-in-Chief of the Army in India; Lord Macmillan, an eminent jurist; and Lord Horne, a former Cabinet Minister.[36] The search for a mediator was also concerning the Prime Minister's Office. That same day, Sir Horace Wilson, officially the Chief Industrial Adviser to the government but more significantly a close friend and confidant of Chamberlain and the *éminence grise* behind the Chamberlain administration, informed the Foreign Secretary of the results of his 'reflections' on the matter.

Wilson's list also consisted of five names, amongst them, for the first time, that of Lord Runciman, whose qualifications were: 'A record that would impress – Ex-Cabinet Minister of wide and varied experience, covering a period which must have made him known internationally. A puzzling demeanour which might, in certain circumstances, be of advantage.' Wilson evidently had some reservations about Runciman, as he added: 'Someone would have to accompany him and do most of the work, but he could be relied on to put the results across.' He concluded, however, by stating that, although Runciman was 'superficially not a model negotiator', he was 'capable of crispness which again might turn out to be what was needed'. Other possible mediators suggested by Wilson were: the jurist Lord Macmillan (who also appeared on the Foreign Office list of possibles), described as 'a tireless mediator with all the necessary tact and pertinacity'; the historian and former Cabinet Minister H.A.L. Fisher who had 'charm of personality' and whose 'reputation as a historian ... might make a considerable appeal to those elements in the controversy who want the situation looked at from the point of view of historical associations'; the industrialist, Lord Riverdale, 'tactful and experienced in elucidating and reconciling conflicting points of view' and who knew Germany well and spoke German; and Sir Norman Raeburn, a barrister, described as 'fully competent, with all the necessary personality, but perhaps too unknown'. In a postscript to the letter, Wilson ranked the candidates in order of preference: Macmillan, Runciman, Riverdale, Raeburn. Fisher was excluded on grounds of ill health.[37]

Despite appearing in second place in Wilson's list of suggested mediators, the proposed assignment was offered to Runciman a week later, on 29 June, possibly on Halifax's initiative.[38] When outlining the scheme to Runciman, the Foreign Secretary stressed that he envisaged the mediator, if sent, going to Czechoslovakia in a 'personal capacity and not as a representative of H.M. Government'. The mediator would 'not therefore receive any official instructions and would not be expected to work on any particular plan'.[39] This formula was adopted in an attempt to circumvent what was seen in the Foreign Office as the major drawback to British mediation – the deepening of British involvement in the Sudeten German problem. As Halifax explained in a despatch to Phipps, he was 'anxious to avoid committing His Majesty's Government to the support of any particular proposals and the mediator would therefore act in a purely independent capacity'.[40]

Runciman's initial response to Halifax's offer was negative, due, at least in part, to a misunderstanding concerning the 'independent' status of the proposed mediator. The day following the discussion, Runciman informed Halifax by letter of his unwillingness to undertake the assignment: 'I have given some thought to the proposal which we discussed yesterday and I feel able to say that for me to go to Prague on no ostensible mission or merely as an intruding watchman, with nothing else to take me there would create poor atmosphere. An Ambassador at large seldom succeeds.' Runciman added the suggestion that, as the economist Lord Stamp would be visiting Prague in September to preside over a meeting of the International Statistical Bureau, 'he could use all his spare time in conciliating – without anyone wondering what mischief he was up to!'[41] This alternative did not appeal to Halifax, who indicated that he would 'greatly prefer' Runciman to Stamp.[42]

On receipt of Runciman's letter, Halifax instructed Sargent to correct the misunderstanding.[43] Sargent's attempts to arrange a further discussion with the reluctant candidate were unsuccessful, as Runciman was leaving London that evening for Scotland. Sargent, therefore, drafted a letter of explanation,[44] which Halifax sent the following day addressed to Runciman's yacht *Sunbeam* at Oban, preceding it by a telegram.[45] Before the letter was actually despatched,[46] however, Runciman reinforced his refusal by telegraphing Halifax: 'Very sorry, but on further reflection am confirmed in my view.'[47]

In his letter to Runciman, Halifax explained that the mission would be undertaken:

> with the concurrence of the Czech[oslovak] Government and the Sudeten leaders, and with the knowledge of the German Government. There would be no reason for keeping it secret or unofficial; on the contrary, it would probably be useful that it should be blazoned abroad. Thus you would not be going to Prague, as you suggest in your letter, 'on no ostensible mission': on the contrary, your status would be official and your mission would be public.

The Foreign Secretary then reiterated that he envisaged the mediator acting in his 'personal capacity' and not officially representing the British government. It was this point, he believed, which had given rise to Runciman's misunderstanding. 'Your position would be', Halifax explained, 'that the Czech[oslovak] Government and the Sudeten leaders had, on the suggestion of H.M. Government, invited you to help them to reach an agreement within the framework of the present Czechoslovak State on the points still at issue between them.' Halifax concluded by holding out the prospect of mediation not being required, adding however, that he would 'certainly feel happier if I knew that I could count upon you in the event of my suddenly having to take action in order to put an end to a dangerous deadlock'.[48] Four days later Halifax again telegraphed Runciman in Oban urging acceptance of the assignment and requesting an early decision.[49]

Runciman received the various Foreign Office messages on his arrival in Oban on 6 July, and reluctantly began to reconsider. He telegraphed Halifax: 'I find it difficult to overcome disadvantages but if you make it dependent on both sides accepting me as mediator I cannot refuse without further talk with you.' Runciman proposed to return to London for this purpose on 12 July.[50] This meeting at the Foreign Office also proved inconclusive, although Runciman asked to see, and was provided with, some papers before he made up his mind.[51] Three days later, Halifax again urged Runciman to send his 'final decision' by the afternoon of 17 July, as he would be seeing Chamberlain that evening.[52] Runciman made a further visit to the Foreign Office on 16 July, where, after lengthy discussion with Cadogan, Sargent and Strang, he conditionally accepted the role of mediator in the Sudeten German dispute.[53] Later that day, Halifax informed Newton of Runciman's appointment 'on the understanding that he will not be asked to proceed unless both sides agree to receive him and to explain to him fully their respective points of view'.[54]

Thus, by mid-July, just as the situation in Czechoslovakia was becoming critical,[55] the British government had a mediator available for action. The conditions on which Runciman agreed to undertake the possible assignment – the consent and co-operation of the two parties directly concerned – were not particularly restrictive, as they were essential prerequisites for any British attempt at mediation. However, as Newton pointed out, it would not be easy to gain the consent of the Czechoslovak government for the proposed British move, despite the fact that such an initiative would commit Britain to a closer interest in the Czechoslovak crisis. The Czechoslovak authorities, he believed, would be reluctant to accept any outside mediation, viewing it as a 'blow to their pride', and, moreover, would be particularly wary of British mediation as they suspected that British policy in Central Europe was directed to 'selfish ends'.[56]

Newton's opinion was shared by Mallet, who added, that it would be particularly difficult to gain the agreement of the Czechoslovak government 'because if the negotiations break down it will be because the Czechs are not prepared to go far enough to meet the Sudetens'. Building on this assumption, Mallet continued: 'This means that in any "compromise" that we are to find we shall have to induce the Czechs to make further concessions on all or some of the three points on which it appears ... that they are still unwilling to meet the Sudetens.' The points at issue were: autonomy for Sudeten German territory; 'the recognition of authoritarian principles in that area'; and, ultimately, the question of Czechoslovakia's foreign policy orientation. Mallet concluded, therefore, that Britain must 'be ready not only to mediate on internal affairs, but also to put forward a scheme for changing the international status of Czechoslovakia'.[57] This frank statement concerning the nature of the projected mediation was, evidently, representative of Foreign Office thinking at the time. Sargent recorded his agreement with Mallet's reasoning, and his minute was in turn initialled by Cadogan and Halifax.[58] Only Vansittart expressed disagreement, pointing out that concessions concerning Czechoslovakia's foreign policy 'will be most difficult from the Czech point of view and most damaging from our own'.[59]

A further sensitive aspect of the proposed mission was the degree of official British involvement – a question that had long troubled the Foreign Office. This is evident from reaction to a related suggestion, made to Newton by a Czechoslovak journalist, that 'a British mission might come to Czechoslovakia in order to investigate thorny questions and give advice as to their treatment'.[60] In the Foreign Office, Roberts reacted strongly against the idea, arguing that it would 'involve this country much more closely in the intricacies of this question than our own proposal to send a British mediator'. He believed that only the two parties directly involved, the Czechoslovak government and the SdP, had sufficient knowledge of local conditions to reach a settlement, and only an individual mediator, and not a mission, could bring them together. A further drawback of a mission, in Roberts' opinion, was that it would have to remain behind to ensure that the solutions reached were implemented. A British mission would therefore commit the British government 'not only to a much closer, but also to a more extended interest in the details of Czech minority problems than seems desirable'. A single British mediator was, therefore, preferable.[61]

Strang was also concerned about this aspect. What troubled him most, however, was the possibility that the British Minister in Prague 'might slip into the position of a mediator'. He was worried by a recent dispatch indicating that Newton was 'beginning to go backwards and forwards between the Czechoslovak Government and his German colleague'. Although preferring either an independent mediator or an advisory mission, Strang was nevertheless concerned about the full implications of any British inspired action, no matter how remote it was officially from the British government. He noted that Britain would 'become a good deal more closely involved in the negotiations and in subsequent developments than might be comfortable', concluding 'that having taken the initiative in this question, we cannot avoid becoming more and more deeply involved if we wish to use our full influence to bring about a solution'.[62]

Strang was, in effect, expressing the basic dilemma which confronted the British government over the Czechoslovak crisis. If, in order to avoid the possibility of war, Britain involved itself directly or indirectly in seeking a solution to the Sudeten German problem, it would inevitably become entangled in the affairs of Central Europe. But if, on the other hand, the British government disinterested itself in the problems of Czechoslovakia, then the nationalities dispute there might well lead to a war, into which Britain would be dragged anyway. Neither of these alternatives was much to the liking of those in charge of formulating British foreign policy, but the danger of war was considered the greater of the two evils. Reluctantly, therefore, it was decided that the risk of deeper involvement in the affairs of Czechoslovakia would have to be taken, though it was hoped that this could be reduced by maintaining that the proposed British mediator would be acting in an independent capacity and not on behalf of the British government. It became increasingly difficult, however, to maintain this assertion, despite its frequent repetition, once details of the composition of the mission became known.

The man chosen by the British government to head the mission of investigation and mediation in the Sudeten German dispute – the first Viscount Runciman of Doxford – was a wealthy shipping magnate and former politician, who listed his recreations as 'yachting, shooting and fishing'.[63] He was then 67 years of age, and cut a pale, diminutive figure with a penchant (shared with Neville Chamberlain) for wing-collars. Earlier in his political career, the combination of his facial pallor and emotional impassivity had earned him, from his colleagues, the description of 'the alabaster statesman'.[64] Another observer of Runciman's appearance, the French diplomat

Robert Coulondre, described him in memorable but less laudatory terms: 'Cold and impassive, dressed in a morning coat with his head perched on top of a high wing-collar, he appeared to have fallen from the pages of Dickens and resented the fall.'[65]

The object of Coulondre's graphic description was born (perchance in the year of Dickens' death) on 19 November 1870, in South Shields on Tyneside. During Runciman's early childhood, his father, also Walter Runciman (later the first Baron Runciman of Shoreston), was first a ship's mate and then a master. Walter Runciman senior claimed to have run away to sea, from a not uncomfortable home, at the age of 12 in 1859. After serving on several sailing ships, he gradually progressed to his first command 12 years later. In 1884, he was forced to give up the sea on medical advice and settled ashore, where he soon demonstrated his remarkable business acumen by developing, despite a depression in the industry, a successful ship-owning business based on the River Tyne. Through this, over the years, he amassed considerable wealth.

The two major formative influences in the early life of young Walter Runciman – in addition to that of the sea – were his parents' ardent Wesleyan Methodism and concomitant teetotalism, and his father's practical demonstration of the benefits (for some) of private enterprise and free trade. His formal education was acquired privately and at South Shields High School and later at Trinity College, Cambridge, where he gained a third class in the historical tripos in 1892. On leaving university, Runciman entered his father's business and soon proved not to lack his parent's commercial ability. Within a year he became his father's partner, conducting business under the name of Walter Runciman and Co. Ltd, founded previously in 1889. The early 1890s were years of rapid growth of the company, renamed the Moor Line Ltd in 1897. This shipping line, consisting of tramp steamers trading throughout the world, became the foundation of the diverse business interests of the Runciman family, and young Runciman contributed considerably to its success. He become managing director of the Moor Line, jointly with his father, on its creation, a position he held until 1905.

But Runciman's interests were not entirely occupied with shipping, and, with the encouragement and assistance of his father, he turned his attention also in the direction of politics. The religious and economic beliefs that influenced his upbringing, not unnaturally, drew him in the footsteps of his father, [66] towards the Liberal Party. Runciman's first contest for a parliamentary seat, in Gravesend in 1898, ended in failure. He was successful the following year, however, in the then two-member constituency of Oldham, where he beat the Conservative candidate Winston Churchill into third place. But this success was short-lived. In the general election of 1900, during the Boer War, Churchill reversed the earlier result. Two years later, however, Runciman again entered Parliament, this time on a more permanent basis, as member for Dewsbury.

In the House of Commons Runciman's speeches, concerned mostly with economic and maritime matters, soon attracted the attention of the Liberal leadership. He gained his first ministerial post, as Parliamentary Secretary to the Local Government Board, in 1905, in the Liberal administration under Sir Henry Campbell-Bannerman. Promotion followed quickly. Within two years, Runciman became Financial Secretary to the Treasury, often a prelude to a post of Cabinet rank. When Herbert Asquith became Prime Minister in 1908, Runciman entered the Cabinet as President of the Board of Education. Three years later, following the reconstruction of the Cabinet, he became President of the Board of Agriculture and Fisheries. Runciman reached the zenith of his early political career in 1914 when, after resignations from the Cabinet at the outbreak of war, he was appointed President of the Board of Trade. He held this post for the first two years of the war, but left office in December 1916 when Asquith resigned the premiership. Two years later, in the general election of 1918, in common with the majority of Asquith's followers, Runciman lost his seat in Parliament.

As a Minister of the Crown, Runciman soon acquired, at least amongst his friends and allies, a reputation for clarity of exposition at Cabinet meetings and for efficient administration in his department. One of his ministerial colleagues, Charles Hobhouse, considered him a candidate for high office, though perhaps not the highest.[67] Setting aside the premiership therefore, Runciman's most probable potential place of destination, in view of his interest in economic affairs, was the Treasury. However, he was destined never to arrive there, which perhaps did not surprise those other observers of his political life who were less generous in their evaluation of his qualities. Pre-eminent amongst Runciman's critics was David Lloyd George – who was, admittedly, far from being an impartial observer of his colleague's career. In his memoirs, written in the 1930s after a prolonged period of unpleasantness between himself and Runciman, Lloyd George conceded that Runciman was a man of 'high intelligence' but who suffered from a 'lack of continuity and persistent application which ... accounted for his failure to achieve any distinguished success in any of the various offices which he has held'.[68]

Even allowing for the fact that when measured against the Olympian standard of Lloyd George's capacity for action many were found wanting, the tangible achievements of Runciman's early ministerial career were certainly not exceptional. Although, whilst at the Board of Education, he succeeded in pacifying the leadership of the Church of England, which had been disturbed by repeated, but unsuccessful, Liberal attempts to loosen the Church's hold on education, he failed to get his proposed legislation on to the statute book. After successful negotiations with the Archbishop of Canterbury and Nonconformist leaders, Runciman introduced his compromise Education Bill in November 1908, but was soon forced to withdraw it in the face of attacks from other prominent churchmen who were dissatisfied with the terms of the Bill.

Despite his failure to achieve a new Education Act, Runciman emerged from the negotiations with credit establishing for himself a reputation as a conciliator. Within a short period of time, however, these gains were negated by his inept handling of the, so-called, 'Holmes circular' affair, concerning a confidential memorandum containing derogatory remarks about elementary school teachers. When its contents became known to the press, it gave rise to predictable protests from educationists. The matter was taken up in Parliament by a young Conservative back-bencher, Samuel Hoare, who succeeded in severely embarrassing the Liberal administration. In response to Hoare's questioning, Runciman first denied the existence of the document and later refused to accept responsibility for it. Runciman's failure to anticipate fully the damaging implications of the affair and to undertake the necessary remedial action in good time, combined with his intemperate treatment of Hoare in the House of Commons (whom he accused of receiving stolen property), did little to enhance his ministerial reputation and he was soon moved to another Cabinet position.[69]

As President of the Board of Agriculture, Runciman's life was less eventful. In that office, which he held for almost three years, Runciman initiated no important legislation although the question of land reform was a live political issue at the time. He was, however, preparing measures to improve the housing of agricultural labourers, but these were abandoned at the outbreak of war. Whilst at the Board of Agriculture, Runciman was, in reality, rather eclipsed by his more dynamic colleague at the Treasury, Lloyd George, who in 1913 launched his Land Campaign aimed at reviving support in the country for the Liberal Party by the promise of radical reform.

Despite Runciman's lack of substantial ministerial achievement, Britain's entry into war in 1914 – which he opposed to the extent of threatening resignation – found him occupying the important office of President of the Board of Trade. In that position he was not only responsible for safeguarding Britain's food and raw materials supplies, but also for industrial relations on the home front. Notwithstanding the generous tribute paid to him by his friend and colleague Sir Edward Grey in his memoirs,[70] Runciman was not particularly successful in that office. Basically, Runciman's effectiveness at the Board of Trade, like that of Asquith's wartime administration in general, was limited by his dedication to *laissez-faire* policies not entirely appropriate to wartime conditions. He was wedded to the principle of private enterprise and resisted repeated demands for greater government control over trade and industry. Despite substantial rises in the price of food in the shops, resulting from wartime disruption, shortages in supply and steeply rising shipping freight charges, Runciman refused to introduce measures to control the distribution of food and to increase the government's control of shipping. Shortly before losing office, however, he reluctantly came to accept the need for stringent food control, although it was left to the succeeding administration to implement the necessary measures.[71]

Undoubtedly Runciman's most significant failure was his inability to find a solution to the wartime shipping problem, resulting from a combination of inefficiencies and enemy action, despite the fact that through his personal experience he was theoretically well qualified for the task. During the autumn of 1916, Runciman considered the situation to be so desperate that he predicted a total breakdown in shipping, but had no suggested solutions to offer. The memoranda on the problem, which he submitted to his fellow ministers at the time, enjoyed the distinction of being described by one critic as 'the most invertebrate and hopeless of any memoranda presented to the Government during the war by a responsible head of a department on a great issue'.[72] However, Runciman's predicted breakdown in shipping did not occur. Tighter government control exercised by Lloyd George's administration resulted in more vessels being brought into service and reduced the volume of imports by restricting non-essential items – both steps which Runciman failed to carry out effectively. The answer found to the submarine menace – the introduction of convoys – had earlier been strenuously resisted, not only by the Admiralty, but also by Runciman, who opposed the measure on grounds of inefficiency.[73]

In the field of industrial relations, Runciman's record was little better, despite the fact that in 1914 he, together with Lloyd George (then Chancellor of the Exchequer) managed to secure the co-operation of most trade unions for the duration of the war by providing for the settlement of disputes in essential industries by arbitration. But the agreement was not comprehensive and failed to prevent a miners' strike in South Wales in March 1915. Eventually, in June, Runciman intervened in the dispute and a compromise settlement was achieved, only to be rejected by the miners who came out on unofficial strike in defiance of a proclamation issued on Runciman's initiative making the stoppage illegal. The law was unenforceable, however, and the government responded by sending a ministerial delegation, including Runciman, to negotiate a new settlement. A month later, when Runciman ruled that the agreement did not apply to craft workers, the dispute erupted anew, forcing him to reverse the ruling. Runciman's critics argued that the crisis was largely of his own making, resulting from his belated intervention and inconsistency, and C.P. Scott, the editor of the *Manchester Guardian*, questioned his competence as a minister.[74]

Runciman's presidency of the Board of Trade was not entirely without success. The commercial experience which he brought with him into office did prove to be of substantial value. Indeed, Runciman devoted considerable attention to stimulating trade in difficult wartime conditions, his major achievement being the negotiation of a comprehensive trade agreement with Italy, which he concluded personally in 1916. More controversial, however, was his involvement in promoting the Paris Resolutions, measures aimed not only at waging economic warfare during the course of the War itself, but also at discriminating against the German economy following the conclusion of the War. Predictably, this earned him few plaudits amongst his fellow free-traders.

Nevertheless, however regarded, Runciman's achievements at the Board of Trade were, on balance, insubstantial. Unlike Lloyd George, he did not enjoy waging war and, indeed, his entire political outlook rendered him unsuited for the task. Moreover, the exigencies of government in wartime placed a considerable strain on Runciman's health, forcing him, in 1914 and in 1916, to take long periods of rest from his ministerial duties. Consequently, when he left office in December 1916, his disappointment was tinged with relief. His friends later pointed out that the burdens of office which Runciman carried during the War were such that, on his departure from government, his responsibilities were divided between four different posts.[75]

Clearly, Runciman's ministerial performance did not measure up to those of the two most brilliant figures of the Liberal and Coalition administrations between 1906 and 1916 – Lloyd George and Churchill. It was subsequently noted by one observer that, although his quality was of 'the first rank', he lacked the 'demonic gifts' possessed by the other two figures.[76] Curiously however, they both, despite their criticisms of Runciman,[77] appear to have had sufficient confidence in his ability to recommend him, on different occasions, for an important government position – though their respective motivations for doing so may have been less than transparent. On the formation of the Coalition government in May 1915, Lloyd George proposed Runciman for the Ministry of Munitions which, in the event, went to Lloyd George himself, as Runciman was considered 'an able man of business' but to lack 'sufficient standing' in the country.[78] Earlier, in October the previous year, when Churchill wished to take command of the forces defending Antwerp, he telegraphed Asquith recommending Runciman as his successor at the Admiralty. The Prime Minister, however, received this advice with derision. Nevertheless, shortly before losing office in December 1916, Asquith himself did contemplate placing Runciman in the Admiralty. This implied estimation of Runciman's ministerial capability contrasted with Asquith's earlier judgement, made in February 1915, when, informing his friend and confidante Venetia Stanley of the order of merit of his Cabinet colleagues, he placed Runciman no higher than joint ninth out of sixteen.[79]

Following his departure from government at the end of 1916 and the loss of his parliamentary seat two years later, Runciman began to concentrate attention on his business affairs. In common with many other British shipowners, the Runcimans found the war years very profitable,[80] despite the fact that their main family business – the Moor Line – lost 26 vessels (over half the entire fleet) during the conflict. Further profits were made from the sale of the remaining vessels in January 1920, at the height of the brief post-war shipping boom. Later that year, the Moor Line went into voluntary liquidation and the assets were distributed. By 1921, however, when the boom had turned to depression, the Runcimans revived the Moor Line, and repeated the spectacular pattern of growth they had achieved in the depressed years of the 1890s. By 1924, their new fleet numbered 23 vessels.

Although shipping continued to play a major role in Runciman's life – in addition to being the Vice-Chairman of the Moor Line up to 1930 and thereafter Deputy Chairman of the Royal Mail Steam Packet Company, he was also Chairman of the International Shipping Conference in 1926 and President of the Chamber of Shipping of the United Kingdom from 1926 to 1927 – his business interests diversified into other areas. He became the principal proprietor of the 'country house' periodical, *The Field*; Chairman of the United Kingdom Provident Institution, a major insurance company; and a director of the Westminster Bank and of the London, Midland and Scottish Railway Company. Runciman was also a considerable landowner. In 1909, he acquired from his father the estate at Doxford, near Alnwick in Northumberland, the title of which he took for his Viscountcy in 1937. In 1926, Runciman also purchased the Hebridean island of Eigg,[81] which he used as a base for his beloved sailing activities off the west coast of Scotland.

The cultivation of his business interests, however, did not prevent Runciman from playing an active role in Liberal Party politics and seeking, and eventually gaining, re-entry into the House of Commons. After fighting unsuccessful contests in Edinburgh North in 1920, Berwick-upon-Tweed in 1922, and Brighton in 1923, he was returned to Parliament as member for Swansea West in 1924. Four years later he was joined in the Commons by his wife Hilda Runciman (herself the daughter of a former Member of Parliament, and whom he had married in 1898[82]) who won a by-election in St Ives. At the general election of 1929, Runciman transferred to his wife's Cornish constituency,[83] which he continued to represent until his elevation to the peerage in 1937. Runciman's move from Swansea West to the St Ives seat was a consequence of his dispute with Lloyd George. Being one of the principal figures in the anti-Lloyd George faction of the Liberal Party, known as the 'Wee Frees', Runciman felt rather vulnerable on his adversary's home territory and sought safer ground for himself outside Wales.

During the early 1920s, with the Liberal Party split between the supporters of Asquith and those of Lloyd George, Runciman remained loyal to his leader, and devoted much of his political activity to combating Lloyd George, whom he disliked personally and whose policies and political methods he detested. In 1921, whilst Lloyd George was Prime Minister of the Coalition Government, Runciman, together with Asquith and others, attempted, unsuccessfully, to persuade the ailing Lord Grey to return to politics to lead a 'centre party' in opposition to Lloyd George. Following the breakup of the Lloyd George Coalition and the 1922 general election, in which the Liberals were pushed into third place by the rising Labour Party, the two warring factions of the Liberal Party became formally reunited – but the differences remained. After his return to the House of Commons in 1924, Runciman participated in several unsuccessful attempts to limit the influence of Lloyd George within the party. However, following Asquith's departure from the leadership in 1926, control of the Liberal Party fell into the hands of Lloyd George, and Runciman, who continued to regard the new leader as a 'millstone'[84] round the neck of the party, found himself increasingly at variance with official Liberal policy. Consequently, by the early 1930s Runciman was again devoting most of his attention to his substantial business interests; he attended the House of Commons less frequently and was on the verge of abandoning politics altogether.

But Runciman's political career was not yet over. Although he was not included in the first National Government formed in August 1931, probably on the insistence of Lloyd George, following the general election in October of that year, Runciman returned to his former position of President of the Board of Trade. He was then aged 60, and had been out of Government office for almost 15 years. On account of this, his critics included him amongst the 'unburied dead', as members of the National government were disparagingly referred to. His supporters, however, considered it only natural that a man of his business talent should be called on to assist the country overcome its economic problems.

In the 1931 general election, Runciman stood not as a Liberal candidate, but as a Liberal National. This break-away group, under the leadership of Sir John Simon, became increasingly less distinguishable from the Conservatives. The Simonites' main disagreement with the official Liberal Party concerned their abandonment of the hitherto fundamental Liberal policy of Free Trade. Although at first sight Runciman appeared an unlikely convert to the Liberal Nationals, being one of the staunchest advocates of Free Trade in British politics, as a businessman he was anxious to see overseas trade brought into balance, if necessary by the introduction of tariffs. His feud with Lloyd George may have been an additional reason for Runciman distancing himself further from the Liberal Party and joining the Simonites.

It appears that, when reconstructing his Cabinet in October 1931, the Prime Minister, Ramsay MacDonald, originally had Runciman in mind for the Chancellorship of the Exchequer.[85] In the event, that office went to Neville Chamberlain; but Runciman's return to the Board of Trade was welcomed by advocates of Free Trade, who depended on his counterbalancing Chamberlain's protectionist policies at the Treasury. He was, however, to disappoint them greatly by performing the major volte-face of his political career. Although still paying lip-service to Free Trade, Runciman supported the imposition of protectionist policies, arguing that they were only a temporary expedient. Nevertheless, when, in 1932, following the introduction of Imperial Preference after the Imperial Economic Conference in Ottawa (which Runciman attended), the Free Trade ministers resigned from the government, Runciman, despite some unease, remained in office. At least one of the departing ministers, Viscount Snowden, considered Runciman to have betrayed the Free Trade cause.[86] Other observers took a more charitable view of Runciman's performance at the Board of Trade, and paid tribute to the measures taken by him to mitigate the full force of protectionism.[87]

When Stanley Baldwin replaced MacDonald as Prime Minister in June 1935, Runciman remained at the Board of Trade. He continued to be regarded as a senior member of the administration, and as such was included in the select inner circle of ministers who were kept fully informed of the events surrounding the abdication of Edward VIII in 1936. Runciman, who was perturbed about the spreading information concerning the King and Mrs Simpson, used his influence as a leading Methodist to pacify the scandalised Free Churches. Indeed, such was his political prominence in the mid-1930s, that Runciman's name featured in speculations concerning possible candidates for the Premiership in succession to both MacDonald and Baldwin.[88]

But that was not to be. Instead, Runciman's ministerial career came to an end for the second time when Chamberlain became Prime Minister in May 1937. Wishing to have 'someone active to reorganise the work' of the Board of Trade, Chamberlain offered Runciman instead the post of Lord Privy Seal.[89] But Runciman, who hoped to become Lord President of the Council, was offended by the offer of an office he regarded as the 'poorest in the Cabinet',[90] and opted instead to withdraw from the House of Commons and take a peerage, while complaining bitterly to others that he had been shabbily treated by Chamberlain.[91] Although not regretting Runciman's departure from the Cabinet, Chamberlain was concerned about the breach in personal relations, which he ascribed to Hilda Runciman's jealousy of Sir John Simon,[92] who was designated to become Chancellor of the Exchequer. Hitherto, relations between Chamberlain and Runciman, although not entirely free from tension, had been generally cordial, despite their differences in political outlook.[93] When informed of Runciman's complaint concerning the Cabinet post offered, Chamberlain endeavoured to heal the breach by a friendly letter.[94] This conciliatory gesture had the desired effect and amicable relations between Chamberlain and Runciman were restored, with Runciman offering to undertake at any time any task in which he could be of assistance.[95] He could not have imagined when making the offer that it would be taken up in little over a year's time, and that it would involve him in the unfamiliar field of international relations.

Throughout his political career prior to 1938, Runciman showed little interest in mainstream foreign affairs, although he did regard international economic relations as something of a speciality. Even when out of office during the 1920s, he devoted considerable attention to international economic affairs, frequently speaking on the subject in the House of Commons, following his re-entry to Parliament in 1924. It was on one such occasion, in 1927, that Runciman showed some concern for the future of Central Europe. He foresaw closer economic co-operation developing amongst the states in that region, possibly in the shape of a customs union under German domination. Believing such a development would be detrimental to British interests, Runciman expressed the hope of 'Great Britain taking the lead rather than leaving it to the Germans to prescribe for Europe what they believe to be best'.[96] His appeal, however, had little effect, and Britain's economic role in Central Europe remained relatively insubstantial and continued to be such even after Runciman's return to government.

During his second term of office at the Board of Trade, Runciman attended the 1932 Lausanne Conference on war reparations, earning generous praise for his supporting work from Chamberlain, who, as Chancellor of the Exchequer, headed the British delegation.[97] Although the Lausanne Conference, in effect, ended Germany's reparation payments, it made little headway on the question of war debts to the United States, which was only resolved later by the default of the debtors. The issue of the British debt lay behind an ostensibly private visit Runciman made to America almost five years later, in January 1937, during which he held discussions with United States government representatives, including President F.D. Roosevelt. Although he appears to have won the lasting friendship and admiration of the President,[98] Runciman failed to make much progress in the negotiations. The outstanding war debt remained an obstacle to improved relations between Britain and the United States, much to the regret of Runciman, who was a strong advocate of closer transatlantic ties.

Outside the economic field, Runciman's limited involvement in foreign policy and related matters resulted mainly from his Cabinet membership and from the inescapable effects of the First World War. On the eve of the outbreak of war in August 1914, he was included amongst those Cabinet Ministers who were opposed to fighting Germany. Unlike some members of the group, Runciman did not sustain his opposition to the point of resignation. He remained in the government in the belief that the war had to be waged to ensure freedom of navigation in the English Channel, but saw his role at the Board of Trade largely as that of attempting to mitigate its harmful effects on the economy. After leaving office he continued to be unenthusiastic about the war, wishing it to be pursued only to the extent of achieving the original 1914 war aim of restoring the frontiers in western Europe to their pre-war positions. Towards the end of 1917, he supported Lord Lansdowne's abortive move for a negotiated settlement with Germany.[99]

Although greatly relieved by the ending of the fighting in November 1918, Runciman was very uneasy about the emerging peace terms. When the details of the proposed Versailles Treaty with Germany became known in May 1919, he was highly critical of its terms, although he refused to sign a public letter of protest. Runciman objected to the treaty on the grounds that it was 'indeterminate', that it failed to achieve an 'element of equilibrium', and that no provision was made for its 'continuous revision'.[100] He was equally critical of the economic clauses of the peace treaty, sharing the misgivings of Maynard Keynes that the reparation payments demanded of Germany would exert a detrimental effect on the post-war economic recovery of Europe.[101]

On the question of the future for the nationalities within the Austro-Hungarian Empire – the effects of which were to concern Runciman 20 years later – his liberal outlook caused him to be sympathetic towards their national aspirations. This is attested to by the fact that during 1915 he allowed his London house, at 8 Barton Street, Westminster, to be used for a meeting in support of the activities of Czechoslovak *émigrés*.[102] But Runciman's sympathy towards the nationalities of Austria-Hungary fell short of supporting their claims for full independence. Particularly during 1917, when there appeared to be some prospect of a separate peace with the Habsburg Empire, with the implied continuation of the Empire's existence, Runciman was eager to promote this.[103] He was motivated not only by his wish to bring the war to a speedy conclusion, but also by his desire to preserve as much as possible of the Austro-Hungarian Empire.

Runciman was also concerned with another consequence of the First World War – the coming to power of the Bolsheviks in Russia and the subsequent war of intervention. Unlike many of his contemporaries, he was not convinced that Bolshevism posed an immediate threat to Western Europe, and therefore regarded the British military incursions into northern and southern Russia as the 'gravest of ... follies' which would lead to 'God only knows where'. Runciman saw parallels between the situation in Russia and that of revolutionary France 120 years previously, with *émigrés* clamouring for foreign intervention which resulted in disaster for those who intervened. If there was a danger of militant Bolshevism spreading across Europe, Runciman argued: 'how much better for us to say to the Bolshevik government: "If you want to fight us you must come to the Rhine to meet us."' His concern was, of course, not for Soviet Russia, but for the 'social, industrial and financial consequences' within Britain of delays in demobilisation arising from the intervention.[104]

Similar considerations caused Runciman to advocate developing trade links with the new Soviet State. On at least two occasions, in 1926 and in 1930, he spoke in the House of Commons in favour of export credit guarantees being made available for trade with the Soviet Union as he saw no reason for refusing to trade 'with those with whom we disagree'.[105] Runciman was able to put this belief into practice on his return to the Board of Trade, securing, in 1934, a trade agreement with the Soviet Union. On the question of the unpaid Russian debts to Britain, he was less consistent. In 1924, Runciman vigorously denounced the Labour government for concluding an agreement with the Soviet Union which amounted to 'capitulation' on the issue of the debts.[106] By 1930 however, he argued that these debts were 'matters of the past' and should not obstruct the improvement of trading relations.[107] As Runciman himself had stated on an earlier occasion, he saw no reason to permit 'political prejudice to stand in the way of sound British business'.[108] Clearly, although Runciman had no great admiration for the Soviet Union, he was prepared to maintain a pragmatic attitude towards it.

At least one aspect of the outcome of the First World War, however, met with Runciman's unqualified approval. That was the creation of the League of Nations, which he later described as 'almost the only unconditionally good thing' to emerge from the Paris Peace Conference.[109] Even before the war was concluded, Runciman, together with other prominent Liberals, was a keen proponent of the League of Nations idea, advocating the creation of an international organisation for the preservation of peace and able to wield strong military and economic sanctions 'against any and every aggressor'.[110] Appalled by the carnage and destruction of the First World War, he saw the League as offering the hope of a new international ethic. Runciman continued to support the League during the 1920s and early 1930s, regarding it as a potentially powerful force for the promotion of peace and disarmament – essential prerequisites, he believed, for prosperity and for social reform – and wished to see its membership extended to all nations, including in particular the United States and the Soviet Union.[111]

However, this enthusiasm for international collective security was not to persist. When, in 1935, consideration was being given to the introduction of economic sanctions against Italy, which was occupying Abyssinia in defiance of the League of Nations, Runciman expressed strong opposition to the plan, believing sanctions to be a 'folly' and preferring to keep out of 'the horrid business'. He was concerned about the probable economic and military costs, believing the measures would be ineffective unless applied by the entire world. In his view, a more 'sensible' way of impressing Mussolini and others would be to display the British fleet in the Mediterranean.[112] Early in 1936, Runciman also opposed the possible introduction of an oil embargo against Italy on the grounds of its ineffectiveness without United States participation. He was one of two Cabinet ministers who dissented from the proposal, and it was no doubt much to his satisfaction that the policy was never implemented.[113]

Runciman's marked reluctance to countenance any challenge to Italian expansion in the mid-1930s was not entirely surprising. Although not sharing his father's almost limitless admiration for Mussolini,[114] Runciman was nevertheless favourably disposed towards Fascist Italy, at least during its early years. Like his father, he was impressed by Mussolini's achievements, particularly the restoration of the Italian economy in the mid-1920s, which caused him to observe in a speech, in 1926, that although the Fascist dictatorship was 'a strange political experience', in terms of commerce 'Italy has never known such prosperity as she does to-day'. He contrasted the depressed state of British engineering and shipbuilding industries with their revival in Italy, where the work-force was 'working more regularly' and even 'their trains run more punctually'. Runciman drew a sharper distinction still with the depressed economic state of France, which was lacking a figure 'forceful enough to do what Mussolini has done for Italy'.[115]

These admiring references were not isolated examples of Runciman's attitude towards Mussolini and similar sentiments were repeated on several other occasions during the 1920s and early 1930s. In the aftermath of the General Strike in 1926, Runciman observed, with evident approbation: 'In Italy a strike of this character, or any other, would not have been permitted.'[116] On a further occasion in the early 1930s, when complaining of the indecisiveness of many elected governments in the face of pressing international problems, Runciman was reported to have expressed the wish: 'Would that there were more Mussolinis in the World!'[117] Runciman was even able to combine, in a jocular remark, his approval of Mussolini with his professed zeal for free trade, declaring that: 'I should like to see some Mussolini wipe out all tariffs, all at once.'[118] Evidently, Runciman admired what he considered to be the efficiency of the Fascist regime and chose to ignore the darker side of Mussolini's rule. This was a point of view not uncommon amongst Conservatives in Britain, but one that was shared by few of his fellow Liberals.

By contrast, Runciman's attitude towards the National Socialist regime in Germany, after it had come into being in 1933, was rather more critical. He was particularly disturbed by the brutal internal policies of the Nazis and observed to Baron von Neurath, the German Foreign Minister, visiting London in 1933, that the persecution of Jews 'signified the collapse of civilisation in Germany'. As President of the Board of Trade, Runciman also told Neurath that, in view of the existing instability in Germany, the establishment of more substantial trade links between their two countries was out of the question.[119]

Nevertheless, shortly after leaving ministerial office in May 1937, Runciman received an invitation to join the Anglo-German Fellowship, described to him as 'a sort of clearing-house where misunderstandings are removed and moderating influences encouraged'.[120] The Fellowship was, in fact, a powerful force for the promotion of Nazi Germany in Britain, its members being drawn primarily from the British political and business elite.[121] Although there is no evidence to indicate that Runciman took up this offer of membership, it suggests that his attitude towards Germany was perceived as being at least sufficiently ambiguous to justify the approach being made, particularly in view of the fact that his elder son Leslie (also a prominent businessman) was a member of the Fellowship.[122]

Certainly, as far as Germany's foreign policy was concerned, Runciman appeared much less censorious than he was towards Nazi anti-Semitism, particularly when breaches of the Treaty of Versailles were involved. When, following Hitler's announced intention to rearm Germany in defiance of the Peace Treaty in 1935, *The Times* saw no reason to object, Runciman praised the newspaper for introducing 'a breath of fresh air' into relations between Britain and Germany. He evidently concurred with the view of the newspaper's editor, Geoffrey Dawson, that the 'dictated' Versailles Treaty was no longer binding.[123]

In his capacity as a member of several Cabinet committees concerned with defence and foreign policy[124] Runciman had a voice in the formulation of the British response to the accelerating pace of Germany's rearmament in the mid-1930s. Although his contribution was relatively modest, it clearly demonstrated his strong opposition to Britain undertaking any European defence commitments. Despite accepting, in 1934, that Germany should be regarded as the 'ultimate potential enemy', he opposed Vansittart's proposals for the containment of that country.[125] Later that year, he also opposed the suggestion that, in the event of Germany rearming, Britain should guarantee France and the Low Countries, considering the proposal to be 'inconsistent with the Treaty of Locarno'. Subsequently, when discussing a specific guarantee to Belgium, he was again far from enthusiastic and also distrustful of France.[126] His general outlook at that time was encapsulated in his expressed hope that 'we should make every effort to keep ourselves clear of commitments which would make our entanglement in a war later inevitable'.[127]

Runciman's preferred course of action was to seek to deter war by strengthening Britain's armed forces, but he was clearly concerned about their all-round inadequacy in 1934. He observed, at a meeting of the Disarmament Committee, that: 'In the air we are weak, in the navy we are weak, and in the army we are in an even worse position.'[128] Reflecting both his personal interests and his ministerial responsibilities as President of the Board of Trade, Runciman's main concern was for the navy. Although considering any rise in national expenditure to be 'extremely undesirable', he supported proposals for naval rearmament in order to strengthen Britain's international standing, which would otherwise, he argued, 'have an unfortunate effect on our industry and trade'.[129] Two years later, in 1936, when again discussing the appropriate response to Germany with fellow ministers, Runciman's remarks were also confined primarily to economic considerations. He endorsed the view that economic concessions alone would not satisfy Germany and would need to be preceded by a political solution.[130]

Evidently, Runciman's general outlook placed him firmly in the mainstream of supporters of British government policy in the late 1930s. The clearest expression of his attitude on the related issues of defence strategy and foreign policy was made, shortly before his departure from the Cabinet in May 1937, in the following note:

i) Our commitments already go far enough
ii) Our defences are inadequate both for defence and for the purpose of adding weight to our foreign policy
iii) For both purposes it is essential that our air force should be as strong as the strongest
iv) For this and for other reasons the Navy must be strengthened no matter what may be done in Naval extension by Germany[131]

Such sentiments could equally well have flowed from the pen of Chamberlain himself.

Runciman also expressed support for another aspect of Chamberlain's foreign policy, the attempt to weaken the Rome–Berlin Axis by achieving a rapprochement between Britain and Italy. During the course of negotiations with the Italian government in March 1938, Halifax encouraged Runciman to visit Mussolini, indicating that such a meeting could 'do nothing but good' and offering the services of the Rome Embassy if required.[132] But Runciman showed little enthusiasm for meeting Mussolini, arguing that it would be wrong for him to visit Rome prior to the conclusion of the agreement. He nevertheless expressed fervent hope for the successful outcome of the negotiations and that 'better things are to be expected for the future all round'. Runciman added the characteristic observation that: 'The world is very wicked and the branches of the green bay trees spread over many lands.'[133] Clearly, he was far from happy with the developing international situation in the early months of 1938.

Irrespective of Runciman's general concern with these issues, resulting largely from his membership of the Cabinet and its committees, foreign policy considerations did not constitute one of his main interests and he was clearly far from being a specialist in that field. Evidently, therefore, it was not for his expertise in international affairs that he was selected for the mission of mediation in Czechoslovakia. On the other hand, during the course of his political career, spanning several decades, Runciman had acquired considerable experience in international negotiations, albeit mainly of an economic and commercial nature. Doubtless more important still was the fact that – despite their different party-political backgrounds, and despite the personal differences between them (which resulted in Runciman's departure from the Cabinet) – Runciman largely shared Chamberlain's world outlook. They were both convinced that Britain was unprepared for war, and that conflict with Germany therefore had to be avoided, particularly if Britain's principal strategic interests were not endangered. They were also in agreement that, in view of Britain's perceived weakness, no further defence commitments could be undertaken –

which precluded, of course, any undertaking to defend Czechoslovakia. The Prime Minister and his advisers could therefore be confident that, in his new-found role of international mediator, Runciman would not subscribe to any recommendations likely to cause distress or embarrassment to the British government. He was not to disappoint them.

Notes

1 Halifax to Newton, 31 May 1938, *DBFP*, 3/I, no. 353.
2 Halifax to Phipps, 30 May 1938, *DBFP*, 3/I, no. 347.
3 Henderson to Halifax, 1 June 1938, *DBFP*, 3/I, no. 359.
4 Henderson to Cadogan, 2 June 1938, C 5617/1941/18, FO 371/21724.
5 Newton to Halifax, 15 June 1938, *DBFP*, 3/I, no. 415.
6 Minute by Roberts, 2 June 1938, C 5297/1941/18, FO 371/21723.
7 Minute by Mallet, 4 June 1938, *ibid.*
8 Minute by Sargent, 7 June 1938, *ibid.*
9 See above pp. 45–6.
10 'Account of Captain Cazalet's Interview with Konrad Henlein at Carlsbad on April 19th, 1938', C 3316/1941/18, FO 371/21716. See also Cazalet's notes on his visit, C 3703/1941/18, FO 371/21717.
11 Minute by Sargent, 30 April 1938, C 3316/1941/18, FO 371/21716.
12 Minute by Cadogan, 3 May 1938, *ibid.*
13 Minute by Halifax, 3 May 1938, *ibid.* See also note 1 to document no. 347, *DBFP*, 3/I, p. 401.
14 Minute by Cadogan, 8 June 1938, C 5297/1941/18, FO 371/21723.
15 Minute by Halifax, 9 June 1938, *ibid.*
16 Cabinet Minutes, 15 June 1938, Cabinet 28 (38), CAB 23/94.
17 FPC Minutes, 16 June 1938, FP (36) 31st Meeting, CAB 27/624. No indication is given of the identities of the persons under discussion, nor of the views of other members of the Committee.
18 Memorandum by Mallet, 'Czechoslovak Mediation', 16 June 1938, C 6005/1941/18, FO 371/21725.
19 Minute by Cadogan, 8 June 1938, C 5297/1941/18, FO 371/21723.
20 Minute by Halifax, 9 June 1938, *ibid.*
21 Minute by Sargent, 13 June 1938, *ibid.*
22 Minute by Halifax, 14 June 1938, *ibid.* No further reference to such a meeting could be traced.
23 Minute by Vansittart, 23 June 1938, C 6167/1941/18, FO 371/21725.
24 Halifax to Newton, 18 June 1938, *DBFP*, 3/I, no. 425.
25 Newton to Halifax, 21 June 1938, *DBFP*, 3/I, no. 431.
26 Minute by Mallet, 22 June 1938, C 6167/1941/18, FO 371/21725.
27 Halifax to Newton, 18 June 1938, *DBFP*, 3/I, no. 425.
28 Newton to Halifax, 21 June 1938, *DBFP*, 3/I, no. 431.
29 Minute by Mallet, 22 June 1938, C 6167/1941/18, FO 371/21725; Halifax to Newton, 22 June 1938, *DBFP*, 3/I, no. 432.
30 Newton to Halifax, 21 June 1938, *DBFP*, 3/I, no. 431.
31 Minute by Mallet, 22 June 1938, C 6167/1941/18, FO 371/21725.
32 Minute by Sargent, 22 June 1938, *ibid.*
33 Minute by Cadogan, 28 June 1938, *ibid.*

34 Minute by Sargent, 27 June 1938, *ibid.*
35 Halifax to Phipps, 29 June 1938, *DBFP*, 3/I, no. 452.
36 Minute by Sargent, 22 June 1938, C 5297/1941/18, FO 371/21723. In the case of the last mentioned person, the typed minute reads 'Lord Hoare' with the name 'Horne', preceded by a question mark, added in what appears to be Sargent's handwriting. (See also Minute by Strang, 16 July, 1938, C 7249/1941/18, FO 371/21728.)
37 Wilson to Halifax, 22 June 1938, H/VI/24, FO 800/309. Wilson added, in passing, the observation: 'I imagine you will have thought of the ex-ambassadors. (Rumbold, Lindley, Macleay and Graham.)' He also disclosed, without explanation, that amongst his 'many rejects' was Lothian – one of Halifax's original candidates, as was Rumbold.
38 R.R. James, *Victor Cazalet: A Portrait*, (London, 1976), p. 204. Halifax told Cazalet that it was 'his idea to send Runciman'.
39 Halifax to Runciman, 1 July 1938, H/VI/29, FO 800/309, and Runciman Papers, WR 292.
40 Halifax to Phipps, 29 June 1938, *DBFP*, 3/I, no. 452.
41 Runciman to Halifax, 30 June 1938, H/VI/27, FO 800/309, and Runciman Papers, WR 292.
42 Halifax to Runciman, 1 July 1938, H/VI/29, FO 800/309, and Runciman Papers, WR 292.
43 Note by Halifax, 30 June 1938 [?], H/VI/27, FO 800/309.
44 Minute by Sargent, 30 June 1938, H/VI/27A, FO 800/309.
45 Halifax to Runciman (telegram), 1 July 1938, Runciman Papers, WR 292.
46 Minute by Caccia, 1 July 1938 [?], H/VI/27A, FO 800/309.
47 Runciman to Halifax (telegram), 1 July 1938, H/VI/30, FO 800/309, and Runciman Papers, WR 292.
48 Halifax to Runciman, 1 July 1938, H/VI/29, FO 800/309, and Runciman Papers, WR 292. Although the letter refers to the meeting of 'yesterday', this took place on 29 June.
49 Halifax to Runciman (telegram), 4 July 1938, Runciman Papers, WR 292.
50 Runciman to Halifax (telegram), 6 July 1938, H/VI/28, FO 800/309, and Runciman Papers, WR 292.
51 Minute by Strang, 16 July 1938, C 7249/1941/18, FO 371/21728.
52 Halifax to Runciman, 15 July 1938, Runciman Papers, WR 292.
53 Minute by Cadogan, 16 July 1938, C 7273/1941/18, FO 371/21728. In a subsequent minute on the same sheet, Halifax responded with the single word 'Good'. Robert Stopford, Secretary to the Mission, recalled later that it was only on the urging of King George VI that Runciman accepted the task. (R.J. Stopford, 'Prague, 1938–1939', p. 9, Stopford Papers, RJS 2/1, and Runciman Papers, WR 354.) No such message could be traced in the Runciman Papers or in the Royal Archive at Windsor.
54 Halifax to Newton, 16 July 1938, *DBFP*, 3/I, no. 493.
55 See below pp. 111–13.
56 Newton to Halifax, 21 June 1938, *DBFP*, 3/I, no. 431.
57 Minute by Mallet, 22 June 1938, C 6167/1941/18, FO 371/21725.
58 Minute by Sargent, 22 June 1938, *ibid.* Initialled by Cadogan and Halifax on the same date.
59 Minute by Vansittart, 23 June 1938, *ibid.*
60 Newton to Sargent, 13 July 1938, C 7249/1941/18, FO 371/21728. The suggestion was made by A. Šašek, foreign editor of the Agrarian Party organ *Venkov*.

61 Minute by Roberts, 15 July 1938, *ibid.*
62 Minute by Strang, 16 July 1938, *ibid.*
63 *Who's Who*, (London, 1938).
64 Lord Riddell, *Intimate Diary of the Peace Conference and After, 1918–1923*, (London, 1933), p. 179. The description originated with John Seeley, Secretary of State for War between 1912 and 1914. See also H.H. Asquith, *Letters to Venetia Stanley*, M. and E. Brock, eds, (London, 1982), p. 409.
65 R. Coulondre, *De Staline à Hitler: Souvenirs de deux ambassades, 1936–1939*, (Paris, 1950), p. 155.
66 Runciman senior, who had been active in Radical politics in South Shields in the late 1880s and early 1890s, chose to concentrate his energies on developing his business interests. Subsequently however, he was active in the Northern Liberal Federation, being its chairman from 1904 to 1926, and between 1914 and 1918 he sat as a Liberal Member of Parliament for Hartlepool.
67 E. David, *Inside Asquith's Cabinet: From the Diaries of Charles Hobhouse*, (London, 1977), p. 122.
68 D. Lloyd George, *War Memoirs*, (6 vols, London, 1933–36), III, pp. 1073–4. Lloyd George also cited Lord Kitchener's assessment that: '"No man in the Cabinet has disappointed me as much as Runciman."'
69 For details of the Holmes circular affair see J.A. Cross, *Sir Samuel Hoare: A Political Biography*, (London, 1977), pp. 17–29.
70 Viscount Grey, *Twenty-five Years, 1892–1916*, (2 vols, London,1925), II, pp. 243–4. Grey referred to Runciman's 'special aptitude, experience and knowledge' which made his work at the Board of Trade 'efficient and valuable'.
71 For details see Sir W.H. Beveridge, *British Food Control*, (London, 1928), pp. 16, 22–9, 341.
72 C. Addison, *Politics from Within*, (2 vols, London, 1924), II, p. 11. Addison, a protégé of Lloyd George, evidently shared his patron's estimation of Runciman.
73 Runciman argued that convoys could only proceed at the pace of the slowest ship and that the simultaneous arrival in Britain of large numbers of vessels would add considerably to the already severe congestion in the ports. To which Lloyd George retorted in his memoirs that Runciman evidently considered it 'better for a ship to be at the bottom of the sea than to arrive late ... [and] the more ships that failed to arrive, the less would be the congestion of the ports'. (Lloyd George, *War Memoirs*, III, pp. 1139–41.)
74 T. Wilson, ed., *The Political Diaries of C.P. Scott, 1911–1928*, (London, 1970), p. 131. For details of the dispute see G.D.H. Cole, *Labour in the Coal-Mining Industry, 1914–1921*, (Oxford, 1923), pp. 27-30.
75 The new posts, in addition to that of the President of the Board of Trade, were those of Minister of Labour, Controller of Shipping, and Controller of Food.
76 S. Gwynn, 'Ebb and Flow', *Fortnightly Review*, vol. 144 (July–December 1938), p. 358.
77 Lloyd George's critical views have been cited previously. Churchill, on one occasion in 1913, expressed relief to have escaped the company of 'little smugs like Runciman'. (R.S. Churchill, *Winston S. Churchill*, (London, 1969), II, Companion, part 3, p. 1884.)
78 See memorandum by Lord Stamfordham (Private Secretary to King George V), 25 May 1915, in M. Gilbert, *Winston S. Churchill*, (London, 1972), III, Companion, part 2, p. 943.
79 Asquith, *Letters*, pp. 263, 452; H.A. Taylor, *Robert Donald*, (London, 1934), p. 139.

80 In 1918, in a letter to Lloyd George, Churchill fulminated against war profits, singling out in particular 'old Runciman's ill-gotten gains'. (Gilbert, *Winston S. Churchill*, IV, pp. 169–70.)

81 For a brief account of the Runcimans' stewardship of Eigg, purchased for £15 000, and which remained in the family's possession until 1966, see J. Urquhart, *Eigg*, (Edinburgh, 1987), pp. 142–50.

82 The Runcimans, who were the first husband and wife to sit together in the House of Commons, had two sons and three daughters.

83 In the 1929 election, Hilda Runciman vacated the seat for her husband and herself stood unsuccessfully in Tavistock.

84 Runciman to Harcourt Johnstone, 3 October 1928, Runciman Papers, WR 218.

85 Roskill, *Hankey: Man of Secrets*, II, pp. 570–1. Hankey, Secretary to the Cabinet, advised MacDonald against appointing Runciman to the Treasury on the grounds that, as Lord Kitchener had pointed out, Runciman failed to achieve results. Hankey added that Runciman was 'not an easy man in a Cabinet' on account of his 'hard uncompromising radical mind that bases itself on principle, but is not easily moved'. He agreed, however, that Runciman 'was firm, had a gift of exposition in Parliament, and [was] competent'.

86 Viscount Snowden, *An Autobiography*, (London, 1934), II, pp. 998–9. Snowden was particularly disappointed as he had recommended Runciman for the Board of Trade on account of his impeccable Free Trade credentials. In fact, shortly before re-entering the government, Runciman had departed from his principles and advocated a tariff on imported luxury goods.

87 See L.S. Amery, *My Political Life*, (London, 1953–55), III, pp. 87–9.

88 Sir C. Petrie, *The Chamberlain Tradition*, (London, 1938), p. 241; James, *Victor Cazalet*, p. 144.

89 Neville Chamberlain's diary, 13 March and 5 May 1937, Chamberlain Papers, NC 2/24A.

90 Runciman to Chamberlain, 7 May 1937, Chamberlain Papers, NC 7/11/30/112, and Runciman Papers, WR 285.

91 Neville Chamberlain's diary, 11 May 1937, Chamberlain Papers, NC 2/24A. See also Chamberlain to Runciman, 6 May 1937, Runciman Papers, WR 285.

92 Neville Chamberlain to Hilda Chamberlain, 30 May 1937, Chamberlain Papers, NC 18/1/1006.

93 'Extract from note of [Cabinet] meeting held in the House of Commons on 26 May 1937', Runciman Papers, WR 285. See also Runciman to MacDonald, 12 August 1933 and Runciman to Chamberlain, 12 August 1933, Runciman Papers, WR 265. Chamberlain recalled that their only notable disagreement over policy in the National Government concerned the subsidies advanced to the Cunard Steamship Company to complete the construction of the liner *Queen Mary*. Runciman opposed this on the grounds that Cunard was receiving preferential treatment not available to its competitors.

94 Chamberlain to Runciman, 6 May 1937, Runciman Papers, WR 285. See also Chamberlain to Runciman, 10 May 1937, Runciman papers, WR 285, and Chamberlain Papers, NC 7/11/30/113.

95 Neville Chamberlain's diary, 11 May 1937, Chamberlain Papers, NC 2/24A.

96 *HC Deb.*, 209, col. 521.

97 Chamberlain to Runciman, 10 July 1932, Runciman Papers, WR 357.

98 See copy of letter from F.D. Roosevelt to A. Murray, 25 February 1937, Runciman Papers, WR 284.

99 Lansdowne to Runciman, 9 October 1917, Runciman Papers, WR 161.
100 Runciman to L.T. Hobhouse (copy), 21 May 1919, Runciman Papers, WR 177.
101 Robert Cecil to Runciman, 2 January 1920, Runciman Papers, WR 185.
102 R.W. Seton-Watson, *Masaryk in England*, (Cambridge, 1943), p. 72.
103 *HC Deb.*, 100, cols 2082–90; and 103, cols 176–84.
104 Runciman to Crewe, 5 January 1919, Crewe Papers.
105 *HC Deb.*, 237, cols 2245–50. See also *HC Deb.*, 192, cols 1105–10.
106 Text of Runciman's speech delivered at Stockton, 30 August 1924, Runciman Papers, WR 195.
107 *HC Deb.*, 237, cols 2247–8.
108 *HC Deb.*, 192, col. 1106.
109 W. Runciman, 'A New International Ethic', *The Methodist Times*, 15 September 1921. (Cutting in Runciman Papers, WR 190.)
110 W. Runciman, 'The Radical Outlook', *Contemporary Review*, vol. 113 (January 1918), p. 4. See also *HC Deb.*, 100, cols 2086–7.
111 W. Runciman, *Liberalism as I See It*, (London, 1927), Runciman Papers, WR 212.
112 Runciman to Wigram, 28 August 1935, Runciman Papers, WR 280. Runciman continued to be greatly concerned about the effects of sanctions on British trade. He informed the Cabinet in May 1936 that 'British traders were sustaining considerable losses owing to the continuance of sanctions, without receiving any compensation'. He added that 'irreparable harm' had been caused to British interests and 'traders were anxious to know how long sanctions were going to continue'. Losses would continue to mount 'to a very serious total' if sanctions were not ended. (Cabinet Minutes, 27 May 1936, Cabinet 39 (36), CAB 23/84.)
113 Cabinet Minutes, 26 February 1936, Cabinet 11 (36), CAB 23/83. In a Cabinet Memorandum, written the previous December, Runciman conceded that although 'complete petroleum sanctions would no doubt quickly and effectively cripple Italian activities', that could only be achieved given the whole-hearted commitment, primarily, of the United States, but also of Romania and the Soviet Union. (Memorandum by Runciman, 'Oil Supplies for Italy', 9 December 1935, CP 236 (35), CAB 24/157.)
114 Runciman senior visited Mussolini whilst cruising in the Mediterranean on his yacht *Sunbeam* during the spring of 1926. He came away with the impression that there was 'nothing of the despot in that man' who had restored 'order, thrift and prosperity' to Italy. This 'great work of regeneration' placed Mussolini in the 'first rank of wise benevolent administrators'. Runciman senior admired the Fascists for their methods of dealing with adversaries (particularly the 'panacea' of administering large doses of castor oil), for defeating the 'Communists', and for the harmony introduced into Italian industrial relations where strikes and unemployment were 'thing[s] of the past'. He expressed the wish that Britain and France might find 'a similar Mussolini spirit'. (Sir W. Runciman, *'Sunbeam' in the Mediterranean during the Regime of Mussolini*, (London, 1926), pp. 17–19, 21-6.)
115 Text of a speech by Runciman (Moor Line speech), 31 March 1926, Runciman Papers, WR 316. Runciman's views were communicated directly to Mussolini by Runciman's father. During the course of his visit to Mussolini in April 1926, Runciman senior read out to his host the relevant passages from his son's Moor Line speech. (Runciman senior to Runciman, 24 April 1926, Runciman Papers, WR 203.)

116 *Alnwick Country Gazette*, 25 December 1926. (Cutting in Runciman Papers, WR 315, vol. 34.)
117 *New York Herald Tribune*, 31 July 1932, feature article by C.P. Thompson, 'England's Key Man at Ottawa'. (Cutting in Runciman Papers, WR 254.)
118 *Sheffield Independent*, 20 January 1927. (Cutting in Runciman Papers, WR 315, vol. 34.)
119 Note of a conversation between Runciman and Neurath, 16 June 1933, Runciman papers, WR 265.
120 Lionel Gall to Runciman, 29 May 1937, Runciman Papers, WR 285.
121 See R. Griffiths, *Fellow Travellers of the Right: British Enthusiasts for Nazi Germany, 1933–39*, (London, 1980), pp. 182–6.
122 S. Haxey, *Tory M.P.*, (London, 1939), p. 209. Also, during the summer of 1937, one of Runciman's sons wrote to the then Foreign Secretary, Anthony Eden, seeking to arrange a possible visit to London by Göring. (See Eden to Runciman, 27 July 1937, Runciman Papers, WR 285.)
123 *The History of the Times*, (London, 1952), IV, part 2, pp. 891–2.
124 Though not a full member of the Ministerial Disarmament Committee (which, in fact, concerned itself largely with rearmament), Runciman did, on occasions, attend its meetings. When this was replaced by the Defence Policy Requirements Committee in 1935, he became a full member, and two years later was also a member of a small sub-committee on air parity with Germany. In 1936, Runciman was a member of a Cabinet Committee on Germany (concerned with responses to German expansion) and, during that year and the year following, intermittently attended meetings of the newly formed Foreign Policy Committee.
125 Reports and Proceedings of the Cabinet Committee on Disarmament, Runciman's observation on Vansittart's memorandum, 'The Future of Germany', 7 April 1934, CP 104 (34), CAB 16/111; Ministerial Committee on Disarmament Minutes, 20 April 1934, DC(M) (32) 38th Cons., CAB 27/506.
126 Ministerial Committee on Disarmament Minutes, 15 May and 11 June 1934, DC(M) (32) 45th and 48th Cons., CAB 27/507.
127 Ministerial Committee on Disarmament Minutes, 19 April 1934, DC(M) (32) 37th Cons., CAB 27/506.
128 Ministerial Committee on Disarmament Minutes, 11 June 1934, DC(M) (32) 48th Cons., CAB 27/507.
129 Ministerial Committee on Disarmament Minutes, 26 June 1934, DC(M) (32) 51st Cons., CAB 27/507. Runciman added, however, the characteristic proviso that naval expansion should not be funded by a defence loan, which he considered a 'pernicious method of finance'.
130 Cabinet Committee on Germany Minutes, 17 February 1936, G (36) 1st Meeting, CAB 27/599. The discussion concerned the transfer of colonies to Germany and the creation of a German customs union in Central Europe.
131 Note by Runciman, [?] May 1937, Runciman Papers, WR 285. (The pencilled note, on the Prime Minister's note paper, is endorsed 'Note by W.R. – probably May 1937.')
132 Halifax to Runciman, 20 March 1938, Runciman Papers, WR 289.
133 Runciman to Halifax, 9 April 1938, Runciman Papers, WR 289. The absence of reports to the contrary would indicate that the meeting with Mussolini did not take place.

5
Deadlock in Prague

Whilst, in London, Halifax and his colleagues were seeking a suitable mediator, in Prague negotiations between the government and the SdP were moving slowly but inexorably towards the feared point of deadlock. The optimistic belief, held in Britain, that the SdP would enter into new negotiations on the basis of the more moderate programme outlined by Henlein in London, was not borne out by events, although this was not immediately apparent. The proposals tabled by the SdP on 30 May were limited to outlining the principles of the territorial autonomy required.[1] Although aspects of the programme were acceptable to the government, the line was drawn at the demand for the creation of a separate Parliament (*Volkstag*) for each nationality, which was considered to endanger the unity of the state.[2]

The initial SdP proposals were not rejected out of hand, but the Czechoslovak authorities requested a fuller statement of the claims. The SdP complied by presenting a detailed 14-point memorandum, dated 7 June, proposing a system of territorial autonomy, based on collective rights, for each nationality. The autonomous administrations were to be responsible for all local government, including policing and education, with only defence, foreign affairs, and finance remaining exclusively in the hands of the central state authorities. Parliamentary deputies from each nationality would also constitute the legislative body of their autonomous administration, electing a president with *ex officio* membership of the central government.[3]

When Newton forwarded these details to London on 15 June, he noted that the SdP's proposals did not entirely bear out the assurances given by Henlein to Vansittart. Although the issues of the control of foreign policy and the collective right to profess National Socialism did not feature overtly in the programme, the question of reparations was included. The general tenor of the proposals confirmed Newton's pessimism and he feared that, even if the SdP modified its stand on some points, agreement would prove impossible.[4] In the Foreign Office, Newton's assessment was shared by Mallet, who noted that the SdP's demands were 'extremely far-reaching'. He was particularly concerned with the proposed system of autonomy, the effect of which, Mallet observed, would be to divide the country 'into racial groups practically independent of the central authority, and liable to fly off and join the neighbouring nations of their own nationality'. He also noted that the government 'would no longer be purely based on a democratic and parliamentary foundation'. Assuming that Britain's objective was to preserve the integrity of Czechoslovakia, Mallet suggested that the SdP should be induced to modify its demands in exchange for a 'readjusting' of Czechoslovakia's external relations. He also expressed sympathy with the SdP's demand for representation in the central government, arguing that 'Czechoslovakia, with its three major and five minor nationalities, is not a country in which the democratic standards of an ordinary national state can easily apply'.[5] Mallet's views caused concern to Sargent, who warned: 'If we are not careful we shall soon get out of our depth in discussing these technical details.' He added, however, that prospects of an agreement would soon hinge on such issues, and concluded therefore (at a time when plans for possible British mediation were under discussion in the Foreign Office), 'if we are not to wash our hands of the whole business we will have shortly to make our proposal to send out an investigator'.[6] But, despite Sargent's advice, some time was yet to elapse before that decision was taken.

The hazards perceived by Mallet in the SdP's demands, caused predictably greater anxiety within the Czechoslovak government. In a commentary prepared on 9 June, Beneš claimed that the SdP's proposals placed in jeopardy the fundamental principles of the constitution, that their complexity was such as to render them unworkable, and that their hidden objective was the partitioning of the state. The President also maintained that the SdP memorandum was based, not on democratic principles, but on those of totalitarian National Socialism.[7] When informing its British counterpart of the proposals, the Prague government drew particular attention to this point, stressing the incompatibility of SdP ideology with a democratic system of government. It was also argued that the implementation of the proposals would disrupt the unity of the state and leave the central authorities virtually powerless. The government nevertheless expressed the belief that compromise was possible on many of the points raised.[8] The Czechoslovak authorities also began preparing counter-proposals of their own, and, at a meeting between Hodža and representatives of the SdP on 14 June, it was agreed that both sets of proposals would provide a basis for further negotiations.[9]

The government's response, known as the Nationalities Statute, was extremely slow to materialise. The evident reluctance of the Czechoslovak authorities to commit their ideas to paper left them exposed to the accusation of deliberate procrastination and cast doubts on the sincerity of their professed desire for an agreement. Such allegations were not only levelled by the SdP and by Germany, but also from London and Paris. The government responded by arguing that, in a democratic society, time was required for a process of consultation prior to a set of proposals being drawn up. In addition, Beneš, who was being personally accused of seeking to avoid a settlement with the SdP and of aiming to establish a military dictatorship, protested vigorously about the 'slanderous' nature of these attacks to the British and French Ministers in Prague.[10]

Despite these explanations, the reluctance of the authorities to formulate their proposals was all too evident, although their tactics were not difficult to understand. Essentially, they were playing for time, hoping that, during the course of the negotiations, Hitler's expansionist aims would become self-evident, resulting in a stiffening of the resolve of Czechoslovakia's allies to resist them. It was also generally believed in Prague that the SdP, on instruction from Berlin, was not interested in conducting genuine negotiations and unwilling to enter into a reasonable, mutually acceptable agreement. Consequently, it was considered unwise to table definite proposals which were likely to be seized upon later in the negotiations by the SdP as minimal demands, thus forcing further concessions.[11] In addition, the government wished to avoid a situation of direct confrontation with the SdP, which would have resulted from a rejection of specific Czechoslovak proposals,[12] and which might well have precipitated a major international crisis. Hence the authorities preferred to deal separately with different aspects of the problem.

The formal negotiations between the government and the SdP commenced on 23 June, when, as was subsequently recalled by one of the SdP negotiators, his side presented their case for 'five solid hours' drawing on 'political, industrial, historical, and psychological arguments'.[13] On the Czechoslovak side, the negotiations were handled by the Political Committee of the Cabinet, headed by the Prime Minister, Hodža.[14] The SdP's negotiating team was led by their Chairman, Ernst Kundt.[15] Henlein, following a meeting with Hodža on 23 May, took no further direct part in the talks.[16] Irregular meetings between the two sides proceeded into July, but progress was negligible, thanks largely to the slow formulation of Czechoslovak counter-proposals. The procedure devised for this purpose was extremely cumbersome. The task of drafting the proposals was undertaken by Beneš in conjunction with the Political Committee of the Cabinet. Assistance was received from two further committees; one, known as the Committee of Six, contained parliamentary representatives of the six political parties forming the government coalition (Agrarians, Social Democrats, National Socialists, Populists, National Democrats, and Small Traders), and the other consisted of legal experts. In addition, limited consultations also took place with several opposition groups, including the autonomist Slovak People's Party and the Communists.[17]

This complex machinery slowly produced results in the form of three interlinked draft parliamentary proposals, which were presented piecemeal to the SdP. The texts of the proposed Language Law and part of the Nationalities

Statute were tabled on 30 June and an incomplete version of the Administrative Reform Law on 28 July.[18] The proposals were developed along the lines which Beneš had indicated to the British and French governments in mid-April. Based on the principle of full equality of all citizens before the law, they defined nationality in terms of language spoken and included measures to prevent the loss of ethnic identity and to ensure the proportionate distribution of government employment, public funds and educational provision. Potentially most far-reaching, but also the least clearly defined, were the proposals for administrative reform. These envisaged some devolution of power from the central authorities to provincial Diets in Bohemia, Moravia and Slovakia, whose electorates would be divided into national *curiae*, coupled with an increase in the functions of local government at the district level.[19]

Although the government proposals were never officially published, details appeared in the press, and their general outline became widely known in Czechoslovakia and elsewhere. As anticipated by the authorities, the SdP lost little time in declaring the proposals to be totally inadequate, arguing that the draft Nationalities Statute did little more than codify existing provisions and that the proposed Language Law not only failed to grant full equality to the German language but also made possible greater encroachment of the Czech language into German areas. The incomplete proposals for administrative reform were also heavily criticised for failing to recognise the collective rights of national groups.[20] The reaction in Berlin was no more positive. Henderson was informed by the State Secretary, on 19 July, that the Czechoslovak proposals constituted a wholly inadequate response to the SdP's Carlsbad demands. Weizsäcker therefore concluded that the Czechoslovak authorities were not seeking genuine reform.[21]

A similar attitude was adopted in the London Foreign Office, where Roberts noted that it was 'difficult to dissent from the view expressed ... at the Wilhelmstrasse'.[22] Two weeks earlier, Sargent had also observed that the proposals, as then known, amounted 'to mighty little in the way of self-government, after all these weeks of so called negotiations and concessions'.[23] Indeed, whilst in Prague the government was laboriously preparing its reform proposals, in London and also in Paris the evident lack of progress in the talks gave rise to growing impatience and anxiety. As usual, it was the British government which showed the greater disquiet, and which took the lead by applying pressure not only directly on the Czechoslovak authorities, but also indirectly by urging France to do likewise.

At the end of May, during the very early stages of the renewed contact between the Czechoslovak government and the SdP, Halifax approached Paris proposing that joint warnings be issued to Beneš in person, drawing attention to the consequences of failing to reach a settlement. Halifax wished France to add further that, if responsibility for this was seen to rest with the Czechoslovak authorities, it 'would be driven to reconsider ... [its] position *vis-à-vis* Czechoslovakia'.[24] In making this suggestion, Halifax was taking advantage of a remark by Bonnet, made in conversation with Phipps at the height of the May Crisis, to the effect that, if the Czechoslovak government behaved unreasonably, France would no longer feel obliged to honour its treaty commitment.[25] Bonnet accepted Halifax's suggestion but preferred the representations to be made separately.[26] The French Minister in Prague saw Beneš on 8 June and duly delivered a warning which, however, did not contain any reference to the possible repudiation of treaty obligations.[27] When news of this reached Halifax, he made a further attempt to persuade Bonnet to issue the agreed warning.[28] The French Foreign Minister explained that he had decided to approach Beneš via the Czechoslovak Minister in Paris, Štefan Osuský. Although Bonnet claimed that the memorandum he had given Osuský was strongly worded,[29] when a copy of it eventually reached Halifax, he was again disappointed by its moderation. It contained no threat to abrogate treaty commitments and merely warned of the possible serious consequences of failure to reach a settlement with the SdP.[30] Nevertheless, Beneš was depressed by the message, and remarked subsequently to de Lacroix that he was beginning to fear that France now considered his country was becoming a burden.[31]

Bonnet's inclination to soft-pedal in his approaches to the Czechoslovak government, which Corbin explained to Cadogan was due to the lack of co-operation from Berlin compared with that of Prague,[32] was certainly not shared by Halifax. British pressure on the Prague government was maintained remorselessly. During a six-week period from early June to mid-July, Newton had four meetings with Beneš, the same number with Hodža and one with Krofta,[33] and Halifax saw Masaryk in London on at least three occasions.[34] At practically every one of these meetings strong pressure was applied on the Czechoslovak side. Within the Foreign Office, the main instigator of this diplomatic saturation bombardment of a friendly country was Vansittart, but he, in turn, was being manipulated by none other than Henlein himself. In almost every case, the diplomatic intervention was made in response to information received from Henlein, relayed mainly through Brand, the SdP's representative in western Europe. This private channel of communication, which Vansittart maintained with the SdP, played a pivotal role in determining the evolving British response to the situation in Czechoslovakia during the early summer of 1938.

The Foreign Office considered the question of establishing direct communications with Henlein towards the end of April, several weeks before his final visit to London. Newton reported that he had not established personal contact with any SdP leaders, and considered that it would be 'a mistake in the present circumstances' to do so, unless asked by the Czechoslovak authorities. He explained that such links might reduce his influence with the government without having any important effect on the SdP, 'for whom the only outside authority is the Reich'.[35] Sargent, however, questioned the assumption that Henlein was simply 'Hitler's mouthpiece', and argued that, in the event of the imminent prospect of Sudeten German territory being ravaged by war, a direct appeal to the SdP leader might possibly secure a last minute settlement. Direct contact between the British Legation and Henlein might therefore be 'very useful'. With Halifax's authority, Sargent's argument was put to Newton on 6 May.[36] Newton, however, remained unconvinced and refused to make direct contact with Henlein against the wishes of Beneš. He suggested instead that the SdP leader might be approached through other channels, such as Brand. This met with the approval of Vansittart, who remarked that this contact was 'sufficient', for although Brand did not live in London, he came over from Paris when required.[37] The direct channel of communication between the British government and Henlein therefore remained in Vansittart's hands. It was to be effectively exploited by the SdP.

The indirect application of pressure on the Czechoslovak authorities by this means commenced in the immediate aftermath of the May Crisis. On 23 May, Vansittart received a message from the SdP, which confirmed his belief that 'the Germans have got their tail down, though only for the time being', and that it was therefore 'of first-class importance to put renewed pressure on the Czechs to come forward and meet Henlein *quickly*'. He was informed that Henlein was 'in urgent need of having his hand strengthened', a service that only the British could provide, 'owing to our known friendliness towards him and the interest that we have always taken in the Sudeten Deutsch question'.[38] Newton was duly instructed to issue a warning that although Germany was likely 'to go slow for the time being ... it might be fatal if [the] Czechoslovak government were to think this a reason for drawing back'. They should therefore come forward with a 'most generous offer and attempt to clinch a settlement'.[39]

Newton appears to have taken no immediate action but, following further despatches from Halifax, made the first of a series of increasingly tough representations during an audience with Beneš on 3 June. His instructions[40] were based on two further messages received by Vansittart. In the first of these, which arrived in London on 25 May, Henlein confirmed he would adhere to his moderated demands in the forthcoming negotiations. He stressed however, that his own support amongst Sudeten Germans was in jeopardy due to disbelief in the goodwill of the government, and urged therefore that 'the strongest representations' be made urgently in Prague. Although Vansittart considered that the SdP leader was 'laying it on thick', he nevertheless stressed to Halifax the importance of the Czechoslovak authorities coming up with a good offer without delay.[41] The second message was delivered to Vansittart by an SdP representative on 31 May. The unnamed emissary reported in pessimistic terms on the previous day's meeting between Hodža and Kundt, adding however, that Hodža had been 'understanding' and willing to reach an agreement but was meeting opposition from Cabinet colleagues and from Beneš in particular.

Vansittart therefore advised Halifax that 'we must now direct our efforts towards strengthening Dr. Hodža's hand and we can best do this by pressing Dr. Beneš very strongly, in conjunction with the French, to go ahead at once with the negotiations on the London lines'.[42]

Before making his representation to Beneš on 3 June, Newton first clarified with the Foreign Office that it was in order for him to disclose the undertaking given by Henlein in London to moderate his demands.[43] Newton also informed Beneš, quoting verbatim from Halifax's instructions, that any delay in achieving a settlement along those lines would increase the danger 'of a serious and perhaps disastrous deterioration in the situation'. He added that, if the Czechoslovak government failed to respond positively, it risked losing the sympathy of Britain. Beneš reacted calmly to Newton's warning and assured his visitor that the government was negotiating in good faith and with urgency.[44]

The Foreign Office, however, was not convinced, and within days Halifax again instructed Newton to see Beneš to inform him of the danger, reported by Henderson from Berlin, that unless the 'moderate' Henlein achieved some success, he might be replaced by a more extremist figure, such as Hans Krebs, the former leader of the German National Socialist Party in Czechoslovakia.[45] This belief was also shared by Vansittart, who had warned of the possibility at the time of Henlein's last visit to London,[46] and who had subsequently received confirmation of it from one of his contacts. He informed Halifax, citing his unnamed source, 'that the pressure on Herr Henlein is so hard "that it is necessary that he should score a *personal* success ... in order ... to retain his moderating influence and personal position against the extremists"'.[47] Vansittart received a similar report, from 'a highly placed German source', a few days previously, indicating that Henlein had 'fallen into disfavour with Hitler', who considered him to be a 'weakling' and merely 'a somewhat useful medium for appeasing foreign opinion'. This informant also vouched for Henlein's integrity and that he was 'playing an honest hand', which caused Vansittart to note, in parenthesis: 'I am glad to have this confirmation of my own opinion.'[48]

Newton spoke to Beneš in the required terms on 11 June,[49] following which Vansittart was informed through his intermediaries of the SdP's gratitude concerning the outcome of British and French pressure on the President, who was considered to be 'now on the right lines'.[50] But this satisfaction was short-lived, and within a week Vansittart was again receiving pessimistic reports from the SdP, describing the situation as 'more serious than ever' (which Vansittart considered an exaggeration) and threatening to publish both sets of proposals in order to draw attention to the alleged inadequacy of the government's offer and to Beneš's policy of procrastination. Vansittart concluded that Beneš was 'backsliding again' and repeated the warning that SdP 'moderates' were in danger of being replaced by 'more extreme elements'.[51] A week later, another pessimistic report arrived from Henlein who claimed to be in 'a state of great depression'. Vansittart, again conceding that Henlein was probably exaggerating, reported nevertheless to Halifax that the SdP leader had 'little confidence in the result of the negotiations', and his party had 'little belief in our ability to help them'.[52]

The receipt of the first of these two reports prompted Sargent to turn to the question of possible British mediation in Czechoslovakia which (as previously discussed) was then under active consideration in the Foreign Office. Foreseeing the possibility of a breakdown in the negotiations, Sargent noted on 22 June, that the time might soon arrive for both sides to be informed 'that the issues are so serious that we cannot allow such a rupture to take place, and that we would be ready to offer a mediator to bring the two parties together again'. He himself did not think that point had yet been reached, but thought it might come suddenly and that Newton should therefore be asked 'to watch the situation with a view to warning us as soon as he sees the moment approaching'.[53] Newton was duly instructed in these terms later that day and was also asked to arrange a further meeting with Beneš.[54] That did not take place until 28 June, when Newton repeated his previous warning that the effect on British public opinion would be 'extremely serious' if the Czechoslovak authorities did not, without delay, do everything possible to secure an agreement. Although authorised by Halifax to hint at the possibility of British mediation being offered if negotiations broke down, Newton appears not to have done so and, indeed, reported that Beneš 'showed no inclination to ask for advice or our services as a mediator'.[55]

The extent of the diplomatic pressure exerted on Prague, however, was not solely the outcome of SdP activity. The British government also received direct encouragement from a very unexpected source – the Czechoslovak Prime Minister himself. During a conversation with Newton on 26 June, Hodža appealed for British assistance, not only in persuading Henlein to be co-operative, but also in influencing his own side into making significant concessions. He requested, in strictest confidence, that further pressure should be brought to bear on the Minister in London and that prominent British individuals should be asked to seek to sway their Czechoslovak counterparts. Hodža also identified two government ministers, Rudolf Bechyně and Emil Franke, whose intransigent attitude might be softened by British pressure.[56] Indication of Hodža's attitude had also reached Vansittart some two weeks earlier, prompting him to report to Halifax that he had 'learned *very confidentially* that Dr. Hodža would not be at all averse to seeing a little more pressure put on Dr. Beneš'.[57] This information was reinforced a few days later by a message from the SdP alleging that Hodža was being obstructed by Beneš and others. Vansittart therefore informed Halifax: 'I am convinced that Hodža is a long way ahead of his other compatriots in the path of wisdom. It is essential to get Beneš pushed along the same path immediately.'[58]

Hodža's surprising approach was followed up the next day, when Masaryk was summoned to the Foreign Office to be told by Halifax of deep British concern over the lack of progress in the negotiations.[59] The Foreign Office also lost no time in seeking to persuade several prominent British personalities, planning to attend the Sokol gymnastic festival in Prague early in July, to apply pressure on their Czechoslovak hosts. Those approached were the chairman of the *News Chronicle*, Sir Walter Layton; the Central European specialist and former journalist, Henry Wickham Steed; the Conservative Member of Parliament, the Duchess of Atholl; and the former diplomat, Sir George Clerk.[60] Newton also did his duty by speaking personally to Bechyně and Franke, as Hodža requested.[61]

The explanation for Hodža's appeal – which he himself indicated might be regarded as treasonable[62] – lay in Czechoslovak domestic party politics. Within the six-party governing coalition there was considerable divergence concerning the attitude to be adopted towards the SdP. In general, it was the political parties on the right of the political spectrum which were prepared to placate Henlein, and it was those on the left which were most intransigent. Hodža, a leading member of the Agrarian Party, belonged to the former category. His approach, favouring significant concessions to the SdP, was opposed within the Cabinet mainly by ministers belonging to the National Socialist Party (to which Beneš had formerly belonged) and, further to the left, the Social Democratic Party. Beneš, although as President bound by the constitution to distance himself from party political considerations, nevertheless shared many of the attitudes of his former party colleagues. Hodža's request for increased British pressure on Masaryk was an indirect means of influencing Beneš. Being the son of the founder-president, the Minister in London had a close personal relationship with Beneš, his father's chosen successor.

Despite the repeated efforts of the British government to persuade its Czechoslovak counterpart of the necessity to reach a speedy agreement with the SdP, there was little immediate evidence of any significant change of attitude in Prague. The majority of the Czech press remained acutely hostile to Henlein and his party, and was implacably opposed to major concessions being made in the negotiations. This attitude added further to the considerable disquiet in the Foreign Office, which concurred with Newton's criticism that the press was 'failing to prepare the public for the large concessions' necessary for an agreement with the SdP.[63] Vansittart also received similar complaints concerning the Czech press through Henlein's intermediaries.[64] Newton was therefore instructed to make 'strong representations' on this matter and did so on at least two occasions during June.[65] In London, Halifax also informed Masaryk of his considerable disquiet concerning the tone of the press.[66]

A new note of urgency was added to the British warnings in the middle of July, when Masaryk and Beneš were separately informed that, unless a settlement was quickly reached, the SdP would demand a plebiscite which, Halifax claimed, British public opinion would almost certainly consider 'not unreasonable'.[67] This assessment of British public opinion was probably correct, at least judging from the influential pages of *The Times*, which, during the previous month, published two leading articles advocating a plebiscite for the Sudeten Germans, arguing that this was a view with which 'the majority of Englishmen probably agree'.[68] Within the Foreign Office, however, this was not the case. Sargent strongly deplored the leader in *The Times* on 3 June, which he described as 'mischievous', fearing that it would undermine the authority of those in the Czechoslovak government who were seeking a negotiated settlement. This view was shared by Vansittart, who termed the article an 'amateurish excursion'. He added that it would be 'unpardonable' if *The Times* pushed Henlein into demanding a plebiscite which, Vansittart believed, the SdP leader did not desire.[69]

Sargent and Vansittart were not alone in the Foreign Office in their hostility towards a plebiscite. A memorandum on 'The Objections to Holding a Plebiscite in the Sudeten Areas of Czechoslovakia', prepared in mid-June by Roberts, examined the drawbacks in some detail. Roberts reasoned that 'a plebiscite undertaken at the present moment would not seem calculated to further the ultimate interests of the Sudeten population' and would also 'not solve the fundamental problem of Czechoslovakia's foreign relations with Germany'. He believed it would certainly be opposed by the Czechoslovak government and possibly also by Germany and that the practical problems of conducting a plebiscite would be 'insuperable'. Moreover, Czechoslovak resistance to a plebiscite would be such that 'it might create the occasion for the war which it is intended to prevent'. Roberts concluded that it was 'inadvisable' for Britain to support the proposal and that it was preferable to continue pressing for 'the widest possible degree of autonomy for the Sudeten Germans within the boundaries of the present Czechoslovak State'. This view was endorsed by Halifax, Cadogan, Sargent and Mallet.[70] Indeed Halifax himself, when issuing the warning to Masaryk, on 13 July, concerning the possibility of a plebiscite being demanded by the SdP, indicated that he was aware of the significant objections to the plan, which made it all the more imperative that a solution be reached by negotiation.[71]

This intensification of British pressure on the Czechoslovak authorities was prompted by a highly alarmist report Vansittart received from Henlein on, or shortly before, 12 July. The SdP leader expressed intense dissatisfaction with the concessions so far offered by the Czechoslovak negotiators and accused them of deliberate procrastination. He also asserted that the government intended to legislate on the minorities question without obtaining the prior agreement of the SdP. Consequently, Henlein maintained, he no longer had any trust in the Czechoslovak leaders and in Hodža in particular – a development which Vansittart considered 'disastrous'. Henlein also claimed that Beneš did not take the diplomatic pressure from Britain and France at all seriously and that the President remained convinced that he could ultimately depend on their support. This caused Vansittart to observe that 'judging from the lack of results up to date and from the amazing way in which the Czechoslovak Government is playing with fire, it would seem that Henlein's convictions are not far wrong'. From this and other confidential information received – which included a remarkably well-informed outline of German military preparations for the invasion of Czechoslovakia, scheduled for the autumn – Vansittart concluded that 'we are rapidly approaching another European crisis' which was likely to be more dangerous than the events of 19 to 22 May. The new crisis would be brought about by the Czechoslovak authorities attempting to impose a solution, in which circumstances, Vansittart argued (underlining his words for emphasis), *'Henlein will have no alternative but to demand a plebiscite for the Anschluss'*, such would be the pressure from his own supporters and from Germany. The SdP leader nevertheless assured Vansittart that he himself wished to avoid a plebiscite and was still seeking a negotiated solution, but, if the government imposed a settlement, 'he will have staked his faith on his friends in London for nothing'. Vansittart therefore advised Halifax that 'we can now only hope to hold him by regaining his confidence, and this can only be done by showing that we really have the power to stop the Czechoslovak Government's clumsy trickery'.[72]

When communicating the essence of Henlein's latest message to Newton, Halifax also sought the Minister's opinion whether a further *démarche*, to be undertaken in Prague jointly with France, was advisable.[73] Newton doubted whether a repetition of the joint initiative of 7 May would have any great effect on the Czechoslovak authorities, and feared that it might well only serve to stimulate the SdP into the adoption of a more provocative attitude.[74] Halifax also indicated that, if a breakdown in the negotiations appeared imminent, the Czechoslovak authorities should be warned about the possibility of the British government's support for a plebiscite and/or of its intention to appoint an independent mediator.[75] Newton evidently believed that the time had not yet come to mention the latter course of action, but immediately sought, and obtained, authorisation from London to use the alternative threat of a possible plebiscite.[76] Despite refuting most of Henlein's criticisms of the Czechoslovak authorities,[77] and despite the fact that he himself had previously been opposed to the idea of a plebiscite,[78] Newton duly issued this warning during the course of a lengthy audience with Beneš on 16 July. Beneš responded by stating forthrightly that, if a plebiscite involved the cession of territory, it would result in war.[79]

Newton emerged from this meeting with the President full of anxiety and pessimism, which he immediately conveyed to London. He was convinced that the negotiations between the government and the SdP were on the verge of breakdown. Although the Czechoslovak authorities were finalising their proposals, which they intended placing before the SdP negotiators the following week, even Beneš did not expect that the SdP would find these acceptable. In that event, the President indicated, the government would promptly present its proposals to Parliament for enactment, without awaiting the prior approval of the SdP, although no date had yet been fixed for this. When Newton pressed for adequate time to be given for the SdP to consider the proposals prior to enactment, Beneš rejoined that by acting without delay the authorities were merely complying with the advice of Britain and France. Newton then raised the possibility of embodying in legislation only those aspects of the problem on which agreement had been reached, reserving the points of disagreement for future negotiations. This, however, was emphatically rejected by Beneš, who argued that the government would be making maximum concessions and additional negotiations would, therefore, be out of the question.[80]

Reporting further to London after two days' reflection on his audience with Beneš, Newton repeated his warning of imminent deadlock. He added, however, that neither Beneš nor his Government could be accused 'of having misled either Sudeten Germans or ourselves in regard to autonomy'. On the contrary, they had 'consistently taken the line that they would accept no territorial division and nothing amounting in fact to federalism nor anything which would jeopardize the integrity of the state'. The apparent differences in attitude between Beneš and Hodža during the negotiations were, in Newton's opinion, probably no more than differences of temperament. As for the attitude of the SdP, the British Minister pointed out that even if, as a result of his most recent conversation with Beneš, the President could 'persuade his Government to go a little further I cannot believe it will be far enough unless Sudeten Germans also make a substantial advance towards a common meeting ground'.[81] Two weeks earlier, Newton had spelled this out more directly by stating that: 'Hitherto there appear to have been no concessions from demands of Sudeten German party.'[82]

However, it was not the failure of the SdP to modify its requirements but the plans of the Czechoslovak authorities that most alarmed the British government. The possibility of reform legislation being enacted without a prior agreement with the SdP had been concerning Newton since the middle of June, when he had been informed of this by Hodža.[83] When Beneš also referred to this possibility on 28 June, Newton stressed that the British government would wish to be consulted in advance of that development.[84] Two days previously, however, Hodža had indicated to Newton that the projected legislation would not constitute the final word but would be followed by further negotiations in the autumn.[85] When Halifax drew Newton's attention to this inconsistency, he naturally expressed a preference for Hodža's plan.[86] In Newton's view however, that alternative gave rise to 'questions of considerable difficulty'. How could the Czechoslovak authorities make maximum concessions and, simultaneously, indicate that their actions were incomplete?[87] Nevertheless, in conversation with Masaryk on 13 July, Halifax strongly urged the Czechoslovak government not to 'shut the door on further negotiations', and to legislate only on points already agreed by both parties.[88]

When it became clear to Newton, during his meeting with Beneš on 16 July, that the government definitely intended to proceed with legislation, irrespective of the attitude of the SdP, he became greatly alarmed. He advised the Foreign Office that the time was rapidly approaching for the implementation of the British plans for mediation, suggesting that the offer might be made immediately following the SdP's rejection of the proposals, but warning that earlier action might prove necessary. Newton, however, added a cautionary note indicating that he would prefer the emphasis being placed 'on investigation rather than on mediation, as the likelihood of bringing the two parties to agreement is not great'.[89]

Newton's reasoning was also influenced by a report from Halifax that the French government had in mind a joint initiative with Britain to overcome the approaching deadlock in Czechoslovakia. In conversation with Cadogan on 9 July, the French Ambassador in London, Charles Corbin, suggested that the two governments might consider preparing some concrete proposals for resolving Czechoslovakia's problems in order to re-start negotiations.[90] Newton was disturbed by this suggestion, foreseeing considerable difficulties. He observed that the question of the administration of Czechoslovakia was 'a highly complicated matter with its roots in history', and was therefore 'unlikely to be solved by random proposals from anyone unacquainted with the technicalities'. Newton was also concerned that the sponsoring governments might well come into conflict with one or other of the protagonists. He believed, therefore, that the British idea of sending out a mediator or investigator offered 'a more profitable line of approach'.[91] This view was shared by the Foreign Office.[92]

Whilst the situation in Czechoslovakia was approaching the point of deadlock, in London, Runciman was being harried for a decision on whether he would accept the assignment of mediator. Runciman's affirmative answer was given on the very day (16 July) that Newton advised in favour of mediation, although this advice, sent by diplomatic bag, did not reach London until two days later.[93] However, Newton's pessimistic report was not the only factor instrumental in influencing Halifax in favour of implementing the plans for mediation. The news from Berlin on 16 July was equally depressing. Henderson reported Weizsäcker's extreme anxiety and that of the Czechoslovak Minister, Vojtěch Mastný.[94] Furthermore, on the same day, rumours began emanating from Germany that Czechoslovakia was again mobilising its armed forces.[95] The combination of these developments convinced Halifax that the situation in Central

Europe was becoming critical and that the time was therefore right for Britain to take the initiative in attempting to bring about a peaceful resolution of the Sudeten German problem.[96]

During the evening of 18 July, Newton was informed that a despatch would be delivered the following day by special messenger. He was also instructed to arrange a meeting with Beneš as soon as possible and to endeavour to ensure, meanwhile, that the Czechoslovak authorities did nothing to exacerbate the situation.[97] The important message from Halifax that followed concerned the offer of British mediation, which Newton was asked to bring to the attention of Beneš immediately. Halifax was particularly disturbed by the possibility of the government legislating on the nationalities dispute without allowing adequate time for further discussion with the SdP. He regarded this as 'quite indefensible' and believed it would not only 'shock public opinion' in Britain, but would also bring about a demand from the SdP for a plebiscite. The authorities were, therefore, strongly to be urged not proceed with their legislative proposals.[98]

Newton's crucial audience with Beneš took place during the morning of 20 July. It lasted for over two hours and was, predictably, far from being a pleasant diplomatic occasion. The British Minister, as instructed from London, issued in effect a threat of moral blackmail. In response to Newton's telephonic request for clarification of this point, Halifax explained that, should Beneš reject the proposal, Britain would 'make public the nature of this suggestion and of the response' given.[99] When addressing the President, Newton expressed strong criticism of the negotiating procedure adopted, particularly of the planned immediate legislation, and indicated the British government's intention of sending an investigator and mediator, namely Lord Runciman. His function would be, Newton explained:

> to acquaint himself with the character of the problem at issue and with the causes of disagreement to which it has given rise, and endeavour by his advice and influence to maintain contact between the Czechoslovak Government and the representatives of the Sudeten German party, or to restore it in the event of a breakdown.[100]

Conscious of the Czechoslovak government's sensitivity about being placed on an equal footing with an opposition political party, Newton made some small but significant changes to the wording of the instructions received, avoiding the use of the phrase 'the two parties', which appeared in the original.[101] In order to make the imposition of a mediator somewhat more palatable, Newton also suggested to Beneš (in this instance in accordance with his instructions) that the government should publicly request British assistance and thus avoid damage to its prestige. Such a move, Halifax argued, would have the additional advantage of creating a favourable impression on public opinion in Britain and counteract to some extent the effects of German propaganda.[102] But these concerns for the President's susceptibilities did little to lessen the impact of the message delivered. Beneš was described by Newton as being 'greatly taken aback and much upset' on being informed of the British action and had not fully regained his composure by the end of the lengthy interview. The President repeatedly pleaded for the matter to be treated only as a preliminary sounding, but Newton insisted on adhering to his instructions.[103]

Despite Newton's assurances that there was no question of arbitration or of the mediator's views being imposed on the government, Beneš considered the proposal to be prejudicial to Czechoslovak sovereignty and likely to exacerbate the situation in the country by leading to the resignation of the government, and possibly also of himself. The President also argued that public and parliamentary opinion in Czechoslovakia would find British mediation unacceptable, and that it would cause the SdP to become even more intransigent. Acutely aware of the fact that the crisis was being managed from Germany, Beneš foresaw that British intervention might force him to negotiate directly with Hitler, which he feared would end his country's close association with the western powers.[104]

In direct reply to Newton's representation, Beneš indicated that, as the matter fell beyond his constitutional competence, the official response would have to be made by the government as a whole. He also wished to consult his country's principal ally, France, before responding to the British initiative. However, the President was able to give Newton a firm undertaking that meanwhile nothing would be done by the authorities to provoke a crisis. Beneš drew attention to an official communiqué of 16 July, issued in response to British pressure, which stated that it was not the intention of the government to present a *fait accompli,* and that further negotiations would take place with interested parties prior to legislation being enacted. He further explained that the government's proposals would shortly be presented to all concerned and that no date had been arranged for Parliament to begin legislating on this issue.[105]

The British offer of mediation, and the form in which it was presented, clearly caused Beneš considerable shock. However, towards the end of the conversation he became less agitated and remarked that if the mediator's role were similar to that of the previously appointed British observers, it might be acceptable to his government.[106] After further reflection, and following a discussion with Hodža, he seemed even less hostile towards the idea. Within a short period of returning to the Legation, Newton received a telephone call from the President indicating he now believed the proposal to be less far-reaching than it had appeared to him at first sight, and that agreement on it might be possible.[107] The day following the interview with Beneš, Newton outlined the British plan directly to Hodža. The Prime Minister's response was markedly different from that of Beneš. Speaking personally, Hodža indicated that, although the proposal was exceptional, he would welcome the arrival of Runciman as soon as possible, as he foresaw an inevitable breakdown in the talks with the SdP. He would therefore endeavour to convince his colleagues in the government that the offer of mediation was evidence of British goodwill and should be accepted.[108]

Two days later, on 23 July, Newton received the formal response to the British initiative. The Czechoslovak government begged Britain 'to be good enough to indicate a person who would be ready with his opinion and advice to help to overcome difficulties which might eventually still arise' before a solution of the nationalities problem was accomplished on the basis of the government's proposals.[109] Although this was substantially what Halifax desired, the request was not made in the exact form he had suggested – a joint approach from the government and the SdP.[110] Newton, however, believed that to have been an unrealistic expectation, as Czech political and public opinion was 'very sensitive to any suggestion that a political party – and the opposition one – should be regarded as on the same footing as [the] Government'.[111] The Foreign Office was, nevertheless, satisfied with the Czechoslovak response and Newton was authorised to express British 'appreciation'.[112]

Although Britain had secured the co-operation of the Czechoslovak government, there remained still the SdP to be approached. Indeed, when Chamberlain officially announced the forthcoming Runciman Mission in the House of Commons on 26 July, he had to admit that the attitude of Henlein's party was not yet known.[113] The approach to the SdP was made in two moves, one in Czechoslovakia and the other in Switzerland. In Prague, Newton, as instructed on 25 July, immediately sought and obtained Hodža's consent to contact directly the SdP leadership.[114] As Henlein and many other party leaders were outside the country attending a German national gymnastic festival in Breslau in Germany (now Wrocław in Poland), it was Kundt who responded to the invitation to visit the Legation the following day. During the course of what Newton described as a 'long and friendly talk', the SdP chief negotiator was informed of the Runciman Mission and urged to co-operate fully with it. Kundt's immediate response was encouraging, indicating that the SdP 'would welcome any objective study of conditions which might in any way help to lead to a positive result'.[115] Halifax was therefore able to announce publicly in the House of Lords the following day that the SdP was favourably disposed towards the Runciman Mission.[116]

The second part of the approach was made directly to Henlein, utilising Vansittart's unofficial channels of communication. As yet unaware of the effectiveness of their pressure, the SdP intermediaries maintained their flow of agitated messages from Henlein. On 21 July, the day after Newton had sprung the news of the Runciman Mission on the hapless Beneš, Vansittart received a visit from one of Henlein's associates, Prince Max Hohenlohe, who reported that the SdP leader was 'very depressed' and 'in rather a desperate mood'. Hohenlohe maintained that Henlein's despondency stemmed from the belief that Germany was no longer interested in a peaceful resolution of the Sudeten German problem but was preparing to attack Czechoslovakia in the near future. He also informed Vansittart that Henlein believed Germany aimed 'to destroy Czechoslovakia and absorb Bohemia and Moravia into the Reich and to bribe Hungary and Poland with the remains'. Vansittart's visitor was particularly concerned about the danger which would arise if reforms were introduced without the prior agreement of the SdP, predicting this would drive the German population into resistance, leading to German military intervention and 'a world war before September'. Actions being considered included a general strike, a refusal to pay taxes, or passive resistance, resulting in an appeal for assistance from Germany. For good measure, Hohenlohe also warned that Henlein now desired a plebiscite, in order to strengthen his position. Reporting the information to Halifax, Vansittart explained that 'Henlein has only been passing very reluctantly under German influence and has no love for his Nazi masters', but believed that by securing a plebiscite with British help, he might be able to retain the leadership of the SdP 'independently of the Reich Nazi Party bosses'. Vansittart added, in parenthesis: 'This of course is a pathetic hallucination.'

Vansittart also learned from Hohenlohe that Henlein would be attending the gymnastic festival in Breslau at the end of July, at which Hitler would be present, and, much alarmed, urged his visitor to bring the SdP leader 'out of his present depressed and angry mood' prior to the meeting taking place. Hohenlohe agreed to do so, but only if he could be furnished with a categorical assurance that the Prague government would not legislate unilaterally.[117] A hurried exchange of telegrams with Newton secured confirmation of the Foreign Office understanding that the authorities had already given the required assurance to the SdP, and also the suggestion from Newton that the SdP, in turn, should be asked for an undertaking to continue the negotiations following the receipt of the Czechoslovak proposals.[118] When Hohenlohe returned the following day, Vansittart made use of some sharp observations supplied by Sargent, drawing attention to the fact that the assurance in question had already been given by the Czechoslovak side and that it was now up to the SdP to make a 'constructive contribution' towards a settlement and to avoid provoking a crisis.[119]

During the course of the earlier conversation with Vansittart, Hohenlohe also observed that the two sides were so entrenched in their attitudes that, left to their own devices, they were unlikely to achieve a negotiated settlement. His proposed solution was precisely what the British government itself had in mind, namely, the despatch of a 'private mediator' with the aim of re-starting the negotiations. He urged that such a person be sent out without delay, and suggested that Group Captain Christie, who was also present at the meeting, would be a suitable candidate. Vansittart did not record any astonishment on hearing this proposal, but noted for Halifax's benefit: 'I need hardly say that I did not give him any indication that we had already embarked on this line.' He did, however, immediately reject Christie's candidacy on the grounds of his known sympathies for the Sudeten Germans. It would appear that Hohenlohe did not make the proposal purely on his own initiative as he disclosed that it had been suggested, by persons unspecified, that he himself might undertake the role of mediator. He added, however, that he had no wish to do so, but would provide assistance to whomever was selected, including the exertion of 'friendly pressure' on Henlein to accept the mediator's recommendations.[120] It is unlikely that Hohenlohe's suggestion was made without the knowledge of Henlein, and it therefore probably resulted from concern felt within the SdP leadership that the Czechoslovak authorities were attempting to bring the dispute to a head and thus precipitate a crisis before Germany was ready to intervene militarily. Hohenlohe's offer to provide assistance to the British mediator was indeed honoured following Runciman's arrival in Czechoslovakia, though not quite in the manner indicated.

When Hohenlohe returned again to London to see Vansittart on 26 July, news of the forthcoming Runciman Mission had already appeared in the press. Hohenlohe expressed himself personally delighted with the idea but suggested it might not be so welcome to Henlein, who might feel upstaged by Runciman's arrival. He also indicated that the development would be most unwelcome in Berlin, as Runciman's presence in Czechoslovakia would frustrate the German invasion planned for August. Vansittart, therefore, sent Hohenlohe flying back to Germany the following day in order 'to speak very strongly' to Henlein about his welcoming the projected Mission. The SdP intermediary was confident of his ability to influence Henlein, but added that strong pressure would be required on both the Czechoslovak and German governments in order to facilitate a satisfactory outcome of the Mission. The pressure on Berlin, Vansittart advised his colleagues, could be administered by a reaffirmation of Chamberlain's Parliamentary statement of 24 March and of the British attitude adopted during the May Crisis. The suggested means for pressuring the Czechoslovak authorities came from the Czechoslovak Prime Minister himself. Hohenlohe, who had met Hodža in Prague the previous day, reported to Vansittart that the Prime Minister had begged him to urge, privately and confidentially, that a 'strong personality' – other than Runciman – should be sent to Czechoslovakia to warn political leaders there of the imminent danger of war and that Britain would not provide support if a fair settlement was obstructed.[121] This suggestion was discussed with Runciman when he visited the Foreign Office on 28 July, but it was decided to take no action for the moment.[122]

Before Hohenlohe's latest return to London, Vansittart had already sent an urgent message to the SdP leader with the aim of preventing an out of hand rejection of the British initiative. By chance, a clandestine meeting between Vansittart's intermediaries – Hohenlohe, Christie, and Brandt – and Henlein himself had been arranged to take place in Switzerland early in August. Vansittart attempted to bring this meeting forward in order to provide an opportunity for advising Henlein 'in a very earnest manner, that he should do his utmost to make a success of the proposals'.[123] In the event, however, it proved impossible to change the date of the meeting that took place in Zurich, as planned, on 5 August, two days after Runciman's arrival in Prague.

During the meeting in Switzerland, Henlein was in a truculent mood, maintaining there was no longer any prospect of a negotiated outcome and restating his demand for a plebiscite. As reported by Christie, Henlein saw 'no other way out', and thought Britain should 'help him and his people to the Anschluss'. Henlein also indicated that he had no confidence in Runciman's ability to achieve a compromise solution. He argued that Runciman, with his English attitude of mind, would be duped by the Czechoslovak authorities and would offer the Sudeten Germans less than the Carlsbad demands, which were the minimum acceptable. Henlein feared that if he were to accept a solution proposed by Runciman, 'possibly in the face of opposition from the Reich and his own people', he would then be abandoned by Britain and France and end up looking 'a fool and a traitor'.

Christie was left in no doubt that Henlein would only accept a solution proposed by Runciman if it embodied the eight Carlsbad points; in effect, if it granted the Sudeten Germans 'a satisfactory measure of self-government'. Henlein was also successful in maintaining the British emissary's belief that he was being subjected to severe pressures from Germany to achieve a radical outcome, although the SdP leader probably found Christie's response to this somewhat unwelcome. Christie warned Henlein that if Germany tried to 'sweep aside the honest attempts of the Runciman mission to solve the problem, and showed herself intent on hostilities by pressing for a plebiscite' the outcome would be 'a grim European war lasting perhaps for two or three years'. Henlein did not react directly to this warning, but Christie concluded that obtaining Henlein's release from 'German pressure' was another essential precondition for a compromise solution. In order to achieve this, he explained to Vansittart, 'Germany must be made to realise that she is up against formidable opposition and that there would be no prospect of a short and successful war'.

Despite Henlein's belligerence and professed pessimism, Vansittart's intermediary did not come away from the Zurich meeting empty handed. The SdP leader gave Christie 'his personal promise that he would for a further four weeks believe in and strive for the success of the Runciman mission'. If, however, on the expiry of that period 'no really successful progress towards a settlement had been achieved, he would feel himself free to press for a plebiscite'.[124] Henlein's behaviour during the meeting seemed to indicate that, despite Hohenlohe's similar suggestion, he was unsure how to react to the Runciman Mission. He could not be certain that Runciman's intervention would further the cause of the SdP. By pointing to the mediator's lack of understanding of the problems of Central Europe, and to the likelihood of his being misled by the Czechoslovak authorities, Henlein was preparing the ground for the rejection of any unpalatable recommendations. However, a total refusal to co-operate with Runciman was out of the question, for not only would it have at once negated the results of three years' work developing contacts in Britain, but it would also have resulted in breaching Hitler's instructions to continue negotiating. Moreover, there remained the possibility that the British government might use the Runciman Mission to apply further pressure for concessions on the Czechoslovak authorities, hence the demonstration of truculence and the threat of a plebiscite in order to convince the British of the acute danger of the situation. Hence also the undertaking to allow Runciman a month in which to attempt his mission before the stakes were raised by the SdP. Clearly, the British initiative had injected an unpredictable, but from the SdP's standpoint not necessarily negative, factor into the situation and for the moment it was prudent to wait and see how events would develop.

In addition to the direct contacts made with the SdP leadership, the British government – being fully conscious of the SdP's relationship with Germany – also approached Berlin. Henderson was instructed, on 25 July, to inform the German authorities, in confidence, of the British plan and to urge them 'to use whatever influence they may have' to secure the acceptance of the SdP. Germany was also asked to indicate to the SdP that these proposals had their 'full approval' and to assist the mediation by advocating 'patience and moderation' at all times.[125] Weizsäcker personally welcomed the initiative, although reserving the judgement of his government.[126] In reality, Weizsäcker was uncertain about the probable outcome of the British move, though he did believe it signalled increased British involvement. He noted that the British government 'hope to find in Runciman a pliable go-between, in order not to have to bear the responsibility themselves for individual proposals'. Weizsäcker observed, however, that the 'idea obviously cuts both ways' and advised Ribbentrop therefore to seek refuge in the fact that reports of the forthcoming Mission had already appeared in the British press.[127] Furnished with this convenient pretext for diplomatic umbrage, Ribbentrop distanced his government from the venture, which, as Henderson was informed two days later, was to be treated as a matter of purely 'British concern'.[128] The German Minister in Prague, Ernst Eisenlohr, was instructed not to co-operate in any form with the Runciman Mission.[129]

Ribbentrop's unhelpful response gave rise to concern in London resulting in a personal letter from Halifax to his German counterpart apologising for the unauthorised press reporting of Runciman's appointment.[130] Halifax also feared that Ribbentrop 'in his present temper'[131] might fail to pass the information to Hitler and hence to Henlein, who was believed to take his instructions directly from Hitler.[132] Chamberlain therefore also wrote personally to Dirksen, who was on leave in Germany at the time, urging the German Ambassador to convey directly to Hitler the contents of Halifax's letter to Ribbentrop.[133] Dirksen responded with a polite but non-committal answer a few days later,[134] whereas Ribbentrop did not reply until 'returning from holiday' on 21 August. In his letter, the Foreign Minister not only adhered to his policy of non-cooperation with the Runciman Mission, on the grounds that Germany was not consulted in advance, but also disclaimed any responsibility for the outcome of the Mission. Ribbentrop added, however, that in view of the fact that the 'tendentious behaviour' of a section of the international press was preventing the world public from realising that the Czechoslovak government, 'strongly influenced by Bolshevik ideas', was the 'only real obstacle' to peace in Europe, he hoped that Runciman's presence in Prague 'would open the eyes of the public in Great Britain' to this.[135]

Alongside the anxiety produced by Ribbentrop's attitude, his apparent pique was also the cause of some self-congratulation within the Foreign Office. Sargent observed that 'Ribbentrop has every reason to be annoyed with us, for once again we have out-manoeuvred him'. Citing the May Crisis and the despatch of British observers to Czechoslovakia as earlier successes, Sargent claimed that the appointment of Runciman would prevent Ribbentrop being able to use deadlock in Czechoslovakia as a pretext for German intervention.[136] Strang likewise believed that the forthcoming mediation had frustrated German plans to invade Czechoslovakia during August.[137] In contrast, Vansittart was much more cautious and warned against an 'orgy of optimism' in the press. He remained convinced that a German attack on Czechoslovakia in late August or early September was still probable, the German military preparations being, he informed Halifax, 'borne out in still more detail by at least half a dozen of our own Secret Service reports'. Vansittart added that 'we are only just going into the wood and are nothing like out of it ... [and] dangerous things may happen when we are in it'. He therefore advised both Halifax and Chamberlain not to issue any optimistic statements, despite recently received assurances from Germany.[138] The assurances in question were, presumably, those brought by Hitler's emissary, Captain Fritz Wiedemann, who had been received privately by Halifax a week previously, on 18 July. Wiedemann assured Halifax that Germany had no plans to use force against Czechoslovakia.[139]

That was, of course, far from being the case and Ribbentrop's displeasure was therefore probably real enough. Britain had, for the moment, seized the initiative over Czechoslovakia. As Weizsäcker indicated to his superior at the end of July, with the attention of the world now focused on that country, plans resorting to a '*coup de force*' would have to be postponed for the present.[140] The directives for 'Operation Green' (as previously mentioned) envisaged the destruction of Czechoslovakia by the end of September. So long as Runciman remained on the scene, that operation would have to wait, for his presence increased considerably the possibility of immediate British involvement in any conflict, an eventuality for which Hitler was not yet prepared. However, this concern was unnecessary. The British mediator was not being sent out primarily to play for time but to seek a resolution of the crisis, and it remained to be seen whether the temporary advantage gained by Britain could be put to good use. There were few in London who had a clear idea how best to exploit the situation. Runciman himself certainly did not. When the proposed assignment was being explained to him, he told Halifax: 'I quite understand; you are setting me adrift in a small dinghy in mid-Atlantic.'[141] Although Runciman's characteristically nautical allusion was made in connection with the professed independence of the Mission, it was in another sense that the metaphor was to prove most apposite.

Notes

1 For a summarised translation of the proposals see *DBFP*, 3/I, appendix III, pp. 636–7.
2 Newton to Halifax, 3 and 4 June 1938, *DBFP*, 3/I, nos 373, 377.
3 Newton to Halifax, 11 June 1938, *DBFP*, 3/I, no. 399. The memorandum, dated 7 June, was published in full in the SdP newspaper, *Die Zeit*, 20 July 1938. For a complete English translation see RIIA, *Documents*, 1938, II, pp. 151–62. See also *DBFP*, 3/I, appendix III, pp. 637–43 for a summarised translation.
4 Newton to Halifax, 15 June 1938, *DBFP*, 3/I, no. 415.
5 Minute by Mallet, 24 June 1938, C 5922/1941/18, FO 371/21724.
6 Minute by Sargent, undated (but probably 24 June 1938), *ibid.*
7 Beneš, *Mnichovské dny*, pp. 110–13, and document no. 13, Notes by Beneš on SdP Memorandum, 9 June 1938, pp. 403–6.
8 Newton to Halifax, 23 June 1938, *DBFP*, 3/I, no. 436 and appendix III, pp. 643–6.
9 Beneš, *Mnichovské dny*, p. 110; RIIA, *Documents*, 1938, II, p. 162.
10 Newton to Halifax, 3, 11 and 13 June 1938, *DBFP*, 3/I, nos 373, 399, 402.
11 Newton to Halifax, 18 June 1938, *DBFP*, 3/I, no. 427.
12 Newton to Halifax, 21 July 1938, *DBFP*, 3/I, no. 528.
13 Minutes of meeting between Beneš, Kundt and Sebekowsky, 24 August 1938, enclosed in Hencke to the Foreign Ministry, 27 August 1938, *DGFP*, D/II, no. 398.
14 Other members of the Committee were Rudolf Bechyně, Jan Černý, František Ježek, Rudolf Mlčoch and Mgr Jan Šrámek.
15 The SdP negotiators in addition to Kundt were Gustav Peters, Alfred Rosche, Wilhelm Sebekowsky and Rudolf Schicketanz.

16 Laffan, in *Crisis over Czechoslovakia*, p. 159, speculates that Henlein kept away from the talks either 'because he had not the mental dexterity necessary for negotiation, or perhaps in order that he might be able to repudiate any concessions made by his colleagues'.
17 *Ibid.*, pp. 180–1.
18 Minute by Roberts, 8 August 1938, C 7930/1941/18, FO 371/21730.
19 For full details of the draft Nationalities Statute, Administrative Reform and Language Laws, as supplied to the Foreign Office by the Prague Legation on 29 July 1938, see C 7930/1941/18, FO 371/21730. For summaries see FO 800/305, ff. 350–67. The measures are summarised more briefly in Beneš, *Mnichovské dny*, pp. 120–8, and in Laffan, *Crisis over Czechoslovakia*, pp. 185–6, 206–8.
20 Newton to Halifax, 2 August 1938, C 7883/1941/18, FO 371/21730.
21 Henderson to Halifax, 20 July 1938, *DBFP*, 3/I, no. 517. Weizsäcker claimed that points 1, 2, 3, 6, and 8 of the Carlsbad demands had been completely ignored and that the responses to points 4, 5, and 7 were wholly inadequate.
22 Minute by Roberts, 8 August 1938, C 7930/1941/18, FO 371/21730.
23 Minute by Sargent, 22 July 1938, C 7216/1941/18, FO 371/21728.
24 Halifax to Newton, 31 May 1938, *DBFP*, 3/I, no. 353; Halifax to Phipps, 31 May 1938, *DBFP*, 3/I, no. 354.
25 Phipps to Halifax, 23 May 1938, *DBFP*, 3/I, no. 286.
26 Phipps to Halifax, 1 June 1938, *DBFP*, 3/I, no. 357.
27 De Lacroix to Bonnet, 8 June 1938, *DDF*, 2/IX, no. 522; Newton to Halifax, 9 June 1938, *DBFP*, 3/I, no. 389.
28 Halifax to Phipps, 11 June 1938, *DBFP*, 3/I, no. 398.
29 Phipps to Halifax, 13 June 1938, *DBFP*, 3/I, no. 406.
30 *Aide-mémoire* for Czechoslovak government, 9 June 1938 [?], *DDF*, 2/IX, no. 535, also enclosed in Phipps to Halifax, 27 June 1938, *DBFP*, 3/I, no. 447; memorandum from Halifax to Bonnet, 7 July 1938, *DBFP*, 3/I, no. 472.
31 Phipps to Halifax, 28 June 1938, *DBFP*, 3/I, no. 450.
32 Halifax to Phipps, 17 June 1938, *DBFP*, 3/I, no. 424.
33 Newton to Halifax, 3, 11 (twice), 18, 22, 17 and 18 June, 13 and 16 July 1938, *DBFP*, 3/I, nos 373, 396, 399, 426, 434, 444, 449, 480, 495. The meetings with Beneš took place on 3, 11, 28 June and 16 July, those with Hodža on 10, 18, 26 June and 13 July, and that with Krofta on 22 June.
34 Halifax to Newton, 16 and 29 June 1938, *DBFP*, 3/I, nos 418, 454; Halifax to Campbell, 14 July 1938, *DBFP*, 3/I, no. 489; Halifax to Newton, 27 June 1938, C 6398/1941/18, FO 371/21725 and 15 July 1938, C 7053/1941/18, FO 371/21727. The meetings with Masaryk took place on 16 and 27 June, and 13 July.
35 Newton to Halifax, 25 April 1938, C 3441/1941/18, FO 371/21716.
36 Minutes by Sargent, 27 April 1938, and Halifax, 2 May 1938, and Strang to Newton, 6 May 1938, *ibid.*
37 Newton to Strang, 24 May 1938, and minute by Vansittart, 17 June 1938, C 5007/1941/18, FO 371/21722.
38 Minute by Vansittart, 23 May 1938, C 4851/1941/18, FO 371/21721. Emphasis in original.
39 Newton to Halifax, 23 May 1938, *DBFP*, 3/I, no. 293.
40 Halifax to Newton, 27 May 1938, C 5260/1941/18, FO 371/21723 and 31 May 1938, *DBFP*, 3/I, no. 353; Newton to Halifax, 3 June 1938, *DBFP*, 3/I, no. 373.
41 Minute by Vansittart, 26 May 1938, C 5260/1941/18, FO 371/21723.

42 Minute by Vansittart, 31 May 1938, C 5261/1941/18, FO 371/21723.
43 Newton to Halifax and Halifax to Newton, 1 June 1938, C 5272/1941/18, FO 371/21723.
44 Newton to Halifax, 3 June 1938, *DBFP*, 3/I, no. 373; Halifax to Newton, 31 May 1938, *DBFP*, 3/I, no. 353.
45 Halifax to Newton, 8 June 1938, *DBFP*, 3/I, no. 384. Krebs fled to Germany in 1935, at the time of the dissolution of the German National Socialist Party in Czechoslovakia.
46 Note by Vansittart, 16 May 1938, *DBFP*, 3/I, appendix II (1).
47 Minute by Vansittart, 7 June 1938, and Halifax to Newton, 10 June 1938, C 5686/1941/18, FO 371/21724. Emphasis in original.
48 Minute by Vansittart, 1 June 1938, C 5342/1941/18, FO 371/21723.
49 Newton to Halifax, 11 June 1938, *DBFP*, 3/I, no. 399.
50 Minute by Vansittart, 14 June 1938, C 6643/1941/18, FO 371/21726.
51 Minute by Vansittart, 21 June 1938, C 6236/1941/18, FO 371/21725.
52 Minute by Vansittart, 27 June 1938, C 6644/1941/18, FO 371/21726.
53 Minute by Sargent, 22 June 1938, C 6236/1941/18, FO 371/21725.
54 Halifax to Newton, 22 June 1938, *DBFP*, 3/I, no. 432.
55 Newton to Halifax, 28 June 1938, *DBFP*, 3/I, no. 449; note 1 to document no. 441, *DBFP*, 3/I, p. 516.
56 Newton to Halifax, 27 June 1938, *DBFP*, 3/I, no. 444. Bechyně, a Social Democrat, was Minister of Railways, and Franke, a National Socialist, was Minister of Education.
57 Minute by Vansittart, 14 June 1938, C 5807/1941/18, FO 371/21724. Emphasis in original.
58 Minute by Vansittart, 21 June 1938, C 6236/1941/18, FO 371/21725.
59 Halifax to Newton, 27 June 1938, C 6398/1941/18, FO 371/21725.
60 Halifax to Newton, 29 June 1938, *DBFP*, 3/I, no. 454. Newton considered that only Clerk would be likely to exert the desired effect. (Newton to Halifax, 27 June 1938, *DBFP*, 3/I, no. 444.)
61 Newton to Halifax, 30 June 1938, C 6689/1941/18, FO 371/21726.
62 Newton to Halifax, 28 June 1938, *DBFP*, 3/I, no. 448.
63 Newton to Halifax, 21 June 1938, C 6125/4770/18, FO 371/21761.
64 Minutes by Vansittart, 21 and 27 June 1938, C 6236/1941/18, FO 371/21725 and C 6644/1941/18, FO 371/21726.
65 Halifax to Newton, 22 June 1938, *DBFP*, 3/I, no. 432. See also Newton to Halifax, 22 and 28 June 1938, *DBFP*, 3/I, nos 434, 449 (annex).
66 Halifax to Newton, 27 June 1938, C 6398/1941/18, FO 371/21725.
67 Halifax to Newton, 14 July 1938, *DBFP*, 3/I, no. 488. See also Halifax to Newton, 15 July 1938, C 7053/1941/18, FO 371/21727.
68 *The Times*, 3 and 14 June 1938. Following the second, less emphatic article, Halifax wrote a note of complaint to the editor, Geoffrey Dawson. (Marginal note by Harvey, undated, C 6643/1941/18, FO 371/21726.) The German Ambassador in London believed that the former article reflected the views of 'authoritative circles', but added that it should not be assumed that a plebiscite would necessarily become British policy. (Dirksen to the Foreign Ministry, 9 June 1938, *DGFP*, D/II, no. 247.)
69 Minutes by Sargent and Vansittart, 3 June 1938, C 5359/1941/18, FO 371/21723.

70 Memorandum by Roberts (dated only June 1938, but received in registry on 21 June) and attached minutes, C 6108/1941/18, FO 371/21725. The memorandum was also printed for the Cabinet Committee on Foreign Policy, see FPC Papers, 4 July 1938, FP 36 (66), CAB 27/627.
71 Halifax to Campbell, 14 July 1938, *DBFP*, 3/I, no. 489.
72 Memorandum by Vansittart, 12 July 1938, C 7009/1941/18, FO 371/21727.
73 Halifax to Newton, 14 July 1938, *DBFP*, 3/I, no. 488.
74 Newton to Halifax, 16 July 1938, *DBFP*, 3/I, no. 497. Newton added: 'It should not be forgotten that our representations on May 7 were followed by increased provocation on the Sudeten German side culminating in the crisis of May 21.'
75 Halifax to Newton, 14 July 1938, *DBFP*, 3/I, no. 488.
76 Newton to Halifax, 15 July 1938, *DBFP*, 3/I, no. 490.
77 Newton to Halifax, 16 July 1938, *DBFP*, 3/I, no. 496.
78 Newton to Halifax, 16 May and 2 June 1938, *DBFP*, 3/I, nos 221, 368.
79 Newton to Halifax, 16 and 17 July 1938, *DBFP*, 3/I, nos 495, 504.
80 Newton to Halifax, 16 July 1938, *DBFP*, 3/I, no. 495.
81 Newton to Halifax, 18 July 1938, C 7216/1941/18, FO 371/21728.
82 Newton to Halifax, 2 July 1938, *DBFP*, 3/I, no. 465.
83 Newton to Halifax, 18 and 21 June 1938, *DBFP*, 3/I, nos 426, 431.
84 Newton to Halifax, 28 June and 4 July 1938, *DBFP*, 3/I, nos 449, 468.
85 Newton to Halifax, 27 June 1938, *DBFP*, 3/I, no. 446.
86 Halifax to Newton, 30 June 1938, *DBFP*, 3/I, no. 457.
87 Newton to Halifax, 3 July 1938, *DBFP*, 3/I, no. 467.
88 Halifax to Newton, 15 July 1938, C 7053/1941/18, FO 371/21727.
89 Newton to Halifax, 16 July 1938, *DBFP*, 3/I, no. 497.
90 See report by Strang, in Halifax to Campbell, 12 July 1938, *DBFP*, 3/I, no. 479.
91 Newton to Halifax, 16 July 1938, *DBFP*, 3/I, no. 497.
92 Minute by Roberts, 18 July 1938, C 7244/1941/18, FO 371/21728; Halifax to Newton, 18 July 1938, *DBFP*, 3/I, no. 508.
93 Newton to Halifax, 16 July 1938, *DBFP*, 3/I, no. 497.
94 Henderson to Halifax, 16 July 1938, *DBFP*, 3/I, no. 494, and note 1 to that document.
95 Newton to Halifax, 16 July 1938, *DBFP*, 3/I, no. 498. The rumours were emphatically denied by the Czechoslovak government and the British observers, returning from the vicinity of the Bavarian frontier, reported no evidence of troop concentrations. (Newton to Halifax, 14 July 1938, *DBFP*, 3/I, no 485.) When the allegation was repeated by the German news agency DNB on 16 July, Newton immediately despatched the observers to the area in question in north–eastern Bohemia. (Newton to Halifax, 16 July 1938, *DBFP*, 3/I, nos 498, 499.) Their report was again negative. (Newton to Halifax, 18 July 1938, *DBFP*, 3/I, no. 506.) In Berlin, however, Weizsäcker rejected the observers' findings, insisting that Czechoslovakia had recently reinforced its garrisons in the frontier regions. (Henderson to Halifax, 21 July 1938, *DBFP*, 3/I, no. 529.)
96 Halifax to Newton, 18 July 1938, *DBFP*, 3/I, no. 508.
97 Halifax to Newton, 18 July 1938, C 7141/1941/18, FO 371/21727.
98 Halifax to Newton, 18 July 1938, *DBFP*, 3/I, no. 508.
99 Halifax to Newton, 19 July 1938, *DBFP*, 3/I, no. 516.
100 Newton to Halifax, 21 July 1938, *DBFP*, 3/I, no. 531.

101 Newton to Halifax, 20 and 21 July 1938, *DBFP*, 3/I, nos 522, 525. For the wording of Newton's original instructions, see Halifax to Newton, 18 July 1938, *DBFP*, 3/I, no. 508.
102 Halifax to Newton, 18 July 1938, *DBFP*, 3/I, no. 508; Newton to Halifax, 20 July 1938, *DBFP*, 3/I, no. 521.
103 Newton to Halifax, 20 July 1938, *DBFP*, 3/I, no. 521. Beneš himself recorded in his memoir that he had been 'extremely surprised and almost dumbfounded' by the approach. (Beneš, *Mnichovské dny*, p. 148.)
104 Newton to Halifax, 20 and 21 July 1938, *DBFP*, 3/I, nos 521, 525.
105 Newton to Halifax, 20 and 21 July 1938, *DBFP*, 3/I, nos 521, 525. For details of the communiqué see RIIA, *Documents*, 1938, II, pp. 1656.
106 Newton to Halifax, 21 July 1938, *DBFP*, 3/I, no. 525.
107 Newton to Halifax, 20 July 1938, *DBFP*, 3/I, no. 521.
108 Newton to Halifax, 21 and 23 July 1938, *DBFP*, 3/I, nos 526, 536.
109 Newton to Halifax, 23 July 1938, *DBFP*, 3/I, no. 537.
110 Halifax to Newton, 18 July 1938, *DBFP*, 3/I, no. 508.
111 Newton to Halifax, 25 July 1938, *DBFP*, 3/II, no. 540.
112 Halifax to Newton, 25 July 1938, *DBFP*, 3/II, no. 542.
113 *HC Deb.*, 338, col. 2959, 26 July 1938.
114 Halifax to Newton, 25 July 1938, *DBFP*, 3/II, no. 542; Newton to Halifax, 26 July 1938, *DBFP*, 3/II, no. 545.
115 Newton to Halifax, 26 July 1938, *DBFP*, 3/II, no. 547.
116 *HL Deb.*, 110, col. 1281, 27 July 1938.
117 Minute by Vansittart, 22 July 1938, C 7512/1941/18, FO 371/21729.
118 Halifax to Newton, 21 July 1938, and Newton to Halifax, 22 July 1938, *DBFP*, 3/I, nos 527, 533.
119 Minute by Sargent, 22 July 1938, C 7512/1941/18, FO 371/21729.
120 Minute by Vansittart, 22 July 1938, *ibid.*
121 Minutes by Vansittart, 26 July 1938, C 7591/1941/18, and 27 July, C 7634/1941/18, FO 371/21729.
122 Minute by Cadogan, 28 July 1938, C 7591/1941/18, FO 371/21729.
123 Minute by Vansittart, 25 July 1938, C 7560/1941/18, FO 371/21729.
124 Memorandum by Christie, (undated), C 8118/1941/18, FO 371/21731.
125 Halifax to Henderson, 25 July 1938, *DBFP*, 3/II, no. 541.
126 Henderson to Halifax, 25 July 1938, *DBFP*, 3/II, no. 544.
127 Minutes by Weizsäcker, 25 and 26 July 1938, *DGFP*, D/II, nos 313, 315.
128 Henderson to Halifax, 27 July 1938, *DBFP*, 3/II, no. 552.
129 Minute by Weizsäcker, 29 July 1938, and note by Ribbentrop, *DGFP*, D/II, no. 325.
130 Halifax to Ribbentrop, 28 July 1938, *DBFP*, 3/II, no. 556.
131 Sargent to Henderson, 4 August 1938, see note to document no. 574, *DBFP*, 3/II, p. 41.
132 Minute by Sargent, 28 July 1938, C 7577/1941/18, FO 371/21729.
133 Chamberlain to Dirksen, 3 August 1938, *DBFP*, 3/II, no. 574.
134 Dirksen to Chamberlain, 7 August 1938, *DBFP*, 3/II, no. 591, and *DGFP*, D/II, no. 343. Ribbentrop subsequently sent a reprimand to London concerning this unorthodox diplomatic approach. (Woermann to Kordt, 14 August 1938, *DGFP*, D/II, no. 357.)
135 Ribbentrop to Halifax, 21 August 1938, *DGFP*, D/II, no. 379, and *DBFP*, 3/II, no. 661.

136 Minute by Sargent, 28 July 1938, C 7577/1941/18, FO 371/21729.
137 Minute by Strang, 27 July 1938, *ibid.*
138 Memorandum by Vansittart, 25 July 1938, C 7614/1941/18, FO 371/21729.
139 Record of Conversation between Halifax and Wiedemann, 18 July 1938, *DBFP*, 3/I, no. 510. Wiedemann was seeking to arrange a goodwill visit to Britain by Göring.
140 Memorandum by Weizsäcker, 31 July 1938, *DGFP*, D/II, no. 329.
141 *HL Deb.*, 110, col. 1282, 27 July 1938. When recounting this to the House of Lords, Halifax substituted the word 'boat' for 'dingy', fearing that 'their Lordships would not know what a dingy was'. (Stopford, 'Prague, 1938–1939', p. 10)

6
The Mission Takes Shape

It was apparent from the outset that Runciman was chosen largely as an illustrious figurehead for the prospective Mission and that he would have to be accompanied by others who would carry out the bulk of the required work. One such person was Frank Trelawny Arthur Ashton-Gwatkin whom Runciman appointed as his chief assistant. Born in 1889, educated at Eton and at Balliol College, Oxford, Ashton-Gwatkin entered the Consular Service in 1913. After six years in the Far East, he joined the Far Eastern Department of the Foreign Office, transferring to the Diplomatic Service in 1921. He remained based in London for the remainder of his career, apart from a short period at the Moscow Embassy in 1929 and 1930, from where he was recalled to serve as secretary to the British–Soviet Debt Committee. Within the Foreign Office, Ashton-Gwatkin specialised in economic affairs, and was instrumental, during the early 1930s, in establishing the Economic Relations Section. Its purpose was to coordinate economic and political information and to liaise with other government departments concerned with international economic affairs. Ashton-Gwatkin became head of this Section on its formal constitution in 1934.[1] Previously, he had participated in several major international conferences including the World Disarmament Conference in Washington in the early 1920s, and, in a more senior capacity, the Imperial Conference at Ottawa in 1932, and the World Economic Conference in London the following year. Away from Whitehall, Ashton-Gwatkin was also a moderately successful writer. Under the pseudonym of John Paris, he published several novels and a collection of poems drawing mainly on his experience of life in the Far East.[2]

Although initially Ashton-Gwatkin's work at the Foreign Office was primarily concerned with developing British policy towards the Far East, during the 1930s he became an ardent exponent of the economic appeasement of Germany.[3] As head of the Economic Relations Section, he made regular annual visits to Germany and repeatedly expressed the belief that German economic domination of Central and South Eastern Europe – or Danubia in his parlance – was an inevitable development and not necessarily damaging to British interests. He maintained this attitude up to (and indeed beyond) the time of his membership of the Runciman Mission. This is evident from his reaction to an approach from the Czechoslovak Prime Minister, made in late March 1938 following the German annexation of Austria, seeking British support for economic arrangements aimed at preventing the countries of Central Europe becoming, in the words of Newton's report, 'mere colonies or satellites of Germany'. Ashton-Gwatkin responded by minuting: 'There is little, if anything, that we can do.'[4] A few days previously, he had commented in greater detail on a proposed speech by the Secretary-General of the League of Nations, Joseph Avenol, aimed at checking Germany's ambition to become 'the metropolis of Central Europe, composed of economic dominions'. Ashton-Gwatkin likened the speech to 'the effort of King Canute', adding that the expansion of the German economy was 'natural and constructive'. He took comfort, however, in his prediction that, because the small states concerned were not rich enough to buy more from Germany: 'The development of the German "economic dominion", will therefore at present be slow.' Struck out from this sentence was a significant final qualifying phrase '– unless Czechoslovakia is taken by force'.[5] Despite the deletion, Ashton-Gwatkin was clearly aware that, at least in the economic sphere, Czechoslovakia was in a key position to resist German expansion. Little did he know at the time that, within a matter of a few months, he himself would play a crucial role in determining the fate of that country.

The inclusion of Ashton-Gwatkin amongst Runciman's staff, although obviously meeting with official approval, was nevertheless the source of some embarrassment for the British government. The Mission was ostensibly independent of the government, yet Runciman's chief assistant in Prague was a senior permanent official in the Foreign Office. This inconsistency was noted in Berlin, where Henderson found that his protestation of the Mission's independence failed to convince the German government.[6] The official explanation was that Ashton-Gwatkin's attachment to the Mission had been made at the personal request of Runciman.[7] Ashton-Gwatkin's work had indeed drawn him into close contact with the Board of Trade, where Runciman served his second term of office as President between 1931 and 1937, and a close working relationship developed between the two men.

Runciman's choice of Ashton-Gwatkin seemed therefore not a surprising one. In fact, his attachment to the Mission appeared to come close to fulfilling the formula, suggested by Newton in mid-June, of sending out a prominent person accompanied by someone with relevant expert knowledge. However, although Ashton-Gwatkin's Foreign Office background, together with his experience of international negotiations, would clearly be helpful, his expertise did not bear directly upon the internal problems of Czechoslovakia. Nevertheless, Ashton-Gwatkin, like Runciman, could be relied on not to say or do anything that might conflict with British policy, and furthermore, should it become necessary – as indeed it did – he could be used to manipulate the outcome of the Mission to the satisfaction of London. He was also expected to keep the Foreign Office supplied with up to date information on developments in Czechoslovakia.[8] But in order to avoid the much feared pitfall of involving Britain too closely in the Sudeten German problem, a little distance was placed between Ashton-Gwatkin and the Foreign Office by his formal secondment to the Runciman Mission.[9] Naturally though, this official explanation cut little ice with sceptical observers in Britain and elsewhere.

The Foreign Office became particularly concerned about reactions in Germany. German newspapers, including the Nazi Party organ, the *Völkischer Beobachter*, taking their cue from articles in the French press, regarded Ashton-Gwatkin's appointment to Runciman's staff as signalling the growth of British resistance to the German economic penetration of Central Europe.[10] Nothing could have been further from the truth. The concern of the Foreign Office was compounded by an incautious remark from Ronald Campbell, Chargé d'Affaires in Paris, who pointed out to the French Foreign Minister that Ashton-Gwatkin's economic expertise could be of direct assistance to the Sudeten Germans concerned about their economic plight inside Czechoslovakia.[11] The British were quick to deny both these interpretations of Ashton-Gwatkin's role. Campbell was instructed to correct the 'misleading impression' left by his conversation with Bonnet, and Berlin was informed that Ashton-Gwatkin was attached to the Mission on Runciman's personal request and not in his capacity as an economic expert.[12] Ashton-Gwatkin himself was also at pains to point out that there was no political significance in his appointment, adding, somewhat disingenuously, that since he had not been engaged in political work at the Foreign Office he could approach the problems facing the Mission 'from an entirely neutral standpoint'.[13]

A similar claim could undoubtedly have been made by one other member of the Mission, Geoffrey Kelsall Peto. Born in 1878, and also an Old Etonian, Peto came from a career background of business and parliamentary politics. He was a director of an industrial firm, the Morgan Crucible Company Ltd, and, on the political side, Conservative Member of Parliament for Frome in the 1920s and for Bilston in the early 1930s. During his second period of service in the House of Commons, Peto became closely associated with Runciman, acting as his Parliamentary Private Secretary between 1931 and 1935. The two men remained friends subsequently and, as in the case of Ashton-Gwatkin, it appeared not unnatural therefore for Runciman to include Peto in his team bound for Prague.

It is surprising therefore, that in a letter to his wife on 24 July, over a week after he had agreed to undertake the task of mediation in Czechoslovakia, Runciman did not include Ashton-Gwatkin or Peto in a 'pretty well complete' list of members of the forthcoming Mission.[14] Clearly, neither Peto's name nor, more significantly, that of Ashton-Gwatkin had sprung quite as readily to Runciman's mind as was officially suggested and, in the case of Ashton-Gwatkin, the idea apparently came from elsewhere. Oliver Harvey, Halifax's Private Secretary, recorded in his diary that Lord Tyrrell, a former Permanent Under-Secretary at the Foreign Office and Ambassador to Paris, claimed credit for advising Runciman to take Ashton-Gwatkin with him to Prague.[15] Runciman himself first raised the possibility of Ashton-Gwatkin's membership of the Mission during a visit to the Foreign Office on 26 July. Cadogan considered the request 'rather objectionable', but Halifax was willing to agree, subject to the approval of the Prime Minister.[16] The matter was discussed by the Cabinet the following day, when Halifax indicated that he himself had 'no doubt as to the great assistance' that Ashton-Gwatkin could provide to Runciman, but wished to know whether other ministers considered the proposal would associate the British government too closely with the forthcoming mediation. The Cabinet raised no objection to Ashton-Gwatkin's membership of the Mission, and Runciman was immediately informed accordingly.[17]

Ashton-Gwatkin was not the only economic expert to accompany Runciman to Prague. At an early stage in the selection of his team, Runciman, then still wishing to avoid obvious links with the Foreign Office, turned to Ivison Macadam, the Secretary of the Royal Institute of International Affairs (RIIA), for advice on staffing his Mission. Macadam recommended Robert Jemmet Stopford, a banker by profession, but with some experience of the affairs of Central Europe and of constitutional problems in general.[18] Stopford was born in Dublin in 1895 and educated as St Paul's School in London and Magdalene College, Cambridge. After serving in the First World War, he embarked on a career in banking but also became associated with the RIIA and its director, Professor Arnold Toynbee. Stopford's experience of constitutional matters was gained through serving as Private Secretary to Sir John Simon during his chairmanship of the Indian Statutory Commission between 1928 and 1930.[19] Subsequently, from 1933 to 1938, Stopford was involved in international financial negotiations as secretary of the Standstill Committee on German, Austrian, Hungarian and Romanian bank debts and participated in talks on the Austrian debt following the *Anschluss* in March 1938. During May and June of that year, he was also involved, together with Vansittart, in contacts with Karl Goerdeler, a prominent member of the anti-Hitler opposition in Germany.[20]

Even Stopford's expert knowledge, however, did not extend to the internal problems of Czechoslovakia, and, clearly, the Mission also required the services of someone familiar with the local situation. Runciman's list of 24 July contained two such persons: John Monro Troutbeck, First Secretary at the British Legation in Prague; and Peter Pares (the son of Sir Bernard Pares, the Russian historian and friend of the Runcimans) who was British Consul in Liberec (Reichenberg) in Czechoslovakia.[21] Troutbeck's candidacy does not appear to have received consideration in the Foreign Office, but, in the case of Pares, advice was sought from Newton. Pares' ability to act as adviser and interpreter was not in doubt, but there was concern about the wisdom of attaching to the Mission someone whose father had been a close friend of T.G. Masaryk.[22]

Whilst Newton was considering this matter, Henderson suggested from Berlin that Pares would more likely be acceptable to the German government if Addison, Newton's predecessor in Prague, were also attached to the Mission.[23] This suggestion prompted an immediate negative response from Newton, who warned that Addison's presence might prove 'disastrous' since he was regarded in Prague as being pro-German and hostile to Czechoslovakia.[24] In the case of Pares, however, Newton concurred with the reservations expressed by the Foreign Office, and shared by Henderson, and advised against his appointment to Runciman's staff. Newton also felt unable to recommend any other member of the British community in Czechoslovakia, but suggested instead Ian Leslie Henderson, one of the British observers appointed in the wake of the May Crisis, providing that his former duties as British Consul in Innsbruck did not render him unacceptable.[25] In the Foreign Office, Roberts was also concerned that Henderson's appointment would link the Mission too closely with the British government[26] but, after further discussion between Runciman and Sargent, it was finally agreed that Henderson would join the Mission as an interpreter.[27]

Henderson was the youngest member of the original Mission staff, born in 1901. After Rugby School and Trinity College, Oxford, he entered the Consular Service in the early 1920s, working in several cities across Europe and in Africa. At the time of Henderson's appointment as an observer in early June, Sargent had noted with approbation that he had proved 'very level-headed and to possess good judgement'.[28] In common with the other members of Runciman's team, Henderson had little prior knowledge of the Sudeten German dispute, although by the time the Mission got under way in early August, he had been exposed to the problems of Czechoslovakia for several weeks. It is probable therefore that, initially at least, he was more familiar with the outstanding issues than any of his senior colleagues.

Towards the end of its activities, the Mission was reinforced by the addition of David Stephens, a Clerk in the House of Lords, on holiday in Czechoslovakia at the time. Stephens, born in 1910, was educated at Winchester and Christ Church, Oxford, followed by a travelling fellowship at Queen's College, Oxford, during which he undertook a study of ethnic minorities. His attachment to the Mission early in September occasioned an uncharacteristic rift in the otherwise harmonious relations between Runciman and Ashton-Gwatkin. Ashton-Gwatkin welcomed Stephens' arrival, believing it to be in response to a request from Runciman for additional staff.[29] In fact, no such appeal had been made, and Runciman was, as Ashton-Gwatkin noted, 'distinctly annoyed', believing that Stephens was being forced upon him.[30] The official staff of the Mission was completed by two secretaries: Rosemary Miller, Runciman's private secretary; and Aline Tillard, a shorthand-typist provided by the British government.

In addition to his official party, Runciman was also accompanied by his wife Hilda. Lady Runciman had often previously travelled with her husband on official visits abroad, and, as a former Member of Parliament, she was herself not unaccustomed to public life. Furthermore, her keen intellect – attested to by her first class degree gained in the historical tripos at Girton College, Cambridge – and linguistic skills, including a knowledge of German, were to be of much value to the Mission, not least from the social point of view. During their stay in Czechoslovakia, the Runcimans also received visits from their sons Leslie and Steven and their daughter Margaret (Mrs Fairweather).[31] The cost of travel for Lady Runciman and her maid was met by Runciman himself.[32] All expenses for the official members of the party were borne by the British government. Two other members of the Mission, Peto and Henderson, were also accompanied by their respective wives.[33]

One further, *de facto*, member of the Mission was Basil Cochrane Newton, the British Minister in Prague. Although officially entirely unconnected with Runciman's activities, he not only provided the Mission's main communications link with London, but also, particularly during the latter part of Runciman's stay in Czechoslovakia, played an active part in the Mission's deliberations. Born in 1889, educated at Wellington and at King's College, Cambridge, Newton entered the Foreign Office in 1912. He was posted to Peking in 1927, moving to Berlin in 1929, and (as previously mentioned) transferring to Prague in March 1937. Newton was, in many respects, the model professional diplomat, acting as the eyes and ears of his government, supplying generally balanced reports and loyally carrying out to the letter instructions received. Although not uncritical of the Czechoslovak authorities, unlike his predecessor Addison, Newton avoided open hostility towards his hosts. He also had few illusions about the expansionist nature of Nazi Germany, being familiar with Hitler's *Mein Kampf*.[34] Nevertheless, as Newton saw it, his role in Prague was to promote British government policy, not to argue against it.

The official party constituting the Runciman Mission to Czechoslovakia was evidently a strong and capable one. Its members between them had a wide experience of public life and considerable expertise in various aspects of politics and international affairs. The Mission however suffered from one obvious and significant drawback – it was largely ignorant of the problems it was being sent to investigate and resolve. Runciman's party did not contain a single person with any detailed knowledge or understanding of the complex issues that had given rise to the conflict between the government and the SdP. This was clearly a major disadvantage – but perhaps an inevitable one, as most experts in the field had established public attitudes, and were therefore unacceptable to one or other of the protagonists or to the British government. One such person was the author and journalist R.H. Bruce Lockhart. His candidacy for membership of the Mission was vigorously canvassed by his friend R.W.A. Leeper, head of the Foreign Office News Section. Not surprisingly, however, Bruce Lockhart was turned down on the grounds of his pro-Czechoslovak bias.[35] Others with specialist knowledge of Czechoslovakia and Central Europe, such as Professor R.W. Seton-Watson or H. Wickham Steed,[36] were evidently also overlooked for the same reason, despite the fact that Chamberlain himself, when announcing the forthcoming Runciman Mission in the House of Commons, admitted that it was 'very difficult' for those who had not made a special study of the matter 'to arrive at a just conclusion as to the rights and wrongs of the dispute'. The Prime Minister was nevertheless confident that Runciman was the right man for the job. Although the task was a 'very exacting, very responsible, and very delicate one', Runciman possessed 'outstanding personal qualifications' to undertake it. He had, Chamberlain added, a long experience of public affairs and of people from all walks of life, and was characterised by 'fearlessness, freedom from prejudice, integrity and impartiality'.[37]

This inevitably generous tribute to the reluctant mediator was widely echoed in the British press, which responded on the whole favourably to the news of the forthcoming Runciman Mission. The general reaction was one of relief, as prospects for peace were considered a little brighter. J.L. Garvin, writing in the *Observer* under the headline 'Relief', hailed Runciman as 'the pilgrim of peace', adding that, although the task ahead of him was a most difficult one, there was 'no better man for the work'. Runciman's 'strong character [and] cogent mind, and [his] rare faculty for the clear and dispassionate analysis of intricate subjects' qualified him admirably for the peacemaking mission.[38] *The Times* shared the view that Runciman was ideally suited for the assignment and was also full of praise for his personal qualities, singling out his extensive experience of public life and his 'able and unbiased mind'.[39] The weekly periodical *Time and Tide* was somewhat less enthusiastic. Whilst not disputing Runciman's personal integrity and devotion to duty, it considered his mind to be of 'a curiously narrow type' which disliked receiving information conflicting with previously established views.[40] The only really discordant note was struck by the Communist *Daily Worker*, which regarded Runciman's role of mediator as 'full of menace' to Czechoslovakia. The *Daily Worker* was not impressed by Runciman's personal qualities and saw him merely as 'Chamberlain's agent', who could 'be trusted not to develop ... any awkward sympathy for the problems of the Czech government'.[41]

Other newspapers, however, including those not noted for their support of the Chamberlain government, commented more favourably on the Mission's objectives as outlined by the Prime Minister. Although unable to guarantee a positive resolution of the Sudeten German crisis, Chamberlain nevertheless indicated to the House of Commons a two-fold benefit to be derived from the initiative; public opinion would be better informed, and the problem itself might prove 'less obstinate' than believed. As for the precise nature of Runciman's role, the Prime Minister explained:

> He is an investigator and mediator ... He will try to acquaint himself with all the facts and the views of the two sides, and he will no doubt see them separately, and perhaps later on he will be able to make some proposals to them which will help them. He is in the position ... of a man who goes down to assist in settling a strike. He has to see two sides who have come to a point when they cannot go any further. He is there as an independent, impartial person.[42]

The Times, which considered the initiative a most interesting 'novel' idea, also saw amongst the principal aims of the Mission the establishment of personal contacts between Runciman and the leaders of the Sudeten Germans, a task that Newton, as an official representative of Britain, was unable to perform.[43] Less predictably, the *News Chronicle* also approved of the decision to send Runciman to Prague, seeing it – incorrectly – as demonstrating British concern for Czechoslovakia, but it warned against the Mission being used to pressure the Czechoslovak side alone into making concessions.[44] Approval for the Mission was also forthcoming from the *Manchester Guardian*, which correctly interpreted what it saw as a 'daring initiative' as indicating that Britain was about to embark on a more active foreign policy. It also regarded the Mission, optimistically, as demonstrating that Britain was not disinterested in the fate of Czechoslovakia, but noted with regret the absence from Chamberlain's statement of any assurance that the vital interests of that country would not be sacrificed in the search for peace. But in any event, the *Manchester Guardian* believed, the Mission would buy time, as Germany was unlikely to bomb Prague whilst Runciman continued his investigations.[45]

One aspect of the official announcement of the forthcoming Runciman Mission – its proclaimed independence of the British government – was received with much scepticism in the press. The claim, made briefly by Chamberlain, was reiterated a little more fully by Halifax, when he explained to the House of Lords that he had made clear to all concerned that Runciman 'is in no way acting as a representative of or on behalf of His Majesty's Government, nor do we take any responsibility for the suggestions that he may make'.[46] *The Times* was virtually alone in accepting this statement at its face value. It observed that Runciman would leave behind the 'direct support' of the British government though he would carry with him the government's 'good will'.[47] The *Observer* considered Runciman's independence to be only nominal, as in his 'unprecedented' role he had 'the prestige of the British Government behind him'.[48] The *Daily Herald*, however, was more uncertain. If Runciman was to be a 'genuinely independent adviser [then] well and good', it argued, but if the British government proposed to use him to coerce the Czechoslovak authorities alone into making concessions, then it was far from satisfactory. Nevertheless, the *Daily Herald* remained optimistic and hoped that 'great good' would come from Runciman's visit.[49] The *News Chronicle* was less guarded in its disbelief and stated bluntly: 'No-one – certainly no Czech and no German – is likely to accept Mr. Chamberlain's bland assurance that the British Government has really nothing officially to do with [Runciman's] success or failure.'[50] This attitude was shared by the *Reynolds News* which wrote disparagingly of 'Chamberlain's travelling circus' and questioned the 'private capacity' of Runciman and his team.[51] The *Star* also considered the Mission's claimed independence to be 'one of those diplomatic circumlocutions which are usually accepted with a large, solemn wink'.[52]

Despite the press scepticism, the British government persisted in maintaining the public front of Runciman's independence. Considerable care was taken to avoid openly associating the Mission with the Foreign Office – except, of course, for the appointment of Ashton-Gwatkin. When Stopford, on joining the staff of the Mission, requested an official briefing on Czechoslovakia, he was refused on the grounds that it would be unwise for him to be seen in the Foreign Office.[53] Runciman himself, however, did visit the Foreign Office on several occasions during the Mission's formation. In addition to the conversations with Halifax and other senior officials, he was also given access to relevant papers.[54] These included a 22-page memorandum, prepared specifically for a possible mediator in early July, describing in some detail the course of negotiations between the Czechoslovak government and the SdP since 1935. The memorandum, written by Roberts, presented a generally balanced account of developments without apportioning responsibility to either side. It noted, however, that the SdP was 'accused, with considerable justification, of taking orders from Berlin' and that, on the Czechoslovak side, 'Dr. Hodža had shown himself more forthcoming and ready to meet Sudeten grievances than Dr. Beneš'.[55] Runciman also requested a briefing from someone with up-to-date firsthand experience of the situation in Czechoslovakia. Troutbeck, from the Prague Legation, brought forward his leave in order to meet Runciman in London for this purpose on 21 July.[56]

There is no evidence to indicate that Runciman had any substantial discussions with Chamberlain at this time, apart from a few words of appreciation uttered by the Prime Minister during the course of a garden party.[57] The task of preparing the reluctant mediator for his arduous assignment appears to have been left to Halifax and his colleagues at the Foreign Office. Little is known about these meetings and what, if any, were the instructions Runciman received prior to his departure for Prague. During the early stages of the negotiations to persuade Runciman to undertake the task of mediation, Halifax did however commit to paper the main objective of the proposed Mission. Writing to Runciman early in July, he explained that the mediator's official and publicly proclaimed task would be to assist the government and the SdP to come to an agreement 'within the framework of the present Czechoslovak State'.[58] This was entirely consistent with official British policy at the time, as was confirmed by the Foreign Secretary in his House of Lords statement concerning the Mission.[59] Halifax himself, however, had expressed doubts about the feasibility of that aim, in the light of Germany's perceived intentions, at a meeting of the Cabinet Foreign Policy Committee in early April,[60] but it is not known whether he repeated these doubts to Runciman.

It is known, however, that, during the conversations between Halifax and Runciman, reference was made to the possibility of resolving the Sudeten German problem by arbitration. At the outset, Runciman was firmly opposed to that solution – although his resolve would subsequently become weakened by events. Nevertheless, before leaving London, he saw his role as essentially that of an intermediary acting to bring the two parties together to achieve an agreement. It was not his intention in any way to arbitrate between them nor, by implication, to design a solution of his own. Halifax was in full agreement with this attitude, fearing that any proposal drafted by Runciman might result in Britain coming under pressure to guarantee the outcome.[61] Vansittart was equally certain that Runciman was not being asked to act as an arbitrator and minuted with emphasis: 'Runciman is *not* binding!'[62]

Further indication of Halifax's thinking is contained in a letter to Henderson, written on 5 August (two days after Runciman's arrival in Prague). Regarding Runciman's role, Halifax explained:

> If he can induce agreement, well and good. If he can't, we must ... be very careful that he does not take any action that would have the effect of committing this country further than it is already committed, to take action in the event of Germany taking military action ... in favour of a solution more drastic than Runciman has recommended.

In the event of failure, Runciman had four alternatives:

1. Merely record the fact with regret, and come away.
2. Record the fact, and say that he thinks such and such a solution was fair and that the blame for disagreement lies with the S.D.
3. As in 2, but that the blame lay with the Czechs.
4. Go a step further, and say that in view of their inability to agree, and the improbability of their being able to settle down together, the only chance was a clean cut – by way of Plebiscite.

Halifax immediately rejected the second option as potentially 'very embarrassing', leading to Germany claiming that Runciman 'had proved either incapable or unwilling to get reason out of Beneš' and that it had no alternative 'but to take justice by force'. That would be done 'in face of an expression of opinion by an impartial investigator which people in this country and in most parts of the world would accept as fair'. In those circumstances, Halifax feared, 'the pressure to intervene actively might be very great'. If, however, Runciman were to blame the Czechoslovak authorities, then 'whatever the Germans did, people would say that the Czechs had had their chance and, however much they condemned the German action, people would incline to feel that the Czechs had brought it on themselves'. The use of a plebiscite, seemed to Halifax 'the devil and as likely to precipitate as to prevent'. Although he did not rule it out as a last resort, the practical difficulties were enormous. It might, however, be used as 'a threat to Beneš'. The situation was full of uncertainties, Halifax continued:

> It is obviously very difficult for anybody to predict how R. is likely to get on, and very difficult, if not impossible, for us to suggest to him as he gets to breaking point what he should say. It will want a good deal of thinking, and we may not have long to think in. ... I am myself slightly disposed to hope that R. may pull it off: but no doubt the odds are long.[63]

Whilst there is no specific evidence to indicate that Halifax put these points directly to Runciman during their conversations prior to the Mission's departure, it is unlikely that the ideas shared with the Berlin Ambassador were not also conveyed to the mediator himself. It is probable therefore, that Runciman was, in effect, advised to avoid placing the blame on the SdP and recommending a plebiscite. In addition, Runciman was almost certainly given access to the (previously mentioned) Foreign Office memorandum analysing the objections to a plebiscite.[64] During his talks with Runciman, Halifax also touched on the question of the possible neutralisation of Czechoslovakia, which had earlier been considered in the Foreign Office. Runciman's reported response was to comment that he did not suppose anyone would wish to raise the question of Czechoslovakia's foreign policy if it could be avoided.[65] Such a remark indicated all too clearly not only that Runciman was not fully aware of the international implications of the problem he was being sent to resolve, but also Halifax's failure to enlighten him.

The briefing Runciman received concerning the Sudeten German problem itself also appears to have been somewhat perfunctory – at least judging from Runciman's notes. Two pages of typescript, probably resulting from his visit to the Foreign Office on 28 July, contain a list of the Sudeten German grievances, some general comments on the situation, and an outline of a possible settlement. The Sudeten German complaints were listed under 11 points:

1. Treated as Minority. No Equality. National State.
2. Promises never fulfilled. Elections put off since 1930.

3. Land Reforms – accepted in principle – were used to denationalise Germans.
4. Tax system used to coerce Germans.
5. Officials in German areas nearly all Czech – Ports – Police – Railways, etc. – some cannot speak German.
6. Contracts given to Czech firms and Czech workmen imported into German districts.
7. German families starving – terrible poverty and underfeeding of children.
8. Complaints to Prague never get beyond Prague. Small officials block everything.
9. German language not accepted outside German districts.
10. Czechs armed in German districts.
11. Censorship and Defence of Realm Act.

This comprehensive list of Sudeten German grievances was not accompanied by any corresponding statement of the Czechoslovak government's case. Nevertheless, the sincerity of the authorities' desire for a settlement was not in question. In his general observations on the situation, Runciman noted: 'Czechs really anxious for settlement – either through fear or sense of justice.' Other points noted were:

> Majority (90%) of Germans in favour of incorporation in Reich.
> Leaders far more moderate than rank and file.
> Germany probably does not want incorporation *Now*.

These were all dubious statements, but nevertheless sincerely believed by many in Whitehall. The third section of Runciman's notes is more cryptic. Under the heading 'Settlement possible' five points are listed:

A. Immediate gesture.
B. Comprehensive Bill giving concessions.
C. 22% of officials – Money – Contracts etc. 50% of officials in German areas.
D. German Nat. inspectorate to consider complaints.
E. Free Election in Municipal and County Elections and nomination in accordance with Majority vote.[66]

Perhaps these points were considered by the Foreign Office as elements of a possible solution to the Sudeten German problem. If that was the case, then those who advised Runciman could be accused of taking an unrealistically optimistic view of the situation.

It is also probable that, under the heading 'immediate gesture', Runciman's attention was drawn to the suggestions which Hohenlohe had conveyed to Vansittart during one of his visits to London in late July. The SdP emissary had proposed that, on arrival in Prague, Runciman should introduce a five-point programme of measures demonstrating 'a new attitude of mind'. The suggested steps were: the start of transfers of German and Czech officials to their respective national territories, the introduction of 'a spirit of conciliation' into the Czechoslovak press, the disarming of Czech political organisations, the gradual withdrawal of the state police from German areas, and the installation of recently elected German mayors.[67] Within the Foreign Office there was little enthusiasm for these measures. Roberts noted that there were obvious Czechoslovak objections to all of them, except for the moderation of the press.[68] Nevertheless, the proposals were forwarded to Newton for advice.[69] He confirmed the objections, pointing out that the exchange of officials could not be carried out overnight, that there was no evidence that Czech political organisations were armed, that the withdrawal of state police was a matter for negotiation, and that the confirmation of new mayors had begun.[70] Although Newton's response itself arrived too late to have been communicated to Runciman before his departure for Prague, the British Minister's observations merely confirmed the views of the Foreign Office which are likely to have been made known to the mediator.

The key question of the Mission's duration was also raised at Runciman's Foreign Office briefing. When the idea of mediation began to be considered in late June, Mallet minuted that 'we need not now, I think, go into the question of whether the mediator should be prepared to stay for a considerable time in Czechoslovakia'.[71] There is little evidence to suggest that much attention was given to this aspect subsequently, although Runciman did recall, on his return to London in mid-September, that Halifax had stated 'that time gained was of importance'.[72] However, when writing to his wife a few days before leaving for Prague, Runciman noted: 'The foreign job may be soon completed because it is hopeless, or it may be necessary to prolong the conference and conversations for three months'.[73] Clearly, Runciman was not being sent to Czechoslovakia with specific instructions to delay until the most favourable season for a German attack had passed, but the possibility of his playing for time until the end of October was not discounted.

At least one member of the Foreign Office, however, was unequivocal in the advice offered on this issue – that was Vansittart. Although there appears to be no record of a meeting between Vansittart and Runciman at this time, Runciman was informed of the contents of the messages received through Vansittart's intermediaries from Henlein.[74] Other members of the Mission certainly did hold discussions with Vansittart. Stopford, (as previously mentioned) having been denied an official Foreign Office briefing, visited Vansittart at his home at Denham to seek advice. He later recalled that Vansittart informed him that a permanent solution of the Sudeten

German problem was not in prospect, and the main purpose of the Mission therefore was that of delay, in order to frustrate any plans Hitler had for invading Czechoslovakia before the autumn. Vansittart believed that by the following spring Britain would be in a stronger position militarily to resist Germany.[75] Ashton-Gwatkin also received advice from Vansittart, though it appears to have been of a rather different nature. Vansittart stressed the importance of establishing good relations with Henlein and suggested that the SdP leader should be approached via Hohenlohe.[76] Both these lines of argument were also used by Vansittart internally within the Foreign Office. He persisted in his view that Henlein was a 'moderate'[77] who sought a compromise with the authorities in Czechoslovakia and also pointed out that, as Germany was unlikely to attack while a British mediator was present, Runciman should be 'in no hurry during his mission'.[78]

In addition to seeking out Vansittart, Stopford also called on the expertise of the Royal Institute of International Affairs during his preparation. He made use of the Chatham House library and sought the personal advice of members of the institute.[79] The institute's director had visited Central Europe, including Czechoslovakia, the previous year and recorded his observations and comments in a paper given at Chatham House in June 1937. Toynbee had been greatly alarmed by the situation in the Sudetenland, he was appalled by the depressed economic condition of the territory and by, what he regarded as, the Czechoslovak authorities' exploitation of this misery to settle historic scores against the formerly ascendant Sudeten Germans. Referring to an ethnographic map of Central Europe, Toynbee likened the areas inhabited by German minorities to 'a train of gunpowder leading up to the powder magazine' of Germany, and the Sudetenland, being closest, was therefore most likely to spark off the disastrous major explosion. The danger was such, he believed, that it was imperative for Britain to intervene with the Czechoslovak authorities in order to create 'tolerable conditions of life' for the national minorities within that country. Toynbee saw Britain in the position of an insurance company 'being asked to issue policies on some very bad lives; she could demand a very stiff premium and lay down stringent conditions' which, he was confident, would be accepted.[80] Stopford's reaction to these ideas is not known and neither is that of Runciman, but the British government, though eager to secure a settlement of the Sudeten German problem, was most certainly not interested in issuing an insurance policy to Czechoslovakia. Runciman, being the chairman of a major life assurance company, most probably shared the view of his political masters that Czechoslovakia was in such a high risk category as to render any form of insurance totally out of the question.

The summer of 1938 also saw the publication, under the auspices of the RIIA, of a more extensive historical analysis of the Sudeten German problem. Elizabeth Wiskemann's book, *Czechs and Germans* – which has stood the test of time as a balanced account of the protracted conflict between Czechs and Germans in Bohemia and Moravia – appeared in the bookshops early in June and was thus available to members of the Mission whilst preparing for their assignment. In the Foreign Office Central Department, both Roberts and Mallet, who read the book in proof, were sufficiently impressed to recommend its acquisition for the Foreign Office library.[81] Runciman also acquired a copy of the book, although his assessment of it is not known. He was photographed reading the volume – still in its dust jacket – as he settled down on the train at London's Victoria Station bound for Prague. If that was the first occasion on which he opened it, he could rightly be accused of leaving an essential piece of background reading until rather late in the day.

In view of the fact that Runciman was approaching the problems of Czechoslovakia from a standpoint of almost total ignorance, the amount of preparatory work undertaken by him was not excessive. The forthcoming Mission was certainly not allowed to interfere with his sailing activities at Cowes during the two weekends preceding his departure for Central Europe. Nevertheless, during the fortnight that elapsed between accepting the assignment and undertaking it, Runciman did visit the Foreign Office several times (as previously discussed), and he also put together his team with little delay. It appears, however, that Runciman did not call a meeting of his entire staff prior to their departure for Prague, and no general briefing took place. Doubtless, thorough preparation for the difficult task ahead was not made any easier by the Mission's hastened departure for Prague. The original intention was for Runciman and his party to leave London on 11 or 12 August, but premature disclosure of the planned Mission in the *News Chronicle* on 25 July, caused the departure to be brought forward by some ten days to 2 August.[82]

Runciman gave away virtually nothing of his thinking at the outset of his reluctantly undertaken Mission. Stopford gained little idea of his superior's general attitude towards the difficulties that would soon confront them in Central Europe, apart from the fact that Runciman considered Beneš to be 'dragging his feet'.[83] A few days before his departure from London, however, Runciman noted with some relief that 'the Czechs are being more reasonable' and that Germany did 'not want a war at present'.[84] Apart from that he left no clues to his proposed approach to the problems awaiting him. Runciman appeared to be travelling to Prague without any particular preconceived solution in mind. He was acutely conscious, however, of the heavy responsibility which rested on him. In a letter to President Roosevelt, written a few days before taking up his Mission, Runciman wrote in sombre terms of the danger of war and of his tenuous hope that it may be possible for him 'to maintain the peace and to relieve Europe from its extreme peril'.[85] He evidently considered that his principal task was to prevent the outbreak of war.

It is certain that Runciman had no relish for the task before him; indeed, he found the prospect of possibly spending the next three months in Central Europe a 'horrible' one.[86] This is understandable, for Runciman's acceptance of the Mission involved forgoing his customary month-long August holiday cruising amongst the Western Isles of Scotland on his yacht *Sunbeam*. The reluctant mediator's sacrifice of his holiday, particularly the associated grouse shooting, was duly acknowledged by the Prime Minister in a brief letter of appreciation sent a few days before Runciman's departure. Chamberlain also expressed his admiration for Runciman's 'courage and public spirit in undertaking such a difficult and delicate task' and his confidence that if anyone could bring off a success it would be Runciman.[87] Halifax addressed similar sentiments to Runciman, wishing him the 'best possible luck' for the 'very difficult adventure', adding that he carried 'a very heavy cargo of good wishes from the world over'.[88] Runciman did, indeed, travel to Prague with the good wishes and earnest hopes of much of the world. These were not only expressed publicly in the press, but in a large number of private messages, including a telegram from his friend, W.L. Mackenzie King, the Prime Minister of Canada, and a note from his former ministerial colleague, Sir John Simon. Runciman also travelled with the blessing of the Archbishop of Canterbury, Cosmo Gordon Lang.[89]

But despite these good wishes, Runciman undertook his Mission with little optimism. Indeed, he appeared to have no illusions about the intractable nature of the situation in Czechoslovakia and the difficulty that faced him in finding a solution acceptable to all. On the eve of his departure for Prague, Runciman expressed his concern in a letter to Chamberlain:

> If only I can make a good beginning with both sides I hope to induce them to talk freely, and indeed this is essential. But what a cockpit Bohemia has always been! For 800 years they have quarrelled and fought: Only one king kept them at peace, Charles IV, and he was a Frenchman! How then can we succeed?[90]

Notes

1 See D.G. Boadle, 'The Formation of the Foreign Office Economic Relations Section, 1930–1937', *Historical Journal*, vol. 20, 4, (1977), pp. 919–36.

2 Ashton-Gwatkin's publications included a trilogy of Japanese novels: *Kimono*, (1921); *Sayonara*, (1924); and *Banzai!*, (1925); and a collection of verses, *A Japanese Don Juan and other Poems*, (1926).

3 See Ashton-Gwatkin's obituary, *The Times*, 31 January 1976; G. Schmidt, *The Politics and Economics of Appeasement: British Foreign Policy in the 1930s*, (Leamington Spa, 1986); D.E. Kaiser, *Economic Diplomacy and the Origins of the Second World War: Germany, Britain, France and Eastern Europe, 1930–1939*, (Princeton, 1980); B.-J. Wendt, *Economic Appeasement. Handel und Finanz in der*

britischen Deutschland-Politik, 1933–1939, (Düsseldorf, 1971); M. Gilbert, *The Roots of Appeasement*, (London, 1966).
4 Newton to Halifax, 22 March 1938 and minute by Ashton-Gwatkin, 31 March 1938, R 3269/94/67, FO 371/22341.
5 Minute by Ashton-Gwatkin, 29 March 1938, R 3319/94/67, FO 371/22341.
6 Henderson to Halifax, 30 July 1938, *DBFP*, 3/II, no. 560.
7 Press notice, 2 August 1938, C 7797/7744/18, FO 371/21782.
8 Halifax to Runciman, 29 July 1938, Runciman Papers, WR 292.
9 Press notice, 2 August 1938, C 7797/7744/18, FO 371/21782.
10 Sargent to Campbell, 11 August 1938, C 8031/7744/18, FO 371/21782.
11 Campbell to Speight, 5 August 1938, *ibid.*
12 Sargent to Campbell, 11 August 1938, and minutes by Roberts, 9 August 1938, and Sargent, 10 August 1938, *ibid.* The implied reprimand issued to Campbell was undeserved as Ashton-Gwatkin had noted, only a week previously, that he would not 'lose sight of the economic side of the problem; it may have considerable importance'. (Minute by Ashton-Gwatkin, 29 June 1938, C 7591/1941/18, FO 371/21729.)
13 Newton to Halifax, 5 August, 1938, C 7992/7744/18, FO 371/21782.
14 Runciman to Hilda Runciman, 24 July 1938, Runciman Papers, WR 303.
15 Harvey, ed., *Harvey Diaries*, p. 167.
16 Dilks, ed., *Cadogan Diaries*, p. 89.
17 Cabinet Minutes, 27 July 1938, Cabinet 35 (38), CAB 23/94; Dilks, ed., *Cadogan Diaries*, p. 89.
18 Stopford, 'Prague, 1938–1939', p. 10.
19 Simon evidently retained a high regard for his former private secretary. On the eve of the Mission's departure for Czechoslovakia he wrote to Runciman: 'So glad you have Bobby Stopford.' (Simon to Runciman, 30 July 1938, Runciman Papers, WR 292.)
20 Stopford, 'Prague, 1938–1939', pp. 1–2.
21 Runciman to Hilda Runciman, 24 July 1938, Runciman Papers, WR 303. Pares had previously been considered for the role of British observer in the frontier districts.
22 Halifax to Newton, 22 July 1938, C 7445/1941/18, FO 371/21729.
23 Henderson to Halifax, 23 July 1938, C 7472/1941/18, FO 371/21729. Henderson received a copy of the telegram to Newton.
24 Newton to Cadogan, 24 July 1938, C 7502/1941/18, FO 371/21719.
25 Newton to Halifax, 25 July 1938, C 7510/1941/18, FO 371/21729.
26 Minute by Roberts, 26 July 1938, *ibid.*
27 Minute by Strang, 27 July 1938, *ibid.*
28 Minute by Sargent, 9 June 1938, C 5582/4839/18, FO 371/21733.
29 Sargent to Ashton-Gwatkin, 1 September 1938, FO 800/304, f. 155.
30 Ashton-Gwatkin to Wilson, 13 September 1938, C 9914/1941/18, FO 371/21738, and also FO 800/304, f. 161. Ashton-Gwatkin observed that 'this affair is the only shadow which has ever fallen on my relations with Lord Runciman, who is a really delightful chief'.
31 *London Evening Standard*, 14 September 1938.
32 Runciman to T.G. Kemp, 26 September 1938, Runciman Papers, WR 296.
33 See entries in Ashton-Gwatkin's diary, 6 and 17 August 1938, FO 800/304.
34 See, for example, Newton to Halifax, 15 March and 16 May 1938, *DBFP*, 3/I, nos 86, 221.

35 K. Young, ed., *The Diaries of Sir Robert Bruce Lockhart, 1915–1938*, (London, 1973), p. 403.
36 On the day that news of the forthcoming Runciman Mission appeared in the press, Steed wrote at length to Halifax expressing his concern and urging that a firm stand be taken against German threats. (Steed to Halifax, 25 July 1939, C 7798/1941/18, FO 371/21730.)
37 *HC Deb.*, 338, col. 2956.
38 *Observer*, 31 July 1938.
39 *The Times*, 27 July 1938.
40 *Time and Tide*, 30 July 1938.
41 *Daily Worker*, 27 July 1938.
42 *HC Deb.*, 338, col. 2958.
43 *The Times*, 27 July 1938.
44 *News Chronicle*, 29 July 1938.
45 *Manchester Guardian*, 27 July 1938.
46 *HL Deb.*, 110, col. 1282.
47 *The Times*, 30 July 1938.
48 *Observer*, 31 July 1938.
49 *Daily Herald*, 27 July 1938.
50 *News Chronicle*, 27 July 1938.
51 *Reynolds News*, 31 July 1938.
52 *Star*, 27 July 1938.
53 Stopford Papers, 'Prague, 1938–1939', p. 11.
54 Minute by Strang, 16 July 1938, C 7249/1941/18, FO 371/21728; Minute by Sargent, 24 July 1938, C 6794/1941/18, FO 371/21726.
55 Memorandum by Roberts, 'Negotiations between the Czechoslovak Government and the Sudeten German Party', 3 June 1938, and unsigned minute attached, C 7038/1941/18, FO 371/21727.
56 Halifax to Newton, 16 July 1938, *DBFP*, 3/I, no. 493; Minute by Roberts, 19 July 1938, C 7205/1941/18, FO 371/21728.
57 Stopford, 'Prague, 1938–1939', p. 9.
58 Halifax to Runciman, 1 July 1938, H/VI/29, FO 800/309, and Runciman Papers, WR 292.
59 *HL Deb.*, 110, col. 1281. It is perhaps significant that Chamberlain did not make that point in his statement to the Commons the previous day. *HC Deb.*, 338, cols 2955–9.
60 See above p. 49.
61 Halifax to Runciman, 18 August, 1938, *DBFP*, 3/II, no. 643.
62 Minute by Vansittart, undated (but probably late July 1938), C 7593/1941/18, FO 371/21729.
63 Halifax to Henderson, 5 August 1938, *DBFP*, 3/II, no. 587.
64 Minute by Sargent, 30 June 1938, C 6108/1941/18, FO 371/21725.
65 Halifax to Campbell, 28 July 1938, *DBFP*, 3/II, no. 557.
66 Notes by Runciman, 28 July 1938, Runciman Papers, WR 296. The notes are typed on two sheets of Runciman's personal headed notepaper and were probably transcribed from manuscript notes made by Runciman during his visit to the Foreign Office that day. (See minute by Cadogan, 28 July 1938, C 7591/1941/18, FO 371/21729.)
67 Minute by Vansittart, 26 July 1938, C 7591/1941/18, FO 371/21729.
68 Minute by Roberts, 27 July 1938, *ibid.*

69 Halifax to Newton, 29 July 1938, *DBFP*, 3/II, no. 559.
70 Newton to Halifax, 1 August 1938, *DBFP*, 3/II, no. 565.
71 Minute by Mallet, 22 June 1938, C 6167/1941/18, FO 371/21725.
72 Cabinet Minutes, 17 September 1938, Cabinet 39 (38), CAB 23/95.
73 Runciman to Hilda Runciman, 24 July 1938, Runciman Papers, WR 303. A few days later, in a letter to President Roosevelt, Runciman indicated only that his task 'may take two or three months'. (Runciman to Roosevelt, 28 July 1938, Roosevelt Papers, PSF, 46, Great Britain, 1937–1938.)
74 Minute by Strang, 27 July 1938, C 7009/1941/18, FO 371/21727.
75 Stopford, 'Prague, 1938–1939', pp. 11–12.
76 Ashton-Gwatkin to Stopford, 5 June 1974, Stopford Papers, RJS (unclassified box); Bruegel, *Czechoslovakia Before Munich*, p. 232.
77 Memorandum by Vansittart, 12 July 1938, C 7009/1941/18, FO 371/21727.
78 Memorandum by Vansittart, 26 July 1938, C 7591/1941/18, FO 371/21729.
79 Stopford, 'Prague, 1938–1939', p. 11.
80 A copy of the paper was supplied to Runciman in 1938. See A. Toynbee, 'Impressions of Central Europe', Runciman Papers, WR 287.
81 Minutes by Roberts, 7 June 1938, and Mallet, 8 June 1938, C 5651/4770/18, FO 371/21761.
82 Runciman to Hilda Runciman, 24 and 25 July 1938, Runciman Papers, WR 303.
83 Stopford, 'Prague, 1938–1939', p. 11.
84 Runciman to Hilda Runciman, 25 July 1938, Runciman Papers, WR 303.
85 Runciman to Roosevelt, 28 July 1938, Roosevelt Papers, PSF, 46, Great Britain, 1937–1938.
86 Runciman to Hilda Runciman, 24 July 1938, Runciman Papers, WR 303.
87 Chamberlain to Runciman, 28 July 1938, Runciman Papers, WR 292.
88 Halifax to Runciman, 29 July 1938, Runciman Papers, WR 292.
89 Mackenzie King to Runciman, 30 July 1938; Simon to Runciman, 30 July 1938; Cosmo Cantuar to Runciman, 27 July 1938; and others, Runciman Papers, WR 292.
90 Runciman to Chamberlain, 1 August 1938, Chamberlain Papers, NC 7/11/31/232. In the letter, Runciman – presumably in error – refers to Charles V.

7
Adrift in Central Europe

The Runciman Mission arrived in Czechoslovakia in two stages. The advance party, consisting of Ashton-Gwatkin, Stopford and Miller, flew to Prague on 2 August, where they were joined by Ian Henderson. Runciman, who preferred not to travel by air, arrived by train the following day, accompanied by Hilda Runciman and the remainder of his team. In order to emphasise the ostensibly unofficial nature of the Mission, the formal reception at Prague's Wilson Station was very low-key, as had been the departure from London's Victoria Station which was observed only by the press and a handful of spectators. No members of the government were present to wish the mediator farewell – that task being performed by the Permanent Secretary at the Board of Trade, who attended in a private capacity as a one-time adviser to Runciman.[1] The welcome in Prague was also conducted in the absence of government ministers, although the reception party there was more numerous. On the Czechoslovak side it consisted of the Mayor of Prague and representatives of leading government figures. The SdP, on Newton's advice,[2] sent two prominent members of the leadership: Ernst Kundt, the party chairman, and Wilhelm Sebekowsky, head of the press department. Henlein himself was not present to greet Runciman. Also at the station were Newton and those members of the Mission who had arrived the previous day.[3]

The Runciman Mission took up residence in the Hotel Alcron, one of Prague's premier hotels, located a short distance from the city's main thoroughfare, Wenceslas Square. A suite of 15 rooms was reserved for an indefinite period for the British party, and was to serve, initially at least, as both living and office accommodation. Prior to his departure from London, Runciman received several offers of private accommodation, but Newton advised against accepting hospitality from either side in the dispute.[4] Runciman and his Foreign Office advisers evidently thought likewise and chose the Hotel Alcron as a suitably neutral base for the Mission.

The first task facing Runciman on his arrival in Prague was to meet representatives of the world's press. Within hours of alighting from the train, he faced 150 or so journalists and cameramen assembled in a reception room of the Hotel Alcron. To the great consternation of members of the Mission, the dais from which Runciman was to speak was located immediately in front of a large nude female statue. Some adroit stage management was therefore required from the British team in order to avoid Runciman – a pillar of non-conformist rectitude – appearing in photographs, printed across the world, in the arms of a nude female figure. Stopford noted that had the statue possessed wings 'she could have been represented as the figure of peace, but even that element of decorum was lacking'.[5]

In his statement to the press Runciman proclaimed, as befitted a leading Methodist, in the words of John Wesley, that he came as 'friend of all and enemy of none'. He expressed thanks for the reception received earlier that day from both parties in the dispute who, prior to his departure from London, had indicated that his 'presence would be welcome'. These carefully chosen words disguised the fact that the initiative behind his Mission came not from the protagonists but from the British government, although Runciman did make it clear that he had 'not asked for the job'. He appealed to the journalists present to assist him in their reporting and expressed the modest expectation that given patience and goodwill some of the problems outstanding might be resolved. Predictably, Runciman gave little away and refused also to answer questions.[6] Although both Runciman and Ashton-Gwatkin felt satisfied with the outcome of the initial press briefing,[7] the Mission would, over the coming weeks, enjoy a somewhat uneasy relationship with the press. Runciman and his staff regarded the nature of their work as necessarily confidential, and released very little information to journalists. This reticence, naturally, failed to please the attendant international press corps, many of whom were hardened veterans of recent trouble spots in Abyssinia, Spain and Austria, and whose very presence in Prague served to heighten further the atmosphere of crisis.[8]

The immediate effect of the Mission's arrival in Prague, however, was an evident relaxation of tension. Even the Prime Minister, Hodža, seized the opportunity, reportedly for the first time since the *Anschluss* in March, to take a weekend break away from the capital.[9] Applying the most favourable interpretation to the Runciman Mission, the Czechoslovak authorities and the bulk of the press presented its arrival as evidence of increased British interest in the fate of their country. Only the Communist Party organ, *Rudé Právo*, observed that Runciman's purpose was to oblige Czechoslovakia to 'commit suicide'.[10] The expressions of optimism concerning perceived British support were, predictably, not to the liking of the Foreign Office in London, particularly if voiced by a government minister. When the Minister for Social Welfare, J. Nečas, spoke publicly in these terms in late July, Newton was instructed to complain about the 'irresponsible' misinterpretation of the British position.[11]

Runciman and his staff formally commenced their duties on the morning of 4 August, when, attired in top hats and tail coats, despite a late summer heat wave (with the temperature reaching 28°C in the shade), they proceeded in a Rolls Royce to pay their official respects, in turn, to Krofta, Hodža, and Beneš.[12] The Prime Minister and the Foreign Minister returned the call the following day, when also Lord and Lady Runciman lunched at the Hradčany Castle as guests of President and Madame Beneš. The luncheon was followed by a 90-minute conversation between Runciman and Beneš.[13]

During this meeting, and also at their shorter formal interview of the previous day, Beneš explained his government's attitude towards the Sudeten German problem and the proposed means for seeking its resolution. The following day, these ideas were presented to the Mission in the form of a memorandum. This emphasised that the Czechoslovak authorities accepted the SdP memorandum of 7 June as a basis for negotiation, but warned that there was little point in discussing the ideological aspects of the document, as the 'two diametrically opposite ideologies involved – the democratic and the totalitarian', would not readily be surrendered by either party. Beneš proposed, therefore, to set aside that element of the problem and to concentrate initially on the 'practical and concrete demands' of the SdP, which fell into two categories. Those in the first category – concerned with achieving greater equality between the nationalities – included demands for linguistic equality; proportionality in state employment, in budgetary distribution and government contracts; and protection from enforced loss of nationality. The demands in the second category – concerning self-administration for the nationalities – called for 'closer investigation' because, Beneš argued, they involved 'the mechanism of state administration', changes to which 'would have far-reaching effects upon the smooth working of the state'. Furthermore, this was a 'complicated question' on which the two sides were very far apart. In those circumstances, he reasoned, the best way forward was to concentrate attention on the soluble practical questions of the first category and thus work by stages towards an agreement.

Beneš maintained that this process had already been initiated by the preparation of new legislation, elements of which, drafts of the Language Law and the Nationalities Statute, would soon be made available to the SdP for comment and criticism. If negotiations were to commence with the Language Law, he argued, a result could be achieved quickly which would 'at once produce a favourable psychological effect on both parties'. Attention could then be turned to the Nationalities Statute and by a process of compromise 'more than nine-tenths of the *practical* German demands in the first category could be met'. The more difficult question of self-administration would be covered in a third piece of legislation, the Administrative Reform Law. That could be discussed, the President hoped, 'in a more satisfactory atmosphere' following the resolution of the two preceding issues, which would have demonstrated goodwill on both sides and established a better working relationship.[14] It is improbable that Beneš, being fully aware of Henlein's links with Berlin, actually believed that the method outlined would achieve the desired results. In the circumstances, however, he had little choice but to proceed with the negotiations in the hope that Czechoslovakia's friends and allies would ultimately provide the diplomatic and material support necessary to resist what he saw as a calculated attempt at the disruption of his country.

But whatever Beneš's motives, Runciman considered the proposed approach to be inadequate and came away from the initial discussions full of disappointment and pessimism. Although conceding that Beneš had 'come on a long way' during the last few weeks, Runciman complained to London that the President did not show much 'understanding or respect' for the German minority. There remained therefore 'a wide gap' in basic principles between the two sides.[15] The attitudes of Hodža and Krofta were regarded as little better, although Runciman believed that all three main figures in the Czechoslovak government did 'intend to be helpful in their own way'.[16] More generally, Stopford described the authorities in Prague during these early stages of the Mission as being 'suave but hostile underneath'.[17] The veiled animosity of Czechoslovak officials was hardly surprising since, despite the diplomatic niceties, the presence of Runciman and his staff had been imposed on them.

The initial contact between the Mission and representatives of the SdP was less formal than that made with the government. An SdP delegation, consisting of Ernst Kundt, Wilhelm Sebekowsky, Rudolf Schicketanz, Alfred Rosche and Gustav Peters (all of whom had earlier participated in the fruitless negotiations with the Czechoslovak authorities), called at the Hotel Alcron during the afternoon of 4 August. The delegation formed the 'political staff', one wing of the machinery created by the SdP for handling the Runciman Mission. It was under the control of the deputy leader of the party, K.H. Frank. The second element of the SdP's response to Runciman's arrival was the establishment of a 'social staff', headed by the great landowner, Prince Ulrich Kinsky.[18] This was to prove a most astute move for influencing Britain's aristocratic mediator by ensuring that much of his cherished leisure time was spent in a milieu sympathetic to the SdP.

At the outset of the discussions with the SdP, Runciman indicated that his objectives were, firstly, to study the problems in detail, and then to seek to obtain a compromise solution to at least some of the issues outstanding. Accordingly, he invited the SdP delegation to present a full account of their requirements. Kundt, the delegation leader, highlighted the fundamental difference between his party and the government, claiming that, whereas the latter thought only in terms of a Czechoslovak 'national state', the SdP aimed to create a 'state of nationalities'.[19] At Runciman's invitation, the SdP team (minus Sebekowsky) returned to the Hotel Alcron later that evening and remained in discussion with members of the Mission, but not Runciman, until the early hours of the morning. A quantity of liquid refreshment was consumed during the talks – which caused Ashton-Gwatkin to note in his diary: 'Such a Bierabend!'[20] – but there was also a serious side to the proceedings. The SdP delegation presented documentation, including the Carlsbad Programme and the memorandum of 7 June, and sought to convince the British mediators of the constructive nature of their proposals and, in particular, that these did not hazard the territorial integrity of the Czechoslovak state.[21]

These introductory discussions were continued at the Mission's headquarters two days later, when the SdP representatives spent a further three hours with Runciman's staff.[22] The process was substantially completed on 9 August, when Runciman himself was present for part of the meeting.[23] During these talks the SdP negotiators sought to inundate the British mediators with a welter of information supporting their cause.[24] From the point of view of the Mission, however, the main purpose was to gain a clear understanding of the SdP standpoint, elements of which, Stopford remarked, were 'so Teutonic and ideological' as to be extremely difficult to comprehend. Particularly challenging to British minds were the concepts of *Rechtspersönlichkeit*, legal personality, and *Siedlungsgebiet*, national territory – contained, respectively, in the second and third Carlsbad demands.[25] The Mission staff prepared a digest of the SdP requirements,[26] but Kundt was dissatisfied with the extent of the draft and undertook to supply additional information.[27] Following the discussions on 9 August, the SdP delegation approved a revised 14-page document which, in effect, summarised their memorandum of 7 June.[28]

During the talks with members of the Mission, the SdP delegates also offered a detailed critique of the government's attitude, complaining that the authorities had failed not only to respond to SdP proposals presented two months previously, but also to supply a complete set of their own plans. Kundt mentioned in particular, that proposals for administrative reform were incomplete, and that conflicting versions had been received of the draft Language Law. In view of these inadequacies, he explained, the SdP could not comment publicly on the government proposals until they had been presented in their entirety.[29] Nevertheless, Kundt did prepare, for Runciman's benefit, a confidential memorandum outlining his party's reaction to the standpoint of the government.[30] The document claimed that the Czechs acted as the predominant nationality, exercised a 'dictatorship' in Parliament, envisaged each self-governing province having a Czech majority, insisted on Czech government officials in all areas, and wanted the Czech language to have priority. In contrast, the SdP maintained it sought equality of status, legislative devolution and self-government for each nationality.[31]

Despite the intensity of their complaints, the SdP negotiators presented their case with considerable skill and moderation and succeeded in creating a favourable impression on the British mediators. Runciman was particularly impressed by Kundt's effective advocacy.[32] Moreover, whereas the first contact with leading members of the government left the British less than satisfied with their attitude, Ashton-Gwatkin noted in his diary, following the initial meeting with the SdP delegates: 'They are not immoderate people.'[33] Similarly, the SdP negotiators were not dissatisfied with the response from the British team. Indeed, Stopford later recalled that 'they seemed to be impressed by the efforts which we had made to understand them and the extent of our success in doing so'.[34] The initial SdP uncertainty about how to respond to the Runciman Mission soon gave way to the realisation that the new situation was potentially advantageous.[35] Through the application of SdP pressure for concessions, the Mission could be used to cause discomfiture to the Czechoslovak authorities, whilst simultaneously ensuring that the crisis continued to simmer as long as Berlin required. Unaware of this, Ashton-Gwatkin believed that the SdP sought to co-operate with the Mission in order to achieve their stated objectives through mediation, rather than as a result of intervention by Germany. He was, however, conscious of the danger that the Mission might thus become 'increasingly identified with one party in the dispute'.[36]

Following the conclusion of the exploratory talks with the SdP, a week was to elapse before a similar series of intensive discussions took place with representatives of the government, although constant contact was maintained at the highest level between Runciman and Beneš and Hodža, mainly over procedural matters. The frequent and lengthy meetings between the Mission staff and the SdP delegates, compared with the limited and formal talks with Czechoslovak leaders, gave rise to some surprised and critical comments amongst journalists and others observing the Mission's activities during its first few days in Prague. The explanation offered was that, whereas the SdP's case was well established and could be fruitfully studied in some detail, the Czechoslovak authorities were still in the early stages of formulating their response, hence detailed negotiations with them would be premature.[37] It was certainly true that the initiative at the time lay with the SdP who, backed by Berlin, were making most of the running, whereas the Czechoslovak authorities were doing little more than attempting to respond to a developing situation. Nevertheless, the British mediators were at least open to the accusation of insensitivity in concentrating their attention at the outset so heavily on the SdP.

Detailed negotiations with the government did not get under way until almost two weeks after the Mission's arrival in Prague. On the Czechoslovak side these discussions were conducted by representatives of the Committee of Six, a semi-official body representing the six political parties of the governing coalition. The chief participant was a former Minister of Justice, Alfred Meissner, a Social Democrat, who had played an important role in drafting the Czechoslovak Constitution. Other prominent representatives of the Committee of Six were: Jan Malypetr (Agrarian), Otakar Klapka (National Socialist), and Alois Rašín (National Democrat). A legal expert was also present on occasions.[38] The discussions between the British and Czechoslovak teams took place at seven meetings, held in

Meissner's house in a Prague suburb, over a period of eight days, commencing on 16 August. They followed a similar pattern to the exploratory talks with the SdP representatives, except that the Czechoslovak hosts plied their British guests not with beer, but with tea, sandwiches and cakes. Runciman, again, did not himself participate in the talks, leaving it to his staff to prepare a paper summarising the government's proposals and approved by them.[39] Documents presented to the Mission included English translations of drafts of the proposed Nationalities Statute, Language Law and Administrative Reform Law.[40]

As had been the case in the discussions between the Mission and the SdP, the Czechoslovak negotiators not only presented their own proposals, but also offered a critical analysis of the SdP's demands. In particular they sought to demonstrate to the British mediators the perceived dangers to the state inherent in the SdP programme. Meissner and his colleagues repeatedly stressed the total unacceptability of demands for legal personality and territorial autonomy for the minority nationalities, pointing out that the Minorities Treaty referred only to the rights of individuals and not of groups. They also drew attention to the considerable practical problems involved, such as the definition of the territories concerned and the inability of some ethnic groups (such as the Poles) to staff, from their limited population, the full institutions required by the SdP for each national territory. More substantially, the government representatives argued that the establishment of virtual states within the state, with separate legislatures, would facilitate secession, thus placing in jeopardy the continued independent existence of Czechoslovakia.[41] They also drew attention to the perceived danger to security arising from the proposal to include heads of the autonomous administrations in the government and the Supreme Council for National Defence.[42]

Meissner and his colleagues also sought to convince the British mediators of the impracticality of the SdP proposals for the transfer of some legislative functions to autonomous units. They argued that matters such as control of the state police, the regulation of currency, the generation of electricity and the provision of public health facilities and social welfare were unsuited for devolution.[43] It was conceded, however, that a degree of autonomy could be granted within the sphere of local government, devolving certain administrative – but not legislative – powers to communes, districts and regions, at which levels there would be no objection from the government side to the creation of sections for each national group.[44] These organisations could be responsible for matters such as education, cultural affairs, and the administration of hospitals and similar institutions.[45] Further concessions concerning language rights could also be granted.[46] In effect, the government indicated its willingness to offer some decentralisation to the minority groups, but limited to measures which, in its judgement, did not endanger the sovereignty and integrity of the state. This attitude was justified on the grounds that although the authorities had accepted the SdP memorandum of 7 June as a basis for discussion, the SdP, for its part, showed no sign of departing from its National Socialist outlook.[47]

However, despite all the efforts by Meissner and his colleagues, the British mediators remained unconvinced and formed a much less favourable impression of the government's attitude than that of the SdP a fortnight earlier. The discussions with representatives of the Committee of Six served to reinforce the view, gained by Runciman and his staff following the initial talks with Beneš, Hodža and Krofta, that the Czechoslovak authorities were not prepared to be sufficiently accommodating towards the SdP and, in particular, were unwilling to undertake any significant constitutional revision. Stopford recalled in his memoir that 'there seemed to be no sign of any willingness to make any serious concessions to the SdP point of view'.[48] Evidently, the Czechoslovak negotiators failed to convince their British guests of the perceived necessity to resist the totalitarian elements of the SdP programme. Members of the Mission were, of course, conscious of this hazard. Indeed, Stopford noted explicitly at the time that the SdP's demands involved a 'totalitarian organisation for their people'.[49] The British mediators, however, did not view this factor with nearly the same degree of concern as did the Czechoslovak authorities.

The detailed talks with the representatives of the Committee of Six also provided Runciman's team with an instructive insight into the politics of Czechoslovakia's coalition administration. Stopford described the situation on the government side as 'most complicated and full of intrigues, personal and party' and detected a divergence of attitudes amongst Czechoslovakia's political leaders concerning their response to the SdP. He noted that Hodža and his Agrarian Party were 'prepared to compromise', but that the Czechoslovak National Socialists, supported by a large section of public opinion, believed that it was 'better to fight and, though defeated at first, ultimately to be restored by their victorious allies'. Beneš, the British perceived, was inclined towards the latter group but nevertheless able to implement a settlement if he so desired.[50] These observations confirmed the impression gained earlier from the SdP negotiators that their intense hostility towards Beneš did not extend to Hodža.[51]

The Prague government and the SdP were not the only parties involved in the complex ethnic and political situation in Czechoslovakia, and representatives of other groups lost little time in pressing details of their respective cases on the British mediators. The first to call on Runciman, only two days after his arrival in Prague, and again on 24 August, was a delegation from the German Social Democratic Party, led by Wenzel Jaksch, the party leader.[52] The German Social Democrats also presented a 43-page memorandum concerning the German minority problem, concluding with the view that 'in the interests of European peace' the Sudeten Germans must remain within Czechoslovakia, but enjoying full equality with the other nationalities, and retaining their own distinctive national identity. The rise in support for the extremism of the SdP was explained as a consequence of the economic depression. The results of the 1929 election were cited as evidence that, in normal political and economic conditions, over two-thirds of German voters supported parties loyal to the Czechoslovak state.

The German Social Democrats also offered a four-point programme for resolving the nationalities conflict – linguistic equality, proportionality in public posts and state contracts, democratic self-administration, and industrial re-construction. Some aspects of this programme were close to the requirements of the SdP. The main difference between the two parties concerned the method of self-government. The Social Democrats rejected the SdP concept of autonomous ethnic sections, with separate legal status, arguing that it would lead to the imposition of totalitarian institutions and deprive Germans of liberties enjoyed by other citizens of Czechoslovakia. They proposed instead that multinational committees should oversee the implementation of the reform programme within democratically elected organs of local government. Their programme also reflected the party's belief that it was the harsh economic climate in the Sudetenland, resulting mainly from the collapse of Czechoslovakia's export trade, that drove Germans into supporting Henlein. Consequently, Jaksch and his colleagues advocated economic relief for the hard-pressed areas, believing it would result in a decline in support for the SdP. The memorandum requested therefore a foreign loan of 'thirty to forty million pounds sterling' to regenerate the industrial base of the German areas and to stimulate foreign trade by financing a Sudeten German export bank.

In their outlook, however, the German Social Democrats were far from optimistic. They shared the view of the government that there was little prospect of reconciliation between the democratic principles of the Czechoslovak constitution and the totalitarian aspirations of the SdP, which was 'subordinate to Berlin'. A permanent solution could only be achieved, the Social Democrats argued, if the German minority itself saw the error of identifying its interests with those of the SdP. It was imperative therefore 'to win back a democratic majority amongst the Sudeten German people'.[53] That was a laudable aspiration but, in the economic and political conditions of Central Europe of the time, a wholly unrealistic one. The German Social Democrats, who during the 1920s had been a major political force amongst the German minority, were, by 1938, completely eclipsed by the SdP. In the general election of 1935 they secured less than 300 000 votes compared with 1.25 million cast for Henlein. The local elections of May and June 1938, in which the SdP gained almost 90 per cent of the vote in German areas, further confirmed the severe decline of the once influential Social Democrats.[54]

Runciman's reaction to the German Social Democrats and to their proposed programme is not known,[55] although he probably regarded them as something of an irrelevance. That is certainly how they were seen in the London Foreign Office, where, on receipt of extracts from their memorandum, Roberts noted that it was 'a very reasonable document' but that unfortunately they 'no longer count for much among the Sudetens'.[56] Nevertheless, Jaksch and his colleagues had demonstrated, much to the chagrin of the SdP, that Henlein and his party were not the sole representatives of the Germans in Czechoslovakia. On his arrival in Prague, Runciman had appeared not even to be aware of their existence.[57] Stopford however, adopted a positive attitude towards the German Social Democrats, subsequently developing a lasting friendship with Jaksch and his family, whom he assisted in leaving Czechoslovakia following the Munich Agreement.[58]

The German Social Democrats were not alone amongst Runciman's visitors in stressing the economic aspects of Czechoslovakia's nationalities problem. A delegation of Sudeten German industrialists, who called on the Mission on 13 August, also drew attention to the depressed condition of the Sudeten territory when, as Ashton-Gwatkin noted, 'they explained at great length the tragic story of their decline and fall'.[59] Members of the delegation, which represented banking and manufacturing interests and included the textile magnate Baron Leibig, being close to the SdP, held the Czechoslovak authorities entirely responsible for causing the economic distress of the German population. They objected to Czech control over the economic life of the German minority, claiming it resulted in Germans suffering higher unemployment than Czechs, receiving no aid to counteract the collapse of their export trade, and disproportionately few government contracts.[60]

Czechoslovakia's other component nationalities also lost little time in making their views known to the British Mission. Indeed, prior to Runciman's departure from London, the Polish and Hungarian governments had approached the Foreign Office with a view to obtaining the mediator's intervention concerning their respective fellow-nationals in Czechoslovakia. Responding to the Polish Chargé d'Affaires, Cadogan pointed out that Runciman would be concerning himself primarily with the Sudeten German question, and that the consent of the Czechoslovak authorities would be required before the Polish case could be taken up.[61] A few days later, Vansittart received similar representations from the Hungarian Minister and replied in identical terms.[62]

Nevertheless, amongst the first to call at the Hotel Alcron, on 4 August, was Count Esterházy, representing the United Hungarian Party, the largest political organisation amongst the Hungarian minority in southern Slovakia, with a role analogous to that of the SdP. Esterházy invited Runciman to shoot on his estate, or that of Count Károlyi, in Slovakia.[63] A delegation from the United Hungarian Party was received by Runciman on 12 August, and a further meeting took place two weeks later. Runciman indicated to Esterházy that although he had no *locus standi* for any intervention, his interest in the situation of the Hungarian minority was demonstrated by his reception of their representatives.[64] At these meetings, the Hungarian's voiced grievances similar to those of the SdP, including complaints of discrimination by the authorities in matters of taxation, in education, in the use of the Hungarian language, and in the staffing of official posts. The party's declared objectives were to gain for the Hungarian minority control over education and land distribution, whilst conceding that foreign affairs, defence and finance should remain in the hands of the central authorities.[65] Ashton-Gwatkin noted that 'if the Sudetens get their prize, the Hungarians will get theirs as well, though it will not satisfy them, for what they really want is to get back to Hungary'.[66]

One other Hungarian political grouping, the Social Democrats, also presented their views to the Mission on a separate occasion. In contrast with their larger political rivals, the Social Democrats indicated their hostility to 'foreign influence' and any form of autonomy leading to the disruption of the state, and insisted that any officials appointed to autonomous institutions should be loyal to Czechoslovakia.[67] Despite the discouragement offered in London, a representative of Czechoslovakia's Polish minority, centred round Těšín (Teschen) in Silesia, called at the Mission headquarters on 25 August.[68] He presented a lengthy memorandum itemising the political, economic and cultural grievances of the Poles against the Czechoslovak authorities, which were very similar in nature to those of the United Hungarian Party.[69]

Two other ethnic groups also made their view known to the Mission. A Ruthenian delegation submitted a memorandum complaining of Czech domination and of inadequate representation in the Czechoslovak Parliament. Lacking the support of a foreign power, their situation was, they claimed, 'incomparably worse' than that of any other minority within the state. They appealed therefore to Runciman for support in attaining autonomy for Ruthenia in accordance with the long-neglected provisions of the Treaty of Saint Germain.[70] The last group to make representations was the Jewish community in Czechoslovakia. Their delegates called on the Mission on 14 September, only days before it left Prague, and pointed out that, if the Sudeten German territories were to receive autonomy, they, as a minority within a minority, would require special protection.[71]

One significant political organisation failed to secure a hearing from Runciman or his staff – the Slovak People's Party, the largest political party in Slovakia, predominantly Roman Catholic in character and autonomist in outlook. At the end of August, the party leadership sought permission for a delegation, including Jozef Tiso (later to become President of the war-time Slovak Republic), to call on Runciman in order to inform him of conditions in Slovakia and of the reasons for the 'quarrels and discord' between the Slovak and Czech nations.[72] The approach was made on the advice of the

Foreign Office, where Roberts saw no reason for Runciman refusing to receive the delegation, provided he did so with the approval of the Czechoslovak authorities. Indeed, Roberts advised a representative of the party that they should approach Runciman directly.[73] Initially, Ashton-Gwatkin was also inclined to receive the Slovak delegation,[74] but nevertheless sought the view of the Legation. Newton advised against a meeting with Tiso, explaining that his party represented 'perhaps less than half' of the Slovaks and that their reception by the Mission would be seen by many as a 'larger and more objectionable intervention in internal affairs' than in the case of the Polish and Hungarian minorities.[75] This advice prevailed and the Slovak People's Party was informed that Runciman could not intervene in the question of Slovak–Czech relations unless invited to do so by the authorities. The proposed delegation would therefore serve no useful purpose and its reception by the Mission might be liable to misinterpretation.[76]

The Slovak autonomists nevertheless persevered and submitted the obligatory memorandum listing their grievances. They maintained that in place of the autonomy promised in the Pittsburg Agreement of 1918, which the Czechoslovak authorities failed to honour, 'Slovakia was gradually occupied and ruled from Prague'. The outcome was 20 years of Czech domination over Slovak life, resulting from Czech control of the Prague-based legislative and executive branches of government. The Slovak People's Party also complained of discrimination against Slovaks in government employment and in public investment, and of restrictions in the fields of education and culture. Many Czechs, the memorandum alleged, regarded Slovakia as a 'colony' to be exploited for the benefit of the Czech people only. The party rejected the argument that Slovak autonomy would weaken the state – they were convinced that Slovakia 'regenerated and strengthened by autonomy' would contribute significantly to its development.[77]

The Mission's ostracism of the Slovak People's Party did not, however, extend to another Slovak autonomist political grouping, the considerably smaller, more moderate and less significant, Slovak National Party. A leading member of this largely Protestant party, Jan Pauliny-Toth, secured an interview with Henderson on 18 August, during which he also argued that the granting of Slovak autonomy would not necessarily be inimical to the integrity of the Czechoslovak state.[78]

The views of the Slovaks and the smaller minority groups were of marginal interest only to the Runciman Mission. They served to confirm the impression of Czechoslovakia's inherent instability, but were not allowed to distract the British mediators from their main focus, the Sudeten German dispute, which occupied the major part of their time. During the early stages of the information gathering exercise with the protagonists in that conflict, a pattern emerged in the respective roles played by members of the Mission staff. The lengthy exploratory meetings, held first with the SdP negotiators and later with the government representatives, were attended, on the British side, mostly by Ashton-Gwatkin, Stopford, Peto and Henderson. Runciman himself dealt mainly with Beneš and Hodža, though he did also personally receive some of the visiting delegations. Subsequently, he also had meetings with Henlein. The bulk of the work, however, was carried out by Ashton-Gwatkin, who acted as the Mission's chief of staff, with substantial authority delegated to him by Runciman, particularly in dealings with the SdP. He also established close links with Hohenlohe, who had previously acted as an intermediary between Vansittart and the SdP, and through him, latterly, maintained contact with Henlein. Ashton-Gwatkin was to prove a tireless mediator, travelling considerable distances for meetings with the SdP leader, and also reporting regularly on progress – or the lack of it – to the Foreign Office in London. Other members of the Mission staff fulfilled different roles. Stopford was mainly active as press officer and in his capacity of constitutional expert; Peto served principally as aide-de-camp to Runciman, accompanying him on social engagements; and Henderson ran the Mission office and acted as interpreter.[79]

The method that Runciman employed in seeking to reconcile the two principal parties to the dispute drew on his previous experience of industrial relations conciliation. At the outset of the initial talks with the SdP delegation, Runciman informed Halifax that he had 'got them into one room' with the Mission staff, explaining that this was 'one of the orthodox manoeuvres for compromise'. He immediately added, however, that he had 'never seen a case less likely to yield to this treatment'.[80] Two weeks later, on 18 August, Runciman reported to London on his procedure in greater detail:

> I have seen nearly everybody who matters in each of the seven parties and a number of persons who have influence in this mixed little world. So far I have gained the confidence, I believe, of both sides and they all come to see me from time to time. We discuss their points of view freely, but I cannot say that we are able to record any progress with the building of the bridge. In a country with seven parties and at least five races, no leader is safe from the risks of desertion or opposition or complicated troubles, so that I am not in a position to report any advance towards agreement or even closer relations.[81]

Runciman's method was evidently not producing the required result and, moreover, was being employed without much expectation of success. Indeed, so self-evident was Runciman's pessimism, that it had even communicated itself to the SdP negotiators. They had noted, a few days previously, not without satisfaction, that 'the British Mission is beginning to doubt its ability to achieve a peaceful solution'.[82]

The early process of familiarisation with the attitudes of the principal protagonists certainly had a depressing effect on Runciman and his staff, as they became acutely aware of the intractable nature of the problem under scrutiny. Within a week of arriving in Prague, Ashton-Gwatkin considered the divergence between the two sides to be 'as deep and deeper than the gulf between England and the Irish republicans at its worst', but with the added complication of the involvement of Germany.[83] Stopford, himself born in Dublin, was also reminded of 'old days in Ireland'.[84] Indeed, both Runciman and Ashton-Gwatkin appear to have been immediately struck by the hopelessness of the situation in Czechoslovakia and the imminence of war – a view also shared in private by Newton.[85] On 8 August, only days after the Mission's arrival in Prague, Ashton-Gwatkin noted in his diary that Runciman was 'beginning to wonder how he is to disengage himself'.[86] Two days later, Runciman sought Halifax's advice as to how much longer he should continue to 'hold the fort' in view of the improbability of a successful outcome since the choice between war and peace lay entirely in Hitler's hands.[87] An equally dispirited Ashton-Gwatkin believed that neither side would 'sacrifice much just to the keep the peace of Europe'. Nevertheless, he considered that the Mission could play a useful role – but one that had 'nothing to do with mediation'. He explained, in a letter to Strang: 'I understand that we must stay here anyhow until the end of September – as a moral influence standing guard over this country and the peace of Europe!'[88] Presumably, Ashton-Gwatkin was relaying Runciman's view of the Mission's role; the significance of the end of September being that climatic conditions would then become unsuitable for invasion. This was an isolated reference by Ashton-Gwatkin to the possibility of playing for time, and over the next few weeks he was to expend very considerable effort towards securing an urgent resolution of the Sudeten German problem. At the time, however, Ashton-Gwatkin considered that there was little prospect of any successful conciliation between Czechs and Germans in Czechoslovakia, for the Mission was drifting, he believed, not in mid-Atlantic, as Runciman had earlier stated, but 'on the edge of Niagara'.[89]

Notes

1 *Daily Telegraph*, 3 August 1938; *Manchester Guardian*, 3 August, 1938. The official was Sir William Brown.
2 Hencke to the Foreign Ministry, 4 August 1938, *DGFP*, D/II, no. 335.
3 Newton to Halifax, 8 August 1938, C 7744/18/8185, FO 371/21728; *The Times*, 4 August 1938.
4 Newton to Halifax, 29 July 1938, C 7744/18/7744, FO 371/21728.
5 Stopford 'Prague, 1938–1939', p. 13.
6 *Manchester Guardian*, 4 August 1938. See also Runciman to Halifax, 4[?] August 1938, *DBFP*, 3/II, no. 583 (enclosure).
7 Runciman to Halifax, 4[?] August 1938, *DBFP*, 3/II, no. 583; Ashton-Gwatkin to Strang, 9 August 1938, *DBFP*, 3/II, no. 598.
8 Stopford, 'Prague, 1938–1939', pp. 17a–18; Thompson, *The Greatest Treason*, pp. 116–17.
9 *Manchester Guardian*, 6 August 1938; *The Times*, 8 August 1938.

10 Newton to Halifax, 28 July 1938, C 7730/4770/18, FO 371/21762; Newton to Halifax, 1 August 1938, C 7821/1941/18, FO 371/21730.
11 Newton to Halifax, 1 August 1938, and Halifax to Newton, 4 August 1938, C 7818/1941/18, FO 371/21730.
12 Ashton-Gwatkin to Strang, 9 August 1938, *DBFP*, 3/II, no. 598; Stopford, 'Prague, 1938–1939', p. 13.
13 Runciman to Halifax, 5 August 1938, *DBFP*, 3/II, no. 588.
14 Memorandum by Beneš, 'General Methods to be adopted in carrying out negotiations between the Czechoslovak government and the Sudeten German Party', 6 August 1938, *Czechoslovak Government Dossier*, item II, FO 800/305, and Stopford Papers, RJS 3/2.
15 Runciman to Halifax, 4[?] August 1938, *DBFP*, 3/II, no. 583.
16 Runciman to Halifax, 5 August 1938, *DBFP*, 3/II, no. 588. Runciman appears not to have kept a minute of these meetings.
17 Stopford to Dudley Ward, 22 August 1938, Stopford Papers, RJS 3/1.
18 Hencke to the Foreign Ministry, 5 August 1938, *DGFP*, D/II, no. 336.
19 Hencke to the Foreign Ministry, 5 and 6 August 1938, *DGFP*, D/II, nos 336 and 339.
20 Ashton-Gwatkin's diary, 4 August 1938, FO 800/304. See also Stopford, 'Prague, 1938–1939', pp. 18–19.
21 Hencke to the Foreign Ministry, 5 and 6 August 1938, *DGFP*, D/II, nos 336 and 339. For the documents in question see *Sudetendeutsch Dossier*, items I–IV, FO 800/305, and Stopford Papers, RJS 3/3. No formal minutes of the introductory meeting with the SdP on 4 August 1938 could be traced in the Mission records.
22 Ashton-Gwatkin to Strang, 9 August, 1938, *DBFP*, 3/II, no. 598.
23 Hencke to the Foreign Ministry, 10 August 1938, *DGFP*, D/II, no. 344.
24 Report dated 13 August 1938, in Bürger to Altenburg, 17 August 1938, *DGFP*, D/II, no. 366.
25 Stopford, 'Prague, 1938–1939', p. 19.
26 'Sudeten German Demands', 5 August 1938, FO 800/305, f. 25 *et seq.*
27 'Minutes of a Conversation held with Herrn. Kundt, Peters, Schicketanz, and Rosche on 6 August 1938', FO 800/305, f. 23.
28 Stopford, 'Prague, 1938–1939', p. 19. For the document itself see *Sudetendeutsch Dossier*, item V, FO 800/305, and Stopford Papers, RJS 3/3.
29 'Minutes of Conversation held with Herrn. Kundt, Peters, Schicketanz, and Rosche on 6 August 1938', FO 800/305, ff. 23–4; 'Minutes of Meeting with Sudeten German Delegation of Five and Herr Ulrich on 9 August, 1938', FO 800/305, ff. 20–2. See also Henderson's record of the meeting of 6 August, *Sudetendeutsch Dossier*, item VII, FO 800/305, and Stopford Papers, RJS 3/3.
30 'Minutes of Conversation held with Herrn. Kundt, Peters, Schicketanz, and Rosche on 6 August 1938', FO 800/305, ff. 23–4.
31 'Memorandum (confidential) of Sudeten German criticism of the general line of the Czechoslovak Government's proposals and of the attitude revealed therein', presented to Runciman on 9 August 1938, *Sudetendeutsch Dossier*, item VI, FO 800/305, and Stopford Papers, RJS 3/3.
32 Memorandum by Mitis, in Hencke to the Foreign Ministry, 10 August 1938, *DGFP*, D/II, no. 344.
33 Ashton-Gwatkin's diary, 4 August 1938, FO 800/304.
34 Stopford, 'Prague, 1938–1939', p. 19. See also Stopford to Alice Wordsworth, 14 August 1938, Stopford Papers, RJS 3/1.

35 See below p. 181.
36 Ashton-Gwatkin to Strang, 16 August 1938, *DBFP*, 3/II, appendix II (III), pp. 661–2.
37 *Observer*, 7 August 1938.
38 Ashton-Gwatkin to Strang, 23 August 1938, *DBFP*, 3/II, appendix II, p. 663. According to Stopford, Jan Šrámek of the People's Party and Minister of Public Administration also attended. (Stopford, 'Prague 1938–1939', p. 23.)
39 'Summary of the proposals of the Czechoslovak Government as agreed with Dr. Meissner's Committee', *Czechoslovak Government Dossier*, item VII, FO 800/305.
40 See *Czechoslovak Government Dossier*, items III–V, FO 800/305, and Stopford Papers, RJS 3/2, and 'Note on the Existing Organisation of the Provinces, Districts, and Municipalities', Stopford Papers, RJS 3/8.
41 'Minutes of Meeting between Lord Runciman's Staff and Coalition Parliamentarians at Dr. Meissner's House', 16 August 1938, FO 800/305, ff. 2–4, and 'Notes on Meeting with Representatives of the Committee of Six', 29 August 1938, FO 800/305, ff. 13–14.
42 'Notes on Meeting with Representatives of the Committee of Six', 23 August 1938, FO 800/305, f. 15 *et seq*.
43 'Czech Criticism of Sudeten German Sketch, Part IV, Given at Meeting with Dr. Meissner and Others', 19 August 1938, FO 800/305, ff. 16–19.
44 'Minutes of Meeting Between Lord Runciman's Staff and Coalition Parliamentarians at Dr. Meissner's House', 16 August 1938, FO 800/305, ff. 2–4, and 'Czech Criticism of Sudeten German Sketch, Part IV, Given at Meeting with Dr. Meissner and Others', 19 August 1938, FO 800/305, ff. 16–19.
45 'Minutes of Meeting between Lord Runciman's Staff and Coalition Parliamentarians at Dr. Meissner's House', 16 August 1938, FO 800/305, ff. 2–4.
46 'Notes on Meeting with Representatives of Committee of Six', 29 August 1938, FO 800/305, ff. 13–14.
47 'Minutes of Meeting between Lord Runciman's Staff and Coalition Parliamentarians at Dr. Meissner's House', 16 August, 1938, FO 800/305, ff. 2–4.
48 Stopford, 'Prague, 1938–1939', pp. 22–3.
49 Stopford to Simon, 9 August 1938, Stopford Papers, RJS 3/8.
50 Stopford to Simon, 22 August 1938, Stopford Papers, RJS 3/8, and Stopford to Dudley Ward, 22 August 1938, Stopford Papers, RJS 3/1.
51 'Minutes of Conversation held with Herrn. Kundt, Peters, Schicketanz, and Rosche', 6 August 1938, FO 800/305, ff. 23–4.
52 Press Communiqué, 5 August 1938, Stopford Papers, RJS 3/7 (c); Ashton-Gwatkin to Strang, 25 August 1938, *DBFP*, 3/II, appendix II (III), p. 665.
53 'Memorandum of the German Social Democratic Workers' Party in Czechoslovakia', Stopford Papers, RJS 3/6. For an abridged translation prepared by the Mission staff see 'The Standpoint and Proposals of the Democratic Sub-Minority Regarding the Sudeten German Problem', FO 800/306, ff. 5–13, and Stopford Papers, RJS 3/6. See also N.M. Wingfield, *Minority Politics in a Multinational State: The German Social Democrats in Czechoslovakia, 1918–1938*, (New York, 1989), p. 175.
54 Newton to Halifax, 23 and 30 May and 13 June 1938, C 4871, C 5153, C 5773/4871/18, FO 371/21775.
55 Laffan, in *Crisis over Czechoslovakia*, p. 217, stated, without citing the source, 'that Runciman was impressed by the sanity and moderation of Jaksch and his colleagues ... is suggested by the fact that he had four interviews with him in

less than three weeks'. However, the Mission records indicate only two meetings, on 5 and 24 August 1938.

56 Minute by Roberts, 1 September 1938, C 8855/1941/18, FO 371/21733.

57 A. Henderson, *Eyewitness in Czechoslovakia*, (London, 1939), p. 145.

58 See Stopford Papers, RJS 3/17 (Jaksch Letters and Pamphlets). Stopford returned to Prague in November 1938 as Liaison Officer for Refugees with the Czechoslovak government.

59 Ashton-Gwatkin to Strang, 16 August 1938, *DBFP*, 3/II, appendix II (III), p. 662.

60 'Notes on Meeting with Sudeten German Industrialists', 13 August 1938, FO 800/306, ff. 183–5.

61 Cadogan to Jazdzewski, 30 July 1938, and Speaight to Norton, 2 August 1938, C 7761/1941/18, FO 371/21730 and FO 800/306, ff. 346–8.

62 Note by Vansittart, 3 August 1938, and Vansittart to de Barcza, 10 August 1938, C 7878/2319/12, FO 371/21567; Speaight to Gascoigne, 4 August 1938, FO 800/306, f. 134.

63 Note by Stopford, 4 August 1938, FO 800/306, f. 148. Subsequently, a further invitation was issued to the Runciman Mission to visit the Slovak capital Bratislava, close to the main Hungarian areas, although neither was taken up. (Note by Stopford, enclosed in Ashton-Gwatkin to Strang, 29 August 1938, *DBFP*, 3/II, appendix II (III), p. 667.)

64 Newton to Sargent, 25 August 1938, C 9241/2319/12, FO 371/21567.

65 'Minutes of Meeting with Delegation of United Hungarian Party', 12 August 1938, and 'Notes on Meeting with the United Hungarian Party', 25 August 1938, FO 800/306, ff. 130, 108.

66 Ashton-Gwatkin to Strang, 16 August 1938, *DBFP*, 3/II, appendix II (III), p. 662.

67 'Notes on Memorandum Presented by Hungarian Social Democrats', 9 September 1938, FO 800/306, f. 112.

68 Note by Stopford, enclosed in Ashton-Gwatkin to Strang, 29 August 1938, *DBFP*, 3/II, appendix II (III), p. 667.

69 'Die Lage der Polnischer Bevölkerung in der Tschechoslowakische Republic', undated memorandum, FO 800/306, ff. 315–48.

70 'Memorandum on Carpathian Russia', 13 September 1938, FO 800/306, ff. 39–45. The 1919 Treaty of St Germain with Austria (and also the Treaty of Trianon with Hungary) recognised the independence of Czechoslovakia, including 'the autonomous territory of the Ruthenians'. (Temperley, ed., *History of the Peace Conference*, V, p. 195.)

71 Note by Stephens, 14 September 1938, FO 800/307, f. 41 and FO 800/304, f. 293.

72 Stano to Runciman, 31 August 1938, FO 800/305, ff. 463–4.

73 Minutes by Roberts, 4 August 1938, C 7976/1941/18 and 6 August 1938, C 7956/1941/18, FO 371/21731.

74 Marginal note by Ashton-Gwatkin, 8 September 1938, on Stano to Runciman, 31 August 1938, FO 800/305, ff. 463–4.

75 Notes by Newton and Troutbeck, 8 September 1938, FO 800/305, ff. 461–2.

76 Ashton-Gwatkin to Stano, 9 September 1938, FO 800/305, f. 459.

77 'Memorandum of Hlinka's Slovak People's Party to the Right Honourable Lord Walter Runciman', FO 800/306, ff. 363–70.

78 'Minute of Meeting between Judr. Pauliny-Toth and Mr. Henderson', 18 August 1938, FO 800/305, ff. 466–8.

79 Stopford, 'Prague, 1938–1939', pp. 17a–18.

80 Runciman to Halifax, 4[?] August 1938, *DBFP*, 3/II, no. 583.

81 Runciman to Halifax, 18 August 1938, *DBFP*, 3/II, no. 644.
82 Report dated 13 August 1938, in Bürger to Altenburg, 17 August 1938, *DGFP*, D/II, no. 366.
83 Ashton-Gwatkin to Strang, 9 August 1938, *DBFP*, 3/II, no. 598.
84 Stopford to Alice Wordsworth, 14 August 1938, Stopford Papers, RJS 3/1.
85 Copy of report from Air Attaché in Prague, 16 August 1938, in Chilver to Caccia, C 8784/1941/18, FO 371/21733.
86 Ashton-Gwatkin's diary, 8 August 1938, FO 800/304.
87 Runciman to Halifax, 10 August 1938, *DBFP*, 3/II, no. 602.
88 Ashton-Gwatkin to Strang, 9 August 1938, *DBFP*, 3/II, no. 598.
89 *Ibid.*

8
A Glimmer of Hope

In addition to familiarising himself with the details of the Sudeten German problem, Runciman had two further initial objectives in mind on his arrival in Prague. The first of these was to obtain a goodwill gesture from the Czechoslovak government in the form of an announcement that additional employment opportunities would be created for the German minority in the public service. During a meeting with Beneš on 10 August, he received an assurance from the President that this would be done imminently.[1] A further sharp intervention from Runciman was required a week later, however, before any action was taken.[2] The government then announced the forthcoming appointment of Sudeten Germans to nine senior positions in the internal administration and the postal service. The SdP regarded the gesture as derisory, but Ashton-Gwatkin noted with satisfaction that the appointments were the 'first fruits' of the Mission.[3]

Runciman's second initial objective was to reopen talks between the government and the SdP, which had reached the point of virtual breakdown prior to the announcement of the British Mission, although he was not in an immediate hurry to achieve this. Indeed, during his first few days in Prague, Runciman sought a hiatus in the contacts in order to avoid 'premature uncompromising statement[s]' from either side.[4] By the beginning of the Mission's second week of activity, however, he felt ready to bring the two sides together again. During the afternoon of Monday, 8 August, Runciman and Ashton-Gwatkin met to plan their strategy[5] and, evidently, decided to attempt to restart the halted negotiations without delay – only to encounter an immediate problem.

Once news of the forthcoming British Mission had become known in late July, there was obviously little point in conducting further bilateral negotiations between the parties concerned prior to Runciman's arrival on the scene. Nevertheless, during that interval, some further exchanges of views did take place. In an open letter to Hodža, on 29 July, Kundt sought answers to five questions concerning the government's attitude towards the negotiations. In his response, the Prime Minister indicated that the government stood by the proposals it had made to date and that additional details would be made available to the SdP. He also confirmed that the government proposals, together with the SdP memorandum of 7 June, would serve as a joint basis for further negotiations.[6]

During a meeting with Hodža on 9 August, Runciman secured the agreement of the Prime Minister to reopen the talks at once. The Czechoslovak side was to be represented by the Committee of Six, consisting (as previously mentioned) of representatives of the governing coalition, in order to secure the widest political participation in the difficult negotiations ahead. When Runciman personally informed the SdP delegation of this development later that day, the arrangement was rejected out of hand. Kundt explained that talks with the Committee of Six, which lacked executive powers, would be pointless, and argued furthermore that the composition of the Committee was such that a complete breakdown would occur within hours. The SdP insisted on negotiating directly with representatives of the government, as had previously been the case, and with whom they considered themselves to be equal in status. Runciman immediately communicated this demand to the Prime Minister.[7] The outcome was a meeting, on 10 August, between Hodža and Kundt, at which the procedural dispute was resolved. The government agreed to participate directly in the talks with the SdP, in addition to the Committee of Six. It was also agreed that negotiations would be held on government premises, not in the parliamentary building, and would be presided over by a government minister.[8]

The two sides eventually came face to face, for the first time in seven weeks, on 11 August. The meeting took place in the Prime Minister's office with Hodža himself in the chair. The Czechoslovak negotiators included a number of government ministers in addition to members of the Committee of Six. The SdP was represented by the usual five-man negotiating team, led by Kundt.[9] Apart from the procedural demands, Kundt had also made two further stipulations to Runciman on 9 August. He demanded a response from the Czechoslovak authorities to the SdP proposals of 7 June and full details of the government's own reform plans.[10] Hodža complied to the extent of presenting a document indicating the government's response to the SdP's memorandum. It rejected the demand for granting legal personality to each of Czechoslovakia's nationalities, but declared a readiness to discuss possible changes in the internal structure of the state.[11] Proposals for achieving this were outlined by Meissner, who argued that these, in effect, granted the Sudeten Germans the territorial and personal autonomy which the SdP demanded, though perhaps not to the full extent sought.[12] Kundt and his colleagues declined to make an immediate response, postponing any discussions until the next meeting, due on 17 August. As the German Chargé d'Affaires in Prague, Andor Hencke, reported to Berlin, this accorded with the SdP's 'tactical design of drawing out negotiations'.[13]

The Czechoslovak negotiators, unaware of Hitler's instructions to the SdP, emerged from the meeting with considerable apprehension. They viewed the SdP's behaviour as uncooperative and feared therefore that the talks would break down when the two sides met again on 17 August.[14] These pessimistic impressions were conveyed to the British mediators. On the day before the scheduled meeting, Hodža appealed to Runciman to prevent the deadlock arising.[15] This anxiety appeared fully justified when, that same evening, the SdP negotiators informed Runciman of their profound dissatisfaction with the current state of the talks. During the course of a lengthy meeting, continuing up to midnight, Kundt and his colleagues were severely critical of the government, accusing it of being uncompromising and of attempting to deceive foreign opinion by the pretence of negotiation. They alleged that, under pressure from Czech nationalist opinion, such as that recently expressed in a manifesto by an association of military officers advocating no surrender, the government was refusing to make any concessions to the SdP viewpoint. Runciman responded by proposing that the planned meeting for 17 August should be postponed. Kundt countered with the suggestion that the meeting should take place, but only in order to agree a suspension of the negotiations, giving time for Runciman and his staff to examine more closely the proposals of both sides.[16]

The meeting duly took place as planned on 17 August. Possibly on Runciman's advice, the Czechoslovak negotiating team on that day did not include the Committee of Six (who were at that time engaged in the earlier mentioned separate talks with the staff of the British Mission). The SdP delegation delivered their response to the government memorandum presented at the previous session. Kundt stressed that the gap between the two sides was virtually unbridgeable but nevertheless indicated a willingness to continue negotiations regarding the reconstruction of the state. Agreement was then reached on the indefinite adjournment of the talks and for arrangements concerning further contacts to be made between Hodža and Kundt.[17] The moderation shown by the SdP delegation at what had been feared would be a critical meeting was unexpected, and caused Newton to remark that Kundt appeared to have been 'at pains not to slam the door' on further discussions.[18]

Although Newton was generally correct in his assessment of the SdP's tactics, the door was being firmly closed on this particular phase of the negotiations. Hitherto, the SdP leadership, mindful of instructions from Berlin, had sought to maintain contact with the authorities, but without reaching an agreement. Runciman's arrival on the scene, whether seeking to resolve the crisis or to play for time, threatened to frustrate that design and some tactical adjustment was therefore required. The SdP's deputy leader, Frank, who directed the political aspects of relations with the Mission, outlined the objective as being to convince Runciman that the nationality problem was insoluble 'within the state' and that the Czechs were 'in no way prepared to make concessions of a kind that could lead to a real pacification'. Frank added:

> His Lordship must take away with him the impression that the situation in this state is so confused and difficult that it cannot be cleared up by negotiation or diplomatic action, that the blame for this lies exclusively with the Czechs, and thus that the Czechs are the real disturbers of peace in Europe.[19]

The SdP had pursued these aims since Runciman's arrival, but would now do so with increased vigour.

The suspension of talks between the government and the SdP on 17 August also marked the virtual culmination of the initial investigative stage of the Mission's work (although the previously discussed exploratory talks with the Committee of Six were not, in fact, completed until a week later) – for, on the following day, Runciman was to meet Henlein. A few days earlier, on 12 August, the first day of the grouse shooting season in Britain, Runciman reported to Halifax that 'on this blessed date we have had our first real encouragement but it is very slender'.[20] The cause of this uncharacteristic outburst of qualified mild elation was the receipt of information that a meeting with Henlein was being arranged.

Almost from the moment of their arrival in Prague, the British mediators had sought to get in touch directly with the SdP leader who, it was believed, held the key to the outcome of the Mission. During the first encounter with the SdP delegation on 4 August, Runciman indicated an interest in meeting other representatives of the SdP, in particular Henlein himself.[21] Ashton-Gwatkin had high hopes that a meeting between Runciman and Henlein, or possibly with his deputy Frank, would be arranged during the talks with Kundt and his colleagues on 9 August.[22] However, the British mediators were to be disappointed. Although Runciman again expressed interest in meeting other representatives of the SdP, no invitation to meet Henlein, or Frank, was issued during the talks. The request for a meeting with Henlein presented Kundt and his negotiating team with a problem and, on the advice of Frank, they gave an evasive answer, claiming that Henlein was still out of the country.[23] Runciman was puzzled by Henlein's absence, finding it difficult to believe that he was abroad, and commented on it in a letter to Halifax the following day, adding that he was 'more than ready' to talk to the elusive SdP leader.[24]

The strength and urgency of Runciman's desire for a meeting with Henlein caught the SdP unprepared and caused them to reconsider their planned response to the Mission. The SdP tactics, initially devised by Frank, involved keeping Henlein in the background whilst the British mediators went about their business and only bringing the SdP leader out, according to Henlein's representative in Berlin, Friedrich Bürger, 'at the final and decisive moment'. Now, however, in order not to give offence to Runciman, which would not have served the interests of the SdP at that juncture, they were forced to revise their plans and make arrangements for a meeting between Henlein and Runciman,[25] although the British mediator was still to be kept waiting a week longer.

The real motivation for maintaining Henlein in isolation not only from the Runciman Mission but also from the SdP negotiators is unclear, but it evidently gave rise to some tensions within the SdP leadership. These were reported to the German Foreign Ministry, on 13 August, by Herbert Kier, the constitutional adviser to the SdP supplied by the *Volksdeutsche Mittelstelle*, who complained of Frank's 'completely negative' attitude towards the negotiations, based on what Frank claimed was 'special information' that the Sudeten German question would be resolved by force. Kundt and his negotiators, on the other hand, were adhering to their instructions to continue with the negotiations in order to avoid giving Runciman the impression that the SdP did not desire a peaceful settlement. Kier believed it essential that this disagreement be resolved.[26]

Evidently, the matter was resolved even before Kier's representation reached Berlin, as arrangements had already been put in train for Runciman to meet Henlein. It would appear that some behind-the-scenes contacts alerted Ashton-Gwatkin to this development, causing him to believe that, at the meeting with the SdP delegation on 11 August, Kundt would issue an invitation for Runciman to visit Prince Ulrich Kinsky's estate near Česká Kamenice (Böhmisch Kamnitz) in the north of Bohemia. Ashton-Gwatkin understood that Henlein might appear 'unostentatiously' at Kinsky's hunting-lodge and, therefore, advised his superior to accept the invitation.[27] The anticipated invitation was duly issued and accepted[28] but the visit to Kinsky's estate was not to be the occasion for Runciman's much desired first meeting with the elusive Henlein.

The day before he set out for Česká Kamenice, 12 August, Runciman received an unexpected visit from Frank, who had also not been in evidence since the Mission's arrival in Prague. The two men talked for three-quarters of an hour, with Henderson acting as interpreter. The atmosphere was cordial and the deputy-leader of the SdP, though preceded by his reputation as an extremist, made a favourable impression on Runciman.[29] Frank's surprise visit was designed to serve a two-fold purpose. First, it was to demonstrate to the British Mission that there was no division within the SdP between the hitherto absent top leadership of the party and Kundt's negotiating team.[30] Frank informed Runciman that during his absence from Prague he had received frequent reports from the negotiators, with whom he was in full agreement, and expressed his thanks for the sympathetic hearing the SdP had received and for the progress achieved so far, particularly the direct involvement of Hodža. Frank also impressed on Runciman the gravity of the situation, by indicating that the current efforts to resolve the Sudeten German problem were, as far as the SdP was concerned, 'the last attempt' to do so within the frontiers of Czechoslovakia. As a sweetener he added that, although he remained pessimistic of the outcome, largely on account of the government's refusal to reform the constitution, he hoped that with the assistance of the British Mission the Sudeten Germans would secure justice. The second and main purpose of Frank's visit, however, was to deliver an invitation for a meeting with Henlein. This was not to take place, as expected, during the coming weekend on Ulrich Kinsky's estate, but on the Thursday of the following week, 18 August, at Hohenlohe's country house, Červený Hrádek (Rothenhaus) near Chomutov (Komotau) in north-western Bohemia.[31]

The visit to Ulrich Kinsky's estate, during which Runciman and his wife were accompanied by Ashton-Gwatkin and Peto, nevertheless went ahead as planned. This was the second occasion on which Runciman accepted the hospitality of the old Austrian aristocracy. The previous weekend, he visited the estate of Count Zdenko Kinsky at Žd'ár in Moravia.[32] This was situated in a Czech-inhabited area, whereas Ulrich Kinsky's estate was located in Sudeten German territory. On their arrival by road in Česká Kamenice, close to the frontier with Germany, the British visitors witnessed evidence of extensive Czechoslovak military preparations.[33] Their weekend host had, nevertheless, gathered together a substantial house party, including Count and Countess Khuen, Count and Countess Clary-Aldringen, Count Westfalen and Hohenlohe. In his capacity as head of the SdP 'social staff' responsible for entertaining Runciman, Ulrich Kinsky provided a congenial setting for exposing the British peer to the pro-German leanings of many of his aristocratic counterparts in Czechoslovakia.[34]

Kinsky also used the opportunity to draw attention to the depressed economic condition of the Sudeten German territory. He personally conducted Ashton-Gwatkin and Peto round the neighbouring area where they were presented with much evidence of unemployment, poverty, bad housing, dereliction, and discrimination by the Czechoslovak authorities.[35] The tour produced the desired effect and Ashton-Gwatkin was reminded of a line from Dante referring to 'the pain of remembering past happiness in present misery'. It was that, he explained in a note to Runciman, 'which made the plight of these people so terribly poignant. It was clearly such a prosperous industrious community until disasters came upon it.' Ashton-Gwatkin conceded that similar conditions could be found in depressed areas of Britain, but argued that 'at home the Government and the rest of the country are doing their best to help', whereas 'here the feeling is that the Prague Government and the Czech people are against them'. He concluded that the Sudeten German population's only remaining hopes rested, firstly, in the SdP which had 'acquired something of the mystical exaltation but not as yet the violence which has accompanied Hitler'; secondly, in the opportunity of well-paid work in nearby Germany; and finally, in the Runciman Mission.[36]

This last point was also made directly to Runciman by a crowd of about 150 people gathered at the gates of the estate who called out to him (in German): 'Please help us in our distress. Give us, Lord Runciman, a just solution.'[37]

Whereas Runciman took full advantage of weekends in the country for relaxation, his chief assistant had little opportunity for rest at Kinsky's hunting-lodge. In addition to his practical introduction to the economic problems of the Sudeten Germans, Ashton-Gwatkin also had an important conversation with Hohenlohe, who assumed the role of intermediary between the British Mission and Henlein. Hohenlohe confirmed arrangements for the meeting with the SdP leader and also disclosed that Henlein's absence hitherto was not accidental but part of the SdP's calculated response to the Runciman Mission. Ashton-Gwatkin summarised Hohenlohe's explanation:

> The intention of Henlein and of the SdP leaders had been for him to ignore the Runciman Mission; to allow it four weeks in which to waste time and to show that it could accomplish nothing; and then to have come out with the demand for a plebiscite, which means in fact demand for Anschluss with Germany.

This attitude, Hohenlohe alleged, had been inspired by Frank, whom he described as a dangerous and mischievous person, and also by some 'vague phrases' uttered by Hitler. He assured Ashton-Gwatkin, however, that Henlein had not rejected the possibility of co-operation with Runciman, and himself claimed credit for persuading the SdP leader to meet the British mediator. Hohenlohe also claimed to have impressed on Henlein earlier, in Ashton-Gwatkin's words, 'the foolishness of losing this opportunity of getting all or most of what he wants by peaceful means and without absorption by Germany'. Conversation then turned to another matter, which Ashton-Gwatkin recorded without comment: 'Henlein, who is both idealistic and rather vain, fancies himself in the role of mediator between Hitler and England; he sees this as his further mission, when he has won freedom for his people.' Ashton-Gwatkin was also informed that Henlein intended visiting Hitler immediately following the meeting with Runciman, causing him to note that 'it is of importance, therefore, what impression he conveys from us'.[38]

It is uncertain whether Ashton-Gwatkin had been previously aware of Henlein's professed ambition to mediate between Britain and Germany, although the Foreign Office in London was alerted to it some days earlier. Christie, reporting on his meeting with Henlein in Zurich, informed Vansittart of the SdP leader's desire to achieve a rapprochement between Britain and Germany. Henlein claimed that the successes of his visits to London had been noted favourably by Hitler and others in Germany and that, as a result, he was sure he could play a useful role in improving relations between London and Berlin. He sought Christie's advice on how to proceed towards that objective. Christie gave a non-committal response, indicating only that he would take soundings on his return to London, but warned that the moment was not propitious for such a development.[39] Vansittart himself probably knew of Henlein's intention earlier. A minute by him, dated 3 August, contains a cryptic reference to Henlein's 'future mission' to be discussed at the Zurich meeting,[40] but Henlein's offer appears to have produced no immediate recorded response within the Foreign Office.[41] However, a copy of Christie's report, which also contained some specific advice for Runciman along the lines of that suggested earlier by Hohenlohe, was sent to the Mission in Prague on 18 August,[42] several days after Ashton-Gwatkin's conversation with Hohenlohe.

Despite the forewarning, Henlein did not refer to the possibility of mediating between Britain and Germany during the course of his first meeting with Runciman which took place, as arranged, at Červený Hrádek on 18 August. Runciman was again accompanied by his wife, Ashton-Gwatkin and Peto. Whilst the other guests strolled in the grounds after lunch, Runciman and Henlein conversed for about an hour, with Ashton-Gwatkin and Hohenlohe acting as interpreters.[43] Subsequently, Ashton-Gwatkin described the discussions as 'friendly but uncompromising',[44] and Runciman was reported to have considered the meeting 'not very encouraging'.[45] The long sought-after meeting with Henlein evidently proved something of a disappointment.

During the conversation, Henlein expressed similar views to those voiced in the talks in Zurich two weeks earlier, but without exhibiting the truculence of that meeting. He complained bitterly of the political and economic mistreatment of the German population, and of the general hostility shown by the Czechs – some of whom, he alleged, had proposed the 'extermination' of the Sudeten Germans – and indicated that the situation would only be remedied by the greatest possible separation of the two peoples. He identified two alternatives in prospect – either a negotiated settlement or a plebiscite. Claiming to prefer the former solution, Henlein undertook to continue negotiations as long as possible, but warned that unless positive results emerged soon, he ran the risk of being unable to further restrain his discontented followers.

Runciman responded by querying some of Henlein's more extreme allegations and observed that the German minority was not alone in experiencing economic hardship. The SdP leader was also made to accept, grudgingly, that the offer being made by the government – on Runciman's insistence – concerning the appointment of German officials, was a constructive first step and evidence of the Mission's positive influence. Henlein nevertheless insisted that the handful of posts in question was insignificant alongside the 50 000 official posts of which, he alleged, the Sudeten Germans had been deprived. He further argued that more significant gestures were required, such as a declaration by the government to appoint only German officials in German areas, and the withdrawal of the state police from those regions.[46]

There was nothing substantially new in what passed between Henlein and Runciman at their first meeting and the disappointment of the British mediators is evident from their record of the event. Summarising the outcome of the conversation, Ashton-Gwatkin noted that all they had obtained from Henlein was:

> a, the statement that he intends to proceed by way of negotiation with the Czech Government;
> b, that he is definitely for peace, since war would fall with immediate impact on the Sudeten German country;
> c, that he is determined to hold his people in order in spite of provocation if he can;
> d, that he is not absolutely pledged to the terms of the Karlsbad speech; or rather, that those terms were definitely left vague in some respects so as to allow room for compromise;
> e, that he has no wish to break up the State frontiers of the Czechoslovak Republic; but rather to obtain a large degree of home rule for his people within these frontiers.[47]

Clearly, despite disappointing his British listeners, Henlein had lost nothing of his ability to convince them of his reasonableness and moderation. Ashton-Gwatkin, in particular, was impressed by Henlein's apparent sincerity, a view that was to be reinforced during a further conversation with the SdP leader a few days later, after which Ashton-Gwatkin noted: 'I like him. He is, I am sure, an absolutely honest fellow.'[48] By contrast, Runciman was less generous in his assessment of Henlein, describing him to his wife as 'a gymnast without much intelligence'.[49]

The SdP not only employed smooth words and an honest face to convince the British of its case, it also staged a practical demonstration of injustices suffered. During the course of Runciman's visit to Červený Hrádek, three Germans arrived from the nearby industrial town of Most (Brüx) with alarming accounts of unrest. As Ashton-Gwatkin noted, they reported that 'owing to the state of uproar and tension in the town and the negligence of the police, lives were no longer safe and they did not know what might happen that very evening'. Runciman at once authorised Ashton-Gwatkin to transmit the complaints over the telephone to Hodža in Prague, who promised an immediate enquiry. Later that day, Ashton-Gwatkin and Peto themselves visited Most to conduct an on the spot investigation.[50] Although the SdP believed that the incident made a 'great impression' on Runciman,[51] the two British mediators reported very differently. They established that the main incident had taken place two days earlier, when clashes occurred between Czechs and Sudeten Germans during the installation of a new mayor. Although several people had been injured in the fighting, Ashton-Gwatkin considered the unrest no more than 'the usual rowdiness in a rough town ... at a time of political excitement' and that police precautions had probably been inadequate. He and Peto concluded that the SdP 'had failed to establish a serious case of negligence against the police and had considerably exaggerated the situation'.[52]

The Most incident itself was not particularly significant, but its exploitation was illustrative of the SdP's method of seeking to influencing the Mission – albeit, on this occasion, unsuccessfully. Despite Kundt's assertion that it clearly demonstrated they were sitting on a 'powder barrel', Ashton-Gwatkin found the episode interesting mainly because it showed the 'nervous tension' which magnified any incident into 'a national insult to the Sudeten Germans'.[53] Nevertheless, it was clearly in the interests of the SdP to arrange for Runciman and his staff to spend as much time as possible in the Sudeten German areas and, conversely, supporters of the government were acutely aware of this hazard. Hence Runciman's visit to Henlein at Červený Hrádek, within predominantly German territory, met with hostile criticism from elements of Czech opinion, which considered that the proper place for the meeting was in Prague.[54]

However, leaving aside the question of protocol, it was not unreasonable for the British mediators to visit the Sudeten German areas in order to become familiar at first hand with local conditions. Further opportunities for doing so arose during the weekend of 20 and 21 August, when Runciman and Peto, accompanied by their wives, were again guests of the old Austrian aristocracy – this time on the estate of Prince Adolf Schwarzenberg near Český Krumlov (Böhmisch Krumau) in southern Bohemia. Ashton-Gwatkin and Stopford, meanwhile, travelled in the opposite direction to visit a German Trade Fair at Liberec (Reichenberg) in the north of Bohemia, fulfilling an invitation that Runciman had declined.[55] Hoping to find 'a little rest',[56] Ashton-Gwatkin and Stopford spent a night at a small spa a few miles to the north of Liberec, close to the border with Germany. However, on arrival the British visitors were immediately taken in hand by the local SdP and municipal leaders and exposed at great length to the now familiar accounts of economic hardship and discrimination. Runciman's assistants received similar treatment the following day in Liberec itself, where they not only visited the Trade Fair, but were also shown many derelict factories in the surrounding countryside. These activities took place to the accompaniment of cheering crowds, chants of '*Sieg Heil*' and Nazi salutes.[57] Stopford later recalled discussing the events with his travelling companion, both agreeing that the orchestrated demonstrations left them 'singularly unmoved'.[58] Nevertheless, when Ashton-Gwatkin met Henlein unexpectedly the following day, he observed that he 'had never felt so like Henlein before'.[59]

This second meeting between Henlein and a senior member of the British Mission took place at the urgent request of the SdP. On 22 August, Ashton-Gwatkin received an invitation from Hohenlohe to travel to Marienbad (Mariánské Lázně) to see Henlein.[60] The SdP leader's sudden desire to meet Runciman's chief assistant was prompted by the receipt, directly from Beneš, of new proposals for resolving the Sudeten German problem, which became known as the 'Third Plan'.[61] Although the German Legation in Prague and the SdP leadership believed the unexpected development was possibly the outcome of Runciman's visit to Beneš on 16 August,[62] the British Mission was equally surprised by the President's initiative. In fact Beneš's action seems to have surprised everyone, and even Hodža was taken unawares by the move and sought an urgent interview with Hohenlohe in order to learn from him details of the President's proposals.[63]

Some days previously, when deadlock appeared imminent, Beneš assumed a direct personal role in the negotiations with the SdP. On the suggestion of the President of the Supreme Court, Jaroslav Krejčí – but without informing Hodža or Runciman – he made contact with Kundt through Fritz Sander, Professor of Law at the German University of Prague.[64] During his conversation with Sander, which took place on 16 or 17 August, Beneš declared himself dissatisfied with Hodža's conduct of the talks, and indicated his intention to take action himself, although constitutionally the initiative rested with the Prime Minister. Beneš also disclosed to Sander that he regarded the concept of the 'National State' adhered to by the government to be a 'mistaken' one, and indicated that he fully understood the Sudeten German desire for self-government. The President added that, in this connection, he would be prepared to consider the establishment of three purely German autonomous districts within Czechoslovakia – those of Silesia, Litoměřice (Leitmeritz) and Carlsbad.[65] As a gesture of goodwill he also proposed to make four preliminary concessions: granting immediate equality for the German language, appointing a greater number of German officials in German areas, special budgetary provision for those areas, and a loan to meet certain claims for damages arising within them. In return, the President demanded a press propaganda truce to create a calmer atmosphere, and some signs of practical co-operation from the SdP including a private meeting between himself and Kundt. If a successful outcome was reached within two months, the state police would be withdrawn from German areas.[66]

The most significant element of Beneš's new plan was the possible creation of purely German self-governing administrative areas within the Czechoslovak state. Such a proposal, despite its tentative presentation, was a major departure from the hitherto maintained position of the government and perhaps explains why the President chose to circumvent the Prime Minister when transmitting the ideas to the SdP. This approach by Beneš marked the first stage in his policy of conceding to the SdP their current demands in order to expose their position and force them into taking up a more extreme standpoint. Beneš was seeking to undermine the SdP's credibility in London and Paris, and thus secure for Czechoslovakia the international support that he believed was the only effective means of resisting Hitler's Germany.

Beneš's unexpected initiative caused concern in the SdP leadership. Kundt's immediate response was to request a delay of two days before replying to the President, while the Chargé d'Affaires in Prague, Hencke, was sent urgently to Berlin, on 17 August, to seek instructions from Ribbentrop. Suspecting Runciman's involvement in the President's surprise proposals, Kundt expected the British mediator to endorse the plan during his meeting with Henlein at Červený Hrádek, arranged for the following day. The SdP therefore wished to know how to react to the new situation. Ribbentrop responded with irritation, observing that:

> Henlein had already received clear instructions, and therefore it was not fitting that one gentleman or another kept appearing from Prague at short intervals to obtain decisions on individual questions. ... The answer to the Beneš proposal was contained in the general instructions given to Henlein, namely, always to negotiate and not to let the link be broken, on the other hand, always to demand more than could be granted by the other side.

Ribbentrop drew attention to the danger that Beneš's proposals might be regarded as 'a magnanimous offer', resulting in international pressure on the SdP to retreat from its Carlsbad demands:

> This must be avoided at all costs. The discussion must be conducted in such a way that Beneš is free to carry out the measures proposed by him, and which the Sudeten German Party, too, hopes will lead to an improvement of the atmosphere. But the demand for fulfilment of the eight Carlsbad points remains as before and is in no way affected by this proposal.[67]

Armed with this advice from Berlin, the SdP leaders met to discuss their response to Beneš's new plan prior to Runciman's arrival at Červený Hrádek. It was agreed that the invitation to private talks with the President would be accepted, although Kundt would not go alone but accompanied by Sebekowsky, and that the negotiations would be conducted in accordance with Ribbentrop's wishes.[68]

Having thus prepared the ground for the meeting with Runciman, Henlein found to his surprise that during the course of their hour-long discussion the British mediator made no reference whatever to Beneš's new proposals.[69] When the SdP leadership held a further meeting the following day, at which Sander himself reported on his conversation with Beneš, particular concern was expressed over the President's remark that the proposed loan for financing compensation claims in the German areas would involve an element of foreign aid. Kier, the SdP's constitutional adviser, drew attention to the 'seriousness of this matter', possibly indicating that Beneš had already secured external support for his plan.[70] The SdP decided to seek answers from the British Mission – hence the urgent summons for Ashton-Gwatkin to meet Henlein in Marienbad, on 22 August.

Although members of the British Mission were probably unaware of the intense activity amongst the SdP leadership prompted by their receipt of Beneš's new proposals, it appears that Ashton-Gwatkin had learned something of the President's ideas before his second meeting with Henlein,[71] but was unsure of their authenticity.[72] The meeting with Henlein in Marienbad, at which Hohenlohe was also present, took place in the Carlton Hotel, described by Ashton-Gwatkin as a 'semi-derelict place', which the SdP used as their headquarters.[73] During their amicable two-hour conversation, Henlein outlined the Third Plan proposals received via Sander from Beneš. It consisted of seven points, noted by Ashton-Gwatkin:

1. Three local autonomous districts in Sudeten German land.
2. Exchange of officials, i.e. Czech officials in German lands to be removed, German officials in Czech lands to be restored to German lands, to begin at once.
3. Independent budget for the 3 districts.
4. Loan from Central Government to the 3 districts.
5. Commission to meet within 1 to 3 months to decide on necessary changes in the constitution.
6. Propaganda and Press armistice.
7. Withdrawal of State police from German districts if all goes quietly.

Henlein professed to be suspicious of the motivation behind Beneš's initiative and wondered if it were not an attempt by the government to 'torpedo' the Runciman Mission. Ashton-Gwatkin replied to that if that were so, 'never [was a] torpedo more welcome to the torpedoed'. Having ascertained the British Mission's positive attitude towards Beneš's new proposals, Henlein indicated his agreement to the immediate reopening of negotiations on the proposed new basis, adding that he did not expect Berlin would make any difficulties. He also requested that Runciman establish the provenance of the new initiative directly from Beneš.[74] Although Ashton-Gwatkin was himself uncertain about the authenticity of the new proposals, he nevertheless enquired of Henlein 'where the capital of his new State would be'. With some amusement, Henlein replied that he had not given the matter any thought yet, though it would probably be Teplice (Teplitz) or perhaps Liberec (Reichenberg).[75]

In order to maintain pressure on the Czechoslovak authorities, Henlein also presented Ashton-Gwatkin with a list of actions for the government to undertake in order to produce a 'better atmosphere'. These were:

1. Immediate withdrawal of the Czech State police and restoration of the local communal police.
2. Strict prohibition of the persecution of Sudeten Germans on account of their nationality and political activity.
3. Strict punishment of excesses by officials, military and police.
4. Prohibition of press violence and incitation of the Czech population living in German districts.
5. Immediate start with the transfer of German officials into German areas.
6. Immediate suspension of the unendurable press censorship.

Ashton-Gwatkin noted that Henlein expected 'that we should recommend these suggestions to the Government'.

In more general terms, Henlein indicated to his British visitor five alternative courses along which the crisis in Czechoslovakia might develop. First, matters could continue as they were – but that was 'impossible'. Secondly, the German areas could receive autonomy as he had proposed. Thirdly, these territories might be detached from Czechoslovakia to form a new independent state. The fourth alternative was *Anschluss* with Germany of the Sudeten German districts. The fifth, and most surprising, possibility mentioned was the incorporation into Germany of the whole of Bohemia and Moravia. Henlein naturally claimed greatly to prefer the option of local autonomy, which would be his objective in the forthcoming negotiations.[76]

Ashton-Gwatkin accepted this assurance without question and also registered no surprise concerning the possible annexation of Bohemia and Moravia – which, in addition to three million Germans, contained over seven million Czechs – although at that time Hitler still publicly maintained that he had no interest in including non-Germans in the Reich. Henlein, however, realised that he had let the cat out of the bag, and, in his account of the conversation submitted to the German Foreign Ministry, he prudently failed to mention this last alternative, as well as that of an independent Sudetenland.[77] But that was the only indiscretion committed by Henlein during the meeting, and he otherwise performed flawlessly. Ashton-Gwatkin noted that the SdP leader 'denied with emphasis' that he was a dictator or that he aimed at 'political totalitarianism or anything other than honourable treatment of opponents and opposition so long as they dealt fairly with him'. Henlein also denied having any sympathy whatever with the violent methods of the German Nazis, and stated he would not permit any persecution of Jews.[78] Ashton-Gwatkin found these assurances utterly convincing, noting in his diary, 'I like him; he is honest and good'.[79]

Indeed, so convinced was Ashton-Gwatkin of the SdP leader's moderation and honesty, that he sought to gain Henlein's services as a mediator between Britain and Germany. The suggestion that Henlein was interested in undertaking that task had been made to Ashton-Gwatkin some days earlier by Hohenlohe, and was no doubt reinforced by Christie's report of his conversation with Henlein in Zurich, which the Foreign Office forwarded to the Mission in Prague.[80] Nevertheless, Henlein did not raise the matter during his talks with members of the British Mission, and Ashton-Gwatkin therefore took the initiative himself. He steered the conversation towards the subject of international relations, remarking that the Sudeten German issue 'was not only a question in itself but part of the problem of peace in Europe'. Henlein, not quite taking the bait, replied that there were two questions – one of relations between Czechs and Sudeten Germans and the second between Czechoslovakia and Germany. Ashton-Gwatkin then supplied a third, that of relations between Germany and the rest of the world, 'especially with England and France'. Henlein immediately responded by indicating that he had always wished to see close relations between Germany and 'England' adding, in strictest confidence, that he thought 'England was a much more suitable friend than Italy'. Having thus created the opening, Ashton-Gwatkin followed through with his proposal:

> I said to him that if he really believed this, and if he was satisfied with our fair and friendly demeanour as regards Lord Runciman's Mission, and if a beginning of peace were made by the starting of negotiations with the Czech Government on a sound basis, then would he himself go to Germany and tell Hitler what his experience had been, and that he believes England desires a settlement and that he believes this would be Germany's best way?

Ashton-Gwatkin stressed that he made the suggestion entirely on his own initiative, without any official authority.[81]

In reply to Henlein's enquiry as to what issues might be discussed between London and Berlin, in addition to that of Czechoslovakia, Ashton-Gwatkin was imprecise but ventured that the talks might cover 'an air pact, the colonial question, and an armament agreement'. The SdP leader responded by indicating his willingness to travel to Berlin for this purpose, but not immediately and only with the prior approval of the British government. Ashton-Gwatkin appears to have anticipated that move and disclosed that he intended visiting London for consultations within the next few days. He undertook to convey to Henlein the British government's response on his return to Prague.[82]

It was a doubtless well-satisfied Ashton-Gwatkin who travelled back to Prague that evening. Not only did it appear that progress was at last underway towards resolving the Sudeten German problem, but he had also made his own personal contribution towards achieving the greater objective of improving relations between Britain and Germany. Nevertheless, he was conscious of the fact that he had overstepped the bounds of diplomatic propriety, and in his report to London did not divulge the full extent of his conversation with Henlein, omitting to mention that he had actually suggested some possible topics for discussion between Britain and Germany. Ashton-Gwatkin was not reluctant, however, to offer general advice to the Foreign Office concerning the SdP leader's proposed visit to Berlin: 'We must be prepared to follow this up very quickly by direct approach to Hitler – so that when he makes his speech at Nuremberg, it will be a peace speech and not a war speech.'[83] The speech in question was the keynote address to be delivered at the Nazi Party Rally (*Parteitag*) in early September.[84]

Runciman himself was also not displeased with the recent turn of events. Reporting to London on the day following Ashton-Gwatkin's Marienbad meeting with Henlein, but before his interview with Beneš due later that morning, Runciman wrote that he detected an improved atmosphere in Prague and saw a 'crack in the clouds'. He was hopeful that, given co-operation from the President, talks might commence immediately, but cautioned that their successful outcome was entirely dependent on Beneš's direct participation. Although he remained optimistic, Runciman was also concerned about the apparent rift which had developed between Beneš and Hodža over the new initiative towards the SdP.[85] The existence of what was, at the very least, a remarkable breakdown in communications between the President and Prime Minister had been confirmed the previous evening on Ashton-Gwatkin's return from Marienbad. Ashton-Gwatkin had travelled back to Prague with Hohenlohe, who was responding to an urgent telephone summons from Hodža. Later that evening, Hohenlohe dined with Ashton-Gwatkin and disclosed that Hodža had been totally unaware of the President's initiative and had threatened to resign unless fully informed.[86]

Runciman's concern was soon dispelled however, when, during the course of the following morning's conversation with Beneš and later in the day over dinner with Hodža, it became apparent that any rift between the two principal figures in the government had been repaired. During his talk with Runciman, the President confirmed his authorship of the new initiative and disclosed that he was already in contact with Kundt. On receipt from Runciman of the list of seven points, which Ashton-Gwatkin had brought from his meeting in Marienbad, Beneš agreed that the document represented an accurate summary of his new proposals. The President also undertook to keep Runciman fully informed of future developments in the negotiations, but offered no explanation as to why the Mission had not been informed in advance of the new initiative. The British assumed that Beneš had wished to be certain of a positive response from the SdP before bringing the matter to their attention.[87] When dining with Hodža that evening, Runciman was assured by the Prime Minister that he fully supported the President's recent action. Hodža also expressed confidence that the Czechoslovak Parliament and public opinion would accept a solution on the lines proposed, but he was somewhat sceptical about the prospect of securing the agreement of the SdP. To Runciman's satisfaction, the Prime Minister nevertheless indicated his awareness of the critical nature of the situation and of the grave repercussions which would inevitably result from a failure to resolve the crisis. Hodža considered that the 'next ten days or so' would be decisive.[88]

Hodža's scepticism concerning the sincerity with which the SdP approached the forthcoming negotiations was not unjustified. On the day of the Marienbad talks between Henlein and Ashton-Gwatkin, 22 August, the SdP leadership also met to review their tactics. At this meeting Henlein ordered his negotiators to adhere 'without compromise' to the eight points of the Carlsbad programme, but at the same time not to allow the talks to break down and, above all, to persuade the British Mission of the SdP's sincere wish to secure an agreement.[89]

The SdP leadership had indeed wasted no opportunity for convincing Runciman and his colleagues of their desire for a negotiated settlement and came to believe that their efforts had met with success. Although initially suspicious of the Runciman Mission, the lengthy and cordial meetings with Runciman and his staff convinced the party leadership that the presence of the British Mission could be turned to their advantage. From the outset, note was taken of individual attitudes of members of the British party. Thus it was observed with satisfaction, that Peto showed 'great understanding' for the SdP's attitude towards the Jews in Czechoslovakia, whom he considered not to be comparable with British Jews.[90] Runciman himself appears to have been more circumspect, but Lady Runciman was less careful. During the course of a dinner at the British Legation, Hilda Runciman, as noted by the German Chargé d'Affaires, Hencke, 'revealed in conversation remarkable understanding for the Sudeten Germans and spoke of Bolshevik influence in Czechoslovakia'.[91] Following the Mission's first meetings with Henlein in mid-August, the SdP leadership came to the conclusion that Runciman himself was 'favourably disposed' towards them. They also observed that the 'active interest of the British in all Sudeten German questions, which is shown by the various journeys to the provinces by His Lordship's colleagues, strikes ... a friendly note'.[92] After three weeks in Czechoslovakia, the presence of the Runciman Mission was perceived by the SdP as advantageous to its aims.

It was not surprising, therefore, that Kundt, when visiting Runciman on 23 August to inform him of the forthcoming renewed contact with the government, sought to involve the mediator more closely in the proceedings. Kundt disclosed that he and Sebekowsky were due to meet Beneš and Hodža the following morning, and indicated that the discussion would cover not only the question of Sudeten German home rule but also

Czechoslovakia's foreign relations. He voiced doubts however, concerning the President's constitutional power to negotiate independently of the government and questioned the utility of conducting simultaneously negotiations with Beneš and with the government negotiators. Kundt also enquired whether Runciman wished to take part in the forthcoming talks or merely to be informed of their progress. Runciman replied emphatically that he had no desire to participate in the talks nor to be involved as an arbitrator on individual points in dispute, but he did ask to be kept fully informed of developments and indicated his willingness, if necessary, to intervene on occasions 'to try to remove obstacles'.[93]

With the stage thus set for the resumption of negotiations between the Czechoslovak authorities and the SdP, and wishing to gain the British government's approval for Henlein's proposed peace mission to Hitler, Ashton-Gwatkin obtained Runciman's permission to return to London for consultations.[94] Despite their initial pessimism, the British mediators were now reasonably satisfied with the outcome of their first three weeks on the ground in Czechoslovakia. Not only had they established good working relations with both parties to the dispute, particularly with the SdP, they had also familiarised themselves with details of the arguments on both sides, and now, at last, meaningful talks were on the horizon. As Ashton-Gwatkin departed for London in the late afternoon of 24 August, he left behind him an uncharacteristically optimistic Runciman. In a letter to Halifax the previous day, reporting on Beneš's new offer to the SdP, the British mediator expressed the hope: 'If only these Beneš balloons drift the right way and in addition we see negotiations proceeding the future for European peace may be comparatively hopeful.'[95]

Notes

1 Runciman to Halifax, 10 August 1938, *DBFP*, 3/II, no. 602; Ashton-Gwatkin to Strang, in Newton to Halifax, 11 August 1938, *DBFP*, 3/II, no. 603.
2 Ashton-Gwatkin to Strang, in Newton to Halifax, 17 August 1938, *DBFP*, 3/II, no. 629.
3 Ashton-Gwatkin to Strang, in Newton to Halifax, 19 August 1938, *DBFP*, 3/II, no. 651.
4 Runciman to Halifax, 5 August 1938, *DBFP*, 3/II, no. 588.
5 Ashton-Gwatkin's diary, 8 August 1938, FO 800/304.
6 Newton to Halifax, 4 August 1938, *DBFP*, 3/II, no. 582.
7 Memorandum by Mitis, in Hencke to the Foreign Ministry, 10 August 1938, *DGFP*, D/II, no. 344; Ashton-Gwatkin to Strang, in Newton to Halifax, 11 August 1938, *DBFP*, 3/II, no. 603; 'Minutes of Meeting with Sudeten German Delegation of Five and Herr Ullrich', 9 August 1938, FO 800/305, ff. 20–2.
8 Hencke to the Foreign Ministry, 12 August 1938, *DGFP*, D/II, no. 349; Ashton-Gwatkin to Strang, in Newton to Halifax, 12 August 1938, *DBFP*, 3/II, no. 609.
9 Ashton-Gwatkin to Strang, 16 August 1938, *DBFP*, 3/II, appendix II (III), p. 662; *Daily Telegraph*, 12 August 1938.

10 Memorandum by Mitis, enclosed in Hencke to the Foreign Ministry, 10 August 1039, *DGFP*, D/II, no. 344; Ashton-Gwatkin to Strang, in Newton to Halifax, 11 August 1938, *DBFP*, 3/II, no. 603; 'Minutes of Meeting with Sudeten German Delegation of Five and Herr Ulrich', 9 August 1938, FO 800/305, ff. 20–2.
11 'To the Executive Committee of the Sudeten German Party', memorandum presented by Hodža on 11 August 1938, *Sudetendeutsch Dossier*, item IX, FO 800/305, ff. 437–44, and Stopford Papers, RJS 3/2 and 3/4.
12 Newton to Halifax, 13 August 1938, *DBFP*, 3/II, no. 622.
13 Hencke to the Foreign Ministry, 12 August 1938, *DGFP*, D/II, no. 349.
14 Newton to Halifax, 13 August 1938, *DBFP*, 3/II, no. 622.
15 Ashton-Gwatkin to Strang, in Newton to Halifax, 17 August 1938, *DBFP*, 3/II, no. 629.
16 'Minutes of meeting with Sudeten German Party Delegation', 16 August 1938, FO 800/305, ff. 9–12; Hencke to the Foreign Ministry, 19 August 1938, *DGFP*, D/II, no. 373. For details of the unofficial Officers' Association manifesto, from which the Czechoslovak government sought to distance itself, see *The Times*, 13 and 16 August 1938.
17 Hencke to the Foreign Ministry, 19 August 1938, *DGFP*, D/II, no. 373; Newton to Halifax, 18 August 1938, *DBFP*, 3/II, no. 642.
18 Newton to Halifax, 19 August 1938, *DBFP*, 3/II, no. 645.
19 Report dated 13 August 1938, in Bürger to Altenburg, 17 August 1938, *DGFP*, D/II, no. 366.
20 Runciman to Halifax, 12 August 1938, *DBFP*, 3/II, no. 611.
21 Hencke to the Foreign Ministry, 6 August 1938, *DGFP*, D/II, no. 339.
22 Memorandum by Ashton-Gwatkin, 9 August 1938, FO 800/304, ff. 277–8. Ashton-Gwatkin believed that the meeting would take place during a planned, but unrealised, weekend visit by Runciman to the mainly German area around Marienbad (Mariánské Lázně)
23 Hencke to the Foreign Ministry, 12 August 1938, *DGFP*, D/II, no. 349.
24 Runciman to Halifax, 10 August 1938, *DBFP*, 3/II, no. 602.
25 Report dated 13 August 1938, in Bürger to Altenburg, 17 August 1938, *DGFP*, D/II, no. 366.
26 Foreign Ministry Memorandum, 13 August 1938, *DGFP*, D/II, no. 350.
27 Note by Ashton-Gwatkin, 11[?] August 1938, FO 800/304, f. 274.
28 Ashton-Gwatkin to Strang, in Newton to Halifax, 12 August 1938, *DBFP*, 3/II, no. 609.
29 Ashton-Gwatkin to Strang, 16 August 1938, *DBFP*, 3/II, appendix II (III), p. 662.
30 Report dated 13 August 1938, in Bürger to Altenburg, 17 August 1938, *DGFP*, D/II, no. 366. See also Hencke to the Foreign Ministry, 13 August 1938, *DGFP*, D/II, no. 352.
31 'Minutes of a conversation between Lord Runciman and Herr Frank', 12 August 1938, FO 800/304, ff. 255-6, and C 8699/1941/18, FO 371/21732. See also Runciman to Halifax, 12 August 1938, *DBFP*, 3/II, no. 611, and report dated 13 August 1938, in Bürger to Altenburg, 17 August 1938, *DGFP*, D/II, no. 366. The meeting with Henlein was originally arranged for 17 August, but, almost immediately, was put back a further day.
32 Ashton-Gwatkin to Strang, 9 August 1938, *DBFP*, 3/II, no. 598; *The Times*, 8 August 1938.
33 Ashton-Gwatkin to Strang, 16 August 1938, *DBFP*, 3/II, appendix II (III), pp. 662–3.

34 Memorandum by Ashton-Gwatkin, 15 August 1938, FO 800/304, ff. 252–4, and C 8699/1941/18, FO 371/21732.
35 Memorandum by Peto, 14 August 1938, C 8688/1941/18, FO 371/21732.
36 Ashton-Gwatkin to Runciman, 16 August 1938, C 8688/1941/18, FO 371/21732.
37 Ashton-Gwatkin to Strang, 16 August 1938, *DBFP*, 3/II, appendix II (III), p. 663.
38 Memorandum by Ashton-Gwatkin, 15 August 1938, FO 800/304, ff. 252–4, and C 8699/1941/18, FO 371/21732.
39 Memorandum by Christie, (undated), C 8118/1941/18, FO 371/21731. Christie assumed at the time that Henlein was merely trying to ingratiate himself with the Berlin government. He subsequently learned, however, that the German authorities had been aware in advance of the Zurich meeting, which gave the matter a 'somewhat different aspect'.
40 Minute by Vansittart, 3 August 1938, C 7877/1941/18, FO 371/21730.
41 The minutes attached to Christie's report make no reference to Henlein's offer. See C 8118/1941/18, FO 371/21731.
42 Mallet to Newton, 17 August 1938, C 8118/1941/18, FO 371/21731. The report was sent out with the instructions that it be burned when read. For Hohenlohe's advice to Runciman, endorsed by Christie, see above p. 140.
43 Note by Ashton-Gwatkin of a conversation between Runciman and Henlein, 19 August 1938, *DBFP*, 3/II, appendix II (I), pp. 656–7; *The Times*, 19 August 1938.
44 Ashton-Gwatkin to Strang, enclosed in Newton to Halifax, 19 August 1938, *DBFP*, 3/II, no. 652.
45 Stopford, 'Prague, 1938–1939', p. 25.
46 Note by Ashton-Gwatkin of a conversation between Runciman and Henlein, 19 August 1938, *DBFP*, 3/II, appendix II (I), pp. 656–7; Notes by Henlein, 19 August 1938, in V. Král, (ed.), *Die Deutschen in der Tschechoslowakei, 1933–1947*, (Prague, 1964), no. 184.
47 Note by Ashton-Gwatkin of a conversation between Runciman and Henlein, 19 August 1938, *DBFP*, 3/II, appendix II (I), pp. 656–7.
48 Ashton-Gwatkin to Strang, 22 August 1938, *DBFP*, 3/II, appendix II (III), p. 664.
49 Stopford, 'Prague, 1938–1939', p. 25.
50 Memorandum by Ashton-Gwatkin[?], 18 August 1938, FO 800/304, f. 144.
51 Hencke to the Foreign Ministry, 19 August 1938, *DGFP*, D/II, no. 373.
52 Memorandum by Ashton-Gwatkin[?], 18 August 1938, FO 800/304, ff. 144–6.
53 *Ibid.*
54 *Manchester Guardian*, 19 August 1938.
55 Note by Ashton-Gwatkin, 11[?] August 1938, FO 800/304, f. 274.
56 Stopford, 'Prague, 1938–1939', p. 25.
57 Ashton-Gwatkin to Strang, 23 August 1938, *DBFP*, 3/II, appendix II (III), pp. 663–4; Stopford, 'Prague, 1938–1939', pp. 25–6.
58 Stopford, 'Prague, 1938–1939', p. 26.
59 Ashton-Gwatkin to Strang, 23 August 1938, *DBFP*, 3/II, appendix II (III), p. 664.
60 *Ibid.*
61 The term 'Third Plan' was derived from the fact that Beneš's new scheme was the third set of proposals produced by the Czechoslovak government following those of 26 April and 30 June 1938. (See Beneš, *Mnichovské dny*, p. 173, note.) Laffan, in *Crisis over Czechoslovakia*, p. 221, offers an alternative, though probably erroneous, explanation that the term signified a compromise between the government's original ideas and those of the SdP.
62 Hencke to the Foreign Ministry, 24 August 1938, *DGFP*, D/II, no. 386.

63 *Ibid.*
64 Hencke to the Foreign Ministry, 27 August 1938, enclosure 1, *DGFP*, D/II, no. 398.
65 Memorandum by Mitis, 20 August 1938, enclosed in Hencke to the Foreign Ministry, 20 August 1938, *DGFP*, D/II, no. 378.
66 Memorandum by Altenburg, 18 August 1938, *DGFP*, D/II, no. 369.
67 *Ibid.*
68 Memorandum by Mitis, 20 August 1938, enclosed in Hencke to the Foreign Ministry, 20 August 1938, *DGFP*, D/II, no. 378.
69 Hencke to the Foreign Ministry, 19 August 1938, *DGFP*, D/II, no. 373.
70 Memorandum by Mitis, 20 August 1938, enclosed in Hencke to the Foreign Ministry, 20 August 1938, *DGFP*, D/II, no. 378.
71 Minute of Conversation between Ashton-Gwatkin and Henlein, 22 August 1938, *Documents and Materials Relating to the Eve of the Second World War*, (2 vols, Moscow, 1948), I, no. 16. (Henlein's notes.)
72 Runciman to Halifax, 23 August, 1938, *DBFP*, 3/II, no. 674.
73 Ashton-Gwatkin's diary, 22 August 1938, FO 800/304.
74 Note of a Conversation between Ashton-Gwatkin and Henlein, 22 August 1938, *DBFP*, 3/II, appendix II (I), pp. 657–9. (Ashton-Gwatkin's notes.) Henlein, in his record of the proceedings, indicated that it was Ashton-Gwatkin who suggested that Runciman should ask Beneš what concrete proposals he had in mind. (Minute of Conversation between Ashton-Gwatkin and Henlein, 22 August 1938, *Documents and Materials*, I, no. 16.)
75 Note of a Conversation between Ashton-Gwatkin and Henlein, 22 August 1938, *DBFP*, 3/II, appendix II (I), pp. 657–9.
76 *Ibid.*
77 Minute of a Conversation between Ashton-Gwatkin and Henlein, 22 August 1938, *Documents and Materials*, I, no. 16.
78 Note of Conversation between Ashton-Gwatkin and Henlein, 22 August 1938, *DBFP*, 3/II, appendix II (I), pp. 657–9.
79 Ashton-Gwatkin's diary, 22 August 1938, FO 800/304. Ashton-Gwatkin also noted that Henlein 'wore a brown suit and has a strong Frank Buchanan look'.
80 See above p. 172.
81 Note of a Conversation between Ashton-Gwatkin and Henlein, 22 August 1938, *DBFP*, 3/II, appendix II (I), pp. 657–9.
82 Minute of Conversation between Ashton-Gwatkin and Henlein, 22 August 1938, *Documents and Materials*, I, no. 16.
83 Note of a Conversation between Ashton-Gwatkin and Henlein, 22 August 1938, *DBFP*, 3/II, appendix II (I), pp. 657–9.
84 The significance of this speech, as perceived by the British government, is discussed in the following chapter.
85 Runciman to Halifax, 23 August 1938, *DBFP*, 3/II, no. 674.
86 Ashton-Gwatkin to Strang, 23 August 1938, *DBFP*, 3/II, appendix II (III), p. 664.
87 *Ibid.* In his memoirs Beneš denied being the originator of the Third Plan. He confirmed that his meeting with Sander had been instigated by Krejčí (whom he described as later becoming a 'quisling' on account of his heading the war-time Protectorate administration) but maintained that it was Sander who suggested the new framework for a settlement, claiming it was acceptable to moderates within the SdP who were genuinely seeking an agreement with the government. Beneš implied that the meeting with Sander took place following his receipt of

the seven point memorandum from Runciman on 23 August which, the President claimed, had been 'literally dictated' to Ashton-Gwatkin by Henlein. Beneš denied having any prior knowledge of the contents of the memorandum and also maintained that Runciman had specifically requested that the origin of the document remain secret. (Beneš, *Mnichovské dny*, pp. 172–6.) The President's account of these developments is not borne out by the other evidence.

88 Ashton-Gwatkin to Strang, 25 August 1938, *DBFP*, 3/II, appendix II (III), p. 665.
89 Hencke to the Foreign Ministry, 24 August 1938, *DGFP*, D/II, no. 386.
90 Hencke to the Foreign Ministry, 6 August 1938, *DGFP*, D/II, no. 339.
91 Hencke to the Foreign Ministry, 19 August 1938, *DGFP*, D/II, no. 373.
92 Hencke to the Foreign Ministry, 24 August 1938, *DGFP*, D/II, no. 386.
93 Ashton-Gwatkin to Strang, 25 August 1938, *DBFP*, 3/II, appendix II (III), p. 665.
94 Ashton-Gwatkin's diary, 24 August 1938, FO 800/304.
95 Runciman to Halifax, 23 August 1938, *DBFP*, 3/II, no. 674.

9
Anxiety in London

The activities of the Runciman Mission were followed with considerable interest across the world, but nowhere more keenly than in London. The British government maintained direct contact with the Mission via the Legation in Prague through which messages were relayed to Runciman and his staff as required. During the early stages of the Mission's residence in Prague little use was made of this facility. August being the height of the holiday season, ministers and civil servants alike were away from their Whitehall desks and the British mediators in Czechoslovakia were left largely to their own devices. This situation persisted until the end of the month, when London began increasingly to influence the Mission's actions.

The flow of information in the other direction was from the outset more plentiful. Not only did Newton keep the Foreign Office fully up to date on all developments concerning the Sudeten German problem in general and the Mission's activities in particular, but members of the Mission themselves also reported back to London. The most assiduous correspondent was Ashton-Gwatkin, who transmitted each week a day-by-day account of developments, and his observations on them, addressed to Strang in the Foreign Office. Runciman himself reported back less frequently in letters to Halifax, which were also seen by Chamberlain.[1] From the start, the Foreign Secretary encouraged the supplementation of the semi-official reports from Ashton-Gwatkin with more impressionistic accounts from Runciman himself, relaying the mediator's judgement of the 'smell' of things.[2] Later, Halifax indicated that he found this double channel of communications 'most useful' and assured Runciman that such contacts did not compromise 'the independent character' of the Mission.[3]

In addition to receiving this direct information from the British mediators in Central Europe, the government in London – and also the public in general – were kept informed of developments by the large international press corps gathered in Prague to observe the Mission at work. Detailed reports were published daily in most of the British press, although, in view of the fact that Runciman's staff disclosed very little to the journalists concerned, these accounts recorded mainly the externally perceived activities of the Mission, rather than its inner workings. The best informed and the most comprehensive were the reports in *The Times*, the *Manchester Guardian* and the *Daily Telegraph*, although the more popular newspapers also provided extensive coverage. The extent of public interest was not surprising, as it was widely believed that the future of peace in Europe was dependent on the successful outcome of the Mission.

Runciman himself was certainly fully aware of the heavy responsibility that rested on him. It was a burden made no lighter by his lack of confidence in the Mission's ability to influence events. In a reflective letter to Halifax, sent only a week after his arrival in Prague and before arrangements had been made for a meeting with Henlein, Runciman wrote: 'It is a pathetic side of the present crisis that the common people here ... are looking to me and my mission as the only hope for an established peace. Alas they do not realise how weak are our sanctions, and I dread the moment when they find that nothing can save them.'[4] Halifax responded with words of encouragement: 'If you do succeed in throwing any planks across the gulf you will have done more for the world than is given to many to do, and I am not at all disposed to let go the hope of your finding a way through. Certainly if you can't, no one else could!'[5]

In addition to these blandishments, the Foreign Secretary also replied to Runciman's previous query about how long he should continue to 'hold the fort'. The response, sent in mid-August, was probably not what the unhappy mediator hoped for. Although Halifax believed it unlikely that Germany would attack whilst Runciman remained in Czechoslovakia, he was to leave if it became clear that Hitler 'means business' or if he made an 'outrageous' speech at the Nuremberg Rally in early September.[6] The Foreign Secretary also supplied more general though wholly inconclusive advice – but which was in some respects significantly different from the views expressed in his (previously mentioned) letter to Henderson a fortnight earlier.[7]

One element of Halifax's advice, however, remained unaltered. He informed Runciman, in words practically identical to those used in his letter to Henderson, that the idea of a plebiscite had 'always seemed the devil, and as likely to precipitate as to prevent a crisis'. Although he did not totally exclude its use as a 'last resort', and indeed anticipated that it would be demanded, he considered the difficulties involved to be 'enormous'.[8] Clearly, the Foreign Secretary remained resolved to avoid a plebiscite if at all possible. Indeed, there had been no change of attitude on this matter in the Foreign Office since June when (as discussed previously) the issue had been thoroughly explored and rejected.[9]

In other respects, however, Halifax was slowly moving his ground. Of the three other options mentioned to Henderson, Halifax had ruled out blaming the SdP for any failure, on the grounds that it might provoke Germany to use force. This left two alternatives, that of blaming no one or of blaming the Czechoslovak authorities only. On mature reflection, however, it was concluded in the Foreign Office that it would be unwise for Runciman to declare either side responsible for the breakdown. An uninitialled minute (probably by Sargent) argued that although Runciman might well be pressed by circumstances into allotting blame, it should 'be withstood at all costs'. Such a step would not only play into the hands of either the German or the Czechoslovak government, but might also be made 'dangerous use of' by France in justifying its policy towards Czechoslovakia and in pressuring Britain into collaboration with it. The remaining alternative of disengagement without blaming anyone was also to be avoided as it was likely to lead to immediate German action 'with incalculable results'.[10]

Halifax incorporated this reasoning in his advice to Runciman:

> No doubt the simplest course open to you in the case of deadlock would be merely to declare that your effort at mediation had failed and therefore your mission must be considered as terminated. The disadvantage of this course would be that such a declaration, standing by itself, would probably by reaction precipitate an acute crisis and might tempt the German Government to immediate action.[11]

The Foreign Secretary also accepted the argument concerning the dangers of placing the responsibility for failure on either of the protagonists. In his letter to Runciman, however, he linked that point with a new alternative raised in the Foreign Office minute, but found equally hazardous – that of Runciman preparing a compromise plan of his own:[12]

> You might, I suppose, in default of agreement, put forward a compromise scheme which each party would have to accept or reject, and from which would emerge a situation where one side or the other would be put definitely in the wrong. Or you might, without putting forward any plan of your own, draw up a report in which you would review the situation generally and assess the blame for a deadlock, but in either case you would seem to be putting yourself in the position of pronouncing judgement, and I must confess that I see great danger, as I fancy would you, in your doing this ... For instance, if you were to put forward a plan of your own, one or other of the parties might accept it on condition that its observance was guaranteed by His Majesty's Government![13]

The Foreign Office minute also raised a further, previously unconsidered possibility, that of attempting to 'mitigate and delay the crisis' by a partial settlement followed by international arbitration.[14] As Halifax explained to Runciman: the points on which agreement had been reached might be brought immediately into force, 'provisionally and experimentally'. If Runciman judged he could make no further progress, the remaining issues might be referred to an international conference. But that would give rise to the 'acute question' of participation. Should those involved be Czechoslovakia, Germany, France and Great Britain only; or, Halifax wondered, should Poland, Hungary, Italy and the Soviet Union also be invited?[15] For the moment the question remained unanswered, but the seeds of the future Munich Conference, which had been sown during Strang's visit to Central Europe in May, were evidently beginning to germinate.

The vague notion of a possible international conference to resolve the Czechoslovak problem had earlier been developed a stage further by the Ambassador in Berlin. Writing to Halifax on 22 July, before Runciman's departure for Prague, Henderson suggested that in the event of the Czechoslovak government refusing to accept the services of a British mediator, or of the mediator's efforts proving fruitless, a four-power conference should be called to settle the crisis. The powers he had in mind were Britain, France and Italy, which were 'chiefly responsible' for creating Czechoslovakia, and Germany which was 'particularly interested'.[16] Henderson's suggestion was vigorously opposed by Vansittart. His objection was not to the principle of a conference but to the suggested participation of Italy – which would only 'stiffen the German attitude' and would be 'the thin end of the German wedge for excluding Russia from Europe'. The Soviet Union, Vansittart argued, 'had just as much right to be interested in the eight million Slavs as Germany to be interested in the three and a half million Germans'. Moreover, being a contingent ally of Czechoslovakia, the Soviet Union could not legitimately be excluded from a conference at which Italy was represented. It would be simpler to have neither Italy nor the Soviet Union participating.[17] Halifax saw 'great force' in Vansittart's reasoning[18] which was communicated by Strang to Henderson on 30 July. Strang added a further point – that of probable Polish objection to a four-power settlement of a problem in which Poland also had an interest.[19] Henderson responded with an explanation of the particular circumstances in which he envisaged a conference being called. He foresaw that coming about in the probable event of a breakdown in the negotiations within Czechoslovakia and the consequent mobilisation by Germany followed by that of France. Italy, 'as the friend of Germany', would then suggest to Britain, 'as friend of France', to offer joint mediation at a four-power conference.[20] Although not accurate in matters of detail, the Ambassador's prediction was to be substantially borne out by events less than two months later.

Of more immediate significance however, was the discussion concerning the possibility of Runciman producing a compromise scheme of his own. Although before his departure for Prague, Runciman had indicated his unwillingness to act as an arbitrator or to draw up his own solution – to which the Foreign Secretary alluded approvingly in his letter of 18 August[21]

– pressure was soon to be applied on the Mission to do just that. This drift towards arbitration was set in motion not by the Foreign Office but by the Ambassador in Berlin. Henderson, in his regular reports to London and in longer more discursive personal letters to Halifax,[22] repeatedly offered comment and advice concerning Runciman's activities. From the outset he was in no doubt whatever as to what the mediator's role should be. Although convinced that Hitler was not seeking an immediate war, Henderson believed that the preservation of peace in Central Europe depended upon Germany retaining confidence in Britain's ability to extract major concessions from the Czechoslovak government. That meant, he argued, 'that we shall have at long last to put our foot down very firmly and say to Beneš "You must"'. The concession required was a 'genuine Nationalities Statute', which involved a 'fundamental change in the Czech proposals'. Even on that basis, however, Henderson considered prospects for a lasting solution not good. He estimated that there was no more than one chance in ten of avoiding the cession of the Sudeten German areas to Germany. Nevertheless, Henderson believed a compromise solution had to be sought and the Runciman Mission was a means towards that end. He did not envy Runciman this 'difficult and thankless' task. 'The Czechs', he explained, undiplomatically, 'are a pig-headed race and Beneš not the least pig-headed among them.' The Ambassador restored the balance somewhat by referring also to the dangers of war arising from 'German stupidity'. He saw advantage, however, in the professed German refusal to exercise any influence over the SdP. It gave the British government, and Runciman, some room for manoeuvre in Prague. In the event of deadlock it could be put to the German government, in Henderson's words: 'If we are prepared to put the thumbscrews on Beneš, you must help by putting pressure on Henlein ...'[23]

The signal, which indicated to Henderson that it was time to apply the 'thumbscrews' on Beneš, came on 1 August, when Germany announced plans to bring several divisions up to war strength in early September.[24] He interpreted this measure of partial mobilisation as a 'mixture of bluff and real menace', signifying that Hitler was preparing for the possible use of force against Czechoslovakia before the winter. The Nuremberg Rally, held at the beginning of September, was therefore seen by Henderson as providing the deadline for a peaceful resolution of the crisis. This gave Runciman 'a month or at most six weeks' to bridge the gulf 'not of detail but of principle' which divided the SdP and the Czechoslovak authorities.[25] Henderson conceded that Germany was unlikely to attack Czechoslovakia whilst the British mediator remained in the country or in advance of the Nuremberg Rally, but unless Runciman succeeded 'by a miracle in achieving an agreed settlement' Britain would be faced with 'Hobson's choice ... between compelling by force either [the] Czechoslovak Government or the German Government to accept terms of which they disapprove'.[26]

Henderson also sought to impress on the Foreign Secretary the necessity of avoiding a repetition of the May Crisis intervention. Although he believed that a direct threat of British involvement would deter Germany from an immediate attack on Czechoslovakia, that would be 'the greatest tragedy of all' – a Pyrrhic victory, making eventual war inevitable.[27] Henderson was therefore most anxious that Britain should not use the threat of war 'unless our case is morally copper-bottomed'.[28]

Indeed, Henderson did not argue his case with Halifax purely in terms of expediency, but also on grounds of principle:

> Personally I just sit and pray for one thing, namely that Lord Runciman will live up to the role of an impartial British Liberal statesman. I cannot believe that he will allow himself to be influenced by ancient history or even arguments about strategic frontiers and economics in preference to high moral principles. The great and courageous game which you and the Prime Minister are playing will be lost ... if he does not come out on the side of the higher principles, for which in fact the British Empire really stands.[29]

The moral principle in question, as he explained in another letter, was national self-determination. The 'great and courageous game' being played by Chamberlain and Halifax was the search for an understanding between Britain and Germany which, Henderson believed, would result in 'world peace for a generation at least'. Such a rapprochement, he argued, was conditional on the prior resolution of the Sudeten German problem. 'Are we to prejudice this prospect [of peace]', he asked rhetorically, 'out of a sentiment for a Czechoslovakia which was constitutionally and initially a mistake?' Although maintaining there remained a 'faint chance' of preserving Czechoslovakia intact, Henderson argued that the Sudeten Germans could not permanently be prevented, as in the case of the Austrians, 'from coming into the Reich if they wish it and undoubtedly the majority to-day do so'. He added, categorically, that 'Czechs and Germans will never harmonize', it was 'either domination or separation' because the problem was primarily 'a racial and national one and not social or economic'.[30]

Henderson's anxious outpouring of advice during August was not without its inconsistencies. Although he clearly believed that autonomy for the Sudeten Germans would be no more than a transitional arrangement, he nevertheless repeatedly urged that Runciman make such a recommendation, applying the formula of the Swiss cantonal system.[31] Indeed, on occasions Henderson implied that autonomy would provide a stable solution. He stated that 'autonomy on Swiss lines', being Hitler's minimal requirement, was the only way of preserving peace, adding the warning that if 'Runciman comes down on the Czech side, I do not ... see how we can avoid trouble sooner or later'.[32] Subsequently, he suggested that following

Runciman's recommendation of Swiss cantonal autonomy, the British government should seek assistance for its implementation from France and Germany.[33] On another occasion, however, Henderson made clear that he envisaged autonomy as purely transitory, and separation as desirable:

> Of course ... the surgical operation would be in the better interests of everybody, even of the patient. That is the tragedy of it all. I wonder if Runciman would get out of Prague alive, if he said so. If I were he ... I should say on general lines: 'absolute autonomy for areas in which Germans predominate with Beneš' minority law applicable in those areas. Self-determination in principle to be exercised if desired after X years.'[34]

Henderson made no effort to disguise his lack of concern for the future integrity of Czechoslovakia. Following autonomy, he openly conceded: 'That the plums thereafter will drop ripe from the tree into the German Reich is another question.'[35] But that caused him little concern, as he regarded the very existence of Czechoslovakia an affront to natural justice and the incorporation of its German population in Germany as unavoidable.

Henderson was greatly concerned, however, that Runciman might fail to make the recommendation he considered essential, which was, in effect, to arbitrate in favour of the SdP. In view of his belief that Germany would accept nothing short of cantonal autonomy for the Sudeten Germans, he warned Halifax, in late August, that 'if Lord Runciman comes out with less and His Majesty's Government regard his proposals as fair and equitable, then *we must make up our minds to fight*. Germany will today listen to nothing except force.'[36] These uncharacteristic sentiments were employed by Henderson in order to spur the Foreign Office into accepting his analysis of the Central European situation. He himself wished to avoid war with Germany, almost at any cost, and he prayed therefore that Runciman would regard 'cantonal autonomy as the only possible solution',[37] but unless the British government persuaded Runciman to say so, Henderson warned, the event it feared most – war with Germany – would become inevitable. He underlined the gravity of the situation by repeatedly pointing out that Germany would be '100 per cent' prepared for war by mid-September.[38]

Henderson also repeatedly stressed the importance of Runciman's plan being announced, at least in outline form, in advance of the Nuremberg Rally in September.[39] He explained that Hitler, who had not yet 'made up his mind irrevocably to employ force against Czechoslovakia',[40] would have to choose, at Nuremberg, between 'moderates' and 'extremists' amongst his supporters. Moderation would only prevail, reasoned the Ambassador, if Hitler received a 'sufficient measure of satisfaction' concerning Czechoslovakia.[41] By mid-August, Henderson claimed that the lack of achievement resulting from the British diplomatic intervention in the

Central European crisis was giving rise to impatience in Germany. Hitler had been patient for four months, but he could not wait indefinitely.[42] If Britain was to retain the initiative, Henderson argued, Runciman must produce 'his epoch-making conception of a just settlement before Hitler's [*sic*] queers his pitch',[43] otherwise Hitler might stipulate his terms for a settlement at Nuremberg, and, Henderson asked rhetorically: 'What will then be Lord Runciman's position and ours?'[44]

The immense responsibility for the peace of Europe that rested on Runciman caused Henderson, in his own words, 'constant nightmares'.[45] Although the nightmares were probably only hyperbolical, his intense anxiety was real enough. That is clear from the incessant stream of agitated advice concerning Runciman's activities kept up by Henderson throughout August in a series of over 20 letters and telegrams addressed to Halifax. Henderson, of course, was fully aware of the excessive attention he was devoting to the problem and apologised for appearing 'over-insistent or over-presumptuous' in writing so much about Runciman. He justified himself on the grounds that 'the stakes for which we are playing are too high to allow me to remain silent on a matter on which I feel so strongly'. The principal stake in question was, of course, that of avoiding war with Germany. Henderson vehemently rejected the views of those in the Foreign Office who considered such a war as inevitable, regarding their attitude as 'nothing short of disastrous'. He denied, however, being defeatist – in his view it was defeatist to regard war with Germany as unavoidable. Henderson added that he 'would fight Germany tomorrow for a good cause but I refuse to contemplate our doing so for the Sudeten'.[46] Even less, of course, would he consider doing so for the Czechs and Slovaks.

The Ambassador's agitation was largely due to the gravity of the international situation, but the state of his mind also left something to be desired, particularly for an incumbent of, arguably, the most important and sensitive posting in the British diplomatic service at that time. Henderson, who was suffering from ill health,[47] found the conduct of diplomacy in the German capital a heavy burden. In one of his manuscript letters to Halifax, written in mid-August, he complained that Berlin was 'nerve racking', adding that 'I get rattled at times and my chart is all ups and downs'. The frequency and tenor of his communications about the crisis in Czechoslovakia certainly testified to his deep concern, but the intensity of the attention he devoted to the issue was verging on the obsessive. He himself admitted: 'I have a one track mind just now and think and eat and sleep on nothing else'.[48] Such a state of mind was hardly conducive to the formulation of the cool and dispassionate advice required of a senior diplomat in a key foreign capital during a grave international crisis.

Henderson's peace of mind was not enhanced by his lack of detailed knowledge of current developments in Prague. 'I suppose it must be so', he complained to Halifax on 17 August, 'but it puts me at a disadvantage here to have no idea whatsoever on what lines of thought Lord Runciman is working.' This ignorance worried him, since he believed Britain would be held responsible for whatever solution the mediator recommended. However, it was not simply a case of the Ambassador wishing to be better informed, he also desired to exercise greater influence over events, and hence offered to fly over to London at any time for consultation.[49] Halifax, who at the time was little better informed of Runciman's activities than was Henderson, did not at that juncture take up the offer for fear of it giving rise to 'all sorts of alarms and rumours'. The Foreign Secretary, however, did supply Henderson with a copy of his lengthy letter to Runciman of 18 August, in order to provide the latest Foreign Office thinking.[50]

Although Henderson failed in his bid to visit London in mid-August, the torrent of advice aimed by him at the Foreign Office did not go unnoticed, particularly concerning the need for Runciman to make a pronouncement of principle in advance of the Nuremberg Rally. So repetitive was this advice that a three-page memorandum was produced summarising the references to this matter from nine letters and telegrams sent by Henderson between 6 and 21 August.[51] Within the Foreign Office, reaction to the Ambassador's insistent advice was mixed. Mallet agreed that there was 'clearly grave danger' that Hitler would 'lose patience' by early September and he therefore saw possible advantages in Runciman making a recommendation before then 'if it were in favour of home rule'.[52] Signs of growing German impatience were also detected by Roberts, who argued for an 'anodyne statement' from Runciman, which would convey 'some encouragement to the Sudeten thesis'. Although his conclusion differed only in terms of degree from that of his colleague, Roberts at least envisaged the possibility of Runciman coming out in support of the Czechoslovak authorities, despite the danger that it might drive Hitler 'to some dangerous gesture'.[53]

The advisability of Runciman assuming the role of arbitrator was explored in greater detail by Sargent, who offered a cogent counter-argument to Henderson's insistent advice. If, he reasoned, 'we believe from other information received (unknown to Sir N. Henderson) that Hitler ... intends to attack Czechoslovakia at the end of September, a great deal of Sir N. Henderson's argument falls to the ground', as Hitler would be unlikely to precipitate a crisis before he was ready to act.[54] Sargent, nevertheless, went on to consider circumstances in which Runciman might make the advocated 'pronouncement'. If negotiations were still proceeding, he argued, Runciman could do no more than report on progress, if any, and appeal for further co-operation, which was unlikely to extend Hitler's reserve of patience. Any more substantial declaration was out of the question: 'For a mediator *publicly* either to blame or to make proposals while negotiations were proceeding would surely be impossible to justify.' In the case of deadlock in the talks, Sargent perceived that it would be difficult to devise a formula that would avoid committing Runciman (and the British government) to a 'definite point of view' without giving Hitler justification for 'taking the law into his own hands'. On the other hand, a general statement from Runciman containing 'only facts and pious sentiments' would be unlikely to influence Hitler, particularly if he had brought about the collapse of the negotiations in order to justify military intervention. In that case, Sargent argued, 'some more direct action by the Governments concerned in the maintenance of peace would surely be necessary to produce any real effect'. Sargent also explored the possibility of seeking to speed up the negotiations by Britain, possibly in conjunction with France, applying pressure on Beneš for an early settlement. He was again unconvinced, arguing that the Czechoslovak authorities were unlikely to grant concessions to the SdP that might jeopardise the integrity and independence of their country without seeking a guarantee from Britain in exchange. 'Are we prepared for the sake of peace to give this guarantee?' he enquired.[55]

Despite Sargent's scepticism concerning Henderson's advice, his memorandum failed to investigate the possibility of Runciman deliberately prolonging his activities beyond the Nazi Party Rally, when climatic conditions would become unsuitable for warfare. A few days earlier, however, during conversation with the Italian Chargé d'Affaires in London, Sargent had suggested that Runciman might remain in Czechoslovakia for a further three months. When news of this exchange reached Henderson via the Italian Ambassador in Berlin, he immediately complained to Halifax.[56] Sargent protested his innocence, claiming that to suggest Runciman intended delaying a settlement was a distortion of his remarks, which only signified that the British mediator was prepared to spend as long as necessary to achieve a solution.[57]

Although it was incautious of Sargent to speak to the Italian Chargé in these terms, the possibility of using the Runciman Mission as a delaying device was self-evident. That was certainly how Runciman's activities were perceived in both Prague and Berlin. The British Air Attaché in Czechoslovakia observed in mid-August that many people there regarded the Mission as a 'time saver for the British rearmament plan'.[58] In Berlin, Weizsäcker and Hitler's emissary, Wiedemann, both accused Runciman of procrastination and of taking no serious steps towards resolving the Sudeten German problem,[59] calculating no doubt that, when this was reported back to the Mission by Hohenlohe, it would result in increased pressure being applied to the Czechoslovak authorities. In London, these German observations were seen as a 'bad sign',[60] although the Foreign Office was not unaware of the possible benefits to be gained by delay. Roberts, in his evaluation of Henderson's advice, noted that the disadvantage of Runciman issuing an early statement of principle would be to put an end to his continuing 'to act as a safety valve or delaying factor until the autumn'.[61] Halifax also alluded to this possibility in his letter to Runciman of 18 August. When enquiring of the prospect of the Mission achieving results before the Nuremberg Rally, the Foreign Secretary stressed that he did not wish Hitler's perceived growing impatience to pressure Runciman into producing a premature judgement, for it was equally valid to argue that so long as he remained in Czechoslovakia it would be difficult for Hitler to resort to any drastic action.[62] Henderson himself had made that point to Halifax a few days previously, observing, in characteristic prose: 'The Germans are damnably stupid but I cannot believe that they will aggress the Czechs so long as Runciman is still in Prague.'[63] At that time, Runciman also appeared to believe that there were benefits to be gained from delay. At least the cryptic observation in his letter to Halifax of 18 August – 'All I can do is to mark time and remember our objective.'[64] – is open to that interpretation. But despite the consensus concerning the benefit to be gained from the mediator's continued presence in Prague, no attempt was made by Britain to exploit this aspect of the situation, nor even to explore further its potential. Indeed, this hitherto underlying assumption was soon to give way to the application of pressure on Runciman for swift concrete action.

For the moment, however, the Foreign Office remained uncertain of the wisdom of accepting Henderson's advice for urgent action in Prague, and it was decided to seek the view of Runciman himself. Newton was instructed to discuss with Runciman the contents of Henderson's despatches, copies of which had been sent to the Prague Legation, and to report back in particular the mediator's response to the suggestion that he should issue a pronouncement in advance of the forthcoming Nuremberg Rally.[65] Runciman was, in fact, already familiar with Henderson's thinking. The Ambassador in Berlin, with Halifax's approval,[66] had written to Runciman, on 11 August, summarising his views on the crisis and enclosing copies of some of his letters to the Foreign Secretary. This was followed by a further letter and enclosures later that month. In the letters to Prague, Henderson reiterated the essential message of the correspondence with London, stressing in particular the acute danger to peace which would arise if the British Mission failed to produce a plan acceptable to Germany before early September. Henderson conceded that this would possibly force Runciman into declaring his views earlier than he wished, but Hitler's hand was also 'being forced' by the forthcoming Nazi Congress. Hitler was convinced, Henderson argued, that Britain was not prepared to exert sufficient pressure on Czechoslovakia, and that Germany would therefore have to do so itself.[67]

Although Runciman was fully aware of the dangers of what he termed an 'awkward speech' at Nuremberg, he found Henderson's unsolicited advice tiresome. In particular, he considered the insistent advocacy of an immediate pronouncement concerning the basis of a settlement 'not useful'. This suggestion, he pointed out to Halifax, was made without knowledge of recent developments in Prague – namely the emergence of the Third Plan – which promised to establish a new basis for effective negotiations. This respectful rejection of Henderson's advice disguised Runciman's true estimation of Britain's Ambassador in Berlin. The additional cryptic remark to Halifax, suggesting that 'someone sent from London to Berlin would find ground for useful conversation', gave little more away, but, Runciman continued, Ashton-Gwatkin would explain all on his return to London later that day.[68] Ashton-Gwatkin himself was less circumspect in the privacy of his diary, where he noted that Runciman had 'no great confidence' in Henderson and would have liked a special envoy sent to Berlin – 'e.g. Rumbold'.[69] Dispatching a retired senior diplomat like Rumbold (who had been briefly considered as a possible mediator a few weeks earlier) was envisaged by Runciman as a follow-up to Henlein's proposed visit to Hitler.[70]

It was left to Newton to relay in greater detail the thinking of the British mediators in Prague. Following consultation with Runciman, Newton explained to Halifax that it was 'unreasonable' to expect the Mission to issue a pronouncement of principle by any given date. Runciman, he continued, had 'steadily and rightly refused the role of judge or arbitrator'. His purpose was 'to mediate and to facilitate direct dealings between the parties'; this he had done 'effectively', securing the confidence of both sides. Although it was still possible that Runciman would announce some measure of success in advance of the Nuremberg Rally, consideration had been given to an alternative. In the event of no significant progress being made by that time, Newton argued – in contrast with the advice offered by Henderson – that

> some statement explaining need for a full examination of the issues and emphasising that Lord Runciman is actively engaged in promoting solution fair to both sides should be sufficient provided Herr Hitler does desire a peaceful solution to enable him to hold his hand.[71]

Evidence gradually accumulating in London during August indicated, however, that Hitler's intentions were far from peaceful. The British government's initial response to the mobilisation measures introduced in Germany early that month was to address an appeal for moderation directly to Hitler, in order to circumvent Ribbentrop and the German Foreign Ministry who were believed hostile to the idea of a German–British understanding.[72] Hence, on 11 August, Henderson was instructed to convey a memorandum from Halifax directly to the Reich Chancellery, requesting Hitler 'to modify his military measures' in order not to 'sterilise Lord Runciman's mission and prematurely and unnecessarily create a fresh crisis in Europe'. Halifax warned that Germany's military preparations, which could only be interpreted 'as a threatening gesture towards Czechoslovakia', might result in Czechoslovak countermeasures and possibly result in a general European war. In addition to pointing out these 'grave and incalculable risks', Halifax offered an incentive, drawing attention to the fact that Germany's action might 'endanger and perhaps even destroy the prospects of a resumption before long of the conversations between our two Governments'.[73] Hitler was not impressed, either by the veiled threat of war or by the inducement of talks with Britain, and German military plans remained unaltered. In fact, this naive British initiative only served to provide an opportunity for the demonstration of German diplomatic umbrage. Hitler pointedly ignored Halifax's appeal and the Foreign Ministry reprimanded Henderson for breaching protocol by directly approaching the office of the Head of State.[74]

Additional indication of Hitler's intentions towards Czechoslovakia reached Britain in mid-August, when a recently retired German general, Ewald von Kleist, visited London claiming to represent moderate opinion within the German General Staff. He was not officially received by the British government but, during a private meeting with Vansittart on 18 August, disclosed that Hitler planned to attack Czechoslovakia in late September and that war was inevitable unless Britain took effective action to prevent it. He offered two suggestions for avoiding the impending conflict: first, that Hitler must be made to realise that Britain would fight in defence of Czechoslovakia and, secondly, that a public appeal must be made by Britain to the German people stressing the horrors and catastrophic repercussions of war.[75] Chamberlain's response was to discount much of von Kleist's message on account of his self-confessed hostility to Hitler. As far as von Kleist's specific advice was concerned, the Prime Minister rejected, for the time being at least, any form of public pronouncement. He was, however, more sympathetic towards the idea of impressing the seriousness of the situation on Hitler and suggested that the public recall of Henderson to London for talks on Czechoslovakia was the most appropriate means of achieving this objective,[76] but even that was not carried out with any urgency. It was almost a week later, on 24 August, that Halifax duly instructed Henderson – no doubt much to the latter's satisfaction – to return to London for consultation on 29 August.[77]

Shortly before Henderson's recall, the Foreign Office received corroboration of von Kleist's warning. On 21 August, Henderson himself reported that the Military Attaché in Berlin, Colonel F. N. Mason-MacFarlane, had learned that Hitler had recently informed his military commanders of the intention to attack Czechoslovakia in late September. The Attaché's unnamed informant urged firm action by Britain and France which would, in his opinion, result in Hitler's downfall. Henderson's response, which closely echoed that of Chamberlain toward von Kleist, was to observe that, although the informant was biased and his view 'largely propaganda', the information itself should be taken seriously.[78]

Further evidence of Germany's menacing attitude towards Czechoslovakia reached London two days later. On 23 August, Sargent was informed by the

French Chargé d'Affaires, Roger Cambon, that the governments of Romania and Yugoslavia – Czechoslovakia's allies in the Little Entente – had received indication from Berlin that Germany would be obliged to intervene if the Sudeten Germans did not receive satisfaction.[79] Coupled with the recent interview between General Joseph Vuillemin, the Chief of the French Air Staff, and Field-Marshal Hermann Göring, German Minister for Air, at which Göring attempted to isolate France from Czechoslovakia,[80] the French government became alarmed and sought Britain's support for a new joint warning to Berlin.[81] Halifax, however, thought otherwise and informed Cambon on 25 August that he considered the letter to Ribbentrop of 28 July and the memorandum to Hitler of 11 August for the moment adequate, as he was wary 'of diluting the effect of warnings by excessive repetition'.[82] Only Sargent was inclined to view the matter differently and urged that the question of how to respond to the latest German diplomatic pressure on Czechoslovakia be 'carefully considered' during the forthcoming consultations with Henderson.[83] Cambon returned to this issue the following day in a letter to Sargent, conveying the suggestion of his Foreign Minister that the warning might take the form of a request to Germany to urge 'moderation and prudence' on the SdP, similar to the advice given by France and Britain to the Prague government.[84] Again, the Foreign Office was not impressed, and Mallet dismissed the suggestion with the remark that it 'would merely provoke a rude reply that it is astonishing that the Sudetens have been so patient in face of Czech procrastination'.[85]

Although the British government was reluctant to take up the French suggestion, a public warning to Germany was nevertheless being planned, despite Chamberlain's rejection of the idea less than a week previously. The Chancellor of the Exchequer was due to address a meeting in Lanark in Scotland on 27 August, and the opportunity was taken to include some carefully phrased remarks regarding the situation in Central Europe. Simon asserted that Britain was pursuing 'a positive policy of peace' and that British rearmament threatened no one. Concerning Czechoslovakia, he stated that the Prime Minister's House of Commons declaration of 24 March was still applicable and that there was 'nothing to add or to vary in its content'. He stressed the independent nature of the Runciman Mission and expressed the conviction that 'all reasonable persons in every nation' would wish to assist Runciman in achieving a just settlement of the Sudeten German problem. The key passages of the Chancellor's speech were those directed at Germany, stressing the danger to all of Europe likely to emanate from any armed conflict over Czechoslovakia, which might spread like 'a fire in a high wind'. In the 'modern world', he added, there was 'no limit to the reactions of war'.[86]

Reactions to the speech itself were mixed. In the Foreign Office, Sargent believed it contained a 'very definite warning'.[87] Halifax's Assistant Private Secretary, F.R. Hoyer-Millar, was much nearer the mark, however, when commenting on a draft version of the speech, that it did not contain 'anything very epoch-making'.[88] Simon's warning to Germany was certainly couched in delicate terms. He avoided any actual repetition of the key passages of Chamberlain's parliamentary statement or even a paraphrase of them. Although the Prime Minister's statement itself had not amounted to a particularly strong warning, it did at least refer to the possible immediate involvement of Britain and France in any war over Czechoslovakia.[89] Simon, however, restricted himself to speaking generally of the contagious nature of modern warfare.

Nevertheless, the French government was impressed by the contents of the Lanark speech; its approval was conveyed to Halifax and the pressure for a joint diplomatic initiative in Berlin abated.[90] Czechoslovak reaction to the speech was also positive, although Krofta indicated to Newton his realisation that Britain was keeping its options open.[91] The German government, to which Simon had addressed his remarks, made no official response, but signalled its displeasure by complaining of the lack of balance in British policy which issued public threats to Germany whilst seeking to influence the Czechoslovak authorities by private means only, thereby creating the impression that it supported the Czechoslovak standpoint.[92] This accusation troubled Halifax who considered making a speech himself, redressing the balance but also repeating the warning to Germany.[93] In the event, the Foreign Secretary decided against such action, and no further public clarification was made of the British position. In terms of issuing a warning to Germany, however, the Lanark speech was ineffective. Ribbentrop certainly made a point of not taking the intended warning to heart and, as reported by Weizsäcker to Henderson on the latter's return to Berlin, remained convinced that Britain would not become militarily involved in the Czechoslovak crisis.[94]

The German Foreign Minister's professed confidence of British non-intervention was doubtless reinforced by the remarks of one of Chamberlain's closest advisers. Only four days before the Lanark speech, Horace Wilson, in conversation with the German Chargé d'Affaires in London, Theodor Kordt, made private observations of a very different nature from Simon's public utterances. Reporting to Berlin on the wide-ranging discussion of German–British relations held at the house of an active pro-German sympathiser, Philip Conwell-Evans, on 23 August, Kordt noted Wilson's view that the present position of Czechoslovakia was 'unnatural and absurd' and also his hope that a peaceful resolution of this question might lead to a more extensive understanding between Britain and Germany. Kordt's record of Wilson's observations continued:

> The Führer had used the simile to an Englishman (he thought it was Lord Halifax) that European culture rested on two pillars which must be linked by a powerful arch: Great Britain and Germany. Great Britain and

> Germany were in fact the two countries in which the greatest order reigned and which were the best governed. Both were built up on the national principle, which had been designed by nature itself as the only working principle of human relationship. The reverse of this, Bolshevism, meant anarchy and barbarism. It would be the height of folly if these two leading white races were to exterminate each other in war. Bolshevism would be the only gainer thereby.[95]

These sentiments must have come like music to the ears of the German government, all the more so as they originated from someone who was, in Kordt's words, 'one of the most influential men in the British Government' and to whom Chamberlain turned for advice 'on all matters'. Remarks such as these certainly did nothing to alert Germany to the possibility of Britain coming to the aid of Czechoslovakia, particularly when coupled with a hint that the British government was preparing for the failure of the Runciman Mission and that a decisive step towards improving British–German relations might result.[96]

Within two days however, Wilson had cause to revise his estimation of Runciman's prospects. When Ashton-Gwatkin returned by air to London for consultations on the evening of 24 August, the news he brought was much better than expected. Runciman's chief assistant spent two days in London discussing the progress of the Mission. His most important meeting was held in the Foreign Office on the morning of 25 August with Halifax, Vansittart, Sargent and Oliphant. Also present were Simon and Wilson.[97] The main outcome of the talks was to deflect attention, for the moment at least, away from the possibility of Runciman acting as an arbitrator in the Czechoslovak crisis, focusing it instead on a very different role for the British mediator.

Ashton-Gwatkin reported on the Mission's activities to date in generally optimistic terms, dividing the problems facing Runciman into three categories. As far as the main constitutional issue was concerned, that of providing some degree of autonomy for the Sudeten Germans, Ashton-Gwatkin was able to report that negotiations were about to commence on the new basis of Beneš's Third Plan, which, he stated, was considered 'rather favourably, on the whole' by the SdP. The political aspect of the crisis involved the future of Czechoslovakia and that of peace in Europe. Regarding the former, Ashton-Gwatkin indicated that the question of Czechoslovakia's foreign policy orientation would be included in the forthcoming discussions between the government and the SdP. On the wider question of European peace, he reported that Henlein was willing, 'if we ask him', to visit Hitler in order to promote an 'Anglo-Franco-German settlement'. The third element was the considerable economic distress of the Sudeten German areas. Ashton-Gwatkin stated that this aspect of the crisis had been brought to the attention of the Mission but that there had been insufficient time to examine it in any detail.[98]

Ashton-Gwatkin then turned to possible future developments. On the constitutional side, if the negotiations made good progress, he foresaw the possibility of an agreement in principle being reached within ten days. If the talks failed, however, Runciman would 'have to intervene with advice' or 'with fresh suggestions', but, Ashton-Gwatkin added, arbitration was firmly ruled out by the mediator himself.[99] On the basis of this information, Halifax and his advisers decided that no intervention in the talks was required from the British government at that moment, apart from a 'telegram of encouragement' which the Foreign Secretary wished to address to Beneš[100] – but which was never sent. Ashton-Gwatkin also drew attention to the importance of withdrawing the Czechoslovak state police from German areas. They were a major irritant to the Germans yet, he conceded, could not be withdrawn without significantly weakening the authority of the government. Ashton-Gwatkin proposed, therefore, that consideration be given to replacing the state police by an international force similar to that deployed in the Saar in 1935. Such a force would not only give reassurance to both sides in the dispute but, it was hoped, would also enable Czechoslovakia to reduce its military preparations.[101] Runciman feared, however, that unspecified 'practical difficulties' would prevent the international agreement necessary to create the force in question.[102] These reservations were shared within the Foreign Office, where it was decided not to pursue the matter any further for the time being.[103]

Under the heading of political developments, Ashton-Gwatkin urged consideration of the possible neutralisation of Czechoslovakia either with or without external guarantees. Such a step would, of necessity, involve the renunciation of Czechoslovakia's treaty with France and the Soviet Union which, he believed, was now under consideration by Beneš. He also suggested that the question of neutralisation, and possibly also that of the creation of the international policing force, might be referred to a conference of interested powers.[104] The Foreign Office was not averse to this idea, particularly as a means of satisfying the possible demand from the Czechoslovak government for international guarantees to protect its neutral status.[105] Possible developments in the economic field outlined by Ashton–Gwatkin were a new external loan to Czechoslovakia to assist in charitable relief and in a programme of public works, and also the reduction of the interest rate on an existing loan. In addition, in the longer term, he envisaged the possible creation of a Czechoslovak-German customs union.[106] The Foreign Office noted these ideas without comment.

Ashton-Gwatkin's progress report was well received by the select audience and he noted with satisfaction 'they seem very pleased with our performance so far'.[107] Wilson reported to the Prime Minister that the meeting had 'turned out to be more pleasant than anyone expected' and that he had found Ashton-Gwatkin's report 'surprisingly encouraging'.[108]

Halifax was also pleased by the account of the Mission's work, which he considered 'most interesting' and, he hoped, 'useful'.[109] News of the agreed new basis for negotiations came as a particularly agreeable surprise to those listening. Halifax found this development 'more encouraging than he had expected' as, in his view, it completely changed the situation.[110] Wilson was also much encouraged by the new formula for talks, which he saw as 'a very considerable advance on the part of the Czechs', and he noted with satisfaction that, providing this progress was maintained, Runciman could make 'some pronouncement in hopeful terms before Nuremberg'. It was conceded by Wilson, however, that any further progress was dependent on Hitler's goodwill, but, in view of the magnitude of the concessions made by the Czechoslovak side, he believed it was possible that Hitler would take a 'favourable view'.[111] After a prolonged period of mounting anxiety in London concerning events in Central Europe, it came as a welcome relief to hear directly from Runciman's chief assistant that a resolution of the vexed Sudeten German problem appeared, at last, in prospect.

Meanwhile, events in Prague did not stand still during Ashton-Gwatkin's absence, and the remaining Mission staff continued with their activities. Whilst in London Ashton-Gwatkin lunched with Wilson following the Foreign Office meeting, and received praise for his good work,[112] his colleagues in the Czechoslovak capital had the previous evening also been mixing business with pleasure when Stopford, Henderson and Peto attended a *Bier-Abend* hosted by the SdP negotiating team and Frank. The evening was a convivial one and, in Stopford's words, 'ended on a very friendly note'. Alternate drinks of beer and neat brandy served even to break down the reserve of the otherwise austere Frank.[113] The potent combination of alcoholic beverages may also have been responsible for Kundt's candid disclosure to Stopford that there were, in reality, two parts to the problem confronting the Runciman Mission. The first element, concerning the future of the Sudeten Germans, was an internal matter, to be settled between the German minority and the Prague government. The second aspect concerned Czechoslovakia's foreign policy orientation. So long as that country remained allied to France and the Soviet Union – and particularly to the latter – there would be no prospect of improved relations between Prague and Berlin. This problem, Kundt stated, could only be settled by the four great powers (Germany, Britain, France and Italy) on the basis of the neutralisation of Czechoslovakia.[114]

Although Kundt's statement of the double nature of the current crisis was substantially no different from what Henlein had told Ashton-Gwatkin at their Marienbad meeting, Stopford's report of his conversation caused a flurry of concern in London. It was feared that Kundt's remarks implied that the SdP regarded the solution of the Sudeten German problem as being contingent on Czechoslovakia's international realignment. This would have amounted to a significant departure from the assurances given by Henlein himself during his last visit to London. The concern felt in the Foreign Office was relayed by telegraph to the Mission in Prague by Ashton-Gwatkin, who, in addition to rebuking Stopford for allowing Kundt to widen the issue in that way, instructed the Mission staff to remind the SdP of Henlein's undertaking not to link the internal and external problems should the matter be raised again.[115] Stopford, who considered the reprimand to be somewhat out of place in view of the recent conversation between Ashton-Gwatkin and Henlein,[116] sought to reassure the Foreign Office that Kundt had not in fact stipulated new preconditions for a settlement but merely indicated 'what would remain to be done ... to secure friendly German–Czech relations' following the resolution of the internal problem.[117]

Back in London, the one element of Ashton-Gwatkin's progress report that generated most interest was his recommendation that advantage should be taken of Henlein's 'offer' to visit Hitler in order to improve relations between Britain and Germany. Wilson explained the plan to the Prime Minister:

> It is proposed ... that Henlein should go to see Hitler before Nuremberg and should tell him that he, Henlein, is impressed by the fair-mindedness of the English (as represented by Runciman) and with their evident desire to assist in a satisfactory settlement of the Sudeten question. He would go on to say that he feels that we are friendly disposed not merely to the Sudetens but to Germany and he will say that in his opinion the line which has been worked out is the best one and should be accepted. He proposes to add that in his view acceptance could be regarded as the first step in improved Anglo-German relations. He would then appeal to Hitler to be reasonable in what he may say at Nuremberg.[118]

Although the Foreign Office meeting approved the idea of using the SdP leader's services as an intermediary with Berlin, a more direct approach from Britain was also considered desirable. Recent experience in that connection, however, had not been encouraging. But despite the conspicuous lack of success of the memorandum of 11 August addressed to Hitler, the view persisted in London that if only contact could be established with the German leader directly, a more favourable outcome would result. As Halifax subsequently explained to Runciman, he remained convinced that the responsibility for the failure lay with the 'hostile and obstructive forces' in the German Foreign Ministry and believed that in order to circumvent that barrier a new channel of communication between London and Berlin was required, one 'so authoritative' that it would overcome any obstacles encountered.[119]

One obvious means of achieving this objective was to send a special emissary to Hitler. Such a step was under active consideration by Chamberlain and his advisers before Ashton-Gwatkin's return to London.

On 23 August, two days before the Foreign Office meeting, Wilson alluded to this possibility during his conversation with Kordt, but did not indicate who the emissary might be.[120] It is possible though that the British already had a definite candidate in mind – namely Runciman – for that was the suggestion that emerged from the Foreign Office meeting with Ashton-Gwatkin. The idea of sending Runciman on a further mission to Berlin did not originate with Wilson, who was far from enthusiastic about it,[121] or with the Foreign Office, but with Simon.[122] Ashton-Gwatkin readily gave his support to the proposal and expressed confidence that Henlein would agree to his projected visit to Hitler being followed up in this way.[123] Runciman himself (as mentioned previously) was thinking along similar lines about sending a British special envoy to Berlin – though without putting himself forward for the task, which he envisaged being undertaken by someone like Rumbold. But that suggestion was either not raised or it failed to find favour with those present at the Foreign Office meeting. It was envisaged, of course, that Runciman would approach Hitler not directly on behalf of the British government but in his capacity as an independent mediator. The main objective of his proposed new assignment, in addition to reinforcing the message which Henlein was to take to Berlin, would be to inform Hitler of the progress of the Runciman Mission, in Wilson's words, 'in the hope that it might thereby be made more difficult for Hitler to interrupt the progress of the negotiations by his Nuremburgh [*sic*] speech'.[124]

Although when informing Runciman of his proposed new task Halifax stated that the idea of sending him to Berlin had been approved unanimously at the Foreign Office meeting as being 'the only really promising course' available,[125] at least one person recalled matters somewhat differently. In his report to Chamberlain, Wilson indicated that during the lengthy discussion of this point 'some risks' were identified, although in view of the optimistic reports from Czechoslovakia these were much reduced. Nevertheless it was, he believed, 'impossible to decide for or against the proposal until more [was] known of the results of the talks' now getting under way in Prague. Consequently, on his return to Czechoslovakia, Ashton-Gwatkin would first ascertain from Henlein how the negotiations had progressed and whether the SdP leader would undertake the proposed visit to Hitler, and then decide whether Runciman should follow.[126] Despite Wilson's reservations, however, the Foreign Office decided to act without delay and proceeded to draft a lengthy message for Runciman.[127] Doubtless delighted with the honour bestowed on his superior, Ashton-Gwatkin telephoned Stopford in Prague that evening to forewarn of the coming telegrams and to urge their immediate decoding as a reply was required in London by noon the following day. When Stopford passed the information to Runciman, he hazarded a guess that the messages from London would urge Runciman to travel to Berlin to see Hitler.[128]

The arrival of the telegrams confirmed Stopford's conjecture. Halifax expressed satisfaction with the Mission's achievements coupled with the hope that the new basis for negotiations would result in a peaceful outcome, but believed it essential to gain German support for this and, in particular, to discourage Hitler from making an intemperate speech at Nuremberg. It was therefore considered necessary to issue a new appeal to Hitler, but it was feared in London that such a move, coming directly from the British government, might be counter-productive and interfere with the Mission's activities. 'In these circumstances', Halifax explained to Runciman, 'I am convinced that you are yourself the most suitable and in fact the only person who can successfully appeal direct to Hitler in the present situation.' Henlein would also be encouraged to see Hitler, but in view of the danger perceived by Halifax, of his being subjected to 'strong ... pressure of a negative character', it was essential for Runciman to move without delay.[129] In order to expedite matters, Halifax even supplied the text of a telegram for Runciman to send to Hitler:

> Your Excellency, I hope that I may count on your sympathetic support in the efforts I am making to help in the search for a satisfactory settlement of the Sudeten German question. I believe that recent developments offer an opportunity for such a settlement if it is quickly taken. I should be grateful therefore if Your Excellency would allow me to call upon you as soon as convenient to you in order that before the Parteitag I may have the honour of explaining to you personally my views on the situation as it now presents itself.[130]

Runciman, far from happy with the idea, turned to Stopford for advice. He also had considerable misgivings, fearing the proposal would destroy the negotiations in Czechoslovakia. Stopford expressed his reservations in a brief five-point memorandum arguing:

1. it would ruin [Runciman's] position in Czechoslovakia as a mediator between the Czechs and the Sudetens,
2. it would broaden his duties as a mediator out of all recognition,
3. it would put him in a false position as middleman between Beneš and Hitler, without having any supporting authority behind him,
4. failure would ruin the chances of any favourable solution of the problem,
5. if war followed, Great Britain would be morally committed to taking part.

The matter was further discussed between Runciman and Newton later in the day. Despite Newton urging acceptance, Runciman resolutely refused, citing Stopford's five reasons and adding a sixth of his own: 'I'm just not going to do it.'[131] Runciman's negative response, explaining that after careful consideration he had concluded that 'the disadvantages of a personal approach by me definitely outweigh the advantages', was immediately conveyed to London. His reasoning was again based on the arguments supplied by Stopford to which Runciman added a further pertinent point, that the SdP negotiations were unlikely to have 'neglected the German factor' or that negotiations would have recommenced against the wishes of Hitler.[132]

News of Runciman's refusal to undertake the new assignment caused disappointment in London, and Ashton-Gwatkin noted with dismay in his diary that 'the Lord has cold feet', adding, 'I must try to warm him up tomorrow'.[133] On his return to Prague by air in the early afternoon of the following day, 27 August, he at once set about attempting to persuade his superior to change his mind. But Runciman remained adamant, leaving Ashton-Gwatkin to record disconsolately, 'he is not to be warmed up'.[134] In addition to the stated reasons for Runciman's refusal to undertake the journey to Berlin, two further factors influenced his decision. The first was Runciman's health. With his mind burdened by the consciousness of the heavy responsibility for peace that he bore, the 67-year-old mediator was beginning to suffer under the strain of the negotiations. The tensions of the political situation combined with the oppressive heat of Prague in August caused Runciman insomnia.[135] He probably concluded, therefore, that he had enough problems to contend with without adding the new venture. The second factor was his irritation by what he saw as the British Government's interference in his ostensibly independent activities. Stopford recalled that when being pressed by Ashton-Gwatkin to undertake the visit to Hitler, Runciman exclaimed with evident exasperation: 'This Government! When they get themselves into a mess, they have to come to a discarded Cabinet Minister to try to get them out of it!'[136]

The matter did not end there, however, for Runciman's refusal to undertake the journey to Berlin was soon to have momentous repercussions. Within a matter of days, Chamberlain and Wilson had conceived an alternative plan. This new idea, which the Prime Minister nevertheless hoped would prove unnecessary, was, in his words, 'so unconventional and daring that it rather took Halifax's breath away'.[137] But Henderson, who had not yet returned to Berlin, responded more encouragingly. When he was informed of the proposal in the strictest confidence on 30 August, he observed (as Chamberlain noted) that 'it might save the situation at the 11th hour'.[138] The object of the new plan, code-named 'Plan Z', was for the Prime Minister himself to undertake the visit to Hitler that Runciman had refused.

Notes

1 Halifax to Runciman, 18 August 1938, *DBFP*, 3/II, no. 643.
2 Halifax to Runciman, 29 July 1938, Runciman Papers, WR 292.

3 Halifax to Runciman, 18 August 1938, *DBFP*, 3/II, no. 643.
4 Runciman to Halifax, 10 August 1938, *DBFP*, 3/II, no. 602.
5 Halifax to Runciman, 18 August 1938, *DBFP*, 3/II, no. 643.
6 *Ibid.*
7 See above pp. 137–8.
8 Halifax to Runciman, 18 August 1938, *DBFP*, 3/II, no. 643.
9 Memorandum by Roberts, June 1938, C 6108/1941/18, FO 371/21725.
10 Minute by Sargent[?], undated, C 8510/1941/18, FO 371/21732.
11 Halifax to Runciman, 18 August 1938, *DBFP*, 3/II, no. 643.
12 Minute by Sargent[?], undated, C 8510/1941/18, FO 371/21732.
13 Halifax to Runciman, 18 August 1938, *DBFP*, 3/II, no. 643.
14 Minute by Sargent[?], undated, C 8510/1941/18, FO 371/21732.
15 Halifax to Runciman, 18 August 1938, *DBFP*, 3/II, no. 643.
16 Henderson to Halifax, 22 July 1938, *DBFP*, 3/I, no. 532.
17 Memorandum by Vansittart, 25 July 1938, C 7375/1941/18, FO 371/21729.
18 Minute by Halifax, 25 July 1938, *ibid.*
19 Strang to Henderson, 30 July 1938, see note 3 to document no. 532, *DBFP*, 3/I, p. 614.
20 Henderson to Strang, 2 August 1938, *DBFP*, 3/II, no. 568.
21 Halifax to Runciman, 18 August 1938, *DBFP*, 3/II, no. 643.
22 Colvin, in *Vansittart in Office*, p. 231, suggests that Henderson resorted to writing privately to Halifax in order to avoid the 'devastating minutes' that Sargent and Vansittart attached to his official despatches.
23 Henderson to Halifax, 26 July 1938, *DBFP*, 3/II, no. 551.
24 Henderson to Halifax, 1 August 1938, *DBFP*, 3/II, no. 564.
25 Henderson to Halifax, 3 August 1938, *DBFP*, 3/II, no. 573.
26 Henderson to Halifax, 15 August 1938, *DBFP*, 3/II, no. 627.
27 Henderson to Halifax, 6 August 1938, *DBFP*, 3/II, no. 590.
28 Henderson to Halifax, 12 August 1938, *DBFP*, 3/II, no. 613.
29 Henderson to Halifax, 6 August 1938, *DBFP*, 3/II, no. 590.
30 Henderson to Halifax, 12 August 1938, *DBFP*, 3/II, no. 613.
31 Henderson to Halifax, 12, 15, 22 (twice), 23 and 25 August 1938, *DBFP*, 3/II, nos 613, 627, 662, 665, 672, 689.
32 Henderson to Halifax, 12 August 1938, *DBFP*, 3/II, no. 613.
33 Henderson to Halifax, 25 August 1938, *DBFP*, 3/II, no. 689.
34 Henderson to Halifax, 17 August 1938, Halifax Papers, H/VI/37, FO 800/309. See also note 2 to document no. 638, *DBFP*, 3/II, p. 108.
35 Henderson to Halifax, 22 August 1938, *DBFP*, 3/II, no. 665.
36 Henderson to Halifax, 23 August 1938, *DBFP*, 3/II, no. 672. (Original emphasis.)
37 *Ibid.*
38 Henderson to Halifax, 19 and 22 (twice) August 1938, *DBFP*, 3/II, nos 647, 665, 666. The British Military Attaché in Berlin, Mason-MacFarlane, was somewhat less categorical in his assessment of Germany's military preparations but nevertheless shared his Ambassador's pessimistic view of the situation. (See report by Mason-MacFarlane, 24 August 1938, in Henderson to Halifax, 25 August 1938, *DBFP*, 3/II, no. 692.)
39 Henderson to Halifax, 6, 8, 17 (twice), 19, 22 (three times), 23 and 25 August 1938, *DBFP*, 3/II, nos 590, 594, 633, 634, 647, 662, 665, 666, 672, 689.
40 Henderson to Halifax, 4 August 1938, *DBFP*, 3/II, no. 577.
41 Henderson to Halifax, 17 August 1938, *DBFP*, 3/II, no. 633.

42 Henderson to Halifax, 19 August 1938, *DBFP*, 3/II, no. 647.
43 Henderson to Halifax, 22 August 1938, *DBFP*, 3/II, no. 666.
44 Henderson to Halifax, 22 August 1938, *DBFP*, 3/II, no. 662.
45 Henderson to Halifax, 12 August 1938, *DBFP*, 3/II, no. 613.
46 Henderson to Halifax, 22 August 1938, *DBFP*, 3/II, no. 665.
47 In November, Henderson underwent an operation for cancer of the tongue. (Dilks, ed., *Cadogan Diaries*, p. 124.)
48 Henderson to Halifax, 17 August 1938, Halifax Papers, H/VI/37, FO 800/309. In this letter, Henderson also conjured up the following improbable scenario which might follow if Runciman took the 'right course' of recommending autonomy for the Sudetenland: 'You could march the Guards up "Unter den Linden" tomorrow and they would get the reception of their lives: and you would have British mediation sought by every country in Europe. There would not be enough Runcimans to go round: and you would get the whole Empire's approval. But dreams never come true and we miserable ants will go on running our heads against stone walls and getting nowhere until Fate relentlessly steps in and teaches us a lesson.' The editors of *Documents of British Foreign Policy* omitted these passages from the abbreviated version of the letter which only gained inclusion as a footnote. (See note 2 to document no. 638, *DBFP*, 3/II, p. 108.)
49 Henderson to Halifax, 17 August 1938, Halifax Papers, H/VI/39, FO 800/309.
50 Halifax to Henderson, 18 August 1938, Halifax Papers, H/VI/40, FO 800/309.
51 Memorandum (unsigned), 22 August 1938, C 9023/1941/18, FO 371/21734.
52 Minute by Mallet, 19 August 1938, C 8435/1941/18, FO 371/21731.
53 Minute by Roberts, 22 August 1938, C 8587/1941/18, FO 371/21732.
54 Memorandum by Sargent, 22 August 1938, C 9023/1941/18, FO 371/21734. The other information in question came from Ewald von Kleist, see below p. 199.
55 Memorandum by Sargent, 22 August 1938, C 9023/1941/18, FO 371/21734.
56 Henderson to Halifax, 19 August 1938, *DBFP*, 3/II, no. 649.
57 Minute by Sargent, 23 August 1938, C 8519/1941/18, FO 371/21732.
58 Copy of report from Air Attaché, Prague, 16 August 1938, in Chilvers to Caccia, C 8784/1941/18, FO 371/21733.
59 Memorandum by Ashton-Gwatkin, 24 August 1938, C 8852/1941/18, FO 371/21733. Ashton-Gwatkin's unnamed informant was Hohenlohe, who visited Berlin on 20 August.
60 Minute by Mallet, undated, *ibid.*
61 Minute by Roberts, 22 August 1938, C 8587/1941/18, FO 371/21732.
62 Halifax to Runciman, 18 August 1938, *DBFP*, 3/II, no. 643.
63 Henderson to Halifax, 11 August 1938, *DBFP*, 3/II, appendix I, pp. 646–7.
64 Runciman to Halifax, 18 August 1938, *DBFP*, 3/II, no. 644.
65 Halifax to Newton, 23 August 1938, *DBFP*, 3/II, no. 668.
66 Halifax to Henderson, 5 August 1938, *DBFP*, 3/II, no. 587.
67 Henderson to Newton, 24 August 1938, Halifax Papers, H/VI/47, FO 800/309. See also Henderson to Newton, 11 August 1938, Halifax Papers, H/VI/35, FO 800/309 and note 3 to document no. 643, *DBFP*, 3/II, pp. 112–13.
68 Runciman to Halifax, 24 August 1938, *DBFP*, 3/II, no. 680.
69 Ashton-Gwatkin's diary, 24 August 1938, FO 800/304.
70 See Ashton-Gwatkin's advice in 'Note of a Conversation between Ashton-Gwatkin and Henlein on 22 August', 23 August 1938, *DBFP*, 3/II, appendix II (I), pp. 657–9.

71 Newton to Halifax, 24 August 1938, *DBFP*, 3/II, no. 677.
72 Halifax to Newton, 25 August 1938, *DBFP*, 3/II, no. 686.
73 Memorandum by Halifax, enclosed in Halifax to Henderson, 11 August 1938, *DBFP*, 3/II, no. 608.
74 Minute by Woermann, 13 August 1938, *DGFP*, D/II, no. 354; Henderson to Halifax, 13 August 1938, *DBFP*, 3/II, no. 620.
75 Note of a conversation between Vansittart and von Kleist, 18 August 1938, *DBFP*, 3/II, appendix IV (i), pp. 683–6.
76 Chamberlain to Halifax, 19 August 1938, *DBFP*, 3/II, appendix IV (ii), pp. 686–7.
77 Halifax to Henderson, 24 August 1938, *DBFP*, 3/II, no. 678.
78 Henderson to Halifax, 21 August 1938, *DBFP*, 3/II, no. 658. Mason-MacFarlane had also reported similar information from another source four days previously.
79 Halifax to Shone (Bled), 23 August 1938, *DBFP*, 3/II, no. 670. See also Shone to Halifax, 23 and 25 August 1938, *DBFP*, 3/II, nos 667, 682, and Newton to Halifax, 25 August 1938, *DBFP*, 3/II, no. 683.
80 Henderson to Halifax, 20 August 1938, *DBFP*, 3/II, no. 653, and Campbell to Halifax, 20 August 1938, *DBFP*, 3/II, no. 655.
81 Halifax to Campbell, 25 August 1938, *DBFP*, 3/II, no. 691; Bonnet to Cambon, 23 August 1938, *DDF*, 2/X, no. 439; Cambon to Bonnet, 25 August 1938, *DDF*, 2/X, no. 455.
82 Halifax to Campbell, 25 August 1938, *DBFP*, 3/II, no. 691.
83 Minute by Sargent, 27 August 1938, C 8792/1941/18, FO 371/21733.
84 Cambon to Sargent, 26 August 1938, *DBFP*, 3/II, no. 699.
85 Minute by Mallet, 27 August 1938, C 8792/1941/18, FO 371/21733.
86 *The Times*, 29 August 1938; Halifax to Newton, 27 August 1938, *DBFP*, 3/II, no. 704.
87 Minute by Sargent, 30 August 1938, C 8792/1941/18, FO 371/21733.
88 Hoyer-Millar to Hardinge, 26 August 1938, Halifax Papers, H/VI/57, FO 800/309.
89 *HC Deb.*, 333, cols 1399–407, 24 March 1938.
90 Halifax to Campbell, 31 August 1938, *DBFP*, 3/II, no. 729. Report of conversation with French Ambassador.
91 Newton to Halifax, 30 August 1938, *DBFP*, 3/II, no. 719.
92 Kirkpatrick to Halifax, 30 August 1938, *DBFP*, 3/II, no. 718.
93 Halifax to Henderson and Newton, 1 September 1938, *DBFP*, II, no. 737.
94 Henderson to Halifax, 1 September 1938, *DBFP*, 3/II, no. 736.
95 Kordt to Weizsäcker, 23 August 1938, and enclosed memorandum, *DGFP*, D/II, no. 382. It is ironic that Kordt's purpose was to warn the British government of Hitler's intentions. See P. Meehan, *The Unnecessary War: Whitehall and the German Resistance to Hitler*, (London, 1992), pp. 150–1.
96 Kordt to Weizsäcker, 23 August 1938, and enclosed memorandum, *DGFP*, D/II, no. 382.
97 Ashton-Gwatkin's diary, 25 August 1938, FO 800/304. No formal minute was kept of the proceedings although Wilson reported on the meeting to the Prime Minister in a lengthy letter. (Wilson to Chamberlain, 25 August 1938, PREM 1/265, ff. 194–8.)
98 Memorandum by Ashton-Gwatkin, 'Sudeten German Question and the Runciman Mission', 24 August 1938, C 8955/1941/18, FO 371/21733. See also Halifax to Henderson, 26 August 1938, *DBFP*, 3/II, no. 696.

99 Memorandum by Ashton-Gwatkin, 'Sudeten German Question and the Runciman Mission', 24 August 1938, C 8955/1941/18, FO 371/21733. The second section of this memorandum is printed in *DBFP*, 3/II, appendix II (II), pp. 660–1.
100 Minute by Mallet, 25 August 1938, C 8955/1941/18, FO 371/21733.
101 Memorandum by Ashton-Gwatkin, 'Sudeten German Question and the Runciman Mission', 24 August 1938, *ibid.*
102 Note by Ashton-Gwatkin, 25 August 1938, *ibid.*
103 Minute by Mallet, 25 August 1938, *ibid.*
104 Memorandum by Ashton-Gwatkin, 'Sudeten German Question and the Runciman Mission', 24 August 1938, *ibid.*
105 Minute by Mallet, 25 August 1938, *ibid.*
106 Memorandum by Ashton-Gwatkin, 'Sudeten German Question and the Runciman Mission', 24 August 1938, *ibid.*
107 Ashton-Gwatkin's diary, 25 August 1938, FO 800/304.
108 Wilson to Chamberlain, 25 August 1938, PREM 1/265, ff. 194–8.
109 Minute by Halifax, 26 August 1938, C 8955/1941/18, FO 371/21733.
110 Halifax to Newton, 25 August 1938, *DBFP*, 3/II, no. 685.
111 Wilson to Chamberlain, 25 August 1938, PREM 1/265, ff. 194–8.
112 Ashton-Gwatkin's diary, 25 August 1938, FO 800/304.
113 Note by Stopford, enclosed in Ashton-Gwatkin to Strang, 29 August 1938, *DBFP*, 3/II, appendix II (III), p. 667. Stopford recalled in his memoir that during the course of the evening an argument broke out between SdP representatives from the Egerland (Chebsko), led by Frank, and the 'more moderate' members from elsewhere in Bohemia. At a suitable moment, Stopford intervened in jest with an offer to mediate between them. (Stopford, 'Prague, 1938-39', p. 33.)
114 Stopford to Ashton-Gwatkin in Newton to Halifax, 25 August 1938, *DBFP*, 3/II, no. 681.
115 Ashton-Gwatkin to Stopford, in Halifax to Newton, 25 August 1938, *DBFP*, 3/II, no. 688.
116 Stopford, 'Prague, 1938–1939', p. 34.
117 Stopford to Ashton-Gwatkin, in Newton to Halifax, 26 August 1938, C 8794/1941/18, FO 371/21733.
118 Wilson to Chamberlain, 25 August 1938, PREM 1/265, ff. 194–8.
119 Halifax to Newton, 25 August 1938, *DBFP*, 3/II, no. 686.
120 Kordt to Weizsäcker, 23 August 1938, *DGFP*, D/II, no. 382.
121 Wilson to Chamberlain, 25 August 1938, PREM 1/265, ff. 194–8.
122 Inskip diary extracts, 30 August 1938, Caldecote Papers, Churchill College, Cambridge, INKP 1. It is unclear whether the proposal emerged during the course of the Foreign Office meeting or in advance of it.
123 Wilson to Chamberlain, 25 August 1938, PREM 1/265, ff. 194–8.
124 *Ibid.*
125 Halifax to Newton, 25 August 1938, *DBFP*, 3/II, no. 686.
126 Wilson to Chamberlain, 25 August 1938, PREM 1/265, ff. 194–8.
127 Ashton-Gwatkin's diary, 25 August 1938, FO 800/304.
128 Stopford, 'Prague 1938–1939', p. 34.
129 Halifax to Newton, 25 August 1938, *DBFP*, 3/II, no. 686.
130 Halifax to Newton, 25 August 1938, *DBFP*, 3/II, no. 687.
131 Stopford, 'Prague 1938–1939', pp. 35–6. Stopford added that Newton 'loyally carried out his instructions; but I think that he really sympathised with Runciman's attitude'.

132 Newton to Halifax, 26 August 1938, *DBFP*, 3/II, no. 695.
133 Ashton-Gwatkin's diary, 26 August 1938, FO 800/304.
134 Ashton-Gwatkin's diary, 27 August 1938, FO 800/304.
135 Runciman to Halifax, 18 August 1938, *DBFP*, 3/II, no. 644.
136 Stopford, 'Prague 1938–1939', p. 36.
137 Neville Chamberlain to Ida Chamberlain, 3 September 1938, Chamberlain Papers, NC 18/1/1066.
138 Memorandum by Wilson, 30 August 1938, PREM 1/266A; Neville Chamberlain to Ida Chamberlain, 3 September 1938, Chamberlain Papers, NC 18/1/1066.

10
Mounting Despair

Ashton-Gwatkin's visit to London marked a watershed in the activities of the Runciman Mission. His return to Prague on 27 August signalled the opening of a new phase in the work of the Mission – one in which London was to play a much more active part than hitherto. As the fear of war over Czechoslovakia intensified, the pretence of Runciman's independence was rapidly abandoned and Halifax and his colleagues began increasingly to seek to influence the outcome of the Mission's work. This is evident from the greater frequency of communications between London and Prague, which is not entirely accounted for by the ending of the holiday season. From the time of his arrival in Prague on 3 August to Ashton-Gwatkin's return to London three weeks later, Runciman received only two direct messages from London. Following Ashton-Gwatkin's return to Prague the telegrams from London began arriving almost daily. This change was brought about by the increasingly menacing international situation. With Germany in a heightened state of military preparedness and the much feared Nazi Party Rally at Nuremberg approaching ever closer, the British government was anxiously seeking some positive results from the Runciman Mission.

Indeed, Ashton-Gwatkin returned to Prague with several urgent objectives resulting directly from his Foreign Office consultations – in addition to the unsuccessful attempt at persuading Runciman to reconsider his refusal to visit Hitler. The most immediate task was for Runciman to issue a new warning to Beneš, emphasising the extreme gravity of the international situation. Within hours of Ashton-Gwatkin's return, Runciman called on the President, implored him 'to go to the limit of concessions ... and even beyond' to satisfy the SdP and urged him to publish his latest proposals – the Third Plan – without delay.[1]

These proposals, which essentially conceded the creation of German self-governing areas within Czechoslovakia, formed the basis of renewed discussions between the government and the SdP that had recommenced three days previously, on 24 August, when Beneš and Hodža secretly met

Kundt and Sebekowsky at the Prague Castle. The exploratory talks were resumed the next day (without Hodža) concentrating on clarifying and developing the proposals earlier outlined by Beneš, who undertook to prepare a detailed memorandum that might serve as a basis for an agreement.[2] Meanwhile, both parties reported to Runciman that some progress had been achieved. He, nevertheless, remained doubtful whether the negotiators would secure the support of their own sides for any agreement.[3] Runciman's scepticism was confirmed by Beneš, who disclosed that although satisfactory progress had been made with Kundt and Sebekowsky, the points agreed had yet to be endorsed by the SdP leadership as a whole. Despite this, Beneš claimed to be optimistic. He planned to meet Kundt again on 30 August and hoped to be able to publish his proposals shortly thereafter. But it was not only the SdP that was reserving its position. The President also confided in Runciman that he too was experiencing difficulties in controlling his own side, but that the threat of an appeal to the British mediator provided an effective restraining influence.[4]

Alas, Runciman's presence did not exert nearly the same salutary effect on some prominent members of the SdP. On 26 August, the day following the second of the new round of meetings between Beneš and SdP representatives, a manifesto appeared declaring that, in view of recent provocations by 'Marxist terrorists', SdP followers would no longer practise restraint but would resort to self-defence, within legal limits, when attacked. The declaration was signed by Henlein's deputy, Frank, and an SdP parliamentary representative, Fritz Köllner.[5] The appearance of this manifesto, which was hardly calculated to exert a calming influence on an already tense situation – and which came as a complete surprise even to the SdP negotiators[6] – caused concern to the British mediators who considered its publication at best inopportune and possibly a deliberate attempt on behalf of Frank to disrupt the negotiations.[7] When Ashton-Gwatkin subsequently raised the matter with the SdP, Frank was found to be 'somewhat shamefaced' and Kundt 'definitely apologetic'. The explanation offered was that the manifesto had been drawn up in response to the Most incident of 16 August, but its publication inadvertently delayed by its appearing in a weekly newspaper. Frank assured Ashton-Gwatkin that it was not designed to wreck the new talks.[8]

Prior to this sign of increased SdP militancy, Ashton-Gwatkin carried out a further task resulting from his London consultations; he informed Henlein of the British government's positive response to his proposed visit to Hitler. This was carried out during a weekend visit by the Mission to the seat of another prominent aristocratic supporter of the SdP. On Saturday evening, 27 August, Lord and Lady Runciman, together with their daughter Margaret Fairweather (who had arrived from Britain for a short stay, piloting her own aircraft) and accompanied by Ashton-Gwatkin and Peto, travelled to the castle of Count Clary-Aldringen at Teplice in northern Bohemia.[9] After dinner, Ashton-Gwatkin left with Hohenlohe for Červený

Hrádek, where, for the second time, a meeting had been arranged with Henlein. Before leaving Teplice, Ashton-Gwatkin recalled that the Clary-Aldringens' castle had witnessed the signing of 'the first Holy Alliance', which caused him to imagine that the ghost of Metternich observed the present company 'rather contemptuously'.[10] The Austrian Chancellor's supposed disdain was surely undeserved, at least as far as Ashton-Gwatkin was concerned. His recently demonstrated capacity for diplomatic intrigue would doubtless have met with Metternich's full approval.

The following morning Ashton-Gwatkin met Frank, who had just returned from Berlin where he had discussed with Hitler Ashton-Gwatkin's suggestion that Henlein might mediate between Britain and Germany. Henlein's deputy had been alarmed by this initiative and reported earlier to Berlin that the issues raised were 'of far-reaching international importance which were dangerous for us'.[11] Frank was probably concerned by the prospect of increased British intervention restraining German freedom of action in Central Europe, but his fears appear to have been allayed by Hitler, who (according to Frank) expressed his determination to wage war against Czechoslovakia.[12] That information was, of course, not passed on to Ashton-Gwatkin, who was assured that Hitler desired a peaceful solution of the Sudeten German problem if it could be achieved without delay. Frank also indicated that Hitler would welcome a visit from Henlein, but with two preconditions. The SdP leader would have to bring a firm indication of Runciman's intention to base a solution on the SdP's Carlsbad programme and also a list of points that the British government desired to discuss with the German government with the object of improving mutual relations.[13] Ashton-Gwatkin was no doubt gratified by this response to his private diplomatic initiative, though perhaps also a little concerned about the wisdom of his candour with Henlein during their previous meeting, which the SdP leadership, with the connivance of Berlin, was now seeking to exploit. In the course of his consultations in London, Ashton-Gwatkin had not divulged to his Foreign Office colleagues the full extent of the encouragement he had given Henlein in Marienbad.

When Henlein arrived at Červený Hrádek later that morning, he confirmed his willingness to undertake the mission to Hitler 'for the sake of world peace' – but at a price. In view of the fact that a more quiescent Germany would weaken his position *vis-à-vis* the Czechoslovak authorities, who under less pressure would likely become more intransigent, he would require increased support from Britain. Henlein requested therefore that the British government should recommend to its Czechoslovak counterpart the adoption of the Carlsbad demands as a 'general basis for the solution of the Sudeten German question', although he would not insist on the Carlsbad programme being officially designated as such.[14] Ashton-Gwatkin judged these developments significant enough to justify bringing in Runciman, but indicated to Henlein that the matters under consideration would require a decision directly from the British government. Runciman came over to Červený Hrádek and during the afternoon, together with Ashton-Gwatkin, conferred with Henlein and Hohenlohe. The mediator's response to Henlein's new demands was predictably cautious. He confirmed the need to consult London and he also wished to discuss the issues with Beneš.[15]

Although Henlein had succeeded in significantly stepping up his demands, the British mediators did not seem in the least disquieted by this. Ashton-Gwatkin, in particular, did not disguise his satisfaction with the turn of events when reporting to Strang:

> The situation is, I think, clearer since we now have direct access to Hitler's intentions; and we know that if he can have the prestige and satisfaction of having secured for the Sudetens a settlement on the Karlsbad 8 Point basis, *there will be peace* – at any rate for this year.[16]

Ashton-Gwatkin was, of course, aware that if the Runciman Mission gave its support to the 'full demands' of the SdP, albeit only in 'general terms', it would be departing from the role of 'strict mediation' that had originally been envisaged by the British government. But as far as the Carlsbad programme itself was concerned, its eight points were, in his estimation, from the British point of view 'unobjectionable'. He admitted, however, that in the view of the Czechoslovak authorities they were 'disagreeable' but, he argued, 'since the Czechs in the end must give way, they should not strain at the Karlsbad gnats after swallowing the Home Rule camel'.

However, as Ashton-Gwatkin realised, some of the 'gnats' were problematical. During the discussions at Červený Hrádek, Frank had identified two points in particular as presenting difficulties. These were the recognition of the German *Volksgruppe* (national group), in order to protect the German population outside the main Sudeten areas, and the granting of *Rechtspersönlichkeit* (legal personality), both concepts which, Ashton-Gwatkin confessed, remained 'very obscure' to him. He also considered two further points to be problematical, the question of reparations and the delimitation of the autonomous German territory. The SdP was seeking a continuous area, whereas Beneš offered three separate districts.

More remarkable still than Ashton-Gwatkin's complete acceptance of the SdP's demands, as perfectly reasonable in the circumstances, was the fact that he appeared to swallow whole their partisan analysis of recent developments. He summarised the situation for Strang:

> 1. Hitler lost prestige seriously on May 21st.
> 2. He has to restore that prestige by announcing that his Sudeten brethren have recovered their freedom on their own terms (Karlsbad) and thanks to his protection.

3. He thought that the Runciman Mission was sent to delay settlement and play for time.
4. He therefore started sabre-rattling in order to frighten the Czechs (and the rest of the world) into accepting his solution; in this he was succeeding very well.
5. He did not, and does not, intend to make war; but a serious incident in Czechoslovakia might compel him to intervene.
6. This danger increases with every day that passes; and that is one reason why Hitler demands a *quick* settlement.
7. Meanwhile, the Sudeten Germans have reported that Lord Runciman is not playing for time and is not unfavourably disposed to their demands, and may be used as a lever to increase pressure on the Czechs.
8. Hitler would welcome this, if it is so, which he still doubts; he has therefore put this request to us through Henlein, in order to find out for certain.[17]

This account was offered by Ashton-Gwatkin not as Henlein's version of events, which it undoubtedly was, but as a true record of recent developments. Evidently, Henlein's charm and perceived integrity had again proved persuasive.

On the Mission's return to Prague, Ashton-Gwatkin reported the weekend conversations to London. He requested an immediate response to the points raised, as Henlein was standing by in readiness to travel at once to see Hitler.[18] Halifax telegraphed his reply that evening. It was uncharacteristically forthright and amounted to a strong disavowal of Ashton-Gwatkin's recent diplomatic manoeuvring. The Foreign Secretary was far from pleased with the outcome of the latest contact between the Mission and the SdP, particularly concerning Henlein's proposed visit to Berlin. He expressed surprise at the suggestion that Henlein should speak on behalf of the British government, stressing it 'would be quite unsuitable and might lead to all sorts of complications'. Halifax added that he had understood from Ashton-Gwatkin that the purpose of Henlein's mission would be 'to assure Hitler that in view of the new proposals made by Beneš he had renewed hopes of reaching an agreed settlement' and that 'he would ask for Hitler's approval and support' for negotiating on the new basis. He continued:

> As regards Anglo-German relations, I had never contemplated using Henlein for anything more than what was suggested in Mr. Gwatkin's memorandum of August 23, namely, that we were very ready for Henlein to tell Hitler that he believed Great Britain desired an Anglo-German agreement, and that he further believed that a settlement of the Czechoslovak question might well open the way for such an agreement. ... It would of course be out of the question for him to be the bearer of a list of subjects

> which His Majesty's Government would be prepared to discuss with Germany. That must, I think, be handled through official channels.[19]

The Foreign Secretary was equally displeased by Ashton-Gwatkin's disclosure to Henlein that an eminent British statesman might also be sent to Berlin to make a direct appeal to Hitler.[20] Halifax flatly denied the existence of such a plan and insisted that Henlein be disabused of any misapprehension on that point.[21]

Halifax was further disturbed by Henlein's second request, that Runciman accept the SdP's Carlsbad demands as a basis for a settlement. He failed to see how that assurance could be given to Hitler, as such a solution was unlikely to be acceptable to Beneš. Although conceding that this was a matter for the Mission to determine in the light of circumstances prevailing in the negotiations, Halifax advised Runciman that the most he could do would be to 'propose to assist both parties to reach a settlement on the basis both of the Karlsbad eight points *and* of Beneš' seven new proposals'. This advice was offered not out of consideration for the Czechoslovak authorities, but purely to avoid increasing direct British involvement in the crisis. Halifax reminded the mediator that the British government remained 'reluctant to pronounce upon the merits of any proposals' from either side in the dispute.

Halifax also registered surprise that Frank had made no reference to Beneš's Third Plan in his conversation with Ashton-Gwatkin, but supposed that Frank had either failed to inform Hitler of this development or had presented the President's plan as being without value. This assumed failure in communication could best be remedied, Halifax suggested, by the publication of the new Czechoslovak proposals, that being 'the only safe way to enable Hitler to form a true estimate of the extent of Beneš' recent concessions'. It was also considered important, of course, that this should be carried out in advance of the forthcoming Nuremberg Rally, at which the British feared a bellicose speech from Hitler. Halifax was confident that the publication of the Third Plan would not only demonstrate that progress was being achieved, but would also make 'intransigence on the part of Hitler more difficult'. Runciman was urged therefore to make immediate representations to Beneš to publish his new offer 'in its most generous and extended form', but preferably not in a tabulated and numbered arrangement which would make for easy comparison with the Carlsbad eight points. Should Runciman himself not wish to do so, Halifax authorised Newton to approach Beneš without delay.[22]

Ashton-Gwatkin's account of the latest conversations with SdP leaders, which met with displeasure in the Foreign Office, had been forwarded to London while Newton was away for the weekend.[23] When the British Minister returned to his desk at the Legation, he at once realised – before the receipt of the Foreign Secretary's admonitory telegram – the unacceptable nature of Frank's preconditions for Henlein's proposed visit to Berlin.

Newton immediately discussed the matter with Runciman, who sought to reassure Halifax that he had neither approved nor accepted the proposals in question. Runciman also made clear that he had not known in advance of Frank's intention to act as a preliminary intermediary with Hitler. The moral Newton drew from this experience was that in matters of British–Czechoslovak–German relations there were 'disadvantages and risks' if any other than a British intermediary were used.[24] This point struck a sympathetic chord with Sargent, who minuted: 'Indeed that was one of the arguments in favour of Lord Runciman going to see Hitler.'[25]

The second part of Newton's despatch, which relayed Runciman's willingness to accept the Carlsbad programme as a basis for a solution, was, however, much less to Sargent's liking. Runciman indicated that he saw 'nothing inherently impracticable' in his doing so, subject to the Carlsbad points 'being defined on suitable lines'. He also expressed a willingness to make that definition himself, if negotiations faltered, and to announce his intention of doing so in advance.[26] Sargent was astonished by this suggestion, observing:

> This surely would completely wreck the negotiations and in present circumstances be nothing short of an ultimatum to the Czech Government. Has Lord Runciman really considered what the effects of such an ultimatum would be (a) on the Czechs; (b) on the Sudeten; and (c) above all on Hitler himself just before the Parteitag.

Sargent conceded, however, that he might be misrepresenting Runciman's intentions. If Runciman was contemplating nothing more than speaking privately to Beneš in the sense indicated, that would be perfectly in keeping with the role of a mediator.[27] Mallet, however, was much less concerned by the proposal, presuming that Runciman would not have considered basing a solution on the Carlsbad programme had he not foreseen it being acceptable to both the Prague and Berlin governments.[28]

A further point in Newton's dispatch which caused comment in the Foreign Office was Runciman's suggestion that, in exchange for advising the Czechoslovak government to accept the substance of the Carlsbad programme, Britain should require some *quid pro quo* from Hitler.[29] Mallet doubted the wisdom of seeking this at that juncture, if what Runciman had in mind was some form of guarantee of Czechoslovak integrity. That could only be achieved, he believed, following the resolution of the problem of Czechoslovakia's foreign relations.[30] Sargent also envisaged the *quid pro quo* being a guarantee by Germany, which would be required by the Czechoslovak authorities in exchange for major concessions. This however, Sargent argued, was something for Runciman to negotiate in Prague, and possibly also personally with Hitler in Berlin, but not via the British government. It would be 'entirely wrong', he argued, for Britain to act as an intermediary between Runciman and Hitler.[31] Sargent's arguments found favour with the Foreign

Secretary, who duly authorised their incorporation into a draft telegram to Prague. In the event this was never sent, for meanwhile a further dispatch arrived from Newton in which Runciman reported his concurrence with Halifax's instructions concerning the response to Henlein's new demands and also the receipt of details of Beneš's Third Plan.[32]

The contacts between Beneš and the SdP, which had resumed on 24 August, continued in secrecy, although in an interview published in the London *Daily Telegraph*, on 26 August, Hodža gave a broad indication that new negotiations had been or were about to be initiated.[33] However, despite the fact that interim reports reaching Runciman from both sides were relatively optimistic, any progress achieved at the three meetings, held on 24, 25 and 30 August at the Prague Castle, soon proved illusory. The initial discussions between the President and Kundt and Sebekowsky, as reported by the SdP representatives, ranged widely over the nature of the Czechoslovak state and its nationalities problem, touching also on Czech–German relations within Austria-Hungary and, indirectly, even on the Hussite wars of the fifteenth century. As had been indicated in advance, the vexed question of Czechoslovakia's foreign policy was raised and Beneš explained that he sought a *modus vivendi* with Germany leading to 'good neighbourly relations' which would cause his country's treaty with the Soviet Union to 'lose all actuality'. Concerning the internal situation, Beneš assured his visitors that he sought a settlement of the nationalities dispute by 'evolutionary methods' and would facilitate such a solution by preparing the population for major concessions.[34]

Details of the President's new proposals – the Third Plan – were presented to the SdP representatives at the meeting on 30 August, Runciman having received a copy the previous evening.[35] When presenting the proposals to Kundt and Sebekowsky, Beneš stated that they amounted to the beginning of the practical fulfilment of the SdP's Carlsbad programme, although he did not himself wish to make that fact explicit to the Czechoslovak people. He would not object, however, to the SdP announcing that their demands had been satisfied. He also requested an unequivocal response by 2 September,[36] and warned the SdP representatives to take cognisance of the internal and external political consequences of their reaction. When later informing Runciman of this exchange, Kundt indicated that he understood the President to have been alluding to the possibility of resistance from the Czech population or army to further concessions being granted to the SdP and to the possibility of war.[37]

The Third Plan was drawn up in the form of a protocol of agreement based on the discussions of 24 August. It consisted of nine points:

1. The objectives were the complete and immediate resolution of the nationalities problem and the preservation of the sovereignty, integrity and unity of the state.

2. Each nationality to receive a proportionate share of government employment (Germans attaining this over a period of 8 to 10 years). Persons previously dismissed from government service to become eligible for re-employment. In districts with German majorities at least 50% of state officials to be German.
3. Funding for educational and cultural matters and for health and social services to be similarly divided.
4. A loan of 700 million crowns to be raised by the end of the year to assist depressed areas and industries (500 million reserved for Germans).
5. A reformed language law to grant equality to German and other minority languages.
6. Policing to be shared between state and local forces, and policing method in German areas to become progressively the same as that in Czech areas.
7. Local government reorganisation into autonomous districts to commence by 15 October. Autonomous representative bodies to be elected by proportional representation. Three districts were envisaged as preponderantly German.
8. Required legislation to be introduced in the forthcoming parliamentary session.
9. Both parties to seek an improved climate of tolerance and co-operation by curtailing propaganda.[38]

Runciman received these details of the Third Plan with very considerable disappointment. He was expecting the document to contain an amplification of the proposals which Beneš had outlined to Sander a fortnight previously and which had been distilled into the seven points given by Henlein to Ashton-Gwatkin in Marienbad on 22 August. In Runciman's estimation, however, the President failed to keep his word. He complained to Halifax the next day that far from expanding the new proposals, Beneš's memorandum seemed 'to dilute them and to put the whole advance back into the realm of academic principles'.[39] Runciman was particularly dismayed that the plan, being 'covered with bolt holes and qualifications', was, in his view, not suitable for publication, as was repeatedly being urged from London in order to pre-empt Hitler's Nuremberg speech. He told Halifax that what he wanted was 'a well condensed' single page combining the SdP's Carlsbad points with Beneš's seven points. Runciman added, with exasperation: 'What we need at present is a little flexibility and someone with the mentality of an Advertising Agent!'[40]

When reports reached Beneš of Runciman's reaction to the Third Plan, he was surprised that the mediator's positive assessment of the main features of the proposals, outlined at their meeting on 23 August, had turned to hostility on receipt of the detailed plan, which, the President contended, was a consistent development of the earlier summary. The accusation that he had reneged on his previously agreed seven point programme led Beneš to believe that either Runciman had failed to understand the full extent of the proposals or it was the result of SdP influence on the Mission. Beneš was also dismayed that Runciman had chosen not to approach him for an explanation, but had complained immediately to London of the President's bad faith, thus souring relations between the British and Czechoslovak governments.[41] In the circumstances it was indeed surprising that, following Runciman's receipt of the Third Plan on 29 August, the two men did not meet again until 1 September. It would appear that during the two intervening days (which were not a weekend) Runciman made no attempt to see Beneš. The explanation may be found in Runciman's report to Halifax of 30 August, in which he stated: 'I suspend final judgement until I know reaction of Sudetens.'[42] The SdP response was given to Runciman by Kundt on 31 August.

The uncharacteristic optimism, displayed by Runciman when Beneš's Third Plan first emerged in embryonic form, was short-lived and soon began to be replaced by growing scepticism concerning the plan's prospects of success. Runciman's changing attitude towards Beneš's new proposals was brought about, at least in part, by information reaching the Mission from the SdP negotiators, who were preparing the ground for rejecting the plan. Despite some mildly encouraging words from Kundt to Stopford, uttered during the course of a '*Bier-Abend*' following the first of the resumed meetings with Beneš,[43] the SdP soon began sending very different signals. After the second meeting between the President and Kundt and Sebekowsky, Ashton-Gwatkin reported to Strang that the SdP leadership did not regard the talks so far 'as adequate in scope or sufficiently clear in their objective' and feared being presented 'with the similitude of a settlement and not the substance'.[44] A few days later, Newton also informed London of his and Runciman's concern regarding the inadequacy of the government's concessions, which, although granting the important principle of territorial autonomy, were judged unlikely to satisfy the requirements of the SdP.[45]

Runciman's trenchant critique of the detailed version of the Third Plan appears to have been somewhat overstated. In particular, his assertion that Beneš had diluted the earlier agreed principles is difficult to sustain. The document, in fact, contained few surprises. It was, as Beneš maintained, essentially an elaboration of the seven basic points with the addition of a general preamble and a further point concerning linguistic equality which, however, had been included in the original proposals supplied to Sander. The most significant aspect of the Third Plan was undoubtedly the proposed creation of three self-governing German districts; although, unlike in the President's original outline, these were not specifically identified. This measure was a major concession by the Czechoslovak authorities who had hitherto resisted granting, in effect, substantial control over territory to the SdP. Nevertheless, the concession did not directly meet the known requirement of the SdP for a single autonomous administration for all the predominantly German areas. Other elements of the SdP's Carlsbad programme which did not receive satisfaction in the Third Plan were: collective legal status for the German nationality, protection for German minorities remaining outside the autonomous area, compensation for previous injustices, and for all state employees in German-inhabited areas to be German. None of these points, however, had been included in the President's outline plan, and Runciman was therefore not justified in accusing Beneš of bad faith. What lay behind the accusation was the British mediator's realisation that Beneš had not moved far enough to satisfy the requirements of the SdP. The SdP, however, were determined to ensure he never would.

Ironically, Runciman's negative assessment of the Third Plan was not shared by the leadership of the SdP – at least not in their private discussions. Kundt, who together with Sebekowsky had become convinced of Beneš's 'sincerity' during the talks with the President,[46] believed that the implementation of the new proposals would fulfil the SdP's Carlsbad demands. Even Frank considered the Third Plan to be 'comparatively far reaching', though of course unacceptable to the SdP, but he conceded it could not be rejected out of hand.[47] Beneš's new offer, which by the SdP's own admission substantially satisfied their demands, was clearly continuing to embarrass the party leadership. In compliance with their instructions from Berlin, to keep open negotiations with the Czechoslovak authorities without actually reaching an agreement, they could neither accept nor reject outright the new proposals. Their response was therefore again to insist on the absolute fulfilment of the Carlsbad programme, which was communicated by Kundt to Runciman on 31 August.

The main thrust of Kundt's report was to complain of the inadequacies of Beneš's proposals which, he maintained, failed to meet the requirements of the SdP. Kundt drew Runciman's attention to six specific shortcomings in the Third Plan. The most significant of these was the SdP's objection to the proposed district basis for autonomy which would result in less than half of the German population being included in the self-governing areas. Kundt was also critical of the proportionality envisaged in government service employment being achieved across the country as a whole, whereas the SdP sought to have only German officials in German areas. The proposed ethnic subdivisions of the Ministries of Education, Health, Social Welfare and Public Works were similarly considered inadequate. The SdP also objected to the conditional withdrawal of the state police from German areas, maintaining that it was the very presence of the police which gave rise to unrest, and linked the question of security with the President's suggested propaganda truce, arguing it could only be achieved following the disarming of Czech civilians in those areas. Kundt's final point was a query concerning the proposed loan; was it to be raised abroad, possibly in Britain? This caused Runciman, the financier, to observe 'that the present state of affairs in Czechoslovakia did not make that country attractive to the investor'.[48]

Kundt's detailed reaction to the Third Plan confirmed Runciman's growing awareness that, despite Henlein's initially positive response, Beneš's new proposals were not acceptable to the SdP. Runciman explained to Halifax the following day that although 'Beneš' main points were, it is true, accepted by Henlein party last week ... they were from the first regarded on Sudeten side as little more than a bridge by which to re-start negotiations'. When it became apparent to Beneš that the SdP had reverted to their Carlsbad demands, Runciman continued, Beneš also began to back-track, doubtless under pressure from other members of the government. Hence the unsatisfactory nature, in Runciman's estimation, of the Third Plan memorandum.[49] Although censorious of Beneš's attitude, Runciman failed to express any overt criticism of the hardened stance adopted by the SdP. Nevertheless, it was at this time that the SdP leadership detected in Runciman, as Hencke reported to Berlin, 'a certain change of opinion in their disfavour'. Kundt ascribed this development to the negative attitude which, he believed, Henlein had exhibited towards Beneš's new proposals at his meeting with Ashton-Gwatkin in Marienbad.[50] The SdP also noted with concern a few days later signs of 'close collaboration' between Beneš and Runciman.[51] However, their fears were unwarranted. Any disapprobation betrayed by Runciman in his dealings with SdP representatives was certainly not translated into action. Despite Runciman's previous observation that it was the Czechoslovak government that was doing 'all the bending',[52] there is no evidence to indicate that he or any of his colleagues applied any pressure whatsoever on the SdP leadership to alter its attitude towards the Third Plan. The British mediator was to show no such inhibitions, however, when it came to dealing with Beneš.

Runciman's acute dissatisfaction with Beneš's Third Plan, evident from his dispatch of 30 August, caused much concern in London. Dropping all pretence of the mediator's ostensible independence of the British government, Halifax sent advice to Runciman by telephone the next day:

> If as your telegram seems to suggest Beneš is playing fast and loose, is it not a case for taking drastic action? His present behaviour will do incalculable harm, and the time at our disposal is too short to permit of these new tergiversations. I would suggest therefore that you should tell him that in the interests of European peace you consider it essential that full substance of the seven proposals ... should be published *at once* as the definite and unalterable basis of all future negotiations and that if he will not publish them as his own unforced offer you will publish them

> forthwith as your own recommendation and communicate them to both parties as the basis on which you propose henceforth to conduct your mediation. If he objects you will know best how to exert pressure on him and in doing so, you can count on fullest support of His Majesty's Government.[53]

Later that day, Halifax also instructed Newton to press Beneš 'with all the earnestness at your command', into publication of the latest proposals. Citing Henderson's advice, that unless some tangible signs of progress became evident in the negotiations, Hitler would make an 'unpleasant pronouncement' at the Nuremberg Rally, which might involve a demand for full autonomy for the German minority or a plebiscite, the Foreign Secretary insisted that the Czechoslovak authorities must

> clear themselves without delay of suspicions which are widely prevalent, to the effect that, counting on foreign support, they are merely manoeuvring for position and spinning out the negotiations without any sincere intention of facing the immediate and vital issue. The only way by which the Czechoslovak Government can remove these suspicions is by offering immediately, publicly, and without reservation, those concessions without which the Sudeten question cannot be solved by peaceful process.

Halifax added that although he was unable himself to judge whether anything less than the Carlsbad programme would be acceptable to the SdP, Beneš must on no account recede from the seven points specified in the initial stages of the formulation of the Third Plan.[54]

The decision to pressure the Czechoslovak government into publishing details of its latest proposals was the outcome, not only of Runciman's depressing report, but also of an extraordinary meeting of the Cabinet held in London on 30 August for the specific purpose of considering the Central European crisis. Although Chamberlain had stated, at the time of von Kleist's visit to London in mid-August, that he was inclined not to believe that Hitler had resolved to attack Czechoslovakia in September, by 24 August the wealth of accumulating evidence had convinced him otherwise. When visiting the Foreign Office that day to finalise the text of Simon's Lanark speech, the Prime Minister left Sargent with the clear indication that he 'took it for granted' that the attack was planned to take place shortly after the end of the Nuremberg Rally on 15 September.[55] As Chamberlain explained when the Cabinet assembled, he now considered the international situation to be 'so grave' as to justify the recall of ministers from vacation.[56] The recall was, however, carried out in a low key with advance publicity being kept to a minimum and the gathering termed merely a 'Meeting of Ministers' rather than a full session of the Cabinet.[57]

Nevertheless, all but four members of the Cabinet attended. One additional person present was Henderson, who had arrived from Berlin for consultations the previous day.

The Foreign Secretary informed the Cabinet of developments since the end of July, giving prominence to the activities of the Runciman Mission. The British mediator received credit for reviving the negotiations in Prague, which had become deadlocked in mid-August. Ministers were also informed of Ashton-Gwatkin's visit to London, bringing news of Beneš's new proposals which included the establishment of autonomous German districts. In addition, Halifax disclosed that the question of a possible visit by an 'eminent person' to Hitler to appeal for a 'reasonable solution' of the crisis had been discussed. Runciman himself was considered ideally suited for the task, but had declined. Turning to the future, the Foreign Secretary outlined two possible alternative developments. If Hitler was determined to use force against Czechoslovakia, Halifax argued, the only possible deterrent would be to announce that Britain would declare war on Germany in that event. He did not advocate such a step, however, as in his view it would divide public opinion in Britain and the Empire. Echoing the arguments first voiced in the Cabinet some five months previously, Halifax added that nothing could be done by Britain, France or the Soviet Union, to prevent Czechoslovakia from being overrun by Germany and, even in the event of ultimate victory over Germany, it was unlikely that Czechoslovakia would be recreated in the form in which it hitherto existed. Halifax also found solace in the belief that Hitler's absorption of parts of Czechoslovakia would influence world opinion, particularly that of the United States, against Germany. If, on the other hand – as was, by implication, more probable – Hitler had not yet decided to use force against Czechoslovakia, the Foreign Secretary advocated the adoption of a two-fold strategy of 'keeping Germany guessing' as to British intentions whilst simultaneously striving for a successful outcome of the Runciman Mission.

The Prime Minister had no doubt which course to follow, arguing that 'no democratic state ought to make a threat of war unless it was both ready to carry it out and prepared to do so' – which he clearly was not. With the sole exception of Duff Cooper, the First Lord of the Admiralty, who argued for some demonstration of the possibility of Britain using force, all the ministers present endorsed the views of the Prime Minister and Foreign Secretary without significant reservation. Henderson also added his opinion that Hitler had not yet decided on war. The outcome was predictable. The Cabinet resolved not to issue any threats of war but to keep Germany 'guessing', to continue with Runciman's attempts at mediation, and to pressure Beneš into publishing his proposals in advance of the Nuremberg Rally. This last decision was made largely at the instigation of Henderson. The presence of an ambassador at a Cabinet meeting was irregular, although that did not inhibit Henderson from playing an active role in the discussions and urging the publication of Beneš's plan in preference to sending Runciman to Berlin. The question of a later visit by Runciman to Hitler would, he suggested, depend on the German government's reaction to the published proposals.[58]

When the instruction to press Beneš to publish the Third Plan was communicated to Runciman and Newton, they were both unconvinced of its wisdom. Runciman resented the British government's intervention and responded tersely and immediately to Halifax's injunction with a single sentence: 'Publication of seven points at present time would be disastrous.'[59] Writing at greater length the following day, he confessed to being puzzled by the Foreign Secretary's desire for publication. He explained that the apparent assumptions behind Halifax's advice, that Beneš's new seven point proposals were acceptable to the SdP, had been overtaken by events. In view of the fact that Kundt and his colleagues now regarded the Third Plan developed from these points as inadequate, its publication at that juncture would, in Runciman's words, exert 'an evil effect' on both the SdP and Hitler.[60]

Runciman's objections were shared by Newton, who was also at a loss to understand why his superiors in London were so insistent on a public declaration from Beneš, which, in his view, could only be counter-productive and possibly dangerous. Newton argued that the German government was unlikely to respond kindly to any publication 'intended to force its hand', and the state control of the mass media ruled out any effective appeal to German public opinion. Moreover, if opinion outside Germany came to regard Beneš's plan as reasonable, whilst it remained unacceptable to the Berlin government, the risk of war would be increased. Newton also pointed out that it was difficult to see what precisely Beneš could usefully publish at that juncture. The public release of his new proposals could only antagonise the SdP, who regarded them as inadequate, and any sudden open espousal by him of the full Carlsbad programme would inevitably undermine his support amongst Czech opinion. In addition, the British Minister argued, two pending developments militated against any immediate publication. Beneš was due to meet Kundt again later that day, 2 September, and on the previous day Henlein had left for Germany to see Hitler.[61]

Even before receiving Newton's more detailed explanations, Halifax accepted the force of Runciman's arguments against publishing Beneš's latest proposals. When responding to Runciman, the Foreign Secretary again explained that his main motive for urging such a step had been 'to take the wind out of Hitler's sails before Nuremberg', but conceded that in view of the 'inadequate' nature of the Third Plan that was no longer appropriate. But the Foreign Secretary did not totally relinquish the idea of publication – only instead of arguing for the release of Beneš's plan, he now urged Runciman to publish proposals which the Mission itself was preparing.[62]

Runciman had first alerted London to the possibility of himself proposing a scheme for resolving the Sudeten German problem, in the event of the protagonists failing to agree amongst themselves, on 30 August – when he obtained permission from Halifax to inform Henlein of this development. The mediator explained that such a step would 'greatly help to convince Henlein and also Hitler that we are sincere in our determination to promote a quick as well as a comprehensive settlement'.[63] It was noted in the Foreign Office that Runciman was, in effect, 'preparing to take up a position which will closely approximate to arbitration'.[64] Although Halifax continued to have some misgivings about Runciman acting in that capacity, he now saw this as a lesser evil than allowing the current situation of mounting tension to continue.[65] Coincidentally, his French counterpart was also showing more enthusiastic support for the idea of British arbitration. In conversation with Campbell on 31 August, Bonnet observed that the key to the peaceful resolution of the Central European crisis lay in British hands. In the event of Britain undertaking to arbitrate between the parties in the Sudeten German dispute on the basis of advice received from Runciman, the Foreign Minister pledged in advance his government's support for the arbitral solution – irrespective of the attitude of the Czechoslovak government.[66] This unsolicited blank cheque from the French nudged the British further along the path towards arbitration. In the Foreign Office, Mallet regarded this unqualified offer of French support as 'extremely valuable' in view of the fact that the time was 'rapidly approaching' when arbitration would become necessary. Halifax concurred with this judgement.[67]

Runciman's willingness to produce his own proposals for resolving the crisis amounted to a major shift in the strategy of his Mission. Hitherto, with the support and encouragement of the British government, he had resolutely resisted playing the role of an arbitrator, despite Henderson's repeated urging from Berlin. Runciman had shown no desire to involve himself directly in sponsoring a settlement of the conflict, limiting his activities first to familiarising himself and his staff with both sides of the argument and then to attempting to mediate between the protagonists. By the end of August, however, he had changed his mind.

One reason for this may be found in the mediator's own frame of mind. After four weeks on the ground in Czechoslovakia with practically nothing to show for it, Runciman was becoming increasingly despondent. The collapse of the initially promising Third Plan, for which he held Beneš responsible, came as a particularly severe blow to the mediator's morale, already sapped by his discomfort and deteriorating health. The oppressive heatwave persisted and Runciman continued to suffer from insomnia. His depression was further intensified by the increasingly overt involvement of Germany in the Czechoslovak crisis and by the limited time available for achieving a solution as the much feared Nuremberg Rally approached. All these considerations came to the surface in Runciman's report to Halifax of 30 August, in which he betrayed his feelings by referring to Czechoslovakia as an 'accursed country'. The unhappy mediator proceeded to pour out his troubles:

> The signs of bad government accumulate day by day and at any moment H[itler] may find an excuse for crossing the frontier in order to maintain order. We are doing everything we can to steer clear of these rocks and if only we could bring B[eneš] to realise how near he is to a cataclysm we could now make some progress – but he is too clever. Time is passing rapidly and we are working against a dead end not much more than a week from today. ... The terrors of war and devastation are weighing on everyone's mind – and yet Europe continues to drift dangerously. I cannot speed up the proceedings to greater pace, and I run some risk of wearing out our little staff. They are at work night and day and during meal times as well. Their spirits are good and they are popular but none of us can keep up this strain much longer – and I have no stop gaps. I must confess to being rather worn myself![68]

Britain's reluctant mediator in Central Europe was clearly under considerable strain and it was therefore hardly surprising that he began to seek the means of bringing his mission to a conclusion – if necessary by producing his own plan for a solution.

A further reason for Runciman's change of attitude concerning arbitration was caused by the fact that a possible 'Runciman plan' had come to hand. It was not, of course, produced by Runciman himself, but by Stopford, who amongst the Mission staff came closest to being a constitutional expert,[69] thanks to having served as private secretary to the chairman of the Simon Commission which investigated the government of India a decade earlier. Stopford also had the foresight to bring with him to Czechoslovakia a volume printed privately by the government of the Irish Free State containing a number of different constitutions. Once the Mission had settled in at the Hotel Alcron in Prague, Stopford found himself minding the office whilst Runciman and Ashton-Gwatkin went about the business of mediating. During quiet periods he was able to put his mind to drafting proposals for a settlement of the Sudeten German dispute in order to forearm Runciman, should it prove necessary for the mediator to propose his own solution.[70]

Stopford began to consider preparing his own plan only a week after arriving in Prague. With Runciman's approval, he wrote to Simon asking him to suggest a suitable constitutional expert to whom the Mission could turn for advice if necessary. Stopford explained to his former superior that the situation in Czechoslovakia was 'both constitutionally and psychologically' similar to the Indian problem, and that, in his view, it would not be possible to achieve a settlement without constitutional changes. He added that 'we may have to devise something like a scheme ourselves and persuade the government to put it forward as theirs'.[71] Simon replied that in his understanding the Mission was not expected 'to pronounce judgement' and with some reluctance suggested that Kenneth Pickthorn, Cambridge historian and Member of Parliament for that University, might be considered as a constitutional adviser should the need arise. Lothian's name was also mentioned but, being in Australia, he was not available.[72]

Although effectively denied additional expert assistance, Stopford persisted in his self-imposed task. His main objective was to reconcile the SdP's Carlsbad demands with the Czechoslovak government's desire to maintain the integrity and security of the state. In consultation with the Swiss Minister in Prague, Charles Brugman, and Count Bost-Waldeck, an Austrian in the service of the Czechoslovak government, who had himself devised a similar constitutional scheme based loosely on the old Austro-Hungarian model, Stopford refined his ideas and presented his blueprint for a solution to Runciman on 30 August. The plan met with the approval of Runciman and Ashton-Gwatkin, who considered it 'a really brilliant effort', and it was agreed to keep it in reserve for possible use in the event of a total breakdown in the negotiations. Stopford also submitted a copy to Bost-Waldeck for transmission to the Czechoslovak authorities.[73]

The 'Stopford Plan' was a ten-point document with two annexures, one providing a gloss for the benefit of the SdP and the other for the Czechoslovak government. The first two Carlsbad demands, the recognition of the equality of Germans and Czechs and the granting of a legal personality to the German ethnic group, were provided for directly in the proposal. Stopford supplemented these by a guarantee of the full equality of the German language. The main part of the plan was concerned with the satisfaction of the third and fourth SdP demands – defining the German areas and granting them full autonomy. This was to be achieved by means of separate provincial Diets for each nationality whose numbers exceeded 10 per cent of the population of the province.[74] Each Diet would elect a President to head the separate ethnic self-administrations of the province, establish an executive body responsible to it, and create its own administrative service. Matters of common concern to all nationalities within a province would be dealt with by joint sessions of the Diets and by joint meetings of the Executives. A Provincial Governor, appointed by the central government, would be responsible for those areas of administration that remained the preserve of the central authorities. At a more local level, the district administration would be organised on a similar basis. The distinct German area demanded by the SdP would comprise all districts within which the German population exceeded 90 per cent.

The central government would remain substantially unaltered, although all legislation affecting any nationality would be referred to a committee of parliamentary deputies belonging to that national group. An advisory State Council containing representatives of all nationalities would advise the President of the Republic. Each self-administration would receive financial grants from the central government proportional to its size and would have the right to levy taxes. All state contracts would be distributed proportionately among the nationalities. Stopford envisaged that the central government would retain control over areas of administration which affected the unity and integrity of the state, such as 'Foreign Affairs, Defence, Civil and Criminal Law, Finance (in principle) and Currency, Railways, Post Office and Customs'. Areas within which the central authorities would legislate only in principle, leaving details to the Diets, might include, he suggested, 'certain aspects of finance, and cultural, social, educational and economic matters'. Other areas of legislation might be devolved entirely to the Diets.

In the annexe addressed to the SdP, Stopford drew attention to four advantages arising from his proposals. It would provide the 'maximum of self-government' to the German population within predominantly German areas; it could be implemented without delay since no territorial reorganisation was required; only a small number of Germans would require special minority protection; and lastly, several 'influential' advisory committees would be established to aid the central government. For the benefit of the Czechoslovak authorities Stopford emphasised that the unity of the central government would remain intact and, moreover, new channels of communication would be developed between the President and the 'more experienced' leaders of the minorities via the advisory State Council. He also pointed out that only a small number of Czechs would come under the direct control of German authorities.

Besides granting territorial autonomy to the German minority, the 'Stopford Plan' also gave satisfaction to two further points from the SdP's Carlsbad demands. Safeguards for minorities outside their main area of habitation would be secured by Minorities Treaty protection and the right of appeal to the Supreme Administrative Court. Replacement of Czech officials by Germans in German areas, phased over an unspecified number of years, would be overseen by a Public Service Commission, with equal representation of all nationalities, attached to the Prime Minister's office. Stopford also made provision for the gradual withdrawal of the predominantly Czech state police from German areas and their replacement by local police. This was additional to the Carlsbad demands enunciated in April, as the introduction of the state police had only taken place during the summer months of 1938 in response to rising tension.

Only two elements of the Carlsbad programme did not receive full realisation in Stopford's proposals. He himself recognised that the SdP's demand for the removal of injustices perpetrated on the German minority since 1918, and for the reparation of damages caused, was only partly met in his plan by the proposed restoration to their posts of all German officials who had been dismissed by the Czechoslovak authorities for other than criminal reasons. Stopford's plan also failed to satisfy the demand by the SdP for the right to profess German nationality and German political philosophy – in other words, National Socialism. In the annexe prepared for the SdP he indicated that this right was 'guaranteed by the terms of the scheme as a whole, so long as it [was] not in conflict with the unity, security and integrity of the state'.[75] Conscious of the political aspirations of the SdP[76] and therefore presumably of the full significance of this demand, Stopford could not fail to be aware of the unreality of his statement. However, since the SdP leaders were not yet prepared to advocate openly their real aims, he was able to capitalise on their reticence and continuing professions of loyalty to Czechoslovakia. Indeed, given the goodwill of both parties in the conflict, Stopford's plan, or something resembling it, might well have offered a workable solution to Czechoslovakia's problems. As far as the SdP was concerned, that goodwill was non-existent. The Czechoslovak government on the other hand, under severe pressure from Britain and France, was soon to produce not dissimilar proposals itself.

Although the existence of Stopford's plan made it possible for Runciman to assume the role of an arbitrator, he was in no immediate hurry to do so, despite his discomfort and ill health. When, on 30 August, he sought Halifax's consent for informing Henlein of the possibility of the Mission proposing its own solution, Runciman envisaged that the plan might be produced by a specific date – 15 September was tentatively suggested – if the current negotiations failed to yield results.[77] The Foreign Secretary was much less inclined to be patient. Whilst approving Runciman's request to inform Henlein – though he assumed, incorrectly, that the mediator's intention was to *publish* his plan by mid September – Halifax indicated that such a step would 'not meet urgent necessity of case in view of the imminence of the Parteitag', and he strongly urged Runciman, once he had decided to sponsor a scheme, to do so 'as soon as you reasonably can'.[78]

Runciman continued to reject this advice. He remained unable to understand London's desire for immediate publication as he could see no advantage arising from this. Responding to a point from an earlier dispatch, in which the Foreign Secretary had argued that the publication of Beneš's Third Plan was the only effective means of informing Hitler of its contents, Runciman conceded that whilst it was possible that the SdP leaders might withhold details of the Third Plan from Hitler, he could not believe that they would fail to inform him of Runciman's own proposals. He also considered it unlikely that Hitler would urge the SdP leadership to accept any solution they themselves did not favour. Moreover, the disadvantages of publishing, as opposed to preparing, a plan were, in Runciman's opinion, considerable: 'It would mean nailing my colours (and of course in the eyes of the world the colours of His Majesty's Government) to the mast and leave me little opportunity for further mediation.'[79]

Despite recognising the force of Runciman's arguments, Halifax continued to press for the public release of at least the general principles of Runciman's plan. He regarded this as essential not only in order to inform Hitler 'in time for him to adapt his language in Nuremberg accordingly' but also in order to inform world opinion. The Foreign Secretary believed this latter consideration to be 'sufficiently important to warrant publication of the scheme immediately after communication to both parties without waiting for their agreement and in spite of objections you feel'.[80] The view persisted within the British government, thanks in no small measure to the earnest advocacy of Henderson endorsed by the Cabinet on 30 August, that some public evidence of progress in Czechoslovakia had to be produced in the desperate hope of moderating Hitler's much feared speech at Nuremberg, which might otherwise signal an intensification of the crisis in Central Europe.[81]

The acute anxiety felt in London about the forthcoming Nazi Party Rally was shared by the British mediators in Prague. On 24 August, Runciman noted with concern that there remained 'barely a fortnight before the Nuremburg [*sic*] oration'.[82] Indeed, Runciman did not dissent from the Foreign Office view that Hitler should be informed of the Mission's intention to produce a solution by mid-September if all else failed, but preferred to do this not by a public announcement but in a private message conveyed to Berlin by Henlein. Having previously secured (during his recent visit to London) Halifax's permission to make such use of the services of the SdP leader, Ashton-Gwatkin duly informed Henlein of this on 31 August.

The meeting took place in the dilapidated Carlton Hotel in Marienbad where, a little over a week earlier, Ashton-Gwatkin had first encouraged Henlein to take up the role of a mediator between Britain and Germany. During this second two-hour-long conversation, conducted in a cordial atmosphere over lunch of sandwiches and white wine, Ashton-Gwatkin conveyed the British government's response to Henlein's terms for undertaking the proposed mission. Most of the meeting was also attended by Hohenlohe, who had been initially responsible for planting the seeds of this enterprise in the receptive mind of Runciman's chief assistant. It is probable that, in addition, Frank was present behind the scenes at the Carlton Hotel, although he appears not to have participated in the discussions with Ashton-Gwatkin.[83]

The British government's response to Henlein's offer was contained in two messages, written in German, which the SdP leader was given to convey to Hitler. The first message concerned the work of the Runciman Mission and closely reflected the contents of Halifax's despatch to Runciman of 29 August. It stated that Runciman's objective was 'to assist both parties to reach a settlement' on the basis of the Carlsbad points and the Third Plan. Henlein's suggestion of direct British intervention was declined with the explanation that London remained 'reluctant to pronounce on the merits of any proposals ...

put forward by either side'. Nevertheless, both Runciman and the British government were 'very anxious' to secure a settlement 'at the earliest possible moment'. Runciman, therefore, wished these sentiments be conveyed to Hitler and hoped that Hitler would 'give approval and support to the continuance of negotiations'.[84]

In effect, Runciman was responding negatively to Henlein's request for the mediator's open support of his Carlsbad programme. Henlein expressed his disappointment,[85] but it was, in fact, superfluous. Despite the wording of the message, developments were, as Ashton-Gwatkin noted, 'leading us gradually on towards the obligation to support full meaning (as Henlein sees it) of Karlsbad eight points'. Ashton-Gwatkin believed this to be 'inevitable', since the programme itself was 'not unreasonable' and constituted 'probably the only way to peace'. He did concede, however, that the Czechoslovak authorities would regard this as a betrayal.[86]

Henlein was probably far more concerned about the second part of the message, marked 'very confidential', which disclosed Runciman's latest proposed *modus operandi*. In order to demonstrate British sincerity 'in their determination to promote a quick as well as a comprehensive settlement', Runciman wished Hitler to be informed that, in the event of failure in the current talks, he would be ready 'by some given date (say September 15)' to produce a scheme of his own.[87] This suggested introduction of a timetable, no matter how tentative, is unlikely to have pleased the SdP leadership. The instructions Henlein received from Hitler in March, to play for time by keeping the negotiations going without agreement until Germany was ready for action, still applied. And although Frank had been informed by Hitler, late in August, that the action in question would be war against Czechoslovakia, the precise date for this remained unspecified. If that was to be later than mid-September, the declaration of Runciman's own proposed solution might create unwelcome complications.

The second message Henlein received from Ashton-Gwatkin concerned the wider question of relations between Britain and Germany, and again closely followed the wording of Halifax's telegram. It requested Henlein to inform Hitler that

> he (Herr Henlein) believes Great Britain desires an Anglo-German agreement and that he further believes that a settlement of the Sudeten question might well open the way to such an agreement. Lord Runciman is not in a position to give any list of subjects which His Majesty's Government would be prepared to discuss; the actual initiation and programme of such discussions would presumably have to be arranged between the two Governments through their own channels.[88]

Henlein expressed no disappointment concerning the rejection of his offer to act as an intermediary with Hitler. On the contrary, choosing to ignore the rebuff, he exhibited considerable enthusiasm for his mission, and, despite suffering from a heavy cold, was eager to depart at once for Berchtesgaden, where Hitler was in residence. The SdP leader omitted to inform his British visitor, however, that he was due to see Hitler within the next two days anyway.[89] Unaware of this arrangement, Ashton-Gwatkin was much impressed with Henlein's enthusiasm, explaining to Strang:

> Henlein is dramatically conscious of the weight upon him personally of responsibility for peace or war. He is I am sure convinced that friendship between England and Germany is the only true basis for world peace. He cannot see what essential questions there are to separate us. He is simple and honest and may succeed with Hitler where the more crafty would fail.[90]

Runciman's chief assistant was well pleased with the way his diplomatic initiative was developing. Despite the reproof from Halifax and the consequent dilution of the significance of Henlein's mission to Hitler, Ashton-Gwatkin remained convinced that good progress was being made[91] and that Henlein was possibly on the brink of performing a 'great service' for the British government.[92] He was equally optimistic about the prospects of resolving the Sudeten German problem, noting in his diary on the day following his meeting with Henlein: 'The corner has probably been turned, if there was a corner.'[93]

Evidently, Henlein's charm and persuasiveness had lost nothing of their force. Indeed, Ashton-Gwatkin also recorded in his diary that '*Poulet*' (the Mission's sobriquet for Henlein) was 'v[ery] friendly as always'.[94] He accepted without question the SdP leader's assurances that, although greatly admiring the achievements of Nazi Germany, he totally rejected persecution and sought to disassociate his party from the Nazi movement in Germany. Ashton-Gwatkin also accepted at face value Henlein's assertion that his presence at the forthcoming Nuremberg Rally would serve as a moderating influence on events.[95] Although Henlein's *bonhomie* was an essential, and most effective, part of his diplomatic armoury, on this occasion it at least in part must have reflected satisfaction derived from successful dissembling. There can be little doubt that, despite the threat of a timetable being imposed by Runciman, Henlein had enjoyed himself immensely at the expense of his credulous British guest. Henlein even succeeded in persuading Ashton-Gwatkin that, in order to avoid the accusation of receiving orders from Hitler, the Czechoslovak authorities be informed that his journey to Berchtesgaden was being undertaken strictly at the request of the Runciman Mission.[96]

Runciman informed Beneš of this the following day. He explained, in a note to the President, that Henlein was going to Berchtesgaden at his request because he believed in Henlein's 'genuine desire for peace' and hoped the SdP leader would influence Hitler in that direction. The British mediator also disclosed that Henlein was bearing a message to Hitler in which Runciman expressed the trust that Hitler would 'give approval and support' for the continuation of the negotiations in Czechoslovakia. The message also indicated that a successful resolution of the problem might result in a rapprochement between Britain and Germany. Runciman added that Henlein had expressly asked that this be explained to Beneš and that he had also voiced the hope that the Czechoslovak press would refrain from distorting the purpose of the journey and that it would not result in adverse repercussions for Henlein.[97]

Beneš received this information with astonished incredulity and, during a meeting with Runciman on 1 September, protested vigorously against this initiative. In the eyes of the President, it amounted to an invitation to Hitler to intervene in the internal affairs of his country. Runciman explained, somewhat disingenuously, that the messages were sent purely on his initiative in order to impress on Hitler that the failure of the negotiations between the Czechoslovak authorities and the SdP would have serious international repercussions leading to the possible involvement of the great powers. Beneš found Runciman's naivety almost beyond belief and recorded in his memoirs that the British mediator patently failed to appreciate 'the derision with which his attempt to "intimidate Hitler" would be met at Berchtesgaden'.[98]

The President's judgement was quite correct. Hitler reacted to the British initiative by contemptuously turning it to his advantage and was certainly neither intimidated nor won over by Runciman's messages. At their meeting on 1 September, Hitler informed Henlein that since the British were seeking to transform the crisis in Czechoslovakia into an international issue, he himself would take the situation in hand. He indicated that the denouement would come before the end of September, and instructed Henlein to keep the negotiations in progress meanwhile.[99] To what extent Hitler further outlined his intentions to Henlein is uncertain, but the SdP leader could have been under no illusion that war was in prospect and that his organisation would have a role to play in the conflict. At a meeting held two days later to review plans for the invasion of Czechoslovakia, Hitler raised in discussion with Generals Brauchitsch and Keitel the possible use of 'Henlein people' in support of the invading German armies. Although the actual date of the operation was not set, it was to be determined by 27 September.[100]

Runciman's goodwill messages conveyed by Henlein to Hitler clearly failed to defuse the situation in Central Europe, nor did they contribute to an improvement in relations between Britain and Germany. Indeed, the entire episode of attempting to use Henlein as an intermediary with Hitler, launched some ten days previously by Ashton-Gwatkin in Marienbad and subsequently approved but tightly circumscribed by Halifax, served only to highlight British diplomatic credulity. The belief persisted, thanks largely to being reinforced by Ashton-Gwatkin, that the SdP leader was a man of peace and moderation and was benevolently disposed towards the British. It was a misjudgement based on a combination of eager credulity and the beguiling effects of Henlein's charm.

This episode also provided a clear demonstration of the starkly distinct attitudes adopted by the British mediators towards Henlein and the SdP on the one hand and towards Beneš and his government on the other. This was a distinction that was only partly accounted for by the obvious differences between the personalities of the two figures and by the fact that contact with Henlein was maintained mostly by Ashton-Gwatkin, whereas dealings with Beneš were conducted by Runciman himself with Newton providing official support when required. Throughout their activities in Czechoslovakia, Runciman and his staff not only regarded Henlein as being virtually equal in standing with the Head of State, they also handled him with far greater indulgence than Beneš. Henlein was accorded the consideration due to a sincere, well-intentioned man of honour – suitable to bear messages to Hitler – whereas Beneš, beneath the niceties of official protocol, was treated as a devious and untrustworthy figure requiring to be kept under constant scrutiny. During the next and final phase of the Mission's activities in Czechoslovakia, this disparity was to become more pronounced as Beneš became increasingly the principal focus of British attention.

Notes

1 Ashton-Gwatkin to Strang, in Troutbeck to Halifax, 27 August 1938, *DBFP*, 3/II, no. 702.
2 Beneš, *Mnichovské dny*, p. 178.
3 Runciman to Ashton-Gwatkin, in Newton to Halifax, 25 August 1938, *DBFP*, 3/II, no. 685; Note by Stopford, 29 August 1938, in Ashton-Gwatkin to Strang, 29 August 1938, *DBFP*, 3/II, appendix II (III), p. 667.
4 Ashton-Gwatkin to Strang, in Troutbeck to Halifax, 27 August 1938, *DBFP*, 3/II, no. 702.
5 Newton to Halifax, 26 August 1938, *DBFP*, 3/II, no. 697.
6 Hencke to the Foreign Ministry, 27 August 1938, *DGFP*, D/II, no. 399.
7 Ashton-Gwatkin to Strang, in Troutbeck to Halifax, 27 August 1938, *DBFP*, 3/II, no. 702.
8 Newton to Halifax, 29 August 1938, *DBFP*, 3/II, no. 713.
9 *Daily Telegraph*, 29 August 1938.
10 Ashton-Gwatkin to Strang, 29 August 1938, *DBFP*, 3/II, appendix II (III), p. 666. Presumably, Ashton-Gwatkin had in mind the formation of the anti-Napoleonic alliance between Austria, Prussia and Russia in September 1813.
11 Hencke to the Foreign Ministry, 24 August 1938, *DGFP*, D/II, no. 387.
12 H. Groscurth, *Tagebücher eines Abwehroffiziers, 1938–1940*, (Stuttgart, 1970), p. 104.
13 Ashton-Gwatkin to Strang, in Troutbeck to Halifax, 29 August 1938, *DBFP*, 3/II, no. 706.

14 *Ibid.*; Ashton-Gwatkin to Strang, 29 August 1938, *DBFP*, 3/II, appendix II (III), p. 666. For Henlein's original German text of the desired statement, see Newton to Halifax, 6 September 1938, enclosure from Ashton-Gwatkin, 29 August 1938, C 9607/1941/18, FO 371/21736.
15 Ashton-Gwatkin to Strang, in Troutbeck to Halifax, 29 August 1938, *DBFP*, 3/II. no. 706; Ashton-Gwatkin to Strang, 29 August 1938, *DBFP*, 3/II, appendix II (III), p. 666. Stopford, who had been spending the weekend with Kundt and his family, also joined the party at Červený Hrádek. He later recalled in his memoir that this, his first meeting with Henlein, left him 'not greatly impressed'. (Stopford, 'Prague 1938–1939', pp. 38–9.)
16 Ashton-Gwatkin to Strang, 29 August 1938, *DBFP*, 3/II, appendix II (III), p. 666.
17 *Ibid.*
18 Ashton-Gwatkin to Strang, in Troutbeck to Halifax, 29 August 1938, *DBFP*, 3/II, no. 706.
19 Halifax to Newton, 29 August 1938, *DBFP*, 3/II, no. 710.
20 Ashton-Gwatkin to Strang, in Troutbeck to Halifax, 27 and 29 August 1938, *DBFP*, 3/II, nos. 702 and 706.
21 Halifax to Newton, 29 August 1938, *DBFP*, 3/II, no. 710.
22 *Ibid.*; see also Halifax to Newton, 30 August 1938, *DBFP*, 3/II, no. 716.
23 Minute by Sargent, 30 August 1938, C 8918/1941/18, FO 371/21733.
24 Newton to Halifax, 29 August 1938, *DBFP*, 3/II, no. 711.
25 Minute by Sargent, 30 August 1938, C 8918/1941/18, FO 371/21733.
26 Newton to Halifax, 29 August 1938, *DBFP*, 3/II, no. 711.
27 Minute by Sargent, 30 August 1938, C 8918/1941/18, FO 371/21733.
28 Minute by Mallet, 30 August 1938, *ibid.*
29 Newton to Halifax, 29 August 1938, *DBFP*, 3/II, no. 711.
30 Minute by Mallet, 30 August 1938, C 8918/1941/18, FO 371/21733.
31 Minute by Sargent, 30 August 1938, *ibid.*
32 Halifax to Newton, undated draft, and minutes by Oliphant, 30 and 31 August 1938, *ibid.*
33 *Daily Telegraph*, 26 August 1938. Extracts cited in RIIA, *Documents*, 1938, II, pp. 1757.
34 Minutes of meetings between Beneš, Kundt and Sebekowsky, 24 and 25 August 1938, enclosed in Hencke to the Foreign Ministry, 27 August 1938, *DGFP*, D/II, no. 398.
35 *Ibid.*; Beneš, *Mnichovské dny*, pp. 178–9. Beneš erroneously recalled the third meeting taking place on 29 August.
36 Hencke to the Foreign Ministry, 30 August 1938, *DGFP*, D/II, no. 407.
37 'Notes of a conversation between Lord Runciman and Herr Kundt on 31 August 1938', FO 800/305, ff. 41–2.
38 'Protocol regarding a modus of negotiation agreed upon on the 24th of August 1938 between the President of the Republic and Deputy Kundt and Herr Sebekowsky regarding national affairs', Stopford Papers, RJS 3/2. For the Czech original see Beneš, *Mnichovské dny*, document no. 27, pp. 445–9.
39 Runciman to Halifax, in Newton to Halifax, 30 August 1938, *DBFP*, 3/II, no. 717.
40 Runciman to Halifax, 30 August 1938, *DBFP*, 3/II, no. 723.
41 Beneš, *Mnichovské dny*, pp. 186–8, 192 and document no. 32, pp. 458–60.
42 Runciman to Halifax, in Newton to Halifax, 30 August 1938, *DBFP*, 3/II, no. 717.

43 Stopford to Ashton-Gwatkin, in Newton to Halifax, 25 August 1938, *DBFP*, 3/II, no. 681.
44 Ashton-Gwatkin to Strang, in Troutbeck to Halifax, 29 August 1938, *DBFP*, 3/II, no. 706.
45 Newton to Halifax, 29 August 1938, *DBFP*, 3/II, no. 711.
46 Hencke to the Foreign Ministry, 26 August 1938, *DGFP*, D/II, no. 391.
47 Hencke to the Foreign Ministry, 30 August 1938, *DGFP*, D/II, no. 407.
48 'Notes of a Conversation between Lord Runciman and Herr Kundt on 31 August 1938', FO 800/305, ff. 36–43.
49 Runciman to Halifax, in Newton to Halifax, 1 September 1938, *DBFP*, 3/II, no. 730.
50 Hencke to the Foreign Ministry, 27 August 1938, *DGFP*, D/II, no. 399. Kundt's reasoning is somewhat difficult to follow particularly since, from the British point of view, the outcome of the Marienbad meeting was far from disappointing. Henlein's report to Berlin also contained no indication of negative comments on Beneš's proposals. (*Documents and Materials*, I, no. 16.)
51 Hencke to the Foreign Ministry, 30 August 1938, *DGFP*, D/II, no. 407.
52 Runciman to Halifax, 24 August 1938, *DBFP*, 3/II, no. 680.
53 Halifax to Newton, 31 August 1938, *DBFP*, 3/II, no. 724.
54 Halifax to Newton, 31 August 1938, *DBFP*, 3/II, no. 727.
55 Memorandum by Sargent, 'Possible German–Czech War', 30 August 1938, C 9041/1941/18, FO 371/21734.
56 Cabinet Minutes, 30 August 1938, extraordinary meeting, CAB 23/94.
57 Hoyer Millar to Hardinge, 26 August 1938, Halifax Papers, H/VI/57, FO 800/309.
58 Cabinet Minutes, 30 August 1938, extraordinary meeting, CAB 23/94; Inskip diary, 30 August 1938, Caldecote Papers, INKP 1.
59 Runciman to Halifax, in Newton to Halifax, 31 August 1938, *DBFP*, 3/II, no. 728.
60 Runciman to Halifax, in Newton to Halifax, 1 September 1938, *DBFP*, 3/II, no. 730.
61 Newton to Halifax, 2 September 1938, *DBFP*, 3/II, no. 740.
62 Halifax to Runciman, in Halifax to Newton, 1 September 1938, *DBFP*, 3/II, no. 739.
63 Runciman to Halifax, in Newton to Halifax, 30 August 1938, *DBFP*, 3/II, no. 717.
64 Minute by Roberts, 31 August 1938, C 8997/1941/18, FO 371/21734.
65 Halifax to Runciman, in Halifax to Newton, 31 August 1938, *DBFP*, 3/II, no. 724.
66 Campbell to Halifax, 31 August 1938, *DBFP*, 3/II, no. 725.
67 Minutes by Mallet and Halifax, 2 and 3 September 1938, C 8997/1941/18, FO 371/21734.
68 Runciman to Halifax, 30 August 1938, *DBFP*, 3/II, no. 723. It was in response to this despondent dispatch that the Foreign Office sent David Stephens to assist the overburdened Mission.
69 In a letter from Prague, Stopford indicated that he was 'busy on the constitutional side ... as no one else knows much about this'. Stopford to Winthrop-Young, 20 August 1938, Stopford Papers, RJS 3/1.
70 Stopford, 'Prague 1938–1939', p. 51.
71 Stopford to Simon, 9 August 1938, Stopford Papers, RJS 3/8.

72 Simon to Stopford, 17 August 1938, Stopford Papers, RJS 3/8.
73 Stopford, 'Prague, 1938–1939', pp. 51–2; Ashton-Gwatkin to Strang, 6 September 1938, *DBFP*, 3/II, appendix II (III), p. 668.
74 Stopford originally proposed a 15 per cent minimum qualification, but the final version of the plan, approved by Runciman and Ashton-Gwatkin, contained the reduced figure. See Stopford, 'Prague, 1938–1939', p. 52.
75 Memorandum by Stopford, 6 September 1938, endorsed 'My constitutional proposals', Stopford papers, RJS 3/8. For a summary of Stopford's proposals telegraphed to London see Runciman to Halifax, in Newton to Halifax, 3 September 1938, *DBFP*, 3/II, no. 756.
76 Stopford to Simon, 9 August 1938, Stopford Papers, RJS 3/8.
77 Runciman to Halifax, in Newton to Halifax, 30 August 1938, *DBFP*, 3/II, no. 717.
78 Halifax to Newton, 31 August 1938, *DBFP*, 3/II, no. 724.
79 Runciman to Halifax, in Newton to Halifax, 1 September 1938, *DBFP*, 3/II, no. 730.
80 Halifax to Runciman, in Halifax to Newton, 1 September 1938, *DBFP*, 3/II, no. 739.
81 Halifax to Newton, 31 August 1938, *DBFP*, 3/II, no. 727.
82 Runciman to Halifax, 24 August 1938, *DBFP*, 3/II, no. 680.
83 Frank reported to the German Legation in Prague that he had participated in the talks alongside Henlein. (Eisenlohr to the Foreign Ministry, 1 September 1938, *DGFP*, D/II, no. 417.) Ashton-Gwatkin, however, made no reference to Frank's presence either in his reports to the Foreign Office (Ashton-Gwatkin to Strang, in Newton to Halifax, 1 September 1938, *DBFP*, 3/II, nos 731 and 734, and Ashton-Gwatkin to Strang, 6 September 1938, *DBFP*, 3/II, appendix II, p. 668) or in his diary (FO 800/304).
84 Newton to Halifax, 1 September 1938, *DBFP*, 3/II, no. 732. See also Halifax to Runciman, 29 August 1938, *DBFP*, 3/II, no. 710.
85 Ashton-Gwatkin to Strang, 6 September 1938, *DBFP*, 3/II, appendix II, p. 668.
86 Ashton-Gwatkin to Strang, in Newton to Halifax, 1 September 1938, *DBFP*, 3/II, no. 731.
87 Newton to Halifax, 1 September 1938, *DBFP*, 3/II, no. 732.
88 *Ibid*. The document refers to 'Anglo-Czech relations', which was evidently entered in error for 'Anglo-German'.
89 Groscurth, *Tagebücher*, pp. 108–9.
90 Ashton-Gwatkin to Strang, in Newton to Halifax, 1 September 1938, *DBFP*, 3/II, no. 734.
91 Ashton-Gwatkin's diary, 31 August 1938, FO 800/304. 'All in order, he will go ...'.
92 Ashton-Gwatkin to Strang, in Newton to Halifax, 1 September 1938, *DBFP*, 3/II, no. 731.
93 Ashton-Gwatkin's diary, 1 September 1938, FO 800/304.
94 *Ibid*., 31 August 1938.
95 Ashton-Gwatkin to Strang, in Newton to Halifax, 1 September 1938, *DBFP*, 3/II, no. 734.
96 Ashton-Gwatkin to Strang, in Newton to Halifax, 1 September 1938, *DBFP*, 3/II, no. 731; Ashton-Gwatkin to Strang, 6 September 1938, *DBFP*, 3/II, appendix II, p. 668. Beneš recorded in his memoirs that Henlein also suggested to Ashton-Gwatkin that Runciman should invite Beneš to use the services of the SdP

leader as a mediator between Czechoslovakia and Germany. Beneš indicated that he was informed of this by Runciman. (Beneš, *Mnichovské dny*, pp. 194–5).

97 Runciman to Beneš, 1 September 1938, in Beneš, *Mnichovské dny*, document no. 33. No copy could be traced in the Mission records.

98 Beneš, *Mnichovské dny*, p. 195. Runciman appears not to have kept an account of this meeting.

99 Groscurth, *Tagebücher*, pp. 111–12.

100 Notes by Schmundt on Conference on Operation Green, 4 September 1938, *DGFP*, D/II, no. 424.

11
Turning the Screw

As September approached, the British mediators had few positive achievements to show for four weeks of activity in Czechoslovakia, apart from establishing personal contacts with the main protagonists and familiarising themselves with the issues in question. Europe still enjoyed an uneasy peace but the dangerous dispute which Runciman was sent to resolve was no nearer being settled, although the Mission did have a possible plan in reserve and had obtained the services of Henlein to convey a message of goodwill to Hitler. Moreover, with Hitler's much dreaded speech at the Nuremberg Nazi Rally less than two weeks away, the fear of war grew more intense by the day and the pressure on Runciman to achieve results increased accordingly. Efforts were therefore redoubled to find a solution – with the attention concentrated principally on Beneš.

Runciman's profound disappointment with the details of the Third Plan resulted in a significant tightening of the screw on the Czechoslovak authorities. This in itself was not a new development, merely an intensified application of the instructions Ashton-Gwatkin received during his consultations in London and subsequently reinforced by Halifax's telegram of 31 August calling for 'drastic action' to be taken against Beneš.[1] In response to that injunction, Runciman indicated that, at his forthcoming meeting with the President, he would draw attention to the inadequacies of the Third Plan, and urge Beneš to go to the 'utmost limits' to meet the requirements of the SdP. He also intended to stress his certain belief that his personal dissatisfaction with the latest Czechoslovak proposals would be shared by British public opinion, were details of the plan to be published. In addition, Runciman proposed to issue a warning that, if the meeting between Beneš and Kundt due the following day failed to make significant progress, he would have no alternative but to produce a scheme of his own 'as a last chance of preserving peace'.[2] When Runciman actually saw Beneš on 1 September (when he also informed the President of Henlein's visit to Hitler), he departed significantly from his indicated intention. Instead of using the threat to impose a solution of his own if the new talks failed, he went considerably further, stating that 'he doubted whether anything less than the substance of the Carlsbad points would suffice to reach a settlement'.[3] Runciman was even more explicit the following day when, during the course of a further meeting, he warned Beneš that given a choice between the SdP's Carlsbad programme and war, Britain would choose the former.[4]

This significant shift in the Mission's policy was confirmed by Newton when he visited Beneš during the morning of 3 September in order to transmit officially Halifax's strictures of 31 August. This was the first occasion since Runciman's arrival in Prague a month previously that Newton had requested to see Beneš, and he drew the President's attention to that fact in order to emphasise the critical nature of the situation as perceived by the British government. In addition to relaying the Foreign Secretary's complaints of protracted Czechoslovak inaction, Newton repeated Runciman's injunction that the Czechoslovak authorities 'ought not to stop short of the eight Karlsbad points if a settlement could not be obtained otherwise'. Newton also drew attention to the increasing danger of war in Central Europe and indicated bluntly that, even in the event of Germany being defeated, it was far from certain that Czechoslovakia would be re-established 'in its present form or in such a re-adjusted form as may now be essential to avert war'.

Beneš was greatly disturbed by Newton's warning, but his vehement protestations that acceptance of Henlein's Carlsbad demands would be tantamount to granting a 'blank cheque' to the SdP, inasmuch as they were open to various interpretations and would ultimately result in the dissolution of Czechoslovakia, cut no ice with the British Minister. Similarly, Beneš's warning of likely internal disorder if his government was pushed too far only elicited the less than sympathetic response from Newton that, in that event, the country would be 'committing suicide'.[5] Such was the impact of Newton's hour-long intervention that the President immediately requested a visit from Runciman to seek clarification of the British attitude. Runciman duly called on the President that afternoon and confirmed Newton's unyielding attitude concerning the SdP's Carlsbad demands, adding further that it was incumbent on Beneš 'to make all sacrifices necessary to preserve the existence of his country'.[6]

Both Runciman and Newton were well satisfied with the immediate outcome of their unprecedented diplomatic assault on Beneš. Although Runciman was aware that his recent daily meetings with the President were viewed with suspicion in Berlin, he explained to Halifax that 'if I do not see him I shall lose my hold of him'. This firm grip achieved the desired effect. The four separate meetings held with the British representatives during the first three days of September resulted in the President being, in Runciman's words, 'shaken severely' by the experience, and Newton also believed they 'had stirred him soundly'. Beneš was greatly distressed by the new turn in

British policy. Runciman described him as being 'much upset' and noted that at the conclusion of their last meeting 'he bid me good-bye sorrowfully'. The President nevertheless indicated to his tormentors an immediate readiness to redouble his efforts in order to achieve the required settlement with the SdP. 'He is now to proceed', Runciman reported with evident satisfaction, 'with the warning ringing in his ears.'[7]

The pressure on Beneš was nevertheless maintained further and no opportunity overlooked for reinforcing the disagreeable message. Runciman even employed his sacrosanct weekend leisure time for this purpose. Mindful of the criticism voiced by Czechoslovak and other observers that he was taking his weekend relaxation exclusively in the company of the pro-SdP Bohemian German aristocracy,[8] Runciman sought to redress the balance by visiting Cardinal Karel Kašpar, the Archbishop of Prague and Primate of Bohemia, at his residence in Dolní Břežany near Prague. The visit was made over the weekend of 3 and 4 September, Runciman being accompanied by Peto and by their respective wives. During his stay at the Archbishop's palace, the mediator prevailed upon his host to write in confidence to Beneš expressing support for Sudeten German autonomy in preference to a destructive war, the outcome of which could not be foreseen. The Archbishop did not disguise the fact that he was writing at Runciman's behest.[9]

Beneš was not alone amongst Czechoslovak leaders being subjected to this latest bout of British pressure. The Prime Minister, Hodža, received similar attention when he dined at the British Legation in the company of Newton and the Runcimans on 2 September. He, however, required little persuading and expressed himself to be in agreement with his British hosts that further major concessions to the SdP were urgently required. Hodža also confided in Newton – not for the first time – that a direct approach from the British Minister, on this occasion to Beneš, would assist in achieving this objective.[10] It was with this encouragement from an unexpected quarter that Newton arranged the fateful audience with Beneš on 3 September.

The intensified British diplomatic offensive against the Czechoslovak government was also conducted in London. Runciman's vehement denunciation of Beneš's Third Plan was received in the Foreign Office during the evening of 30 August. The following morning, Vansittart immediately summoned the Czechoslovak Minister to issue a strong warning of the grave dangers of delay. Masaryk was informed in no uncertain terms of the British government's particular displeasure concerning Beneš's perceived retreat from his previously indicated proposals. His attention was also drawn to Runciman's considerable disappointment.[11] In addition, indirect pressure was brought to bear on the Czechoslovak authorities via Paris. Availing himself of an offer made by the French Ambassador during a routine meeting earlier that day, Halifax requested the French government to instruct its Minister in Prague to concert with his British counterpart in applying pressure on Beneš.[12] Bonnet willingly complied, instructing de Lacroix, on 1 September, to liaise at once with Newton. Following a conversation with the British Minister, de Lacroix visited Beneš that afternoon to convey the required message.[13]

When, three days later, Halifax learned of Runciman's and Newton's espousal of the SdP's Carlsbad demands, he sent a further request to Paris for this new direction to be supported by de Lacroix. Newton was also instructed to inform the French Minister of this development.[14] That, however, was superfluous since, following his distressing conversation with Newton during the morning of 3 September, in addition to asking to see Runciman, Beneš summoned de Lacroix to his office to seek the attitude of the French government. The French, however, refused to follow Runciman's lead and despite the British Ambassador in Paris strongly urging Bonnet to instruct de Lacroix to fall in line with the new British stand, the Foreign Minister declined to issue such instructions, though he did agree to ensure that Beneš was again pressed in more general terms. Bonnet also indicated, paradoxically, that ultimately France would accept Runciman's verdict – whatever it might be.[15] The French government's reluctance to force acceptance of the SdP's Carlsbad programme on the Czechoslovak authorities was confirmed by its Ambassador in London. Corbin, in conversation with Halifax on 5 September, indicated his government's perplexity over Runciman's change of attitude in Prague, particularly since Beneš had already moved a considerable distance but that the SdP had hitherto shown little sign of compromise. The French conceded that it was incumbent on Beneš to make substantial concessions to the SdP, but they depended on Runciman's 'spirit of impartiality and justice' to protect the position of the Czechoslovak authorities. Halifax confessed that he too was 'somewhat puzzled' by Runciman's change of policy, but explained that, finding it difficult to make its own assessment of particular proposals, the British government had no alternative but to place its trust in Runciman's judgement.[16]

Despite Halifax's professed puzzlement over Runciman's action, the new policy direction of the Mission in Prague appears to have caused few raised eyebrows within the Foreign Office. Roberts merely minuted in passing that Runciman had 'more or less committed himself to the Carlsbad points', adding that Beneš would have to accept this 'provided he can be satisfied [that] the integrity of the state can be preserved'[17] – which was precisely the point at issue. The question of granting the SdP's demands in full had been raised in the Central Department some ten days previously by Michael Creswell in connection with the visit to London by von Kleist. Creswell argued that the only effective means of avoiding the outbreak of war, of which von Kleist warned, was 'to get Lord Runciman to produce recommendations containing all that the Sudetens could reasonably desire', including '"self-determination"' and for Britain to offer Czechoslovakia 'a definite public commitment if they are accepted'. He added: 'Unfortunately the corollary to this is very strong pressure on the Czechs, amounting to a statement that we would leave them to their fate if they do not accept the Runciman proposals.'[18] This suggestion was remarkably close to the action taken in Prague by Runciman and Newton in early September – though there was, of course, no question of any British commitment being offered in exchange for concessions. Despite this similarity, there is no evidence to indicate that Runciman's acceptance of the Carlsbad demands as a basis for a settlement had taken place at the behest of London, although in applying severe pressure on Beneš he was undoubtedly carrying out the wishes of the British government.

It is unclear precisely why Runciman chose to put his weight behind the SdP's Carlsbad programme during his meeting with Beneš on 1 September. Only the previous day, his declared intention was to threaten Beneš with the production of his own plan – or more accurately that prepared by Stopford – in the event of the Czechoslovak side failing to make further concessions to the SdP. Stopford's plan (as discussed previously), although based substantially on the eight Carlsbad points, sought to reconcile them with the Czechoslovak government's objective of maintaining the integrity of the state. Its entire credibility depended upon it being presented as a compromise solution, but there appears to have been no question of any compromise in the threats issued by Runciman and repeated by Newton during their meetings with Beneš between 1 and 3 September. At least part of the explanation for this unplanned change of approach probably lies in Runciman's state of health, as was the case with his preparedness to resort to arbitration which he had first indicated to Halifax on 30 August. The tiredness he complained of on that occasion persisted, and a week later he wrote again of being 'almost exhausted' by insomnia.[19] There is also some evidence that Runciman himself was conscious of overreacting to events at about this time. In a draft note to Halifax (undated and almost certainly never sent, but probably written on 2 September) Runciman explained that his telegram of 30 August – in which he expressed his intense dissatisfaction with the Third Plan – had been written when he was 'impatient' with the Czechoslovak government.[20] It is therefore probable that it was the combined effects of stress and fatigue that caused Runciman to go beyond his original intention in pressing Beneš on 1 September.

Curiously though, Beneš appears not to have been unduly alarmed by this at the time. Runciman reported that the President did not consider the acceptance of the Carlsbad demands as being impossible and described his attitude as being 'conciliatory and encouraging'. Beneš even asked Runciman to continue to pay him frequent visits[21] – an invitation he was soon bitterly to regret. Even when Runciman repeated his warning the following day Beneš remained unperturbed, and it required Newton's forceful intervention on 3 September to drive the message home fully to the disconsolate President, who then sought immediate clarification from Runciman and de Lacroix. Precisely why Newton's words should have had so much greater impact than Runciman's is puzzling, particularly when Newton did little more than reiterate emphatically what he believed Runciman had stated earlier. But for one reason or another, Runciman initially failed to get his message across with sufficient clarity. Possibly he may not have made a clear distinction between Stopford's proposals and the Carlsbad demands and was in actual fact still considering using the former as a basis for a settlement. That was certainly the indication given when, transmitting a brief outline of Stopford's plan to London on 3 September – the day of maximum pressure on Beneš – Runciman prefaced his dispatch by describing the contents as 'a summary of the proposals which I am preparing', adding that they were 'of course subject to alteration in the light of developments here'.[22] But whatever the reason behind the differing interpretations of the conversations conducted in Beneš's office during the early days of September, and whatever the motivation for words uttered by the British representatives, the outcome was clear. By the evening of 3 September, Beneš was left in no doubt that what the British government required of him was to grant the SdP the substance of their Carlsbad demands.

The previous day, Beneš had also been informed of the SdP's reaction to the Third Plan. During the morning of 2 September, in the course of a four-hour meeting, Kundt and Sebekowsky indicated that the President's proposals failed to fulfil their party's requirements. Their views were presented to Beneš in writing the following day in the form of counter-proposals set out in a lengthy 14-point memorandum.[23] The document did not amount to an outright rejection of the Third Plan but proposed some significant extensions of it. Four of its points, the preamble and the sections concerning proportionate government funding for areas such as health and education, linguistic equality, and measures for reducing tension, differed little from the President's proposal. Four further points referred to matters not raised in Beneš's plan. Overdue local elections were to take place within three months; government departments were to be divided into ethnic sections and the internal administration of the state reorganised to correspond with the new autonomous areas; all discrimination against the SdP was to cease; and restitution made for damages caused to the German population.

The remaining six points required changes, some substantial, to Beneš's plan. The SdP sought to achieve proportionality in government service within five years and for official employees in each district to reflect exactly the national composition of the local population. The Third Plan envisaged an 8–10 year period and for at least 50 per cent of state employees in German districts to be German. The counter-proposal for economic relief in depressed areas sought to increase the proposed government loan from

700 million crowns to 1000 million crowns, of which 700 million crowns (as opposed to 500 million) would be earmarked for the benefit of the German population. The SdP also required the agreement to be treated as an indivisible whole and to be implemented without delay, the necessary legislation being drafted jointly by the government and the SdP. In his plan, Beneš aimed to place legislative proposals before Parliament during the forthcoming autumn session. Concerning security, whereas the President proposed to return to the sharing of responsibilities between state and local police forces only as conditions within each area permitted, the SdP sought an immediate return to the previous arrangements. On the crucial issue of autonomy, the SdP required the area to be determined on a historical basis, thus providing for a more extensive self-governing territory than proposed by Beneš, and for the granting of legal personality to each nationality in order to protect minorities outside the autonomous area.[24]

The SdP's response to the Third Plan came as no surprise to Beneš, who anticipated counter-proposals,[25] nor was it unexpected by the British mediators, although it did give rise to disappointment when Runciman learned of it during his meeting with the President on 2 September.[26] Further information, of a more positive nature, reached Runciman and his colleagues later that day, when Kundt visited the Mission headquarters in order to explain his party's attitude to current developments. He did so at some length, arriving at the Hotel Alcron at 6.30 p.m. and not leaving until midnight.[27] In his conversation with Ashton-Gwatkin, Kundt conveyed an essentially optimistic message, emphasising the points of agreement with the President's plan. The only major problem, he indicated, concerned the central question of Sudeten German autonomy. The proposed creation of three autonomous German districts was unacceptable to the SdP because Germans living outside these areas would remain, as Ashton-Gwatkin reported to London, 'at the mercy of the Czech majority'.[28]

Kundt proceeded to explain that, although no compromise was possible between the demands of the SdP and the government's present proposals, because the latter 'represented the hitherto existing system with certain reforms', compromise was possible between the principles behind the President's position, 'unity, sovereignty, [and] integrity of the State', and the principles of the SdP's eight Carlsbad points. He challenged the government's contention that the SdP's demand for autonomy was incompatible with the unity of the state, pointing out that Swiss cantons enjoyed a wider measure of autonomy than that demanded by the SdP. The desired unity of the state, Kundt maintained, would be preserved by the unity of the Army, foreign policy, and political and financial administration.[29]

Judging from Ashton-Gwatkin's report to London that agreement was 'well within reach on everything except "Selbstverwaltung"' – though he conceded this was 'all important'[30] – Kundt's detailed report on his and Sebekowsky's conversation with Beneš did not give rise to undue alarm in the British Mission. It is therefore improbable that it was news of the SdP's effective rejection of the Third Plan which caused Runciman to step up the pressure on Beneš the following day. Likewise, the assertion made by Kundt in his earlier conversation with Runciman on 31 August, that Beneš had conveyed the impression of being confident of forthcoming British, French and Soviet support,[31] appears, surprisingly, not to have perturbed the Mission. It was not immediately reported to London, and there is no evidence to suggest that it significantly influenced Runciman. More probably, it was the belief, stimulated by Kundt, that an agreement appeared to be within grasp, which gave rise to the hope that one final push against Beneš might secure it without delay.

This belief, that an agreement on the basis of the Third Plan was attainable, had been brought to the attention of the British Mission in a telephone despatch from Halifax on 1 September, the day before Ashton-Gwatkin's lengthy conversation with Kundt. Citing a source 'in close contact with Sudeten leaders', the Foreign Secretary indicated that 'moderates' within the SdP, Kundt in particular, wished to negotiate seriously with Beneš but were being held back by their distrust of the President. Halifax advised therefore that Runciman should encourage Kundt, that very day, to proceed with negotiations, whilst at the same time applying the strongest possible pressure on Beneš.[32] The British mediators lost little time in applying Halifax's advice, and their actions appear to have been substantially underpinned by the belief that an agreement was within reach. The contents of the memorandum drawn up by Ashton-Gwatkin during his talk with Kundt on 2 September, which minimised the differences between the two sides, were employed by Runciman in his meetings with Beneš, Hodža and Kašpar in the following days.[33] Moreover, Runciman himself confirmed this attitude when informing Halifax on 5 September, a Monday, that: 'I cannot be sure of an agreement this week but that is what I am working for.'[34] It is probable therefore that this belief in the relative closeness of the two sides was a further factor – additional to the pressure from London, personal disillusionment with Beneš, and impatience and fatigue due to illness – responsible for prompting Runciman into applying extreme pressure on the President for more extensive concessions to the SdP.

Unpleasant though it was for Beneš to receive such unceremonious handling from representatives of a friendly power, who sought (in Ashton-Gwatkin's words) 'to keep him up to the scratch',[35] the situation might have been, from his point of view, even more humiliating. The President could draw a small crumb of comfort from the fact that the exertion of pressure on him was conducted behind closed doors and not in the full glare of international publicity. Such consideration was not due to any concern on the part of Runciman and Newton for Beneš's susceptibilities, but to the belief that private pressure on the Czechoslovak government was more likely to achieve the desired results than that exerted in public. In his letter to Halifax of 5 September, reporting on the effects of the concerted pressure on Beneš, Runciman complained of the President's dilatoriness in negotiating with the SdP, but observed that 'nothing can be said in public about this unfortunate defect in his methods'. He added that, despite the severe private warnings to Beneš, 'we are not giving him away' as a 'stiff back' was essential in his dealings with the SdP 'up to the last moment'.[36]

A similar consideration is also evident in the response of the British mediators to an enquiry from Halifax concerning the contents of a proposed speech, to be delivered in early September, following up Simon's Lanark address. The Foreign Secretary's principal intention was to counter the German government's accusation that the Lanark speech had not been even-handed.[37] Runciman's advice, given the day before his crucial conversation with Beneš on 3 September, was to soft-pedal. Newton reported that Runciman now considered the Czechoslovak authorities to be sufficiently aware that they would 'have to go a long way' and that 'to hammer them further might provoke resentment and make them less disposed to listen to him'. Some public recognition of the efforts made by the government might, however, be helpful in securing further concessions. Newton cautioned that it had to be borne in mind that the 'Czechs are an obstinate people [who] react unfavourably to threats' and that care should therefore be taken to address the speech to Germany as well as Czechoslovakia. In particular, he advised the Foreign Secretary to avoid the use of the expression 'concessions which are essential for a settlement', which Halifax had included in his dispatch. Newton argued that such a phrase 'would be unfair as logical conclusion would be that Czechs must give way on every point whether reasonable or unreasonable which Germans may consider essential for a settlement'.[38] This laudable public sensitivity was not reflected, however, in Newton's private dealings with Beneš. Halifax also sought the views of the Ambassador in Berlin. Henderson advised that the Foreign Secretary acknowledge Hitler's 'goodwill' and his 'declared love of peace' and that a sympathetic reference be made to Henlein. He further suggested that Halifax should point out that the Czechoslovak government was urged to make concessions for the sake of peace and the 'principle of self-determination'.[39]

In the event, the views of the British representatives in Central Europe proved superfluous, as Halifax decided not to follow up the Lanark speech, but besides throwing light on an aspect of Runciman's thinking, the episode also served to demonstrate the extent of his active involvement in the British diplomatic process. Although on this occasion it was purely Runciman's advice which was being sought by the Foreign Office, more important still was the role he played in the actual execution of British policy in Czechoslovakia. In doing so Runciman did not, of course, slavishly follow every detail of the frequently arriving communications from London. As previously mentioned, he resolutely refused to travel to Germany to meet Hitler and also declined to accept Halifax's repeated urging that the details of Beneš's Third Plan be published. However, the differences between Runciman and the British government were essentially limited to matters of tactical detail and did not concern the main thrust of diplomatic strategy. Being on the spot and more immediately involved in developments, Runciman sometimes judged the situation somewhat differently from the way it was perceived in London. This, in due course, became recognised in the Foreign Office. Having sent a flurry of anxious telegrams to Prague in late August, Halifax conceded, on 1 September, that in view of the rapidly developing situation in Czechoslovakia, Runciman was in a better position than the Foreign Office to determine the most appropriate action he should take.[40]

A week later Halifax confirmed that view. In a reflective letter, sent via the diplomatic bag on 6 September and intended primarily to raise the mediator's flagging morale, the Foreign Secretary indicated that Runciman had won the argument against the publication of his own or any other proposed solution. Moreover, Halifax's earlier doubts concerning the wisdom of the mediator himself proposing a settlement had began to resurface. The Foreign Secretary disclosed to Runciman that, 'from time to time', he experienced the feeling, which he had expressed in a letter some three weeks previously, 'that the position might become very embarrassing if you were to produce a scheme that you deemed reasonable, which was then immediately rejected by Hitler'. The confused signals emanating from London were due to the fact that, as Halifax explained, 'we live from day to day digesting or expecting what comes from you or making suggestions that I fear are generally belated and sometimes irrelevant'. He nevertheless added the hope that the 'suggestions' offered might sometimes prove useful.[41]

At the receiving end of the communications from London, Ashton-Gwatkin was much less circumspect in his choice of words, noting that same day that because of the rapid movement of events in Czechoslovakia: 'F.O. instructions are sometimes out of date when they reach us.'[42] The term 'instructions' was indeed apposite when used in connection with the campaign of intense pressure exerted on Beneš in early September. This action was instigated at the behest of the Foreign Secretary in London and carried out by Runciman in close co-ordination with Britain's official diplomatic representative in Czechoslovakia. It is ironic that Runciman's professed independence was exercised only in going beyond the instructions from London in forcing acceptance of the Carlsbad demands on the President, thus committing Britain to an even harder line against the Czechoslovak government than was being pursued by the Foreign Office. Arguably, however, in doing so Runciman was merely following his instructions through to their logical conclusion – a development which Halifax himself baulked at. Nonetheless, irrespective of the issue of the Carlsbad demands, the extreme pressure applied by Runciman on Beneš was clearly not the action of an independent mediator but that of an agent of the British government.

By coincidence, it was also at this time that the Runciman Mission publicly abandoned its hitherto much proclaimed insistence on being entirely independent of London. It did not do so for any diplomatic purpose, but for practical reasons – and because members of the Mission judged it no longer necessary to maintain that fiction. The official residence of the Mission, at the Hotel Alcron in the centre of Prague, had been deliberately chosen not only as neutral territory, but also to demonstrate Runciman's professed independence of the British government. But the luxury hotel proved an uncomfortable base for the 67-year-old mediator who, owing to the combined effects of a late-summer heatwave and the noise of passing traffic, experienced (as previously mentioned) considerable difficulty sleeping. Neither the installation of air conditioning in Runciman's suite nor the closure of the street outside the hotel to traffic – both carried out shortly after the Mission's arrival in Prague[43] – did much to ease the situation and, despite his regular weekend breaks away from the city, Runciman's insomnia persisted. This, together with the perception of the heavy responsibility for the preservation of peace resting on his shoulders, took a considerable toll of the reluctant mediator's none-too-robust constitution. By early September, Runciman's health reached such a low ebb that he moved his residence from the Hotel Alcron to the more tranquil atmosphere of the British Legation on higher ground beneath the Prague Castle. The move was made possible by the altered role of the Mission – now overtly acting in concert with the British Minister. As Ashton-Gwatkin observed, there was 'absolutely no need now to maintain the figment that we hardly know the Legation'.[44] The Mission office, however, remained located in the Hotel Alcron.

Whilst Runciman, with Newton's forceful assistance, was turning the metaphorical thumbscrews on Beneš, the other party to the dispute, the SdP, received very different treatment. No instructions came from the Foreign Office to apply corresponding pressure for concessions on the SdP negotiators, nor were Runciman and his staff inclined to use their initiative in that direction. None of the available evidence concerning several meetings which took place at that time – that between Runciman and Kundt on 31 August, and between Ashton-Gwatkin and Henlein in Marienbad that same day and at Aš (Asch) on 4 September, and his meeting with Kundt on 2 September – contains so much as a hint of a suggestion from the British side that the SdP might be more accommodating in their attitude towards Beneš's most recent proposals. Arguably, of course, there was little point in doing so, for the British in London and in Prague were under no illusion concerning the SdP's independence of Berlin.

When it came to seeking to influence Germany itself, however, the situation was not dissimilar. The British government restricted itself to the vague formula of the Lanark speech, which was nevertheless subsequently largely contradicted by Runciman's personal goodwill messages sent via Henlein to Hitler. Even Halifax's contemplated follow-up to the Lanark speech was aimed more at redressing the perceived imbalance in that pronouncement – arising, it was believed, from a failure to admonish the Czechoslovak government – than at reissuing a warning to Germany. However, the draft text prepared by the Foreign Secretary proved unacceptable to his colleagues who met to consider it on 1 September. Present at the meeting were Wilson, Vansittart, Oliphant and Sargent, who were later joined by Malcolm MacDonald, now the Colonial Secretary. One notable absentee was Cadogan, on holiday in Le Touquet. Reporting by letter to the Prime Minister, who was also on holiday (in his case in Scotland), Wilson indicated that it was the feeling of the meeting that the Foreign Secretary was both too critical of the Czechoslovak authorities and too menacing towards the German government. For his part, Wilson was primarily concerned about the severity of the proposed threat to Germany, which he considered most unwise.[45] A further meeting took place in the Foreign Office three days later, on Cadogan's return to London. Halifax was also present on that occasion. Again, no firm decision was taken on any action pending the anxiously expected report from Ashton-Gwatkin on the outcome of Henlein's visit to Hitler. During the discussion, Cadogan added his objection to a public declaration being made, supporting instead, as he noted in his diary, 'the idea of a *private* warning to Hitler' that Britain would protect France.[46] This particular avenue was to be pursued somewhat further in due course. Meanwhile, accepting the critical observations of his colleagues, and also influenced by positive reports of Henlein's meeting with Hitler, Halifax had, by 6 September, abandoned the idea of delivering his proposed speech. Explaining his decision to Henderson, the Foreign Secretary candidly confessed to being at a loss as to how to deal with Hitler:

> I am constantly reminding myself of the importance of not getting wrong with the psychology of this strange man, but all said and done one is all the time groping like a blind man trying to find his way across a bog, with everybody shouting from the banks different information as to where the next quagmire is![47]

As a result of this bewilderment, the British government issued no warning to Berlin to counter-balance the pressure being applied on Prague. Indeed, on his return to Berlin on 1 September, Henderson specifically informed Weizsäcker that he had no instructions to issue any warning to the German government.[48] He also disclosed that British pressure on Beneš was about to achieve results, and drew attention to the importance of Henlein making a positive response, adding by way of encouragement (according to Weizsäcker) the observation that: 'Cherries are not swallowed whole, but eaten in two bites.'[49]

The outcome of Henlein's visit to Hitler, which had influenced Halifax's decision not to warn Germany, was awaited just as keenly by Runciman and his colleagues in Prague as it was in the Foreign Office. Being informed by Hohenlohe that Henlein was expected back from Berchtesgaden imminently, Ashton-Gwatkin travelled to Červený Hrádek during the evening of 3 September to be on hand for a meeting with the SdP leader. Early the following morning he left with Hohenlohe for Henlein's home at Aš, where, on arrival, Ashton-Gwatkin was left to cool his heels in the office accommodation downstairs. Whilst waiting, he was much impressed by the smart uniformed appearance of Henlein's personal staff ('clean, decent-looking fellows') and observed a bust of Henlein in one corner and a plaque of Hitler on the wall above it. After 20 minutes, Runciman's chief assistant was ushered upstairs to meet an exceedingly jovial Henlein who was, Ashton-Gwatkin noted, 'clearly very pleased at the outcome of his mission'. In the modest living quarters, which impressed Ashton-Gwatkin by their simplicity and which he described as a 'village schoolmaster sort of dwelling', he also met Henlein's family. He was introduced to Henlein's wife and young boy and also to his aged mother, whom Ashton-Gwatkin congratulated on her 'famous son'.[50]

Predictably, Henlein's account of his meeting with Hitler bore little resemblance to reality. The SdP leader reported that he conveyed to Hitler the two messages from Runciman and also a verbal commendation of the Mission's work. He claimed, however, that Hitler chose not to discuss relations between Britain and Germany, but enquired of Henlein what his policy was. Henlein maintained that he stressed at the outset his desire to avoid war – with which Hitler firmly concurred – and then indicated two policy options: either autonomy within Czechoslovakia or a plebiscite leading to, as Ashton-Gwatkin noted, 'solidification with the Reich'. Henlein added that he expressed a preference for autonomy, but that in either case he wished to achieve his objective by peaceful means. Hitler reportedly shared the desire for a peaceful solution, but expressed considerable scepticism concerning the likely success of Henlein's preferred policy.

Ashton-Gwatkin was delighted by what he heard during the two-hour-long conversation and ascribed particularly great significance to Henlein's cheerful demeanour. In addition, he was much impressed by Henlein's impudent request not to give 'too rosy an account' of the meeting to the Czechoslovak authorities, lest it might make them more intransigent. Ashton-Gwatkin was also greatly relieved by Henlein's repeated – but nonetheless disingenuous – assurance that Hitler had not set a time limit for a resolution of the crisis. Henlein did, however, set such a limit himself. He explained to his British visitor that the SdP was due to hold its first rally in Česká Lípa (Böhmisch Leipa) in Northern Bohemia in mid-October, at which, Ashton-Gwatkin noted, 'it would be necessary for him to make a big speech ... and be able to announce that all had been satisfactorily arranged'. In order to be able to do so, Henlein added, an agreement would have to be reached by the end of September[51] – which, unknown to Ashton-Gwatkin, was near enough the date Hitler had in mind for launching 'Operation Green' against Czechoslovakia.

Henlein's account of his meeting with Hitler was a skilful misrepresentation of the truth which once again succeeded in duping his British visitor. In view of the instructions from Hitler to continue for the time being the negotiations with the Czechoslovak authorities, Henlein was bound to tell Ashton-Gwatkin what the British wished to hear – namely, that a peaceful outcome of the Czechoslovak crisis was still possible. In addition, Henlein used the opportunity to increase the pressure on the Czechoslovak authorities by representing Hitler as being sceptical concerning the prospects for success of Henlein's professed preferred solution of autonomy within Czechoslovakia. Hitler, by implication, favoured the alternative policy of a plebiscite and the subsequent incorporation of the Sudeten German territory into Germany. This device, of course, also served to reinforce Henlein's moderate reputation in British eyes. The message of reasonableness and moderation was further reinforced by Hohenlohe, who expressed great relief over the outcome of Henlein's visit to Berchtesgaden and, for Ashton-Gwatkin's benefit, put an optimistic gloss on certain aspects of Henlein's report. Hohenlohe presented Henlein's display of satisfaction at his visit as evidence of Hitler's endorsement of Henlein's 'peaceful' policy, and the fact that Hitler did not impose a time limit as indicating that he did not intend bringing matters to a head at Nuremberg.[52]

In addition to having his view of Henlein's moderation reinforced by this skilful performance, Ashton-Gwatkin had once again been beguiled by the SdP leader's considerable charm. Confirming his earlier assessment of his host, Ashton-Gwatkin noted that Henlein was 'an honest unpretentious man' free from 'any complexes', and forgave him his momentary inclination 'to rant a bit about the grievances of his people and to thump the arm of his chair'. During the course of their conversation, over glasses of cherry brandy, Runciman's principal assistant and the leader of the SdP drank, in Ashton-Gwatkin's words, 'with growing friendship to a happy future'.[53] Despite the bonhomie, however, a note of unease crept into Ashton-Gwatkin's assessment of his latest conversation with Henlein causing him to record, in the privacy of his diary, 'a very friendly talk ... but very little concrete'.[54] Ashton-Gwatkin also alluded to the lack of substance in the outcome of Henlein's visit to Hitler in a brief telephone call to the Prague Legation from Aš,[55] although he did not develop or even repeat the point in his more detailed reports to London. Clearly, Ashton-Gwatkin felt some disappointment that his private diplomatic initiative, launched two weeks previously in Marienbad, had yielded such meagre results.

Ashton-Gwatkin's eagerly awaited report of Henlein's visit to Hitler was received with mixed feelings in the Foreign Office. The first reaction, that of

Roberts, was one of concern. He regarded Hitler's response as 'extremely non-committal' and also viewed as 'not very promising' Hitler's reported scepticism concerning prospects for the achievement of Sudeten German autonomy. He nevertheless took some comfort from the fact that Hitler appeared prepared to give Henlein and Runciman 'a little longer in which to obtain concessions from the Czechs' by keeping the demand for a plebiscite in reserve. Roberts was also surprised by Hitler's failure to respond to Runciman's goodwill messages, especially to the overtures concerning British–German relations.[56] This last point also troubled Sargent, who, before going on leave, left word that he too wished to draw attention to the fact that Hitler had not replied to Runciman. But others in the Foreign Office assessed matters differently. A meeting held in Halifax's room on 5 September took a more sanguine view, concluding that the 'general effect is rather better than might have been expected'. It was argued – with unintended irony – that 'Herr Hitler could hardly be expected to show his hand to so relatively insignificant a person as Herr Henlein, particularly if what he said was to be passed on to Lord Runciman'.[57] No one, it would appear, thought to question the veracity of Henlein's report.

This optimistic collective assessment of the Berchtesgaden meeting was, however, at variance with a further comment from Roberts the following day, which again betrayed some disappointment. Responding to a report from the Ambassador in Berlin, Roberts noted that Henlein had been 'singularly uninformative' concerning his conversation with Hitler. Henderson had learned from his Italian counterpart that Hitler had made some unspecified counter-proposals to Henlein, for immediate implementation and for the longer term. Roberts noted that Henlein had reported differently to Ashton-Gwatkin, but added that the new information was probably correct, as 'the obvious Sudeten game is to obtain the principle of autonomy now and work out the details later'.[58] However, irrespective of Hitler's views concerning SdP policy, his silence on the issue of relations between Britain and Germany came as a considerable disappointment to the Foreign Office. Cadogan admitted as much when he minuted that the outcome of Henlein's mission to Berlin had to be 'noted and remembered', but there was 'nothing to be done about it'.[59] The British government was left to draw the inescapable conclusion that yet another overture to Hitler – albeit a somewhat unorthodox one, initiated not in London but by Ashton-Gwatkin in Czechoslovakia – had run into the sands. This concern was reflected in an urgent request to Runciman, on 5 September, for an assessment of the situation following Henlein's meeting with Hitler. Halifax's request was coupled with a sharp reminder that, as the Nuremberg Rally was already then under way, it was imperative that 'some sort of concrete step ... registering definite advance' was made by the negotiators or by Runciman himself before Hitler's closing speech, due on 12 September.[60] Henlein's visit to Hitler had clearly done nothing to reduce British anxiety.

One other person who had been on tenterhooks awaiting the outcome of Henlein's visit to Hitler was Britain's Ambassador to Berlin. 'What did Hitler say to Henlein? That is the question.' So mused Henderson in a dispatch to London, while still awaiting reports of the meeting. He also supplied his own supposed answer; 'not less than the Karlsbad programme and I wonder if that is now going to suffice'. He also supplied, in passing, a prescient suggestion for breaking the deadlock, should Runciman's attempts at mediation fail – namely, an international conference to revise the Treaty of Versailles. The participants would be Britain, France, Germany and Italy with Czechoslovakia attending as the '"corpus delicti"'. Poland and Hungary might also attend as observers, but the Soviet Union, being a non-signatory of the Versailles settlement, would be excluded.[61] However, Henderson had not given up hope of assuaging Germany by other means. Following his return from London in late August, Henderson continued to argue that a military confrontation would only be avoided if major concessions were forthcoming from the Czechoslovak authorities. The Ambassador became particularly concerned about the possibility of Hitler demanding a plebiscite for the Sudeten Germans in his Nuremberg speech, following an indication by Weizsäcker that he strongly favoured that solution. Henderson was surprised that this alternative had not hitherto received more publicity within Germany and feared that it was being reserved for Hitler's speech.[62] In a postscript to a letter to Cadogan sent on 4 September, before receiving any news of Henlein's meeting with Hitler, Henderson outlined the situation as he saw it: 'Either the Karlsbad programme and a State of Nationalities or (a) a Plebiscite or (b) a war after which C.S. could never be reconstituted as it is today.'[63]

Henlein's report of his Berchtesgaden meeting, as given to Ashton-Gwatkin, confirmed Henderson's fears concerning a plebiscite and he lost no time in pointing out that the risks to the territorial integrity of Czechoslovakia arising from the acceptance of the Carlsbad programme were preferable 'to the certainty of losing Sudeten areas as a result of a plebiscite ... or of war'. Henderson also interpreted Henlein's reported satisfaction with the outcome of his conversation with Hitler as proof of the fact that Hitler still favoured a 'pacific solution'. He warned, however, that Hitler's attitude might change rapidly if Beneš could not be induced to accept the Carlsbad programme without delay.[64] The Ambassador conceded that Hitler was under pressure to resort to military action, although he remained hopeful that, thanks to 'Hitler's own love of peace, dislike of dead Germans and hesitation of risking his regime', war would be avoided if he were to secure a diplomatic victory over Czechoslovakia and become regarded as the preserver of peace in Europe.[65]

The arrival of the Nuremberg Nazi Party Congress, at which Hitler was expected to deliver his much feared verdict on the Sudeten German problem, added further to the Ambassador's concern. Henderson was keen to attend the festivities together with other members of the Berlin diplomatic corps as he believed they would provide a useful opportunity for meeting prominent members of the German government and possibly even Hitler himself. He also hoped that his own presence at the Nazi rally might have 'some restraining value'.[66] Although rating the chances of either peace or war being declared at Nuremberg at about even, Henderson continued to cling to his belief that Hitler would choose the former. In a personal letter to Cadogan, written on the eve of his departure for Nuremberg, Henderson also expressed the view that prospects for peace would be enhanced if Hitler were to receive a better press in Britain. He therefore suggested that the Foreign Office News Department influence the British press to present Hitler 'as the apostle of Peace'. Positive results would only be achieved, he argued, if abuse of Hitler ceased and he were given the opportunity of being a 'good boy'.[67]

However, no such consideration was to be extended to Beneš – he was to be forced into granting concessions to the SdP. Henderson continued to argue that Beneš was still failing to make sufficient progress and that only 'direct compulsion' would make him 'see realities'. He suggested that Beneš might possibly be inviting such compulsion in order to save face with his own people and in the hope of obtaining guarantees from Britain and France, but urged nevertheless that the necessary pressure be brought to bear.[68] 'Beneš will never go far enough till he is *made* to do so', Henderson argued in his letter to Cadogan, adding that, as the entire world was looking to Britain 'to save civilisation', action was imperative. 'We *must* take the bull by the horns', he urged.[69] In the light of these views, Newton's telegrams to London concerning his and Runciman's meetings with Beneš in early September, copies of which were also sent to the Berlin Embassy, doubtless provided satisfying reading for Henderson.

The unprecedented pressure Runciman and Newton brought to bear on Beneš between 1 and 3 September left the President in absolutely no doubt that the Runciman Mission, with the British government behind it, was neither seeking a compromise solution nor playing for time, but was actually endeavouring to placate the SdP at the inevitable expense of Czechoslovakia. Runciman's declared intention of forcing the acceptance of the Carlsbad programme on the Czechoslovak authorities amounted to moral blackmail. If the government failed to grant the required concessions, Czechoslovakia would be abandoned by Britain and France and forced to come to terms as best it could with the SdP and Nazi Germany under the threat of military annihilation. Pursuing the alternative course, of bowing to Runciman's pressure and accepting the SdP's Carlsbad programme, also placed the security of the state in jeopardy, though hopefully retaining the support of the western powers. In those circumstances Beneš had little choice but to resort to the latter alternative, especially since, he considered, it did still hold out a slim prospect of success. As the President noted in his memoirs, he set out, with Hodža's agreement, 'to provide the British and French Governments with a final demonstration of our goodwill and simultaneously provide evidence that all concessions would be in vain, even if we went to the extreme limits'.[70] Beneš's hopes, however, were to prove utterly futile.

Notes

1 Halifax to Runciman, in Halifax to Newton, 31 August 1938, *DBFP*, 3/II, no. 724.
2 Runciman to Halifax, in Newton to Halifax, 1 September 1938, *DBFP*, 3/II, no. 730.
3 Newton to Halifax, 2 September 1938, *DBFP*, 3/II, no. 740.
4 Newton to Halifax, 3 September 1938, and Runciman to Halifax, 5 September 1938, *DBFP*, 3/II, nos 753 and 783.
5 Newton to Halifax, 4 September 1938, *DBFP*, 3/II, nos 758 and 759. See also Beneš, *Mnichovské dny*, pp. 201–3.
6 Newton to Halifax, 4 September 1938, and Runciman to Halifax, 5 September 1938, *DBFP*, 3/II, nos 759 and 783.
7 Runciman to Halifax, 5 September 1938, *DBFP*, 3/II, no. 783.
8 See below pp. 330–3.
9 Kašpar to Beneš, 4 September 1938, *Mnichov v dokumentech*, (2 vols, Prague, 1958), II, no. 101; Runciman to Halifax, 5 September 1938, *DBFP*, 3/II, no. 783; Beneš, *Mnichovské dny*, pp. 203–4.
10 Newton to Halifax, 2 and 3 September 1938, *DBFP*, 3/II, nos 740 and 752. Hodža (as mentioned previously) had requested a similar British intervention in conversation with Newton in late July.
11 'Minute of conversation between Mr. R.J. Stopford and Dr. Smutný', 1 September 1938, FO 800/304, f. 131.
12 Halifax to Campbell, 31 August 1938, *DBFP*, 3/II, nos 726 and 729.
13 Campbell to Halifax, 1 September 1938, and Newton to Halifax, 2 September 1938, *DBFP*, 3/II, nos 733 and 740; Bonnet to Corbin and de Lacroix, 1 September 1938, *DDF*, 2/X, no. 520.
14 Halifax to Phipps, 4 September 1938, and Halifax to Newton, 4 September 1938, *DBFP*, 3/II, nos 763 and 762.
15 Phipps to Halifax, 5 September 1938, *DBFP*, 3/II, no. 781. See also Beneš, *Mnichovské dny*, p. 203.
16 Halifax to Phipps, 5 September 1938, *DBFP*, 3/II, no. 782; Corbin to Bonnet, 5 September 1938, *DDF*, 2/XI, no. 8.
17 Minute by Roberts, 5 September 1938, C 9169/1941/18, FO 371/21734. No minutes directly concerned with Runciman's change of policy could be found in the Foreign Office records.
18 Minute by Creswell, 22 August 1938, C 8520/1941/18, FO 371/21732. Creswell also speculated that von Kleist's warning of impending conflict may have been contrived in order to induce greater British pressure for concession on the Czechoslovak authorities, but added that this was no reason for not taking all possible action to avoid war.
19 Runciman to Halifax, 5 September 1938, *DBFP*, 3/II, no. 783.
20 Note by Runciman, undated, Runciman Papers, WR 296. Internal evidence suggests that the note was written on 2 September.
21 Newton to Halifax, 2 September 1938, *DBFP*, 3/II, no. 740.

22 Runciman to Halifax, in Newton to Halifax, 3 September 1938, *DBFP*, 3/II, no. 756.
23 Beneš, *Mnichovské dny*, pp. 198–9.
24 *Ibid.*, document no. 35, pp. 463–70. See also Laffan, *Crisis over Czechoslovakia*, p. 236, n. 1.
25 Beneš, *Mnichovské dny*, pp. 185–6.
26 Newton to Halifax, 2 September 1938, *DBFP*, 3/II, no. 746.
27 Ashton-Gwatkin to Strang, 6 September 1938, *DBFP*, 3/II, appendix II (III), p. 668.
28 Ashton-Gwatkin to Strang, in Newton to Halifax, 3 September 1938, *DBFP*, 3/II, no. 755.
29 Memorandum by Ashton-Gwatkin, 2 September 1938, C 9613/1941/18, FO 371/21736. In an accompanying note, dated 6 September, Ashton-Gwatkin explained that the memorandum had been drawn up by himself following the conversation with Kundt, 'who agreed to it as representing his views'.
30 Ashton-Gwatkin to Strang, 6 September 1938, *DBFP*, 3/II, appendix II, (III), p. 668.
31 'Notes of a conversation between Lord Runciman and Herr Kundt on 31 August 1938', FO 800/305, f. 41.
32 Halifax to Runciman, in Halifax to Newton, 1 September 1938, *DBFP*, 3/II, no. 735. The report probably came via Vansittart though it could not be traced in the Foreign Office records.
33 Note by Ashton-Gwatkin, 6 September 1938, C 9613/1941/18, FO 371/21736.
34 Runciman to Halifax, 5 September 1938, *DBFP*, 3/II, no. 783.
35 Ashton-Gwatkin to Strang, 6 September 1938, *DBFP*, 3/II, appendix II (III), p. 668.
36 Runciman to Halifax, 5 September 1938, *DBFP*, 3/II, no. 783.
37 Halifax to Henderson and Newton, 1 September 1938, *DBFP*, II, no. 737. See also Wilson to Chamberlain, 1 September 1938, PREM 1/265.
38 Newton to Halifax, 2 September 1938, *DBFP*, 3/II, no. 742. Newton also demonstrated his talents as a political speech-writer by supplying Halifax with some choice phrases for inclusion in the proposed address. These included the following appeal: 'Not to shrink from such far-reaching adjustments or even sacrifices as may be necessary on one side, and on the other to show spirit of compromise and to make a real response and show genuine intention to collaborate in building up a State in which all nationalities concerned can co-operate in a spirit of loyal partnership.' (Newton to Halifax, 2 September 1938, *DBFP*, 3/II, no. 743.)
39 Henderson to Halifax, 2 September 1938, *DBFP*, 3/II, no. 745.
40 Halifax to Runciman, in Halifax to Newton, 1 September 1938, *DBFP*, 3/II, no. 735.
41 Halifax to Runciman, 6 September 1938, Halifax Papers, H/VI/61, FO 800/309. For the earlier letter, see Halifax to Runciman, 18 August 1938, *DBFP*, 3/II, no. 643.
42 Ashton-Gwatkin to Strang, 6 September 1938, *DBFP*, 3/II, appendix II (III), p. 670.
43 *The Sunday Times*, 7 August 1938.
44 Ashton-Gwatkin to Wilson, 13 September 1938, C 9914/1941/18, FO 371/21738 and FO 800/304. See also Runciman to Halifax, 5 September 1938, *DBFP*, 3/II, no. 783.
45 Wilson to Chamberlain, 1 September 1938, PREM 1/265. Wilson enclosed a copy of the draft text with his letter.

46 Dilks, ed., *Cadogan Diaries*, p. 94.
47 Halifax to Henderson, 6 September 1938, *DBFP*, 3/II, no. 792. See also Halifax to Runciman, 6 September 1938, Halifax Papers, H/VI/61, FO 800/309.
48 Henderson to Halifax, 1 September 1938, *DBFP*, 3/II, no. 736.
49 Minute by Weizsäcker, 1 September 1938, *DGFP*, D/II, no. 419.
50 Ashton-Gwatkin to Strang, 6 September 1938, *DBFP*, 3/II, appendix II (III), p. 669.
51 Ashton-Gwatkin to Strang, in Newton to Halifax, 4 September 1938, *DBFP*, 3/II, no. 765. Ashton-Gwatkin also considered significant Hitler's reported amiability towards Henlein. Henlein indicated that Hitler had conversed at length on matters outside politics and had showed the SdP leader round his farm where, in the cowsheds, he declared: 'Here are the members of the National Socialist Bovine Movement.' Ashton-Gwatkin noted with satisfaction: 'So the Führer has his lighter moments.' (Ashton-Gwatkin to Strang, 6 September 1938, *DBFP*, 3/II, appendix II (III), p. 669.)
52 Ashton-Gwatkin to Strang, in Newton to Halifax, 5 September 1938, *DBFP*, 3/II, no. 777; Ashton-Gwatkin to Strang, 6 September 1938, *DBFP*, 3/II, appendix II (III), p. 669. Hohenlohe also drew attention to Henlein's denigration of Frank, whom the SdP leader characterised to Ashton-Gwatkin as a '"treue soldat" but an ass' and unsuitable therefore for inclusion in the SdP's negotiating team. Hohenlohe added that Hitler recently called Frank a 'damned fool' and offered Ashton-Gwatkin the interpretation that the 'extremist' Frank was not being pushed by Berlin to challenge Henlein for the leadership of the SdP.
53 Ashton-Gwatkin to Strang, 6 September 1938, *DBFP*, 3/II, appendix II (III), p. 669.
54 Ashton-Gwatkin's diary, 4 September 1938, FO 800/304.
55 Newton to Halifax, 4 September 1938, C 9173/1941/18, FO 371/21734.
56 Minute by Roberts, 5 September 1938, C 9182/1941/18, FO 371/21734.
57 Minute by Strang, 6 September 1938, *ibid.* Halifax also received some unspecified secret information, concerning Henlein's meeting with Hitler, which reinforced his optimism. (Halifax to Henderson, 6 September 1938, *DBFP*, 3/II, no. 792.)
58 Minute by Roberts, 6 September 1938, C 9215/1941/18, FO 371/21735. For Henderson's report, see Henderson to Halifax, 5 September 1938, *DBFP*, 3/II, no. 776.
59 Minute by Cadogan, 7 September 1938, C 9182/1941/18, FO 371/21734.
60 Halifax to Runciman, in Halifax to Newton, 5 September 1938, *DBFP*, 3/II, no. 778.
61 Henderson to Halifax, 4 September 1938, *DBFP*, 3/II, nos 767 and 771.
62 Henderson to Halifax, 1, 4 and 5 September 1938, *DBFP*, 3/II, nos 738, 767 and 776.
63 Henderson to Cadogan, 4 September 1938, DBFP, 3/II, no. 772.
64 Henderson to Halifax, 6 September 1938, *DBFP*, 3/II, no. 785.
65 Henderson to Halifax, 5 September 1938, *DBFP*, 3/II, no. 776.
66 Henderson to Halifax, 2 September 1938, *DBFP*, 3/II, no. 748.
67 Henderson to Cadogan, 6 September 1938, *DBFP*, 3/II, no. 793.
68 Henderson to Halifax, 4, 5 and 6 September 1938, *DBFP*, 3/II, nos 771, 779 and 785.
69 Henderson to Cadogan, 6 September 1938, *DBFP*, 3/II, no. 793.
70 Beneš, *Mnichovské dny*, p. 205.

12
The Last Resort

Runciman and his colleagues did not have long to wait for signs to emerge that their decisive intervention with Beneš in early September had proved effective. During the morning of 5 September, Ashton-Gwatkin visited the Prime Minister to deliver an account – as he knew it – of Henlein's recent meeting with Hitler. Encouraged by his visitor to resume contacts with the SdP, Hodža then disclosed the outline of a new proposal for Sudeten German self-government, the basis of which was to be announced that evening. Initially, it was unclear to the British mediators who was behind the new initiative, particularly since Beneš did not refer to it during his conversation with Runciman later that day. It was also speculated that the new proposal might closely resemble the plan prepared by Stopford, which had been communicated unofficially to the Czechoslovak authorities a few days previously.[1] That assumption was reinforced the following day when Stopford was invited to accompany Ashton-Gwatkin to visit Hodža. In the event, no reference was made to Stopford's plan,[2] although Hodža did provide some further details of the emergent proposals, stressing in particular that they were envisaged as a basis for a settlement rather than as a rigid plan, and that additional points would be open for discussion.[3]

The new proposals were, in fact, prepared by Beneš as a direct consequence of Runciman's and Newton's pressure. The Fourth Plan, as the proposals inevitably became known, was approved by the Czechoslovak inner cabinet, under the chairmanship of the President, during the evening of 5 September, although the details did not reach the SdP negotiators until the morning of 7 September. The British Mission was informed of the plan the previous day. In addition to Ashton-Gwatkin and Stopford receiving some details from Hodža during the morning, Runciman was presented with the complete version, in German, by Beneš late that afternoon.[4] The delay in informing the SdP appears to have resulted from the desire on the part of the government to secure Runciman's endorsement for the Fourth Plan in advance of its presentation to the SdP negotiators. Hodža's attempt to obtain this over the telephone, during the evening of 6 September, was rebuffed by the Mission. Runciman declined to accept any responsibility for the proposals and urged that they be handed to the SdP without further delay.[5]

The Fourth Plan was a direct development of Beneš's Third Plan and of the SdP's response to it, and had evidently been produced in great haste. Two of its 11 points, concerning, respectively, the allocation of state funds and a propaganda truce, were substantially identical with components of the Third Plan and the SdP's counter-proposals. Five further points were developments of Third Plan proposals incorporating items from the SdP's response. These proposals included: the provision for further negotiation; the proportional distribution of all state employee posts and the eligibility for re-employment of dismissed political activists; increasing the loan to one thousand million crowns (with 700 million crowns going to German areas); the restoration of local police responsibility for security alongside that of the state police; and the involvement of the SdP in drafting the necessary legislation. One new aspect of the Fourth Plan, added in response to the SdP, was the proposed creation of special departments responsible for ethnic issues within central state authorities and the establishment of special courts to resolve disputes. Two further points went some way towards meeting the SdP's requirements, without satisfying them entirely. One proposed that the resolution of cases of hardship resulting from earlier discrimination should be the subject of further negotiation, and the other that the projected autonomous territories should be defined in accordance with the nationality of the population. The SdP had sought restitution for damages suffered during the nationalities conflict and a consolidated autonomous territorial unit determined on a historical basis. Finally, one other element of the Third Plan was extended (though not at the behest of the SdP) by proposing equality for all minority languages. An annex to the Plan also proposed an amnesty for previously disciplined official employees, speedy elections to public bodies and an assurance of no discrimination against members of the SdP.[6]

When informing Runciman of the Fourth Plan, Beneš stressed that it amounted to capitulation which, he believed, Britain and France would come to regret.[7] Allowing for an element of hyperbole in the President's words, the concessions made were nevertheless considerable. Subsequently, Beneš claimed that he believed the implementation of the Fourth Plan would result in the establishment within Czechoslovakia of a territory governed not on democratic constitutional principles but on a totalitarian basis, which would, sooner or later, become detached. He nevertheless made the proposal partly in order to convince Britain and France of his good faith, and partly because he was confident that the SdP would reject the deal. Beneš explained that he sought to demonstrate to his allies 'that even the greatest concessions ... would not halt Pan-Germanism, whether emanating from Berlin or the so-called Sudetenland'. He also saw the

Fourth Plan as offering the last remaining opportunity for attempting to secure for Czechoslovakia the support of Western Europe and the rest of the world in the event of war with Germany.[8] Under severe pressure from Britain and France to make concessions, Beneš sought to call the bluff of the SdP and turn the situation to his advantage, even at this eleventh hour.

The first reactions to Beneš's initiative from British representatives was not unfavourable. Indeed, Runciman's response to the Fourth Plan was in marked contrast to the bitter disappointment he had expressed on receipt of its predecessor only eight days earlier. The crucial question in the mediator's mind was whether the new proposals amounted to a fulfilment of the SdP's Carlsbad demands, any prospect of a compromise solution having long since been abandoned. The Czechoslovak government certainly claimed that its latest proposals substantially complied with the SdP's requirements, and furnished the Mission with supporting arguments in two additional memoranda. The government maintained that it had fully met six of the eight Carlsbad demands – concerning equality between Czech and Germans, the definition of German territory, the granting of full autonomy to this territory, legal protection for minorities in other areas, reparation for injustices suffered by Germans since 1918, and the appointment of German officials in German areas. As far as one of the two remaining demands was concerned – the freedom to profess allegiance to the German nationality and political philosophy – the government argued that this question did not arise as the state recognised the full political rights of all citizens.[9] The last outstanding demand – for legal personality to be granted to the German population – was covered in greater detail in the second explanatory document, which drew attention to the vague nature of the concept and to the possible dangers to the unity of the state that might arise from it. The government pointed out, however, that the new proposals not only recognised the rights and interests of nationalities, and established machinery for their protection, but that they also contained specific references to nationalities as groups. The explanatory document also argued that the SdP's demand for ethnic proportionality in government employment be achieved within five years was unrealistic, a period of 'at least ten years' being considered necessary.[10]

An additional, but formally unspecified, aspect of the SdP's demands was the requirement for the autonomous territory to comprise a single consolidated unit. Although this point was not addressed in the Fourth Plan itself nor in the supplementary memoranda, the government took care not to exclude the possibility. During his explanation of the proposals to the British mediators on 6 September, Hodža indicated (as reported by Runciman) that the proposed autonomous districts 'might be united by some kind of committee which would give a form of unity to the whole national area and thus provide a single self-government for over two million Germans'.[11] Although not quite providing what the SdP was seeking, the

Prime Minister's words nevertheless indicated a willingness on the government's behalf to go some way towards meeting their requirement.

The British mediators were largely convinced by the exposition of the government's case. Even before the complete details of the Fourth Plan had been fully studied by the Mission staff, Runciman reported favourably to London on the new proposals. Whilst cautioning that the situation remained 'very delicate and ... uncertain' he stated, unequivocally: 'This basis represents a very great advance, in fact a real self-government.' Providing the SdP accepted the plan, he added, the way was 'at last clear to an agreement', although many difficulties would doubtless still arise.[12] The following day, Ashton-Gwatkin also reported that the new proposals went 'a very long way to meet the eight Karlsbad points'.[13] Writing at greater length a day later, after a discussion with the SdP negotiators, Ashton-Gwatkin repeated that assessment indicating that, although 'much clarification' was required, the proposals were 'sufficiently near the eight points to serve as an adequate basis for resuming official negotiations'.[14] Even after the vicissitudes to come in the following weeks, Runciman persisted in his positive assessment of the Fourth Plan. In his formal report on the outcome of the Mission, sent to Chamberlain and Beneš on 21 September, he maintained that the plan 'embodied almost all the requirements' of the Carlsbad demands.[15]

Runciman's and Ashton-Gwatkin's uncharacteristically positive reports concerning the latest proposals caused some surprise in London. When Runciman first alerted the Foreign Office to the new initiative from Beneš, Cadogan wondered whether it was in fact Runciman's plan (prepared by Stopford) that was being put forward. He requested clarification from the Prague Legation, being anxious to know 'whether we – or L[or]d R[unciman] – have another shot in our locker'.[16] Further analysis of the outline report of the new proposals led to the conclusion that they differed in certain important respects from Runciman's plan, although an enquiry was nevertheless addressed to Newton.[17] However, a more detailed study of the advance summary of the new Czechoslovak initiative left Roberts less than impressed with its content. He observed that, at first sight, the proposals did not seem to be 'such an advance towards the Karlsbad points' as press reports had indicated, because key elements of the SdP's demands remained unsatisfied. Nevertheless, Roberts noted with approval Hodža's offer of further negotiations and also Runciman's positive assessment of the plan, observing: 'Lord Runciman is really in a better position than we are to form a judgement on these new proposals and I do not think we can express any opinion upon them until we know the Sudeten reaction.'[18]

On receipt of the full version of the Fourth Plan the Foreign Office was somewhat reassured and Roberts minuted that it was 'quite clear that they do go a very long way to meet the 8 Karlsbad demands and are in fact a much more satisfactory offer than at first sight appeared'. He added that 'some attempt has been made to meet all the Karlsbad points except 8' – the freedom to profess German political philosophy – but noted that there was 'really nothing very much to interfere with such freedom at present in Czechoslovakia' and there would be even less if the new proposals were adopted. Regarding two other outstanding points, the issue of legal personality and the question of reparations, Roberts noted with approval that 'an attempt has after all been made to meet the German point of view'. Although not disguising the fact that difficulties remained, particularly concerning the proposed limits of the autonomous areas and the retention of the state security forces alongside the local police, Roberts concluded that 'the Czech offer seems a very reasonable basis for negotiations and I do not think that Lord Runciman and Mr. Gwatkin have taken too favourable a view of it'.[19] Strang concurred with this assessment, noting with surprise: 'Yes these proposals are a nearer approximation to the Karlsbad programme – or a reasonable interpretation of that rather equivocal document – than I thought the Czechs would ever be brought to offer.'[20]

Evidently, the British evaluation of Beneš's Fourth Plan, both within the Foreign Office in London and on the ground in Prague – though tempered with anxiety concerning the SdP's response – was that it offered the SdP the substance of their demands. To their considerable embarrassment the SdP leadership thought likewise. Indeed, Beneš was subsequently to claim that Kundt and Sebekowsky had themselves drawn up the Fourth Plan at his invitation. In an interview with the journalist G.E.R. Gedye, published in the *Daily Herald* in 1945, the President recalled that at a meeting with the SdP negotiators he invited Kundt and Sebekowsky to write down on paper their full demands, which he would grant immediately. The negotiators declined the invitation, but dictated their requirements to Beneš, who wrote them down and signed the document. Beneš also claimed in the interview that he had informed Runciman of this incident the following day.[21] Sebekowsky, however, subsequently denied such an occurrence had taken place,[22] and there is no evidence to indicate that Runciman had been informed of it by Beneš. Ashton-Gwatkin and Stopford also did not come to hear of the incident at the time.[23] Moreover, Beneš himself made no reference to this episode in his memoirs, in which he specifically claimed authorship of the Fourth Plan.[24] In all probability therefore, the meeting as described to Gedye had become embellished over the years in the President's imagination. Nevertheless, although the SdP negotiators may not have actually dictated the Fourth Plan to Beneš, it was certainly drawn up with the specific intention of meeting their demands.

The SdP obtained their first indications of the new Czechoslovak proposals when Hohenlohe visited the Hotel Alcron in the morning of 6 September. He was urgently dispatched to inform the SdP negotiators of the development and, in Ashton-Gwatkin's words, 'to persuade Kundt to persuade Henlein that the Eight Points really are in the new proposal'.[25]

Kundt and Rosche duly arrived at the Mission offices that afternoon to seek further information and to question Hodža's re-entry into the negotiations.[26] Runciman joined the discussions on his return from visiting the President, and in addition to reassuring the SdP representatives concerning Beneš's continuing key role, the British spent some time outlining the government's new proposals as they understood them.[27] Kundt's immediate reaction was non-committal. He expressed scepticism concerning the practicability of the proposed self-governing districts, which, he claimed, would result in expensive duplication of administration, and also foresaw the need for some form of judicial tribunal to enforce the implementation of any settlement. Kundt stressed however that these were his personal views, and that it would be for Henlein himself to determine whether the Fourth Plan fulfilled the requirements of the Carlsbad programme.[28]

The SdP negotiators formally received details of the Fourth Plan the following morning, 7 September, when Kundt accompanied by Kier, the party's legal adviser, visited Hodža. The Prime Minister explained that the new plan was based on the Carlsbad demands, and indicated that he was aware of the importance Henlein attached to securing that programme. He also repeated the statement made to the British mediators the previous day, that the proposals were not yet in their final form, and that, in particular, details concerning arrangements for self-government would require further elaboration in discussion between the two sides. The SdP representatives appear to have made no immediate comment on the new initiative, except to complain of the premature publication of the proposals.[29] A brief summary of the Fourth Plan had been released by the government, appearing in the press the following day.[30]

The full SdP negotiating team, with Frank in the chair, met that afternoon to discuss the unexpected new situation. They came to the unanimous view that, particularly in the light of the Prime Minister's statement that the proposals were open for further discussion, they had no alternative but to accept the Fourth Plan. Kier considered that the government's proposals granted the Carlsbad demands in theory, although it remained to be seen how they would be carried out in practice.[31] Frank also believed the proposals to be very far-reaching, conceding 90 per cent of the SdP's demands; others put the figure at 95 per cent.[32] A confidential resolution was adopted accepting that the Fourth Plan covered all the substantial points of the Carlsbad programme, although three demands – those concerning the equality of national groups, the question of legal personality, and recognition of the self-governing area – were only partially satisfied. The resolution concluded that, subject to these issues, the new proposals formed a 'theoretically suitable basis for agreement', though 'exceptional difficulties' were to be anticipated in their implementation.[33]

The views of two members of the SdP negotiating team were elaborated further in separate memoranda sent via the German Legation in Prague to

Nuremberg, where members of the German government were gathered for the Nazi Party Rally. In the first memorandum, Kier set out the perceived alternatives. In the event of rejection:

a) Strongest possible support from Britain and France for the Czechs.
b) The Czech people united behind the Government.
c) Removal of all dissension in the Czech Government camp.
d) No new *point de départ* for the Sudeten Germans and elimination of all possibilities of a solution, not involving the use of force.

In the event of acceptance:

a) The State undoubtedly greatly weakened.
b) Great difficulties for the Government with the Czech people and increase in internal Czech differences.
c) Extraordinary difficulties in necessary negotiations in the Parliament.

In Kier's view the balance of advantage clearly lay in accepting the proposal. During the implementation of the agreement, he argued, ample opportunity would arise for the SdP to demonstrate the failure of the Czechoslovak authorities to fulfil their promises. He added, moreover: 'Even in the unlikely event of a *complete realisation* of the eight points, there is no danger in acceptance, since by skilful carrying out of this policy by the Sudeten German Party ... the power of the State can be completely undermined from within.' He therefore saw no benefit in further delay, and advised immediate acceptance of the Fourth Plan.[34]

Even less circumspect in tone was the second memorandum, drawn up by Kundt, who headed the negotiating team. He also advised acceptance of the government's proposals, arguing: 'If the Sudeten German Party does not wish to put itself, and thus also the German Reich, in the wrong, the Sudeten German Party must eventually accept such an agreement which, outwardly and in its essential content, covers the most important principles of the Karlsbad demands.' The offer being made by Beneš under British and French pressure was, Kundt believed, a device to gain time and the Czechoslovak authorities would inevitably seek to evade its implementation. Kundt reasoned, in terms most revealing of the objectives of the Carlsbad demands, that it must be assumed that Beneš and his colleagues were

> fully aware that, if such an agreement actually materialises, the Germans will acquire such a position within the Bohemian-Moravian area, in conjunction with the encircling of this area by the greater German Reich and full cooperation between Sudeten German and Reich German forces

> made possible by the treaty, that though the State remains in form a sovereign, independent, and to a certain extent unified State, enclosed by State frontiers, in practice it will come, in a very short space of time, not only to economic and intellectual, but also diplomatic and military subjection.

Kundt therefore argued that the aim of German and SdP policy should be 'to demonstrate to world opinion the dishonesty of ... Beneš, as we succeeded in doing in the case of the more clumsy stupidity of Schuschnigg, in such a way that the Western Powers were no longer prepared to take up arms for such a politician'. The main danger Kundt saw in rejecting the Fourth Plan was the probability that Runciman would come forward with a proposal of his own, which he knew was already in preparation. Such a development would, he argued, enhance the political significance of the Runciman Mission and 'thereby establish the British in the Central European region', thus making 'political intervention by the Reich more difficult'. Kundt concluded therefore that by accepting the Fourth Plan 'the Bohemia-Moravia-Silesia area would either come unobtrusively under the exclusive influence of the Reich, or that, on the sudden violation of this agreement by the Czechs, there would remain the possibility of a solution by other means'. Ultimately, however, this was a decision for Hitler himself, but Kundt urged that it be taken without delay to avoid both Germany and the SdP being placed at a disadvantage.[35] Aiming, no doubt, to expedite such a decision, Frank and Schicketanz travelled to Nuremberg to join Henlein, who was already attending the Nazi festivities.[36]

Kundt's memorandum amounted to an unequivocal statement of the real objectives of SdP policy. It is not surprising, therefore, that although Hohenlohe supplied Ashton-Gwatkin with a copy of the SdP delegation's confidential resolution and also allowed him to read, but not retain, a presumably bowdlerised version of Kier's memorandum,[37] he was not granted similar access to Kundt's report. Ashton-Gwatkin was informed, however, that it strongly advocated the resumption of negotiations and the desirability of an agreement, and also that a summary of the memoranda was being sent to Henlein at Nuremberg for transmission to Hitler. This information caused Ashton-Gwatkin to report to London that 'the Sudeten German leaders themselves appear to be doing their utmost to convince the German government and Herr Hitler himself that the way of negotiation is the best way and that [the] Czechoslovak Government's offer is in general adequate'.[38]

The main thrust of the documents Ashton-Gwatkin did see differed little from the view that he himself had expressed to Hohenlohe, that the new proposals came close to satisfying the Carlsbad demands, which could be met fully through additional negotiations. Ashton-Gwatkin had added – as reported to Berlin by the German Legation in Prague – that Britain and

France would not allow the Czechoslovak authorities to 'make difficulties over ... implementation' of the plan. He was also reported to have indicated that if the Czechoslovak government failed to fulfil its undertakings, 'Britain would regard herself as being under no obligation'.[39] It was doubtless welcome to the SdP negotiators to learn from Ashton-Gwatkin that further British pressure on the Czechoslovak authorities was available should it be required. Nevertheless, for the moment the SdP was on the defensive and needed to play for time pending the arrival of fresh instructions from Germany. Fortunately for the SdP, a solution to their dilemma was immediately to hand.

On the day the SdP negotiating delegation met to consider its response to the Fourth Plan, 7 September, a group of other prominent party figures visited Moravská Ostrava (Mährisch Ostrau), an industrial town in northern Moravia, to investigate the alleged mistreatment of German prisoners. Over 80 SdP members and sympathisers had recently been arrested there on charges of smuggling arms and other security offences. A sympathetic German crowd gathered to greet the delegation, and a hostile Czech counter-demonstration soon materialised. During police intervention to disperse the demonstrators a mounted officer struck a member of the visiting delegation – the SdP parliamentary deputy Franz May – with a riding whip, which resulted in SdP accusations of police brutality and breaches of parliamentary immunity. There were no serious injuries and only six people were briefly detained by the police.[40]

The incident itself was relatively minor and lasted less than half an hour, but it provided the SdP with a convenient pretext for suspending all negotiations with the government pending an enquiry and punishment of the alleged police offenders. This decision was justified on the grounds that the authorities were not sufficiently in control of the situation to hold out any prospects of success for concluding a settlement of the nationalities problem.[41] The Moravská Ostrava incident, in fact, only offered the SdP leadership a temporary respite, and it reported with some concern to the German Legation in Prague that following the resolution of the incident it saw 'for the present no possibility of refusing acceptance of Government proposals and avoiding negotiations for its implementation'.[42] Nevertheless, the SdP sought to make the most of the situation and the entire negotiating team, under Frank's leadership, called at the Hotel Alcron during the afternoon of 7 September to inform Runciman in person of the new crisis.[43] The British mediator expressed great concern and offered to assist in any way he properly could. He also observed that a general settlement of the nationalities problem would provide the best means of avoiding disorder and appealed to the SdP not to allow a local incident to prejudice world peace.[44]

The SdP delegation's dramatic visitation succeeded in alarming the British mediators[45] and prompted Ashton-Gwatkin to issue a stern warning via

Hohenlohe that Runciman would consider it 'extremely provocative' if the SdP used the incident as a pretext for abandoning further discussions with the Czechoslovak authorities.[46] This was the first occasion on which such a message was given to the SdP. The reports of the Moravská Ostrava incident also caused much alarm in London. Indeed, so concerned was Halifax that he considered making a personal appeal to Hitler in the event of a breakdown in negotiations, and an urgent request for advice was therefore telegraphed to Runciman in the early hours of 8 September.[47] Following a meeting with Beneš later that morning, during which the President assured his visitor that the government was intent on resolving the incident without delay, Runciman was able to send a calming message back to London. He also added the observation that Beneš showed no further sign of resenting British and French pressure expressed the week before.[48]

The previous evening, following their conversation with Runciman, two members of the SdP delegation, Kundt and Rosche, called on the Prime Minister to communicate formally the party's intention of suspending negotiations 'until the Moravská Ostrava incidents had been liquidated'. Hodža was able to give them an immediate assurance that a rigorous investigation of the events in question was already under way and that appropriate steps would be taken to punish any police officers found guilty of breaches of discipline. The SdP representatives agreed to reconsider the situation the following day in the light of this statement.[49] Meanwhile, the Runciman Mission initiated an intensive round of dinner-table diplomacy. During the evening of 7 September, Kundt returned again to the Hotel Alcron where he joined members of the Mission for dinner. Hohenlohe was also present. The following evening Frank dined with the British mediators, and remained in conversation with Ashton-Gwatkin and Stopford until 2 a.m. Ashton-Gwatkin noted that 'he was in a nervous and apprehensive state'. Stopford recalled that, during dinner, Frank was 'being very difficult' over the resumption of negotiations. In subsequent discussions, however, after emphatic warnings from Ashton-Gwatkin concerning the dangers for peace arising from the situation, Frank disclosed the SdP's terms for resolving the Moravská Ostrava incident, authorising Ashton-Gwatkin to convey these directly to Hodža.[50]

The following morning, 9 September, Ashton-Gwatkin duly called on the Prime Minister to deliver the SdP's conditions for resuming negotiations.[51] The demands included the immediate arrest and punishment of those police officers who had assaulted the SdP delegation in Moravská Ostrava, and an enquiry into the conduct of the police chief in the town. A further immediate enquiry was demanded into the cases of those recently detained in Moravská Ostrava for security offences, leading to their being charged or released without delay. Lastly, an independent post-mortem examination was demanded on a prisoner who died as a result of a fall from a train while being transported to prison.[52] Hodža at once accepted the terms, and

Ashton-Gwatkin relayed this information to the SdP when Kundt called again at the Hotel Alcron in the late afternoon. A timetable was immediately drawn up for the resumption of contacts between the government and the SdP. Informal talks about talks were arranged for the following day, 10 September, a Saturday, with full negotiations recommencing on 13 September. Later that evening Kundt visited Hodža to confirm these arrangements, and word subsequently came to the Mission headquarters that the Moravská Ostrava incident had been satisfactorily resolved.[53]

The Czechoslovak government immediately announced that the police chief in Moravská Ostrava had resigned from his post and that several other police officers, including the officer accused of striking the SdP parliamentary deputy, had been suspended pending disciplinary investigation.[54] In effect, the government had capitulated to the demands of the SdP. Adapting Ashton-Gwatkin's turn of phrase, used earlier in a different situation, having swallowed a substantial camel in the shape of the Fourth Plan, the Czechoslovak authorities were not going to strain at the gnat of a relatively minor local incident, thus offering the SdP a pretext for breaking off negotiations and an easy escape from the dilemma that Beneš, under British pressure for concessions, had constructed for them.

By accepting responsibility for the Moravská Ostrava incident the government had, for the moment, retained the initiative in its dealings with the SdP, but it had done so at a price in terms of Czech public opinion. When informing the Czechoslovak representatives in London and Paris of the outcome of the Moravská Ostrava incident, the Foreign Minister reported that for the first time in several months considerable public disquiet was evident amongst the Czech population.[55] The extent of the disquiet may be gauged from a petition of more than one million signatures presented to the government at this time, urging that no further concessions be made to the SdP.[56] Beneš also disclosed to Runciman that the concessions offered in his latest proposals were meeting with opposition from some of his own supporters.[57]

Criticism of Beneš's action, particularly in offering the Fourth Plan, came mainly from the centre and the left of the political spectrum, prompting the declaration from Bechyně, the Social Democrat leader and Deputy Prime Minister, that the government would not go 'one millimetre further' in granting concessions to the SdP.[58] Another prominent Social Democrat, Meissner, who headed the Committee of Six, which officially negotiated with the Runciman Mission on behalf of the government, complained to Ashton-Gwatkin of the President's intervention in the negotiations and was critical of the extensive nature of the concessions proposed in the Fourth Plan.[59] However, it was not only the political left that was unhappy with developments even before Beneš's latest offer to the SdP. Tomáš Bat'a, the shoe manufacturer, also made public statements urging the government not to surrender. Consequently, when he called at the Mission offices at the end of August, Ashton-Gwatkin advised him, bluntly, 'to stick to his last'.[60] Not all Ashton-Gwatkin's Czech acquaintances however disapproved of the government giving way to the SdP. Another prominent Czechoslovak business figure, Jaroslav Preiss, the head of one of the country's largest banks, the Živnostenská banka – to whom Ashton-Gwatkin awarded the supreme accolade of 'an objective Czech, which is not usual'[61] – argued that further concessions would need to be made to achieve peace. He believed that the present government proposals might have secured a settlement some five months before, but that they were now inadequate.[62] Preiss, however, was not representative of the majority of Czechs. The belief that no further concessions should be made to the SdP was widespread amongst Czech opinion and, as Ashton-Gwatkin observed, the proposed Fourth Plan was generally 'looked upon as a national misfortune to be endured for the sake of peace'.[63] The mood of the nation was accurately expressed by one government official, who observed disconsolately to members of the Runciman Mission, concerning the Fourth Plan: '*Mon coeur tchèque pleure.*'[64]

In an attempt to calm public anxiety, Beneš addressed the people of Czechoslovakia on radio during the evening of 10 September. The President appealed for peace and calm and sought to reassure his audience that although the pace of change towards securing a nationalities settlement would accelerate, the country's democratic spirit would be preserved. He promised full equality for all national groups, whether Czech, German, Slovak, Hungarian, Ruthenian or Polish. Addressing the Czechs, though not by name, Beneš spoke of 'making no small sacrifice for the preservation of world peace'. The objectives were, he stated, to establish good relations with all neighbouring states, particularly with Germany, and to prove to the world, especially to Britain and France, 'that we understand our duty with regard to general collaboration'.[65]

Members of the Runciman Mission were greatly relieved by Beneš's conciliatory attitude, believing that an agreement between the government and the SdP was now attainable, though by no means certain. Runciman himself indicated to Halifax, on the day before Beneš's speech, that he did not now anticipate a breakdown in the negotiations, 'unless brought on by some external influence or internal incident'.[66] Two days after the President's broadcast Stopford was more explicit, stating in a letter to a relative, 'we have to all intents and purposes got agreement here', though, he added, substantial dangers remained from Hitler's forthcoming speech and from violent incidents.[67] Ashton-Gwatkin struck a similar note the following day when writing to Horace Wilson. Referring to Wilson's allusion to a 'gap' between the two sides, Ashton-Gwatkin explained: 'With the last proposals of the Czech Government the "gap", as we know it, practically disappears.' Ashton-Gwatkin also shared Stopford's concern over incidents, concluding that 'whereas progress towards settlement is now on the right lines, the atmosphere has become troubled and the visibility dim'. Responsibility for the incidents, he maintained, was shared by both sides.[68]

In the case of the Moravská Ostrava incident, however, the British representatives in Prague were in no doubt as to which party was responsible. One of the British observers monitoring unrest in Czechoslovakia, who visited the scene immediately following the incident, placed the blame unequivocally on the SdP. Sutton-Pratt concluded that the incident was 'greatly exaggerated' and did not justify the suspension of negotiations.[69] In a later, more detailed report, Sutton-Pratt indicated that even if the police acted impetuously they were, in his view, justified in dispersing the German crowd in order to avoid clashes between Czechs and Germans. He also found no evidence to support the allegation that the German prisoner who died in a fall from a train had been murdered. The British observer did, however, find that several of the German prisoners had been ill-treated by the Czechoslovak authorities, some very badly.[70] Sutton-Pratt's final report on the incident itself concluded that it was 'yet another "put-up job"' to publicise the 'police mishandling scandal'.[71] The view of the Runciman Mission concurred with Sutton-Pratt's assessment. Runciman himself, in his letter of report to Chamberlain and Beneš, merely accused the SdP of exploiting the incident to suspend or sever the negotiations then in progress, without holding them responsible for its actual instigation.[72] Ashton-Gwatkin, however, not often critical of the SdP, was in no doubt that the Moravská Ostrava incident had been intentionally provoked by the SdP in order, he believed, to interrupt negotiations until after Hitler's speech at Nuremberg.[73]

Wherever the cause of the Moravská Ostrava incident lay, it appeared at the time that, thanks largely to the activities of the Runciman Mission, the issue had been satisfactorily resolved and contact re-established between the Czechoslovak authorities and the SdP. The British mediators, not unnaturally, believed they had achieved a considerable success. In conversation with Lord Stamp, who was visiting Czechoslovakia for an international meeting (doubtless unaware that some three months previously he had been proposed by Runciman as an alternative mediator), Stopford characterised the Mission at this time as 'an island of self-satisfaction in a sea of panic'.[74] Ashton-Gwatkin noted in his diary on Saturday, 10 September, with a mixture of complacency and relief 'so we got this world a rather better weekend'.[75]

Feeling well pleased with the fruits of their diplomacy, the British mediators dispersed into the Bohemian countryside for the weekend. The Runcimans were once again the guests of the German aristocracy, visiting the seat of Count Edmund Czernin, at Petrohrad (Petersburg) near Jesenice (Jechnitz) west of Prague. At the castle on the Sunday morning, Runciman received an SdP delegation headed by one of the party's parliamentary deputies, Georg Wollner, who spent an hour talking about their grievances.

Meanwhile a crowd of several thousand SdP supporters had gathered outside, chanting Nazi slogans, singing the German national anthem and the Horst Wessel song, and calling for a plebiscite. The crowd also chanted:

> *'Lieber Runziman mach uns frei*
> *Von der Tschechoslovakei.'*

Runciman was prevailed upon to appear on the balcony and briefly addressed the crowd with the words: 'Good men and women, you are living in a wonderful country, perhaps one of the finest in the world. I pray God that He will give peace to this fine country.' The words were translated into German by Czernin.[76] Stopford, accompanied by a member of the Prague Legation, headed further westwards to the vicinity of Carlsbad, and also encountered SdP activity. On the Sunday evening they came across a night exercise being carried out, 'very openly and efficiently' by SdP para-military units, and their vehicle was stopped at several check-points. Stopford and his companion returned to Prague both refreshed and relieved.[77]

Ashton-Gwatkin remained in the capital on the Saturday, having lunch and tea, respectively, with the Polish and French Ministers, noting that it was 'the first easy day since we came'.[78] The following day he too headed for the country, in the company of the Swiss Minister and his wife, to visit the castle of Prince Max Lobkowicz at Roudnice (Raudnitz), north of Prague. After lunch Ashton-Gwatkin proceeded to Hohenlohe's seat at Červený Hrádek, where he met Kier, the SdP's legal adviser. Their discussion centred on the Fourth Plan, particularly on those aspects of it which, in the view of the SdP, required further development. Kier identified these as being a clearer definition of the German national group and its acquisition of legal personality; the need for a head (an individual or a committee) for the German group; the delineation of responsibilities between the central parliament and the autonomous authority; and the establishment of a distinct German representation in the central parliament.[79]

On his return to Prague later that morning Ashton-Gwatkin had no reason to doubt that a major obstacle had been overcome. His satisfaction was doubtless all the more exquisite, as the apparent resolution of the Moravská Ostrava incident had been almost entirely his own work. Except for receiving the SdP delegation during the afternoon of 7 September and making one visit to Beneš the following morning, Runciman had played no part in the intensive round of diplomacy at the end of the previous week. The two previous days, in fact, marked a new low point in Runciman's state of health. His recent move from the Hotel Alcron to the calmer atmosphere of the British Legation had not brought about the hoped for relief from insomnia, and on the morning of 8 September he felt too ill to travel from the Legation to the Mission office. Runciman did, nevertheless, respond to a summons from Beneš and later arrived at the Hotel Alcron, Stopford recalled, somewhat 'refreshed'.[80] The recovery was short-lived, however, and Ashton-Gwatkin noted in his diary the following day that Runciman was 'very tired'.[81] Stopford also reported, in a letter on 12 September, that 'the Lord has been more or less hors-de-combat with tiredness for 3 or 4 days'. In addition, Stopford was full of admiration for Ashton-Gwatkin, whom he described as 'amazingly good', as he had 'carried things lately even more than before'.[82]

News of Runciman's indisposition also reached the German Legation, which reported to Berlin on 8 September that the British mediator 'almost suffered a nervous collapse the day before yesterday'.[83] A subsequent report from Hencke noted that only Ashton-Gwatkin was still playing an 'active part', and that he had indicated to Hohenlohe that Runciman 'was no longer studying the situation, and was annoyed by the methods of negotiation of both parties'. Hohenlohe believed that Runciman wished to return to London without delay.[84] Ashton-Gwatkin's aristocratic friend was indeed well informed, for it was at this time that Britain's mediator came closest to abandoning his Mission. In a pencilled note on British Legation notepaper, undated but from internal evidence probably written on 9 September, Runciman recorded:

> I am feeling strain and cannot expect to be able to keep up successfully my efforts to conciliate actively. We shall have to deal with a new situation next week. When time comes for renewed action I shall have to carry a great burden and I would like you to consider whether and at what stage I ought to hand over to Newton and Gwatkin.[85]

The note was evidently intended for Halifax, and almost certainly never sent, but was nevertheless clearly indicative of Runciman's very troubled state of mind in early September.

A further considerable contribution to Runciman's discomfort at this time was undoubtedly made by rumours of his planned assassination.[86] Although Runciman himself appears not to have made any reference to the reported threats, they did reach the attention of the British government, which gave consideration to dispatching two British detectives to Prague to protect the mediator. Newton, however, advised against such a step arguing it was likely to be seen as implying that the Czechoslovak authorities could not maintain order within their own country.[87] It was also considered by British security advisers that the arrangements for Runciman's protection made by the Czechoslovak police were adequate. The Cabinet was therefore informed, on 12 September, that no action would be taken for the moment, although the situation would be kept under review. The rumoured threats to Runciman's life, and also to that of Henlein, coincided with reports of German plans to attack Czechoslovakia in the near future, for which they would serve as a pretext.[88] More probably, however, the reports were linked with a cryptic offer by Hohenlohe, reported by the German Legation in Prague on 9 September, to 'force the ... speedy departure' of the Runciman Mission if required.[89]

In addition to the combined personal and political pressures to which he was being subjected within Czechoslovakia, Runciman also felt himself being buffeted by developments elsewhere. In his letter to Halifax of 5 September, he noted that: 'This afternoon we are upset by the French communiqué on mobilisation. Tomorrow some fresh news will doubtless emerge from the fog.'[90] That indeed did occur, although it was not the next day but the one after when such unwelcome news arrived from London. That morning, 7 September, *The Times* newspaper appeared with a leading article, entitled 'Nuremberg and Aussig', commenting, not unfavourably, on Beneš's Fourth Plan, but concluding that

> it might be worth while for the Czechoslovak Government to consider whether they should exclude altogether the project, which has found favour in some quarters, of making Czechoslovakia a more homogeneous State by the secession of that fringe of alien populations who are contiguous to the nation with which they are united by race.[91]

This suggestion by an authoritative London newspaper – considered by many outside Britain to reflect the views of the British government – that the Sudeten German problem should be resolved by the transfer of territory, was most unwelcome to Runciman at that juncture. The contents of the article had been drawn to the attention of the Mission early that morning by *The Times'* correspondent in Prague, who had received a telegraphed summary from London. The newspaper's Political Correspondent, Iverach McDonald, who was also present in Prague, was greatly distressed by the development. He had no prior knowledge of the article in question, and considered resigning from *The Times* in protest, but was dissuaded from doing so by Runciman.[92]

The contents of *The Times* article caused major embarrassment to the Runciman Mission. With what was widely considered to be the authority of the British government, it proposed a solution inimical to the Czechoslovak state which was at that time ostensibly not even desired by the SdP. Later that day Runciman telegraphed Halifax with the understated complaint that the leading article had 'added to our difficulties'. He went on to explain: 'We are dealing with the matter here but it would be useful to caution them against adventurous speculations at a time when we are hoping to make some progress. The last paragraph of article is a recommendation of an Anschluss.'[93] The Foreign Office was, of course, perfectly aware of that. Moreover, they had earlier received a vigorous protest from Masaryk, who requested that the British government disassociate itself from the article.[94] A formal *démenti* was duly issued, but in the absence of a public denial from a prominent Cabinet minister doubts continued to linger, and the damage could not be undone.[95]

The offending article was not, in fact, inspired by the Foreign Office, where Roberts minuted that *The Times* was 'quite incorrigible', having published, on the day following the appearance of the leading article in question, a collection of its previous statements concerning self-determination for the German minority in Czechoslovakia. Roberts also noted that Halifax had, some months ago, sent privately to Dawson, the Editor of *The Times*, a Foreign Office memorandum 'showing the objections to a plebiscite, so the "Times" can hardly plead ignorance or lack of guidance'. Nevertheless, it was agreed that no further action would be taken with *The Times*, as Roberts expressed it, 'to prevent them putting their foot still further in'.[96] The considerable impact achieved by *The Times* leading article was due essentially to the intervention of Dawson himself who had intensified the thrust of a draft prepared by another leader writer, by adding the phrase 'which has found favour in some quarters'.[97] It was this statement which convinced many readers that *The Times* was speaking on behalf of the British government.

By coincidence, a telegram had arrived at the Foreign Office only the previous day, confirming the credibility of such an interpretation. The Ambassador in Berlin contributed one of his frequent exhortations concerning the British press, arguing that it would be most helpful if newspapers 'could be persuaded to emphasise Hitler's love of peace and confidence in his will to ensure it' and to point out that neither the SdP nor Hitler were asking for plebiscite but were 'ready to accept autonomy', which was significantly short of full self-determination. He also wished the Czechoslovak authorities to be warned that failure to settle now would soon result in a demand for a plebiscite. Henderson added that it was his firm belief that an article, 'say in the "Times" on the above lines, would be far more profitable to peaceful and equitable solution than constant praise of Monsieur Beneš who ... does not yet face up to harsh realities of his position'.[98] Despite the somewhat self-righteous minute from Strang, doubting 'whether we could – or ought to – influence the press in this sense',[99] using *The Times* as a vehicle for furthering the objectives of British foreign policy was evidently not inconceivable.

One trenchant assessment of the damage done by *The Times* article came from the pen of Harvey, Halifax's Private Secretary, who noted in his diary that it had a 'calamitous effect in spite of *démenti* from Foreign Office'. He added: 'It was broadcast in Germany and it has been interpreted everywhere as a *ballon d'essai* and as foreshadowing a fresh surrender by H.M.G., especially in U.S.A.'[100] Some indication of the German interpretation of this episode may be gauged from the report of the German Chargé d'Affaires in London. Kordt reported to Berlin that it required two visits from the

Czechoslovak Minister before the Foreign Office agreed to follow up an initial denial given at a press briefing with an official *démenti*. Nevertheless, Kordt believed that the Foreign Office had not inspired the article, but added that it possibly derived 'from a suggestion which reached *The Times* editorial staff from the Prime Minister's entourage'.[101]

Whatever the origin of the suggestion, its effects on the Czechoslovak crisis were profound. The possibility of the transfer of Sudeten German territory had been firmly placed on the agenda, not by the SdP or the German government, but by a prominent newspaper widely believed to reflect the views of the British government. Such a move effectively cut the ground from beneath Beneš's Fourth Plan, which still sought to preserve the territorial integrity of Czechoslovakia.

Notes

1 Ashton-Gwatkin to Strang, 6 September 1938, *DBFP*, 3/II, appendix II (III), p. 669, and also in Newton to Halifax, 5 September, *DBFP*, 3/II, no. 773. See also note by Ashton-Gwatkin on Henlein's visit to Hitler, 6 September 1938, C 9612/1941/18, FO 371/21736.

2 Stopford, 'Prague, 1938–1939', p. 53.

3 Runciman to Halifax, in Newton to Halifax, 6 September 1938, *DBFP*, 3/II, nos 788 and 789; Ashton-Gwatkin to Strang, 6 September 1938, *DBFP*, 3/II, appendix II (III), p. 670.

4 Ashton-Gwatkin to Strang, 6 and 17 September 1938, *DBFP*, 3/II, appendix II (III), pp. 669–71, and in Newton to Halifax, 7 September 1938, *DBFP*, 3/II, no. 796.

5 'Minute of conversation between Dr. Preiss and Mr. Gwatkin', 6 September 1938, C 9801/1941/18, FO 371/21737 and FO 800/304, ff. 171–4.

6 'Protocol regarding the modus of negotiation agreed upon between the Czechoslovak Government and the Sudeten German Party regarding the settlement of national affairs', C 9426/1941/18, FO 371/21735 and Stopford Papers, RJS 3/8. For the Czech original see Beneš, *Mnichovské dny*, document no. 36, pp. 471–9, and for an English translation, without the annex, see RIIA, *Documents*, 1938, II, pp. 178–84.

7 Newton to Halifax, 7 September 1938, C 9354/1944/18, FO 371/21735. See also Newton to Halifax, 6 September 1938, DBFP, 3/II, no. 788, n. 4.

8 Beneš, *Mnichovské dny*, pp. 212–13.

9 'The Government proposal and the eight Carlsbad points', C 9426/1941/18, FO 371/21735 and Stopford Papers, RJS 3/8. For a detailed analysis of the extent to which the Fourth Plan met the requirements of the Carlsbad demands see Laffan, *Crisis over Czechoslovakia*, pp. 240–8.

10 'Explanations of certain concrete and detailed questions of the protocol', C 9426/1941/18, FO 371/21735 and Stopford Papers, RJS 3/8.

11 Runciman to Halifax, in Newton to Halifax, 6 September 1938, *DBFP*, 3/II, no. 789.

12 Runciman to Halifax, in Newton to Halifax, 6 September 1938, *DBFP*, 3/II, nos 788 and 789.

13 Ashton-Gwatkin to Strang, in Newton to Halifax, 7 September 1938, *DBFP*, 3/II, no. 796.
14 Ashton-Gwatkin to Strang, in Newton to Halifax, 8 September 1938, *DBFP*, 3/II, no. 803.
15 'Letter from Lord Runciman to President Beneš [and Mr. Chamberlain]', 21 September 1938, *DBFP*, 3/II, appendix II (IV), pp. 675–6. For analysis of this letter, see below pp. 310–16 and Appendix 1.
16 Minute by Cadogan, 7 September 1938, C 9285/1941/18, FO 371/21735.
17 Minute by Strang, 7 September 1938, C 9323/1941/18, FO 371/21735. See Halifax to Runciman, in Halifax to Newton, 8 September 1938, *DBFP*, 3/II, no. 804.
18 Minute by Roberts, 7 September 1938, C 9323/1941/18, FO 371/21735.
19 Minute by Roberts, 9 September 1938, C 9426/1941/18, FO 371/21735.
20 Minute by Strang, 9 September 1938, *ibid.*
21 *Daily Herald*, 8 October 1945. Wheeler-Bennett was also informed of the incident by Beneš in 1946. See Wheeler-Bennett, *Munich*, pp. 90–1, where the date of the meeting is given as 4 September 1938.
22 Sebekowsky made the denial to Jaksch in 1957 and repeated it later to another enquirer. See Jaksch to Stopford, 3 February and 10 March 1963, Stopford Papers, RJS 3/17 and copy of letter from Slánský to Ashton-Gwatkin, undated (but probably January 1963), Stopford Papers, RJS (unclassified box). See also Thompson, *Greatest Treason*, p. 125.
23 Stopford, 'Prague, 1938–1939', p. 55. Runciman did report to London at the time, however, that the new proposals had been 'privately discussed with Kundt and Sebekowsky', implying that these discussions had been held with Beneš. (Runciman to Halifax, in Newton to Halifax, 6 September 1938, *DBFP*, 3/II, no. 789.)
24 Beneš, *Mnichovské dny*, p. 205.
25 Ashton-Gwatkin to Strang, 6 September 1938, *DBFP*, 3/II, appendix II (III), p. 670.
26 Ashton-Gwatkin's diary, 6 September 1938, FO 800/304.
27 *Manchester Guardian*, 7 September 1938.
28 Ashton-Gwatkin to Strang, in Newton to Halifax, 8 September 1938, *DBFP*, 3/II, no. 803.
29 Hencke to the Foreign Ministry, 7 September 1938, *DGFP*, D/II, no. 438; Newton to Halifax, 7 September 1938, C 9396/4839/18, FO 371/21774.
30 See *The Times*, 8 September 1938.
31 Hencke to the Foreign Ministry, 7 September 1938, *DGFP*, D/II, no. 438.
32 Hencke to the Foreign Ministry, 8 September 1938, *DGFP*, D/II, no. 441. Beneš recorded in his memoirs, without citing a source, that 'one naive participant at the meeting exclaimed: "My God, he has given us everything!"' (Beneš, *Mnichovské dny*, p. 218.) Wheeler-Bennett, improbably, ascribes the exclamation to Frank. (Wheeler-Bennett, *Munich*, p. 92.)
33 Hencke to the Foreign Ministry, 8 September 1938, *DGFP*, D/II, no. 442.
34 Memorandum by Kier, in Hencke to the Foreign Ministry, 8 September 1938, enclosure 2, *DGFP*, D/II, no. 440. (Emphasis in original.)
35 Memorandum by Kundt, in Hencke to the Foreign Ministry, 8 September 1938, enclosure 1, *DGFP*, D/II, no. 440.
36 *Sunday Times*, 11 September 1938.

37 Ashton-Gwatkin to Strang, in Newton to Halifax, 9 September 1938, *DBFP*, 3/II, no. 812, and 17 September 1938, *DBFP*, 3/II, appendix II (III), p. 671.
38 Ashton-Gwatkin to Strang, in Newton to Halifax, 9 September 1938, C 9513/1941/18, FO 371/21736.
39 Hencke to the Foreign Ministry, 8 September 1938, *DGFP*, D/II, no. 441.
40 *The Times*, 8 September 1938.
41 Hencke to Ribbentrop, 7 September 1838, *DGFP*, D/II, no. 438.
42 Hencke to the Foreign Ministry, 8 September 1838, *DGFP*, D/II, no. 441.
43 Ashton-Gwatkin to Strang, 17 September 1938, *DBFP*, 3/II, appendix II (III), p. 671.
44 Newton to Halifax, 7 September 1938, C 9396/4839/18, FO 371/21774; Ashton-Gwatkin to Strang, 17 September 1938, *DBFP*, 3/II, appendix II (III), p. 671.
45 Ashton-Gwatkin's diary, 7 September 1938, FO 800/304.
46 Hencke to Foreign Ministry, 8 September 1938, *DGFP*, D/II, no. 441.
47 Halifax to Runciman, in Halifax to Newton, 8 September 1938, *DBFP*, 3/II, no. 799.
48 Runciman to Halifax, in Newton to Halifax, 8 September 1938, *DBFP*, 3/II, no. 800, Ashton-Gwatkin to Strang, in Newton to Halifax, 8 September 1938, *DBFP*, 3/II, no. 801.
49 Ashton-Gwatkin to Strang, in Newton to Halifax, 8 September 1938, *DBFP*, 3/II, no. 801. For the official communiqué see *The Times*, 8 September 1938.
50 Ashton-Gwatkin to Strang, 17 September 1938, *DBFP*, 3/II, appendix II (III), p. 671; Stopford, 'Prague, 1938–1939', pp. 60–1. Stopford described the scene as concluding with 'Frank having his head scrubbed by Gwatkin (with flashing eyes) at 1 a.m.'. (Stopford to Winthrop-Young, 12 September 1938, Stopford Papers, RJS 3/1.)
51 Ashton-Gwatkin to Strang, 17 September 1938, *DBFP*, 3/II, appendix II (III), p. 671.
52 Ashton-Gwatkin to Strang, in Newton to Halifax, 9 September 1938, C 9501/4839/18, FO 371/21774.
53 Ashton-Gwatkin to Strang, 17 September 1938, *DBFP*, 3/II, appendix II (III), p. 671.
54 *The Times*, 10 September 1938.
55 Krofta to Masaryk and Osuský, 9 September 1938, in Beneš, *Mnichovské dny*, document no. 38, pp. 482–3.
56 *Sunday Times*, 11 September 1938; *The Times*, 12 September 1938. Czechs comprised an estimated 7.4 million out of a total population of 14.7 million. (*Statistická ročenka Československé republiky*, (Prague, 1935), p. 7. Census of 1930.)
57 Ashton-Gwatkin to Strang, in Newton to Halifax, 8 September 1938, *DBFP*, 3/II, no. 801.
58 H. Ripka, *Munich: Before and After*, (London, 1939), p. 37.
59 Ashton-Gwatkin to Strang, in Newton to Halifax, 8 September 1938, *DBFP*, 3/II, no. 803. Ashton-Gwatkin also reported Meissner's observation that 'Czechs would blame England and say we had made a "Kuhhandel" in sacrificing Czechoslovakia in order to retain British colonies'.
60 Ashton-Gwatkin to Strang, 6 September 1938, *DBFP*, 3/II, appendix II (III), p. 668.
61 *Ibid.*

62 Ashton-Gwatkin to Strang, in Newton to Halifax, 8 September 1938, *DBFP*, 3/II, no. 803. Preiss also claimed that he had been approached by Eisenlohr, the German Minister in Prague, to obtain an offer from the government that would satisfy the SdP's Carlsbad demands. (Ashton-Gwatkin to Strang, in Newton to Halifax, 7 September 1938, *DBFP*, 3/II, no. 796.)
63 Ashton-Gwatkin to Strang, in Newton to Halifax, 8 September 1938, *DBFP*, 3/II, no. 803.
64 Ashton-Gwatkin to Strang, 6 September 1938, *DBFP*, 3/II, appendix II (III), p. 670.
65 Broadcast speech by Beneš, 10 September 1938, extracts in RIIA, *Documents*, 1938, II, pp. 184–8. For the original text, see Beneš, *Mnichovské dny*, document no. 39, pp. 484–91.
66 Runciman to Halifax, in Newton to Halifax, 9 September 1938, *DBFP*, 3/II, no. 813.
67 Stopford to Winthrop-Young, 12 September 1938, Stopford Papers, RJS 3/1.
68 Ashton-Gwatkin to Wilson, 13 September 1938, C 9914/1941/18, FO 371/21738 and FO 800/304.
69 Report from Sutton-Pratt, in Newton to Halifax, 9 September 1938, C 9435/4839/18, FO 371/21774. Sutton-Pratt added: 'Deputies May and Köllner appear to have intervened unwarrantably and got what they deserved.' See also note 1 to document no. 801, *DBFP*, 3/II, p. 265.
70 Newton to Halifax, 9 September 1938, C 9454/4839/18, FO 371/21774. Sutton-Pratt estimated that five prisoners had been mildly ill-treated, six fairly badly and two or three very badly.
71 Report by Sutton-Pratt, 10 September 1938, C 9924/4839/18, FO 371/21774.
72 'Letter from Lord Runciman to President Beneš [and Mr. Chamberlain]', 21 September 1938, *DBFP*, 3/II, appendix II (IV), p. 676.
73 Ashton-Gwatkin to Strang, 17 September 1938, *DBFP*, 3/II, appendix II (III), p. 671. Ashton-Gwatkin observed that the alleged victim of the police brutality, May, was 'known among his comrades as "Siegfried" – a well-known bruiser'.
74 Stopford to Winthrop-Young, 12 September 1938, Stopford Papers, RJS 3/1.
75 Ashton-Gwatkin's diary, 10 September 1938, FO 800/304.
76 Ashton-Gwatkin to Strang, 17 September 1938, *DBFP*, 3/II, appendix II (III), p. 672; *Daily Express*, *Daily Mail*, *Daily Telegraph*, and *Manchester Guardian*, 12 September 1938. The correspondent of *The Times*, however, considered the incident to have been 'much exaggerated'. (*The Times*, 13 September 1938.)
77 Stopford, 'Prague, 1938–1939', p. 63. A week previously, Stopford had contracted what he termed 'a severe liver-chill and the local foot and mouth disease', but felt fully recovered after his weekend in the country. (Stopford to Wordsworth, 8 September 1938, and Stopford to Winthrop-Young, 12 September 1938, Stopford Papers, RJS 3/1.)
78 Ashton-Gwatkin's diary, 10 September 1938, FO 800/304.
79 Ashton-Gwatkin to Strang, 17 September 1938, DBFP, 3/II, appendix II (III), p. 671–2.
80 Stopford, 'Prague, 1938–1939', p. 59.
81 Ashton-Gwatkin's diary, 9 September 1938, FO 800/304.
82 Stopford to Winthrop-Young, 12 September 1938, Stopford Papers, RJS 3/1.
83 Hencke to the Foreign Ministry, 8 September 1938, *DGFP*, D/II, no. 441.
84 Hencke to the Foreign Ministry, 9 September 1938, *DGFP*, D/II, no. 446.

85 Note by Runciman, undated (but probably 9 September 1938), Runciman Papers, WR 296.
86 Stopford, 'Prague, 1938–1939', p. 56.
87 Newton to Halifax, 12 September 1938, C 9560/1941/18, FO 371/21736.
88 Cabinet Minutes, 12 September 1938, Cabinet 37 (38), CAB 23/94; Cabinet Committee on Czechoslovakia Minutes, 12 September 1938, CS 38 (1), CAB 27/646.
89 Hencke to the Foreign Ministry, 9 September 1938, *DGFP*, D/II, no. 446.
90 Runciman to Halifax, 5 September 1938, *DBFP*, 3/II, no. 783. The French communiqué concerned the mobilisation of specialist forces required for the Maginot Line. (See *The Times*, 6 September 1938.)
91 The title of the article, 'Nuremberg and Aussig', referred to the respective venues of the German Nazi Party Rally, then taking place, and of a projected rally of the SdP. The Czech name for Aussig is Ustí nad Labem.
92 Stopford, 'Prague, 1938–1939', p. 58. See also I. McDonald, *A Man of The Times*, (London, 1976), pp. 32–3.
93 Runciman to Halifax, in Newton to Halifax, 7 September 1938, C 9356/4770/18, FO 371/21764. See also note 1 to Halifax to Chilston, 6 September 1938, *DBFP*, 3/II, no. 808.
94 Masaryk to Halifax, 7 September 1938, C 9362/4770/18, FO 371/21764.
95 Halifax to Chilston, 8 September 1938, *DBFP*, 3/II, no. 808. Reporting on a conversation between Halifax and the Soviet Ambassador, Ivan Maisky.
96 Minute by Roberts, 8 September 1938, C 9356/4770/18, FO 371/21764.
97 *The History of the Times*, IV, part 2, pp. 929–30.
98 Henderson to Halifax, 6 September 1938, C 9290/4770/18, FO 371/21764.
99 Minute by Strang, 7 September 1938, *ibid.*
100 Harvey, ed., *Harvey Diaries*, p. 171.
101 Kordt to the Foreign Ministry, 8 September 1938, *DGFP*, D/II, no. 443.

13
The Collapse of Mediation

The first week of September saw the arrival of the event that had been the cause of increasing concern for the British government throughout the late summer of 1938 – the Nazi Party Rally at Nuremberg. The Rally itself got under way on 5 September, but the particular element that gave rise to so much anxiety in London, Hitler's closing address, did not take place until 12 September. As that date drew inexorably closer, attempts to head off the feared approach of war intensified, resulting in a flurry of diplomatic activity in London and other capitals.

The French government made two attempts to influence its British counterpart into taking preventive action. On 7 September, Bonnet sent a request to London for a renewed warning to be issued to Germany concerning possible British involvement in any war over Czechoslovakia. Halifax undertook to give the suggestion full consideration.[1] Two days later France also sought to use Runciman as a direct means of avoiding the crisis. In conversation with Halifax, Corbin urged that Runciman 'be ready to formulate his own proposals and conclusions' in order to forestall the possibility of Hitler demanding a plebiscite in his speech. Halifax was unenthusiastic about the proposal, drawing attention to the fact that Runciman saw his role as purely that of a mediator.[2]

In London meanwhile, minds were being applied to the same problem. The idea of issuing a warning to Germany had received inconclusive consideration from Halifax and his colleagues a few days earlier, but was given fresh impetus by the receipt, on 6 September, of a secret warning from the German Chargé d'Affaires of Hitler's intention to attack Czechoslovakia in two weeks time. Kordt urged that a public warning be broadcast to Germany.[3] The receipt of this information coincided with the first reports of the Moravská Ostrava incident and led to the Foreign Office urgently contacting Runciman for advice in the early hours of 8 September. In the telegram however, Halifax referred only to making a 'personal appeal to Hitler' and gave no indication of a possible warning.[4] Runciman (as indicated previously) advised against such an appeal being issued.

Further consultations took place in London later that day. Chamberlain, who had returned from holiday the previous evening, was concerned to find that Halifax, believed to be influenced by Vansittart, was considering sending a warning note to Hitler.[5] During a meeting in Downing Street, attended by Halifax, Simon, Cadogan, Wilson and Vansittart, the Prime Minister countered by unveiling his plan for a possible visit to Hitler. Predictably, this met with strong opposition from Vansittart, who argued instead for a warning to be given to Germany. The meeting eventually settled on an alternative suggestion from Vansittart that Chamberlain should make a statement to the British press, commending Beneš's Fourth Plan, and including an endorsement from Runciman.[6]

That evening, a draft of the proposed press statement was telegraphed to Runciman. It spoke of the British government's previously held belief that the 'Czech problem, difficult and complicated as it is, should be capable of peaceful and agreed solution'. In the light of the latest Czechoslovak proposals, the draft statement continued, the British government was 'yet more clearly convinced that it should be possible to arrive at an agreed solution by way of friendly discussion and negotiation'. Chamberlain proposed to add that Runciman also held this view.[7] Anodyne though the draft statement was, Runciman's response was again negative. He believed that the proposed statement might not only hinder the resumption of negotiations, but his association with it might also compromise his position as an impartial mediator. Runciman also argued that, with regard to Hitler's speech at Nuremberg, the statement might 'act as irritant and even incitement rather than a deterrent'.[8] Runciman's refusal to co-operate forced the abandonment of the proposed Prime Ministerial press statement, although a confidential press briefing did take place on 11 September. In this, Chamberlain paid generous tribute to Runciman's efforts to date and drew attention to his continuing availability to overcome further difficulties.[9]

Meanwhile, the attitude in London appeared to harden in favour of a warning being issued to Germany. During a further meeting of the small group of ministers and advisers, on 9 September, a telegram was drafted to Henderson at Nuremberg, containing a message for Hitler to be relayed via Ribbentrop. This stated that the British government regarded the Fourth Plan as going 'far to meet the claims' of the Sudeten Germans and affording therefore 'a reasonable and hopeful basis for negotiations'. If, however, force was resorted to, France would honour its treaty obligations towards Czechoslovakia, and, in the ensuing conflict, Britain 'could not stand aside'.[10] Henderson reacted with extreme alarm to the message, claiming to have already made the British position 'as clear as daylight' to prominent members of the German government. In view of the unbalanced state Hitler was in, he argued, 'any solemn warning which he will regard as repetition of May 21 ... will drive him to the very action which we seek to prevent'.[11] The Ambassador's vehement representations achieved their desired effect. Following another Downing Street meeting, on 10 September, at which Hoare was also present, the instruction to Henderson was withdrawn.[12]

While the British government was vacillating over its warning to Hitler, the celebrations at Nuremberg were gradually approaching a climax. The tone towards Czechoslovakia was set on 10 September in a speech by Göring, who referred to 'that little fragment of a nation ... goodness knows where it hails from' oppressing 'a highly civilised people'. He added that 'these absurd pygmies' were acting on behalf of 'Moscow and the ... Jewish-Bolshevik rabble'.[13] On the same day Josef Goebbels also described Prague as the 'organising centre of Bolshevik plots against Europe'.[14] Two days later, came the leader's keynote speech. As anticipated, Hitler turned the spotlight on Czechoslovakia, condemning the treatment of the German minority, declaring: 'This misery of the Sudeten Germans is undescribable. It is sought to annihilate them. As human beings they are oppressed and scandalously treated in an intolerable fashion.' Later, he demanded that 'the oppression of three and a half million Germans in Czechoslovakia shall cease and that its place shall be taken by the free right of self-determination'. Hitler added that it was 'the business of the Czechoslovak government to discuss matters with the representatives of the Sudeten Germans and in one way or another to bring about an understanding'. He also pledged his support for the Sudeten Germans, declaring he would not tolerate, 'in the heart of Germany', the creation of a 'second Palestine'.[15]

Despite the vehemence of Hitler's rhetoric, the contents of the speech brought a modicum of relief in London. Hitler had been menacing towards Czechoslovakia, but his demand for 'self-determination' was unspecific, no deadline was attached to it and there was no direct reference to a plebiscite. The speech also appeared to hold out the hope that a negotiated solution remained a possibility. The main concern in the Foreign Office was that a demand for a plebiscite would soon follow and Halifax therefore sought the views of Runciman and Newton on the probable consequences.[16] On balance, however, it was generally considered by the British government that although the speech had changed nothing, at least Hitler had not brought the crisis to an immediate head. In Cadogan's words, it pulled 'no triggers'.[17]

Henderson, who had returned to Berlin before Hitler's speech, anticipating that he 'would burn no boats',[18] was also generally relieved by the outcome. Despite 'certain violence and ill mannerisms', Henderson considered it a 'good debating speech' that emphasised Hitler's 'sacrifices for and love of peace'. Nevertheless, the Ambassador was in no doubt that Hitler meant business over Czechoslovakia and that 'failing [the] immediate grant of autonomy to the Sudetens he will march'. The speech amounted to an 'ultimatum without a definite time limit and without mention of a plebiscite in words'. Henderson therefore considered it imperative for the

Czechoslovak authorities to act without delay and he persisted in his belief that a solution should come from Runciman, and forced on Beneš under the threat of British abandonment.[19]

Amongst the British mediators in Prague, the initial reaction to Hitler's speech was also one of relief. Members of the Mission had gathered anxiously round a radio in the Hotel Alcron to listen to the broadcast from Nuremberg. What they heard was less bellicose than feared, and Stopford recalled years later that at the end they all 'breathed a little more easily'.[20] Earlier that day, however, Stopford appeared much less concerned, stating in a letter, 'I don't believe Adolf will say anything terrible tonight'.[21] Runciman's view is not known but Ashton-Gwatkin characterised the speech as 'thunder without lightning', adding 'I do not think it will alter the situation greatly'.[22] This belief, however, was soon proved to have been misplaced. Indeed, at the very time that Ashton-Gwatkin made this observation in a letter to Horace Wilson on 13 September, the first signs of this change were already evident from two directions.

The previous day, the Mission had received clear indication from the Czechoslovak side that the situation was deteriorating. Prior to Hitler's speech that evening, Runciman and Ashton-Gwatkin visited Hodža, who informed them that, in view of the recent increase in tension within the country, he proposed to introduce emergency regulations to calm the situation, such as a ban on public meetings. The Prime Minister added that in the event of unrest following Hitler's speech, special military measures might also prove necessary to restore order. He made it clear, however, that the contemplated measures excluded mobilisation as that would provoke war with Germany. Runciman responded with a warning against police interference with public meetings, but was content with Hodža's additional suggestion that at his meeting with the SdP negotiators, scheduled for 13 September, a joint appeal should be issued to avoid provocations.[23] The second indication of imminent change came from the SdP. Late in the evening of 12 September, following Hitler's speech, Kundt paid a visit to the Mission offices, leaving Ashton-Gwatkin with the impression that 'something is going wrong' as his visitor was clearly 'an unhappy man',[24] although at the time he did not understand why.[25] Kundt rejected Ashton-Gwatkin's appeal, following up Hodža's suggestion, that a '"gentleman's truce" be publicly announced', but he did request a meeting between the SdP's full negotiating delegation and the British Mission for the following day.[26]

Although not connecting them directly with Hitler's speech, the British mediators began increasingly to fear the outbreak of violent incidents, which, Stopford noted, 'the extremists on both sides seem to be engineering'.[27] Ashton-Gwatkin also voiced rising concern over 'incidents' (almost invariably, in his reports, enclosing the word in inverted commas), explaining in his letter to Wilson that he perceived an 'apparent lack of will or ability on either side to stop them', although he seemed to regard the SdP as the main culprit. In Ashton-Gwatkin's opinion the SdP had scored 'a great victory' over the Moravská Ostrava incident, which was possibly giving it an appetite for more. He also surmised, from the unhappiness he had perceived in Kundt, 'that the power to stop "incidents" may (intentionally or unintentionally) be slipping from the hands of the Sudeten leaders'. Ashton-Gwatkin concluded that 'Berlin may have a finger in this', and went on to suggest to Wilson, uncharacteristically, that 'we may have to warn the German Government that if they want peace they must allow it to be'. Equally out of character, Ashton-Gwatkin was also complimentary about the Czechs, stating that it was their 'great quality that they seem to remain calm and keep their heads', consequently, the Mission had not been affected by any 'local "jitters"'. Later in the letter, however, Ashton-Gwatkin sought to redress the balance somewhat by stressing that it was 'not only the Sudetens who commit incidents, the Czechs and "Communists" are also guilty'. He added that he believed it was not 'the higher command on either side' that was responsible but 'subordinates', who would not or could not be controlled.[28]

Clear indication of the SdP's responsibility for causing much of the unrest came from the British observers in Czechoslovakia. Sutton-Pratt and Pares (who, as previously mentioned, had been rejected for membership of the Runciman Mission in late July, but had replaced Henderson as an observer when he was attached to the Mission), in addition to investigating the Moravská Ostrava incident, also visited other reported trouble-spots. The most notable of these was at a village near Trutnov (Trautenau), where, the SdP alleged at the end of August, the local German population were being terrorised by a force of 1000 Czech workmen.[29] After investigating the alleged incident, Sutton-Pratt reported that it was 'a put-up job by the Sudetens', who outnumbered the Czechs in the locality.[30] In London, Roberts noted that 'the observers' reports have in almost all cases born[e] out the official Czech version of incidents'. Sargent added that the observers were evidently 'cramping the style of the German propagandists'.[31] Although not all the observers' reports exonerated the Czech community,[32] most concluded that it was the SdP and not the Czechs who were responsible for causing unrest or making alarmist accusations.

The underlying tension between the Czech and German communities exploded into open violence following Hitler's Nuremberg address on 12 September. The main flash-points were in Cheb, Carlsbad and Falknov (Falkenau; now Sokolov) where large crowds of SdP supporters took to the streets in response to Hitler's speech. Sutton-Pratt, who witnessed the events in Cheb, reported that the crowd was orderly, although breaking windows of Jewish shops, and that swastika flags were much in evidence. Shooting broke out the following morning, and the Czechoslovak authorities called in military assistance.[33] Martial law was proclaimed in eight districts in western Bohemia, and the government reported that several attempts had been made to seize public buildings.[34] On 14 September, Czechoslovak security forces captured the SdP's fortified headquarters in Cheb after a three-hour long battle,[35] and calm was restored throughout the area. The extent of casualties is uncertain, though Runciman later stated that the number of dead on both sides did not exceed 70.[36] The Czechoslovak authorities claimed that 27 people had been killed during the period of unrest from 12 to 15 September.[37]

Although the available evidence cannot provide irrefutable indication of responsibility, the balance of probability suggests that it was SdP activists, rather than the Czechoslovak authorities, who initiated the violence. The government is unlikely to have risked throwing away the advantage, so painfully gained by the production of the Fourth Plan, by ordering military action against the SdP without provocation. Nevertheless, uncertainty surrounds the degree of involvement of the SdP leadership in causing the unrest. In view of the fact that Hitler did not go to the brink in his Nuremberg speech, probably because plans for 'Operation Green' were not yet finalised,[38] it is unlikely that Henlein would have attempted to stage an insurrection at that juncture. The events in question, therefore, did not constitute the planned incident providing the pretext for German military intervention, referred to in a General Staff memorandum on 24 August.[39] More probably, the unrest arose either out of the spontaneous response of SdP activists to Hitler's speech, or was stimulated in order to avoid the SdP having to negotiate with the government on the Fourth Plan. During his meeting with Hitler on 26 August, Frank had received instructions to create incidents in the Sudetenland in order to maintain a high degree of tension.[40]

However, if the unrest was deliberately provoked by the SdP, its organisation left much to be desired. Eisenlohr reported to Berlin on 14 September that calm had been restored almost everywhere and that there was 'general helplessness and nervousness' amongst the German population. He added that the SdP leadership – minus Henlein – were meeting in Aš 'as a sort of revolutionary committee without any revolution'.[41] A few days later, Kundt complained to the German Legation of the 'lack of leadership' in the SdP, which had resulted in 'a state of complete panic and uncertainty in the Sudeten German area'.[42] Henlein certainly did not hurry back to Czechoslovakia following the Nuremberg Congress, going instead to Selb, just over the border in Bavaria, to await developments, returning only briefly to his home in Aš on 14 September.[43]

Beneš, at the time, did not believe that the outbreak of violence had been instigated by Germany or by the SdP leadership. He suggested to Newton, on 14 September, that, if not spontaneous, the events may have been directed by local leaders.[44] Hodža expressed a similar view in conversation with Newton the previous day, though he also thought it possible that the SdP was deliberately fomenting a revolution.[45] Within the London Foreign

Office some sympathy was felt for the way the Czechoslovak authorities responded to the situation. Commenting on official casualty figures listing 13 Czech dead and 61 injured compared with 10 German dead and 14 injured, Roberts observed that the government appeared justified 'especially in view of Herr Hitler's speech, in treating these incidents as incipient armed uprisings'.[46] Nevertheless, he was little inclined to support the Prague government, minuting: 'Everything points to the Sudeten as having been mainly responsible for the latest incidents. But as Mr. Gwatkin pointed out, the situation has got beyond a question of rights or wrongs. Czechs and Sudetens can hardly now be expected to live happily side by side.'[47]

With one of the principal members of the Runciman Mission adopting this attitude, the prospects for a successful conclusion of British mediation within the framework of the Czechoslovak state were virtually extinguished. Indeed, although the origins of the unrest remain obscure, the outcome was clear cut – it brought about the termination of negotiations between the government and the SdP, and the consequent removal of the very reason for the Mission's continued existence. Clear evidence of the deteriorating situation reached the Mission staff during 13 September, when the SdP delegation called off their meeting with Runciman, which had only been arranged the previous day, and also cancelled their scheduled reopening of talks with Hodža. Instead, the entire SdP negotiating team travelled to Cheb for consultations with Henlein and Frank, who were due back from Nuremberg.[48] The reports of spreading unrest in the western border region of Bohemia prompted the Runciman Mission to dispatch Henderson to the area to act as an additional observer and to liaise with Sutton-Pratt, who was already on the scene. Immediately before the SdP negotiators' departure from Prague, Ashton-Gwatkin impressed on Kundt that the Mission was relying on him to do his utmost to restore order.[49] But Ashton-Gwatkin did not have much confidence in the effectiveness of his appeal, observing in his letter to Wilson: 'Kundt is all right, I think; but I am not so sure of some of the others, e.g., Sebekowsky, Frank.' He added: 'If things get worse, it will mean civil war in the Sudeten country.'[50] This concern is also evident from a note in Ashton-Gwatkin's diary on 13 September (contradicting his earlier assessment): 'Things are going very wrong – mainly the fault of Hitler's speech.'[51]

The Czechoslovak authorities, nevertheless, remained anxious to re-establish contact with the SdP. Unable to communicate with the party's headquarters in Cheb on 13 September, Hodža turned to the Runciman Mission for assistance.[52] Later that day, Ashton-Gwatkin succeeded in speaking to Frank, who dictated over the telephone his conditions for the restoration of contact.[53] He demanded the withdrawal of Czechoslovak police from German areas, the return of the military to their normal duties, and the cancellation of martial law. For its part the SdP would undertake to instruct local mayors to maintain order. Frank also demanded compliance by midnight, six hours later.[54] Ashton-Gwatkin immediately contacted Hodža, who accepted the terms on behalf of the government, stipulating only that the SdP send a representative to Prague without delay to discuss the restoration of order. The British mediator duly relayed this response by telephone to Frank, who indicated that he would reply directly to the Prime Minister following consultation with Henlein. At 11 p.m. Frank telephoned Hodža rejecting the offer to renew talks.[55] Shortly after midnight, the government received a further telephone message from the SdP headquarters declaring that negotiations within the existing framework were no longer possible, and announcing the dissolution of the SdP negotiating delegation.[56]

Earlier in the evening, before the SdP's rejection of the Prime Minister's terms had been communicated to Prague, the indefatigable Ashton-Gwatkin – prompted by a suggestion from Hodža – set off once again in pursuit of Henlein. His purpose was to convey personally to the SdP leadership the Prime Minister's response to Frank's ultimatum together with a recommendation from Runciman that this should be accepted.[57] Accompanied by Peto, Ashton-Gwatkin left Prague at 7 p.m., calling en route at Carlsbad, where they were joined by Henderson. The mediators arrived at their destination in Aš at 1.30 a.m., but on this occasion the SdP leader was not there to welcome them. Instead, Ashton-Gwatkin was handed the notice announcing the severing of negotiations with the government. The British mediators immediately headed back to the SdP headquarters in Cheb, described by Ashton-Gwatkin as 'quite a fortress with steel doors', and where they were received by a 'chorus of toughs with "Heil Hitler"'. The visitors found Frank, dressed in SdP paramilitary uniform, seated at a table with a revolver placed in front of him. Ashton-Gwatkin noted however, that the area was quite peaceful, though there was evidence of Czechoslovak military activity. In Cheb itself, at 3.30 a.m., Runciman's chief assistant together with Frank strolled through the streets observing soldiers conducting searches. Not being one to miss an opportunity for demonstrating his historical knowledge, Ashton-Gwatkin drew Frank's attention to the fact that Albrecht Wallenstein (or Waldstein), the great general of the Thirty Years' War, had been murdered in that city. Frank's response was not recorded, though Ashton-Gwatkin noted that his companion was outwardly friendly but 'so inflated with the eloquence of Nuremberg and his own importance that no commonsense or sense of responsibility were to be got out of him'.[58] What the British mediator did get out of Frank, however, was a restatement of the SdP's new demands, which he immediately telephoned to the Legation in Prague. Frank added that if these requirements were met, the SdP would issue an appeal for calm and recommence negotiations for a settlement, but, he added ominously, not on the basis considered hitherto.[59]

Later that morning the mediators returned to Aš, where they met Henlein at his home. The conversation turned out to be no more successful than had been Ashton-Gwatkin's nocturnal discussions with Frank. The SdP leader assured his visitors that he did not wish to sever relations with the Runciman Mission, and would indeed instruct Kundt to maintain close contact.[60] However, Ashton-Gwatkin noted that Henlein was 'otherwise uncompromising',[61] reiterating the SdP's refusal to send a representative to Prague to reopen negotiations with Hodža unless the party's new demands were first unconditionally implemented. As foreshadowed by Frank, Henlein then significantly raised the stakes by indicating that any resumption of talks would have to be on a new basis – that of a plebiscite.[62] Reporting to London, Ashton-Gwatkin observed: 'I think ... Sudetens hope Lord Runciman's Mission may make attainment of this policy easier for them.' He added that they were 'genuinely enraged at defence measures taken by the Government and at incidents for which they denied all responsibility'. Ashton-Gwatkin found it 'useless to argue with them' and stressed instead that efforts should be made 'to find a way to internal peace and to avoid international war', but even that 'did not appeal to the mood of the moment'.[63] Nevertheless, as Ashton-Gwatkin informed Strang, he and Henlein 'parted friends'.[64] It was to be their last meeting.

The stepping-up of the SdP's demands was confirmed in a communiqué issued following Ashton-Gwatkin's visit to Aš. It emphasised that in the event of any further negotiations with the Czechoslovak authorities, the Carlsbad programme would no longer suffice, 'but account would have to be taken of the Sudeten German right to self-determination'. The statement also noted that Henlein had thanked the representatives of the Runciman Mission for their efforts, but held the Czechoslovak government responsible for the Mission's lack of success.[65] The *Volksdeutsche Mittelstelle* reported to the German Foreign Ministry on the exchange between Henlein and members of the Mission in more robust language, claiming that the SdP leader had declared 'that the Sudeten Germans wanted to return to the Reich and that no power on earth could deter them from this purpose'.[66] Henlein himself reported to Hitler in similar terms, stating that he had informed the British that the Carlsbad points were no longer relevant and that any further negotiations could only be conducted on the basis of union with Germany. Contrary to what he had told Ashton-Gwatkin, Henlein advised Hitler against a plebiscite suggesting instead that all areas with over 50 per cent German population (according to 1918 figures) should be ceded to Germany and occupied within 48 hours.[67]

No matter how the sentiment was expressed, however, the British mediators were left in no doubt of a fundamental transformation in the SdP's public attitude. The requirement for autonomy within Czechoslovakia, which the SdP had ostensibly pursued since its inception in 1935, and which had been re-emphasised during April 1938 in the Carlsbad programme, was replaced by a demand for a plebiscite followed by secession, with inevitable profound consequences for the continued existence of the state. As Kundt explained on 15 September to Professor André Brunet – whom the French government had dispatched to Prague in order to be better informed of Runciman's activities – an immediate plebiscite, aiming at uniting the Sudetenland with Germany, was the 'only method still practicable of maintaining peace'.[68] This message was also brought home to the British mediators by Hohenlohe, whom Ashton-Gwatkin met briefly at the German frontier following his last meeting with Henlein. Hohenlohe argued that a plebiscite now provided the only prospect of a peaceful outcome, and offered to visit Vansittart to explain the new situation. Ashton-Gwatkin was also informed that Henlein had gone to Germany to see Hitler.[69]

Henlein did indeed leave Czechoslovak territory, but not until the following day, and not for the purpose of seeing Hitler. Accompanied by other members of the SdP leadership, he crossed into Germany on 15 September and returned to his base in Selb.[70] Before leaving Henlein issued a proclamation accusing the government of brutal oppression, which demonstrated that Czechs and Germans could no longer co-exist within one state. He concluded with the declaration: 'We wish to live as free Germans! We want peace and work again in our homeland! We want to return to the *Reich*!'[71] Although clarifying beyond doubt the SdP's intentions, the proclamation had little impact on the German population of Czechoslovakia. The combined effects of the introduction of martial law in certain areas and the flight of the party leadership abroad, left SdP supporters depressed and demoralised and the Czechoslovak authorities firmly in control.[72] The creation, within Germany, two days later of the Sudeten German Legion, or *Freikorps*, which immediately began small-scale attacks on targets in Czechoslovakia, did little to alter the situation.[73] However, despite the fact that within a matter of days following Hitler's Nuremberg speech the Czechoslovak authorities had succeeded in restoring calm in the predominantly German areas, developments were destined not to end there.

Apart from Ashton-Gwatkin's dogged pursuit of Henlein, the British mediators did not react to the upsurge of violence in the Sudetenland following Hitler's speech. In London and Paris, however, where the unrest in Czechoslovakia was viewed with considerable alarm, these events gave rise to intense activity. Most immediate was the reaction of the French government. Around midday on 13 September, the Foreign Minister personally telephoned the British Ambassador in Paris to express grave concern over the situation in Central Europe which, he feared, might lead to war in minutes rather than days. Bonnet urged that Runciman should immediately declare his intention to arbitrate.[74] In London that afternoon, the French request was considered at a meeting of the inner group of foreign policy makers – now constituted as the 'informal' Cabinet Committee on

Czechoslovakia. Halifax was far from keen and concerned that any plan produced by Runciman was likely to be considered a 'British plan'.[75] This view was shared by Chamberlain, who explained to a meeting of the full Cabinet the following day that 'we did not want the responsibility of sponsoring any particular scheme'.[76] The French request was nevertheless passed on to Runciman with a note from Halifax advising against arbitration as this would indicate that 'all prospect of further negotiation on present lines is exhausted'. Moreover, the Foreign Secretary added, any such British proposal might prejudice 'other possibilities'.[77] However, Halifax need not have worried about Runciman frustrating Chamberlain's plan to meet Hitler. The British mediator had no intention of producing his own solution at that juncture because, as he explained to Halifax, he could not be certain 'that any plan however favourable would now be accepted by Sudeten Party'.[78]

Britain's response to the new situation in Czechoslovakia had, in fact, already been set in train before the outbreak of unrest in the Sudetenland. The informal meeting of ministers and advisers, which met in Downing Street on 10 September, not only endorsed Henderson's unwillingness to deliver a direct warning to Hitler, but also began the preparation for the Prime Minister's preferred alternative – his possible visit to Germany. In two memoranda, written that day, Horace Wilson outlined Chamberlain's proposed approach. He would suggest to Hitler that the Fourth Plan should serve as the basis for further negotiations and offer British assistance towards achieving and implementing a just settlement, thus dispensing with the need to use force. Nevertheless – in Wilson's words, 'according to circumstances' – a warning would be given of the consequences if force were used. It was considered undesirable, however, for the British government to become directly involved in negotiations with Germany on behalf of Czechoslovakia, and Chamberlain would suggest therefore, that Runciman should be invited by all parties concerned to 'become the arbitrator'. In addition, some form of international police force might be employed to maintain order during the interim period. More generally, Wilson noted that Chamberlain would indicate to Hitler his appreciation of the view 'that Germany and England form the two pillars that between them support orderly civilisation against the onslaught of disruptive Bolshevism', and that it was therefore his desire to 'do nothing that shall weaken the resistance that we can jointly offer to those who threaten our civilisation'.[79]

Two days later, on 12 September, Chamberlain confirmed these ideas in a discursive five-page letter sent by special messenger to Runciman, which contained a remarkably candid statement of the Prime Minister's intentions. Chamberlain congratulated Runciman on the 'patience, tact, and skill' with which he was pursuing his 'thankless task' and on succeeding in narrowing the gap between the two sides to 'what looks like manageable proportions'. Assuring Runciman that 'if you could be left to finish your task alone, I should feel confident of a settlement', the Prime Minister explained that 'the question which agitates our minds here without ceasing is whether Hitler will make some irruption that will put an end to peaceful negotiations'. This uncertainty was compounded by conflicting information concerning Germany's intentions. Chamberlain disclosed that many reports 'declare positively that Hitler has made up his mind to attack Czecho-Slovakia ... after the 20th [September]'. These reports argued that Hitler was not really interested in the Sudeten Germans but that he planned 'to swallow up Czecho-Slovakia and then to proceed further East'. Hitler's intention being to achieve a *fait accompli* before Britain and France could react. The alternative opinion, by implication, came from a single source – the British Ambassador in Berlin. Chamberlain explained that 'Henderson steadily maintains that Hitler has not yet made up his mind to violence' and that if a solution 'which must be satisfactory to himself, can be obtained peacefully, well and good'. In the light of these contradictory views, Chamberlain stated that he intended acting 'on the basis of the latter and more optimistic forecast'. The letter was written before Hitler's speech, and although he doubted whether that would clarify matters, the Prime Minister nevertheless wished to be prepared for a possible sudden deterioration in the situation by having a contingency plan to hand.

Chamberlain explained that he had in mind a 'dramatic step which might change the whole situation', and proceeded to outline his proposal to visit Hitler. He stressed the very secret nature of the plan by indicating that even the Cabinet would not be informed until the last moment. Disclosing his intention of appealing to Hitler's vanity, the Prime Minister confided that he hoped to persuade the German leader that he had 'an unequalled opportunity of raising his own prestige and fulfilling what he has so often declared to be his aim, namely the establishment of an Anglo-German understanding, preceded by a settlement of the Czecho-Slovakian question'.

The Prime Minister then indicated Runciman's possible role in the proceedings, as foreshadowed by Wilson:

> After sketching out the prospect of Germany and England as the two pillars of European peace and buttresses against communism, I should suggest that the essential preliminary was the peaceful solution of our present trouble. Since I assume that he will have declared that he cannot wait and that the solution must come at once, my proposal would be that he should agree that, after both sides had laid their case before you and thus demonstrated the points of difference, you should act as final arbitrator.

Chamberlain noted that he would be unable to guarantee Beneš's acceptance, but would 'undertake to put all possible pressure on him to do so', adding that the French government had already agreed to accept any plan approved by Runciman. Other points to be discussed with Hitler would include Czechoslovakia's treaties with France and the Soviet Union, and although Chamberlain again anticipated that he would not be able to give definite assurances, he would nevertheless 'not despair of finding a solution acceptable to all, save perhaps Russia'. The Prime Minister concluded by stressing that the plan was a last resort, for use only if the situation was 'otherwise desperate', but one that, if implemented, would impose on Runciman 'a final task which no one else could fulfil'. He therefore hoped that Runciman would be prepared to accept it and thus bring about the successful conclusion of his work.[80]

Runciman shared the secret of 'Plan Z' with Newton and also with his wife, who observed that the two men 'rather shook their heads over it'.[81] Her husband's response to the Prime Minister's scheme certainly appeared less than enthusiastic. In a brief telegram to Chamberlain, sent on 13 September, Runciman replied: 'With great reluctance and as the last resort I would do as you suggest. It would of course mean an end to my mediation here.' He added that as a result of the unrest that had broken out the previous evening the situation was 'very obscure'. Negotiations were stalled but, striking a note of uncharacteristic optimism, Runciman concluded that 'it would be premature to abandon hope of their resumption'.[82] Clearly, Runciman was unenthusiastic about the new role Chamberlain wished him to undertake. That was hardly surprising as, on the advice of the British government, Runciman had consistently, over the previous six weeks, resisted being placed in the position of an arbitrator. Now however, in the event of the implementation of the Prime Minister's secret plan, he was being invited to perform just such a function, for which he had little appetite.

Runciman's response was immediately conveyed to a meeting of the Cabinet Committee which noted that the Czechoslovak government would be unlikely to agree to Runciman acting as arbitrator if he were to be given powers to transfer territory to Germany.[83] At a meeting of the full Cabinet the following day, 14 September, during which the Prime Minister first disclosed his plan to visit Hitler, he outlined Runciman's proposed role as arbitrator and indicated the intention of inviting him also to the talks in Germany. The ministers who contributed to the subsequent discussion all expressed enthusiasm for Runciman's proposed new task, except for MacDonald, who argued it was now too late for such action. Simon repeated the observation, made at the previous day's Committee meeting, that Beneš would certainly object if Runciman were granted powers to hand over territory, which would, in turn, give rise to the issue of a plebiscite. Earlier in the discussion, Chamberlain argued that were Hitler to demand a plebiscite this could not reasonably be opposed by Britain.[84] That point had also been noted at the previous day's meeting of the Cabinet Committee, when it was agreed that the British government would not initiate any discussion of a plebiscite and would draw attention to the inherent difficulties if it were raised by others.[85]

The problems associated with a plebiscite had been troubling British policy-makers since May, when (as previously discussed) the idea was explored and rejected. The fear that this step would be demanded by Germany persisted and received fresh impetus from Hitler's Nuremberg speech, even though this did not contain an explicit reference to a plebiscite. Halifax was aware of the Czechoslovak government's strong objections to that eventuality, but sought to ascertain from Runciman and Newton, on 13 September, whether these could be overcome if 'reasonable and fair' conditions were assured.[86] The Prague government's views on a plebiscite had been vigorously represented to Newton on the eve of Hitler's speech by the Foreign Minister who explained that there was no provision in the Czechoslovak constitution for such a measure – an argument that cut no ice with Newton. Krofta also drew attention to the Åland Islands precedent of 1921 (when an international commission ruled against the islanders' wish for secession from Finland) and referred to the practical problems of determining the area within which a plebiscite would be held. The intimidation of voters in the German areas, he argued, would inevitably distort the outcome of a plebiscite and, if the result were for secession, the remainder of Czechoslovakia would be left defenceless against Germany. For good measure, Krofta also warned that, far from preventing war, a plebiscite might precipitate it, as most Czechs would rather fight than accept the dismemberment of their country.[87]

Responding to Halifax's query, Runciman and Newton confirmed that the authorities would reject a plebiscite 'in any circumstances', except possibly if it were very strongly urged by France as well as Britain. The effects of this on the Czech population, Newton warned, would be 'to raise their temper still further', although he added that their attitude remained 'remarkably restrained'. He also noted the view of the Military Attaché, Colonel H.C.T. Stronge, that if the government were to agree to a plebiscite it might precipitate a military *coup d'état*. Amongst the Czech objections, Runciman and Newton drew attention to the perceived difficulty of devising a fair question, the unwillingness to accept the destruction of a historic territory the remainder of which would be left exposed to Germany, and the belief that a plebiscite would not resolve the main issue – that of relations between Germany and Czechoslovakia. The British representatives also feared that a plebiscite might itself precipitate widespread bloodshed and advised therefore that if it became necessary, in order to preserve peace, 'to force [the] Czechoslovak Government to surrender their German provinces, it might be preferable to use the rough and ready basis of recent communal elections'.[88]

The question of the cession of territory – albeit on a very limited scale – also began to feature for the first time in the thinking of the Czechoslovak government. Hodža mentioned to Newton, on 16 September, the possibility, 'in the last resort', of surrendering to Germany certain areas, such as that round Aš and Cheb (the Egerland) in western Bohemia. The Prime Minister, who did not wish to be identified as the source of the idea, believed that Czech resistance to it could be overcome by pointing out that the Czechoslovak delegation at the Paris Peace Conference in 1919 had not expected these areas to be included in the new state. Moreover, their removal, with up to one million German inhabitants, could be presented as having the effect of strengthening the Czechoslovak frontier.[89] The previous day, Beneš had referred to the same possibility in discussion with Newton, but rejected the idea out of hand on the grounds of it creating a dangerous precedent and being unacceptable to public opinion.[90] Nevertheless, policy-makers in Prague were evidently beginning to consider the limited transfer of territory as a preferable alternative to a plebiscite.

The Czechoslovak objections to a plebiscite had also been communicated to the Foreign Office, on 12 September, by the Minister in London.[91] The note was delivered personally by Masaryk to Vansittart, whom he regarded as 'a very old friend', and to whom he wished to speak frankly about the current situation. Masaryk did so in characteristic terms:

> France and England have squeezed us like a lemon. Newton's language to Beneš was such as has never been employed before by a Minister to a Head of State. ... But because you have squeezed us so hard and because we have done what you asked us, we take it for granted that you will not attempt to squeeze us further, because there are limits. For some time past the impression has been gaining ground in Czechoslovakia that you are going to sell us, and I, Masaryk, get many hundreds of hard spoken communications in this sense, because I am thought likely to be cast for the role of salesman. I beg you not to under-rate the growth of this feeling of desperation in Czechoslovakia.

Masaryk added that everything had been done to avoid incidents, but if Hitler was determined to create a pretext for invasion, it could not be prevented.[92] No reaction to Masaryk's plea was recorded in the Foreign Office, but he was soon to discover that the Czechoslovak lemon would be squeezed considerably further.

The precise method to be applied was foreshadowed, with remarkable accuracy, in a lengthy minute by Mallet on 15 September. Noting the dangers inherent in a plebiscite and also the probable extreme difficulty in persuading the Prague government to accept such a course of action, Mallet cast around for an alternative method of achieving 'the Anschluss of the Sudeten districts to the Reich', in the anticipated event of autonomy no longer being acceptable to the SdP. He also noted the difficulty of justifying, to both the Czechoslovak and the British public, the cession of territory to Germany without a clear demonstration of the principle of self-determination. However, Mallet argued, with uncanny prescience:

> were several of the great Powers, including England and France, as a result of a Four-Power Conference, together to inform the Czechoslovak Government that the cession of the Sudeten districts was essential for the preservation of peace it would be extremely difficult for the Czechs to resist.

Although conceding that such a solution would be 'less palatable' than a plebiscite, Mallet believed it could be more easily justified than a settlement imposed by Germany alone.[93]

The idea of a four-power conference had been included amongst the options discussed by Strang during his visit to British diplomatic representatives in Central Europe following the May Crisis. It was rejected at that time on the grounds that it would probably not be acceptable to Germany. During August, however, Newton had detected growing German interest in the idea, should the Runciman Mission fail to find an acceptable solution.[94] The SdP leadership also alluded to that possibility in conversation with a British journalist at the end of that month.[95] These reports prompted Roberts to observe that the four-power conference was 'a kite' being flown by Germany, 'intended as a device to convict the Czechs of unreasonableness and so permit them to settle the Sudeten question by force without outside intervention'.[96] Mallet, however, by 2 September, was already warming to the idea of an international conference. He reasoned that the German destruction of Czechoslovakia by force, with Britain standing aside, would be 'a bitter humiliation and lead to a tremendous loss of prestige', but the imposition of a plebiscite by a four-power conference would be much less damaging to British susceptibilities.[97] Two weeks later (as mentioned), Mallet envisaged the conference dispensing with the formality of a plebiscite and proceeding directly to the cession of territory. The composition of the conference under consideration in the Foreign Office did not, however, please Vansittart. He restated his opposition to the participation of Italy, arguing that the Soviet Union had a stronger claim to representation as the population of Czechoslovakia was largely Slav. His preferred alternative was to include Czechoslovakia but exclude both Italy and the Soviet Union.[98]

Vansittart's attempt to rule out Italian participation in a possible conference was destined to failure. By chance, the future promoter of the Munich Agreement issued, at this time, an appeal not for a four-power conference but for a plebiscite. In an open letter to Runciman, published in the newspaper *Popolo d'Italia*, Mussolini urged the British mediator to propose a plebiscite not only for the Sudeten Germans, but for all the minorities in Czechoslovakia, which he termed 'a monstrous fiction even in its geographical conformation, so much so that it has been called sometimes a crocodile, sometimes a sausage state'.[99] Runciman, predictably, made no response. Ironically, when the Runciman Mission was first announced in late July, Sargent advised against a letter of explanation being sent to Mussolini on the grounds that he might 'use it as a pretext for suggesting that the Czechoslovak question should be considered by the four Great Powers'.[100]

The chain of events that would lead directly to that eventuality had already begun to unfold. The first sign of this reached Runciman during the evening of 13 September, when he received a copy of Chamberlain's message to Hitler, giving notice of the intended visit in search of a 'peaceful solution'.[101] Twenty-four hours later, a brief message arrived from Chamberlain disclosing his intention of travelling to see Hitler at Berchtesgaden the following day. The Prime Minister added: 'I may want to ask you if you will come and join me there – and hope if I do so you would be able and willing to come at short notice.'[102]

Whilst Runciman and Ashton-Gwatkin (who was to accompany him) stood by at the British Legation all day on 15 September awaiting the summons to travel to Germany,[103] Stopford busied himself drafting a paper, for possible use at Berchtesgaden, outlining the available policy alternatives. Starting from the premise that there was little point in pursuing further the scheme he himself had prepared earlier, since it closely resembled the Fourth Plan on which negotiations had broken down, Stopford explored six other possibilities, four of which involved the transfer of territory. The first option, that of a plebiscite, was rejected on the grounds that it would 'scarcely be a free expression of opinion' and that the inevitable delays would only increase the danger of the situation. However, the alternative of ceding territory without a prior plebiscite was even more dangerous. Stopford considered this 'the most difficult solution for the Czechoslovak Government', and believed it was 'probable that the Czechs would fight sooner than accept this'. The third option, creating an independent 'Sudeten State', would avoid the dangers of a plebiscite and facilitate a two-stage transfer to Germany, since there was no means of permanently preserving the new state's independence. Stopford observed, however, that considerable difficulties would arise if the extent of the area in question were to be left to the SdP alone to determine. The alternative which appeared to present the least number of difficulties was an international conference. Stopford reasoned that it might be easier for Czechoslovakia to transfer territory to the four powers – Britain, France, Germany and Italy – than to Germany alone. That, he argued, 'would probably ensure a fairer decision as to the areas to be handed over than any other method', though it would involve 'a considerable assumption of responsibility' by the governments concerned.

Stopford's remaining two options, which did not involve pressing the Czechoslovak government into the surrender of territory, were added as something of an afterthought. The first, a federal model, involved the division of the country into independent 'national areas', with certain functions, such as defence and foreign policy, delegated to a central government. The last possibility – which was, in fact, proposed by the Czech financier Preiss – involved not only the full implementation of the Carlsbad demands, but also the suppression of the Communist Party, the renunciation of the treaty with the Soviet Union, the conclusion of a commercial agreement with Germany, and a permanent seat in the Cabinet for a representative of the Sudeten Germans. Although not mentioned by Stopford, Preiss's proposal, despite nominally preserving the integrity and independence of Czechoslovakia, would inevitably have resulted in its domination by Germany. Of all the alternatives considered, only one therefore – the federal solution – offered any prospect of continued Czechoslovak independence, and that option, Stopford indicated, would only be relevant if the Berchtesgaden talks determined 'that a solution was possible within the Czechoslovak State'.[104]

Preiss's plan for the implementation of the Carlsbad programme, with the addition of the other points mentioned, was essentially an unofficial and unrepresentative last-minute attempt to come to terms with Germany and thus preserve the territorial integrity of Czechoslovakia – but at the inevitable expense of its independence. In conversation with the German Minister in Prague, Preiss (as reported to London by Newton) drew attention to the fact that the 'removal of German districts would leave a united Czechoslovak State attached by race with Russia and by sentiment with Social Democracy'. Eisenlohr agreed that such a state would be a 'continuing anxiety' for Germany, and expressed the belief that Hitler would therefore prefer Preiss's alternative. The Minister, however, advised against Preiss's offer to put his plan in person to Hjalmar Schacht, the President of the *Reichsbank*, arguing instead that it would only be acceptable in Berlin if proposed by the British government.[105]

These suggestions were communicated by Preiss to the Runciman Mission during the evening of 14 September[106] and Newton transmitted them to London the next day. Preiss, whom Newton described as an 'intelligent Czech banker', added that he had also spoken to Hodža, who supported the proposal, considering it preferable to a plebiscite or to war. Hodža had also urged that maximum pressure be applied on Beneš by Britain and France as the President, allegedly, remained convinced that Czechoslovakia and its allies would emerge victorious from war with Germany. Preiss therefore appealed for the matter to receive the most urgent consideration by the British government as he believed that in two or three days war would be almost inevitable.[107] Within the Foreign Office, however, Preiss's proposals attracted little attention apart from a lengthy minute from Robert Hadow (who had previously served in the Prague Legation) drawing attention to Preiss's close links with Hodža's Agrarian

Party, and concluding that they had both come together to save Czechoslovakia from 'the utter ruination of war'.[108]

Despite the advance warning received from Chamberlain, Runciman's invitation to Berchtesgaden did not materialise. Instead, doubtless to the mediator's intense relief, he received a summons to return immediately to London. The message arrived from the Prime Minister's entourage in Germany during the evening of 15 September, as members of the Mission were attending an official dinner at the French Legation, described by Stopford as 'a grand – if nervous – affair'.[109] In addition to summoning Runciman to London for 'essential' consultations the following day, Chamberlain requested that it should be announced that 'Runciman was not abandoning his Mission, but going to London at the Prime Minister's invitation'. The suggestion was also made that Runciman should appeal to both parties 'to refrain from any action which might give rise to further incidents', pending the outcome of a second meeting between Chamberlain and Hitler.[110] Runciman indicated immediately that he would 'gladly come to London', with Ashton-Gwatkin, the following day.[111]

The British mediators spent a busy night informing the Czechoslovak authorities of the latest development, preparing the required communiqué,[112] and making the necessary travel arrangements. In order to demonstrate that the Runciman Mission was not abandoning its task, two of its senior members, Stopford and Peto, were to remain in Prague with other Mission personnel, though Stopford noted that this was a device 'which deceived nobody'.[113] The arrival of a telegram of thanks addressed to Runciman from King George VI only added to the air of finality. In this, the King recorded 'how greatly the patient and untiring efforts of yourself and your staff to bring about a peaceful solution are appreciated by your fellow countrymen' and added his 'warmest wishes for a successful issue to your labours'.[114]

Runciman and Ashton-Gwatkin left Prague at noon on 16 September on a Czechoslovak Airlines flight bound for London. It was the first time Runciman had travelled by air, and this overcoming of his known aversion to flying added further to the drama of the occasion.[115] As his departure was ostensibly only temporary, Runciman left the Czechoslovak capital without ceremony. Before leaving he did, however, pay a lengthy call on Beneš, who spoke of his fear that Czechoslovakia would be sacrificed. The mediator's response was far from sympathetic. He blamed the President for his failure to accept the Carlsbad demands when first articulated, arguing therefore that the prime responsibility for sacrificing his country rested with Beneš himself.[116] For his part, Beneš recorded in his memoir that he asked Runciman to inform Chamberlain that, were Britain and France to attempt to impose a settlement without the prior agreement of the Czechoslovak authorities, neither he nor his government would be able to implement it.[117] Also that morning, Runciman summoned Kundt to the British Legation to take leave of him and thank him for his assistance. In response to a direct question, Kundt, the sole member of the SdP leadership remaining in Prague, claimed to have severed all connections with his party.[118] This was no more than a device enabling Kundt to remain at liberty in Prague, and he nevertheless reported on the meeting to the German Legation, imparting the impression that Runciman and Ashton-Gwatkin would not be returning to Czechoslovakia.[119]

Runciman flew back to a tense and anxious Britain, his aircraft touching down at Croydon Airport in the late afternoon at about the same time as Chamberlain, returning from his visit to Hitler, landed at Heston. The returning mediator informed waiting journalists that he had enjoyed his flight, but otherwise divulged little apart from noting that the situation was 'very delicate', and adding: 'It is in the lap of the gods.' Runciman also disclosed that he did not know when he would be returning to Prague.[120] An hour later, described by one journalist as looking 'composed but distinctly tired and pale',[121] Runciman arrived at Downing Street where he joined a meeting of the Cabinet Committee on Czechoslovakia. In addition to three senior Cabinet Ministers – Halifax, Simon and Hoare – also present were Wilson, Cadogan and Vansittart. The meeting had gathered not only to receive Runciman's views but also to hear Chamberlain's account of his conversation with Hitler.[122]

With Britain's mediator back in London, the Runciman Mission to Czechoslovakia had been effectively concluded. Its outcome, however, was yet to be determined.

Notes

1 Halifax to Phipps, 7 September 1938, *DBFP*, 3/II, no. 798; Bonnet to Corbin, 7 September 1938, *DDF*, 2/XI, no. 33.
2 Halifax to Phipps, 9 September 1938, *DBFP*, 3/II, no. 814; Bonnet to Corbin, 8 September 1938, *DDF*, 2/XI, no. 45.
3 Dilks, ed., *Cadogan Diaries*, pp. 94–5. Kordt made a clandestine visit to Downing Street the following day to appeal to Halifax in person.
4 Halifax to Runciman, in Halifax to Newton, 8 September 1938, *DBFP*, 3/II, no. 799.
5 Inskip diary extracts, 8 September 1938, Caldecote Papers, INKP 1.
6 Dilks, ed., *Cadogan Diaries*, pp. 95–6; Harvey, ed., *Harvey Diaries*, pp. 171–2.
7 Halifax to Newton, 8 September 1938, *DBFP*, 3/II, no. 806.
8 Newton to Halifax, 9 September 1938, *DBFP*, 3/II, no. 809.
9 Prime Minister's Press Statement, 11 September 1938, *DBFP*, 3/II, appendix III, pp. 680–2.
10 Halifax to Henderson, in Halifax to Kirkpatrick, 9 September 1938, *DBFP*, 3/II, no. 815.
11 Henderson to Cadogan, in Ogilvie-Forbes to Halifax, 10 September 1938, *DBFP*, 3/II, no. 819; Henderson to Halifax, 10 September 1938, *DBFP*, 3/II, no. 823.
12 Halifax to Henderson, 10 September 1938, *DBFP*, 3/II, no. 825; Harvey, ed., *Harvey Diaries*, p. 174; Note by Wilson of meeting held at 10 Downing Street on 10 September 1938, PREM 1/266A, ff. 339–40.

13 Speech by Göring, 10 September 1938, extract in RIIA *Documents*, 1938, II, p. 189.
14 Speech by Goebbels, 10 September 1938, *ibid.*, p. 191.
15 Baynes, ed., *Speeches of Adolf Hitler*, II, pp. 1487–99.
16 Halifax to Newton, 13 September 1938, C 9659/9572/18, FO 371/21782.
17 Dilks, ed., *Cadogan Diaries*, p. 97. See also Harvey, ed., *Harvey Diaries*, pp. 176–7.
18 Henderson to Halifax, 12 September 1938, *DBFP*, 3/II, no. 837.
19 Henderson to Halifax, 13 September 1938, *DBFP*, 3/II, no. 849.
20 Stopford, 'Prague, 1938–1939', p. 63.
21 Stopford to Winthrop-Young, 12 September 1938, Stopford Papers, RJS 3/1.
22 Ashton-Gwatkin to Wilson, 13 September 1938, C 9914/1941/18, FO 371/21738 and FO 800/304.
23 Runciman to Halifax, in Newton to Halifax, 13 September 1938, *DBFP*, 3/II, no. 845.
24 Ashton-Gwatkin's diary, 12 September 1938, FO 800/304. See also Ashton-Gwatkin to Strang, 17 September 1938, DBFP, II, appendix II (III), p. 672.
25 Ashton-Gwatkin to Wilson, 13 September 1938, C 9914/1941/18, FO 371/21738 and FO 800/304.
26 Ashton-Gwatkin to Strang, 17 September 1938, *DBFP*, 3/II, appendix II (III), p. 672.
27 Stopford to Winthrop-Young, 12 September 1938, Stopford Papers, RJS 3/1.
28 Ashton-Gwatkin to Wilson, 13 September 1938, C 9914/1941/18, FO 371/21738 and FO 800/304.
29 Newton to Halifax, 30 August 1938, C 8946/4839/18, FO 371/21774.
30 Newton to Halifax, 31 August 1938, C 9015/4839/18, FO 371/21774. See also report from Sutton-Pratt, 31 August 1938, C 9603/4839/18, FO 371/21774.
31 Minutes by Roberts, 1 September 1938; Sargent, 2 September 1938; and Halifax, 4 September 1938, C 9015/4839/18, FO 371/21774.
32 See undated report from Pares concerning an incident near Liberec, C 9105/4839/18, FO 371/21774.
33 Report from Sutton-Pratt, in Newton to Halifax, 13 September 1938, C 9677/4839/18, FO 371/21774. See also note 3 to document no. 867, *DBFP*, 3/II, pp. 319–20. When Sutton-Pratt approached one of the military vehicles, to remonstrate about indiscriminate firing, he himself was shot at by the officer in command. Sutton-Pratt added: 'I consider the tank personnel quite lost their heads.'
34 Newton to Halifax, 14 September 1938, *DBFP*, 3/II, no. 867.
35 Ashton-Gwatkin to Strang, 17 September 1938, *DBFP*, 3/II, appendix II (III), p. 673. Although not mentioned by Ashton-Gwatkin, press reports indicated that a substantial cache of arms was found in the building. (*The Times*, 15 September 1938.)
36 'Letter from Lord Runciman to President Beneš [and Mr. Chamberlain]', 21 September 1938, DBFP, 3/II, appendix II (IV), p. 677.
37 Hencke to the Foreign Ministry, 16 September 1938, *DGFP*, D/II, no. 502.
38 Notes by Schmundt, 9 and 10 September 1938, *DGFP*, D/II, no. 448. Although the notes are not explicit, the invasion appeared to be planned for early October.
39 Memorandum by the General Staff, 24 August 1938, *DGFP*, D/II, no. 388. The memorandum was submitted to Hitler, who accepted the proposed line of action.
40 Groscurth, *Tagebücher*, p. 104.

41 Eisenlohr to the Foreign Ministry, 14 September 1938, *DGFP*, D/II, no. 481.
42 Hencke to the Foreign Ministry, 17 September 1938, *DGFP*, D/II, no. 518.
43 Smelser, *Sudeten Problem*, pp. 237–9.
44 Newton to Halifax, 14 September 1938, *DBFP*, 3/II, no. 884.
45 Newton to Halifax, 13 September 1938, C 9714/4839/18, FO 371/21774.
46 Minute by Roberts, 17 September 1938, C 9800/4839/18, FO 371/21774.
47 Minute by Roberts, 16 September 1938, C 9837/4839/18, FO 371/21774.
48 Newton to Halifax, 13 September 1938, *DBFP*, 3/II, no. 846; Ashton-Gwatkin's diary, 13 September 1938, FO 800/304.
49 Newton to Halifax, 13 September 1938, *DBFP*, 3/II, no. 846.
50 Ashton-Gwatkin to Wilson, 13 September 1938, undated post-script (probably 14 September), C 9914/1941/18, FO 371/21738 and FO 800/304.
51 Ashton-Gwatkin's diary, 13 September 1938, FO 800/304.
52 Stopford, 'Prague, 1938–1939', pp. 64–5.
53 Ashton-Gwatkin's diary, 13 September 1938, FO 800/304; Ashton-Gwatkin to Strang, 17 September 1938, *DBFP*, 3/II, appendix II (III), p. 672.
54 Circular dispatch from Krofta, 14 September 1938, in Beneš, *Mnichovské dny*, document no. 41, p. 494; Memorandum by Altenburg, 13 September 1938, *DGFP*, D/II, no. 466; Newton to Halifax 13 and 14 September 1938, *DBFP*, 3/II, nos 860 and 870. Newton made no reference to Ashton-Gwatkin's initial intermediary role in his reports.
55 Ashton-Gwatkin to Strang, 17 September 1938, *DBFP*, 3/II, appendix II (III), p. 672; Newton to Halifax, 13 September 1938, *DBFP*, II, no. 860.
56 Telephone message for the President, 14 September 1938, in Beneš, *Mnichovské dny*, document no. 43, p. 497; Newton to Halifax, 14 September 1938, *DBFP*, 3/II, no. 869.
57 Ashton-Gwatkin's diary, 13 September 1938, FO 800/304; Newton to Halifax, 13 September 1938, C 9714/4839/18, FO 371/21774.
58 Ashton-Gwatkin to Strang, 17 September 1938, *DBFP*, 3/II, appendix II (III), p. 672; F.T.A. Ashton-Gwatkin, 'The Personal Story of the Runciman Mission', *The Listener*, 21 October 1948, p. 596.
59 Newton to Halifax, 14 September 1938, *DBFP*, 3/II, no. 871. For the full text of the SdP's ultimatum see Memorandum by Altenburg, 13 September 1938, *DGFP*, D/II, no. 467.
60 Ashton-Gwatkin to Strang, in Newton to Halifax, 15 September 1938, *DBFP*, 3/II, no. 889.
61 Ashton-Gwatkin's diary, 14 September 1938, FO 800/304.
62 Ashton-Gwatkin to Strang, 17 September 1938, *DBFP*, 3/II, appendix II (III), p. 673.
63 Ashton-Gwatkin to Strang, in Newton to Halifax, 15 September 1938, *DBFP*, 3/II, no. 889.
64 Ashton-Gwatkin to Strang, 17 September 1938, *DBFP*, 3/II, appendix II (III), p. 673. See also Ashton-Gwatkin to Strang, in Newton to Halifax, 15 September 1938, *DBFP*, 3/II, no. 889.
65 Newton to Halifax, 14 September 1938, *DBFP*, 3/II, no. 880. See also the *Manchester Guardian*, 15 September 1938.
66 Memorandum by Altenburg, 14 September 1938, *DGFP*, D/II, no. 472.
67 Henlein to Hitler, 15[?] September 1938, *DGFP*, D/II, no. 489. Henlein also informed Hitler of the probability that Chamberlain would propose the transfer of territory. He did not indicate the source of this information.

68 Hencke to Foreign Ministry, 16 September 1938, *DGFP*, D/II, no. 497. Brunet, a former professor of law and Socialist Party politician, had been standing by from early August to work alongside Runciman as a French mediator. According to Kundt, Brunet, who had been closely acquainted with the Sudeten German problem for over 20 years, had shown 'remarkable understanding' for the Sudeten Germans. (Hencke to Foreign Ministry, 6 August 1938, *DGFP*, D/II, no. 340.) For details of Brunet's visit see *DDF*, 2/XI, nos 102, 123, 178 and 224.
69 Ashton-Gwatkin to Strang, 17 September 1938, *DBFP*, 3/II, appendix II (III), pp. 672–3.
70 Beneš, *Mnichovské dny*, p. 237; Hencke to the Foreign Ministry, 17 September 1938, *DGFP*, D/II, no. 520.
71 Proclamation by Henlein, 15 September 1938, *DGFP*, D/II, no. 490.
72 Hencke to the Foreign Ministry, 17 September 1938, *DGFP*, D/II, nos 513, 515 and 520.
73 Hencke to the Foreign Ministry, 17 and 19 September 1938, *DGFP*, D/II, nos 520 and 528.
74 Phipps to Halifax, 13 September 1938, *DBFP*, 3/II, no. 848. Later that day, Daladier repeated the suggestion in a telephone message to Chamberlain. (Daladier to Chamberlain, *DDF*, 2/XI, no. 122.)
75 Cabinet Committee on Czechoslovakia Minutes, 13 September 1938, CS (38) 2, CAB 27/646.
76 Cabinet Minutes, 14 September 1938, Cabinet 38 (38), CAB 23/95.
77 Halifax to Runciman, in Halifax to Newton, 13 September 1938, *DBFP*, 3/II, no. 850.
78 Runciman to Halifax, in Newton to Halifax, 13 September 1938, *DBFP*, 3/II, no. 859.
79 Notes by Wilson, in Wilson to Cadogan, 10 September 1938 (twice), PREM 1/266A, ff. 342–3, 345–8.
80 Chamberlain to Runciman, 12 September 1938, PREM 1/266A, ff. 320–4.
81 Lady Runciman's diary, 12 September 1938, notes by Stopford, Stopford Papers, RJS 3/24.
82 Runciman to Chamberlain, 13 September 1938, PREM 1/266A, f. 319.
83 Cabinet Committee on Czechoslovakia Minutes, 13 September 1938, CS (38) 2, CAB 27/646.
84 Cabinet Minutes, 14 September 1938, Cabinet 38 (38), CAB 23/95.
85 Cabinet Committee on Czechoslovakia Minutes, 13 September 1938, CS (38) 2, CAB 27/646.
86 Halifax to Newton, 13 September 1938, C 9659/9572/18, FO 371/21782.
87 Newton to Halifax, 11 September 1938, C 9572/9572/18, FO 371/21782. In the Foreign Office, Roberts did not accept the Åland Islands as a relevant precedent, arguing that the two cases were quite different. The Åland Islands dispute was between two members of the League of Nations willing to accept its ruling, whereas the Sudeten German problem involved a non-member of the League prepared to use force against its smaller neighbour. (Minute by Roberts, 12 September 1938, *ibid.*)
88 Newton (and Runciman) to Halifax, 14 September 1938, C 9811/9572/18, FO 371/21782.
89 Newton to Halifax, 16 September 1938, *DBFP*, 3/II, no. 902. The other territories Hodža probably had in mind were the two northern salients round Rumburk

(Rumburg) and Frýdlant (Friedland). For the discussion of these areas at the Paris Peace Conference, see Perman, *Shaping of the Czechoslovak State*, p. 144.

90 Newton to Halifax, 15 September 1938, *DBFP*, 3/II, no. 888.

91 Masaryk to Halifax, 12 September 1938, C 9725/9572/18, FO 371/21782.

92 Memorandum by Vansittart, 12 September 1938, *ibid.*

93 Minute by Mallet, 15 September 1938, C 9811/9572/18, FO 371/21782.

94 Newton to Halifax, 23 August 1938, *DBFP*, 3/II, no. 675.

95 Troutbeck to Mallet, 23 August 1938, C 8857/1941/18, FO 371/21733.

96 Minute by Roberts, 31 August 1938, C 8820/1941/18, FO 371/21733.

97 Minute by Mallet, 2 September 1938, *ibid.*

98 Minute by Vansittart, 13 September 1938, C 9966/1941/18, FO 371/21738. Vansittart was concerned about the exclusion of the Soviet Union, arguing that it would first 'retire into sulky isolation' and then 'be penetrated by Germany, and Bismarck's traditional policy of close Russo-German relations' would follow.

99 Translation of Mussolini's open letter to Runciman in Charles to Halifax, 15 September 1938, C 10148/9572/18, FO 371/21782. See also enclosure in Woermann to Weizsäcker, 15 September 1938, *DGFP*, D/II, no. 488.

100 Minute by Sargent, 28 July 1938, C 7765/1941/18, FO 371/21730.

101 Chamberlain to Hitler, in Halifax to Henderson, 13 September 1938, (repeated to Prague), *DBFP*, 3/II, no. 862.

102 Chamberlain to Runciman, in Halifax to Newton, 14 September 1938, *DBFP*, 3/II, no. 882.

103 Ashton-Gwatkin's diary, 15 September 1938, FO 800/304.

104 Memorandum by Stopford, undated (but probably 15 September 1938), Stopford Papers, RJS 3/8.

105 Newton to Halifax, 15 September 1938, C 9787/1941/18, FO 371/21737.

106 Ashton-Gwatkin to Strang, 17 September 1938, *DBFP*, 3/II, appendix II (III), p. 673.

107 Newton to Halifax, 15 September 1938, C 9787/1941/18, FO 371/21737.

108 Minute by Hadow, 15 September 1938, *ibid.*

109 Stopford, 'Prague, 1938–1939', p. 71. Stopford recalled: 'That message broke up the party; and one was inevitably reminded of the Waterloo Ball!' See also Ashton-Gwatkin to Strang, 17 September 1938, *DBFP*, 3/II, appendix II (III), p. 673.

110 Telephone message from Strang, 15 September 1938, FO 800/304. See also note 1 to document no. 882, *DBFP*, 3/II, p. 329.

111 Runciman to Halifax, in Newton to Halifax, 15 September 1938, C 9844/1941/18, FO 371/21737.

112 See Newton to Halifax, 16 September 1938, C 9982/4770/18, FO 371/21766; *The Times*, 16 September 1938.

113 Stopford, 'Prague, 1938–1939', p. 71.

114 Telegram from King George VI to Runciman, 15 September 1938, Runciman Papers, WR 293. The Prime Minister had written to the King in terms very similar to those addressed to Runciman. See Chamberlain to King George VI, 13 September 1938, PREM 1/266A.

115 Ashton-Gwatkin's diary, 16 September 1938, FO 800/304. A month earlier, Runciman had written to his son 'getting out is going to be difficult ... I won't fly'. (Runciman to Leslie Runciman, 15 August 1938, Runciman Papers, WR 296.)

116 Cabinet Committee on Czechoslovakia Minutes, 16 September 1938, CS (38) 5, CAB 27/646.

117 Beneš, *Mnichovské dny*, p. 249, footnote.
118 Cabinet Minutes, 17 September 1938, Cabinet 39 (38), CAB 23/95.
119 Hencke to the Foreign Ministry, 16 September 1938, *DGFP*, D/II, no. 497.
120 *The Times*, 17 September 1938.
121 *Manchester Guardian*, 17 September 1938.
122 Cabinet Committee on Czechoslovakia Minutes, 16 September 1938, CS (38) 5, CAB 27/646.

14
The Reckoning

With Runciman's return to London, British policy towards Czechoslovakia passed entirely under the control of the Prime Minister and his close advisers. Nevertheless, Runciman's role was not quite concluded. In addition to participating in a series of top level discussions, including attending a special meeting of the Cabinet held on Chamberlain's return from visiting Hitler at Berchtesgaden, the British mediator prepared a report on his activities in Czechoslovakia. This formal conclusion of the Runciman Mission consisted of two, substantially identical, letters from Runciman addressed, respectively, to Beneš and to Chamberlain, dated 21 September.[1]

The 2000-word report commenced with a brief definition of the problem the Mission had been sent to resolve, and summarised the main developments during its residency in Czechoslovakia. The dispute in question was characterised as a problem that had been in existence for 'many centuries', although 'new factors' had recently appeared alongside the historic ones. The main body of the report was divided into three sections reflecting what Runciman saw as the essential components of the problem: constitutional, political and economic. It was the constitutional issue which most immediately commanded his attention on arrival in Czechoslovakia, and the bulk of the report was therefore concerned with this aspect. As Runciman noted: 'At the time it implied the provision of some degree of home rule for the Sudeten Germans within the Czechoslovak Republic; the question of self determination had not yet arisen in an acute form.'

Having familiarised himself with the initial standpoints of both sides, it became evident – Runciman recorded – that no compromise between the two positions was possible. Talks were therefore suspended in mid-August, but a new basis for discussion, the Fourth Plan, was established in early September. In Runciman's opinion:

> this plan embodied almost all the requirements of the Karlsbad eight points, and with a little clarification and extension could have been made to cover them in their entirety. Negotiations should have at once

> been resumed on this favourable and hopeful basis; but little doubt remains in my mind that the very fact that they were so favourable operated against their chances with the more extreme members of the Sudeten German party.

Runciman also believed that the Moravská Ostrava incident:

> was used in order to provide an excuse for the suspension, if not for the breaking off, of negotiations. The Czech Government, however, at once gave way to the demands of the Sudeten German party in this matter and preliminary discussions of the 4th Plan were resumed on the 10th September.

The mediator was again convinced that 'Sudeten extremists ... provoked and instigated' the unrest that broke out on 11 and 12 September, as a result of which:

> Herr Henlein and Herr Frank presented a new series of demands – withdrawal of State police, limitation of troops to their military duties, &c. – which the Czechoslovak Government were again prepared to accept on the sole condition that a representative of the party came to Prague to discuss how order should be maintained. On the night of the 13th September this condition was refused by Herr Henlein, and all negotiations were completely broken off.

This account accurately reflected actual developments and placed the responsibility for the collapse of the negotiations unequivocally on the SdP. The point was reiterated even more explicitly in a subsequent paragraph: 'Responsibility for the final break must, in my opinion, rest upon Herr Henlein and Herr Frank and upon those of their supporters inside and outside the country who were urging them to extreme and unconstitutional action.'

Runciman then noted that with the collapse of negotiations, 'my functions as a mediator were, in fact, at an end'. The key element of the new situation was the 'connexion between the chief Sudeten leaders and the government of the Reich', and as a consequence 'the dispute was no longer an internal one'. 'It was not part of my function', Runciman observed, 'to attempt mediation between Czechoslovakia and Germany.' Thus far, Runciman's report was substantially unexceptionable. In an earlier paragraph, however, he noted (writing on 21 September): 'It is quite clear that we cannot now go back to the point where we stood two weeks ago, and we have to consider the situation as it now faces us.'

The mediator's report progressed to an examination of the grievances of the Sudeten Germans. In doing so, and indeed throughout the entire document, Runciman totally equated the views of the SdP with those of the German minority as a whole. (Although in terms of electoral support that was substantially accurate, the German Social Democrats nevertheless remained independent of the SdP, but failed to receive a mention in the report.) Runciman declared that he had 'much sympathy ... with the Sudeten case', explaining:

> It is a hard thing to be ruled by an alien race, and I have been left with the impression that Czechoslovak rule in the Sudeten areas for the last twenty years, though not actively oppressive, and certainly not 'terroristic', has been marked by tactlessness, lack of understanding, petty intolerance and discrimination, to a point where the resentment of the German population was inevitably moving in the direction of revolt.

Again, Runciman's description of the attitude of the Czechoslovak authorities was in itself accurate enough, although his conclusion that the transgressions listed fully explained the arousal of revolt was perhaps open to question. Runciman proceeded to itemise what he termed the 'local irritations' suffered by the German population (with the variations in the letter to Chamberlain given in parenthesis):

> Czech officials and Czech police, speaking little (or no) German, were appointed in large numbers to purely German districts; Czech agricultural colonists were encouraged to settle on land transferred (confiscated) under the Land Reform in the middle of German populations; for the children of these Czech invaders Czech schools were said to have been built (were built) on a large scale; there is a very general belief that Czech firms were favoured as against German firms in the allocation of State contracts and that the State provided work and relief for Czechs more readily than for Germans.

Runciman added that he believed these complaints were 'in the main justified', and observed that even during his stay in Czechoslovakia, the authorities were reluctant 'to remedy them on anything like an adequate scale'.

In addition to listing the perceived malpractices, Runciman noted the claim that the Czechoslovak authorities had made frequent promises to the Sudeten Germans, but that 'little or no action had followed'. This experience, he explained, 'had induced an attitude of unveiled mistrust of the leading Czech statesmen'. Runciman added that he himself was unable to judge how far this mistrust was 'merited or unmerited', but it certainly existed and resulted in a lack of confidence in the minds of the German minority towards Czechoslovak leaders 'however conciliatory their statements'. Doubtless, the statesmen in question included Beneš, and if the worst iniquity he was alleged to have committed was a failure to fulfil his promises, deplorable though this was, he was certainly not alone amongst political leaders of any nation in being so accused.

The third of the SdP's 'major grievances' itemised by Runciman concerned the parliamentary system. He pointed out that following its success in the 1935 elections, the SdP formed the largest single party in the Czechoslovak parliament, but 'they can always be outvoted, and consequently some of them feel that constitutional action is useless', adding, in the version addressed to Chamberlain, the phrase, 'and that the Czech democracy is a farce'. Safeguarding the interests of minorities has presented problems in many parliamentary systems, including the British, and Czechoslovakia was not alone in having less than perfect representative institutions, but they were nevertheless considerably less farcical than those of neighbouring Nazi Germany, the object of the SdP's admiration. This irony, however, escaped Runciman's notice, as he proceeded to explain that it was indeed the rise of Nazi Germany which 'gave them new hope'. He added, moreover: 'I regard their turning for help towards their kinsmen and their eventual desire to join the Reich as a natural development in the circumstances.'

Runciman claimed credit for seeking, unsuccessfully, to head off this 'natural development':

> At the time of my arrival the more moderate Sudeten leaders still desired a settlement within the frontiers of the Czechoslovak State. ... I did my best to promote it, and up to a point with some success, but, even so, not without misgiving as to whether, when agreement was reached, it could ever be carried out without giving rise to a new crop of suspicions, controversies, accusations and counter-accusations. I felt that any such arrangement would have been temporary, not lasting.

The collapse of the Fourth Plan, Runciman added, terminated all hopes of such a solution. This reasoning, however, is less than convincing. The question of self-determination and the consequent transfer of territory had not formally arisen until Hitler's speech on 12 September, and it is difficult to believe that Runciman had devoted the previous six weeks to pursuing a solution he regarded as no more than temporary.

The report proceeded to the central task of making recommendations. Turning first to the security situation, Runciman noted that by the time of his departure from Prague on 16 September, the unrest in the German areas, which, in his view, 'had never been more than sporadic', had subsided; that a state amounting to martial law had been imposed by the government in many districts; and that 'the more extreme' SdP leaders had fled to Germany. The limited nature of the unrest was given credence by Runciman's claim that the number of deaths on both sides did not exceed

70. 'Unless, therefore,' he continued, 'Herr Henlein's Freikorps are deliberately encouraged to cross the frontier, I have no reason to expect any notable renewal of incidents and disturbances.' In those circumstances, Runciman believed, the presence of the state police in the German areas was no longer necessary, and in view of their extreme unpopularity among the German population, 'they should be withdrawn as soon as possible', thus reducing the causes of unrest.

Runciman's second recommendation constituted the crux of his report:

> Further, it has become self-evident to me that those frontier districts between Czechoslovakia and Germany where the Sudeten population is in an important majority should be given full right of self-determination at once. If some cession is inevitable, as I believe it to be, it is as well that it should be done promptly and without procrastination. There is real danger, even a danger of civil war, in the continuance of a state of uncertainty. Consequently, there are very real reasons for a policy of immediate and drastic action.

The mediator added that a plebiscite would be 'a sheer formality' in the predominantly German areas and the inevitable delay potentially dangerous:

> I consider, therefore, that those frontier districts should at once be transferred from Czechoslovakia to Germany, and further that measures for their peaceful transfer, including the provision of safeguards for the population during the transfer period, should be arranged forthwith by agreement between the two Governments.

Here Runciman could at the very least be accused of inconsistency. Having argued previously that, failing an attack by SdP *Freikorps* from Germany, there would be no reason to anticipate continuing unrest, and thus justified his recommended withdrawal of the state police from the areas concerned, he then raised the spectre of possible civil war to justify cession of territory. By his own reasoning, such an event would only have arisen as a result of external attack, making the use of the term 'civil war' somewhat questionable. Moreover, Runciman further undermined his own argument in the following paragraph, when he expressed the conviction that 'history has proved that in times of peace the two peoples can live together on friendly terms' and that this was 'the real desire of the average Czech and German', who were 'alike in being honest, peaceable, hard-working and frugal folk'.

Runciman's third constitutional recommendation concerned the protection of national minorities remaining after the transfer of territory was accomplished. He accurately observed that even if all the areas with a German majority were ceded to Germany, 'there would still remain in

Czechoslovakia a large number of Germans and in the areas transferred to Germany there would still be a certain number of Czechs'. In the case of the former, Runciman recommended 'that an effort be made to find a basis for local autonomy ... on the lines of the "Fourth Plan", modified so as to meet the new circumstances'. He remained totally silent concerning the future of Czechs within the areas to be handed to Germany, nor did he make any reference to members of the German minority who might not wish to be transferred to Nazi Germany.

The two remaining sections of the report, concerned respectively with political and economic matters, were relatively brief but no less controversial. Runciman defined the political aspects of the problem as involving the security and integrity of Czechoslovakia, particularly in relation to Germany. The issue, he believed, was 'one of removing a centre of intense political friction from the middle of Europe'. His objective in that direction was, on the surface, unexceptionable: namely, 'permanently to provide that the Czechoslovak State should live at peace with all her neighbours and that her policy, internal and external, should be directed to that end'. However, Runciman's proposed means of achieving it went far beyond the original terms of reference of his Mission. Citing the precedent of neutral Switzerland, he argued that 'an analogous policy is necessary for Czechoslovakia – not only for her own future existence, but for the peace of Europe'. In order to achieve this neutralisation, Runciman made four recommendations. The first two – a ban on political activity 'antagonistic to Czechoslovakia's neighbours' and a realignment of foreign policy in order to ensure no 'aggressive action against them' – amounted to major intrusions into the affairs of a friendly sovereign state. Their impact would be to limit the freedom of political expression and cause the abandonment of Czechoslovakia's alliances with France and the Soviet Union, and with Romania and Yugoslavia. The third recommendation sought to compensate for the loss of these alliances through a collective guarantee of Czechoslovakia against unprovoked aggression. However, Czechoslovakia's independence would inevitably be further circumscribed by the, albeit tentatively proposed, fourth recommendation for a commercial treaty with Germany.

This last recommendation led directly into the economic aspect of the problem under investigation, which, in Runciman's opinion, centred on the 'distress and unemployment' in the German areas which 'constituted a suitable background for political discontent'. He stressed, however, that it was 'misleading' to claim that the Sudeten German question was 'entirely or even in the main an economic one'. Nevertheless, Runciman had earlier asserted that the grievances he listed 'were intensified by the reactions of the economic crisis on the Sudeten industries' and that the Czechoslovak government was 'blamed for the resulting impoverishment'. However, Runciman made no recommendations concerning the economic situation, merely observing that, if a transfer of territory took place, it would become a matter mainly for Germany to resolve.

Runciman added three further recommendations almost as an afterthought. The first of these amounted to another major violation of Czechoslovakia's sovereignty, placing in jeopardy the security of the state, by advising that 'a representative of the Sudeten German people' should be given a permanent seat in the Czechoslovak cabinet. The remaining recommendations were essentially of a practical nature concerned with details of the proposed territorial transfer. One advised the establishment of 'a commission under a neutral chairman' to determine the precise areas for transfer to Germany and to resolve any difficulties that might arise. The last proposed the creation of 'an international force' to keep order in the territory to be transferred, thus facilitating the withdrawal of Czechoslovak security forces.

The Runciman report amounted to one of the most hostile communications ever delivered from a representative of one friendly country to another. Not only was Czechoslovakia to lose unspecified strategically important frontier districts to Germany, but what remained of the country was to be so weakened as to reduce it inevitably to a total dependency of that powerful neighbour. Yet, despite its devastating contents, Runciman concluded his report with customary expressions of gratitude for 'personal courtesy, hospitality and assistance' received from the Czechoslovak government, especially from Beneš and Hodža, and also from representatives of the SdP, and from many others with whom the Mission had come into contact.

Runciman began his report with a declaration of independence, claiming 'I was ... left perfectly free to obtain my own information and to draw my own conclusions'. In retrospect, that proved an unfortunate statement and was subject to challenge following the report's publication at the end of September.[2] In view of the circumstances of its production, even with the aid of Foreign Office facilities, it was hardly surprising that the Runciman report was not the most coherent piece of diplomatic prose ever written. It was produced over a period of five days between Runciman and Ashton-Gwatkin returning to London on 16 September and 21 September, the date on the report, which was a period of some of the most feverish activity hitherto undertaken in the field of international diplomacy. Nevertheless, the extent of the internal contradictions and inconsistencies combined with the ferocity of the recommendations it contained, caused some observers to question the authorship of the report, and to wonder to what extent the views it expressed were genuinely those of Runciman himself.

One such critical commentary was published in the *News Chronicle*. The article was not concerned with the authorship of the report but did question the logic of Runciman's conclusions. It noted that although Runciman considered his function as a mediator to have ended with the breaking off of negotiations by the SdP, he nevertheless proceeded to produce 'certain recommendations'. The *News Chronicle*, not inaccurately, summarised Runciman's findings:

> That self-determination was not a burning issue in August ...;
> That the disorders in Sudetenland were stimulated by Hitler's speech;
> That the last thing the Sudeten leaders wanted was a peaceful settlement; and
> That the Czech Government bears no responsibility whatsoever for the final break.

The article then posed a rhetorical question concerning Runciman's deductions: 'On the basis of his findings, what would you expect the recommendations to be?'[3]

An even more devastating assessment of the report appeared on the other side of the Atlantic in the *New York Herald Tribune*, where the journalist Dorothy Thompson termed it 'a remarkable and illogical document'. She detected a point in the report, just before Runciman's recommendation of territorial transfer, where, 'the whole nature and tenor of the argument changes', which led her to ask whether the last part of the document 'may not have been dictated by Hitler'.[4] In an earlier issue of the same newspaper, Thompson argued that the Runciman report was 'apparently made to order to fit the agreement which had already been reached between Hitler and Chamberlain' at Berchtesgaden. She added that the tenor of the report did not correspond with one of Runciman's last public pronouncements in Czechoslovakia, made during his visit to Czernin's castle at Petrohrad on 11 September, which she interpreted (perhaps somewhat dubiously) as indicating that he had no thoughts at that time of recommending the transfer of territory to Germany. Thompson concluded therefore, that the report was 'rigged' and a 'piece of propaganda'.[5]

The appearance of these criticisms in a leading American newspaper caused concern in the British Library of Information in New York, and guidance was sought from the Foreign Office News Department regarding the response to inevitable questions. The Library's Director, Angus Fletcher, agreed with Thompson's textual analysis but was confident of 'a perfectly simple explanation' for the hiatus.[6] In the Foreign Office the query was passed to Ashton-Gwatkin who responded with a five page memorandum refuting Thompson's allegations.

Ashton-Gwatkin insisted at the outset that the document in question was 'in no sense of the word a report', but a letter, 'partly narrative ..., partly explanatory ..., partly advisory'. Its intention was simply to provide Beneš and Chamberlain with 'Runciman's "final views" and with "certain suggestions"', as indeed was stated in the opening paragraph of the document itself. Within what Ashton-Gwatkin termed the 'advisory portion' of the letter, beginning with the 'suggestion' that Czechoslovak state police should be withdrawn from German areas, where the break in continuity had been detected, he conceded that 'perhaps these paragraphs are badly arranged', but he considered the meaning quite clear:

> (a) By 16th September the revolt in the Sudetenland had died down; the State Police should be withdrawn;
> (b) Transfer should follow 'promptly and without procrastination';
> (c) Otherwise delay and uncertainty may lead to civil war.

Ashton-Gwatkin also failed to see any inconsistency between Runciman's brief address from the balcony at Petrohrad castle and his advised transfer of territory ten days later. He argued that this and the other proposals were 'made on the basis of the breakdown and complete change of scene during 11th–13th September, which is all clearly explained in Lord Runciman's letter'. Earlier in the memorandum, Ashton-Gwatkin set out the sequence of events as he perceived it:

> The alternative solutions of the Sudeten question were:-
> (a) Local autonomy within Czechoslovak frontier
> (b) Plebiscite
> (c) Transfer to Germany without plebiscite.
> Lord Runciman did his best to promote a settlement on basis (a). Such a settlement appeared possible up to and including 11th September which was the day when he received the demonstrators at Petersbourg castle .... It was on this afternoon and evening of 11th September that the incidents broke out which destroyed any hope of a settlement on basis (a). This impression was reaffirmed by Herr Hitler's speech on 12th September demanding 'self-determination'; and on 13th September by the Sudeten delegation's refusal to meet the Czech authorities. By this date therefore, Lord Runciman had come to the conclusion that a solution could now be found only on basis (b) plebiscite or (c) transfer.

Ashton-Gwatkin added that this 'change in the situation' was telegraphed to London following his last conversation with Henlein on 14 September, and was therefore known to Chamberlain before his meeting with Hitler at Berchtesgaden on 15 September.[7]

Ashton-Gwatkin appears, in fact, to have sent two telegraphic reports to London concerning his visit to Aš on 14 September. The first, sent before his meeting with Henlein, reported only Frank's belief that the reference to self-determination in Hitler's speech 'meant more than the existing basis would give'.[8] It contained no specific reference to a plebiscite nor to the transfer of territory. Henlein's declaration to Ashton-Gwatkin that negotiations with the Czechoslovak authorities would only be resumed 'on the basis of a plebiscite' was reported to London in a second dispatch, which was actually telegraphed from Prague in the early hours of 15 September, and received at the Foreign Office at 9.30 a.m.[9] The Prime Minister left Heston Aerodrome for Germany at 8.30 that morning.[10] Unless the information was relayed to him on arrival in Munich by the British Embassy in Berlin (which received a copy of the telegram from Prague), it is improbable that Chamberlain was aware of Ashton-Gwatkin's message before meeting Hitler. Moreover, in the unlikely eventuality of the message reaching the Prime Minister, it was certainly not expressed in terms of Runciman's advice but in terms of Henlein's requirements. Contrary to Ashton-Gwatkin's assertion, it is therefore improbable that the Prime Minister believed himself to be in possession of Runciman's latest advice unless, of course, Henlein's wishes were considered tantamount to Runciman's recommendations – which was not very far removed from the point made by Thompson in her *New York Herald Tribune* article.

Ashton-Gwatkin also addressed the issue of the dating of the report. He explained that on 18 and 19 September, Runciman was 'resting in the country', and on his return to London the following day 'decided to put together his views and suggestions' for the benefit of both Beneš and Chamberlain. He continued: 'The letter was therefore composed, in its entirety, on 20th and 21st September; but many of the views therein expressed had already been given to Mr. Chamberlain and the Cabinet before that date.'[11] Runciman had indeed been involved in an intensive round of Whitehall discussions following his return from Prague on 16 September, but the nature of his initial advice was not quite as Ashton-Gwatkin implied.

Within an hour of flying into London on 16 September, Runciman attended a meeting of the Cabinet Committee on Czechoslovakia in Downing Street. The meeting (as previously mentioned) was attended by Halifax, Simon, Hoare, Vansittart, Cadogan and Wilson, who had gathered to receive Chamberlain's report of his conversations with Hitler at Berchtesgaden. Runciman arrived after the meeting had commenced and immediately gave an account of his interview with Beneš that morning, particularly concerning the President's views on a plebiscite. Beneš had described it as a 'most explosive weapon' that would probably meet with resistance from the Czechoslovak army, but had indicated nevertheless that under severe pressure from Britain he would accept that course. Runciman was also highly critical of the President's general attitude, speaking of his 'fatal habit' of only responding to pressure when it was too late, but nevertheless conceded that the government had the internal security situation 'well in hand'. Commenting on the recent unrest, Runciman observed that this had been grossly exaggerated, adding that it was 'not without significance that more Czechs than Germans had been killed'. As far as his role as investigator and mediator was concerned, Runciman stated that 'he had come to the end of the proposals which he could usefully make'. Only one further possibility remained of which 'something might be made' – that was the proposal by Preiss, for the full implementation of the Carlsbad points and the reorientation of Czechoslovakia towards Germany, which Runciman briefly outlined.

Discussion then turned to the issue of a plebiscite. Chamberlain observed that Hitler had indicated 'plainly what was in his mind, namely, that self-determination was now the only possibility'. In view of the fact that Hitler was prepared to risk war to secure an early settlement, and that France and therefore Britain would not intervene, Chamberlain 'had no doubt that a plebiscite offered the only solution'. Runciman merely rejoined that 'in the long run this was what would weigh with ... Beneš'. Prompted by an observation from Simon, referring to Runciman's and Newton's recently expressed objections to a plebiscite, Runciman confirmed that their alternative suggestion, of using the results of recent local government elections, would serve as a 'very good guide'. Runciman added later, however, that Ashton-Gwatkin, after studying the question of self-determination in considerable detail, had concluded that once that principle was accepted, 'there was no alternative to a plebiscite'.

Runciman also expressed severe criticism of the Czechoslovak government's attitude towards the national minorities, describing it as 'outrageous' and constituting an 'ugly story'. In response to a question from Chamberlain, he anticipated that the Hungarian and Polish minorities would also demand self-determination but considered the situation a 'little different' concerning the Slovaks. Answering a further query, about the viability of Czechoslovakia shorn of its German, Hungarian and Polish districts, Runciman observed that the country would be reduced to 'a very small area'. At this point the Prime Minister disclosed that he had received a categorical assurance from Hitler at Berchtesgaden that Germany was not interested in the remainder of Czechoslovakia. Looking to the future, Runciman was pessimistic. He believed there was 'no hope of a negotiated settlement' and that Czechs and Germans were unlikely ever to settle down peacefully. Moreover, he 'did not see how anything could now be achieved except by force in one form or another'.[12]

Clearly, during the first meeting on his return to London with those directing British foreign policy, Runciman had surprisingly little concrete advice to offer, apart from a less than whole-hearted endorsement of a plebiscite. Although such a policy could logically be seen to imply the cession of territory to Germany where the German population was in a majority, it was far from being presented as a positive recommendation for adoption by the British government. Moreover, during a meeting of the full Cabinet the following morning, Runciman appeared to retreat from that implication.

Runciman informed the Cabinet of his disappointment that he had been unable to resolve the Sudeten German problem, but considered that the time gained was of importance. He again made no specific recommendations apart from stating, in answer to a question, that 'he had reached the conclusion that Czechoslovakia could not continue to exist as she was today', adding: 'Something would have to be done, even if it amounted to no more than cutting off certain fringes.' Earlier, when discussing several possible solutions, Runciman indicated that the 'fringes' in question were areas round Cheb and Aš, containing an overwhelmingly German population of 800 000. He stated that the 'transfer of these areas to Germany would almost certainly be a good thing', although it would meet with the very strong opposition of the Czechoslovak Army. Runciman mentioned this possibility when discussing the question of a plebiscite, which presented 'very great' but, in his view, not insurmountable difficulties, and which he also linked with a possible four-power conference. The other options touched on by Runciman, but considered impractical in the circumstances, were the Preiss plan, a federal solution (favoured by Newton, he claimed), and an independent Sudeten-German state.[13] Evidently, Runciman's report to the Cabinet was essentially negative in tone and he put forward no firm proposals. One minister present, Duff Cooper (who was, admittedly, a critic of government policy and who resigned from the Cabinet over the terms of the Munich Agreement less than two weeks later), noted at the time that though 'interesting', Runciman was 'quite unhelpful, as he was unable to suggest any plan or policy'.[14]

Nevertheless, several other observations Runciman made to the Cabinet are worthy of note. He made the clear declaration that, in his view, 'there was a considerable percentage of people in the German areas who did not wish to be incorporated in the Reich'. He was also much less critical of Beneš than he had been the previous evening, describing him as 'rather more honest then he allowed himself to appear to be'. Runciman explained that Beneš was 'much cleverer than anyone else in the country, and this gave him a reputation for slipperiness'. Even more remarkable, however, were his comments on Henlein, described as a 'genial, good-tempered person', though 'nothing much could be got out him'. Runciman informed the Cabinet that he 'had since learned that, even before his own arrival in Prague, Herr Henlein had been in frequent communications with Berlin'. At another point in the discussion, he also alluded to a stage in the negotiations some two weeks previously when 'he had not fully realised the close connection between the Sudeten-German leaders and Berlin'.[15] It would appear that towards the end of his stay in Czechoslovakia, Runciman had been supplied with convincing evidence of the SdP's real relationship with Nazi Germany.[16]

Henlein's ties with Berlin were, however, of little interest to Chamberlain and his advisers at that juncture. The Prime Minister was more concerned with preparing the ground for his return visit to Germany. During his conversation with Hitler at Berchtesgaden on 15 September, Chamberlain had personally accepted the principle of Hitler's demand that the $3\frac{1}{2}$ million

Sudeten Germans should 'return to the *Reich*'. The Prime Minister had spoken of the possible transfer of territory 'containing 80 per cent of Germans' but Hitler indicated that he had in mind all areas that had a German majority, possibly accompanied by population transfers from other districts. Chamberlain also held out the prospect of abrogating Czechoslovakia's alliance with the Soviet Union, but Hitler seemed unconcerned about the rump that would remain following the expected secession of the other minorities. The conversation concluded with Chamberlain's undertaking to consult his ministerial colleagues, the French government and Runciman concerning these issues.[17]

Chamberlain and his colleagues immediately set about seeking to persuade their French counterparts of the drastic action considered necessary, and Daladier and Bonnet were summoned to London on 18 September for urgent discussions. After some token resistance, the French ministers accepted the principle of Czechoslovakia ceding territory to Germany and the British side agreed to depart from previous policy by participating in an international guarantee of the remaining Czechoslovak state.[18] A telegram was drafted communicating the joint decision to Beneš, indicating that, in view of the President's known objections to a plebiscite, a 'direct transfer' of territory would be preferable. The territory in question 'would probably have to include areas with over 50 per cent of German inhabitants'. Although some minor adjustments of frontier might be possible, the two governments were 'satisfied that the transfer of smaller areas based on a higher percentage would not meet the case'.[19] Chamberlain had abandoned his previously suggested 80 per cent limit, accepting instead Hitler's demand for all areas with a simple German majority.

The unwelcome message was delivered to Beneš jointly by Newton and de Lacroix on 19 September. Not surprisingly, Newton reported that the President was 'greatly moved and agitated' and complained bitterly about being abandoned.[20] The initial Czechoslovak reply, which proposed recourse to the Czechoslovak-German arbitration treaty of 1926,[21] was deemed unacceptable in London and Paris and the two Ministers made a further stern representation to Beneš in the early hours of 21 September.[22] Later that day the Czechoslovak government bowed to the pressure and formally accepted the Franco-British terms.[23] The path was now clear for Chamberlain to return to see Hitler.

During the discussions with the French ministers, Chamberlain made good – but selective – use of Runciman's advice. He indicated that Runciman believed there was now no prospect of achieving a mediated settlement between Czechs and Germans in Czechoslovakia and that adoption of the principle of self-determination offered the only possible solution.[24] Halifax's Private Secretary, Harvey (who was not actually present at the discussions), noted in his diary that Chamberlain made 'great point' of this advice from Runciman.[25] Evidently, the British government considered it important to be seen to be acting in accordance with the views of the person whom it sent to investigate and mediate in the Sudeten German dispute. Indeed, when the Prime Minister subsequently reported to the House of Commons, on 28 September, he detailed the advice given to the Cabinet on the mediator's return from Prague:

> Runciman informed us that although, in his view, the responsibility for the final breach in the negotiations at Prague rested with the Sudeten extremists, nevertheless, in view of recent developments, the frontier districts between Czechoslovakia and Germany where the Sudeten population was in a majority, should be given the full right of self-determination at once. He considered the cession of territory to be inevitable and thought it should be done promptly.

Chamberlain also stated that Runciman suggested that the German minority remaining on Czechoslovak territory should receive 'local autonomy on the basis of the Fourth Plan' and that Czechoslovakia should be neutralised 'as in the case of Switzerland'. Two further recommendations ascribed to Runciman were the establishment of an international commission to delimit the precise area to be transferred to Germany and the creation of an international force to keep order in the area concerned, thus facilitating the withdrawal of Czechoslovak troops and police as soon as possible.[26] However, as discussed above, neither the Cabinet minute nor that of the Committee on Czechoslovakia record Runciman's advice in these precise terms.

Four of these five proposals were duly put by Chamberlain to Hitler at their second meeting, held at Godesberg on 22 September, the exception being the suggested creation of an international force.[27] Hitler, however, demanded considerably more. All German areas of Czechoslovakia, up to what he termed the 'nationalities frontier',[28] were to be handed over to Germany by 1 October and plebiscites were to be held in certain additional localities. Both categories of territory were marked on a map of Bohemia and Moravia which Hitler presented to Chamberlain on 23 September together with a memorandum outlining his 'proposals'.[29] The British reaction to the map was mixed. A general report from the British delegation expressed the view that the proposed new boundary was drawn so 'as to give the most favourable results to Germany'.[30] Chamberlain, however, informed Halifax over the telephone that the boundary marked on Hitler's map 'corresponded very closely to the line we have been examining'.[31] In his conversation with Hitler, the Prime Minister had suggested that the 65 per cent line should serve as the new frontier, but in view of the fact that the British government had already accepted the 50 per cent line, this was presumably no more than an opening negotiating position. During their exchanges, Hitler also disclosed that the Hungarian and Polish minorities likewise sought to secede from Czechoslovakia.[32] Although apparently unconcerned about the extent of the territory to be ceded, Chamberlain baulked at the related demand for near immediate German military occupation of the Sudeten German areas. Following an inconclusive exchange of letters and a further meeting with Hitler late on 23 September, the Prime Minister returned to London the next day with Hitler's memorandum for transmission to the Czechoslovak government.[33] Prior to Chamberlain's second conversation with Hitler, Britain and France had given Czechoslovakia the green light to mobilise – which was implemented without delay.[34]

The proposals Chamberlain had taken to Godesberg, and which he later claimed had originated from Runciman, were, in fact, drawn up in a flurry of meetings, held between Chamberlain's return from Berchtesgaden on 16 September and his departure for Godesberg six days later. The principal input concerning Czechoslovakia at these meetings came not from Runciman but from Ashton-Gwatkin. On his return to Britain, Runciman was unstinting in praise of his chief assistant on the Mission, commending him strongly to the foreign policy makers, who 'should be able to get a good deal of useful information out of him'.[35] Full advantage was indeed taken of Ashton-Gwatkin's experience and he became a key adviser in the final stages of the crisis over Czechoslovakia, attending the Munich conference as a member of the British delegation.

More immediately, Ashton-Gwatkin was given the task of drafting Runciman's report. The original idea was to set down Runciman's detailed advice in a letter to the Prime Minister, which would be published after Chamberlain had shown it to Hitler on his return trip to Germany.[36] At a later stage it was decided to address a similar letter to Beneš, though neither Runciman nor Ashton-Gwatkin had suggested doing so.[37] Ashton-Gwatkin probably worked on the report over the weekend of 17 and 18 September, whilst Runciman was relaxing in the country following his attendance at the Cabinet meeting on the Saturday morning and lunch with the King at Buckingham Palace.[38] By midday on Monday, Runciman had been supplied with a draft letter which he took with him to Downing Street, where he lunched with Chamberlain and Halifax.[39]

Two days later, during the afternoon of 21 September, Chamberlain informed the Cabinet that he had seen a draft of the letter, 'in an incomplete form'.[40] It would appear that, in its original form, the letter did not meet with the Prime Minister's approval, because that same day Ashton-Gwatkin spent some time redrafting the document. He did so in consultation with Runciman, who approved the amended version in the early evening, following which it was, as Ashton-Gwatkin noted, 'at last' sent off to the Prime Minister.[41] Two copies were also sent to Horace Wilson,[42] who had evidently been previously involved in the preparation of the report as, earlier that day – before the revised version was completed – he had informed the Cabinet Committee on Czechoslovakia of the satisfactory outcome of the revision. Wilson stated that: 'Lord Runciman's draft Report now took the line that the time had gone past when a settlement could be made on the basis of the Carlsbad points, and that it was no use talking about a plebiscite. In effect, his Report supported the action taken by His Majesty's Government.'[43] The statement is unambiguous. It was the Runciman report which was being brought into line with British policy, rather than that policy being determined by the report.

What is less certain, however, is the nature of the advice offered in the original draft of Runciman's report, although it clearly was more concise than that contained in the revised version. The Foreign Office records contain a ten-page typed draft of the letter, originally dated 20 September, from which page 5 is missing and is replaced by eight pages of typescript on Foreign Office minute paper. Both parts of the draft contain revisions in Ashton-Gwatkin's handwriting. The inserted section, consistent with Wilson's remark, contained both the rejection of the Fourth Plan (which is presumably what Wilson had in mind when referring to the 'Carlsbad Points' basis), as it was no longer relevant, and also of a plebiscite, on the grounds that it would be 'a sheer formality' and that the associated delay might have 'most dangerous results'. The immediate transfer of the territories concerned was, therefore, proposed. These were defined, with a surprising lack of precision, as 'those frontier districts between Czechoslovakia and Germany where the Sudeten population is in an important majority'.[44]

The fact that even the revised version of the report is imprecise in defining the territory to be transferred suggests that this might have been, at least in part, the cause of the difference between Runciman and Chamberlain. This is confirmed by Harvey, who recorded in his diary on 19 September, that Runciman's letter advocated the cession of territory with over 80 per cent German population and the application of the Fourth Plan to the German minority remaining in Czechoslovakia. Harvey also noted that Ashton-Gwatkin regarded this as 'an ideal solution which would give Germany $1\frac{1}{2}$ million more Germans and would preserve to some extent the strategic and economic unity of Czechoslovakia'.[45] In a letter to a former political colleague, Viscount Samuel, written the same day, Runciman not only disclosed that he was 'being kept at work by the Government', but added also the observation 'that self-determination (however that can be achieved) combined with neutralisation would go a long way to satisfying the reasonable Germans and the minorities'.[46] This remark appears to fall short of a direct recommendation for the total cession of the German areas.

This, however, was not the view of the British government, which only the previous day, 18 September, had taken the joint decision with its French counterpart to transfer to Germany all Czechoslovak territory with a German majority of over 50 per cent. Although Runciman visited the Foreign Office that evening,[47] he appears not to have taken full cognisance of the development, and, four days later, he reportedly told Masaryk over the telephone that he believed only territory with over 75 per cent German population was to be ceded. The Czechoslovak Minister, when reporting this to Beneš in Prague, added: 'When I told him about the 50% he collapsed and wept.'[48] Ashton-Gwatkin, however, despite the indication given to Harvey of his agreement with Runciman, in the privacy of his diary was much more philosophical. Referring to the adoption of the 50 per cent line, he noted, on the 18 September: 'A sad capitulation, but was there really an alternative? The Czechs have delayed too long.'[49]

A further reason, additional to the requirement for Runciman's report to be brought into line with the policy of the British government concerning the territory to be ceded by Czechoslovakia, was perhaps the need to strengthen the case for the principle of cession itself. The dismembering of Czechoslovakia could best be justified by drawing attention to the failings of the authorities in their treatment of the German minority. Indeed, Harvey noted in his diary on 19 September that Runciman 'now had nothing good to say of the Czechs and adds his influential voice to the chorus of blame and abuse which is now their lot'.[50] That assertion appears to be borne out by the revised version of the report, which contains a lengthy catalogue of complaints against the Czechoslovak authorities (analysed previously) too long to have been part of the original draft.[51]

The original draft report nevertheless appears to have recommended some transfer of land. The section immediately following the insertion is concerned with the Germans who would remain behind – even if 'all the areas where the Germans have a majority were transferred to Germany' – for whom Runciman recommended the application of the Fourth Plan. Moreover, most of Runciman's other recommendations, which sought fundamentally to transform the nature of the Czechoslovak state and its foreign policy orientation, appear in the original section of the report.[52] As Ashton-Gwatkin himself admitted,[53] they resembled many of the provisions contained in the Preiss Plan, received by the Mission shortly before Runciman's return to London. Elements adopted from that proposal included the suppression of political activity antagonistic towards Germany (Preiss had singled out the Communist Party for suppression), the permanent addition of a Sudeten German representative to the Czechoslovak Cabinet, the effective neutralisation of Czechoslovakia, and the conclusion of a commercial treaty with Germany.[54]

The degree of severity of the report caused considerable dismay to one member of Runciman's staff. Stopford, who returned from Prague by air on 23 September[55] – thus effectively winding up the Mission's activities on the ground in Czechoslovakia[56] – read a copy of the report in the Foreign Office the following day. He immediately communicated his 'distress' to Ashton-Gwatkin and enquired whether Runciman could be persuaded to revise the document. Before leaving Czechoslovakia, Stopford had discussed the desired nature of the Mission's report with Newton. Stopford recalled in his memoir that, believing war to be inevitable 'next week or next year', they both agreed that the Runciman report 'ought to be the great moral document of the War, showing that even when it was possible to solve local problems by negotiation Hitler would reject them in favour of a solution either by arms or the threat of arms'.[57] Stopford's request for a revision of the report was briefly considered in the Foreign Office, and Ashton-Gwatkin drafted a letter to Runciman (who had by then returned to Northumberland) seeking his views. This stressed there could be 'no question of the alteration of facts', merely of 'emphasising one point rather than another', adding that the object of any revision would be 'to avoid providing Germany with any material that might be quoted against us in justification of her policy'.[58] That, indeed, was the main thrust of Stopford's objection, as minuted by Mallet, who, however, advised against rewriting the report, particularly in view of the fact that the version addressed to Beneš had been handed to Masaryk on 22 September. Sargent agreed, and the request to Runciman was never sent.[59]

Stopford's last-minute attempt to revise the Runciman report having failed, plans for its publication in a government White Paper went ahead.[60] The appearance of the report on 28 September, coincided with the dramatic announcement of Chamberlain's flight to Munich, and it was inevitably eclipsed by the unfolding events. Nevertheless, the report's clear purpose was to support British government policy for resolving the Sudeten German problem – and thus avoiding the danger of war – by the cession to Germany of territory with a majority German population. That is how Runciman perceived his role on his return to London, being motivated not only by a general sense of duty to the government but also by personal loyalty to Chamberlain. He explained, within Harvey's hearing in the Foreign Office on 18 September: '"I feel I must do everything to make the P.M.'s position easier."'[61] Ashton-Gwatkin also recalled, many years later, that he had been instructed by Runciman to draft a report that would '"support the Prime Minister's policy"'.[62]

That indeed was the function the Runciman report performed, its publication paving the way for the decisions taken at the Munich Conference. The Godesberg meeting between Chamberlain and Hitler on 22 and 23 September was followed by further intense diplomatic activity. The Godesberg memorandum and the accompanying map were handed to the Czechoslovak government by Newton late on 24 September.[63] The Czechoslovak response was given by Masaryk the following day: Hitler's demands were 'absolutely and unconditionally unacceptable' to his government.[64] Later that day, Daladier and Bonnet again visited London for talks. The French Ministers were opposed to the acceptance of Hitler's Godesberg terms but readily agreed that Wilson should visit Hitler with a further appeal.[65] In this, Chamberlain urged adherence to the 'Anglo-French plan' and suggested direct talks between Germany and Czechoslovakia to arrange the transfer of territory.[66] This attempt to revert to Chamberlain's original proposals was also prompted by Halifax's reluctance to impose Hitler's Godesberg terms on the Czechoslovak government.[67]

Wilson, who visited Berlin on 26 and 27 September, met with a tirade from Hitler and the insistence that the 1 October deadline for occupation of the Sudetenland remained in force and that a response was required from the Czechoslovak government by 2 p.m. on 28 September.[68] During the previous evening Chamberlain sent Beneš a personal message stressing that if he failed to accept Hitler's terms, nothing could be done to save his country.[69] Simultaneously, a new British plan was communicated to Berlin proposing the immediate cession of the territory round Aš and Cheb and a gradual Czechoslovak withdrawal from the other areas to be completed, under international supervision, by the end of October.[70] That same evening Hitler replied to the message Wilson had brought from Chamberlain, holding out the prospect of further negotiations.[71] Chamberlain responded with an offer to come to Berlin for talks with French, Italian and Czechoslovak representatives.[72] The invitation to Munich arrived on the afternoon of 28 September,[73] and the conference itself took place on the two following days.

The Munich Agreement provided for the gradual German occupation of the Sudeten German territory between 1 and 10 October. The precise extent of that territory, 'of preponderatingly German character', would be determined by an International Commission consisting of representatives of the four signatories plus Czechoslovakia. Although not defined in the Agreement, Mussolini's proposal made clear that the territory in question was that indicated on the map accompanying Hitler's Godesberg memorandum. The Agreement also provided for a guarantee of the remainder of Czechoslovakia by the four signatory powers, following the resolution of similar Hungarian and Polish claims to Czechoslovak territory.[74] The Czechoslovak representatives present in Munich – Mastný, the Minister in Berlin, and Hubert Masařík, Private Secretary to the Foreign Minister – did not participate in the discussions. They were handed a copy of the Agreement at a subsequent meeting with Chamberlain and Daladier. However, the honour of actually delivering the *coup de grâce* fell, appropriately, to Ashton-Gwatkin, who was a member of the British delegation at the Conference. He accompanied Mastný and Masařík in their private aircraft to Prague on 30 September, in order to convey the appropriate instructions to Newton.[75] Beneš and the new Prime Minister, General Jan Syrový, who had replaced Hodža a week previously, accepted the inevitable. Five days later, Beneš himself resigned from office.

Runciman's report, recommending the cession of territory, provided the perfect justification for the Munich Agreement. Indeed, one member of Chamberlain's inner Cabinet, Simon, confirmed the pivotal role of Runciman's contribution. In a letter written in early October, following the implementation of the Munich Agreement, Simon expressed great admiration for the work of the Mission, adding, 'your Report was *the* conclusive document and every decision flows from it'.[76] On another continent, however, a leading political figure reacted to Runciman's report with a certain degree of scepticism. Following his visit to the United States President in 1937, Runciman maintained contact with Roosevelt via Arthur Murray, a former Liberal Member of Parliament. Roosevelt's initial reaction on Runciman's return to Britain was to send a message of appreciation for the work done in preventing the outbreak of war.[77] However, some months later, in January 1939, following the receipt of an autographed copy of Runciman's report, Roosevelt requested Murray to pass on his thanks adding '"I only wish I had his real inside thoughts about Henlein and the latter's Master"'.[78]

Unfortunately, it is impossible to gauge Runciman's inner thoughts with any certainty. Despite the invaluable support for Chamberlain's foreign policy which his report provided, there is sufficient evidence to indicate at least a degree of disquiet in Runciman's mind. In addition to the previously mentioned ambiguities in the advice given to the British government and to his reported conversation with Masaryk, Runciman's conspicuous public silence following his return to Britain indicated perhaps some unhappiness concerning his role in recent events. As Harvey had noted on Runciman's return to London, 'he was very anxious to keep out of any row over Czechoslovakia at any cost'.[79] Runciman's reticence was deliberate,[80] and he made only one characteristic exception, granting an interview to the *Methodist Recorder*. This reluctance to comment on the work of his Mission could, at least in part, be explained by Runciman's state of health. After six uncomfortable weeks spent in crisis-torn Central Europe, Britain's mediator had returned home in a state of utter exhaustion. Harvey was 'horrified' by his appearance, noting that he looked 'ten years older' and was 'quite broken down and ... rather pathetic'.[81] Equally, however, Runciman's silence possibly indicated some unease over the outcome of his Mission. Runciman hinted at this to his son Steven, later that autumn, when he explained that the report had been prepared under considerable pressure and, had more time been available for reflection, he would perhaps have been less harsh in his judgement of the Czechoslovak government.[82]

It is also perhaps significant that in the one press interview Runciman did grant, he was considerably less censorious of the Czechoslovak government than he had been in his formal report. In the interview, published in the *Methodist Recorder* on 13 October, Runciman repeated his criticism of the Czechoslovak authorities for their 'lack of understanding, petty acts of intolerance, and discrimination against the German population', but declined to enter into, what he termed, 'the long argument, mainly of a technical nature, as to what territories were suitable for amputation and other operations'. He did not, however, hold the Czechs entirely responsible for the problem and placed some of the blame also on the makers of the Versailles settlement. Runciman argued that it was the peacemakers' over-hasty determination of the frontiers of Czechoslovakia that created a situation in which the Czechs began behaving like 'conquerors'. He also added a tribute to Czechoslovakia's founder-president, T.G. Masaryk, referring to his 'fine tolerant spirit', and expressing the belief that, were Masaryk still alive, 'a natural and generous settlement could and would have been reached'. It also clearly emerges from the interview, however, that Runciman's primary motivation was the preservation of peace. To have gone to war over Czechoslovakia, he argued, 'would have been one of the most stupendous sins ever committed'. Runciman was clearly at one with Chamberlain on this issue, and, in characteristic terms, expressed his gratitude 'to the good providence of God that He gave us a peace-loving Prime Minister'.[83]

Despite his general reluctance to comment publicly on any aspect of the Mission to Czechoslovakia, Runciman did respond, in private, to one particular criticism voiced by journalists and other observers. This criticism concerned Runciman's choice of company for his weekend leisure activities. Throughout his political and business career, Runciman had regarded his weekends as sacrosanct[84] and he saw no reason for departing from this practice whilst mediating in Czechoslovakia. Indeed, by his own admission, he derived much welcome relief from relaxing on the sabbath, away from the oppressive climate of Prague[85] and from the considerable stresses of the task in hand, which he considered 'even more strenuous than a hard election campaign'.[86] Nevertheless, in the circumstances of Runciman's presence in Czechoslovakia, it was impossible for him totally to separate work from leisure, even at weekends. This was precisely the thrust of his critics' arguments, who accused him of spending a disproportionately large amount of his leisure time in the company of the Bohemian German aristocracy, many of whom were actively involved in, or sympathetic towards, the SdP.[87]

Runciman spent a total of six weekends in Czechoslovakia, five of which were spent on the estates of the German aristocracy. In contrast, only part of one weekend was spent in the company of a prominent Czech figure. The venues for most of Runciman's weekend retreats from Prague were not accidental but the result of careful planning by the SdP. Shortly after Runciman's arrival in Czechoslovakia the SdP leadership established a 'social committee', under the leadership of Prince Ulrich Kinsky,[88] the purpose of which was to provide suitable recreational activities for the British mediator, within a milieu sympathetic towards the aspirations of the SdP. Runciman's initial contact with the Bohemian nobility was established by visiting Count Zdenko Kinsky's estate at Žd'ár, in Moravia, during his first weekend in Czechoslovakia only three days following his arrival on 3 August. On that first occasion the British mediator was entertained in a

Czech-inhabited area, but most of his subsequent weekends in the country were spent in a predominantly German environment.

The following weekend, that of 13 and 14 August, Runciman and his wife visited the estate of Prince Ulrich Kinsky himself, near Česká Kamenice in the north of Bohemia, in predominantly German territory. He was enticed there with the promise of a meeting with the then elusive Henlein. The SdP leader failed to materialise, but the pattern had been set for Runciman's subsequent weekends – to the advantage of the SdP. Other aristocratic guests on that occasion included Count Clary-Aldringen, who invited the British mediator to visit his castle at Teplice also in northern Bohemia. This invitation was taken up two weeks later, on 27 and 28 August. During the intervening weekend, the Runcimans were the guests of Prince Adolf Schwarzenberg on his estate near Český Krumlov in southern Bohemia, again in a mainly German area. Runciman's last weekend in Czechoslovakia was spent at Count Czernin's castle at Petrohrad, west of Prague on the edge of predominantly German territory. The single day of leisure spent in the company of a prominent Czech figure was Sunday, 4 September, when the Runciman's visited the residence of Cardinal Kašpar, the Primate of Bohemia, at Dolní Břežany, outside Prague.[89]

It could, of course, be argued that the fault lay with the Czech nation for having the carelessness to lose most of its aristocracy following the Battle of the White Mountain in 1620, and that a British peer, wishing to associate with his social equals, had little choice but to seek the only suitable company available, which happened to be German. However, being insensitive to the attendant risk of compromising the neutrality of his Mission amounted to a significant error of judgement on Runciman's part. Taking into consideration Runciman's age, his state of health, the magnitude of the responsibility he bore, and even the oppressive climate of the Central European late summer, it was not unreasonable of him to seek weekend recreation away from the uncomfortable bustle of Prague. He did not, however, need to do so almost exclusively in the company of those perceived to be closely associated with one of the parties in the dispute he was seeking to resolve. He would no doubt have been able to enjoy similar standards of comfort and relaxation as the guest of members of the Czechoslovak business and cultural elite, as indeed did Ashton-Gwatkin. Runciman's chief assistant much enjoyed dining at the home of the industrialist Otakar Kruliš-Randa, in the company of other prominent business personalities, describing the event as 'all rather sumptuous; good music – Firkuský playing Chopin etc.'. Ashton-Gwatkin was also favourably impressed by the hospitality received from the financier, Preiss. He likened Preiss's country retreat near Písek, south of Prague, to a 'super-log-cabin', and at a later date noted in his diary an 'excellent dinner' provided by the same host.[90] Runciman himself did not shun Czech society, but his acceptance of Czech hospitality was limited. With his wife, he attended a dinner given by Zdeňa Havránková, a prominent business woman and society hostess, at which most of the Czechoslovak Cabinet was present, and the couple also attended the opening night of a production of Smetana's opera *The Bartered Bride*.[91] However, an invitation to Runciman and his party to visit the shoe-making centre at Zlín in Moravia as guests of the proprietor Tomáš Bat'a,[92] was not taken up.

There is no question of members of the Mission being unaware of the political partisanship of at least some of their aristocratic hosts. Following the visit to Ulrich Kinsky's shooting-lodge on 14 August, during which he accompanied the Runcimans, Ashton-Gwatkin noted in some detail the views of the assembled company. In addition to Kinsky and his wife, this consisted of Count and Countess Khuen, Count and Countess Clary-Aldringen, Count von Westfalen and Prince Hohenlohe. Ashton-Gwatkin recorded that they were all 'strong supporters' of the SdP and 'personally very fond of "the Chicken"' (i.e. Henlein), in addition to being 'pro-German and (with reservations) pro-Hitler', but preferring 'on the whole that the Sudetenland should not be absorbed' into Germany. He also noted that they thought 'poorly and contemptuously of the Czechs', had a 'horror of Russia and "Bolshevism"', which they considered a threat to their life-style, but admired 'England and the English', believing that 'friendship between England and Germany' could 'save the world'.[93] With views such as these in circulation, combined with the material comforts on offer, it is perhaps hardly surprising that Runciman chose to spend his relaxation in this company. Ashton-Gwatkin subsequently claimed that only one of Runciman's weekend hosts, Ulrich Kinsky, was a 'real pro-Nazi', adding for good measure that Hohenlohe was positively 'pro-British'.[94] In view of the fact that another of Runciman's hosts, Clary-Aldringen, openly supported the SdP whilst the Mission was in residence in Prague,[95] this statement could only be justified if a distinction is made between pro-Nazi and pro-SdP sympathies. Moreover, although not all of Runciman's hosts were active supporters of the SdP, and, as the crisis deepened in mid-September, Zdenko Kinsky, Schwarzenberg and Czernin associated themselves with the declaration of Bohemian aristocrats supporting the historic frontiers of the Bohemian Crown,[96] their estates were mostly located in predominantly German-inhabited regions of Bohemia, where Runciman, inevitably, was perceived as being exposed to SdP influence.

Runciman himself sought to rebut the criticism of lack of balance on at least two occasions. Shortly after his return from Prague, he responded to the charge, levelled at a private meeting, by the Berlin correspondent of the *News Chronicle*, H.D. Harrison, that Runciman had refused hospitality from Czechs. Through his Private Secretary, Runciman stated that 'he made every endeavour either to dispose his weekends equally between families of Czech and German sympathy, or to accept invitations from non-political people', such as Cardinal Kašpar.[97] Some six months later, Runciman again responded to the same accusation following the publication of a book by

Mary Borden in 1939. The book, *Passport for a Girl*, a work of fiction set against the background of then recent events, contained the allegation of an American journalist, that the British mediator spent 'so much of his time with Henlein and the Sudetens that he didn't have much left for Beneš', and that he 'spent his week-ends in the country talking to the German aristocrats'.[98] In a letter to the author, Runciman pointed out that on the evidence of his engagement list he had met Henlein on only three occasions while having had at least twelve meetings with the President. He added, that while in Prague: 'I was able to arrange my numerous interviews and conferences with Czechs and Sudetens scrupulously and evenly.'[99]

The scrupulous parity with which Runciman claimed to conduct his official negotiations was itself a further subject of critical comment particularly from the Czechoslovak authorities themselves, who were most unhappy that, throughout his activity in Czechoslovakia, Runciman treated a single opposition political party on the basis of full equality with the legitimate government of the state.[100] Though legalistically a valid point, it was perhaps inevitable that this should have been the case in view of the fact that the express purpose of the Runciman Mission was to mediate in a dispute between precisely two such disparate parties.

Some of Runciman's critics went a step further still and accused him of openly supporting Nazi activity. The Communist *Daily Worker* published a photograph, taken during Runciman's visit to Czernin's castle at Petrohrad on 10 and 11 September, when he briefly addressed a crowd of several thousand SdP supporters from the castle balcony, with the accusing caption: 'Runciman giving the Hitler salute to a crowd of Nazi demonstrators. This is Chamberlain's "impartial" mediator in Czechoslovakia.'[101] The British mediator was certainly captured on film with his right arm raised and palm downturned, but the bend of the elbow suggested that he had, more probably, been simply waving to the crowd.

Although some of the points raised by Runciman's critics – particularly those relating to the contents of his report – were, in retrospect, to be fully justified; at the time, these views were unrepresentative of the majority. Immediately following Runciman's return from Czechoslovakia, expressions of criticisms concerning his role were greatly outweighed by the amount of praise heaped upon him from many quarters. His name was frequently linked with that of Chamberlain as great practitioners of 'appeasement' – which had saved humanity from a devastating war. Loud cheers broke out in the House of Commons on 28 September when the Prime Minister mentioned his name and there was much support, both inside and outside Parliament, for the tribute that followed. Chamberlain declared that 'we, and indeed all Europe must ever be grateful to him and to his staff for their long and exhausting efforts on behalf of peace'.[102] Amongst the messages of congratulations Runciman received was one from Stanley Baldwin, who bestowed blessings on the mediator's noble effort. The former Prime Minister also added the interesting parallel: 'It must have been about as hopeful as dealing with the miners in [19]26.'[103]

Perhaps most appreciated was the reward received from Chamberlain – reappointment to the Cabinet. Runciman took up his seat round the familiar table, for the third time in his career, at the end of October, on this occasion as Lord President of the Council (a position to which he had aspired some 18 months previously). When approaching Runciman with the offer, the Prime Minister stressed the need 'to strengthen the personnel of the present Cabinet' in order to further promote his policy of seeking reconciliation with Germany.[104] The offer was accepted with some reluctance and for a limited period only, partly, no doubt, on account of Runciman's state of health, but partly also because, as he explained to Halifax, Runciman was 'uneasy' about the quality of the Cabinet.[105] That view appeared to be shared by the King who reportedly told Lord Wigram, Lord in Waiting to the King, that Runciman would be 'a great strength to the P.M.' as some of his colleagues were 'a bit vacillating and weak'.[106] Notwithstanding any qualms Runciman may possibly have felt concerning his contribution to the destruction of Czechoslovakia, he evidently continued to be perceived as a staunch and loyal supporter of Chamberlain's policy. Whatever his private views, Runciman was happy to be seen in that light.

Ashton-Gwatkin, however, had no reservations whatsoever concerning the outcome of the Mission, although he would later claim otherwise. With the benefit of over 30 years' hindsight, he argued that had the truth been known of Hitler's intentions 'we would have known that the Mission was absolutely useless from the very beginning'.[107] He also maintained, however, that the Munich Agreement, though 'inglorious', was nevertheless 'right', as it bought valuable time to prepare Britain for war against Germany.[108] Earlier, in a radio broadcast made in 1948, Ashton-Gwatkin regretted that the Mission had failed 'in its unavowed object of spinning out negotiations until the dangerous months of 1938 were over'. The Mission had been wrecked, he argued, '[by] Germany's ambition to expand, to break the independence of the Slav state of Czechoslovakia, to control its armaments industries and to dominate central Europe'.[109] However, that is not what he believed at the time.

In a lengthy Foreign Office memorandum surveying aspects of the European scene following the dismembering of Czechoslovakia, written within a month of the event, Ashton-Gwatkin observed, with a note of triumphalism: 'The German victory over Czechoslovakia is probably one of the decisive events of history. ... Taken in connection with the incorporation of Austria, of which it is the logical consequence, it reconstitutes a middle European Empire, which has not existed since the Reformation.' Ironically, Ashton-Gwatkin shared with some opponents of 'appeasement' the belief that, had war broken out in the autumn of 1938, the Nazi government in Germany might have been overthrown, but he did not consider that a desirable objective, adding approvingly, that 'this was saved by the British intervention'. With a characteristic historical flourish, he declared that, 'Once again (after the White Mountain, Austerlitz, Königgratz) the fate of Central Europe has been decided probably for many years to come, in the "Historische Länder"'. The German economic domination of East Central Europe, which would inevitably follow the defeat of Czechoslovakia, provided opportunities he considered 'economically advantageous for the world at large', though he conceded that it would be regarded as 'politically alarming' by many people. Ashton-Gwatkin, however, was not amongst them, foreseeing instead the possibility of 'an Anglo-German policy of economic co-operation' whereby Britain would provide financial support for the German development of this area.[110]

Even though Ashton-Gwatkin's was an extreme expression of this attitude, the achievement of a settlement with Nazi Germany was nevertheless the general objective of those directing British foreign policy in 1938. To this end Czechoslovakia was sacrificed, and the Runciman Mission played a not insignificant role in bringing that about. But the peace being sought was a chimera and the sacrifice made was in vain.

Notes

1 'Letter from Lord Runciman to President Beneš [and Mr. Chamberlain]', 21 September 1938, *DBFP*, 3/II, appendix II (IV), pp. 675–9. See also Appendix 1 below.
2 The report was published in a White Paper, 'Correspondence Respecting Czechoslovakia; September 1938', Cmd. 5847, on 28 September 1938 and appeared in the press the following day.
3 *News Chronicle*, 30 September 1938. The article was by William Forrest. Another British journalist observing events in Czechoslovakia, G.E.R. Gedye, offers a similar critique in *Fallen Bastions*, pp. 454–9. Gedye adds a spoof conclusion observing that the Sudeten Germans were in an 'excellent situation – as compared with all other minorities in Europe', and recommending Germany be warned that Britain, France and the Soviet Union would defend Czechoslovakia.
4 *New York Herald Tribune*, 3 October 1938. Thompson's criticism may, of course, have been based on inside information from the Foreign Office. See R. Lamb, *The Drift to War, 1922–1939*, (London, 1989), p. 271.
5 *New York Herald Tribune*, 1 October 1938. For an account of Runciman's words at Petrohrad, as reported in the British press, see above p. 276.
6 Fletcher to Leeper, 10 October 1938, C 12633/1941/18, FO 371/21745.
7 Memorandum by Ashton-Gwatkin, enclosed in Ashton-Gwatkin to Fletcher, 28 October 1938, *ibid.*
8 Newton to Halifax, 14 September 1938, *DBFP*, 3/II, no. 871. The dispatch relayed the contents of a telephone report from Ashton-Gwatkin in Aš.
9 Ashton-Gwatkin to Strang, in Newton to Halifax, 15 September 1938, *DBFP*, 3/II, no. 889.

10 Dilks, ed., *Cadogan Diaries*, p. 98.
11 Memorandum by Ashton-Gwatkin, enclosed in Ashton-Gwatkin to Fletcher, 28 October 1938, C 12633/1941/18, FO 371/21745.
12 Cabinet Committee on Czechoslovakia Minutes, 16 September 1938, CS (38) 5, CAB 27/646.
13 Cabinet Minutes, 17 September 1938, Cabinet 39 (38), CAB 23/95.
14 A. Duff Cooper, *Old Men Forget*, (London, 1953), p. 229.
15 Cabinet Minutes, 17 September 1938, Cabinet 39 (38), CAB 23/95.
16 This information may have been supplied by Hans Neuwirth, a legal adviser to the SdP negotiators, who informed the Mission on 14 September that Kundt and his colleagues had, in reality, 'not been free agents for many months, although they did not know it'. (Minute of conversation with Dr. Neuwirth, 14 September 1938, FO 800/304, ff. 78–9.)
17 Chamberlain's notes of conversation with Hitler on 15 September 1938, *DBFP*, 3/II, no. 895; Schmidt's notes of conversation between Chamberlain and Hitler on 15 September 1938, *DBFP*, 3/II, no. 896.
18 Record of Franco–British conversations, 18 September 1938, *DBFP*, 3/II, no. 928; *DDF*, 2/XI, no. 212.
19 Message to Beneš, in Halifax to Newton, 19 September 1938, *DBFP*, 3/II, no. 937.
20 Newton to Halifax, 19 September 1938, *DBFP*, 3/II, no. 961; de Lacroix to Bonnet, 19 September 1938, *DDF*, 2/XI, no. 217.
21 Newton to Halifax, 21 September 1938, *DBFP*, 3/II, no. 986; Note from Czechoslovak government, 20 September 1938, *DBFP*, 3/II, no. 987.
22 Newton to Halifax, 21 September 1938, *DBFP*, 3/II, no. 992.
23 Newton to Halifax, 21 September 1938, *DBFP*, 3/II, no. 1002; Note from Czechoslovak government, 21 September 1938, *DBFP*, 3/II, no. 1005.
24 Record of Franco–British conversations, 18 September 1938, *DBFP*, 3/II, no. 928; *DDF*, 2/XI, no. 212.
25 Harvey, ed., *Harvey Diaries*, p. 186. Harvey recorded Runciman's advice as: '"Sudeten and Czechs could not live together any more."'
26 *HC Deb.*, vol. 339, cols 15–16, 28 September 1938.
27 Notes of conversation between Chamberlain and Hitler on 22 September 1938, *DBFP*, 3/II, no. 1033; Minute of conversation between Hitler and Chamberlain on 22 September 1938, *DGFP*, D/II, no. 562.
28 Hitler to Chamberlain, 23 September 1938, in *DBFP*, 3/II, no. 1053.
29 Memorandum from Hitler (with attached map), in British Delegation (Godesberg) to Newton, 24 September 1938, *DBFP*, 3/II, no. 1068.
30 British Delegation (Godesberg) to Halifax, 23 September 1938, *DBFP*, 3/II, no. 1040.
31 Halifax to Phipps and Newton, 23 September 1938, *DBFP*, 3/II, no. 1038.
32 Notes of conversation between Chamberlain and Hitler on 22 September 1938, *DBFP*, 3/II, no. 1033; Minute of conversation between Hitler and Chamberlain on 22 September 1938, *DGFP*, D/II, no. 562.
33 Notes of conversation between Chamberlain and Hitler on 23–4 September 1938, *DBFP*, 3/II, no. 1073; Memorandum on conversation between Hitler and Chamberlain on 23 September 1938, *DGFP*, D/II, no. 583.
34 Halifax to Newton, 22 and 23 September (twice) 1938, *DBFP*, 3/II, nos 1027, 1049, 1062; Newton to Halifax, 28 September 1938, *DBFP*, 3/II, no. 1170.

35 Cabinet Committee on Czechoslovakia Minutes, 16 September 1938, CS (38) 5, CAB 27/646.
36 Harvey, ed., *Harvey Diaries*, p. 187.
37 Notes by Ashton-Gwatkin, undated (but probably c. 1970), Stopford Papers, RJS (unclassified box).
38 *The Times*, 17 September 1938.
39 Ashton-Gwatkin's diary,18 and 19 September 1938, FO 800/304; Entry for 19 September 1938, Lunch Book 1937–40, Chamberlain Papers, NC 12/1/3. Stopford claimed that Ashton-Gwatkin drafted the report during the evening of 16 September, in order to make it available to Chamberlain for his meeting with the French ministers on 18 September. (Stopford, 'Prague, 1938–1939', p. 76.) Ashton-Gwatkin's diary, however, indicates otherwise.
40 Cabinet Minutes, 21 September 1938, Cabinet 41 (38), CAB 23/95.
41 Ashton-Gwatkin's diary, 21 September 1938, FO 800/304.
42 Minute by Roberts, 22 September 1938, C 10677/1941/18, FO 371/21741.
43 Cabinet Committee on Czechoslovakia Minutes, 21 September 1938, CS (38) 8, CAB 27/646.
44 Runciman to Chamberlain, draft originally dated 20 September 1938 but revised to 21 September, C 10677/1941/18, FO 371/21741. First to draw attention to this revision of the Runciman Report was J.W. Bruegel, in *Czechoslovakia before Munich*, pp. 275–6. The hiatus noted by Thompson (see above p. 317) falls within the revised section of the report.
45 Harvey, ed., *Harvey Diaries*, p. 187.
46 Runciman to Samuel, 19 September 1938, Samuel Papers, A/110 (10). Runciman was responding to a suggestion from Samuel for the neutralisation of Czechoslovakia 'preceded by plebiscites in the border districts'. (Samuel to Runciman, 15 September 1938, Samuel Papers, A/110 (4).)
47 Ashton-Gwatkin's diary, 18 September 1938, FO 800/304.
48 Transcript of telephone conversation between Masaryk and Beneš, 23 September 1938, enclosed in Kirkpatrick to Strang, 27 September 1938, C 1102/1941/18, FO 371/21742. The transcript of the intercepted telephone conversation was supplied to the British Embassy in Berlin by the German authorities.
49 Ashton-Gwatkin's diary, 18 September 1938, FO 800/304.
50 Harvey, ed., *Harvey Diaries*, p. 187.
51 The Runciman report, with details of the textual alterations, is attached as Appendix 1. The single missing page from the typescript of the draft report, page 5, probably contained no more than 200 words, whereas the part of the inserted section (in its entirety consisting of 1200 words) which details the complaints against the Czechoslovak government is itself 500 words long.
52 See Appendix 1.
53 Ashton-Gwatkin stated in a radio broadcast, in 1948, that the report was based on 'a solution which we had already submitted to the Foreign Office in London before leaving Prague', claiming that it 'was less drastic (in terms of population and economic life) than the solution thrust in Chamberlain's pocket by Hitler at Berchtesgaden'. (Ashton-Gwatkin, 'Personal Story', p. 597.)
54 Laffan, commenting on the recommendation for permanent Sudeten German representation in the Czechoslovak Cabinet, states – without citing a source – that this 'was only made because Runciman expected the amputation of territory would be small and would remove the extremist Sudeten Germans to the

Reich, while the remainder would be well content to be citizens of Czechoslovakia, enjoying local autonomy and to be trusted in the innermost councils of the state'. (Laffan, *Crisis over Czechoslovakia*, p. 336.)

55 Stopford returned to London in the 'Heracles' aircraft summoned to Prague, without Newton's authority, by the emergency radio of the Legation's 'Passport Officer' – in reality intelligence officer – who feared the imminent outbreak of war and arrival of Soviet forces. (Stopford, 'Prague, 1938–1939', p. 88–9, 91.)

56 Stopford, who had been left in charge of the remainder of the Mission in Czechoslovakia, judged the situation to be sufficiently menacing on 18 September to justify the recall of Lady Runciman and her party from their weekend in the country. They set off by train for Britain that afternoon, together with the two secretaries attached to the Mission, and accompanied by Stephens. Peto followed two days later. (Stopford to Ashton-Gwatkin, 19 [?] September 1938, C 10546/1941/18, FO 371/21740 and Stopford Papers, RJS 3/8.) The remaining member of the Runciman Mission, Ian Henderson, was reassigned to the British Legation in Prague. (Henderson to Runciman, 25 September 1838, Runciman Papers, WR 293.)

57 Stopford, 'Prague, 1938–1939', p. 79.

58 Draft letter by Ashton-Gwatkin, undated (but probably 26 September 1938), C 10677/1941/18, FO 371/21741.

59 Minutes by Mallet, 26 September 1938, and Sargent, 27 September 1938, *ibid.*

60 The question remained, which version should be published, the one addressed to Chamberlain or the one to Beneš? Mallet's preference was for the latter version, because it was marginally less likely to cause offence to the Czechoslovak government. Chamberlain, however, ruled in favour of the letter addressed to himself, which was duly published with minor modifications. Minutes by Mallet, 23 and 27 September 1938, *ibid.*

61 Harvey, ed., *Harvey Diaries*, p. 187.

62 Ashton-Gwatkin to Stopford, 22 January 1970, Stopford Papers, RJS (unclassified box).

63 Newton to Halifax, 24 September 1938, *DBFP*, 3/II, no. 1080.

64 Note from Masaryk to Halifax, 25 September 1938, *DBFP*, 3/II, no. 1092.

65 Record of Franco-British conversations, 25 and 26 September 1938, *DBFP*, 3/II, nos 1093, 1096; *DDF*, 2/XI, nos 356, 375.

66 Chamberlain to Hitler, 26 September 1938, *DBFP*, 3/II, no. 1097.

67 See A. Roberts *'The Holy Fox': A Biography of Lord Halifax*, (London, 1991), pp. 114–22.

68 Notes of Conversations between Wilson and Hitler, 26 and 27 September 1938, *DBFP*, 3/II, nos 1118, 1129.

69 Chamberlain to Beneš, in Halifax to Newton, 27 September 1938, *DBFP*, 3/II, no. 1136.

70 Halifax to Henderson, 27 September 1938, *DBFP*, 3/II, no. 1140.

71 Hitler to Chamberlain, in Henderson to Halifax, 27 September 1938, *DBFP*, 3/II, no. 1144.

72 Chamberlain to Hitler, in Halifax to Henderson, *DBFP*, 3/II, no. 1158.

73 Note by Cadogan, 28 September 1938, *DBFP*, 3/II, no. 1174.

74 Text of Munich Agreement, in United Kingdom Delegation to Halifax, 30 September 1938, *DBFP*, 3/II, no. 1224; Note by Wilson on Munich Conference, 29–30 September 1938, *DBFP*, 3/II, no. 1227. The determination of the post-Munich frontier of Czechoslovakia by the International Commission is

analysed by E. Wiskemann in 'Czechs and Germans after Munich', *Foreign Affairs*, vol. 17, no. 2, January 1939, pp. 291–304.

75 Note by Wilson on Munich Conference, 29–30 September 1938, *DBFP*, 3/II, no. 1227; Ashton-Gwatkin's diary, 29 and 30 September 1938, FO 800/304.

76 Simon to Runciman, 9 October 1938, Runciman Papers, WR 293.

77 Murray to Runciman, 24 October 1938, Runciman Papers, WR 284.

78 Murray to Runciman, 1 February 1939, Runciman Papers, WR 284.

79 Harvey, ed., *Harvey Diaries*, p. 186.

80 Copy of note to the *British Weekly*, 3 October 1938, Runciman Papers, WR 293. The note contained the statement 'Lord Runciman not writing about Czechoslovakia'.

81 Harvey, ed., *Harvey Diaries*, pp. 186–7.

82 Stopford, 'Prague, 1938–1939', p. 79. Stopford was informed of this conversation by Sir Steven Runciman.

83 *Methodist Recorder*, 13 October 1938; typescript copy of interview also in Runciman Papers, WR 296.

84 J.H. Thomas, *My Story*, (London, 1937), p. 262.

85 Runciman to Halifax, 18 August 1938, *DBFP*, 3/II, no. 644.

86 *Daily Telegraph*, 13 September 1938.

87 See Henderson, *Eyewitness*, pp. 146–9 and G.E.R. Gedye, *Fallen Bastions: The Central European Tragedy*, (London, 1939), p. 435.

88 See above, p. 150.

89 Details of these visits are covered in Chapters 8, 10 and 12.

90 Ashton-Gwatkin to Strang, 6 September 1938, *DBFP*, 3/II, appendix II (III), p. 668; Ashton-Gwatkin's diary, 6 September 1938, FO 800/304.

91 Note by Stopford, enclosed in Ashton-Gwatkin to Strang, 16 August 1938, *DBFP*, 3/II, appendix II (III), p. 667.

92 Ashton-Gwatkin to Strang, 16 August 1938, *DBFP*, 3/II, appendix II (III), p. 662.

93 Memorandum by Ashton-Gwatkin, 15 August 1938, C 8699/1941/18, FO 371/21732 and FO 800/304. Ashton-Gwatkin also recorded the following observation by Khuen: '"A Czech can be a good fellow – yes; I had many in my regiment in the War; but a gentleman – never!"'

94 Ashton-Gwatkin, 'Personal Story', p. 595. Laffan, in *Crisis over Czechoslovakia*, p. 218, also argues that only Ulrich Kinsky was a 'professed member of the SdP', the others being 'well known in London society, and remote from any political affinity'.

95 *Observer*, 28 August 1938.

96 *The Times*, 17 September 1938.

97 Chandler to Runciman, 29 October 1938, and Runciman's Private Secretary to Chandler, 7 November 1938, Runciman Papers, WR 296.

98 M. Borden, *Passport for a Girl*, (London, 1939), p. 301. The author subsequently explained in a letter to Runciman that although the journalist to whom the views in question were ascribed was fictitious, the views were representative of several American journalists whom she had met in Prague. (Spears [*née* Borden] to Runciman, 22 June 1939, Runciman Papers, WR 296.)

99 Runciman to Spears [*née* Borden], 17 June 1939, Runciman Papers, WR 296. The engagement list to which Runciman referred could not be found amongst his available papers.

100 Newton had drawn attention to this sensitivity before the Mission's arrival in Czechoslovakia. (Newton to Halifax, 20 July 1938, *DBFP*, 3/I, no. 522.)

101 *Daily Worker*, 15 September 1938.
102 *HC Deb.*, vol. 339, col. 6, 28 September 1938; *The Times*, 29 September 1938.
103 Baldwin to Runciman, 7 October 1938, Runciman Papers, WR 293.
104 Chamberlain to Runciman, 20 October 1938, Runciman Papers, WR 289.
105 Runciman to Halifax, 25 October 1938, Runciman Papers, WR 289.
106 Wigram to Runciman, 27 October 1938, Runciman Papers, WR 289.
107 Ashton-Gwatkin to Stopford, 22 January 1970, Stopford Papers, RJS (unclassified box).
108 Ashton-Gwatkin to Stopford, 21 December 1973, Stopford Papers, RJS (unclassified box).
109 Ashton-Gwatkin, 'Personal Story', p. 597.
110 'Notes on Germany and Central Europe', memorandum by Ashton-Gwatkin, 27 October 1938, C 13864/772/18, FO 371/21705; copy also in Runciman Papers, WR 296. Ashton-Gwatkin also expressed the view that Göring possibly represented 'the only effective opposition party in Germany' and suggested therefore that he be invited to Britain for a 'courtesy visit' similar to the one made by Halifax to Germany in November 1937.

Conclusion

Viewing events over a period of thirty years, Ashton-Gwatkin observed that the Runciman Mission had been 'a by-water to the great stream; but very significant of many things ... '.[1] Indeed, although the Mission formed only one, relatively small, element of British foreign policy in the late 1930s, it was nevertheless characteristic of the broader picture, to which it also contributed some revealing points of detail. Between March and September 1938, the British government sought, with rising anxiety, to avoid the perceived danger of becoming engulfed in a disastrous war with Germany, precipitated by Czechoslovakia's German minority problem. In order to achieve that aim, it resorted to increasingly radical means of attempting to defuse the situation in Central Europe – culminating in the Munich Agreement. The Runciman Mission formed a significant stage in that process.

Britain's attitude was founded on the belief that Czechoslovakia was indefensible against a German attack; that due to its heterogeneous ethnic composition it was inherently unstable and unworthy of support; and that it was not necessarily inimical to British interests to allow Germany to extend its influence further into Central Europe. There can be no question of the British government not being conscious of the real relationship between the SdP and Nazi Germany. British policy-makers repeatedly indicated their awareness that Henlein was being controlled from Berlin, whilst simultaneously clutching optimistically to the contrary belief in the SdP leader's moderation and freedom from Hitler's influence.

Equally, there can be no doubt concerning the British government's understanding of Germany's intentions towards Czechoslovakia. Hitler's stated objective of bringing all Germans into the *Reich* was accepted in Whitehall at its face value, and it was realised that the Sudeten Germans were included in that aim. The disruption of Czechoslovakia was an inevitable consequence, but that was considered not necessarily detrimental to Britain, particularly if it helped to secure the desired understanding between Britain and Germany, and only caused alarm because it involved the danger of armed conflict. The main imperative was to avoid war – not to limit German expansion in Central Europe.

The concept of a British mission of investigation and mediation in the Sudeten German dispute was the outcome of policy drift rather than a bold incisive initiative. It was conceived in the immediate aftermath of the *Anschluss*, further developed following the May Crisis, and resorted to in the absence of preferable alternatives. The proclaimed independence of the Mission, devised in a futile attempt to reduce the risk of British involvement, was transparently implausible. Nevertheless, Runciman arrived in Czechoslovakia with no clear instructions from the British government and, more fundamentally, with little comprehension of the complex problems he confronted. However, the Mission was not contrived primarily as a means of buying time, but in the optimistic expectation that it would, somehow, achieve a solution.

As tension rose with the approach of Hitler's Nuremberg speech, which was expected to bring the crisis to a head, Runciman's main function in Prague became the application of increasing pressure on the Czechoslovak authorities for immediate and significant concessions. Consequently, the Mission's mediating activities in Prague constituted little more than a cruel charade. Whilst Henlein was considered to be a moderating force in the crisis, and employed as a trusted emissary to Hitler on behalf of the Runciman Mission, Beneš was regarded as stubborn and obstructive and a danger to the preservation of peace – and was repeatedly subjected to intense pressure for further concessions.

From the onset of the crisis, Chamberlain was keen to involve Germany directly in any solution, although this view was not shared by the Foreign Office which sought to avoid giving undue encouragement to Berlin. However, the Prime Minister's approach ultimately prevailed, and the fate of Czechoslovakia was determined in direct negotiation with Hitler. The Runciman Mission contributed directly to that development. It was Ashton-Gwatkin's conversation with Henlein on 22 August, combined with Runciman's refusal to visit Hitler, that set in train the events that took Chamberlain, via Berchtesgaden and Godesberg, to Munich.

Ashton-Gwatkin was certainly well pleased with the turn of events. He regarded the Munich Agreement as clearing the ground for the German domination of Central and Eastern Europe from Bohemia to the Balkans, providing considerable opportunities for the growth of closer economic ties between Britain and Germany as the two countries co-operated in the development of the region. In contrast with Ashton-Gwatkin's buoyant satisfaction, Runciman was remarkably reticent about the outcome of his Mission. He continued loyally to support British government policy, but his silence, which could not entirely be explained by illness, indicated at least a modicum of unease concerning the harsh consequences of his, albeit initially reluctant, intervention in the affairs of Czechoslovakia.

The task Runciman had been set by the British government was an impossible one. Within the context of the geo-political realities of Central Europe in 1938, there was no prospect of a successful negotiated outcome of the Sudeten German problem which preserved the integrity of Czechoslovakia. Despite being fully aware of this, the British government nevertheless persisted in its search for an illusive compromise. It did so, primarily, because it not only perceived the resolution of the Sudeten German problem as a means of extinguishing a volatile potential flash-point, but also in order to provide a demonstration of British goodwill towards Germany which might serve as a foundation for a lasting rapprochement. The Runciman Mission was thus part of a policy of wishful thinking and drifting improvisation, constituting a wholly inadequate response to the dynamic system in the ascendant in Germany, which, whether or not actually desiring war, was certainly seeking expansion. This, ultimately, could only be detrimental to Britain's interests.

It is not surprising therefore, that the Runciman Mission failed to secure the peace of Europe, as did the Munich Agreement which immediately followed it. In reality, the Mission's activities served only to pave the way towards the British government's central participation in the destruction of a friendly country – an act which (not least by enriching the English language with a dishonourable connotation for the name of the Bavarian capital) will long haunt the political conscience of Britain. Moreover, it left Runciman himself with the cruel epitaph, chanted by SdP supporters confident that his intervention would prove advantageous to their cause:

Wir brauchen keinen Weihnachtsmann,
Wir haben unseren Runciman.[2]

It was, indeed, an inglorious episode all round.

Notes

1 Ashton-Gwatkin to Stopford, 17 December 1969, Stopford Papers, [additional papers]. (Ellipsis in original.)

2 *The Times*, 3 September 1938; *News Chronicle*, 30 September 1938. ('We don't need Father Christmas, we have our Runciman.') See also Gedye, *Fallen Bastions*, p. 459.

Appendix 1: The Runciman Report

The Runciman Report, in the form of a letter to Chamberlain, was first published in a White Paper 'Correspondence respecting Czechoslovakia: September 1938' (Cmd. 5847), on 28 September 1938. The published text was, in fact, in some respects closer to the version of the letter addressed to Beneš, omitting several words and short passages critical of Czechoslovak government policies.[1] These differences between the two letters are noted in the text published in *Documents on British Foreign Policy*, Third Series, vol. 2, appendix II (IV), 'Letter from Lord Runciman to President Beneš', pp. 675–9.

The text reproduced below is that of a typed draft of the letter from Runciman to Chamberlain held in the Public Record Office (C 10677/1941/18, FO 371/21741). The original typescript consisted of ten pages, but page 5 is missing, being replaced by eight pages of typescript on Foreign Office minute paper.[2] Both sections of the letter contain manuscript alterations in Ashton-Gwatkin's handwriting. These modifications are indicated in the following text. Ashton-Gwatkin's manuscript additions are given in italic and his deletions in strikethrough type. The letter was originally dated 20 September 1938, but altered to 21 September.

My dear Prime Minister,

When I undertook the task of mediation in the controversy between the Czechoslovak Government and the Sudeten German party, I was, of course left perfectly free to obtain my own information and to draw my own conclusions. I was under no obligation to issue any kind of report. In present circumstances, however, it may be of assistance to you to have the final views, which I have formed as a result of my mission, and certain suggestions which I believe should be taken into consideration, if anything like a permanent solution is to be found.

The problem of political, social and economic relations between the Teuton and Slav races in the area which is now called Czechoslovakia is one which has existed for many centuries, with periods of acute struggle and periods of comparative peace. It is no new problem, and in its present stage there are at the same time new factors and also old factors which would have to be considered in any detailed review.

When I arrived in Prague at the beginning of August the questions which immediately confronted me were (1) constitutional, (2) political, and (3) economic. The constitutional question was that with which I was immediately and directly concerned. At that time it implied the provision of some degree of home rule for the Sudeten Germans within the Czechoslovak Republic; the question of self-determination had not yet arisen in an acute form. My task was to make myself acquainted with the history of the question, with the principal persons concerned and with the suggestions for a solution proposed by the two sides, viz. by the Sudeten German party in the 'Sketch' submitted to the Czechoslovak Government on the 7th June (which was by way of embodying the eight points of Herr Henlein's speech at Karlsbad), and by the Czechoslovak Government in their draft Nationality Statute, Language Bill and Administrative Reform Bill.

It became clear that neither of these sets of proposals was sufficiently acceptable to the other side to permit further negotiations on this basis, and the negotiations were suspended on the 17th August. After a series of private discussions between the Sudeten leaders and the Czech authorities, a new basis for negotiations was adopted by the Czechoslovak Government and was communicated to me on the 5th September and to the Sudeten leaders on the 6th September. This was the so-called 4th Plan. In my opinion – and I believe in the opinion of the more responsible Sudeten leaders – this plan embodied almost all the requirements of the Karlsbad eight points, and with a little clarification and extension could have been made to cover them in their entirety. Negotiations should have at once been resumed on this favourable and hopeful basis; but little doubt remains in my mind that the very fact that they were so favourable operated against their chances with the more extreme members of the Sudeten German party. It is my belief that the incident arising out of the visit of certain Sudeten German Deputies to investigate into the case of persons arrested for arms smuggling at Mährisch-Ostrau was ~~provoked~~ *used* in order to provide an excuse for the suspension, if not for the breaking off, of negotiations. The Czech Government, however, at once gave way to the demands of the Sudeten German party in this matter and preliminary discussions of the 4th Plan were resumed on the 10th September. Again, I am convinced that this did not suit the policy of the Sudeten extremists and that incidents were provoked and instigated on the 11th September and, with great effect after Herr Hitler's speech, on the 12th September. Herr Henlein and Herr Frank presented a new series of demands – withdrawal of state police,[3] limitation of troops to their military duties, etc., which the Czechoslovak Government were again prepared to accept on the sole condition that a representative of the party came to Prague to discuss how order should be maintained. On the night of September 13th this condition was refused by Herr Henlein, and all negotiations were completely broken off.

It is quite clear that we cannot now go back to the point where we stood two weeks ago*; and we have to consider the situation as it now faces us.*

With the rejection of the Czech Government's offer on September 13th and with the breaking off of negotiations by Herr Hitler, my functions as a mediator were in fact at an end. Directly and indirectly, the connection between the chief Sudeten leaders and the Government of the Reich had become the dominant factor in the situation; the dispute was no longer an internal one. It was not part of my function to attempt mediation between Czechoslovakia and Germany.

Responsibility for the final break must, in my opinion, rest upon Herr Henlein and Herr Frank and upon those of their supporters inside and outside the country who were urging them to the extreme and unconstitutional action ~~with a view to obtaining annexation by Germany~~.

I have much sympathy, however, with the Sudeten case. It is a hard thing to be ruled by an alien race; and I have been left with the impression that Czechoslovak rule in the Sudeten areas for the last twenty years, though not actively oppressive and certainly not 'terroristic', has been marked by tactlessness, lack of understanding, petty intolerance and discrimination, to a point where the resentment of the German population was inevitably moving in the direction of revolt. ~~They~~ *The Sudeten Germans* felt too that in the past they had been given many promises by the Czech Government, but that little or no action had followed these promises. This experience had induced an attitude of unveiled mistrust of the leading Czech statesmen. *I cannot say how far this mistrust* ~~was~~ *is* merited or unmerited*; but it certainly exists with the result* ~~so~~ that, however conciliatory their statements they inspire~~d~~ no confidence *in the minds of the Sudeten population.* ~~In the Parliament, the Sudeten German party has been since 1935, the largest individual party; but as the~~

~~Czechoslovak parties could and did unite to outvote, they felt~~[4] *Moreover, in the last elections of 1935 the Sudeten German Party polled more votes than any other single party; and they actually formed the second largest party in the State Parliament. They then commanded some 44 votes in a total Parliament of 300. With subsequent accessions, they are now the largest party. But they can always be outvoted; and consequently* ~~*they*~~ ***some of them*** *feel*[5] that constitutional action ~~was~~ *is* useless *for them,* and that ~~for them at least~~ the Czech democracy ~~was~~ *is* a farce.

Local irritations were added to these major grievances. Czech officials and Czech police, speaking little or no German, were appointed in large numbers to purely German districts; Czech agricultural colonists were encouraged to settle on land confiscated under the Land Reform in the middle of German populations; for the children of these Czech invaders schools were built on a large scale; there ~~was~~ *is* a very general belief that Czech firms were favoured as against German firms in the allocation of State ~~orders~~ *contracts,* and that the State provided work and relief for Czechs more readily than for Germans. I believe these complaints to be in the main justified. Even as late as the time of my Mission, I could find no readiness on the part of the Czech Government to remedy them on anything like an adequate scale.

All these, and other, grievances were intensified by the reactions of the economic crisis on the Sudeten industries, which ~~are~~ *form* so important a part ~~(roughly estimated at 70%)~~ of the life of the people. Not unnaturally, the Government ~~was~~ *were* blamed for the resulting impoverishment.

For many reasons, therefore, including the above, the feeling amongst the Sudeten Germans until about 3 or 4 years ago was one of hopelessness. But the rise of Nazi Germany gave them new hope. I regard their turning for help towards their kinsmen [across the frontier][6] and their eventual desire to join the Reich as a natural development in the circumstances.

At the time of my arrival, the more moderate Sudeten leaders still desired a settlement within the frontiers of the Czechoslovak State. They realised what war would mean in the Sudeten area, which would itself be the main battlefield. Both nationally and internationally such a settlement would have been an easier solution than territorial transfer. I did my best to promote it, *and up to a point with some success,* but even so not without ~~some~~ misgiving as to whether, when agreement was reached, it could *ever* be carried out without giving rise to a new crop of suspicions, controversies, accusations and counter-accusations. ~~Probably~~ *I feel that* any such arrangement would have been temporary, not lasting.

This solution, in the form of what is known as the 'Fourth Plan', broke down in the circumstances narrated above; the whole situation, internal and external, had changed; and I felt that with this change my mission had come to an end.

When I left Prague on September 16th, the riots and disturbances in the Sudeten areas, which had never been more than sporadic, had died down. A considerable number of districts had been placed under a regime called Standrecht, amounting to martial law. The Sudeten leaders, at any rate the more extreme among them, had fled to Germany and were issuing proclamations defying the Czech Government. I ~~was~~ *have been credibly* informed ~~before leaving~~ that, *at the time of my leaving,* the number of killed on both sides was not more than 70. ~~I have no reason to discredit this figure.~~

Unless, therefore, Herr Henlein's Freikorps are deliberately encouraged to cross the frontier, I have no reason to expect any notable renewal of incidents and disturbances. In these circumstances the necessity for the presence of ~~a~~ State Police in these districts should no longer exist. As the State Police are extremely unpopular among the German inhabitants, and ~~even perhaps the~~ *have constituted one of their* chief grievances for the last three years, I consider that they should be withdrawn as soon as possible. I believe that their withdrawal would reduce the ~~cases~~ *causes* of wrangles and riots.

Further, it has become self evident to me that those frontier districts between Czechoslovakia and Germany where the Sudeten population is in an important majority should be given full right of self-determination at once. If some cession is inevitable, as I believe it to be, it is as well that it should be done promptly and without procrastination. There is real danger, ~~both from within and from without,~~ *even a danger of civil war,* in the continuance of a state of uncertainty.~~,~~ ~~and consequently~~[7] Consequently there are very real reasons for a policy of immediate and drastic action. Any kind of plebiscite or referendum would, I believe, be a sheer formality in respect of these predominantly German areas. ~~An immense~~ A very large majority of their inhabitants ~~unquestionably~~ desire amalgamation with Germany. The inevitable delay involved in taking a plebiscite vote would only serve to excite popular feelings, with perhaps most dangerous results. I consider, therefore, that these frontier districts should *at once* be transferred from Czechoslovakia to Germany, and further that measures for their peaceful transfer, including the provision of safeguards for the population during the transfer period should be arranged ~~at once~~ *forthwith* by agreement between the two Governments.

The transfer of these frontier districts does not, however, dispose finally of the question how Germans[8]

and Czechs are to live together peacefully in future. Even if all the areas where the Germans have a majority were transferred to Germany there would still remain in Czechoslovakia a large number of Germans and in the areas transferred to Germany there would still be a certain number of Czechs. Economic connections are so close that an absolute separation is not only undesirable but inconceivable; and I repeat my conviction that history has proved that in times of peace the two peoples can live together on friendly terms. I believe that it is in the interest of all Czechs and of all Germans alike that these friendly relations should be encouraged to re-establish themselves; and I am convinced that this is the real desire of the average Czech and German. They are alike in being honest, peaceable, hard-working and frugal folk. ~~when~~ When political friction has been removed on both sides I believe that they can settle down quietly.

For those portions of the territory*, therefore,* where the German majority is not so important, I recommend that an effort be made to find a basis for local autonomy within the frontiers of the Czechoslovak Republic on the lines of the '4th Plan', modified so as to meet the new circumstances created by the transfer of the predominantly German areas. *As I have already said, there is always a danger that agreement reached in principle may lead to further divergencies in practice. But I think that in a more peaceful future this risk can be minimised.*

This brings me to the political side of the problem which is concerned with the question of the integrity and security of the Czechoslovak Republic, especially in relation to her immediate neighbours. I believe that here the problem is one of removing a centre of intense political friction from the middle of Europe. For this purpose it is necessary permanently to provide that the Czechoslovak State should live at peace with all her neighbours and that her policy internal and external should be directed to that end. Just as it is essential for the international position of Switzerland that her policy should be entirely neutral, so an analogous policy is necessary for Czechoslovakia – not only for her own future existence but for the peace of Europe.

In order to achieve this, I recommend

(1) That those parties and persons in Czechoslovakia who have been deliberately encouraging a policy antagonistic to Czechoslovakia's neighbours should be forbidden by the Czechoslovak Government to continue their agitations; and that if necessary legal measures should be taken to bring such agitations to an end.

(2) That the Czechoslovak Government should so remodel her foreign relations as to give assurance to her neighbours that she will in no circumstances attack them or enter into any aggressive action against them arising from obligations to other states.

(3) That the *principal* Powers ~~interested in maintaining~~, *acting in the interests of the peace of Europe,* should give to Czechoslovakia guarantees of assistance in case of unprovoked aggression against her.

(4) That a commercial treaty on preferential terms should be negotiated between Germany and Czechoslovakia if this seems advantageous to the economic interests of the two countries.

This leads me to the third question which lay within the scope of my enquiry, viz. the economic problem. This problem centres on the distress and unemployment in the Sudeten German areas, a distress which has persisted since 1930, and is due to various causes. It constitutes a suitable background for political discontent. It is a problem which exists; but to say that the Sudeten German question is entirely or even in the main an economic one is misleading. If a transfer of territory takes place it is a problem which will for the most part fall to the German Government to solve.

If the ~~above suggestions recommend themselves~~ *policy which I have outlined above recommends itself* to those concerned in the present situation, I would further ~~add that in my opinion~~ suggest (a) *that* a representative of the Sudeten German people should have a permanent seat in the Czechoslovak Cabinet. (b) That a Commission under a neutral chairman should be appointed to deal with the question of the delimitation of the area to be transferred to Germany and also with controversial points immediately arising from the carrying out of any agreement which may be reached. (c) That an international force be organised to keep order in the districts which are to be transferred pending actual transfer, so that ~~Czechoslovak troops and~~ Czechoslovak State police ~~may at once~~, *as I have said above, and also Czechoslovak troops may* be withdrawn from this area.

I wish to close this letter by recording my appreciation of the personal courtesy, hospitality and assistance which I and my staff received from the Government authorities, especially from Dr. Beneš and Dr. Hodža, from the representatives of the Sudeten German party with whom we came into contact, and from a very large number of other people in all ranks of life whom we met during our stay in Czechoslovakia.

Yours very sincerely,
Runciman of Doxford

Notes

1 The version published in the White Paper, in common with the letter addressed to Beneš, omits (in addition to some other stylistic phrases) the words 'Czech democracy is a farce' when describing the views of some in the SdP, and substitutes the word 'transferred' for 'confiscated' when referring to land gained by Czechs under the Land Reforms.

2 First to draw attention to this was J. W. Bruegel in *Czechoslovakia before Munich*, pp. 275–6.

3 End of page 4 of original typescript and beginning of inserted text.

4 Some minor stylistic changes made by Ashton-Gwatkin to this section before its deletion have not been reproduced.
5 Manuscript marginal insertion by Ashton-Gwatkin. Some minor stylistic changes and alteration in word order have not been reproduced. Words in bold type inserted in a different, unidentified, handwriting.
6 Square brackets inserted in ink.
7 The following text in Ashton-Gwatkin's handwriting, but struck out, appears in the margin: (~~*If Herr Henlein's Freikorps were to cross the frontier, there would*)~~
8 End of inserted text and beginning of page 6 of original typescript.

Appendix 2: Ashton-Gwatkin's Parodies[1]

The New Wenceslas

Good Lord Runciman looked out
   On the street of Stephen;[2]
Nobody was round about,
   Not a p'liceman even.
He was thinking how he might
   This and that determine,
When a poor man came in sight,
   A Sudeten German.

'Hither, Peto, stand by me;
   If thou know'st it telling
Yonder poor man who is he?
   Where and what his dwelling?'
'Sire, he lives a long way hence
   Underneath the mountain,
Right against the forest fence
   By Saint Mary's fountain.'[3]

'Bring me sausages and wine,
   Bring an eight course dinner;
German troops come marching ein,
   If he gets much thinner.'
Lord and Peto forth they went
   Towards Prince M-x's castle[4]
With the poor man's nourishment
   Tied up in a parcel.

'Sire, the way is hard to find,
   And my heart is thumping,
And I'm getting sore behind,
   In this motor bumping.'
'Come, my Peto, take my place;
   And, my calm observing,
Thou shalt find this fearful pace
   Less and less unnerving.'

In the Master's corner, Peto
   Felt once more elated;
Warmth was in the very seat
   By the Lord vacated.
Wherefore, German folk, be sure

He's your best vermittler;
He will all your troubles cure,
And himself meet H——r.[5]

*

In his state-room Ashton-Gwatkin
Solved the problems of the Mission,
Clad in gorgeous shirt of blue silk,
Shirt of blue and carpet slippers.
Off he journeyed to Marienbad,
To the far and healthful waters,
There to meet with Konrad Henlein
(there to see the bust of Hitler)
Used his manner Diplomatic,
Chatted with the aged mother
– lunched with them, and toyed with Chicken.[6]

With his brown eyes tensely staring,
Ian Leslie did interpret,
Listened to the guttural German,
Reproduced it in plain English,
Lest the meaning should be losed,
Lest the Lord should be misguided.

Let us not forget our Stopford,
Friend and confidant of all men,
Working on his constitution
(on a diet of tepid fruit juice),[7]
That the Gaus might be successful,
That the Volksgruppe long might flourish.

In one room there dwelt the maidens,
Dwelt the maidens of the Mission,
Sweated on a mean subsistence,
That they might remain more humble,
That the men might be more wealthy.

And the Lord, the man of learning,
Man of years and vast experience,
Daily travelled to the Castle,
There to feel political pulses,
There to talk to Monsieur Beneš
– Talk to him with words of wisdom,
Tell him how to rule more justly,
That his country might be saved,
That the Hun might not o'er run it.

*

To the Lord of the Red House,[8] 'twas Gwatkin who spoke:
'Now where is the Chicken, that Sudeten bloke?
I've sought him in Eger, I've sought him in Asch
To tell him freiwillig the tale of my pash.
He's dined with the Führer; and now it's my turn
To sit at his feet and all wisdom to learn.
For the charm of the Chicken is greater by far
Than the lure of White Russia's beloved samovar'.[9]

*

Runciman, Runciman, where have you been?
I've been to Hradcin to shampoo the Bean.[10]
Runciman, Runciman, what did you there?
I frightened a Schramek[11] hid under his chair.
Runciman, Runciman, what did you say?
I told him the British weren't going to play.

*

(With apologies to Lewis Carroll.)

I passed Berchtesgaden and saw with one eye
How Adolf and Eddy were sharing a pie.
Adolf took piecrust and gravy and meat,
While the dish remained Eduard's share of the treat;
But later (his hunger a bit to console)
He was kindly allowed a stale slice of Swiss roll,
While Adolf, demanding more meat and more greens,
Concluded his feast with Prague bacon and benes.

Notes

1 Stopford Papers, RJS 3/7 and Runciman Papers, WR 296.
2 Štěpánská ulice in Prague, location of the Hotel Alcron, the official residence of the Runciman Mission.
3 Marienbad or Mariánské Lázně.
4 Hohenlohe's country seat Červený Hrádek (Rothenhaus).
5 Evidently written before Runciman's declared refusal, on 25 August 1938, to visit Hitler.
6 'Chicken' was the Mission's sobriquet for Henlein. The journey in question was the visit to Henlein's home in Aš (Asch) on 4 September 1938.
7 Stopford suffered a stomach infection.
8 Hohenlohe.
9 Evidently written before the Mission's first direct meeting with Henlein on 18 August 1938.
10 Beneš.
11 Jan Šrámek, the Czechoslovak Minister of Public Administration and leader of the People's Party.

Bibliography

Unpublished sources

Public Record Office, London

CAB 16 Committee of Imperial Defence
CAB 23 Cabinet Minutes
CAB 24 Cabinet Papers
CAB 27 Cabinet Committees
FO 371 General Correspondence
FO 800/269 Nevile Henderson Papers
FO 800/275 Sargent Papers
FO 800/293–294 Cadogan Papers
FO 800/304–308 Runciman Mission
FO 800/309 Halifax Papers
PREM 1/264–266A Chamberlain Papers

University of Newcastle upon Tyne, Robinson Library – Runciman Papers

WR 280 Abyssinian crisis, 1935
WR 284 Visit to the USA, 1937
WR 285 Letters and papers, 1937
WR 287 'Impressions of Central Europe' speech by Toynbee to RIIA, 17 June 1937
WR 289 Letters and papers, 1938
WR 292 Letters etc. on eve of Mission to Czechoslovakia, 1938
WR 293 Letters etc. at end of Mission to Czechoslovakia, 1938
WR 296 Letters about Mission to Czechoslovakia
WR 303 Letters between Walter Runciman and Hilda Runciman
WR 315 Press cuttings of speeches, 1894–1931
WR 316 Press cuttings, personal and family
WR 354 Memorandum by Stopford on Mission to Czechoslovakia
WR 357 Additional documents and letters, 1897–1941
(Other papers consulted for biographical material)

Imperial War Museum Library, London – Stopford Papers

RJS 2 Unpublished writings
RJS 3 Documents
RJS 4 Press cuttings
Unclassified additional papers

University of Birmingham Library – Neville Chamberlain Papers

NC 2 Political diaries
NC 4 Drafts and notes for speeches
NC 7 Miscellaneous correspondence
NC 8 Germany, 1938

NC 18 Correspondence with Ida and Hilda Chamberlain

Other private papers

Caldecote Papers (Thomas Inskip) – Churchill College, Cambridge
Christie Papers – Churchill College, Cambridge
Crewe Papers – University of Cambridge Library
Lothian Papers – National Archives of Scotland, Edinburgh
Mason–Macfarlane Papers – Imperial War Museum, London
Samuel Papers – House of Lords Record Office, London
Stronge Papers – Imperial War Museum, London
Templewood Papers (Samuel Hoare) – University of Cambridge Library
Vansittart Papers – Churchill College, Cambridge

Thesis

Palmer, K.M., 'The Runciman Mission to Czechoslovakia: August 1938', PhD, University of Belfast, 1989

Published sources

Documents

Das Abkommen von München, 1938. Tschechoslowakische diplomatische Dokumente 1937–1939, (V. Král, ed.), Prague, 1968.
'Correspondence Respecting Czechoslovakia; September 1938', Cmd. 5847, London, 1938.
Die Deutschen in der Tschechoslowakei, 1933–1947, (V. Král, ed.), Prague, 1964.
Documents and Materials Relating to the Eve of the Second World War, 2 vols, Moscow, 1948.
Documents Diplomatiques Française, 1932–1939, Série 2, vols VII, VIII, IX, X, XI, Paris, 1972–77.
Documents on British Foreign Policy, 1919–1939, Second Series (1929–38), vols XII, XVIII, XIX, London, 1946–85.
Documents on British Foreign Policy, 1919–1939, Third Series (1938–39), vols I, II, London, 1949.
Documents on German Foreign Policy, 1918–1945, Series C (1933–37), vols III, IV, V, London, 1957–83.
Documents on German Foreign Policy, 1918–1945, Series D (1937–45), vols I, II, London, 1949–56.
Europäische Politik, 1933–1938 im Spiegel der Prager Akten, (F. Berber, ed.), Essen, 1942.
Foreign Relations of the United States, Diplomatic Papers, 1938, vols I and II, Washington, 1955.
'Further Documents Respecting Czechoslovakia Including the Agreement Concluded at Munich on September 29, 1938', Cmd. 5848, London, 1938.
International Military Tribunal, *Trial of the Major War Criminals*, XLII vols, Nuremberg, 1947–49.
Mnichov v dokumentech, 2 vols, Prague, 1958.
New Documents on the History of Munich, Prague, 1958.
Parliamentary Debates, 5th series, *House of Commons*, vols 100, 103, 110, 192, 209, 237, 333, 336, 338, 339.

Parliamentary Debates, 5th series, *House of Lords*, vol. 110.
Politické strany a Mnichov; dokumenty, (V. Král, ed.), Prague, 1961.
'Protocols Determining the Frontier Between Germany and Czechoslovakia, Berlin, November 20/21, 1938', Cmd. 5908, London, 1938.
Royal Institute of International Affairs, *Documents on International Affairs*, 1935, vol. I, 1938, vol. II, London, 1936–43.
Statistická příručka Československé republiky, vol. III, Prague, 1928.
Statistická ročenka Československé republiky, Prague, 1935.
Winston S. Churchill, (M. Gilbert, ed.), vol. V (1922–39), *Companion*, part 3 (Documents), London, 1982.

Diaries, speeches and memoirs

Ashton-Gwatkin, F.T.A., 'The Personal Story of the Runciman Mission', *The Listener*, 21 October 1948.
Beneš, E., *Mnichovské dny*, Prague, 1968.
Bruce Lockhart, Sir R., *The Diaries of Sir Robert Bruce Lockhart*, vol. 1, *1915–1938*, (K. Young, ed.), London, 1973.
Cadogan, Sir A., *The Diaries of Sir Alexander Cadogan, O.M., 1938–1945*, (D. Dilks, ed.), London, 1971.
Chamberlain, N. *In Search of Peace; Speeches 1937–1938*, (A. Bryant, ed.), London, 1939.
Channon, Sir H., *Chips: The Diaries of Sir Henry Channon*, (R.R. James, ed.), London, 1967.
Churchill, W.S., *The Gathering Storm*, (*The Second World War*, vol. I), London, 1948.
Conwell-Evans, T.P., *None so Blind*, London, 1947.
Coulondre, R., *De Staline à Hitler: Souvenirs de deux ambassades, 1936–1939*, Paris, 1950.
Duff, S. Grant, *The Parting of Ways: A Personal Account of the Thirties*, London, 1982.
Duff Cooper, A. (Viscount Norwich), *Old Men Forget*, London, 1953.
Eden, A. (Earl of Avon), *Facing the Dictators*, (*Memoirs*, vol. 1), London, 1962.
Fierlinger, Z., *Ve službách ČSR*, 2 vols, Prague, 1947–48.
Groscurth, H., *Tagebücher eines Abwehroffiziers, 1938–1940*, Stuttgart, 1970.
The Guardian Book of Munich, (R.H. Haig, D.S. Morris and A.R. Peters, eds), Aldershot, 1988.
Halifax, Viscount, *Fullness of Days*, London, 1957.
Halifax, Viscount, *Speeches on Foreign Policy*, (H.H.E. Craster, ed.), London, 1940.
Harvey, O., *The Diplomatic Diaries of Oliver Harvey, 1937–1940*, (J. Harvey, ed.), London, 1970.
Henderson, Sir N., *Failure of a Mission*, London, 1940.
Henlein, K., *Heim ins Reich. Reden aus den Jahren 1937 und 1938*, Reichenberg, 1939.
Hitler, A., *The Speeches of Adolf Hitler*, (N.H. Baynes, ed.), 2 vols, London, 1942.
Hoare, Sir Samuel (Viscount Templewood), *Nine Troubled Years*, London, 1954.
Hore-Belisha, L., *The Private Papers of Hore-Belisha*, (R.J. Miney, ed.), London, 1960.
McDonald, I., *A Man of The Times*, London, 1976.
Moravec, F., *Master of Spies. The Memoirs of General Frantisek Moravec*, London, 1975.
Nicolson, H., *Diaries and Letters*, vol. 1, *1930–1939*, London, 1966.
Roberts, F., *Dealing with Dictators: The Destruction and Revival of Europe, 1930–1970*, London, 1991.
Schuschnigg, K., *Austrian Requiem*, London, 1947.
Simon, Sir J. (Viscount Simon), *Retrospect*, London, 1953.

Stopford, R.J., 'Was Czech-Sudeten Agreement Possible?', *Sudeten Bulletin*, vol. X (1962).
Strang, Sir W. (Lord Strang), *Home and Abroad*, London, 1956.
Stronge, H.C.T., 'The Czechoslovak Army and the Munich Crisis: A Personal Memorandum', in B. Bond, and I. Roy, eds, *War and Society*, vol.1, London, 1976.
Thomas, J.H., *My Story*, London, 1937.
Vansittart, Sir R. (Lord Vansittart), *Bones of Contention*, London, 1945.
Vansittart, Sir R. (Lord Vansittart), *The Mist Procession*, London, 1958.
Vansittart, Sir R. (Lord Vansittart), 'A Morally Indefensible Agreement', *The Listener*, 4 November 1948.

Newspapers and periodicals

The Daily Express
The Daily Herald
The Daily Mail
The Daily Telegraph
The Daily Worker
The Evening Standard (London)
The Manchester Guardian
The Methodist Recorder
The New York Herald Tribune
The News Chronicle
The Observer
Reynolds News
The Star
The Sunday Times
The Times (London)

Books and pamphlets

Adamthwaite. A., *France and the Coming of the Second World War*, London, 1977.
Ashton-Gwatkin, F.T.A., *The British Foreign Service*, Syracuse, 1951.
Bachstein, M.K., *Wenzel Jaksch und die Sedetendeutsche Sozialdemokratie*, Munich-Vienna, 1974.
Barnett, C., *The Collapse of British Power*, London, 1972.
Beaumont, M., *The Origins of the Second World War*, New Haven and London, 1978.
Beckman, R., *K diplomatickému pozadí Mnichova*, Prague, 1954.
Bell, P.M.H., *The Origins of the Second World War in Europe*, London, 1986.
Birkenhead, Earl of, *The Life of Lord Halifax*, London, 1965.
Bond, B., *British Military Policy Between the Two World Wars*, Oxford, 1980.
Braddick, H.B., *Germany, Czechoslovakia and the 'Grand Alliance' in the May Crisis, 1938*, Denver, 1969.
Bruegel, J.W., *Czechoslovakia Before Munich: The German Minority Problem and British Appeasement Policy*, Cambridge, 1973.
Bruegel, J.W., *Tschechen und Deutsche, 1918–1938*, Munich, 1967.
Calder, K.J., *Britain and the Origins of the New Europe, 1914–1918*, Cambridge, 1976.
Campbell, F.G., *Confrontation in Central Europe; Weimar Germany and Czechoslovakia*, Chicago, 1975.
Carr, W., *Arms, Autarky, Aggression*, London, 1979.
Celovsky, B., *Das Münchener Abkommen: 1938*, Stuttgart, 1958.
Charmley, J., *Chamberlain and the Lost Peace*, London, 1989.

Cockett, R., *Twilight of Truth. Chamberlain, Appeasement and the Manipulation of the Press*, London, 1989.
Colvin, I., *The Chamberlain Cabinet*, London, 1971.
Colvin, I., *Vansittart in Office*, London, 1965.
Cowling, M., *The Impact of Hitler: British Politics and British Policy, 1933–1940*, Cambridge, 1975.
Cross, J.A., *Sir Samuel Hoare: A Political Biography*, London, 1977.
'Diplomaticus', *The Czechs and their Minorities*, London, 1938.
Douglas, R., *In the Year of Munich*, London, 1977.
Duff, S. Grant, *Europe and the Czechs*, London, 1938.
Duff, S. Grant, *German and Czech: A Threat to European Peace*, (New Fabian Research Bureau pamphlet), London, 1937.
Dutton, D., *Simon*, London, 1992.
Dutton, D., *Neville Chamberlain*, London, 2001.
Eubank, K., *Munich*, Norman, 1963.
Feiling, K., *The Life of Neville Chamberlain*, London, 1946.
Fuchser, L.W., *Neville Chamberlain and Appeasement: A Study in the Politics of History*, London, 1982.
Franke, R., *London und Prag: Materialien zum Problem eines multinationalen Nationalstaates, 1919–1938*, Munich, 1982.
Furnia, A.H., *The Diplomacy of Appeasement: Anglo-French Relations and the Prelude to World War II*, Washington, 1960.
Gajanová, A., *ČSR a středoevropská politika velmocí*, Prague, 1967.
Gannon, F.R., *The British Press and Germany*, Oxford, 1971.
Gedye, G.E.R., *Fallen Bastions: The Central European Tragedy*, London, 1939.
Gilbert, M., *Britain and Germany between the Wars*, London, 1964.
Gilbert, M., *The Roots of Appeasement*, London, 1966.
Gilbert, M., *Winston S. Churchill*, vol. V, *1922–1939*, London, 1976.
Gilbert, M. and Gott, R., *The Appeasers*, London, 1963.
Haig, R.H. and Turner, P.W., *The Hall of Mirrors – An Examination of the Diplomatic and Political Influences Affecting the Events of the Munich Crisis: Autumn 1938*, Sheffield, 1978.
Haslam, J., *The Soviet Union and the Struggle for Collective Security in Europe, 1933–1939*, London, 1984.
Henderson, A., *Eyewitness in Czechoslovakia*, London, 1939.
Hildebrand, K., *The Foreign Policy of the Third Reich*, London, 1973.
Hinsley, F.H. *et al.*, *British Intelligence in the Second World War*, vol. I, London, 1979.
The History of The Times, vol. IV, part 2, London, 1952.
Hochman, J., *The Soviet Union and the Failure of Collective Security, 1934–1938*, Ithaca, 1984.
Hoffmann, P., *The History of the German Resistance, 1933–1945*, (translated by R. Barry), Cambridge, Mass., 1977.
Howard, M., *The Continental Commitment: The Dilemma of British Defence Policy in the Era of Two World Wars*, London, 1972.
James, R.R., *Victor Cazalet: A Portrait*, London, 1976.
Jordan, N., *The Popular Front and Central Europe*, Cambridge, 1992.
Kaiser, D.E., *Economic Diplomacy and the Origins of the Second World War: Germany, Britain, France and Eastern Europe, 1930–1939*, Princeton, 1980.
Kalvoda, J., *The Genesis of Czechoslovakia*, New York, 1986.
Karlgren, A., *Henlein–Hitler a československá tragedie*, Prague, 1945.

Kennedy, P.M., *The Realities Behind Diplomacy: Background Influences on British External Policy, 1865–1980*, London, 1980.
Kershaw, I., *The Nazi Dictatorship: Problems and Perspectives of Interpretation*, London, 1985.
Kitchen, M., *Europe Between the Wars*, London, 1988.
Kokoška, J., *Plan 'Grün'. Reportážní kronika zářijových událostí roku 1938*, Prague, 1968.
Král, V., *Dny které otřásly Československem*, Prague, 1975.
Král, V., *Plán Zet*, Prague, 1973.
Král, V., *Zářijové dny, 1938*, Prague, 1971.
Krejčí, J., and Machonin, P., *Czechoslovakia, 1918–1992; A Laboratory for Social Change*, London, 1996.
Křen, J., *Do emigrace. Západní zahraniční odboj, 1938–1939*, Prague, 1967.
Kváček, R., *Nad Evropou zataženo: Československo a Evropa 1933–1937*, Prague, 1966.
Kváček, R., *Osudná mise*, Prague, 1958.
Laffan, R.G.D., *The Crisis over Czechoslovakia, January to September 1938*, (*Survey of International Affairs, 1938*; volume II), London, 1951.
Lamb, R., *The Drift to War, 1922–1939*, London, 1989.
Lisický, K., *Československá cesta do Mnichova*, London, 1958.
Lukes, I., *Czechoslovakia between Stalin and Hitler: The Diplomacy of Edvard Beneš in the 1930s*, Oxford, 1996.
Luža, R., *The Transfer of the Sudeten Germans: A Study of Czech-German Relations, 1933–1962*, New York, 1964.
Lvová, M., *Mnichov a Edvard Beneš*, Prague, 1968.
Mack Smith, D., *Mussolini's Roman Empire*, London, 1977.
MacDonald, C.A., *The United States, Britain and Appeasement, 1936–1939*, London, 1981.
Mckenzie, C., *Dr Beneš*, London, 1946.
Macleod, I., *Neville Chamberlain*, London, 1961.
Meehan, P., *The Unnecessary War: Whitehall and the German Resistance to Hitler*, London, 1992.
Michie, L.W., *Portrait of an Appeaser: Robert Hadow, First Secretary in the British Foreign Office, 1931–1939*, London, 1996.
Middlemas, K., *Diplomacy of Illusion: The British Government and Germany, 1937–39*, London, 1972.
Morrell, S., *I Saw the Crucifiction*, London, 1939.
Murray. W., *The Change in the European Balance of Power 1938–1939*, Princeton, 1984.
Néré, J., *The Foreign Policy of France from 1914–1945, London*, 1975.
Northedge, F.S., *The Troubled Giant: Britain among the Great Powers, 1916–1939*, London, 1966.
Offner, A.A., *American Appeasement, 1933–38*, Cambridge, Mass., 1969.
Olivová, V., *The Doomed Democracy: Czechoslovakia in a Disrupted Europe, 1914–1938*, London, 1972.
Ovendale, R. *'Appeasement' and the English Speaking World. The United States, the Dominions, and the Policy of 'Appeasement', 1937–1939*, Cardiff, 1975.
Overy, R.J. and Wheatcroft, A., *Road to War*, London, 1989.
Parker, R.A.C., *Chamberlain and Appeasement: British Policy and the Coming of the Second World War*, London, 1993.
Parker, R.A.C., *Europe, 1918–1939*, London, 1969.
Parkinson, R., *Peace for Our Time*, London, 1971.
Pearson, R., *National Minorities in Eastern Europe, 1848–1945*, London, 1983.

Peden, G.C., *British Rearmament and the Treasury: 1932–1939*, Edinburgh, 1979.
Perman, D., *The Shaping of the Czechoslovak State: Diplomatic History of the Boundaries of Czechoslovakia, 1914–1920*, Leiden, 1962.
Peroutka, F., *Budování statu*, 4 vols, Prague, 1933–36.
Peters, A.R., *Anthony Eden at the Foreign Office, 1931–1938*, Aldershot and New York, 1986.
Polonsky, A., *The Little Dictators: The History of Eastern Europe since 1918*, London, 1975.
Prażmowska, A.J., *Eastern Europe and the Origins of the Second World War*, London, 2000.
Ripka, H., *Munich: Before and After*, London, 1939.
Reynolds, D., *The Creation of the Anglo-American Alliance, 1937–1941*, London, 1981.
Robbins, K., *Munich 1938*, London, 1968.
Roberts, A., *'The Holy Fox': A Biography of Lord Halifax*, London, 1991.
Rock, W.R., *British Appeasement in the 1930s*, London, 1977.
Rock, W.R., *Chamberlain and Roosevelt, 1937–1940*, Columbus, Ohio, 1978.
Rönnefarth, H.K.G., *Die Sudetenkrise in der internationalen Politik: Entstehung, Verlauf, Auswirkung*, 2 vols, Wiesbaden, 1961.
Rose, N., *Vansittart: Study of a Diplomat*, London, 1978.
Roskill, S., *Hankey: Man of Secrets*, 3 vols, London, 1970–74.
Rothschild, J., *East Central Europe between the Two World Wars*, Seattle, 1974.
Schmidt, G., *The Politics and Economics of Appeasement: British Foreign Policy in the 1930s*, (translated by J. Bennett-Ruete), Leamington Spa, 1986.
Seton-Watson, R.W., *A History of the Czechs and Slovaks*, London, 1943.
Seton-Watson, R.W., *From Munich to Danzig*, London, 1939.
Shay, R.P., *British Rearmament in the Thirties: Politics and Profits*, Princeton, 1977.
Smelser, R.M., *The Sudeten Problem, 1933–1938: Volkstumspolitik and the Formulation of Nazi Foreign Policy*, Folkestone, 1975.
Taborsky, E., *President Edvard Beneš: Between East and West, 1938–1948*, Stanford, 1981.
Taylor, A.J.P., *The Origins of the Second World War*, London, 1961.
Taylor, T., *Munich: The Price of Peace*, London, 1979.
Teichová, A., *An Economic Background to Munich: International Business and Czechoslovakia, 1918–1938*, Cambridge, 1974.
Temperley, H.W.V., ed., *A History of the Peace Conference of Paris*, 6 vols, London, 1920–24.
Thompson, L., *The Greatest Treason: The Untold Story of Munich*, New York, 1968.
Thompson, N., *The Anti-Appeasers. Conservative Opposition to Appeasement in the 1930s*, Oxford, 1971.
Thorne, C., *The Approach of War, 1938–1939*, London 1967.
Wallace, W.V., *Czechoslovakia*, London, 1976.
Wark, W.K., *The Ultimate Enemy: British Intelligence and Nazi Germany, 1933–1939*, Oxford, 1986.
Watt, D.C., *How War Came. The Immediate Origins of the Second World War, 1938–1939*, London, 1989.
Watt, D.C. *Personalities and Policies: Studies in the Formulation of British Foreign Policy in the Twentieth Century*, London, 1965.
Watt, D.C., *Too Serious a Business: European Armed Forces and the Approach to the Second World War*, London, 1975.
Weinberg, G.L., *The Foreign Policy of Hitler's Germany*, 2 vols, Chicago, 1970 and 1980.

Weisskopf, K., *The Agony of Czechoslovakia '38/'68*, London, 1968.
Wendt, B.-J., *Economic Appeasement. Handel und Finanz in der britischen Deutschland-Politik, 1933–1939*, Düsseldorf, 1971.
Wheeler-Bennett, J.W., *Munich: Prologue to Tragedy*, London, 1966.
Wingfield, N.M., *Minority Politics in a Multinational State: The German Social Democrats in Czechoslovakia, 1918–1938*, New York, 1989.
Wiskemann, E., *Czechs and Germans: A Study of the Struggle in the Historic Provinces of Bohemia and Moravia*, (2nd edn), London, 1967.
Wrench, J.E., *Geoffrey Dawson and Our Times*, London, 1956.
Young, R.J., *In Command of France: French Foreign Policy and Military Planning, 1933–1940*, Cambridge, Mass., 1978.

Collections of essays

Boyce, R., and Robertson, E.M., eds, *Paths to War: New Essays on the Origins of the Second World War*, London, 1989.
Craig, G. and Gilbert, F., eds, *The Diplomats*, 2 vols, New York, 1972.
Latynski, M., ed., *Reappraising the Munich Pact: Continental Perspectives*, Washington, 1992.
Lukes, I. and Goldstein, E., eds, *The Munich Crisis, 1938: Prelude to World War II*, London, 1999.
Mamatey, V.S. and Luža, R., eds, *A History of the Czechoslovak Republic, 1918–1948*, Princeton, 1973.
Mommsen, W.J. and Kettenacker, L., eds, *The Fascist Challenge and the Policy of Appeasement*, London, 1983.
Robertson, E.M., ed, *The Origins of the Second World War: Historical Interpretations*, London, 1971.

Articles

Adamthwaite, A., 'The British Government and the Media, 1937–1938', *Journal of Contemporary History*, vol.18 (1983).
Aulach, H., 'Britain and the Sudeten issue, 1938: The Evolution of a Policy', *Journal of Contemporary History*, vol. 18 (1983).
Baker, V.B, 'Selective Inattention: The Runciman Mission to Czechoslovakia, 1938', *East European Quarterly*, vol. 29 (1990).
Black, N., 'Decision-making and the Munich Crisis', *British Journal of International Studies*, vol. 6 (1980).
Boadle, D.G., 'The Formation of the Foreign Office Economic Relations Section, 1930–1937', *Historical Journal*, XX (1977).
Boadle, D.G., 'Vansittart's Administration of the Foreign Office in the 1930s', in R.T.A. Langhorne, ed., *Diplomacy and Intelligence during the Second World War*, London, 1985.
Chalupa, A., 'Pražsky rok Roberta J. Stopforda: Vzpomínky na léta 1938–39', *Sborník národního muzea v Praze: Řada A: Historie*, vol. 42 (1988).
Cornwall, M., 'Dr Edvard Beneš and Czechoslovakia's German Minority, 1918–1943', in J. Morison, ed., *The Czech and Slovak Experience*, London, 1992.
Cornwall, M., 'A Fluctuating Barometer: British Diplomatic Views on the Czech-German Relationship in Czechoslovakia, 1918–1938', in S.B. Winters and E. Schmidt-Hartmann, eds, *Grossbritannien, die USA und die böhmischen Länder, 1848–1938*, Munich, 1991.

Cornwall, M., 'The Rise and Fall of a "Special Relationship"?: Britain and Czechoslovakia, 1930–1948', in B. Brivati and H. Jones, eds, *What Difference Did the War Make?*, Leicester, 1993.

Dilks, D., 'Appeasement and "Intelligence"', in D. Dilks (ed.), *Retreat from Power: Studies in Britain's Foreign Policy of the Twentieth Century*, vol. 1 (1906–1939), London, 1981.

Dilks, D., 'Flashes of Intelligence: The Foreign Office, the SIS and Security Before the Second World War', in C. Andrew and D. Dilks (eds), *The Missing Dimension: Governments and Intelligence Communities in the Twentieth Century*, London, 1984.

Dilks, D., '"We must hope for the best and prepare for the worst." The Prime Minister, the Cabinet and Hitler's Germany, 1937–9', *Proceedings of the British Academy*, vol. 73 (1987).

Goldman, A.L., 'Two Views of Germany. Nevile Henderson vs. Vansittart and the Foreign Office, 1937–1939', *British Journal of International Studies*, vol. 6 (1980).

Haslam, J., 'The Soviet Union and the Czech Crisis 1938', *Journal of Contemporary History*, vol. 14 (1979).

Král, V., 'Anglická politika před schůzkou v Berchtesgadenu v září 1938', *Československý časopis historický*, vol. 21 (1973).

Král, V., 'Československo a Mnichov', *Československý časopis historický*, vol. 7 (1959).

Král, V., 'Historická literatura o Mnichovu 1938', *Československý časopis historický*, vol. 22 (1974).

Lammers, D., 'From Whitehall after Munich: The Foreign Office and the Future Course of British Policy', *Historical Journal*, vol. 16 (1973).

Lukes, I., 'The Czechoslovak Partial Mobilisation in May 1938: A Mystery (Almost) Solved', *Journal of Contemporary History*, vol. 31 (1996).

Luh, A., 'Grossbritannien, die Sudetendeutsche Partai und das Dritte Reich', in S.B. Winters and E. Schmidt-Hartmann, eds, *Grossbritannien, die USA und die böhmischen Länder, 1848–1938*, Munich, 1991.

MacDonald, C.A., 'Economic Appeasement and the German "Moderates", 1937–1939', *Past and Present*, vol. 56 (1972).

Richter, K., 'Sudetoněmecký separatismus v úloze páté kolony Hitlerovského Německa', *Historie a Vojenství*, vol. 37 (1988).

Robbins, K.G., 'Konrad Henlein, the Sudeten Question and British Foreign Policy', *Historical Journal*, XII (1969).

Seton-Watson, C., 'R.W. Seton-Watson and the Czechoslovaks, 1935–1939', in S.B. Winters and E. Schmidt-Hartmann, eds, *Grossbritannien, die USA und die böhmischen Länder, 1848–1938*, Munich, 1991.

Wallace, W.V., 'The Foreign Policy of President Beneš in the Approach to Munich', *Slavonic and East European Review*, XXXIX (1960–61).

Wallace, W.V., 'The Making of the May Crisis of 1938', *Slavonic and East European Review*, XLI (1962–63).

Wallace, W.V., 'A Reply to Mr. Watt', *Slavonic and East European Review*, XLIV (1965–66).

Watt, D.C., 'Appeasement: The Rise of a Revisionist School?', *Political Quarterly*, vol. 36 (1965).

Watt, D.C., 'British Intelligence and the Coming of the Second World War in Europe', in E.R. May, ed., *Knowing One's Enemies: Intelligence Assessment Between Two World Wars*, Princeton, 1986.

Watt, D.C., 'Hitler's Visit to Rome and the May Weekend Crisis: A Study in Hitler's Response to External Stimuli', *Journal of Contemporary History*, vol. 9 (1974).

Watt, D.C., 'The May Crisis of 1938: A Rejoinder to Mr. Wallace', *Slavonic and East European Review*, XLIV (1965–66).
Weinberg, G.L., 'The May Crisis, 1938', *Journal of Modern History*, XXIX (1957).
Weinberg, G.L., Rock, W.R., and Cienciala, A.M., 'The Munich Crisis Revisited', *International History Review*, vol. 11 (1989).
Wiskemann, E., 'Czechs and Germans after Munich', *Foreign Affairs*, vol. 17 (1939).
Young, R.J., 'French Military Intelligence and Nazi Germany, 1938–1939', in E.R. May, ed., *Knowing One's Enemies: Intelligence Assessment Between Two World Wars*, Princeton, 1986.
Zorach, J., 'The Nečas Mission during the Munich Crisis: Nečas' Own Account from the Hoover Institute Archives', *East Central Europe*, vol. 16 (1989).

Principal biographical sources on Runciman

Addison, C., *Politics from Within*, 2 vols, London, 1924.
Amery, L.S., *My Political Life*, 3 vols, London, 1953–55.
Asquith, H.H., *Letters to Venetia Stanley*, (M. and E. Brock, eds), London, 1982.
Beaverbrook, Lord, *Politicians and the War*, London, 1928.
Beveridge, Sir W.H., *British Food Control*, London, 1928.
Churchill, R.S., *Winston S. Churchill*, II (1901–14) and Companion vols, London, 1969.
Cole, G.D.H., *Labour in the Coal-Mining Industry, 1914–1921*, Oxford, 1923.
David, E., *Inside Asquith's Cabinet: From the Diaries of Charles Hobhouse*, London, 1977.
Gilbert, M., *Winston S. Churchill*, III (1914–16), IV (1916–22), V (1922–29), and Companion vols., London, 1972–76.
Grey, Viscount, *Twenty-five Years, 1892–1916*, 2 vols, London, 1925.
Griffiths, R., *Fellow Travellers of the Right: British Enthusiasts for Nazi Germany, 1933–39*, London, 1980.
Harrison, R.A., 'The Runciman Visit to Washington in January 1937', *Canadian Journal of History*, vol. XIX (1964).
Haxey, S., *Tory M.P.*, London, 1939.
Hurwitz, S.J., *State Intervention in Great Britain: A Study of Economic Control and Social Response, 1914–1919*, London, 1949.
Lloyd George, D., *War Memoirs*, 6 vols, London, 1933–36.
Petrie, Sir C., *The Chamberlain Tradition*, London, 1938.
Riddell, Lord, *Intimate Diary of the Peace Conference and After, 1918–1923*, London, 1933.
Riddell, Lord, *War Diary, 1914–1918*, London, 1933.
Runciman, Sir W., *'Sunbeam' in the Mediterranean during the Regime of Mussolini*, London, 1926.
Runciman, W. (Viscount Runciman), *Liberalism as I See It*, London, 1927.
Runciman, W. (Viscount Runciman), 'A New International Ethic', *Methodist Times*, 15 September 1921
Runciman, W. (Viscount Runciman), 'The Radical Outlook', *Contemporary Review*, vol. 113 (1918).
Sacks, B., *The Religious Issue in the State Schools of England and Wales, 1902–1914*, Albequerque, 1961.
Seton-Watson, R.W., *Masaryk in England*, Cambridge, 1943.
Snowden, Viscount, *An Autobiography*, London, 1934.

Taylor, H.A., *Robert Donald*, London, 1934.
Thompson, C.P., 'England's Key Man at Ottawa', *New York Herald Tribune*, 31 July 1932.
Turner, J., *British Politics and the Great War: Coalition and Conflict, 1915–1918*, New Haven and London, 1992.
Urquhart, J., *Eigg*, Edinburgh, 1987.
Wilson, T., ed., *The Political Diaries of C.P. Scott, 1911–1928*, London, 1970.

Index

Abyssinian crisis, 91
'Activism' (Sudeten German), 5, 7–8, 11, 17–18
Addison, Sir Joseph, 9–10, 12, 20, 132, 133
administrative reform (in Czechoslovakia), 104, 149, 153
Aga Khan, 27, 33
Agrarian Party (Czechoslovak), 103, 109, 154, 302–3
Agrarian Party (Sudeten German), 5, 11, 18
agrarian reform *see* land reform
'Agreement of 18 February 1937', 11, 15
Åland Islands, 298, 307
Alcron, Hotel (Prague), 147–8, 253
Anglo-German Fellowship, 92
'appeasement', 94–5, 333
arbitration by Britain in Sudeten German dispute, 71, 137
Aš (Asch), viii, 253, 255–6, 290, 292–3, 318, 321
Ashton-Gwatkin, Frank, 158, 159, 165, 187, 231, 288, 320, 331, 332, 341
  appointment to Runciman Mission, 128–31
  assessment of Henlein, 173, 178–9, 185, 236, 256, 293
  attitude to Central Europe, 128–9
  breakdown of mediation, 291
  career background, 128–9
  contacts with SdP, 169–71, 172–4, 215, 249–50, 271–3, 276, 282, 288
  'Fourth Plan', 266, 267, 270–1, 273–4, 276
  'Franco-British Plan', 325–6
  Henlein's mediation between Britain and Germany, 179–80, 202, 205–6, 218–19, 234–6, 256, 262
  'independence' of Mission, 129–31, 136
  judgement of SdP, 151–2
  in London for consultations, 182, 202–4, 205, 208, 227
  meeting with Frank, 291–2
  meetings with Henlein, 172–3, 174–5, 177–80, 204, 215–18, 222, 225, 234–6, 237, 253, 255–6, 292–3, 342
  Munich Conference, 324, 328, 334
  'Notes on Germany and Central Europe', 334–5, 340, 342
  objectives of Mission, 159–60
  preparation for Mission, 141, 144
  return to London, 303–4, 316
  Runciman's proposed visit to Hitler, 206–8
  Runciman Report, 317–19, 324–6, 327, 337
  unrest in Sudetenland, 288–9
  see also John Paris
Asquith, H.H., 82, 85, 86–7
Atholl, Duchess of, 109
Austria, *Anschluss* of, 13, 17–18, 342
Austria-Hungary, 2, 90, 221, 231
autonomy (for Sudeten Germans), 11–12, 15, 27, 33, 46, 52–3, 56, 59, 153, 173, 217, 224, 231–2, 248–50, 293–4, 310, 313, 318, *see also* 'Third Plan'; 'Fourth Plan'
  Czechoslovak memorandum of 7 June 1938, 101
Avenol, Joseph, 129

Baldwin, Stanley, 88, 333–4
Bat'a, Tomáš, 273–4, 332
Bechyně, Rudolf, 108–9, 122, 124, 273
Belgium, 93
Beneš, Edvard, 8, 57, 64, 73, 105, 108, 109, 142, 290, 302, 310, 312–13, 316, 342
  'Franco-British Plan', 322
  Henlein's visit to Hitler (1 September 1938), 236–8, 241
  interview with the *Sunday Times* (March 1938), 32–3
  meetings with Newton (1937), 14–15
  meetings with Runciman, 149–50, 165, 180, 214, 243–8, 249–51, 259, 272, 273, 303

negotiations with SdP, 214–15, 221–2
Paris Peace Conference, 3–4, 47
pressured by Britain, 105–8, 110–13
proposals for reform, 52, 54, 59, 102–4, 110–13, *see also* 'Third Plan', 'Fourth Plan'
radio address (10 September 1938), 274
reaction to British policy statement of 24 March 1938, 44, 46
resigns from presidency, 328
Bentinck, Charles, 12
Berchtesgaden, 33–4, 42, 58, 236
Chamberlain–Hitler meeting, 310, 319–20, 321–2, 342
Bohemia and Moravia, 2–3, 4, 12, 16, 17, 19, 26, 29, 52, 59–60, 104, 117, 142, 143, 178, 323
see also Historic Provinces
Böhmisch Kamnitz *see* Česká Kamenice
Böhmisch Krumau *see* Český Krumlov
Böhmisch Leipa *see* Česká Lípa
Bolshevism *see* Communism
Bonnet, Georges, 57, 105, 130, 229, 246, 294, 322, 327
Borden, Mary, 332–3, 339
Bost-Waldeck, Count, 231
Bramwell, Christopher, 14
Brand, Walter, 13, 21–22, 105–6, 119
Brauchitsch, General Walter von, 237
Breslau *see* Wrocław
Britain *see* Great Britain
British Commonwealth, 26
British Library of Information (New York), 317
British Legation (Prague), 253, 276
Bruce Lockhart, R.H., 133–4
Bruegel, J.W., 337
Brugman, Charles, 231
Brunet, André, 294, 307
Brüx *see* Most
Bürger, Friedrich, 168–9
Butler, Sir Montagu, 76
Butler, R.A., 40, 67

Cabinet (British), 37, 48, 58, 69, 73, 131, 226–8, 277, 297, 310, 320–1, 323, 324, 334
Cabinet Committee on Czechoslovakia, 294–5, 297–8, 304, 319–20, 323, 324–5
Cabinet Committee on Foreign Policy, 24–8, 35–7, 48–50, 73–4, 137
Cadogan, Sir Alexander, 28, 30–1, 42, 73–4, 78, 79, 105, 110, 113, 131, 156, 254, 257, 259, 286–7, 304, 319
Campbell, Ronald, 130, 144, 229
Campbell-Bannerman, Sir Henry, 82
Cambon, Roger, 199–200
Cambridge, Trinity College, 81
Carlsbad (Karlovy Vary), viii, 175, 276, 289–90
Carlsbad Programme (April 1938) *see* Sudeten German Party
Cazalet, Captain Victor, 73
Černý, Jan, 122
Červený Hrádek (Rothenhaus), viii, 170, 173, 176, 215–17, 239, 255, 276
Česká Kamenice (Böhmisch Kamnitz), viii, 169–71, 331
Česká Lípa (Böhmisch Leipa), viii, 255
Český Krumlov (Böhmisch Krumau), viii, 174, 331
Chamberlain, Neville, 40, 87–8, 94–5, 121, 131, 187, 199, 327, 330, 333, 342
announcement of Runciman Mission, 1, 116, 134–5
concerned about attack on Czechoslovakia, 226–7, 296
favours negotiating with Germany over Czechoslovakia, 17, 27, 34–5, 39, 44, 48
favours rapprochement with Germany, 34–5
House of Commons statement on 24 March 1938, 36, 43–4, 200–1
meetings with Hitler, 304, 310, 319–20, 321–2, 323–4, 342
Munich Conference, 327–8
opposed to guarantee of Czechoslovakia, 26, 31
Runciman, 88–9, 94–5, 98, 134, 143
urges settlement between Czechoslovak government and SdP, 15–16, 37
visit to Hitler, 208, 295–7, *see also* 'Plan Z'
Charles IV (of Bohemia), 143
Chatham House *see* Royal Institute of International Affairs (RIIA)

Chautemps, Camille, 15–16
Cheb (Eger), viii, 57, 289–90, 291–2, 321
Chebsko (Egerland), 212, 299, 321
Chetwod, Field Marshal Sir Philip, 76
Chiefs of Staff (UK) report (1938), 26, 28, 36–7
Christian Social Party (Sudeten German), 5, 11, 18
Christie, Group Captain Grahame, 10, 21, 55, 117–20, 171–2, 179, 184
Churchill, Winston S., 24, 55–6, 67, 68, 81, 85, 97–8
Claridge's Hotel (London), 67, 68
Clary-Aldringen, Count and Countess, 170, 215–16, 331, 332
Clerk, Sir George, 109
commission of enquiry (considered for Czechoslovakia), 24–5, 32–3, 40, 44, 62–3
'Committee of Six' (Czechoslovak), 103, 152–4
Communism (Soviet), 16, 90–1, 121, 181, 201–2, 287, 295–6, 332
Communist Party (Czechoslovak), 103, 302, 326
Constitution (Czechoslovak), 4, 43, 46–7, 52
Conwell-Evans, Philip, 201
Cooper, A. Duff, 227, 321
Corbin, Charles, 42, 105, 113, 245–6, 285
Coulondre, Robert, 80–1
Cranborne, Viscount, 9, 13
Creswell, Michael, 246–7, 260
Cunard Steamship Company, 98
'Czechoslovak' nationality, 4
Czechoslovakia
  advised by Britain to reach settlement with SdP, 38–9, 40, 49, 52, 54, 57, 105–8
  alliance with France (1925), 6–7, 105, 115, 203–4, 297, 315
  alliance with the Soviet Union (1935), 6–7, 16, 190, 203–4, 221, 297, 302, 315, 322
  arbitration treaty with Germany (1925), 6, 33, 322
  border fortifications, 7
  British mediation imposed, 113–16
  British observers in Sudetenland, 63–4
  commercial treaty with Germany, 302, 315, 326
  exploratory discussions with Runciman Mission, 149–50, 152–4
  foreign policy orientation, 47, 60–2, 70, 138, 203, 204–5, 221, 297, 302, 315, 322
  formation of, 2–3, 192
  informed of British refusal of guarantee, 38–9, 44
  international guarantee of, 322
  May Crisis, 57–8
  memorandum of 7 May, 101
  mobilisation, 324
  negotiations with SdP, 103–4, 110–13, 166–8
  proposals for reform, 52, 54, *see also* 'Third Plan' and 'Fourth Plan'
  'sort of Switzerland', 3, 47
  State Defence Law 1936, 7
Czechs, 3, 191–2,
  in Austria-Hungary, 2
Czernin, Count Edmund, 275–6, 317, 331, 332, 333

Daily Herald, 135–6, 267
Daily Telegraph, 8, 13, 188, 221
Daily Worker, 134, 333
Daladier, Edouard, 53–4, 322, 327, 328
Dawson, Geoffrey, 68, 93, 124, 279
Delbos, Yvon, 12, 15–16
Dewsbury, 81
Dirksen, Herbert von, 56, 121, 124
Dolní Břežany, viii, 245, 331
Doxford, 86
Duff Cooper A. *see* Cooper A. Duff

economic depression, 5, 141, 155, 156, 170–1, 174, 202–3, 312, 315
Economic Relations Section of the Foreign Office (London), 128
Eden, Anthony, 8, 9–10, 15–16, 17, 21, 22, 43
education (Czechoslovakia), 4–5, 52, 312
Edward VIII, 88
Eger *see* Cheb
Egerland *see* Chebsko
Eigg, Isle of, 86, 98
Eisenlohr, Ernst, 19, 283, 290, 302

elections (in Czechoslovakia),
general elections (1920, 1925, 1929), 5, 7–8, 155
local elections (1919, 1938), 5, 155, 298, 320
Emerson, Sir Herbert, 74
Esterházy, Count, 156–7
Evening Standard (London), 8

Fairweather, Margaret, (*née* Runciman – daughter), 133, 215
Falkenau, *see* Falknov
Falknov (Falkenau), viii, 289–90
Feetham, Richard, 74
Field, The, 86
Fisher, H.A.L., 76–7
Fletcher, Angus, 317
Foreign Ministry (Berlin), 198–9, 205
Foreign Office (London), 187
Ashton-Gwatkin's report of progress, 202–4, 205
attitude towards Czechoslovakia, 10, 11, 12, 28–36
breakdown of mediation, 291
Czechoslovak-SdP negotiations, 104–8
Henderson's advice on Mission outcome, 195–7
international conference, 300
mediation between Czechoslovakia and SdP imposed, 113–16, 121
mediation in Czechoslovakia, 62, 71–6, 79–80
neutralisation of Czechoslovakia, 60–2
'Possible Measures to Avert German Action in Czechoslovakia', 24–5
preparation of Runciman Mission, 136–41, 147, 156, 240
Runciman's activities, 229, 246–7, 252–3, 266–7
Runciman Report, 316
'The German Minority in Czechoslovakia: The Next Step', 45–7, 51
'The Objections to Holding a Plebiscite in the Sudeten Areas of Czechoslovakia', 110, 138
The Times leading article of 7 September 1938, 278–80
Foreign Office News Department (London), 317
Foreign Policy Committee *see* Cabinet Committee on Foreign Policy
Forrest, William, 335
'Fourth Plan', 259–70, 273–4, 280, 286, 310–11, 315, 323, 325
France, 93, 190, 200, 201, 278, 284
alliance with Czechoslovakia (1925), 6–7, 105, 115, 203–4, 286, 315
attitude towards Czechoslovakia, 3, 12, 38, 44
'Franco-British Plan', 322, 325, 327
ministerial meetings with Great Britain, 15–16
pressure on Czechoslovakia to settle with SdP, 105, 113
Runciman Mission, 18, 115, 229, 245–6, 285, 294–5, 297
warning to Germany during May Crisis, 57–8
Frank, Karl Herman, 18, 150, 167–70, 171, 204, 212, 215, 216–17, 219–20, 224, 234, 235, 241, 262, 268, 270, 271, 282, 290, 291, 311
Franke, Emil, 108–9, 124
Free Trade, 87–8, 98
Freikorps (Sudeten German), 294, 314
Friedland *see* Frýdlant
Frýdlant (Friedland), 307–8

Gallop, R.A., 11
Garvin, J.L., 68, 134
Gedye, G.E.R., 267, 335
general election *see* elections
George VI, 96, 303, 334
German minority (in Czechoslovakia) *see* Sudeten Germans
Germany, 5–6
British Observers in Sudetenland, 63
Czechoslovak-SdP negotiations, 104, 176
informed of Runciman Mission, 120–2
links with SdP, 11, 18, 176, 321 *see also* Henlein, Konrad
military preparations, 191, 198–9
see also international conference considered on Czechoslovakia; Munich Agreement

Godesberg, Chamberlain–Hitler meeting, 323–4, 327–8, 342
Goebbels, Josef, 287
Goerdeler, Karl, 131
Göring, Field Marshal Hermann, 99, 127, 200, 287, 340
government service *see* Sudeten Germans
Graham, Sir Ronald, 96
'Grand Alliance' against Germany, 24, 26, 29–30
Gravesend, 81
Great Britain, 190
  appoints observers in Sudetenland, 64
  considers mediation between Czechoslovakia and SdP, 44–5, 49, 51
  and Czechoslovakia, 8, 14, 341
  Czechoslovakia considered indefensible, 26–7, 227, 341
  'Franco-British Plan', 322, 325, 327
  guarantee of Czechoslovakia rejected, 27–8, 31, 35, 40, 43, 51, 53
  informs France that Czechoslovakia would not be guaranteed, 37–8
  mediation between Czechoslovakia and SdP imposed, 113–16
  ministerial meetings with France, 15–16, 53–4
  possible guarantee of Czechoslovakia, 15, 27–8, 29, 31–2
  possible indirect commitment to Czechoslovakia via France, 24–6, 29, 31
  pressure on Czechoslovakia to settle with SdP, 38–9, 40, 49, 52, 53–4, 57, 65, 105–8
  proposed concerted action with France over Czechoslovakia, 50–1, 54
  proposed emissary to Hitler, 219–20, 227–8
  seeks rapprochement with Germany, 201–2, 235, 236, 295–6, 341–2
  seeks to involve Germany in Sudeten German problem, 38–9, 40, 48, 50–1, 54
  The Times leading article of 7 September 1938, 278–80
  warning to Germany during May Crisis, 57–8
Great Depression *see* economic depression
Grey, Sir Edward (Lord), 83, 86–7, 97

Habsburg Monarchy *see* Austria-Hungary
Hadow, Robert, 67, 302–3
Hailey, Lord, 74
Hailsham, Lord, 40, 49
Halifax, Viscount, 18, 40, 59, 79, 124, 131, 143, 187, 272, 304, 319
  appeals to Hitler for moderation, 198–9, 206–7
  arbitration by Runciman, 229, 233–4
  British mediation between Czechoslovakia and SdP, 45, 48–9, 71, 73
  candidates for mediator, 74–7
  continues pressure on Czechoslovakia, 245–6
  duration of Runciman Mission, 196–7
  favours Czechoslovakia negotiating with Germany, 25, 34–5, 39
  Godesberg terms, 327–8
  Henderson recalled for consultations, 194–5, 199
  neutralisation of Czechoslovakia, 61
  objectives of Runciman Mission, 136–40, 188–90
  opposes commitment to Czechoslovakia, 24–8, 35
  outlines situation to Cabinet (30 August 1938), 227
  plebiscite in Sudetenland, 110
  pressures Czechoslovakia for concessions, 105–8
  proposes follow-up to Lanark speech, 251, 253–4
  proposes warning to Hitler, 285–7
  restrains Ashton-Gwatkin, 218–20, 237
  Runciman Mission imposed, 113–16
  urges publication of 'Third Plan', 225–6, 228, 244
  view of German intentions towards Czechoslovakia, 49
  visits Berlin in November 1937, 17
Hammond, Sir Laurie, 74
Hankey, Sir Maurice, 26, 40, 41, 98
Harrison, H.D., 332

Harvey, Oliver, 41, 131, 279, 322, 325–6, 327, 329
Havránková, Zdeňa, 331–2
Hencke, Andor, 166, 176, 181, 225, 277
Henderson, Ian Leslie, 64, 132, 159, 204, 289, 291–2, 338
Henderson, Sir Nevile, 54, 57, 188, 199, 209, 210, 251, 254, 257, 279
  arbitration by Runciman, 229, 287–8
  conversations with Strang (May 1938), 59–63
  Henlein's visit to Hitler (1 September 1938), 258–9
  ill health, 194
  mediation in Czechoslovakia, 62–3, 71–2, 74
  objectives of Runciman Mission, 137–8, 190–5, 196–7, 226
  recalled to London for consulations, 194–5, 199, 227–8
  Runciman Mission, 132
  warning to Hitler, 286–7
Henlein, Konrad, 6, 20, 73, 123, 270, 277, 290, 291, 311, 321, 332, 342
  Carlsbad Programme, 52–3, *see also* Sudeten German Party
  contact with Vansittart, 105–8, 110–11, 119–20, 171–2, 179, 184
  demands plebiscite and self-determination, 293–4, 318–19
  destruction of Czechoslovakia, 16
  leaves Czechoslovakia, 294
  mediating between Britain and Germany, 171–2, 179–80, 198, 202, 205–6, 216–17, 218–20, 229, 234–6
  meeting with Hitler in August 1936, 11
  meeting with Hitler in March 1938, 18, 55, 176
  meeting with Hitler (1 September 1938), 228, 234–7, 255–8
  meetings with Ashton-Gwatkin, 174–80, 215–18, 222, 225, 237, 293, 318–19
  meetings with Runciman, 168–73, 216–17, 331
  seeks clarification from Hitler of SdP role (1937), 16
  visits London in December 1935, 8, 10–11
  visits London in July 1936, 8, 10–11
  visits London in October 1937, 13–14
  visits London in May 1938, 55–7, 65, 67, 71, 101, 204–5
Hess, Rudolf, 18
'Historic Provinces' (of the Bohemian Crown), 2–3, 19, 335
  see also Bohemia and Moravia
Hitler, Adolf, 121, 198–9, 342
  approached by Henlein for clarification of SdP role (1937), 16
  attitude to Czechoslovakia, 17, 27
  meeting with chiefs of armed services (1937), 16–17
  meeting with Frank (26 August 1938), 216–17, 290
  meeting with Henlein in March 1938, 18
  meeting with Henlein (1 September 1938), 228, 234–7, 255–6, 262
  meetings with Chamberlain, 304, 310, 319–20, 321–2, 323–4, 342
  reaction to May Crisis, 58–9
  speech at Nuremberg (12 September 1938), 287–8, 291, 318
Hoare, Sir Samuel, 36, 40, 44, 48, 49, 52, 65, 66, 287, 304, 319
Hobhouse, Charles, 82
Hodža, Milan, 64, 73, 112, 115, 173, 175, 180–1, 221, 259–60, 290, 302–3, 316, 328
  conciliatory towards SdP, 108–9, 154
  contacts with SdP negotiators, 165–8, 268, 272
  meetings with Runciman Mission, 149, 166, 245, 288
  meetings with SdP in May 1938, 65, 103, 106
Hohenlohe, Prince Max, 159, 177, 210, 215–17, 255–6, 262, 267, 272, 277, 278, 332
  contacts with Vansittart, 116–20, 139–40, 294
Hoover, President Herbert, 32, 41
Horne, Lord, 76, 96
'Hossbach Memorandum', 16–17
Hoyer-Millar, F.R., 200
Humphrys, Sir Francis, 76
Hungary, 117, 190

Hungarian minority (in Czechoslovakia), 3, 156–7, 320, 323, 328
Hussite Wars, 1, 221

India Office, 74
industry (in Czechoslovakia), 5
Inskip, Sir Thomas, 40
international commission considered for mediation in Czechoslovakia, 62–3, 71–3
international conference considered on Czechoslovakia, 189–90, 203, 300, 321
  see also Munich Agreement
international loan (for Czechoslovakia), 222, 225
Ireland, 160
Italy, 91–2, 190, 300

Jaksch, Wenzel, 13, 154–6, 162–3
Jebb, Gladwyn, 30
Jews, 16, 92–3
Jewish minority (in Czechoslovakia), 3, 157, 181
Ježek, František, 122

Kameradschaftsbund (KB), 6, 11
Karlovy Vary *see* Carlsbad
Karlsbad *see* Carlsbad
Károlyi, Count, 156
Kašpar, Cardinal Karel, 245, 250, 331, 332
Keitel, General Wilhelm, 59, 237
Keynes, Maynard, 90
Khuen, Count and Countess, 170, 332, 339
Kier, Herbert, 169, 177, 268–70, 276
Kinsky, Prince Ulrich, 150, 169–70, 330–1, 332, 339
Kinsky, Count Zdenko, 170, 330, 332
Kitchener, Lord, 97, 98
Klapka, Otakar, 152
Kleist, Ewald von, 199, 226, 246–7, 260
Köllner, Fritz, 215, 283
Kordt, Theodor, 201–2, 206, 211, 279–80, 285
Krebs, Hans, 107, 124
Krejčí, Jaroslav, 175
Krofta, Kamil, 44, 54, 149, 201, 273, 298
Kruliš-Randa, Otakar, 331
Kundt, Ernst, 103, 106, 116, 122, 165–6, 175–6, 224, 268–70, 294, 307
  contacts with Mission, 147, 150–2, 167, 168, 174, 181–2, 204–5, 215, 224–5, 228, 239, 240, 249–50, 267–8, 272, 288–9, 293, 303–4
  negotiations with Beneš and Hodža, 214–15, 221, 228, 248–50, 267–8, 272, 281

Lacroix, François de, 54, 105, 246, 248, 322
Lanark speech *see* Simon, Sir John
land reform (in Czechoslovakia), 4–5, 312
Lang, Archbishop Cosmo Gordon, 143
language law (in Czechoslovakia), 4, 52, 103, 149, 153, 175, 222, 231, 248, 264
Lansdowne, Lord, 89
Layton, Sir Walter, 109
League of Nations, 36, 43, 44
Leeper, R.W.A., 134
Leibig, Baron, 156
Leitmeritz *see* Litoměřice
Liberal Nationals (Simonites), 87
Liberal Party (UK), 81, 86–7, 97
Liberec (Reichenberg), 64, 174, 177
Lindemann, Professor F.A., 55–6
Lindley, Sir Francis, 96
Litoměřice (Leitmeritz), viii, 175
'Little Entente', 200, 315
Lloyd George, David, 82–7
Lobkowicz, Prince Max, 276
local elections *see* elections
Locarno, Treaty of, 6, 36, 93
Lockhart, R.H. Bruce *see* Bruce Lockhart, R.H.
London, Midland and Scottish Railway Company, 86
Lorenz, Werner, 18
Lothian, Lord (Philip Kerr), 74, 96, 231

Macadam, Ivison, 131
McDonald, Iverach, 278
MacDonald, Malcolm, 36, 40, 67, 254, 297
MacDonald, Ramsay, 87–8, 98
McDermott, G.L., 21

Mackenzie King, W.L., 143
Macleay, Sir Ronald, 96
Macmillan, Lord, 76
Magyars *see* Hungarians
Mährisch Ostrau *see* Moravská Ostrava
Malkin, Sir William, 32
Mallet, Ivo, 32–3, 53, 72, 74, 79, 101–2, 110, 140, 142, 195, 200, 220, 229, 299–300, 327, 338
Malypetr, Jan, 152
Manchester Guardian, 135, 188
Mariánské Lázně *see* Marienbad
Marienbad (Mariánské Lázně), viii, 175–80, 183, 234, 253
Masařík, Hubert, 328
Masaryk, Jan, 9, 22, 44, 45, 49, 56, 61, 65–6, 105, 109, 245, 278–80, 299, 327
 conversation with Runciman, 325–6, 329
Masaryk, Tomáš Garrigue, 4, 132, 330
Mason-MacFarlane, Colonel F.N., 199, 209, 211
Mastný, Vojtěch, 57, 113, 328
May, Franz, 271, 283
'May Crisis' (1938), 57–9, 64–5, 69, 121, 342
mediation in Czechoslovakia (evolution of British policy), 37, 40, 44–5, 49, 51–2, 62–3, 64–5, 71–4, 79–80, 108
Mein Kampf, 133
Meissner, Alfred, 152–4, 166, 273, 282
Methodist Recorder, 329–30
Metternich, Prince, 216
Miller, Rosemary, 133, 147, 338
Minorities Treaty (Czechoslovak, 1919), 4 8, 46, 153, 232
Mlčoch, Rudolf, 122
Montmorency, Sir Geoffrey de, 74
Moor Line Ltd, 81, 85–6, 99
Moravia *see* Bohemia and Moravia
Moravská Ostrava (Mährisch Ostrau), viii, 271–3, 275, 276, 283, 285, 289, 311
Most (Brüx), viii, 173–4, 215
Munich Agreement, 39, 327–9, 343
Mussolini, Benito, 91–2, 94, 300–1, 328
Murray, Arthur, 329

National Democratic Party (Czechoslovak), 103
National Socialism (in Sudetenland), 16, 53, 55, 67, 102, 154, 233, 236, 264–5, 333
National Socialist Party (Czechoslovak), 103, 109, 154
National Socialist Party (Sudeten German), 5–6, 107, 124
'National State' (Czechoslovak), 4, 150, 175
Nationalist Party (Sudeten German), 5–6
Nationalities Statute, 102–4, 149, 153
Nečas, J., 148
Neurath, Constantin von, 11, 92
neutralisation of Czechoslovakia, 47, 60–2, 70, 138, 203, 204–5, 315, 325, 326
Neuwith, Hans, 336
New York Herald Tribune, 317, 319
News Chronicle, 1, 135–6, 316–17, 332
Newton, Basil, 12, 14, 38, 52, 54, 64, 101, 133, 187, 207, 251, 261, 300, 302
 conversations with Strang (May 1938), 59–63
 'Franco-British Plan', 322
 German policy towards Czechoslovakia, 15, 58
 mediation in Czechoslovakia, 62–3, 72, 74–5, 79, 113
 meetings with Beneš, 244–8, 259
 neutralisation of Czechoslovakia, 60, 70
 plebiscite in Sudetenland, 59–60, 298, 320
 position of Czechoslovakia, 17, 25, 60
 pressures Czechoslovakia for concessions, 105–8, 111–12
 Runciman Mission, 132, 140, 147, 158, 197–8, 212, 219–20, 223 228, 277
 Runciman Mission imposed, 113–16
 Runciman Report, 326–7
 Sudeten German autonomy, 15
Nicolson, Harold, 56, 67
Noel-Baker, Philip, 62–3
Noel-Buxton, Lord, 32–3
Norton, Clifford, 8
Nuremberg Nazi Congress (1938), 258–9, 268–9, 270, 285, 287–8
 British fear of, 180, 188, 191, 193–4, 197–8, 207, 214, 219, 222, 226, 228, 229, 234, 236, 243, 257, 342

Hitler's speech (12 September 1938), 287–8, 291, 318

Oban, 77, 78
Observer, The, 134–5
Observers (British) in Sudetenland, 62–4, 73, 121, 125, 275, 289, 291
Oliphant, Sir Lancelot, 202, 254
Oldham, 81
O'Malley, Owen, 10, 13
'Operation Green', 58–9, 122, 199, 237, 255–6, 285
Ormsby-Gore, W., 40
Osuský, Štefan, 105
Ottawa, Imperial Economic Conference (1932), 88, 128

Palacký, František, 1
Pares, Sir Bernard, 131–2
Pares, Peter, 64, 131–2, 144, 289
Paris, John (Ashton-Gwatkin's literary pseudonym), 128
Paris Peace Conference, 3–4, 26, 59–60, 90, 299
parliament (Czechoslovak, Chamber of Deputies), 5, 7–8
parliament (UK),
  House of Commons, 1, 36, 43–4, 323, 333
  House of Lords, 116, 137
Paul-Boncour, Joseph, 38
Pauliny-Toth, Jan, 158
Peters, Gustav, 122, 150
Petersburg *see* Petrohrad
Peto, Geoffrey, 130, 159, 170, 172–3, 174, 181, 204, 215, 245, 292, 303, 338
Petrohrad (Petersburg), viii, 275–6, 317, 331, 333
Phipps, Sir Eric, 37–8, 246, 294
Pickthorn, Kenneth, 231
Piłsudski, Marshal, 17
Písek, viii, 331
Pittsburg Agreement (1918), 4, 158
'Plan Z', 208, 295–7
plebiscite (in Sudetenland), 25, 33–4, 56, 59–60, 110–11, 117, 138, 279, 297–9, 314, 318–19, 320–1, 325
Poland, 6, 17, 117, 190
Polish minority (in Czechoslovakia), 3, 153, 156–7, 320, 323, 328
Political Committee of Cabinet (Czechoslovak), 103, 263
Popolo d'Italia, 300
population census (Austrian 1910; Czechoslovak 1921), 3
Populist Party (Czechoslovak), 103
postal service (Czechoslovak), 7, 165
Preiss, Jaroslav, 274, 283, 331
  'Preiss Plan', 302–3, 320, 321, 326
press, 147–8, 152, 177–8, 187
  British, 110, 124, 134–6, 143, 278–80, 286
  Czechoslovak, 109, 148, 237
  German, 57, 125, 130, 175
propaganda, 222, 224
public opinion
  in Britain, 110, 227, 243, 299–300, 333
  in Czechoslovakia, 273–4, 299–300

Raeburn, Sir Norman, 77
Rašín, Alois, 152
Raudnitz *see* Roudnice
Rechtspersönlichkeit (legal personality for Sudeten Germans), 217, 231, 265, 267, 268, 276
refugees from Nazi Germany, 6, 16
Reichenber *see* Liberec
reparations, sought by SdP, 53, 55, 101, 217, 232–3, 267
Reynolds News, 136
Rhineland (German reoccupation), 7
Ribbentrop, Joachim von, 18, 54, 55, 57, 120–2, 176, 198–200, 201
Riverdale, Lord, 77
Roberts, Frank, 53, 72, 79–80, 104, 110, 140, 142, 155–6, 158, 195, 196, 246, 257, 266–7, 289, 300, 307
Romania, 200, 315
Roosevelt, President Franklin D., 89, 142, 146, 329
Rosche, Alfred, 122, 150, 268
Rothenhaus *see* Červený Hrádek
Roudnice (Raudnitz), viii, 276
Royal Institute of International Affairs (RIIA), 8, 13, 131, 141
Royal Mail Steam Packet Company, 86
Rudé Právo, 148
Rumbold, Sir Horace, 74, 96, 198, 206
Rumburk (Rumburg), 307–8

Runciman, Baron (father), 81, 91–2, 97, 98, 99
Runciman, Hilda (*née* Stevenson – wife), 86, 88, 98, 133, 170, 172, 174, 181, 245, 297, 338
Runciman, Leslie (son), 92, 133
Runciman, Stephen (son), 133, 329
Runciman, Viscount (biographical details),
  abdication crisis, 88
  Abyssinian crisis, 91
  'appeasement', 94–5, 333
  assumes peerage (1937), 86, 88
  Austria-Hungary, 90
  business career, 81, 85–6, 87
  Central Europe, 89
  Chairman of the International Shipping Conference (1926), 86
  childhood and education, 81
  educational reform, 82–3
  estimations of, 81–2, 83, 84, 85, 88, 97–8
  Fascist Italy, 91–2, 94, 99
  Financial Secretary to the Treasury (1907–8), 82
  Free Trade, 87–8, 98
  'Holmes circular', 83
  ill health, 85
  Imperial Economic Conference, Ottawa (1932), 88
  industrial relations, 84
  international trade, 84–5
  Lausanne Conference (1932), 89
  League of Nations, 91
  Lord President of the Council (1938–39), 334
  Member of Parliament for Dewsbury (1902–18), 81, 85
  Member of Parliament for Oldham (1899–1900), 81
  Member of Parliament for St Ives (1929–37), 86, 130
  Member of Parliament for Swansea West (1924–29), 86
  Nazi Germany, 92–3
  Parliamentary Secretary to the Local Government Board (1905–7), 82
  political career, 81–5, 86–8
  President of the Board of Agriculture and Fisheries (1911–14), 82, 83
  President of the Board of Education (1908–11), 82–3
  President of the Board of Trade (1914–16), 82, 83–5, 89
  President of the Board of Trade, (1931–37), 87–8, 92, 93, 129
  President of the Chamber of Shipping of the United Kingdom, (1926–27), 86
  rearmament, 93–4, 100
  relations with Chamberlain, 88
  relations with Lloyd George, 86–7
  Rome–Berlin Axis, 94
  shipping control, 84, 97
  Soviet Union, 90–1
  war debts, 89
  wartime administration, 83–5
Runciman, Viscount (Mission to Czechoslovakia), 32, 187, 335, 341–3
  appointed mediator in Czechoslovakia, 76–8, 96, 113
  arbitration, 229–31, 233, 234–5, 294–5, 297
  arrival in Prague, 147–8
  assassination threat, 277–8
  assessment of Beneš, 150, 244–5, 250–1, 321
  assessment of Henlein, 173, 321
  assessment of progress, 180, 182, 188
  breakdown of mediation, 291
  Chamberlain's visit to Berchtesgaden, 295–7, 301, 303
  compromise proposal, 189–91, 193
  espousal of Carlsbad programme, 243–8, 249–50, 252–3, 258–9
  exploratory discussions with Czechoslovak government, 149–50, 152–4, 158–60
  exploratory discussions with SdP, 150–2, 158–60
  formation of Mission, 128–34
  'Franco-British Plan', 322, 325
  Henlein's visit to Hitler (1 September 1938), 236–8
  ill health, 208, 229–30, 247, 253, 276–7, 329
  'independence' of Mission, 129–31, 135–6, 147, 187, 200, 214, 252–3, 316

meetings with Beneš, 149–50, 165, 180, 214, 243–8, 249–51, 259, 272, 273, 303, 319, 333
meetings with Henlein, 168–73, 216–17, 333
meetings with Hodža, 149, 166, 180–1
meetings with other national groups, 154–8, 162–3
meetings with SdP negotiators, 181–2, 253, 303
Mission announced in House of Commons, 1, 116, 134–5
Mission imposed on Czechoslovakia, 113–20
nature of Mission, 78–80, 122
objectives of Mission, 136–40, 142–3, 145, 146, 159–60, 188–94, 196–7
plebiscite, 298, 320
pressure for urgent resolution, 197–8
promotes negotiations between Czechoslovak government and SdP, 165–8,
proposed visit to Hitler, 206–8, 214, 227–8, 252, 342
proposed warning to Hitler, 286
reaction to 'Fourth Plan', 265–6, 274
reaction to 'Third Plan', 222–6, 228, 243, 252
return to London, 303–4, 316, 319–21, 338
Runciman Report, 266, 275, 290, 310–19, 324–7, 328–9, 337, 338
self-determination for German minority, 322–3
supporting Chamberlain, 327, 330, 334
The Times leading article of 7 September 1938, 278–80
unrest in Sudetenland, 288–91, 319
visits to Bohemian aristocracy, 169–71, 172–4, 215–17, 245, 275–6, 330–3
Rutha, Heinrich, 9, 13, 22
Ruthenia (Sub-Carpathian Ukraine), 3
Ruthenian minority (in Czechoslovakia), 3, 157, 163

Saar, 203
St Germain, Treaty of, 157, 163
Samuel, Viscount, 325, 337
Sander, Professor Fritz, 175, 177, 222
Sargent, Orme (Sir), 8, 10, 22, 44, 51, 77, 78, 117, 121, 132, 189, 199–200, 202, 209, 226, 254, 257, 289, 327
arbitration by Runciman, 195–6
British mediation in Czechoslovakia, 72–3, 74, 79, 102, 108, 220, 301
contact with Henlein, 105–6
Czechoslovak–SdP negotiations, 104
duration of Runciman Mission, 196
mobilising international support against Germany, 29–30, 31
opposes neutralisation of Czechoslovakia, 60–1
opposes pressure on Czechoslovakia, 34, 39–40
plebiscite in Sudetenland, 110
Šašek, A., 96
Schacht, Hjalmar, 302
Schicketanz, Rudolf, 122, 150, 270
Schuschnigg, Kurt von, 12, 42, 270
Schwarzenberg, Prince Adolf, 174, 331, 332
Scott, C.P., 84
SdP *see* Sudeten German Party
Sebekowsky, Wilhelm, 122, 147, 150, 176, 181, 214–15, 221, 223–4, 248–50, 267, 281, 291
Seeley, John, 97
Selb (Bavaria), 290
self-determination *see* Sudetenland
Seton-Watson, Robert William, 134
Seyss-Inquart, Artur, 42
Silesia, 175
Simon, Sir John, 27, 40, 49, 87, 88, 131, 143, 144, 202, 206, 230–1, 286–7, 297, 304, 319–20, 328–9
Lanark speech (27 August 1938), 200–1, 226, 251, 253–4
Sinclair, Sir Archibald, 55–6, 67
Slovak National Party, 158
Slovak People's Party, 103, 157–8
Slovakia, 3, 52, 104, 158
Slovaks, 3, 157–8, 320
Small Traders Party (Czechoslovak), 103
Snowden, Viscount, 88, 98
social conditions *see* 'Sudetenland'
Social Democratic Party (Czechoslovak), 5, 103, 109, 273

Social Democratic Party (Sudeten German), 5, 11, 18, 154–6, 312
Sokol gymnastic festival, 109
South Shields High School, 81
Soviet Union, 90–1, 190, 300, 308
alliance with Czechoslovakia, 6–7, 190, 203–4, 221, 315, 322
Šrámek, Mgr Jan, 122
Stamp, Lord, 77, 275
Stanhope, Lord, 8
Stanley, Oliver, 26, 36, 40
Stanley, Venetia, 85
Star, The, 136
'State of Nationalities' (Czechoslovakia), 52, 54, 150
state police (in Czechoslovakia), 7, 175, 177–8, 203, 222, 224, 232, 249, 264, 267, 311, 314, 318
Steed, H. Wickham, 109, 134, 145
Stephens, David, 132, 240, 338
Stopford, Robert J., 96, 131, 144, 156, 159, 163, 174, 204–5, 212, 223, 239, 267, 272, 275, 276, 277, 283, 288, 303, 308, 338
draft proposals for Berchtesgaden meeting, 301–2
preparation for Mission, 136, 140–1
progress of Mission, 150, 151, 154, 160, 274
Runciman Report, 326–7, 337
Runciman's proposed visit to Hitler, 206–8, 212
'Stopford Plan', 230–3, 247–8, 263
Strang, William, 28–29, 32–3, 34, 41, 78, 80, 121, 190, 267, 279
receives reports from Ashton-Gwatkin, 187, 217, 223, 293
visits Central Europe after May Crisis, 59–63, 73, 300
Stronge, Colonel H.C.T., 298
Sub-Carpathian Ukraine *see* Ruthenia
Sudetendeutsche Partai see Sudeten German Party
Sudeten German industry, 5, 156
Sudeten German Home Front (*Sudetendeutche Heimatfront*), 6, 7
Sudeten German Party (SdP), 7, 19, 311–14, 316
in 1935 general election, 7–8,
autonomist programme, 11–12
breakdown of mediation, 291, 292
Carlsbad Programme (April 1938), 52–3, 54, 55–6, 67, 119, 123, 151, 173, 176, 216–17, 219, 224–5, 231–3, 234–5, 243–8, 252–3, 258, 259, 266–7, 269, 270, 293–4, 302, 310
exploratory discussions with Runciman Mission, 150–2, 158–60
informed of Runciman Mission, 116–20
links with Nazi Germany, 8, 11
Moravská Ostrava incident, 271–3
negotiating strategy, 167–70, 171, 176, 181
negotiations with Beneš, 214–15, 221–2, 248–50, *see also* 'Third Plan'; 'Fourth Plan'
negotiations with Czechoslovak authorities, 65, 103–4, 110–13, 166–8
proposals of 7 June 1938, 101, 147, 151, 166
'six parliamentary bills', 11–12
unrest in Sudetenland, 288–91, 311
Sudeten Germans
in government service, 7, 52, 165, 172–3, 175, 177–8, 222, 224, 232, 264, 312
resisting formation of Czechoslovakia (1918–19), 2–3, 19
'Sudetenland', 19
economic assistance proposed, 222, 224–5, 248–9, 264
martial law declared, 289–90, 291, 313–14, 319
social conditions, 7, 11, 141, 155, 156, 170–1, 202–3, 315
transfer to Germany, 278–80, 298–300, 314, 318–19, 320, 321–2, 322, 325
Sunbeam (yacht), 77, 99, 143
Sunday Times, 32
Sutton-Pratt, Major R., 64, 275, 283, 289–91, 305
Syrový, General Jan, 328

Teplice (Teplitz), viii, 14, 22, 177, 215–16, 331
'Third Plan', 175–7, 180–1, 184, 185–6, 202–3, 214–15, 219, 221–6, 227–8, 234–5, 264

Thirty Years' War, 1, 292
Thompson, Dorothy, 317, 319, 335, 337
Tillard, Aline, 133, 338
The Times, 93, 110, 124, 134–5, 188
  leading article of 7 September 1938, 278–80
Time and Tide, 134
Tiso, Jozef, 157–8
Toynbee, Arnold, 131, 141
Trautenau *see* Trutnov
Trianon, Treaty of, 163
Troutbeck, John Monro, 131
Trutnov (Trautenau), viii, 289
Turnverband, 6
Tyrrell, Lord, 131

unemployment (in Czechoslovakia), 5, 7
United Hungarian Party, 156–7
United Kingdom Provident Institution, 86
United States of America, 89, 91, 227, 279
USSR *see* Soviet Union

Vansittart, Sir Robert (Lord), 13, 22, 31, 36, 41, 69, 74, 110, 131, 190, 202, 209, 245, 254, 299, 300, 304, 308, 319
  assessment of Henlein, 9, 13, 53, 55–7, 107, 117, 141
  contact with Henlein, 105–8, 110–11, 116–20, 139–40
  critical of British policy towards Czechoslovakia, 50–1,
  intelligence reports, 10, 111, 121
  meetings with Henlein, 8–9, 13, 55–7, 65, 67–8
  neutralisation of Czechoslovakia, 61, 79
  objectives of Runciman Mission, 137, 140–1, 156
  plebiscite in Sudetenland, 110–11
  warning to Germany, 286
Venkov, 96
Versailles, Treaty of, 90, 93, 330
Völkischer Beobachter, 130
Volksdeutsche Mittelstelle, 18, 169, 293
Volksgruppe (Sudeten German), 217
Vuillemin, General Joseph, 200

Wallenstein, Albrecht, 292
Walter Runciman and Co. Ltd *see* Moor Line Ltd
'Wee Frees', 86–7
Weizsäcker, Ernst von, 63, 104, 113, 120–2, 125, 196, 201, 254
Wesleyan Methodism, 81, 88, 148
Westfalen, Count, 170, 332
Westminster Bank, 86
White Mountain, battle of, 331
Wiedemann, Captain Fritz, 121, 127, 196
Wilson, Sir Horace, 76–7, 96, 201–4, 206, 208, 254, 274, 286–7, 295–6, 304, 319,
  report from Ashton-Gwatkin, 288–9, 291
  Runciman Report, 324–5
  visit to Hitler (26 and 27 September 1938), 328
Wigram, Lord, 334
Wiskemann, Elizabeth, 141–2
Wollner, Georg, 275–6
Wrocław (Breslau), gymnastic festival, 116–17

Yugoslavia, 200, 315

Žd'ár, viii, 170, 330
Živnostenská banka, 274
Zlín, 332
Zurich, meeting with Henlein (August 1938), 119–20, 171–2, 179, 184